DEFENSIO FIDEI NICÆNÆ.

A

DEFENCE OF THE NICENE CREED,

OUT OF

THE EXTANT WRITINGS

OF THE

CATHOLICK DOCTORS,

WHO FLOURISHED DURING THE THREE FIRST CENTURIES
OF THE CHRISTIAN CHURCH;

IN WHICH ALSO
IS INCIDENTALLY VINDICATED

THE CREED OF CONSTANTINOPLE;

CONCERNING THE HOLY GHOST.

BY

GEORGE BULL, [D.D.,]

A PRIEST OF THE ENGLISH CHURCH,
[AFTERWARDS LORD BISHOP OF ST. DAVID'S.]

A NEW TRANSLATION.

VOL. I.

WIPF & STOCK · Eugene, Oregon

Wipf and Stock Publishers
199 W 8th Ave, Suite 3
Eugene, OR 97401

Defensio Fidei Nicaenae, vol. 1
A Defence of the NIcene Creed, out of the Extant Writings of the Catholick Doctors, Who Flourished During the Three First Centuries of the Christian Church; in which also is incidentally Vindicated the Creed of Constantinople; Concerning the Holy Ghost.
By Bull, George
ISBN 13: 978-1-60608-137-2
Publication date 2/10/2009
Previously published by John Henry Parker, 1851

ADVERTISEMENT.

The circumstances which led to the composition of this Work, and the history of its completion and publication, are fully narrated by Bp. Bull in the Preface to the Reader, pp. i. &c., and by Nelson in his life of Bp. Bull, pp. 239, &c., in which there is also a valuable review of the state of the controversy at that time. An account of the successive editions will be found in Dr. Burton's Preface to the 8vo. edition of the Works, first published in Oxford in 1827. The text of that edition has been followed in the present Translation, and the additional notes which it contains have also been translated; those of Dr. Burton being distinguished by the letter B. His notes, and the references added by him, as well as the few additional references and observations which are introduced in the notes to this Translation, are included in brackets. Grabe's longer Annotations are removed from the places which they occupy in the Oxford edition, at the ends of the several chapters, to an Appendix at the end of the Work, in order not to interrupt the continuity of the original Treatise. The paging of the folio edition of Grabe, and of the 8vo. of 1827, are retained in the margin, the latter being included in brackets.

The passages quoted from the fathers are preserved in

the original language as notes, and in a few places the context has been added.

There was a translation of this and of Bp. Bull's other Works on the Trinity by Dr. F. Holland, in two volumes 8vo. A.D. 1725. This has been consulted by the translator, but so little use has been made of it, that the present must be considered as an independent version.

The Indices and List of Authors for this and the other Works on the Holy Trinity, will be placed at the end of the volumes, as in Dr. Burton's 8vo. edition of the originals.

TO THE MOST LEARNED AND HOLY

PRELATE,

THE CHOICEST ORNAMENT OF OUR CHURCH, UNIVERSITY, AND AGE,

THE RIGHT REVEREND FATHER AND LORD IN CHRIST,

JOHN,

LORD BISHOP OF OXFORD,

AND

DEAN OF THE

MOST NOBLE COLLEGE AND CATHEDRAL CHURCH

OF CHRIST CHURCH IN OXFORD;

THIS

VINDICATION OF THE NICENE FAITH

IS DEDICATED AND CONSECRATED,

AS A PLEDGE AND MEMORIAL SUCH AS IT IS

OF GRATITUDE AND OF THE UTMOST RESPECT,

BY THE MOST DEVOTED ADMIRER OF HIS VIRTUES,

GEORGE BULL

TO THE READER.

In the Apology[a], which I sent out in defence of a work entitled the *Harmonia Apostolica,* the first-fruits of my theological studies, I said[b],—being forced to do so by a very grave and unjust calumny of my opponents,—"that I had drawn out certain historico-ecclesiastical propositions concerning the divinity of the Son, in which, as I trusted, I had clearly shewn[c] the agreement of the ancient doctors, who preceded the Nicene council, with the Nicene fathers, as well concerning the consubstantiality of the Son of God as His co-eternity, the tradition having been derived from the very time of the Apostles; but that, owing to ill health, and other cares and business of sundry kinds, it had not yet been in my power to put together my scattered sheets, and bring to a completion my imperfect work." Upon this I was assailed on all sides with entreaties from learned friends, that I would apply both mind and hand, to finish, as speedily as possible, a work which was absolutely needed. For they gave me to understand that the writings of Christopher Ch. Sandius[d] were

[a] [Apologia pro Harmonia, &c. Lond. 1676.]

[b] i. 8. [p. 317. See Bp. Bull on Justification, Pt. ii. and iii.: Anglo-Cath. Library, p. 238.]

[c] [Bp. Bull here omits the words "against Petavius and others" which occur in the Apologia. The calumny to which he refers was a charge of Socinianizing on the doctrine of justification.]

[d] Of the treatise of Christopher Christopher Sandius: the first edition had been sent out A.D. 1668, the second—so much enlarged and corrected as, except from its retaining the original title, to be a new work, (ibid.,)—was published A.D. 1676, with the following title, Christoph. Christophori Sandii Nucleus Historiæ Ecclesiasticæ, exhibitus in Historia Arianorum, tribus libris comprehensa: Quibus præ-tina est Tractatus de Veteribus Scriptoribus Ecclesiasticis, secunda editio ab Authore locupletata et emendata. Coloniæ apud Joannem Nicolai, 1676. Prefixed is a Præfatio ad Lectores, by Christophorus Philippi Sandius the father of the writer. The volume contains 432 pages (besides Addenda and Index); of these 49 pages are occupied by the tract *de Scriptoribus Ecclesiasticis:* the heading of the pages of the rest is *Enucleatæ Historiæ Ecclesiasticæ*, lib. i., &c., though the title-page, as has been said, bears the name *Nucleus H. E. exhibitus*, &c. Bp. Bull throughout refers to both these tracts, and to the Nucleus under both titles.]

every where in the hands of our students of theology and others, a writer who openly and unblushingly maintains the blasphemy of Arius as the truly catholic doctrine, and as supported by the voices of all the ancients who preceded the council of Nice. Overcome at last by their reiterated requests, (although I had not even then sufficient leisure, nor was my health strong enough for so arduous a task,) I again read over the works of the primitive fathers; the testimonies out of them, bearing on my subject, which I had collected into my note-books, I again submitted one by one to a fresh and most searching examination; I added several others to them; the passages alleged by Sandius and others in support of the opposite side I weighed with increased care; and lastly, I put in order the whole of this, as it were, rude and confused mass of my observations, disposing and arranging them in the easiest and clearest method that I could; and it is now more than five years since I finished the work, in the state in which it now comes out.

If you ask, why then has the publication been so long delayed? I will tell you plainly. As soon as I had put the finishing hand to my MS., I immediately offered it to three booksellers in succession, for publication, on the fairest terms: they all, however, on different grounds, declined to undertake the care and expense of printing the work; apprehensive, I suppose, that few would be found to buy a book, of which the author was little known, and the subject difficult, and which very few indeed would care to bestow pains in examining. Nor was I myself,—a person of narrow income and with a large family,—able to bear the expense of the press.

In consequence, I brought home again my neglected work, to be laid up on the shelves of my bookcase; content to have had the will at least to do something for the defence of divine truth, and to have complied, so far as lay in my power, with the wishes of my friends.

After I had for some time consoled myself with these reflections, at length, at the suggestion of a friend, I submitted my papers, raised as it were from the grave, to the judgment of a most distinguished man and consummate theologian, Dr. William Jane, the very worthy Regius Pro-

fessor of Divinity in Oxford, who, with his usual kindness, did not decline the trouble of reading them through, and when he had read them through, and honoured them with his approval, he further recommended them to the favour and patronage of the great bishop of Oxford[e], and easily obtained from his singular kindness and zeal for catholic truth, that this Defence of the Nicene Creed should at last come out from the press at the Sheldonian Theatre, which the bishop had fitted up at his own expense. But as that press was occupied with different works of other writers, there was for a considerable time no opportunity whatever, and afterwards only occasionally, for mine; and hence delay has arisen in bringing this treatise through the press.

If I could have foreseen that it would have been so long before this treatise of mine was published, you should have certainly had it much more carefully finished, more polished, and more rich in matter. But, as I have already said, I completed this work at the request of friends, who were keenly pressing and unceasingly spurring me on, to revise and enlarge the collections which I had by me in defence of the catholic faith, made from the reading of ancient authors, and, having enlarged them, to publish them as speedily as possible, as an immediate antidote to the poisonous writings of Sandius. When, however, I had lost all hope of publishing it through the booksellers, what object was there for further enlarging and improving a work, which was now condemned to the moths and worms? And at last, when an unexpected opportunity was afforded for my papers being printed, and I had placed them in the printer's hands, they were no longer under my controul.

It were, indeed, to be wished, that this most important subject had been treated by some one very much more learned than myself, on whom the providence of God had withal bestowed more uninterrupted leisure, a better furnished library, and all requisites in more abundant measure. Very many such persons our English Church has, and such I pray Almighty God that she may ever continue to have. But no one hitherto, so far as I know, has undertaken to work out this subject with the care it deserves. Do not,

[e] [Bp. Fell, to whom the work is dedicated.]

therefore, disdain to use and profit by what I have done, till such time as one appears, who shall have brought out from a more ample store a better and more complete work. You have here all that it was in my power to do, a man of moderate abilities and learning, the possessor of a limited store of books, in poor health, hindered by domestic cares, and, whilst writing this work, tied to the cure of souls in a country parish, and lastly, living far from the society of learned men, an exile, as it were, from the literary world. This one thing, however, I may venture to assure you of, and most solemnly to declare, that in the whole course of this work I have observed the utmost good faith. Not a passage have I adduced from primitive antiquity in support of the decisions of the council of Nice, which, after a careful examination both of the passage itself and its context, I did not seriously think really made for the cause which we are maintaining; not a passage have I garbled, but have put before you all entire. The opinions of the Greek fathers I have cited not only in Latin, but in the Greek also, in order that those who know Greek may be able themselves to form a surer judgment of their genuine meaning. Of those passages which the modern defenders of Arianism have adduced from the ancient doctors in support of it, I have not knowingly and designedly kept back any; nor have I ever attempted any how to salve over the harder sayings of the ancients by cunning artifices; but have endeavoured, by observing the drift and purpose of each author, and by adducing other clearer statements from their several writings, to establish on solid grounds that they not only admit, but actually require, to be understood in a catholic sense. To end the matter in one word,—while I willingly confess that it is indeed possible that I may be mistaken, I resolutely deny that I have wished to deceive any one.

As regards the chief point, of which I wish to persuade others,—I myself am quite convinced, and that on no hasty view, that, What the Nicene fathers laid down concerning the divinity of the Son, in opposition to Arius and other heretics, the same in effect (although sometimes, it may be, in other words, and in another mode of expression) was taught, without any single exception, by all the fathers

and approved doctors of the Church, who flourished before the council of Nice, even from the very times of the Apostles.

I pray you kindly to excuse the mistakes of the printer, and the occasional slips of a careless corrector of the press. It has been my misfortune, that I have had the opportunity of examining and correcting, in person, one sheet only, and that the last, of this work, as it passed through the press. As the only thing I can do, you will find that all the errors of the press that are of any moment, are carefully brought together and set down in a table prefixed to the work[f].

And now, reader, whose object is truth and piety, if these labours of mine are of any service towards confirming your faith on the primary article of the Christian religion, there will be good cause both for you and myself to give thanks to Almighty God. This only do I ask of you as a recompense for my labours, (and this I earnestly request,) that in your prayers you would sometimes remember me, a sinner, and mine.

Farewell in Christ our Saviour, our Lord and our God.

f [There was a table of errata prefixed to the first edition of the original work.]

AN INDEX

OF THE

PROPOSITIONS DEMONSTRATED IN THIS WORK.

BOOK I.

ON THE PRE-EXISTENCE OF THE SON OF GOD.

THE PROPOSITION.

THE CATHOLIC DOCTORS OF THE FIRST THREE CENTURIES ALL WITH ONE ACCORD TAUGHT THAT JESUS CHRIST, THAT IS, HE WHO WAS AFTERWARDS CALLED JESUS CHRIST, (BEFORE HE WAS MADE MAN, THAT IS, BEFORE HIS BIRTH, ACCORDING TO THE FLESH, OF THE MOST BLESSED VIRGIN,) EXISTED IN ANOTHER NATURE FAR SURPASSING THE HUMAN; THAT HE APPEARED TO HOLY MEN, AS A PRELUDE TO HIS INCARNATION; THAT HE ALWAYS PRESIDED OVER AND PROVIDED FOR THAT CHURCH, WHICH HE WAS AFTERWARDS TO REDEEM WITH HIS OWN BLOOD; AND THAT THUS FROM THE BEGINNING THE "WHOLE ORDER OF THE DIVINE ADMINISTRATION" (AS TERTULLIAN EXPRESSES IT) "HAD ITS COURSE THROUGH HIM;" AND THAT, MOREOVER, BEFORE THE FOUNDATIONS OF THE WORLD WERE LAID HE WAS PRESENT WITH GOD HIS FATHER, AND THAT THROUGH HIM THIS UNIVERSE WAS CREATED.

BOOK II.

ON THE CONSUBSTANTIALITY OF THE SON.

THE PROPOSITION.

IT WAS THE SETTLED AND UNANIMOUS OPINION OF THE CATHOLIC DOCTORS, WHO FLOURISHED IN THE FIRST THREE CENTURIES, THAT THE SON OF GOD WAS OF ONE SUBSTANCE, OR CONSUBSTANTIAL WITH GOD THE FATHER: THAT IS, THAT HE WAS NOT OF ANY CREATED OR MUTABLE ESSENCE, BUT OF ALTOGETHER THE SAME DIVINE AND UNCHANGEABLE NATURE WITH HIS FATHER, AND, THEREFORE, VERY GOD OF VERY GOD.

CORD TAUGHT THAT THE DIVINE NATURE AND PERFECTIONS BELONG TO THE FATHER AND THE SON, NOT COLLATERALLY OR CO-ORDINATELY, BUT SUBORDINATELY; THAT IS TO SAY, THAT THE SON HAS INDEED THE SAME DIVINE NATURE IN COMMON WITH THE FATHER, BUT COMMUNICATED BY THE FATHER; IN SUCH SENSE, THAT IS, THAT THE FATHER ALONE HATH THE DIVINE NATURE FROM HIMSELF, IN OTHER WORDS, FROM NO OTHER, BUT THE SON FROM THE FATHER; CONSEQUENTLY THAT THE FATHER IS THE FOUNTAIN, ORIGIN, AND PRINCIPLE OF THE DIVINITY WHICH IS IN THE SON.

THE SECOND PROPOSITION.

THE CATHOLIC DOCTORS, BOTH THOSE WHO PRECEDED, AND THOSE WHO LIVED AFTER, THE COUNCIL OF NICE, WITH UNANIMOUS CONSENT DETERMINED THAT GOD THE FATHER, EVEN IN RESPECT OF HIS DIVINITY, IS GREATER THAN THE SON; THAT IS TO SAY, NOT IN NATURE INDEED, OR IN ANY ESSENTIAL PERFECTION, SO THAT IT SHOULD BE IN THE FATHER, AND NOT IN THE SON; BUT IN AUTHORSHIP ALONE, THAT IS TO SAY, IN ORIGIN; FORASMUCH AS THE SON IS FROM THE FATHER, NOT THE FATHER FROM THE SON.

THE THIRD PROPOSITION.

THIS DOCTRINE RESPECTING THE SUBORDINATION OF THE SON TO THE FATHER AS TO HIS ORIGIN AND PRINCIPLE, WAS REGARDED BY THE ANCIENT DOCTORS AS VERY USEFUL AND ABSOLUTELY NECESSARY TO BE KNOWN AND BELIEVED, FOR THIS REASON, THAT BY MEANS OF IT ESPECIALLY THE DIVINITY OF THE SON IS SO ASSERTED, AS THAT THE UNITY OF GOD AND THE DIVINE MONARCHY, IS NEVERTHELESS PRESERVED UNIMPAIRED. FOR ALTHOUGH THE NAME AND THE NATURE BE COMMON TO THE TWO, NAMELY THE FATHER AND THE SON OF GOD, STILL, INASMUCH AS THE ONE IS THE PRINCIPLE OF THE OTHER, FROM WHICH HE IS PROPAGATED, AND THAT BY AN INTERNAL, NOT AN EXTERNAL, PRODUCTION, IT FOLLOWS THAT GOD IS RIGHTLY SAID TO BE ONLY ONE. THIS REASON THOSE ANCIENTS BELIEVED TO BE EQUALLY APPLICABLE TO THE DIVINITY OF THE HOLY GHOST.

CONTENTS

OF THE

CHAPTERS OF EACH BOOK.

INTRODUCTION.

BOOK I.

ON THE PRE-EXISTENCE OF THE SON BEFORE [HIS INCARNATION OF] THE BLESSED VIRGIN MARY, NAY RATHER BEFORE THE FOUNDATION OF THE WORLD, AND ON THE CREATION OF THE UNIVERSE THROUGH HIM.

CHAPTER I.

CHAPTER II.

BOOK II.

ON THE CONSUBSTANTIALITY OF THE SON.

CHAPTER I.

CHAPTER II.

CHAPTER III.

CHAPTER IV.

CHAPTER V.

CHAPTER VI.

CHAPTER VII.

CHAPTER VIII.

CHAPTER IX.

CHAPTER X.

CHAPTER XI.

CHAPTER XII.

CHAPTER XIII.

CHAPTER XIV.

A

DEFENCE

OF THE

NICENE CREED, &c.

INTRODUCTION.

IN WHICH THE OCCASION, DESIGN, AND ARRANGEMENT OF THE ENTIRE WORK ARE SET FORTH.

1. THE first Œcumenical Council, which was held at Nice[a], has ever been regarded by all Catholics as of the highest authority and esteem, and indeed deservedly so. For never, since the death of the Apostles, has the Christian world beheld a synod with higher claims to be considered universal and free, or an assembly of bishops and prelates more august and holy. "For at that council," as Eusebius says[b], "there were assembled out of all the Churches, which had filled the whole of Europe, Asia, and Africa, the very choicest[1] from amongst the ministers of God: and one sacred building, expanded as it were by the divine command, embraced at once within its compass both Syrians and Cilicians, Phœnicians and Arabians, and Christians of Palestine; Egyptians too, Thebans and Libyans, and some who came out of Mesopotamia. A bishop also from Persia was present at the council, and even Scythia was not wanting to that company. Pontus also and Galatia, Pamphylia and Cap-

[1] τὰ ἀκροθίνια.

[a] A.D. 325. Cave, Hist. Lit. Sec. Arian.—BOWYER.

[b] [Bp. Bull only gave the Latin of this extract; and the translation has been made according to that Latin; but it is thought best to add the Greek original. *τῶν γοῦν ἐκκλησιῶν ἁπασῶν, αἳ τὴν Εὐρώπην ἅπασαν, Λιβύην τε καὶ τὴν Ἀσίαν ἐπλήρουν, ὁμοῦ συνῆκτο τῶν τοῦ Θεοῦ λειτουργῶν τὰ ἀκροθίνια· εἷς τὲ οἶκος εὐκτήριος, ὥσπερ ἐκ Θευῦ πλατυνόμενος ἔνδον ἐχώρει κατὰ τὸ αὐτὸ Σύρους ἅμα καὶ Κίλικας, Φοίνικάς τε καὶ Ἀραβίους καὶ Παλαιστινοὺς καὶ ἐπὶ τούτοις Αἰγυπτίους, Θηβαίους, Λίβυας, τούς τ' ἐκ μέσης τῶν ποταμῶν ὁρμωμένους· ἤδη δὲ καὶ Πέρσης ἐπίσκοπος τῇ συνόδῳ παρῆν· οὐδὲ Σκύθης ἀπελιμπάνετο τῆς χορείας· Πόντος τε καὶ Γαλατία καὶ Παμφυλία, Καππαδοκία τε καὶ Ἀσία καὶ*

INTROD. padocia, with Asia and Phrygia, contributed the choicest

[2] of their prelates. Moreover Thracians, Macedonians, Achaians and Epirotes, and inhabitants of still more remote districts, were, notwithstanding their distance, present. Even from Spain itself, that most celebrated man, [Hosius,] took his seat along with the rest. The prelate of the imperial city[c]" (of Rome, that is,) "was indeed absent on account of his advanced age, but presbyters of his were present to supply his place. Constantine is the only emperor from the beginning of the world, who, by convening this vast assembly, an image, as it were, of the company of the Apostles, presented to Christ his Saviour a garland such as this, twined and knit together by the bond of peace, as a sacred memorial of his gratitude for the victories which he had gained over his foreign and domestic enemies.... In this company more than two hundred and fifty bishops were present[d]," (Athanasius, Hilary, Jerome, Rufinus, Socrates, and many others, assert that three hundred and eighteen bishops sat in this council,) "whilst the number of the presbyters who accompanied them, with the deacons, acolytes, and crowds of others, can scarcely be computed. Moreover of these ministers of God some were eminent for their wisdom and eloquence, others for their gravity of life and patient endurance of hardships, whilst others again were adorned with modesty and gentleness of demeanour. Some also among them were held in the highest honour from their advanced age; others were young and vigorous in body and mind," &c.

2. The subject treated of in this council concerned the

Φρυγία τοὺς παρ' αὐταῖς παρεῖχον ἐκκρίτους. ἀλλὰ καὶ Θρᾶκες καὶ Μακεδόνες Ἀχαιοί τε καὶ Ἡπειρῶται τούτων θ' οἱ ἔτι πορρωτάτω οἰκοῦντες ἀπήντων. αὐτῶν τε Σπάνων ὁ πάνυ βοώμενος εἷς ἦν τοῖς πολλοῖς ἅμα συνεδρεύων· τῆς δέ γε βασιλευούσης πόλεως, ὁ μὲν προεστὼς ὑστέρει διὰ γῆρας· πρεσβύτεροι δὲ αὐτοῦ παρόντες τὴν αὐτοῦ τάξιν ἐπλήρουν. τοιοῦτον μόνος ἐξ αἰῶνος εἷς βασιλεὺς Κωνσταντῖνος Χριστῷ στέφανον δεσμῷ συνάψας εἰρήνης, τῷ αὐτοῦ Σωτῆρι τῆς κατ' ἐχθρῶν καὶ πολεμίων νίκης θεοπρεπὲς ἀνετίθει χαριστήριον· εἰκόνα χορείας ἀποστολικῆς ταύτην καθ' ἡμᾶς συστησάμενος. . . . . ἐπὶ δὲ τῆς παρούσης χορείας, ἐπισκόπων μὲν πληθὺς ἦν, πεντήκοντα καὶ διακοσίων ἀριθμὸν ὑπερακοντίζουσα· ἑπομένων δὲ τούτοις πρεσβυτέρων καὶ διακόνων ἀκολούθων τε πλείστων ὅσων ἑτέρων, οὐδ' ἦν ἀριθμὸς εἰς κατάληψιν. τῶν δὲ τοῦ θεοῦ λειτουργῶν οἱ μὲν διέπρεπον σοφίας λόγῳ· οἱ δὲ βίου στερρότητι καὶ καρτερίας ὑπομονῇ· οἱ δὲ τῷ μέσῳ τρόπῳ κατεκοσμοῦντο. ἦσαν δὲ τούτων οἱ μὲν χρόνου μήκει τετιμημένοι· οἱ δὲ νεότητι καὶ ψυχῆς ἀκμῇ διαλάμποντες.—Vit. Const. iii. 7—9. [pp. 579—581.]

[c] See Valesius's notes on the passage.

[d] Ibid.

chief doctrine[1] of the Christian religion, namely, the dignity
of the Person of Jesus Christ our Saviour; whether He is to
be worshipped as true God, or to be reduced to the rank and
condition of creatures and of things subject to the true God. [3]
If we imagine that in this question of the very utmost
moment the whole of the rulers of the Church altogether
erred, and persuaded the Christian people to embrace their
error, how will the promise of Christ our Lord hold good, 2
who engaged to be present, even to the end of the world,
with the Apostles, and consequently with their successors?
For, since the promise extends to the end of the world[e], and
yet the Apostles were not to continue alive so long, Christ
must most certainly be regarded as addressing, in the persons of the Apostles, their successors also in that office.

3. I cannot but feel indignation, nay even a degree of horror, so often as I reflect on these things, and consider the amazing ignorance, or rather the impious madness of those writers who have not shrunk from openly raving against the venerable fathers, as if they had, with settled evil purpose[2], or, at all events, through ignorance and rashness, corrupted the catholic doctrine respecting the Person of Jesus Christ, which had been taught by the Apostles and preserved in the Church during the first three centuries, and had obtruded a new faith on the Christian world. Not to mention the early Arians, the most notorious enemies and calumniators of the Nicene Creed,—it was on this account that Sabinus was infamous in former times, a follower of the faction of Macedonius, whose rash and shameless judgment concerning the Nicene council is mentioned and refuted by Socrates[f]. That excellent Church historian, after saying that he had related the history of the Nicene council, in order that, if any persons should be disposed to condemn that council as having fallen into error in a matter of the faith, we should give them no heed at all, subjoins these words[g]; "Let us not believe Sabinus, the follower of Macedonius, who calls those who assembled in that council
unlearned and simple men. For this Sabinus, bishop of the [4]

[1] capite.

[2] malitia.

[e] Matt. xxviii. 20.—Bowyer.

[f] Eccl. Hist., i. 8.

[g] [The translation is based on the Latin, which alone was given by Bp. Bull: the Greek is; *μηδὲ πιστεύσωμεν Σαβίνῳ τῷ Μακεδονιανῷ ἰδιώτας αὐτοὺς καὶ ἀφελεῖς καλοῦντι τοὺς ἐκεῖσε συν-ελθόντας. Σαβῖνος γὰρ ὁ τῶν ἐν Ἡρα-*

INTROD.

[1] synodorum acta.

[2] ἰδιώτην.

Macedonians at Heraclea, a city of Thrace, who collected into one work the acts of different synods[1], treated with derision the prelates of the council of Nice as unlearned and simple men, and perceives not that he is herein charging as unlearned[2] even Eusebius himself, who after a long and searching enquiry embraced that Creed. There are some things which he has purposely passed over, and others which he has perverted and altered, but still he has drawn all to his own purpose and views: and yet he praises Eusebius Pamphili[h] as a most trust-worthy witness, and also bestows encomiums on the emperor himself, as one who was exceedingly well acquainted with the doctrines of the Christian faith; at the same time he finds fault with the Creed, which was set forth at Nice, as if it were compiled by ignorant and unlearned men; and thus does he knowingly despise and neglect the express declaration of an author whom he acknowledges to be a wise man and a truthful witness; for Eusebius declares, that of the ministers of God who were present at the Nicene synod, some were eminent for their eloquence and wisdom, others for the firmness and fortitude of their life; and that the emperor himself, who was present, by leading all to concord, made them to be of one mind and of one consent." At the same time, however, Socrates[i], in the ninth chapter of the same book, censures Sabinus, because he did not also reflect, "that, even if the members of that council were unlearned men, and yet were illuminated by God and by the grace of the Holy Ghost, they could by no means have erred from the truth." For Socrates seems to have thought that the illuminating grace of the Holy Ghost is always present with a council of bishops truly uni-

κλείᾳ τῆς Θρᾴκης Μακεδονιανῶν ἐπίσκοπος συναγωγὴν, ὧν διάφοροι ἐπισκόπων σύνοδοι ἐγγράφως ἐξέδωκαν ποιησάμενος, τοὺς μὲν ἐν Νικαίᾳ ὡς ἀφελεῖς καὶ ἰδιώτας διέσυρε, μὴ αἰσθανόμενος, ὅτι καὶ αὐτὸν Εὐσέβιον, τὸν μετὰ πολλῆς δοκιμασίας τὴν πίστιν ὁμολογήσαντα ὡς ἰδιώτην διαβάλλει. καὶ τινὰ μὲν ἑκὼν παρέλιπεν· τινὰ δὲ παρέτρεψε. πάντα δὲ πρὸς τὸν οἰκεῖον σκοπὸν μᾶλλον ἐξείληφεν. καὶ ἐπαινεῖ μὲν τὸν Παμφίλου Εὐσέβιον ὡς ἀξιόπιστον μάρτυρα· ἐπαινεῖ δὲ καὶ τὸν βασιλέα ὡς τὰ Χριστιανῶν δογματίζειν δυνάμενον· μέμφεται δὲ τῇ ἐκτεθείσῃ ἐν Νικαίᾳ πίστει ὡς ὑπὸ ἰδιωτῶν καὶ οὐδὲν ἐπισταμένων ἐκδεδομένῃ· καὶ ὃν ὡς σοφὸν καὶ ἀψευδῆ καλεῖ μάρτυρα, τούτου τὰς φωνὰς ἑκουσίως ὑπερορᾷ· φησὶ γὰρ ὁ Εὐσέβιος, ὅτι τῶν παρόντων ἐν τῇ Νικαίᾳ τοῦ Θεοῦ λειτουργῶν οἱ μὲν, διέπρεπον σοφίας λόγῳ· οἱ δὲ βίου στερρότητι· καὶ ὅτι ὁ βασιλεὺς παρὼν πάντας εἰς ὁμόνοιαν ἄγων, ὁμογνώμονας καὶ ὁμοδόξους κατέστησεν.—p. 21.]

[h] [The friend of Pamphilus.]

[i] ὡς εἰ καὶ ἰδιῶται ἦσαν οἱ τῆς συνόδου, κατελάμποντο δὲ ὑπὸ τοῦ Θεοῦ καὶ τῆς χάριτος τοῦ ἁγίου πνεύματος, οὐδαμῶς ἀστοχῆσαι τῆς ἀληθείας ἐδύναντο.—Ibid., p. 31.

versal, to keep them free from error, at least in the necessary articles of the faith. And if any one is unwilling to admit this supposition, the argument of Socrates may still be stated and presented to him thus; suppose the Nicene fathers to have been unlearned and unlettered men, still they certainly were for the most part men of piety; and it is incredible that so many holy and approved men, meeting together out of all parts of the Christian world, could possibly have dishonestly conspired for the purpose of making an innovation on the received faith of the Church, respecting the primary article of Christianity; especially as, whatever may have been their lack of learning in other respects, they could not have been ignorant of the elementary doctrine of the most holy Trinity, which was wont to be taught even to catechumens, nor of what they themselves had received from their fathers concerning that subject.

§ 3, 4.

[5]

4. But to come to more modern writers; within the memory of our fathers, Faustus Socinus of Siena, in his second letter to Radecius[k], asserts, that the knowledge of the true doctrine concerning God, namely, that the Father alone is very God, continued down to the time of the council of Nice. "This knowledge[l]," he says, "without any controversy ceased not to exist even until the period of the council of Nice, and for some time afterwards, among those who professed the name of Christ. For throughout the whole of that period, as is clear from the writings of all who then lived, the Father of Jesus Christ alone was believed to be that one true God, of whom the Holy Scriptures every where make mention." In this passage, when he says, that this was the belief of all the ancients down to the council of Nice, "that the Father of Jesus Christ alone is the one true God," if it be understood of that special prerogative of the Father, by which He alone is of Himself[1] very God, then we acknowledge it to be most true. But this does not make any thing in favour of Socinus; and it is certain that the knowledge of this doctrine not only "continued until the time of the council of Nice, or some time after," but has ever continued in the Church of Christ. But if, on the

[1] ipse solus a seipso.

[6]

k [Opera, ed. 1656. vol. i. p. 375.]

l [The knowledge of the Father, as "the only true God, and Jesus Christ whom He had sent," S. John xvii. 3, according to the Socinian interpretation.]

 other hand, this proposition, "The Father of Jesus Christ alone is the one true God," be taken altogether exclusively, so as to take away from Christ His true divinity, and to deny what was defined by the Nicene council, namely, that the Son is very God of very God, (and it is but too evident
3 that this was what Socinus meant,) then we contend that it is manifestly false, that "all the ancients, down to the council of Nice, did so believe;" nay, we shall shew that they all taught that the Son is of the same nature with the Father, and therefore is very God, equally with the Father. Accordingly even Socinus himself in another place, i.e. in his third letter to this same Matthew Radecius[m], (contradicting himself, as he is apt to do,) confesses, "that almost from the very earliest period of the existence of the Church[1], even to our own times, so many men most distinguished for piety no less than for learning, so many most holy martyrs of Christ, as to be past numbering, have followed that error, in other respects most serious, that Christ is the one true God, who created all things, or, at least, was begotten of His proper substance." But surely, that the Son of God was begotten of the proper substance of God, and is, therefore, very God of very God, is the sum and substance of the doctrine, which the Nicene fathers asserted against Arius.

[1] initio nascentis ecclesiæ.

5. M. Simon Episcopius, a most learned theologian in all other respects, but an utter stranger to ecclesiastical antiquity, although he held different views from those of Socinus, and even publicly maintained, in opposition to him, the preexistence of the Son, not only before [His birth of] the blessed Virgin, but also before the creation of the world, still has spoken in his works in a way altogether shameful and intolerable concerning the Creed authoritatively put forth by the Nicene fathers. For he inveighs (whether with greater want of learning or of modesty is not easy to say) against
[7] the Nicene Creed, and those, framed and composed after the third century, which agreed with it; "As regards the other Creeds" (he says[n]) "which followed after, which were framed at so-called general councils, as they are of more recent date, they are not worthy to be compared with these"—

[m] Ibid., p. 391.

[n] Institutiones Theologicæ, iv. 34. [sect. 2.]

§ 4, 5.

that is, with the creeds and confessions of faith, by which, as by marks and watch-words, Christians and Catholics, during the first three centuries, used to be distinguished from unbelievers and heretics—"And if the truth must be spoken, they ought to be regarded as precipitately framed from excitement, if not fury, and a maddened and unblessed[1] party spirit, on the part of bishops who were wrangling and contending with one another with excessive rivalry, rather than as what issued from composed minds." And that you may understand that the Nicene Creed, especially, is glanced at by him in this passage, he presently adds, "Who does not know, what keen contests, and obstinate bickerings, were raised amongst the bishops at the Nicene council?" Nay, rather I would say, who is there that does not perceive that all this issues from a mind far from sound or composed? Was it so clearly the part of a sober and moderate man, to tear and rend with revilings the venerable prelates of that most august council? But to proceed to the matter itself. He is not ashamed to say that the Nicene Creed was "precipitately framed by the bishops out of fury and maddened and unblest party spirit." Yet Constantine the emperor, who himself presided as moderator in the Nicene council, expressly testifies of it, in his Epistle to the Churches, that in his presence[o] "every point had there received due examination." Again, in the letter which he specially addressed [8]
to the Church of Alexandria, he says, that being present amongst the bishops assembled at Nice, as though he were one of their number, and their fellow-servant, he had undertaken the investigation of the truth, in such a way, as that[p] "all points, which appeared to raise a plea either of ambiguity[2]," (for it is clear that this is the true reading from the same clause being soon after repeated by Socrates,) "or difference of opinion, were tested and accurately examined." On this letter of Constantine, Socrates makes these observations[q]; "This account the emperor wrote to the people of

[1] malefe-riato.

[2] ἀμφιβο-λίας.

[o] ἅπαντα τῆς προσηκούσης τετύχηκεν ἐξετάσεως.—Euseb. de Vita Constant. iii. 17.

[p] ἠλέγχθη ἅπαντα, καὶ ἀκριβῶς ἐξήτασται, ὅσα ἢ ἀμφιβολίαν, [Bull read ἀμφιβολίας, as Socrates has it in commenting on the letter, p. 31,] ἢ διχονοίας πρόφασιν ἐδόκει γεννᾷν.—Socrat. Eccl. Hist. i. 9. p. 30. ed. Vales.

[q] ὁ μὲν δὴ βασιλεὺς τοιαῦτα ἔγραφε τῷ Ἀλεξανδρέων δήμῳ, μηνύων ὅτι οὐχ' ἁπλῶς, οὐδὲ ὡς ἔτυχε γέγονεν ὁ ὅρος τῆς

Alexandria, to inform them that the definition of the faith had not been made lightly[1] or carelessly, but that they had put it forth after much discussion and strict testing; and it was not the case that some points had been mentioned at the council, whilst others had been passed over in silence, but that all things, which were meet to be alleged for establishment of the doctrine[2], had been mooted, and that the matter had not been hastily[3] defined, but had been first discussed with exact accuracy." Nay, Eusebius himself, an author of the utmost integrity, and of temperate disposition, and not unfair towards the Arian party, and who seems to have had the chief place next to the emperor in the Nicene council[r], expressly states, that all the bishops subscribed with unanimous agreement to the creed drawn up in that council, *οὐκ ἀνεξεταστῶς*, "not without examination," not hastily and inconsiderately, but after an exact, deliberate, and careful in-
[9] vestigation, in presence of the emperor, of each separate proposition, (and, as he specifies by name, of the clause relating to the homoousion, "of one substance.") See Eusebius' letter to his own diocese, in Socrates, Eccles. Hist. i. 8. [pp. 22, 23.] At the opening of the council, indeed, there were considerable disputes among some of the bishops, but, as Eusebius also informs us, they were soon and easily settled and lulled by the pious and mild address of the emperor.

[1] ἁπλῶς.
[2] πρὸς σύστασιν τοῦ δόγματος.
[3] ἁπλῶς.

6. The anonymous author[s] of a book published some time ago under the title of 'Irenicum Irenicorum,' &c., boldly proclaims, that the Nicene fathers "were the framers of a new faith;" and this he labours to prove, throughout his work,
4 by heaping together such testimonies, out of the remains of the ante-Nicene fathers, as have the appearance of being inconsistent with the Nicene Creed. This book is said by Stephen Curcellæus[t] to contain "irrefragable testimonies and arguments." The like web has been woven over again, very lately, by Christopher Sandius, in what he calls his 'Kernel[4] of Ecclesiastical History,' now in the second edi-

[4] Nucleus Eccl. Hist.

πίστεως· ἀλλ' ὅτι μετὰ πολλῆς συζητήσεως καὶ δοκιμασίας αὐτὸν ὑπηγόρευσαν· καὶ οὐχ' ὅτι τινὰ μὲν ἐλέχθη, τινὰ δὲ ἀπεσιγήθη, ἀλλ' ὅτι ὅσα πρὸς σύστασιν τοῦ δόγματος λεχθῆναι ἥρμοζε, πάντα ἐκινήθη· καὶ ὅτι οὐχ' ἁπλῶς ὡρίσθη, ἀλλ' ἀκριβῶς ἐξητάσθη πρότερον.—Ib., p. 31.

[r] Vid. not. Vales. ad Euseb. iii. de Vita Const., c. 11.

[s] Page 84. [Daniel Zuicker. See the Introduction to the Primitive and Apostolical Tradition, § 2.—B.]

[t] Quat. Dissert. Theol. Dissert. i. 118. in fine.

tion, and enriched by a very copious addition of fables and contradictions. In this book, the shameless author is entirely bent upon persuading such readers as are unlearned, and have very little acquaintance with the writings of the ancients, that the ante-Nicene fathers, without exception, simply held the same doctrine as Arius. §5—7.

7. There is, however, one great man fully furnished with learning of every kind, Dionysius Petavius, at whom I cannot sufficiently wonder; for, whilst he professes the utmost reverence for the Nicene council, and on all occasions declares that he receives the faith therein affirmed against the Arians, as truly catholic and apostolic, still he freely gives up to the Arians, that which (if true) would very greatly tend to [10] confirm their heresy, and to disparage, nay, rather, utterly to overthrow, the credit and authority of the council of Nice; I mean, that almost all the bishops and fathers before the council of Nice held precisely the same opinions as Arius. For thus he writes, (Of the Trinity, i. 5. 7.) "Accordingly there was this settled opinion in the minds of some of the ancients, touching the Godhead and the diversity of Persons in It, viz., that there is One supreme, unbegotten, and invisible God, who put forth, without, from Himself, as vocal and sounding, that Logos[u], that is, that Word, which He had laid up within (*ἐνδιάθετον*), yet not, like a voice or sound, passing away and capable of being dissipated, but of such sort, as that, as though embodied and subsisting, It might in turn afterwards create all other things. Moreover, they said, that the Word was put forth by the Supreme God and Father at the time when He determined on creating this universe, in order that He might use Him as His assisting Minister. This opinion some intimate more clearly, others more obscurely. But these may be specially mentioned[1]; Athenagoras, Tatian, Theophilus, Tertullian, and Lactantius. Both these authors, however, and the rest[x], whom

[1] sed isti fere.

[u] [Qui λόγον, id est, *Verbum*, vel *Sermonem*, quem ἐνδιάθετον, *intus inclusum* tenebat, ex sese foras produxerit, vocalem et sonantem.—Petav. de Trin. i. 5. 7.]

[x] [Instead of the words, *reliqui, quos commemoravi*, "the rest, whom I have mentioned," Petavius, at the end of the volume, substituted *aliqui alii, ut Origenes*, "some others, as Origen." And the passage thus amended is cited by Bp. Bull, iii. 4. 10.—B. It is so amended in the later editions of Petavius. Bp. Bull, however, in the passage referred to, cites only part of Petavius' correction. See iii. 4. 10. and Dr. Burton's note on it.]

INTROD. I have mentioned," (and which of the primitive fathers had he not before mentioned?) "thought that the Father was superior to the Word, in age, dignity, and power; and, although they asserted, that the Son was of the substance or nature of the Father, (in which point alone they made His mode of existence[1] to differ from that of all other beings, which are properly called creatures;) still they conceived that He had a beginning no less than the creatures; in other words, that He had by no means been a distinct Person[2] from eternity." But in the second section of the eighth chapter of the same book he speaks still more plainly. "It is most clear," he says, "that
[11] Arius was a genuine Platonist, and that he followed the opinions of those ancient writers, who, while as yet the point had not been developed and settled[3], had fallen into the same error. For they also taught that the Word was produced by God the Father, yet not from eternity, but before He formed the world, in order that He might use Him as His assisting Minister for the accomplishment of that work. For they conceived that He had not created all things by Himself, and without the intervention of any one[4]; a doctrine which Philo also followed in his book on the Creator of the World. And therefore I take it to have been in a rhetorical and exaggerated way of expression, that Alexander, in his epistle, and others of the fathers, who wrote against this heresy, complained that Arius had been the author of that opinion[5], the like to which had been unheard of before his time; inasmuch as we have brought forward a great number of early writers who previously taught the same doctrine as Arius."

[1] conditionem.
[2] hypostasim.
[3] nondum patefacta constitutaque re.
[4] sine interjecto aliquo.
[5] architectum dogmatis.

8. If, therefore, reliance is to be placed on Petavius, we shall have to lay down, first, that the heresy of Arius, which was condemned by the Nicene fathers, agreed, in the most important point, with the commonly received view of the ancient Catholic doctors, who preceded him; secondly, that the doctrine concerning the true divinity of the Son was not settled and developed[6] before the council of Nice; thirdly, that Alexander, and the other Catholics, who accused Arius, as the author of a doctrine which was new and unheard of previously in the Catholic Church, said this in a rhetorical and an exaggerated way; that is to say, (if the thing is to be

[6] constitutum et patefactum.

more plainly stated,) that they uttered a notable falsehood, § 7, 8.
I suppose in the Jesuit fashion, to subserve the Catholic cause. Unlucky Arius! that Petavius was not yet born, to become the patron and advocate of his cause in the conflict at Nicæa. It is not, however, easy to say, what Petavius had in view when he wrote thus. Some suspect [12]
that in his heart he cherished the Arian heresy himself, and wished craftily to pass on the cup to others. This was the opinion of Sandius[y], whom I have just before mentioned, who thus remarks of Petavius; "But when I recollect that Petavius asserts, that the ante-Nicene fathers taught the same doctrines as Arius, and, also, that the articles of the faith are to be proved by traditions, I think it impossible but that Petavius must have been persuaded of the truth of the conclusion, which infallibly follows from these premises, namely, that the Trinity which the Arians hold, and not the consubstantial Trinity[1], is an article of the faith. And as to his wresting the argument to a contrary conclusion, I presume he did this with a twofold view; 1. To escape the inconveniences[2] which commonly fall on those who secede from the Roman Catholic to the Arian party; 2. That the Arians might be able to derive a stronger proof of their doctrine from a father of the Society of Jesus, as from an adversary; especially since it is sufficient to prove premises, from which any person of sound mind can draw such a conclusion, as will make it plain what his opinion is about the Trinity." These are the words of Sandius; in my opinion, however, it is most clear from the writings of Petavius himself, that the conjecture of this most vain writer is entirely false. If indeed 5
it must be said that Petavius wrote thus with any sinister purpose, and not merely from that bold and reckless temper which is his wont in criticising and commenting on the holy fathers, I should say that, being a Jesuit, he wished to promote the papal, rather than the Arian, interest. For, from the fact (for which Petavius contends) that almost all the Catholic doctors of the first three centuries fell into the selfsame error which the Nicene council afterwards condemned as heresy in the case of Arius, these two things will easily follow; 1. That little authority is to be assigned to the

[1] Trinitatem ὁμοούσιον.

[2] adversa.

[y] Sandius' Nucl. Hist. Eccl. i. p. 156. last edition [1676.]

INTROD. fathers of the first three centuries,—to whom Reformed
[13] Catholics are wont to make their chief appeal,—as being persons to whom the principal articles of the Christian faith were not as yet sufficiently understood and developed[1]; 2. That œcumenical councils have the power of framing[2], or, as Petavius says, of settling and developing[3] new articles of faith; by which principle it may seem that sufficient provision is made for those additions, which the fathers of Trent patched on to the rule of faith, and thrust upon the Christian world; though not even in this way will the Roman faith stand good; since the assembly at Trent is to be called any thing rather than a general council.

[1] satis perspecta et patefacta.
[2] condendi.
[3] constituendi et patefaciendi.

But so it is: the masters of that school have no scruples in building their pseudo-catholic faith on the ruins of the faith which is truly catholic. The divine oracles themselves, must, forsooth, be found guilty of too great obscurity, and the most holy doctors, bishops, and martyrs of the primitive Church be accused of heresy, in order that, by whatever means, the faith and authority of the degenerate Roman Church may be kept safe and sound. And yet these sophists (of all things) execrate us as if we were so many accursed Hams, and deriders and despisers of the venerable fathers of the Church; whilst they continually boast that they themselves religiously follow the faith of the ancient doctors, and reverence their writings to the utmost. That Petavius, however, wrote those passages with this wicked design, I would not venture to affirm for certain, leaving it to the judgment of that God who knoweth the hearts. At the same time, what the Jesuit has written, as it is most pleasing to modern Arians, (who on this account with one consent look up to and salute him as their patron,) so we confidently pronounce it to be manifestly repugnant to the truth, and most unjust and insulting to the holy fathers, whether those of the council of Nice, or those who preceded it.

9. For this is the plan of the work which I have undertaken, —to shew clearly that what the Nicene fathers laid down
[14] concerning the divinity of the Son, in opposition to Arius and other heretics, was in substance (although sometimes perhaps in other words and in a different mode of expression) taught by all the approved fathers and doctors of the Church, without a single exception, who flourished before the

period of the council of Nice down from the very age of the Apostles. § 8—10.

And, O most holy Jesus, the co-eternal Word of the eternal Father, I, the chief of sinners, and the least of Thy servants, do humbly beseech Thee that Thou wouldest vouchsafe to bless this labour of mine, undertaken (as Thou, O searcher of hearts, dost know) for Thine honour and the good of Thy holy Church; and to succour and help mine infirmity in this most weighty work, for Thine infinite mercy and most ready favour towards them that love Thee. Amen!

10. The Nicene Creed, as it is quoted by Eusebius[z] in his epistle to his own diocese of Cæsarea, by Athanasius in his letter to Jovian[a] *De Fide*, and by other writers, is as follows:

Πιστεύομεν εἰς ἕνα Θεὸν Πατέρα, παντοκράτορα, πάντων ὁρατῶν τε καὶ ἀοράτων ποιητήν· καὶ εἰς τὸν ἕνα Κύριον Ἰησοῦν Χριστὸν, τὸν υἱὸν τοῦ Θεοῦ, γεννηθέντα ἐκ τοῦ Πατρὸς μονογενῆ, τουτέστιν ἐκ τῆς οὐσίας τοῦ Πατρός· Θεὸν ἐκ Θεοῦ, φῶς ἐκ φωτὸς, Θεὸν ἀληθινὸν ἐκ Θεοῦ ἀληθινοῦ, γεννηθέντα οὐ ποιηθέντα, ὁμοούσιον τῷ Πατρὶ, δι' οὗ τὰ πάντα ἐγένετο, τά τε ἐν τῷ οὐρανῷ, καὶ τὰ ἐπὶ τῆς γῆς· τὸν δι' ἡμᾶς τοὺς ἀνθρώπους καὶ διὰ τὴν ἡμετέραν σωτηρίαν κατελθόντα, καὶ σαρκωθέντα, ἐνανθρωπήσαντα, παθόντα, καὶ ἀναστάντα τῇ τρίτῃ ἡμέρᾳ, καὶ ἀνελθόντα εἰς τοὺς οὐρανοὺς, ἐρχόμενον κρῖναι ζῶντας καὶ νεκρούς· καὶ εἰς τὸ Πνεῦμα τὸ Ἅγιον. Τοὺς δὲ λέγοντας, Ἦν ποτε, ὅτε οὐκ ἦν, καὶ πρὶν γεννηθῆναι, οὐκ ἦν, καὶ ὅτι ἐξ οὐκ ὄντων ἐγένετο, ἢ ἐξ ἑτέρας ὑποστάσεως ἢ οὐσίας φάσκοντας εἶναι, ἢ κτιστὸν, ἢ τρεπτὸν, ἢ ἀλλοιωτὸν [15] *τὸν υἱὸν τοῦ Θεοῦ, τούτους ἀναθεματίζει ἡ καθολικὴ καὶ ἀποστολικὴ ἐκκλησία·* i. e., "We believe in one God the Father, Almighty, Maker of all things visible and invisible. And in one Lord Jesus Christ, the Son of God, begotten of the Father, only-begotten, that is, of the substance of the Father; God of God, Light of Light, very God of very God, begotten not made, of one substance with the Father, by whom all things were made, both which are in heaven and which are on earth; who, for us men and for our salvation, came down, and was incarnate, and was made Man, and suffered, and rose again the third day, and ascended into

[z] Socrates Eccles. Hist. i. 8. pp. [21, 22.]

[a] [§ 3. vol. i. p. 781. Bp. Bull follows Athanasius.—B.]

the heavens, who cometh to judge the quick and the dead. And in the Holy Ghost. But as for those who say, There
6 was a time when He was not; and, Before He was begotten He was not, and, He was made out of what existed not; or who assert that the Son of God is of another hypostasis or essence, or that He was created, or is capable of change or alteration, them the Catholic and Apostolic Church doth anathematize."

11. The doctrine respecting the Son of God, contained in this Creed, so far as it concerns our present design, may be reduced to these heads.

The First; concerning the *προύπαρξις*, or Pre-existence, of the Son of God, before [His Incarnation of] the blessed Virgin Mary, nay, rather, before the foundation of the world; and concerning the creation of the universe through the Son.

The Second; concerning the *ὁμοούσιον* ("of one substance") or Consubstantiality, of the Son; that He is not of any such essence as is created or subject to change; but of a nature altogether the same with His Father, that is, that He is very God.

The Third; concerning the *συναΐδιον*, the Co-eternity of the Son; that is, His existence co-eternal with His Father.

The Fourth; concerning the subordination of the Son to the Father, as to Him who is His author and principle[1], which is expressed by the Nicene fathers in two ways, in that, first, they call the Father "One God;" and then, in that they say
[16] that the Son is "God of God, Light of Light," &c.

On all these points we shall make it manifest, that the faith of the ante-Nicene fathers is quite in harmony with the Nicene Creed; going through each particular in the order in which we have just proposed them.

[1] sui auctorem ac principium.

BOOK I.

ON THE PRE-EXISTENCE OF THE SON OF GOD; BEFORE [HIS INCARNATION OF] THE BLESSED VIRGIN MARY, NAY RATHER, BEFORE THE FOUNDATION OF THE WORLD; AND ON THE CREATION OF THE UNIVERSE THROUGH HIM.

CHAPTER I.

THE PROPOSITION STATED; AND THE FORMER PART OF IT, NAMELY, THE PRE-EXISTENCE OF THE SON BEFORE [HIS INCARNATION] OF THE BLESSED VIRGIN MARY, DEMONSTRATED.

1. WHAT the opinion of the Catholic fathers, who preceded the council of Nice, was concerning the Pre-existence of the Son of God, we will unfold in the following

BOOK I. CHAP. I. § 1.

PROPOSITION.

The Catholic Doctors of the first three centuries all with one accord taught that Jesus Christ, that is, He who was afterwards called Jesus Christ, (before He was made man, that is, before His birth, according to the flesh, of the most blessed Virgin,) existed in another nature far surpassing the human; that He appeared to holy men, as a prelude to His Incarnation; that He always presided over and provided for that Church, which He was afterwards to redeem with His own blood; and that thus from the beginning the "whole order of the divine administration[1]" (as Tertullian expresses it[a]) "had its course through Him;" and that moreover, before the foundations of the world were laid He was present with God His Father, and that through Him this universe was created.

[1] dispositionis.

[a] [A primordio omnem ordinem divinæ dispositionis per ipsum decucurrisse. —Adv. Prax., c. 16. p. 510.]

ON THE PRE-EXISTENCE OF THE SON.

Though this was never denied by the Arians, it may still perhaps be worth while to demonstrate it briefly against other opposers of the catholic doctrine concerning our Saviour. [18] In this proposition we assert two things (in a kind of climax[1]) concerning the primitive fathers, namely, that they believed and taught, I. That Jesus Christ, before He became man, existed, appeared to holy men, &c.: II. That He was present with God the Father before the foundations of the world were laid, and that through Him this universe was created.

[1] quasi per incrementum quoddam.

2. As to the former part of the proposition, the fathers of the first centuries agree in teaching, that the Son of God frequently appeared to holy men under the Old Testament; and further they expound of the same Son of God Himself all those appearances, in which the name of Jehovah and divine honours are attributed to Him who appears, although at other times perhaps He is called an angel. One who is ignorant of this, is a stranger to the writings of the fathers. For the sake, however, of students in divinity, who perhaps have not yet advanced to the reading of the fathers, (with which certainly, next after the holy Scriptures, they ought to have commenced their theological studies,) I wish to produce here some testimonies out of the writings of those ancient authors.

3. Justin Martyr, in his Dialogue with Trypho, shews at length that it was Christ who appeared to Abraham at the oak in Mamre[b]; that He was that Lord, who received from the Lord in Heaven, *ἐκ Πατρὸς τῶν ὅλων*, that is, from the Father of all, to send down upon Sodom a shower of fire and brimstone[c]; who appeared in dreams to Jacob, wrestled with him in the form of a man, comforted him in his exile; who, lastly, appeared to Moses in the burning bush[d].

[19] 4. Irenæus held the same opinion as Justin concerning Him who appeared to Moses and Abraham: for he thus writes[e]; "He, therefore, who was worshipped by the prophets as the living God, is the God of the living, and His Word[2],

[2] Λόγος.

[b] Page 275. [56. p. 150.]

[c] Page 277. [p. 152.]

[d] Page 280—282. [58, 59. pp. 155, 156.]

[e] Qui igitur a prophetis adorabatur Deus vivus, hic est vivorum Deus, et Verbum (Λόγος) ejus, qui et locutus est Moysi, qui et Sadducæos redarguit, qui et resurrectionem donavit.—Adv. Hæres. iv. 11. ed. Paris. 1639. [c. 5. p. 232.]

who also spake unto Moses, and confuted the Sadducees, and also bestowed [the gift of] resurrection." And in the twelfth chapter of the same book, he says of Abraham; "In Abraham man had before learnt and had been accustomed to follow the Word of God. For Abraham according to his faith, following the command of the Word of God, with a ready mind yielded up his only-begotten and beloved son as a sacrifice to God[e]." And a little farther on he writes, "The Lord therefore, whose day he desired to see, was not unknown to Abraham; nor again was the Father of the Lord [unknown to him], for he had learned from the Word of the Lord and believed in Him," &c. &c.

5. Theophilus of Antioch (writing to Autolycus, book ii.[f]) asserts, that it was the Son of God who appeared to Adam shortly after the fall, and that "assuming the person of the Father and Lord of all, He came into paradise in the person of God and conversed with Adam." I confess that in this passage Theophilus seems to speak less honourably than he ought of the Son of God; but this I shall notice elsewhere[g].

6. Clement of Alexandria teaches almost the same as Justin, (*Pædag.* i. c. 7)[h]; where he asserts, that the Instructor[1] (by whom he every where means Christ) appeared to Abraham, was seen by Jacob, with whom also He wrestled, and lastly shewed Himself to Moses. He also in another place teaches, that Christ gave to the world the written law of Moses as well as the law of nature, (*Strom.* vii.)[i]; "Wherefore the Lord" (here also he means Christ, as is evident from what goes before) "gave His precepts, both the former and the latter, drawing them from one fountain, neither through neg- [20]

[1] pædagogum.

[e] In Abrahamo prædidicerat et assuetus fuerat homo sequi Verbum Dei. Etenim Abraham secundum fidem suam secutus præceptum Verbi Dei prono animo unigenitum et dilectum filium suum concessit sacrificium Deo. . . . Non incognitus igitur erat Dominus Abrahæ, cujus diem concupivit videre: sed neque Pater Domini: didicerat enim a Verbo Domini, et credidit ei, &c.—Ibid. [A few of these words are extant in the Greek, *προθύμως τὸν ἴδιον μονογενῆ καὶ ἀγαπητὸν παραχωρήσας θυσίαν τῷ Θεῷ*.—B.]

[f] *ἀναλαμβάνων τὸ πρόσωπον τοῦ Πατρὸς καὶ Κυρίου τῶν ὅλων [οὗτος] παρεγίνετο εἰς τὸν παράδεισον ἐν προσώπῳ τοῦ Θεοῦ, καὶ ὡμίλει τῷ Ἀδάμ.*—Ad calc. Justin. Martyr., ed. Paris. 1615. p. 100.

[g] [Book iii. ch. 7. sect. 1 sqq.]

[h] Edit. Paris. 1641. p. 110.

[i] *διὸ καὶ τὰς ἐντολὰς ἃς ἔδωκεν, τάς τε προτέρας τάς τε δευτέρας ἐκ μιᾶς ἀρυττόμενος πηγῆς ὁ Κύριος, οὔτε τοὺς πρὸ νόμου ἀνόμους εἶναι ὑπεριδὼν, οὔτ' αὐτοὺς* [*αὖ τοὺς* Sylburg.] *μὴ ἐπαΐοντας τὰ βαρβάρου φιλοσοφίας ἀφηνιάσαι συγχωρήσας. τοῖς μὲν γὰρ ἐντολὰς, τοῖς δὲ φιλοσοφίαν παρασχὼν, συνέκλεισεν τὴν ἀπιστίαν εἰς τὴν παρουσίαν κ. τ. λ.*—[cap. ii. p. 834.]

ON THE PRE-EXISTENCE OF THE SON.

ligence allowing those who lived before the law to be without law, nor yet permitting those who heard not the teaching of barbarian philosophy to be without restraint, for having given precepts to the one, philosophy to the other, He shut up their unbelief unto His coming."

7. In like manner Tertullian writes, (Against the Jews[j], chap. 9;) "He who used to speak to Moses, was the Son of God Himself, and it was He that at all times appeared[k]." But he speaks most openly and fully on this point in his treatise against Praxeas, chap. 16[l]; "It is," he says, "the Son who hath executed judgment from the beginning, throwing down the haughty tower, and dividing the tongues, punishing the whole world by the violence of waters, raining upon Sodom and Gomorrah fire and brimstone, 'the Lord from the Lord.' For He Himself it was, who also at all times came down to hold converse with men, from Adam on to the patriarchs and the prophets, in vision, in dream, in mirror, in dark saying; ever from the beginning laying the foundation of the course [of His dispensations[1]], which He meant to follow out unto the end. Thus was He ever learning[2], and the God who conversed with men upon earth could be no other than the Word, which was to be made flesh. But He was learning, in order to level for us the way of faith[3], that we might the more readily believe that the Son of God had come down into the world, if we knew that in times past also something similar had been done."

[1] ordinem suum præstruens.

[21]

[2] or "practising."

[3] fidem sterneret.

8. Let it suffice, as I am anxious to be brief, simply to refer to the remaining testimonies. See Origen against Celsus, iii.[m]

[j] Qui ad Mosen loquebatur, ipse erat Dei Filius, qui et semper videbatur.—Cont. Jud., p. 194.

[k] See also his book de Carne Christi, c. 6. [p. 311;] and his Treatise against Marcion. ii. 27. [p. 395;] and iii. 6. [p. 400;] and his Treatise against Prax. c. 14. [p. 507.]

[l] Filius est qui ab initio judicavit, turrim superbissimam elidens, linguasque dispertiens, orbem totum aquarum violentia puniens, pluens super Sodomam et Gomorram ignem et sulphurem, Dominus a Domino. Ipse enim et ad humana semper colloquia descendit, ab Adam usque ad patriarchas et prophetas in visione, in somnio, in speculo, in ænigmate, ordinem suum præstruens ab initio semper, quem erat persecuturus in finem. Ita semper ediscebat, et Deus in terris cum hominibus conversari non alius potuit, quam Sermo, qui caro erat futurus. Ediscebat autem, ut nobis fidem sterneret, ut facilius crederemus Filium Dei descendisse in seculum, si et retro tale quid gestum cognosceremus. — Adv. Prax., p. 509.

[m] Ed. Cant. 1658. [§ 14. p. 456.]

BOOK I. CHAP. I. § 6—9.

p. 119, and vi. p. 329[n]; Novatian on the Trinity, cc. 25—27[o]; Cyprian, Tract 3. *De Simplicitate Prælatorum*[p]. The Catholic Doctors of the Church after the council of Nice agree on this point with the ante-Nicene Fathers. See Athanasius, (Orat. iv. against the Arians;) Hilary, (books iv. and xii. on the Trinity;) Philastrius, (Heresy 84;) Chrysostom, (Homily to the people of Antioch, chap. 8, and on the seventh chapter of the Epistle to the Hebrews;) Ambrose, (book i. On those who are Initiated, chap. 3;) Augustine, (Epistles 99, 111, 112;) Leo, (Epistle 17;) Theodoret, (Question 68. on Genesis, &c.)

9. I am aware that there are some who ridicule these views, as the mere dreams and dotings of the good fathers, and who are too self-satisfied, laying it down as certain, that the Angel who appeared of old to the patriarchs and holy men and was worshipped by them, was only a created angel, fulfilling the office of an ambassador in behalf of[1] the most high God, and bearing His name and character[2]. To such I answer; 1. Supposing that the fathers were in error on that point, still this remains fixed and certain, that they themselves believed that our Saviour Jesus really 9 existed before His birth, according to the flesh, of the most blessed Virgin; which is enough for our purpose. But it will be said, it is very likely that they, who erred in [22] their premises, were also deceived in their conclusion. I grant it, if they had built their conclusion only upon these premises, which are supposed to be false. But in this instance the case is quite different. For the fathers, although they sometimes establish the pre-existence of the Son of God by this argument, do yet throughout their writings[3] intimate that they were led to this view from other very plain testimonies of Scripture, as well as from the tradition of the Apostles; this we shall hereafter shew clearly in its own time and place. But, 2ndly, I have, and always shall have, a religious scruple in interpreting the Holy Scriptures against the stream of all the fathers and ancient doctors, except when the most evident proofs compel me to do so; this, however, I do not believe will ever happen. For certainly the consentient judgment of antiquity, especially of primitive antiquity, ought

[1] pro.
[2] personam sustinentem.
[3] passim.

n [§ 78. p. 691.]
o [Page 723, &c.]
p [This treatise is not believed to be Cyprian's.—B.]

to outweigh the force of many probabilities and reasonings from likelihood. But it will be said, there are in this instance the most evident reasons for thinking otherwise. Well then, let us see.

10. The first objection they urge is, that in Exodus iii. 4 we read, that God spoke to Moses out of the burning bush; and, in Exod. xix. 20, and xx. 1, that God gave him the law; whilst yet it is clear from other passages of Scripture, that it was a created angel, who in each case appeared and spoke to Moses. For by the author of the Epistle to the Hebrews, ii. 2, the law is called "the word spoken by angels," with which compare Gal. iii. 19. Stephen also, Acts vii., clearly says that an angel appeared to Moses in the bush, ver. 30, and that the law was ministered by the dispensation of angels, ver. 53. They add, that in that well-known appearance to Abraham in Mamre, Gen. xviii. 1, 2, although one of the three is distinguished by the name of Jehovah, yet it is certain that all the three were angels; since the author of the Epistle to the Hebrews expressly says, that they were angels whom Abraham and Lot hospitably entertained, xiii. 2.

11. My answer is; when the fathers agree in asserting,
[23] that the angel who appeared to Abraham and Moses, and to whom the name of Jehovah and divine honours are attributed, was the Son of God, their statement admits of two senses; namely, either that it was God, (that is, the Son of God,) designated by the name of an angel, inasmuch as He assumed a body or visible appearance[1] such as angels are accustomed to use; or that the Son of God was in the angel; that is, that it was an angel who assumed the bodily shape, and that the Son of God was in the angel; I mean, by a special mode of accompaniment[2] and presence. On the former hypothesis, the objection alleged is met by saying that the Son of God is called an angel also, that is to say, "the Angel of the covenant;" and that in these appearances He is called an angel, because He imitated the manner and way in which angels used to appear to men; moreover, that it is not true that it was a created angel who spoke to Moses in the bush and on mount Sinai; nor is this proved from its being said both by Stephen and the author of the Epistle to the Hebrews, that the law of Moses was "given by angels," in the plural number; because

[1] speciem.

[2] per assistentiam singularem.

nothing hinders but that God might have been Himself present on Sinai, although, to set forth His majesty, He was attended by a multitude of angels: nay, from Deut. xxxiii. 2, and Ps. lxviii. 17, it most certainly appears that God Himself was present by a special presence on mount Sinai amongst those myriads of angels. And in the case of the appearance of the three, who turned aside to [visit] Abraham, [we should say] that two of them indeed were created angels, and that this is quite enough to preserve the truth of the Apostle's words in Heb. xiii. 2; but that the third was the Son of God, since even Abraham recognised in Him the marks of the Divine Majesty, and therefore interceded with Him as with the supreme Judge, that, if it were possible, He might delay the destruction of the five cities [of the plain]. And very much in this way does the celebrated Andrew Rivet (among others) answer the ob- [24]
jection in his Commentary on Hosea xii. 4—6. The second hypothesis, however, is adopted by many ancient writers, both Jewish and Christian. Trypho the Jew, in Justin[q], contends, that in the appearance to Moses in the burning bush, two were present together, God and an angel; that it was the angel which appeared in the flame of fire, whilst it was God, (that is to say, in the angel,) who spoke with Moses. Justin answers him, that this may be allowed without affecting the truth of his hypothesis—that it was the Son of God, I mean, who spoke to Moses; although he afterwards tries to shew that the Son of God alone appeared to Moses. And indeed the view of Trypho seems to have been received and approved amongst the more ancient Jews. For even Stephen himself clearly teaches that it was an angel which appeared to Moses in the bush, Acts vii. 30, but that it was God Himself who spoke these words to Moses, "I am the God of thy fathers," &c., Acts vii. 31, 32. Compare Exod. iii. 2, with verses 4—6. Clement of Alexandria, the same who affirms that He who was over the children of Israel in the wilderness, was the Instructor[1], that is, the Son of God, expressly teaches, and that in the very same passage[r],

[1] Pædagogum.

[q] Dialog. cum Tryphon., pp. 282, 283. [c. 60. p. 156, &c.]

[r] τὴν εὐαγγέλιον καὶ ἡγεμόνιον ἐπιστήσας τοῦ λόγου δύναμιν, . . . τὸ ἀξίωμα τὸ κυριακὸν φυλάττων.—Pædagog. i. 7. pp. 110, 111, [p. 133.]

that He who conducted Moses was an angel, "setting over him the evangelizing[1] and guiding power of the Word," and "reserving the dignity of the Lord." And a little afterwards he adds, that, under the Old Testament, "the Word was an angel[s]," that is, appeared to men by means of angels. In which sense also he, by and by, calls the Son "the mystic Angel[t]," as concealing, as it were, at that period, His divine majesty under the guise of an angel. The same view was entertained by many of the fathers who wrote [25] after the council of Nice. Thus Athanasius (Orat. iv. against the Arians[u]), speaking concerning the angel which appeared to Moses in the bush, says, "He who appeared was an angel, but it was God who spoke in him." Jerome (on chap. iii. of the Epistle to the Galatians) says[x], "But in that he asserts that the law was ordained by angels, this is what he would have understood, that, whenever throughout the Old Testament an angel is first said to appear, and afterwards God, as it were, is introduced speaking, it is really an angel, one of many ministering spirits, whoever he is, who appears, but it is the Mediator who speaks in him, who says, 'I am the God of Abraham,'" &c. Augustine (against Maximinus, book iii. near the end[y]) says, "Who was it, I ask, that appeared to Moses in the flame, when the bush is burning, but was not consumed? Although Holy Scripture itself declares, that in this case also it was an angel which appeared, in the words, 'But there appeared unto him an angel of the Lord in a flame of fire out of the bush,' yet who doubts that God was in the angel?" Gregory (Preface to Job, ii.[z]) says,

[1] εὐαγγέλιον.

[s] λόγος ἄγγελος ἦν.—[Id. ibid.]

[t] μυστικὸς ἄγγελος.—[Id. ibid.]

[u] ὁ μὲν φαινόμενος ἦν ἄγγελος· ὁ δὲ Θεὸς ἐν αὐτῷ ἐλάλει.—Tom. i. p. 467. [Orat. iii. 14. p. 563.]

[x] Quod autem ait, *lex ordinata per angelos*, hoc vult intelligi, quod in omni Veteri Testamento, ubi angelus primum visus refertur, et postea quasi Deus loquens inducitur, angelus quidem vere ex ministris pluribus, quicunque sit, visus; sed in illo Mediator loquatur, qui dicat, *Ego sum Deus Abraham*, &c.—Ed. Par. 1627. [tom. vii. p. 441.]

[y] Quæro, inquit, quis apparuerit Mosi in igne, quando rubus inflammabatur et non urebatur? quanquam et illic angelum apparuisse Scriptura ipsa declarat, dicens, *Apparuit autem illi angelus Domini in flamma ignis de rubo;* in angelo autem Deum fuisse quis dubitat?—[Lib. ii. 11. vol. viii. p. 742.]

[z] Angelus, qui Mosi apparuisse describitur, modo angelus, modo Dominus memoratur; *angelus* videlicet propter hoc, quod exterius loquendo serviebat; *Dominus* autem dicitur, quia interius præsidens loquendi efficaciam ministrabat. Cum ergo loquens ab interiori regitur, et per obsequium angelus, et per inspirationem Dominus nominatur.—[Greg. M. vol. i. p. 8.]

BOOK I. CHAP. I. § 11.

"The angel which is described as appearing to Moses, is sometimes mentioned as an angel, at other times as the Lord; as an angel, that is, as it seems, by reason of his doing service by outward speech; but yet he is called the Lord, because it was He who, presiding within, supplied the power[1] of speech; as then he who speaks is guided by Him who is within, he hath both the name angel by reason of his service, and the name Lord by reason of His inspiration." With these agree Fulgentius (against Maximus) and other writers; and this opinion of the ancients seems to me to receive complete confirmation from that passage in Exodus xxiii. 20, where God, that is, the Son of God, according to the opinion of all primitive antiquity, speaking to Moses, promises that He will send His [26] angel before His people, through the wilderness, and that "His Name shall be בקרבו, in the midst of him[2]." It was, therefore, in very truth an angel who went before the people of Israel to the promised land; but yet an angel in whom the Son of God placed His name, that is, His own divine virtue and power; in whom, that is to say, He was Himself present in some peculiar manner. However, from the words of Trypho in Justin, which we have just now quoted, it is clear that that notion never entered into the minds of the ancient Jews, which in our age has been entertained by certain learned men among Christians; namely, that He who appeared and spoke to Moses in the bush and on mount Sinai was a mere angel, who called himself the God of Abraham, and willingly permitted divine worship to be paid to him under the name of God. Surely such an opinion is too absurd, and is simply horrible. For it is impious to suppose that angels ever practised the art of actors, and that God ever communicated to them His incommunicable Name, or such a representation as that by it a creature should take to himself[3] all that belongs to God. Rightly also does the learned Cameron remark[a]; "It is true advocates do often personate their clients; but it has never been even heard of that any ambassador, in setting forth the mandates of his prince, spoke in any other than the third person, 'My sovereign says this.' Of which usage we have a remarkable testimony in the prophets, with whom, as it is

1 efficacia.

2 in medio ejus.

3 sibi attribuet.

a In Annot. ad Heb. ii. 2.

ON THE PRE-EX-ISTENCE OF THE SON.

well known, the customary formula of expression is, 'Thus saith the Lord.' Nay, even in visions angels acknowledge that they are sent[b]." Hence Grotius himself allows in one
[27] place[c], that he, who promulgated the ancient law on Sinai, was indeed a special[1] angel, accompanied by a retinue of others; not however a mere angel, but one with whom the Word was present.

1 singularem.

12. Let it be granted then, you will say, that it was God who by an angel, or under the figure of an angel, appeared and spake to holy men in the Old Testament; yet by what reasoning, we ask, were the (ancient) doctors led to believe that this was the Son of God? I answer, by the best of reasoning, if I am not mistaken, which they had learnt from apostolical tradition. I mean this; God the Father, as He at first framed and created the world through His Son, so through the same Son did He afterwards manifest Himself to the world. Therefore the Son of God, although in the last times, through the dispensation of His incarnation, He has at length held familiar intercourse with mankind, still always, even from the very earliest period of its existence, presided over the Church; and even under the Old Testament, though by a hidden and secret dispensation, shewed Himself[2] to holy men. Clement of Alexandria (*Pædagog.* i. 11[d]) says; "Of old time, then, the Word performed the office of instructor[3] through Moses, and afterwards also through the prophets." Origen (against Celsus, lib. vi.[e]) writes thus; "It was not as if God had awaked out of a long sleep, and sent Jesus to the human race; for although He (for good reasons) assigned unto[4] this time the dispensation of the Incarnation, yet had He
[28] always been a benefactor to mankind; for nothing of what is good among men was ever done, except by the Word of God visiting the souls of those who, even for a little while, were capable of receiving such influences of the Divine Word."

2 ingessit sese.

3 ἐπαιδαγώγει.

4 [al. "fulfilled at."]

b Vide Athanas. Orat. iv. cont. Arian., p. 466. [Orat. iii. 12. vol. i. p. 561.]

c Ad Gal. iii. 19.

d πάλαι μὲν οὖν διὰ Μωσέως ὁ λόγος ἐπαιδαγώγει, ἔπειτα καὶ διὰ προφητῶν.—Pag. 132. [p. 155.]

e οὐχ' ὥσπερ ἀπὸ μακροῦ ὕπνου διαναστὰς ὁ Θεὸς ἔπεμψε τὸν Ἰησοῦν τῷ γένει τῶν ἀνθρώπων, τὴν μὲν κατὰ τὴν ἐνσωμάτωσιν οἰκονομίαν νῦν δι' εὐλόγους αἰτίας ἐπικληρώσαντα [πληρώσαντα, ed. Ben.], ἀεὶ δὲ τὸ γένος τῶν ἀνθρώπων εὐεργετήσαντα· οὐδὲν γὰρ τῶν ἐν ἀνθρώποις καλῶν γεγένηται, μὴ τοῦ θείου λόγου ἐπιδημήσαντος ταῖς ψυχαῖς τῶν κᾂν ὀλίγον καιρὸν δεδυνημένων δέξασθαι τὰς τοιάσδε τοῦ θείου λόγου ἐνεργείας.—Pag. 329. [§ 78. p. 691.] Vide et lib. iii. p. 119. [§ 14. p. 456.] et lib. iv. p. 165. [§ 6. p. 506.]

11

Tertullian, however, expresses himself most plainly and fully (against Praxeas, c. 15. [p. 509[f]]); "It was the Son who was always seen, and the Son who has always worked by the authority and will of the Father, for 'the Son can do nothing of Himself, but what He seeth the Father do,' &c.... Thus, 'all things were made by the Son, and without Him was not any thing made.' And think not that only the works which pertain to the [creation of the] world were made through the Son, but also whatever since that time has been done by God." Afterwards, c. 16[g], follow the words which we have quoted above; "The God, who conversed with men upon earth, could have been no other than the Word, which was to be made flesh."

13. There remains a second objection, which is held up by certain very learned men as unanswerable[1], and it shall be discussed by me in but few words. They urge then, that this opinion of the fathers is diametrically opposed to most express words of Holy Scripture. For, say they, the inspired author of the Epistle to the Hebrews, i. 1, 2, plainly says that "God, who in divers manners spake in times past unto the fathers and prophets, hath at length in the last days spoken [unto men] through His Son:" but it is evident that by the last days is meant the age of the Gospel; therefore before that time the Son of God had never spoken, or God through His Son; otherwise, the author would not have been correct in opposing the last days of the Gospel to the early period of the ancient law, if the Son of God, or God through the Son, has appeared and spoken in both.

[1] invictam.

14. Ludovicus de Tena proposes this objection, and answers it in words to the following effect[h]; "Paul only makes a difference between this last appearance of the [29]

[f] Filius visus est semper, [Filius conversatus est semper] et Filius operatus est semper, ex auctoritate Patris et voluntate, quia Filius nihil a semetipso potest facere, nisi viderit Patrem facientem, &c. . . . Sic omnia per Filium facta sunt, et sine illo factum est nihil. Nec putes sola opera mundi per Filium facta, sed et quæ a Deo exinde gesta sunt.—Tert. adv. Praxeam, c. 15. p. 509.

[g] Deus in terris cum hominibus conversari non alius potuit, quam Sermo, qui caro erat futurus.—[Ibid. c. 16.]

[h] Respondeo Paulum solum ponere discrimen inter hanc ultimam apparitionem Filii Dei, et priores V. T. quia istæ fiebant in creatura corporali, non hypostatice unita Filio Dei; et ita medio supposito creato corporeo, imo et angelico, loquebatur Filius Dei. At vero in illa apparitione Verbi incarnati, de qua asserit, *novissime locutus est nobis in Filio*, non mediat aliquod suppositum creatum, neque corporeum, neque angelicum; sed Verbum divinum

ON THE PRE-EXISTENCE OF THE SON.

Son of God, and the earlier ones of the Old Testament, in that those were made in a created body, not united hypostatically to the Son of God; and so the Son of God spoke through the medium of a subject[1], created, corporeal, nay rather angelic. But in that appearance of the incarnate Word, of which he asserts, 'He hath in these last days spoken unto us by His Son,' no created subject intervenes, either corporeal or angelic, but the Divine Word immediately, without the intervention of any subject, spoke unto men. Nor is it any difficulty that this had been done through the medium of His human nature, because that nature was without any subject of its own, and was immediately united to the Word as its subject. Now this is the legitimate sense of the words, and thus the contrast spoken of, when rightly explained, holds good, and the superiority of the gospel over the ancient law." This answer of the very learned writer, though barbarous so far as the expressions are concerned, (after the fashion of the schools,) is nevertheless sound and solid in sense, and, as is evident from the testimonies adduced a little above, in agreement with the mind of the ancient fathers. To this may be added the following: Justin Martyr in the Apology for the Christians, which in the common editions is called the first, though in reality it is the second, speaks thus of the Word or Son of God[1]; "For He was and is the Word, who is in every thing; who foretold what should come to pass, both through the prophets, and through Himself, when He had become of like passions with us, and had taught us these things." In this passage Justin teaches, that the Word or Son of God under the Old Testament manifested Himself to the prophets in a certain manner, and through them to others; but that in the last days, having taken our nature unto Himself, He by Himself[2] delivered unto us His heavenly doctrine; and that herein especially consists the excellence of the gospel over the old law. To this agrees Clement of Alexandria,

[1] supposito.

[2] per seipsum.

[30]

immediate immediatione suppositi loquebatur hominibus. Neque obstat, quod hoc fuerat media humana natura, quia hæc caruit proprio supposito, et immediate fuit unita supposito Verbi. Et hic est legitimus sensus horum verborum, et sic manet recte explicata dicta contrapositio, et excellentia evangelii supra legem veterem.—In cap. i. Epist. ad Heb. difficult. 2. § 2. [p. 32.]

[1] λόγος γὰρ ἦν καί ἐστιν ὁ ἐν παντὶ ὢν, καὶ διὰ τῶν προφητῶν προειπὼν τὰ μέλλοντα γίνεσθαι, καὶ δι' ἑαυτοῦ ὁμοιοπαθοῦς γενομένου καὶ διδάξαντος ταῦτα.—Pag. 48, 49. [Apol. ii. 10. p. 95.]

BOOK I. CHAP. I. § 14, 15.

(*Pædag.* i. 7[k];) "For the Lord was, indeed, the Instructor[1] of His ancient people by means of Moses, but by Himself is He the guide of His new people, face to face." And a little after; "Previously indeed for the elder people there was an elder covenant, and the law schooled the people with fear, and the Word was an angel; but now unto His new and younger people a new and younger covenant has been given, and the Word has come to be [unto us], and fear has been turned into love, and that mystic Angel is born, even Jesus." And no other was the meaning of Tertullian, when, in the passage which we have quoted a little above[l], he teaches, "That the Son of God came down to converse with men, from Adam to the patriarchs, in vision, in dream, in mirror, in dark saying," &c.

[1] Pædagogus.

15. Thus no solid objection can be brought out of Holy Scripture against this opinion of the ancient fathers. Let us now enquire, whether the Holy Scriptures do not plainly enough favour this view. Concerning the angel who led the people of Israel in the wilderness, (of whom it is written, "Beware of His face, and obey His voice, provoke Him not, for He will not spare thee, nor pardon thy transgressions; for My name is in Him,") St. Paul expressly teaches, that He was the Son of God, who afterwards was called Christ. "Neither let us tempt Christ," he says, "as some of them also tempted, and were destroyed of the serpents[m]." At least these words shew that Christ was present with the children of Israel in the wilderness, and was tempted by them. The heretic Socinus, indeed, here objects, that it is written by St. Paul, "Let us not tempt Christ, as some of them also tempted," but that it is not written, "as some of them tempted Christ;" and therefore that the sentence may be very suitably filled up with another word, for instance "God;" but this is clearly futile. For very many instances of this elliptical mode of expression are to be found in the Scriptures; thus St. John viii. 56, "Abra-

Exod. xxxiii. 20, &c.

1 Cor. x. 9.

[31]

12

[k] καὶ γὰρ ἦν ὡς ἀληθῶς διὰ μὲν Μωσέως παιδαγωγὸς ὁ Κύριος τοῦ λαοῦ τοῦ παλαιοῦ· δι' αὐτοῦ δὲ, τοῦ νέου καθηγεμὼν λαοῦ, πρόσωπον πρὸς πρόσωπον. . . . τὸ μὲν οὖν πρότερον τῷ πρεσβυτέρῳ λαῷ πρεσβυτέρα διαθήκη ἦν, καὶ νόμος ἐπαιδαγώγει τὸν λαὸν μετὰ φόβου, καὶ λόγος ἄγγελος ἦν· καινῷ δὲ καὶ νέῳ λαῷ καινὴ καὶ νέα διαθήκη δεδώρηται, καὶ ὁ λόγος γεγένηται, καὶ ὁ φόβος εἰς ἀγάπην μετατέτραπται, καὶ ὁ μυστικὸς ἐκεῖνος ἄγγελος Ἰησοῦς τίκτεται. — Pag. 110, 111. [p. 132.]

[l] [§ 7.]

[m] μηδὲ ἐκπειράζωμεν τὸν Χριστὸν, καθὼς καί τινες αὐτῶν ἐπείρασαν, καὶ ὑπὸ τῶν ὄφεων ἀπώλοντο. 1 Cor. x. 9.

ON THE PRE-EXISTENCE OF THE SON.

ham rejoiced to see My day, and he saw;" there is no repetition of "and he saw My day," but that is understood. But we have a most apposite instance of this kind of expression in Deut. vi. 16; "Thou shalt not tempt the Lord thy God,
[Massah.] as thou temptedst in the place of temptation;" where it is obvious that the latter clause refers to Him, whose name was just before mentioned, "the Lord thy God," without any repetition of it. Besides, we might ask the heretic in turn, why it was not added, "as some of them tempted God[n]?" Surely, if that be the sense of this verse, which the heretic fixes on it, no reason can be given for the ellipsis; but, if the meaning of the passage be that which we give it, as it certainly is, the reason for the ellipsis may most easily be given. For it would have been a much more unusual form of expression if the name of Christ had been repeated. Lastly, the particle *καὶ*, "also," in this place is of great force; as shewing that the words of the Apostle must necessarily be so taken, as if he meant, "that Christ was tempted in the wilderness by the Israelites." For to what purpose would it have been for him to have said, "as also," when in the former clause there was no mention made of God, but
[32] only of Christ? Accordingly Grotius[o], perceiving with his usual acuteness that this quibble of the Socinians is clearly absurd, himself cast about for some other way of escaping [the force of the words.] "The clause," he says, "must ne-
[1] omnino. cessarily[1] be read *μηδὲ ἐκπειράζωμεν τὸν Θεὸν*, 'neither let us tempt God.'" Is it really so? must it be so read "necessarily?" Let us have a reason. "Because," he says, "that most ancient MS." (the Alexandrine[p]) "so reads the passage." But surely those most ancient MSS., which were
[2] vetus Latinus. used by the Syriac, Arabic, and the old Latin[2] translators, and by Ambrose, Chrysostom, and Theophylact, all have *Χριστὸν*, (Christ,) not *Θεὸν*, (God:) and this reading too

[n] Vide Cameron in loco.

[o] In loco.

[p] And the Ethiopic version of the New Test. (*Mill in loco.*) Certainly as there agree with the printed text, not only Irenæus, Theodotus *in ἐπιτομαῖς*, and very many Greek and Latin writers, but also all the manuscript copies without exception, and particularly the *Codex Claromontanus* and the *Codex Germanensis*, both Greek-Latin MSS., and that Vulgate which seems to have been earlier than the time of Marcion; I am quite of opinion that the Apostle himself wrote Χριστὸν, which was altered into Θεὸν by some daring critic, who could not see the truth of the common reading, that the Israelites tempted Christ in the wilderness. *Id. ib.*—BOWYER.

is followed by all those other copies which are presented to us in the Polyglott Bibles, except that the Lincoln has *Κύριον*, which also is in the New Testament a name of Christ[q]. And the *Codex Alexandrinus* is not of so great authority as that it should be set against so general an agreement. This very distinguished man, however, adduces another reason; "Christ," he says, "is the name of a man, who, it is certain, did not exist at that time." The answer is most easy. Christ is here put for the Son of God, who afterwards in the fulness of time, when He had taken unto Him human nature, was called Christ; so that there is here a synecdoche, as it were, of the whole, as in other passages of Scripture[r]. By the same sophism, Grotius also eludes the force of a most express testimony to the divinity of the Son of God, that in Col. i. 16. ["By Him were all things created, that are in heaven, and that are in earth, visible and invisible, whether they be thrones, or dominions, or principalities, or powers; all things were created by Him, and for Him."] "It is certain," he says, "that all things were created by the Word; but the preceding context shews that the Apostle is speaking of Christ, which is the name of a man. So that it would be more correct to render the word ἐκτίσθη, *ordinata sunt*—were placed in a new condition." But if these words of the Apostle do not speak of a creation, properly so called, I should believe that Holy Scripture laboured under inexplicable difficulty, and that no certain conclusion could be deduced from its words, however express they might seem to be. [33]

16. From these things, however, it is clear, that, what the primitive fathers taught concerning the appearances of the Word, or Son of God, to the patriarchs and saints under the Old Testament, were no vain imaginations of their own, but derived from the very teaching of the Apostles. There is this further (which I put before the reader as especially useful for him to observe) that neither were the Apostles of Christ the first to teach these truths, but that they derived them from the ancient *cabala* or tradition of the Jews; or, at least, that those

q MS. in the possession of Dr. J. Covel; Theodoret and Epiphanius have Κύριον.—BOWYER. [The Slavonic version confirms Θεὸν; and Griesbach shews that Κύριον is found in several MSS.—B.]

r See Vossii Instit. Orat. iv. 7.

ON THE PRE-EXISTENCE OF THE SON.

things which the Apostles were taught on this subject, by the [inspiration of] the Holy Ghost, agrees well with that tradition. Thus Philo the Jew, just like St. Paul, explains the angel, who led the children of Israel in the wilderness, of the Word and first-begotten Son of God, through whom God directs and governs the universe. In his book Of Agriculture[s] there is a most express passage; "For God as a shepherd and king guides by a certain order[1] and law, as if they were a flock, earth and water, air and fire, and again whatsoever they contain, plants and living beings, whether mortal or divine; the nature of the heavens too, and the circuits of the sun and moon, as well as the turnings and harmonious movements of
[34] the other stars; having set over them His true Word[2], even His first-begotten Son, to undertake the care of this sacred flock, as some vicegerent of a powerful king; for in a certain place it is said, 'Behold I am, and I will send My angel before thy face to keep thee in the way.'" (Ex. xxiii. 20.) Philo also understands, as the ancient Christians did, that God, who appeared to Adam in paradise after his fall, to Moses in the bush, and also to Abraham, was the Word. For thus he writes in his work
13 Of Dreams[t]; "The sacred Word to some enjoins as a king with authoritative command what they ought to do; whilst others He instructs in what will profit them, as a teacher his intimate disciples; to others as a counsellor suggesting the best advice, He greatly aids such as of themselves know not what will be for their good; again, to others as a friend,

[1] δίκην.

[2] ὀρθὸν λόγον.

[s] καθάπερ γάρ τινα ποίμνην, γῆν, καὶ ὕδωρ, καὶ ἀέρα, καὶ πῦρ, καὶ ὅσα ἐν τούτοις φυτά τε αὖ καὶ ζῶα, τὰ μὲν θνητὰ, τὰ δὲ θεῖα, ἔτι δὲ οὐρανοῦ φύσιν, καὶ ἡλίου καὶ σελήνης περιόδους, καὶ τῶν ἄλλων ἀστέρων τροπάς τε αὖ καὶ χορείας ἐναρμονίους, ὡς ποιμὴν καὶ βασιλεὺς ὁ Θεὸς ἄγει κατὰ δίκην καὶ νόμον, προστησάμενος τὸν ὀρθὸν αὐτοῦ λόγον πρωτόγονον υἱὸν, ὃς τὴν ἐπιμέλειαν τῆς ἱερᾶς ταύτης ἀγέλης, οἷά τις μεγάλου βασιλέως ὕπαρχος διαδέξεται. καὶ γὰρ εἴρηταί που· Ἰδοὺ ἐγώ εἰμι, ἀποστελῶ ἄγγελόν μου εἰς πρόσωπόν σου τοῦ φυλάξαι σὲ ἐν τῇ ὁδῷ.—De Agric., p. 195. edit. Par. 1640. [vol. i. p. 308.]

[t] ὁ ἱερὸς λόγος τοῖς μὲν ὡς βασιλεὺς ἃ χρὴ πράττειν ἐξ ἐπιτάγματος παραγγέλλει· τοῖς δὲ ὡς γνωρίμοις διδάσκαλος τὰ πρὸς ὠφέλειαν ὑφηγεῖται· τοῖς δὲ ὡς σύμβουλος γνώμας εἰσηγούμενος τὰς ἀρίστας. τοὺς τὸ συμφέρον ἐξ ἑαυτῶν οὐκ εἰδότας μέγα ὠφελεῖ: τοῖς δὲ ὡς φίλος ἐπιεικῶς καὶ μετὰ πειθοῦς πολλὰ καὶ τῶν ἀρρήτων ἀναφέρει, ὧν οὐδὲν αὐτῶν ἀτέλεστον ἐπακοῦσαι θέμις· ἔστι δ' ὅτε καὶ πυνθάνεταί τινων, ὥσπερ τοῦ Ἀδὰμ τὸ, ποῦ εἶ; . . . ἐπειδὰν μέν τοι πρὸς τὸ τῶν φίλων ἔλθῃ συνέδριον, οὐ πρότερον ἄρχεται λέγειν, ἢ ἕκαστον αὐτῶν ἀνακαλέσαι καὶ ὀνομαστὶ προσειπεῖν, ἵνα τὰ ὦτα ἀθροίσαντες, [ἀνορθιάσαντες MSS. et Potter,] ἡσυχίᾳ καὶ προσοχῇ χρώμενοι, τῶν θεσμῳδουμένων εἰς ἄληστον μνήμην ἀκούωσιν· ἐπεὶ καὶ ἑτέρωθι λέγεται, σιώπα καὶ ἄκουε· τοῦτον τὸν τρόπον ἐπὶ τῆς βάτου Μωσῆς ἀνακαλεῖται. ὡς γὰρ εἶδε, φησὶν, ὅτι προσάγει ἰδεῖν, ἐκάλεσεν αὐτὸν ὁ Θεὸς ἐκ τῆς βάτου, λέγων· Μωϋσῆ, Μωϋσῆ· ὁ δὲ εἶπε· τί ἐστίν; Ἀβραάμ δὲ, κ.τ.λ.—De Somn., pp. 593, 594. [vol. i. p. 649.]

with gentleness and persuasion, He communicates many even of His secrets, none of which is it lawful for the uninitiated to hear; at times also He enquires of some, as He did of Adam, saying, Where art thou?... But when the Word has come into the assembly of His friends, He does not begin to speak, until He has called each of them, and addressed him by name, that with ears intent and with quietness and attention they may lay up His oracles in never-failing memory; as in another place also it is written, 'Be still, and listen.' In this way Moses is called at the bush, 'For when the Lord,' he says, 'saw that he drew near to see, God called him out [35] of the bush, and said, Moses, Moses; and he answered, What is it?' &c. So also Abraham," &c.

In the same book[u] also he was of opinion[1], with the holy fathers of the Church, that the Lord who rained brimstone and fire upon Sodom and Gomorrah was the Word; for after quoting those words out of Genesis, "The sun was risen upon the earth when Lot entered into Zoar[2], and the Lord rained upon Sodom and upon Gomorrah brimstone and fire;" he immediately adds, "For when the Word of God visits our terrestrial system, He gives help and succour to such as are akin to virtue and incline to it, so as to afford to them a [36] refuge and complete security; whilst upon His enemies He sends irremediable destruction and ruin."

17. This testimony is not weakened by the observation, which Grotius has made, that the created angels themselves are called by Philo throughout, the Words, *τοὺς λόγους*; doubtless because they also are, according to their measure, the messengers and interpreters of God's will to men. For although this is most true, still it is evident that Philo, in the passages quoted, (to which it would be easy to add many others,) designates as the Word, one certain individual being[3], so called by way of pre-eminence, who is the first-begotten Son of God, superior to all the angels, and even to the whole universe. And if this same Philo has, in some instances, used expressions concerning the Word and first-begotten Son of God, which are not worthy of His majesty,

[1] sensit.

[2] Segor.

[3] singularem quendam.

[u] *ὁ γὰρ τοῦ Θεοῦ λόγος, ὅταν ἐπὶ τὸ γεῶδες ἡμῶν σύστημα ἀφίκηται, τοῖς μὲν ἀρετῆς συγγενέσι καὶ πρὸς ἀρετὴν ἀποκλίνουσιν ἀρήγει καὶ βοηθεῖ, ὡς καταφυγὴν καὶ σωτηρίαν αὐτοῖς πορίζειν παντελῆ· τοῖς δὲ ἀντιπάλοις ὄλεθρον καὶ φθορὰν ἀνίατον ἐπιπέμπει.*—Pag. 578. [p. 633.]

ON THE PRE-EXISTENCE OF THE SON.

this is easily to be excused in an age in which the mystery of the most Holy Trinity had not, as yet, been fully revealed to the Jews. Nay, it is rather to be wondered at that a man should have seen so clearly in so great a darkness. For in Book ii. Of the Allegories of the Law [x], he says, that this Word of God is "above the whole world, the oldest and most universal [1] of all things which have been made." And in his work Of the Creation of the World [y], he calls the same being "the Word of God that created the world." And, afterwards [z], he speaks of "the divine Word, and the Word of God, invisible
[37] and perceived by the mind, a supercelestial star, the fountain of the stars which are perceived by sense." Also in his book On the Confusion of Tongues [a], he calls Him not only "the most ancient and the most sacred Word of God," but likewise "His eternal image."

18. Lest, however, any one should suspect that Philo Platonizes [2] in these expressions, (an opinion which many have entertained who are not acquainted with Jewish literature, whereas it should rather be thought that Plato Philonizes [3], that is, that he derived his notions concerning the Logos from the doctrines of the Jews, which were, I may say, the mother tongue of Philo,) the Jewish author of the book intitled "the Wisdom of Solomon," (who it is certain from most evident proofs, was much more ancient than Philo, and not, as some have imagined, Philo himself,) propounds the same doctrines concerning the Word. For in xviii. 15, speaking of the Angel who smote the first-born of the Egyptians, he says, "Thine almighty Word leaped down out of heaven from off Thy royal throne, as a fierce man of war, into the

[1] γενικώτατον.

[2] πλατωνίζειν.

[3] φιλωνίζειν.

x ὑπεράνω παντὸς τοῦ κόσμου, καὶ πρεσβύτατον καὶ γενικώτατον τῶν ὅσα γέγονε.—Leg. Allegor. p. 93. [lib. iii. vol. i. p. 121.]

y Θεοῦ λόγον κοσμοποιοῦντα.—De Opif. Mundi, p. 5. [vol. i. p. 5. So quoted by Bp. Bull; Dr. Burton says; "In citing these words this great man has made a slight mistake. Philo's words are: εἰ δέ τις ἐθελήσειε γυμνοτέροις χρήσασθαι τοῖς ὀνόμασιν, οὐδὲν ἂν ἕτερον εἴποι τὸν νοητὸν εἶναι κόσμον ἢ Θεοῦ λόγον ἤδη κοσμοποιοῦντος."]

z τὸν ἀόρατον καὶ νοητὸν θεῖον λόγον, καὶ Θεοῦ λόγον, ὑπερουράνιον ἀστῆρα, πηγὴν τῶν αἰσθητῶν ἀστέρων.—Ibid., p. 6. [So quoted by Bp. Bull; Dr. Burton says; "He here also cites Philo's words inaccurately: τὸν δὲ ἀόρατον καὶ νοητὸν θεῖον λόγον καὶ Θεοῦ λόγον εἰκόνα λέγει Θεοῦ, καὶ ταύτης εἰκόνα τὸ νοητὸν φῶς ἐκεῖνο, ὃ θείου λόγου γέγονεν εἰκὼν τοῦ διερμηνεύσαντος τὴν γένεσιν αὐτοῦ· καί ἔστιν ὑπερουράνιος ἀστὴρ, πηγὴ τῶν αἰσθητῶν ἀστέρων."]

a [The whole passage is, καὶ γὰρ εἰ μήπω ἱκανοὶ θεοῦ παῖδες νομίζεσθαι γεγόναμεν, ἀλλά τοι τοῦ ἀϊδίου εἰκόνος αὐτοῦ, λόγου τοῦ ἱερωτάτου· Θεοῦ γὰρ εἰκὼν, λόγος ὁ πρεσβύτατος.]—De Conf. Ling., p. 341. [vol. i. p. 427.]

midst of a land of destruction;" where it is clear that the author is speaking of a personally-subsisting Word[1]. And it is no less evident that it is not some ministering angel, as Grotius would have it, but a Divine Person, that is designated in this place; for the author calls this Word[2] "Almighty," and also assigns to Him "a royal throne in heaven." We may further add what he afterwards says of the same Being
in the 16th verse; "And standing up, He filled all things with 14
death; and He touched the heaven, but He walked upon [38]
the earth;" in these words are signified the greatness and power of Him who filleth all things, and displays His power in heaven and on earth. The author possibly erred in this point, (I say, possibly, for I will not venture to assert certainly that he has erred,) in expounding the destroying angel of the Word, inasmuch as learned commentators in general have thought that he was a mere angel. However, it is clear from this passage that this ancient and venerable writer believed that the Word Himself, being sent by God the Father, sometimes came down from His royal throne in heaven unto men in the form of an angel, and that on this account He is in Scripture called by the name of an Angel. For the same view Masius quotes, out of the Jewish Rabbis, the very ancient book Tanchumah, and the Rabbi Gerundensis; whose words he cites at some length in his commentary on Joshua v. 13, 14.

19. It is, however, to be especially observed here, (as has been long ago remarked by learned men,) that almost always in the Scriptures of the Old Testament, when God is mentioned as speaking to us, assisting us, or in short holding any sort of intercourse with us, the Chaldee Paraphrases render the name of God by מימרא or מימר, *Verbum,* the Word; no doubt signifying hereby, that in such passages it is the Son of God who is spoken of, who is called the Word, and whose peculiar office it is to hold converse with us. Thus in Gen. iii. 8, instead of "They heard the voice of the Lord God," the Targum of Onkelos, and the Targum ascribed to Jonathan, have, "They heard the voice of the Word of the Lord God." In the same chapter, verse 9, instead of, "And God called unto Adam," the Jerusalem Targum has, "And the Word of the Lord called unto Adam;" just as we have

[1] λόγος ἐνυποστάτος.

[2] Sermonem.

before seen that Philo understood the passage. In Gen. xxi. 20, instead of, "And God was with him," Onkelos has, "And the Word of the Lord was with him, to help him;"
[39] and in the 22nd verse, instead of "God is with thee," Onkelos has, "The Word of the Lord is with thee for a help." So in Hosea i. 7, instead of, "And I will save them by Jehovah their God," the Targum of Jonathan has, "I will save them by the Word of the Lord their God[1]." This passage the ancient Christian writers also agreed in explaining of the salvation of God's people to be obtained through Christ. To elude the force of these places, (similar ones to which are contained in the Targums throughout[b],) some writers remark, that מימרא or מימר is occasionally used for *αὐτὸς*, "himself[c]." But this is to no purpose, for though we should allow the fact, we yet on good grounds deny that that mode of expression applies to the passages before us. For, besides that it is plain from the evidence alleged above out of Philo and the book of Wisdom, that the ancient Hebrews recognised a certain Word of God the Father, [as] a Person really distinct from God the Father Himself, who used to come down [from heaven] to men and converse[2] with them; there are also in the Chaldee Paraphrases some passages which altogether refuse to admit the interpretation in question. In Gen. xx. 3, where the Hebrew text has, "And God came to Abimelech," the Targum of Onkelos (with which the Targum of Jonathan agrees) translates it, "And מימר מן קדם יי the Word from the face of God came to Abimelech;" which cannot, certainly, be understood to mean, "And God Himself came from the face of God," &c. So, according to the testimony of Petrus Galatinus, iii. 28, and that writer of very great learning and integrity, Paulus Fagius, on Deut. v., the Targum of Jonathan, on Ps. cx. 1, (for the part of that Targum which is on the Psalms has now either altogether perished, or at all events is
[40] not extant in print,) paraphrases the words thus, "The Lord said למימרה, unto His Word, Sit Thou on My right hand;" which cannot possibly be understood to mean, the Lord said unto Himself, &c. But enough on this point.

[1] Dei Domini sui.

[2] loqui.

[b] On this see more in Poole's Synopsis on Joh. i. 1.—BOWYER.

[c] For the reason of this expression see Jacob. Capellus in his Annotations on John i. 1.

20. From all that has been said, it is now manifest on how great authority the ancient doctors of the Church affirmed that it was the Son of God who in former times, under the Old Testament, appeared to holy men, distinguished by the Name of Jehovah, and honoured by them with divine worship. But the attentive reader will observe, that here, whilst I have aimed at proving by the testimonies adduced the pre-existence of the Son before [His birth of] the Virgin Mary, I have at the same time furnished no inconsiderable confirmation, also, of His consubstantiality. Inasmuch as from what we have thus far said, it is most evident, that the ante-Nicene fathers, with one consent, taught, (in accordance with the Holy Scripture of the Old Testament, and the teachers of the ancient Jews,) that He who appeared and spoke to Moses, in the burning bush and on Mount Sinai, who manifested Himself to Abraham, &c., was the Word, or Son, of God. It is, however, certain, that He who appeared is called Jehovah, I am[1], the God of Abraham, of Isaac, and of Jacob, &c., titles which clearly are not applicable to any created being, but are peculiar to the true God. And this is the very reasoning which the fathers all employ to prove, that in such manifestations it was not a mere created angel, but the Son of God, who was present; that the Name of Jehovah, namely, and divine worship are given to Him who appeared; but that these are not communicable to any creature, and belong to the true God alone; whence it follows that they all believed that the Son was very God. This, however, I must simply pass over, until I come to the proof of the second proposition. Meanwhile let us proceed to what remains bearing on the division already before us.

[1] Eum qui est.

CHAPTER II.

THE SECOND PART OF THE PROPOSITION IS ESTABLISHED, RESPECTING THE PRE-EXISTENCE OF THE SON BEFORE THE FOUNDATION OF THE WORLD, AND THE CREATION OF ALL THINGS THROUGH HIM.

ON THE PRE-EXISTENCE OF THE SON.

1. I PASS to the second portion of our Proposition, that is, to shew that the Doctors of the first ages of the Church believed that the Son was begotten of God the Father before the foundations of the world were laid, and that this universe was created through Him. It will not be necessary to spend much time on this; since in the following books we shall adduce many passages out of these writers, which declare far more excellent things of the Son of God. At present, therefore, I shall be content with a few testimonies from such writers as flourished either in the very age of the Apostles, or in that of their first successors[1]; during which times especially, our modern Photinians impudently aver, that their tenets obtained in the Church of Christ.

[1] in prima apostolorum διαδοχῇ.

2[d]. An Epistle is extant, which was printed[e] for the first time in our own days, bearing the name of St. Barnabas. That the Apostle Barnabas was the author of it, was the opinion of our own very learned Hammond, the illustrious Isaac Vossius, and others[f]; and chiefly on the ground that Clement of Alexandria, Origen, and other ancient writers, frequently quote it under his name. Nor have the patrons of the opposite opinion[g] any thing else to advance against them, except that the author of the Epistle appears to have interpreted some passages of the Old Testament too mystically. A probable reason for this, however, is given by Hammond in his first Dissertation against Blondel[h]; where, after having, in the preceding chapters, drawn the character of the Gnos-
[42] tics, he says, "The Epistle of the Apostle Barnabas, which was published not long ago, will admit of easy explanation from

[d] [Grabe's annotations on this section will be found in an Appendix at the end of the work.]

[e] [Paris. 1645, cum notis Menardi et Dacherii.—B.]

[f] [Pearson, Cave, Du Pin, Wake.—B.]

[g] [Basnage, Jones (on the Canon of the N. T. q. v.)—B.]

[h] Chap. 7. §§ 4, 5, pp. 22, 23.

BOOK I. CHAP. II. § 1, 2. BARNABAS.

this one characteristic of the Gnostics: whereas otherwise (as a complicated and lengthy riddle) it will most certainly create a difficulty to its readers. Those disciples of Simon (Magus) arrogating to themselves knowledge (*γνῶσιν*), that is, the power of interpreting Holy Scripture mystically, were in the habit of accommodating many mysteries of the Old Testament to their own impure uses. Hence Barnabas, almost throughout the whole of this Epistle of his, opposes to the doctrines of the Gnostics very many passages, also mystically and cabalistically interpreted." And in the following chapters he shews how well the whole Epistle serves to refute the wild notions[1] of the Gnostics. Be that however as it may, at any rate he is proved to have been an author of the very earliest antiquity, by the testimonies of the ancients cited above, by his use of expressions which are peculiar to the apostolic age, by the simplicity of his style, and lastly, by the heresies which he opposes, and which are such only as sprung up[2] in the time of the Apostles themselves. Now this author, not far from the beginning of the Epistle, according to the old Latin translation, (for the Greek original in that part is lost,) thus speaks of our Saviour, chap. 5[i]; "And for this end the Lord endured[3] to suffer for the salvation of our souls, though He is the Lord of all the earth, to whom He said on the day" (perhaps we should read "to whom God said") [*Deus* for *die*] "before the creation of the world, 'Let us make man in our own image, and after our own likeness.'" And a little afterwards he calls the sun the handy-work[4] of the Son of God. It is a remarkable passage in the same chapter, which runs thus[k]; "He at that time manifested Himself to be the Son of God; for if He had not come in the flesh, how could men have been saved by looking on Him? For in looking on the sun, which will one day cease to be, and which is His handy-work, they cannot endure to fix their eyes full upon its rays." Lastly, in chap. 12 he [43]

[1] deliriis.

[2] pullularunt.

[3] sustinuit.

[4] opus manuum.

[i] Et ad hoc Dominus sustinuit pati pro anima nostra, cum sit orbis terrarum Dominus, cui dixit die (forte legendum, Deus) ante constitutionem sæculi, *Faciamus hominem ad imaginem et similitudinem nostram.*—Pag. 217, 218. ed. Voss. ad calcem Ignat. Lond. 1680. [p. 60.]

[k] τότε ἐφανέρωσεν ἑαυτὸν υἱὸν Θεοῦ εἶναι· εἰ γὰρ μὴ ἦλθεν ἐν σαρκὶ, πῶς ἂν ἐσώθημεν ἄνθρωποι βλέποντες αὐτόν; ὅτι τὸν μέλλοντα μὴ εἶναι ἥλιον, ἔργον χειρῶν αὐτοῦ ὑπάρχοντα, βλέποντες οὐκ ἰσχύουσιν εἰς ἀκτῖνας αὐτοῦ ἀντοφθαλμῆσαι.—Pag. 218, 219. [p. 16.]

ON THE PRE-EXISTENCE OF THE SON.

speaks thus of our Saviour[l]; "Herein also you have the glory of Jesus, because by Him and for Him are all things."

3. Hermas, or the author of the book entitled the Shepherd, most expressly delivers the same doctrine concerning our Lord. If you enquire about the antiquity of this author, hear the opinion of Grotius[m]; "Hermas," he says, "whatever his authority may be, is certainly of the highest antiquity, as is evident from Irenæus and Clement, who quote his words." Indeed it is clear that this author was contemporary with Clement of Rome[n]; for in his second Vision[o], towards the end, the old woman thus addresses him; "You shall then write two books, and send one to Clement, and the other to Grapta; and Clement will send it to the foreign cities, for it is permitted him," &c. But as to the credit and authority which are due to this author, Blondel[p], indeed, as if stung with madness, raves against
16 him and his writings in a strange way, calling them "the dreams of an insane prophet," and the author himself "an impure dogmatist, the fountain-head of the Novatians and of the Pelagians, and the sink of Montanist superstitions." If you ask what made him so angry, I imagine that it will be found that the man was vexed, (though he avow it
[44] not,) because in more than one place the Shepherd[q] has expressly acknowledged that the order of bishops is above [that of] presbyters, contrary to what Blondel wished. The primitive Church, however, thought very differently of both, and in comparison of her judgment, we justly consider the criticism of Blondel, notwithstanding his very great learning, as of little weight, or rather of none. By Irenæus[r] the tract called the Shepherd, is quoted as Scripture; "Well, then," he

[l] ἔχεις καὶ ἐν τούτῳ τὴν δόξαν τοῦ Ἰησοῦ, ὅτι ἐν αὐτῷ πάντα καὶ εἰς αὐτόν. —P. 238. [p. 40.]

[m] Annot. ad Marc. ii. 8.

[n] Dodwell conceives that Clement occupied the see of Rome from the year 64, or 65, to the year 81. The bishop of Chester [Pearson] from the year 69 to 82. Cave, Hist. Lit. in Herm.—BOWYER.

[o] Scribes ergo duos libellos; et mittes unum Clementi, et unum Graptæ. Mittet autem Clemens in exteras civitates; illi enim permissum est, &c. [Lib. i. p. 78.]

[p] Apol., pp. 16, 17.

[q] See Hermas, Vis. iii. et Simil. ix. [i. e. lib. i. Vis. iii. 5. p. 80. et lib. iii. Sim. ix. 15. p. 119.]

[r] Bene ergo, inquit, pronuntiavit Scriptura: Primo omnium crede, quoniam unus est Deus, qui omnia constituit et consummavit, et fecit ex eo quod non erat; &c. [c. 20. p. 253. The Greek is given by Eusebius, v. 8, and others: καλῶς οὖν εἶπεν ἡ γραφὴ, ἡ λέγουσα, πρῶτον πάντων πίστευσον, ὅτι εἷς ἐστὶν ὁ Θεὸς, ὁ τὰ πάντα κτίσας καὶ καταρτίσας, καὶ ποιήσας ἐκ τοῦ μὴ ὄντος εἰς τὸ εἶναι τὰ πάντα.—B.]

says, "has the Scripture spoken, which says, 'Before all things believe that God is one, who created and perfected all things, and made them out of that which did not exist,'" &c. Where by Scripture Eusebius (E. H. v. 8) observes, that the treatise called the Shepherd is meant: and the passage quoted by Irenæus is found, word for word, in the writings of Hermas, which are now extant, (Book ii. Mand. 1;) and on this Bellarmine appositely remarks, that "Irenæus would not have given the title of Scripture simply[1] to the book of an author of his own age, who had neither been an Apostle, nor a hearer of the Apostles[s]." Hermas is also quoted frequently by Clement of Alexandria, who also in express terms acknowledged "the power, which spoke by revelation to Hermas, as speaking divinely." (Strom. i. near the end[t].) Tertullian, whilst yet a Catholic, in the twelfth chapter of his treatise On Prayer, [p. 134,] replies to certain men who alleged the writings of Hermas in favour of a custom of which he himself disapproved, in such a way as by no means to reject the authority of the writing[2], but to endeavour to evade the force of his words by a suitable explanation of them, as is usually done in weighing the sense of other Holy Scriptures. Nay more, in his treatise On Chastity, c. 20, [p. 572,] after he had fallen into the heresy of Montanus, although he is somewhat bitter against the Shepherd, and, therefore, with want of modesty enough calls him "an apocryphal shepherd of adulterers," (because in accordance with the whole of Scripture he allowed a second repentance to the adulterer and fornicator,) and consequently denies his canonical authority, he yet does it in such a way that all persons of sound judgment must think that he bestows on it no despicable character. He says[u]; "The Epistle of Barnabas" (meaning the Epistle to the Hebrews, which he attributed to Barnabas) "is a more received book in the Churches than that apocryphal Shepherd of adulterers." Well, indeed, will it be for the Shepherd, if the second place after the

[1] absolute.

[2] scripturæ.

[45]

[s] Bellarm. de Script. Eccles., concerning the author of the book called the Shepherd, [vol. vii. p. 25. Op., ed. 1601—1617.]

[t] θείως τοίνυν ἡ δύναμις ἡ τῷ Ἑρμᾷ κατ' ἀποκάλυψιν λαλοῦσα . . . φησὶ κ.τ.λ.—[P. 426.]

[u] [Et utique receptior apud Ecclesias Epistola Barnabæ illo apocrypho Pastore mœchorum.—Tert. de Pudicitia, c. 10. p. 572.]

Epistle to the Hebrews be given it! When, therefore, Tertullian (in the tenth chapter of the same book[x]) calls the writing of the Shepherd "false and spurious[1]," he must certainly be so understood as to be thought only to deny that that treatise "was worthy to be inserted in the divine Canon[2];" as indeed he explains himself in so many words in that very passage. The Shepherd is also very frequently quoted by Origen, who (on Rom. xvi.[y]) even pronounced it to be not only a "very useful writing[3]," but also "divinely inspired." It is also quoted by Eusebius, out of Irenæus, Eccl. Hist. v. 8[z]; also by Athanasius[a], On the Incarnation of the Word, who likewise calls it a "most useful" treatise; and this judgment of the great doctor will be readily assented to by any one who peruses the work attentively and without prejudice. Rufinus (On the Creed, c. 38[b]) allows to the Shepherd the same place in the New Testament which the books of Tobit, Judith, and the Maccabees, had in the Old. Lastly, Jerome in his Prologus Galeatus [to the book of Kings[c]] reckons the treatise, [46] called the Shepherd, among the ecclesiastical books, with the book of Judith and Tobit: and in his treatise On the Ecclesiastical Writers[d], he says, "The Shepherd is at this time publicly read in some of the churches of Greece; it is a really profitable book; and many of the ancient writers have employed testimonies out of it." Whoever would know more concerning the antiquity and authority of this book, may consult the Vindication of the Epistles of St. Ignatius, by the very learned J. Pearson, the present most worthy bishop of Chester[e].

1 adulteram.

2 instrumento.

3 scripturam.

4. As however I think it of no small moment, that the authority and estimation with which this apostolic writer was regarded in the ancient Church should be maintained, I have deemed it fit, in passing, briefly to weigh the princi-

x [Sed cederem tibi, si scriptura Pastoris, . . . divino instrumento meruisset incidi, si non ab omni concilio Ecclesiarum etiam vestrarum inter apocrypha et falsa judicaretur, adultera et ipsa, &c.—c. 10. p. 563.]

y [Puto tamen quod Hermas iste sit scriptor libelli illius qui Pastor appellatur, quæ Scriptura valde mihi utilis videtur, et ut puto divinitus inspirata. —Vol. iv. p. 683.]

z [See p. 38. note r.]

a [ἡ δὲ ἔνθεος διδασκαλία, καὶ ἡ μετὰ Χριστὸν πίστις . . . φησὶ διὰ Μωσέως . . . διὰ δὲ τῆς ὠφελιμωτάτης βίβλου τοῦ ποιμένος· πρῶτον πίστευσον, κ.τ.λ.—De Incarnatione Verbi, § 3. vol. i. p. 49.]

b [Opusc., p. 189.]

c [Vol. ix. p. 454.]

d Pastor, inquit, apud quasdam Græciæ ecclesias jam publice legitur: revera utilis liber, multique de eo scriptorum veterum usurpavere testimonia. —[c. 10. vol. ii. p. 833.]

e Pearson, Vindic., part i. [c. 4.] p. 39, &c.

pal reasons which have influenced certain modern theologians, especially amongst the reformed, to cast him out entirely from the catalogue of approved doctors of the Church, and to drive far off from the fold of the Church that very excellent Shepherd, as if he were a wolf and an enemy to the flock of Christ. They allege as objections against him sundry doctrines, little befitting one who was a disciple of the Apostles. What then are these doctrines? First, says Scultetus, who is followed by Rivetus, "Purgatory is brought forward by a certain old woman in the third Vision." But (let me say it, with all deference to men so great) they are very much mistaken. Let the words of the passage be produced. Hermas is enquiring, whether the grace of repentance and a place within the tower can be again accorded to such as in the vision had been cast forth out of the tower into the fire? The aged woman replies[f], "They have [the grace of] repentance, but they cannot meet in this tower[1]; but they shall be put into another place, much lower, and this after they
have been tormented, and have fulfilled the days of their 17
sins. And for this cause shall they be transferred, because [47]
they have known the Word of righteousness. And then it shall befall them to be transferred from their punishments, if the evil deeds which they have done shall arise up in their hearts; but if they do not arise in their hearts, they shall not be saved, by reason of the hardness of their heart." Precisely akin to this is a passage[g] at the end of the sixth Similitude, [lib. iii.]; "For the passionate man, gratifying his habitual feelings, receives therein his pleasure; the adulterer also, and the drunkard, and the slanderer, and the liar, and the covetous man, and the fraudulent, and whosoever commits any thing like unto these, yielding to his disease[2], derives pleasure from what he does[3]. All these delights and pleasures[4] are hurtful to the servants of God;

[1] convenire in hac turre.

[2] morbo.

[3] ex ea re.

[4] πράξεις, dulcedines ac voluptates.

[f] Habent pœnitentiam; sed in hac turre non possunt convenire. Alio autem loco ponentur multo inferiore, et hoc, cum cruciati fuerint et impleverint dies peccatorum suorum. Et propter hoc transferentur, quoniam perceperunt Verbum justum. Et tunc illis continget transferri de pœnis, si ascenderint in corda ipsorum opera, quæ operati sunt scelesta. Quod si non ascenderint in corda ipsorum, non erunt salvi propter duritiam cordis sui.—[§ 7. p. 80.]

[g] Etenim iracundus satisfaciens moribus suis percipit voluptatem suam (τρυφᾷ); et adulter, et ebriosus, et detractor, et mendax, et cupidus, et fraudator, et quicunque iis simile aliquid admittit, morbo suo parens, percipit ex ea re voluptatem (τρυφῶσι ἐν

ON THE PRE-EXISTENCE OF THE SON.

on account of them therefore they are tormented and endure punishments. There are, moreover, pleasures which bring salvation unto men. For many in performing good works find pleasure in them, being drawn on by the sweetness thereof. Such pleasure, then, as this, is profitable to the servants of God, and procures for such persons life; but those hurtful pleasures, which were before mentioned, produce torments and punishments. And, whosoever shall continue in them, and not repent of what they have done, shall bring death upon themselves." I regard it as certain that, in these passages, the thing spoken of is not the popish purgatory, (that is a mere figment of the monks, which none of the ancients who flourished in the three first centuries even dreamed of[h],) but only to those cleansing punishments, or afflictions, which God, in His mercy, is wont to send upon sinners, for their amendment, in this present life. For so the Shepherd most clearly explains himself in the same sixth Similitude[i], in a passage before that just cited. Hermas there relates, that he saw some sheep, which a certain shepherd
[48] "was driving into a place full of precipices, and thorns, and briars, so that they could not extricate themselves from the briars and thorns; but they fed there, entangled, as they were, in the briars and thorns, and were grievously tortured with his lashes[1]; for he continued to drive them about, and allowed them neither space nor time to rest." Hermas then

[1] verberibus, δερόμενα.

τῇ πράξει αὐτῶν). Hæ omnes dulcedines ac voluptates noxiæ sunt servis Dei: propter has itaque cruciantur et patiuntur pœnas. Sunt etiam voluptates, salutem hominibus afferentes. Multi enim opera bonitatis facientes percipiunt voluptatem, dulcedine sua tracti. Hæc ergo voluptas utilis est servis Dei, et vitam parat hujusmodi hominibus. Illæ vero noxiæ, quæ supra dictæ sunt, tormenta et pœnas pariunt. Quicunque vero permanserint in illis, nec admissorum suorum egerint pœnitentiam, mortem sibi acquirent. [§ 5. p. 110. The text of the old Latin version is given, being that which Bull used. Of some portions only has the original Greek been recovered, and that since he wrote: it has been used in this translation to determine the sense of the Latin, and in one instance to correct it. The variations do not affect any doctrinal point.]

[h] [Dr. Burton here refers to his note on Bp. Bull's first Sermon, (Works, vol. i. p. 33,) which is as follows; "For the opinion of the ante-Nicene fathers on this passage, (i. e. 1 Pet. iii. 19, 20,) see Hermas, iii. sim. 9. c. 16; Irenæus, iv. 27; Clem. Alex. Strom. iii. 4. p. 526, vi. 6; Excerpta. Theod. ad fin. Clem. Alex., p. 973; Tertull. de Anima, c. 7. 55; Origen, c. Cels. ii. 43; In Exod., § 6; In Reg. Hom. ii. vol. ii. p. 497; in Psalm., p. 553; Hippol. de Antichristo, § 26, 45."]

[i] Visa sibi pecora, quæ pastor quidam compellebat in præcipitem locum quendam ac spinosum, tribulisque consertum, usque adeo ut de spinis et tribulis se non possent explicare; sed implicita ibi pascebantur spinis et tribulis, et graves cruciatus experiebantur ex verbis (s. verberibus) ejus (δερόμενα ὑπ' αὐτοῦ): agebat enim ea, et nec consistendi eis locum ante (s. aut.) tempus

BOOK I. CHAP. II. § 4.

HERMAS.

goes on to say; "When, therefore, I saw that they were thus lashed, and suffering such misery, I was grieved for them, because they were greatly tormented, and no rest was given them, and I said to the Shepherd[1] that was with me, Who, Sir, is this shepherd that is so unmerciful and cruel, and is not at all moved by compassion towards these sheep? He answered, This shepherd is indeed the angel of vengeance, and he is one of the righteous angels, but is appointed over the punishment [of sinners]. To him, accordingly, are handed over those who have strayed from God, and served the desires and pleasures of the present world. For this cause doth he punish them, as they have each deserved, with varied and cruel punishments. Sir, was my reply, I would fain know of what sort are these various punishments? Hear then, said he; these are the various penalties and torments which men suffer daily IN THEIR LIFETIME[2]. For some suffer losses, others poverty, and others divers sicknesses. Some of them suffer from unsettledness[3], others suffer injuries at the hands of unworthy men, and many other trials and inconveniences. . . . When, therefore, they shall have endured every vexation and discomfort, then they are delivered over to me for good instruction, and are strengthened in the faith of the Lord, and serve Him the rest of the days of their life with a pure mind. And when they have begun to repent for their sins, then their deeds

[1] *τῷ ἀγγέλῳ* pastori.

[2] in vita sua *βιωτικαί εἰσι βάσανοι.*

[3] *ἀκαταστασίαις.*

permittebat (*καὶ ὅλως ἀπάπαυσιν αὐτοῖς οὐκ ἐδίδου, οὐδ' ἵσταντο.*) Cum viderem ergo sic ea flagellari, et miserias experiri, dolebam pro eis, quia valde cruciabantur, nec ulla requies eis dabatur. Dico ad Pastorem illum, qui erat mecum (*τῷ ἀγγέλῳ τῷ μετ' ἐμοῦ λαλοῦντι*). Quis est, Domine, hic pastor tam implacabilis, et tam amarus, qui nullo modo miseratione movetur adversus hæc pecora? Hic, inquit, Pastor pro justis quidem nuntius est, (*οὗτός ἐστιν ὁ ἄγγελος τῆς τιμωρίας· ἐκ δὲ τῶν ἀγγέλων δικαίων ἐστὶ,*) sed præpositus pœnæ. Huic ergo traduntur qui a Deo aberraverunt, et servierunt desideriis ac voluptatibus sæculi hujus. Punit ergo eos, sicut meruit unusquisque eorum, sævis variisque pœnis. Vellem, inquam, nosse, Domine, varias has pœnas, cujusmodi sunt. Audi, inquit; variæ pœnæ atque tormenta hæc sunt, quæ homines quotidie IN VITA SUA patiuntur. Alii enim (*βιωτικαί εἰσιν βάσανοι, ἐπὰν γὰρ ἀποστῶσι τοῦ Θεοῦ, νομίζοντες ἐν ἀναπαύσει εἶναι καὶ πλούτῳ*) detrimenta patiuntur; alii inopiam alii diversas ægrimonias (*ἀσθενείαις*). Quidam inconstantiam (*ἀκαταστασίαις*), alii injurias ab indignis patientes, multaque alia exercitia et incommoda . . . Cum igitur perpessi fuerint omnem vexationem et omne incommodum, tunc traduntur mihi ad bonam admonitionem, et firmantur in fide Domini, et per reliquos dies vitæ serviunt Domino mente pura (*καὶ λοιπὸν αἰτιῶνται τὸν κύριον καὶ οὐκ ἀνέχονται τὰς λοιπὰς ἡμερὰς αὐτῶν ἐπιστρέψαντες δουλεῦσαι τῷ Θεῷ ἐν καθαρᾷ καρδίᾳ*). Et cum cœperint delictorum agere pœnitentiam, tunc ascendunt in præcordia eorum opera sua, in quibus se nequiter exercuerunt (*τότε συνιῶσι, ὅτι διὰ τὰ ἔργα αὐτῶν τὰ πόνηρα οὐκ*

ON THE PRE-EXISTENCE OF THE SON.

in which they have wickedly exercised themselves, rise up in their hearts; they then give honour to God, confessing that He is a just judge, and that they have deservedly
[49] suffered all according to their doings. And for the time to come they serve God with a pure mind, and have success in all they undertake, obtaining of the Lord whatsoever they ask. And then they give thanks to the Lord, that they have been handed over unto me; and do not henceforward suffer any thing of cruelty," &c. &c. Now what can be clearer than this explanation? Nay, you may read statements in our Hermas which utterly overthrow the popish purgatory. For he writes thus in his third Vision[k]; "They, therefore, who have yet to repent, if they shall have repented, will be strong in the faith; that is, provided they shall repent NOW, whilst the tower is in building. For if the building shall have been finished, from that time no one hath a place left wherein he may be put, but he will be a reprobate. That man alone will have this, who is ALREADY placed on the tower."

Another objection of these same learned persons, that free-will is asserted by Hermas, is a frivolous one. For a free-will, acting with and under divine grace, which alone Hermas maintains, is equally[1] asserted both by Holy Scripture, and by all the Catholic doctors of the first ages.

[1] pariter.

There is a graver charge which is made against him both by reformed and popish theologians, to the effect that he allows but one repentance to such as have lapsed into the more heinous sins, after receiving the grace of the Holy Ghost in baptism. But let us once more hear the very words of the Shepherd; thus then does he write (in the second book, in the fourth Mandate, near the end[l];) "I tell thee, if any one,

εὐοδοῦντο). Et tunc dant Deo honorem, dicentes justum Judicem eum esse, meritoque se omnia esse perpessos secundum facta sua. In reliquum vero serviunt Deo mente pura, et successum habent in negotiis suis omnibus, accipientes a Domino quæcunque poscunt. Et tunc gratias agunt Domino, quod sint mihi traditi, nec jam quidquam crudelitatis patiuntur, &c.—[§ 2. p. 109. See the Greek in ed. Coteler.—B.]

[k] Qui ergo pœnitentiam acturi sunt, si egerint pœnitentiam, fortes erunt in fide, si NUNC pœnitentiam egerint, dum ædificatur turris. Nam si consummata fuerit structura, jam quis non habet locum, ubi ponatur, sed erit reprobus. Solummodo autem hoc habebit, qui JAM ad turrim positus est.—[§ 5. p. 80.]

[l] Dico tibi, quod post vocationem illam magnam et sanctam siquis tentatus fuerit a Diabolo, et peccaverit, unam pœnitentiam habet. Si autem subinde peccet, et pœnitentiam agat, non proderit homini talia agenti; difficile enim vivit Deo."—[§ 3. p. 91.]

BOOK I. CHAP. II. § 4. HERMAS.

after that great and holy calling, shall have been tempted of the devil, and shall have committed sin, he hath one repentance. But if from time to time[1] he sin and repent, it shall not profit the man that doeth so; for hardly will he live unto God." The Shepherd seems to be speaking of such as, after receiving the grace of regeneration, having fallen away, and having been restored through repentance, again relapse, *subinde*, that is, often, into the same or similar grievous sins, [50]
and, as often, repent. That this desultory repentance, so to call it, profits a man nothing, he does with good reason affirm. He does not, however, altogether despair of the salvation of such persons, he only declares that "it is difficult" for men of such a character, who thus, as it were, sin and repent by 18
turns, "to live unto God;" and this is most true. So also in an earlier part of the same chapter[m] the Shepherd opposes to one repentance the "sinning often." For shewing how a husband ought to behave towards a wife, who has been put away because of adultery, and who repents of her sin, and seeks to be received back again by her husband, he says, "He ought to receive the offending woman who has repented, but not often; because to the servants of God there is but one repentance." But if you interpret *subinde* by *deinde*, ["from time to time" by "afterwards," see above,] and so understand the mind of the Shepherd as if he meant indeed to allow repentance to such as had only once lapsed, after they had received the grace of the Holy Ghost, but not to those who had fallen a second time, (i. e. into the more grievous sins,) then the Shepherd must be regarded as speaking of the penance to be performed before the Church, and of the absolution consequent upon it, which the severer discipline of that age in many places used to allow once only to such lapsed persons; although, at the same time, it did not entirely exclude such as had repeatedly lapsed, from the hope of obtaining remission with God. In this way Acesius in Socrates explains the opinion of the Novatians themselves concerning such as had once only after baptism fallen into sin which is unto death[n]; "How that it is not fit that they who, after bap- [51]

[1] subinde.

[m] [§ 1. pp. 88, 89.]

[n] ὡς ἄρα οὐ χρὴ τοὺς μετὰ τὸ βάπτισμα ἡμαρτηκότας ἁμαρτίαν, ἣν πρὸς θάνατον καλοῦσιν αἱ θεῖαι γραφαί, τῆς κοινωνίας τῶν θείων μυστηρίων ἀξιοῦσθαι· ἀλλ' ἐπὶ μετάνοιαν μὲν αὐτοὺς

ON THE PRE-EXISTENCE OF THE SON.

tism, have committed a sin which the Holy Scriptures call 'a sin unto death,' should be admitted to the participation of the divine mysteries; still they ought to be exhorted to repentance, and to look for the hope of remission, not from the priests, but from God, who is able and has full power to forgive sins." Indeed, in whatever other way you interpret the passage of the Shepherd, this is certain, that the lapsed, of whom he is speaking, are not by him wholly shut out from the hope of living with God; forasmuch as he only says, as I have remarked already, that "it is difficult for them to live unto God." On account of a similar passage, however, it was a long time before the Epistle to the Hebrews was received into the canon by the Church of Rome. See the learned annotations of Grotius on the fourth and following verses of the sixth chapter of that Epistle. I thought that I ought, by the way as it were, once for all, to say thus much in defence of Hermas, whose authority we shall hereafter use in contending against the Arians.

5. Let us now hear the very remarkable testimony of this venerable and apostolic writer respecting the pre-existence of the Son. In the ninth Similitude[o], then, he thus speaks concerning the Son of God; "The Son of God indeed is more ancient than any creature, so that He was present in counsel with His Father, in order to the creation of the world." This passage of Hermas is allowed by the author of the Irenicum Irenicorum, who agrees with me respecting the antiquity and authority of the writer. For the purpose, however, of defending his own most absurd opinion, (by which he lays down that it was Justin who first introduced into the Christian Churches, out of the school of Plato, the doctrine of the pre-existence of the Son before the formation of the world, and of the creation of the world through Him,) he endeavours to elude
[52] the testimony of Hermas in this manner; "It is altogether uncertain," he says[p], "whether by the Son of God he means Christ, when, in the ninth Similitude, he says that the Son of God was more ancient than any creature." What? Is it un-

προτρέπειν· ἐλπίδα δὲ τῆς ἀφέσεως μὴ παρὰ τῶν ἱερέων, ἀλλὰ παρὰ τοῦ Θεοῦ ἐκδέχεσθαι, τοῦ δυναμένου καὶ ἐξουσίαν ἔχοντος συγχωρεῖν ἁμαρτήματα.—Socrates, E. H. i. 10.

[o] Filius quidem Dei omni creatura antiquior est, ita ut in consilio Patri suo adfuerit ad condendam creaturam.—[Lib. iii. § 12. l. Sim. ix. 12. p. 118.]

[p] Iren. Irenic., p. 21.

certain? Is it altogether uncertain? Then, say I, sceptics are the wisest of men, and there is nothing certain in human affairs! "Nay," says this anonymous author, "the Holy Spirit is called by Hermas the Son of God, both in the fifth Similitude, and in other places." Here, however, the heretic is wholly mistaken, and but too manifestly displays, as is his wont, his ignorance of "primitive antiquity, and of the faith of the early Christians," which, nevertheless, he boasts[q] of "having set before men's eyes, more clearly than it ever was before." Hermas nowhere calls the Holy Spirit, the third Person of the Godhead, the Son of God. The words of his in the fifth Similitude[r], to which the anonymous author refers, are as follows; "The Son of God is the Holy Spirit[s]." Where, it is true, the Son of God is called the Holy Spirit; but the Holy Spirit, if you understand the third Person of the Godhead, is not called by the title of the Son of God, which will be easily seen by one who examines the passage. The truth is, the whole discourse of Hermas in that place relates to the Son of God, who for our salvation became a servant, and assumed a body, in which He[1] conversed as a servant. You will, however, ask on what principle Christ, the Son of God, is by Hermas called the Holy Spirit? I answer, in respect of His divine nature[2], or Godhead; inasmuch as He, being Himself a most Holy Spirit, hath His being from God the Father, who is a most Holy Spirit. In which sense the designation of Holy Spirit may be applied to each Person of the most Holy Trinity. The appellation of Holy Spirit is given, indeed, peculiarly to the [53]
third Person of the Godhead, not in regard of nature[3], (for in this respect both the Father[t] is a Holy Spirit and the Son also,) but by reason of that ineffable spiration[4], whereby He[u] proceeds from the Father, through the Son. 19
The ancient ecclesiastical writers, however, did not always so

[1] quod.

[2] τῆς θείας φύσεως.

[3] φύσεως.

[4] spirationis.

[q] P. 13.

[r] [§ 5. p. 107.]

[s] [Hermas' words are, *Filius autem Spiritus Sanctus est. Servus vero ille Filius Dei.* Whoever reads the entire similitude, will perceive that "the Son" and "the Servant" are two persons. Hermas therefore does not say that "the Son of God is the Holy Spirit." The reader, however, should consult the passage.—B.]

[t] τῷ πατρὶ καὶ τῷ υἱῷ κατὰ τὸ ἴσον ἥ τε τοῦ πνεύματος καὶ ἡ τοῦ ἁγίου κλῆσις παρὰ τῆς γραφῆς ἐφαρμόζεται.—Gregor. Nyssen. Orat. i. contr. Eunom. p. 57. ed. Paris. 1615. [Orat. ii. vol. ii. p. 485.]

[u] ["Ipsa" scil. tertia Divinitatis ὑπόστασις, the third Person of the Godhead just mentioned.]

accurately keep[1] up this distinction between the generation of the Son, and the procession of the Holy Spirit by the mode of spiration[2]; as the great Grotius has most truly remarked, in his notes on Mark ii. 8; "The divine nature in Christ is called Spirit, not merely on account of its incorporeality[3], in the sense in which that name is suitable to the Father, but also because they used to designate that which, for the purpose of distinguishing between the Word and the Holy Ghost, is expressed by the word *generare*, and sometimes among the Greek fathers by the word ἀπαυγάζειν also, by the more wide expression *spirare;* meaning by this word an emanation[4] of whatever kind, or, as Tertullian designates it, προβολή; for in his treatise against Praxeas he has spoken of the Son as 'proceeding,' no less than as 'derived.'" Be that, however, as it may, it is most certain that the Son of God, the second Person of the Godhead[5], is in the writings of the Fathers[x] throughout called by the title of "Spirit," "Spirit of God," and "Holy Spirit." If there be any one so much a stranger to the works of the ancients as not to know this, he may consult the author I have just quoted, Hugo Grotius, in the passage referred to, where he will find this very point demonstrated by many most evident testimonies; and in that numerous collection of quotations our Hermas is expressly mentioned as one who had sanctioned this mode of expression. To the passages adduced by Grotius, I will my-
[54] self add two remarkable passages out of the most ancient writers of the Church, viz., the author of the Epistle attributed to Barnabas, and Ignatius. The former in the seventh chapter of his Epistle, [p. 21,] thus speaks concerning Christ[y]; "He Himself was about to offer up the vessel of the Spirit[6] as a sacrifice for our sins." Where "the vessel of the Spirit" is the human nature of Christ, in which His Divinity, which is called Spirit, was received as in a vessel. For the author afterwards expressly expounds this vessel of the flesh of Christ. Whence (to remark it in passing) may be easily gathered, if it were not otherwise clear, the meaning of the author of the Epistle to the Hebrews, chap. ix. 14,

[1] tenuerunt.
[2] spirationis.
[3] διὰ τὸ ἀσώματον.
[4] emanationem.
[5] secundam Deitatis hypostasin.
[6] σκεῦος τοῦ πνεύματος.

[x] With which agree the Holy Scriptures. See Mark ii. 8; Rom. i. 3, 4; 1 Tim. iii. 16; Heb. ix. 14; 1 Pet. iii. 18—20. See also John vi. 63, compared with 56.

[y] αὐτὸς ὑπὲρ τῶν ἡμετέρων ἁμαρτιῶν ἤμελλε σκεῦος τοῦ Πνεύματος προσφέρειν θυσίαν.

wherein Christ is said to have offered Himself without spot to God, "through the eternal Spirit[1]." That is to say, the meaning of the words is that the eternal Godhead of Christ, or the Divine Person of the Son of God, offered up to God on the altar of the cross, the human nature, which was personally[2] (as they express it) united to Himself. Ignatius again, in the very inscription of his Epistle to the Smyrneans[z], wishes to them "fulness of joy through the immaculate Spirit, the Word of God." Where the Word, who is the Son of God, is plainly called the "immaculate," or holy, "Spirit[a]."

[1] διὰ Πνεύματος αἰωνίου.

[2] personaliter, or "hypostatically."

6. But what need is there of many words on a point which is clear? If any one is moved by this most perverse difficulty, raised by this anonymous writer, so as still to doubt what Hermas meant, in the passage quoted, by "the Son of God, who is more ancient than every creature," let him consult the passage itself, as it occurs entire in the ninth Similitude, [§ 12;] and if I am not mistaken he will at once lay aside all doubts. Near the beginning of that Similitude, Hermas's shepherd had exhibited to him a very large plain, surrounded by twelve mountains; and in the midst of the plain a huge and very ancient rock, higher than those twelve mountains, which had a new gate, that seemed to have been lately hewn out, [55] and exceeded the sun in brightness. When the shepherd had finished the entire similitude, Hermas at last asks for the interpretation, and first enquires concerning the rock and the gate; "First of all, Sir," he says, "shew me what this rock and gate are?" "This rock and this gate," answered the shepherd, "is the Son of God." Hermas proceeds in his enquiries, "How is it, Sir, that the rock is old, but the gate new?" To whom the shepherd replies[b], "Hear, O simple one! and understand. The Son of God, indeed, is more ancient than any creature, inasmuch as He was present in counsel with His Father in order to the formation of all created things. But the gate is therefore new, because at the end

[z] [p. 33.]

[a] [See infra, ii. 10. 2.]

[b] Primum omnium, domine, inquam, hoc mihi demonstra; petra hæc et porta quid sunt? Audi, inquit, petra hæc et porta Filius Dei est. Quonam pacto, inquam, domine, petra vetus est, porta autem nova? Audi, inquit, insipiens, et intellige. Filius quidem Dei omni creatura antiquior est, ita ut in consilio Patri suo adfuerit ad condendam creaturam. Porta autem propterea nova est, quia in consummatione in novissimis diebus apparuit, ut qui assecuturi sunt salutem, per eam intrent in regnum Dei.—[§ 12. p. 118.]

ON THE PRE-EXISTENCE OF THE SON.

[of the world,] in the last days[c], He hath appeared, that they who shall attain unto salvation, may by it enter into the kingdom of God." Then, to illustrate the similitude of the gate, he proposes the example of a city surrounded by a wall, and having only a single gate; and adds[d]; "As, therefore, one cannot enter into that city but by its gate, so neither can one enter into the kingdom of God, otherwise than by the name of His Son, who is most dear unto Him;" and a little afterwards; "But the gate is the Son of God, who is the only way of access unto God; for no man shall enter in unto God otherwise than by His Son." Immortal God! is it possible that in so clear a light any one can fail to see! Is there any one who bears the name of Christian, who knows not who is that Son of God, most dear to His Father, who has appeared in these last days, who is the only gate through which there is open to us sinners an access unto God the Father, and an entrance into the kingdom of heaven? And yet many other expressions follow presently in the same
[56] similitude, which also most plainly shew who that Son of God is, of whom the Shepherd is speaking. For instance,
20 the Shepherd shews that upon the rock—the Son of God—the tower, which is the Church, is built. And having spoken concerning the various gifts and graces of the Holy Spirit, (which he had in the similitude[e] shadowed forth under the figure of virgins,) he says, "They who have believed in God, through His Son, have put on this Spirit;" where also he plainly distinguishes the Son from the Spirit of God, that is, from the third Person of the Godhead. He then, a little after, makes mention of the Apostles and doctors (represented in the similitude by stones) who preached the coming of the Son of God. Lastly, concerning the Gentiles converted to the faith of the Son of God, (whom he had in the similitude symbolised by mountains,) he speaks in these words[f]; "All the nations, which are under heaven, have heard

[c] [Cf. Heb. ix. 26: ἅπαξ ἐπὶ συντελείᾳ τῶν αἰώνων semel in consummatione sæculorum.—Vulg. Once in the end of the world hath He appeared, &c.]

[d] Sicut ergo in illam urbem non potest intrari, quam per portam ejus; ita nec in regnum Dei potest aliter intrari, nisi per nomen Filii ejus; qui est ei carissimus; . . . Porta vero Filius Dei est, qui solus est accessus ad Deum; aliter ergo nemo intrabit ad Deum, nisi per Filium ejus.—[§ 12. p. 118.]

[e] Ii, qui crediderunt Deo per Filium ejus, induti sunt Spiritum hunc.—[§ 13. p. 118.]

[f] Universæ nationes, quæ sub cœlo sunt, audierunt et crediderunt, et uno

and believed, and have been called by the one name of the Son of God." Who is there then, I ask again, so blind as not to see at once that all this is spoken of that Son of God which is Christ? Surely there can be no one of any piety, but must from his heart detest the extreme shamelessness of the anonymous writer, when he asserts, that "It is altogether uncertain whether Hermas, when he says, in the ninth Similitude, that the Son of God is more ancient than any creature, by the Son of God means Christ." Thus much of the testimony of Hermas. HERMAS.

7. After Hermas let Ignatius come, who was appointed bishop of Antioch[g] by the Apostles themselves. That the seven Epistles mentioned by Eusebius,—which were first published in Latin by the most reverend Abp. Ussher, from two MSS. discovered here in England, and afterwards in Greek by the very learned Isaac Vossius from the Medicean MS., (with the single exception of the Epistle to the Romans,)—are his genuine remains, has been sufficiently proved against Blondel by Vossius and Hammond; and the bishop of Chester[h], whom I have mentioned above, has so [57] very clearly and fully demonstrated the fact in reply to Daillé, that in the view of fair judges the question about the writings of Ignatius and the whole controversy is considered to be settled. For no lover of truth, who is even moderately versed in this sort of learning, will be in the least degree induced to doubt respecting those Epistles, by the sophistical "Observations" which an anonymous author[i], in the year 1674, published at Rouen in reply to Pearson. Altogether useless is the attempt of this writer to rally and put again in array the broken and scattered forces of his friend Daillé. Ignatius, then, in his Epistle to the Magnesians, having before spoken of Christ, adds as follows[k]; "Who was with the Father before all ages, and in the end appeared." IGNATIUS.

nomine filii Dei vocati sunt.—[§ 17. pp. 120, 121.]

[g] About the year 67. *Cave in Ignat.* —BOWYER.

[h] [Bp. Pearson, in his "Vindiciæ Ignatianæ."]

[i] [The title of the book is, "Observationes in Ignatianas Pearsonii Vindicias, et in Annotationes Beveregii in Canones S. Apostolorum, Rothomagi, 1674." The anonymous author was for a time unknown; Dr. Allix was afterwards suspected, as appears from a copy in the Bodleian library. Placcius, however, (i. p. 149,) has sufficiently proved that the true author was Matthew Larroque.—B.]

[k] ὃς πρὸ αἰώνων παρὰ Πατρὶ ἦν, καὶ ἐν τέλει ἐφάνη.—p. 33. [§ 6. p. 19.]

ON THE PRE-EXISTENCE OF THE SON.

We shall, however, adduce from Ignatius in a later part of the work more numerous and more marked[1] testimonies.

[1] illustriora.

8. Justin the philosopher lived and wrote[l] and was crowned with martyrdom[m] some years before the close of the generation immediately succeeding that of the Apostles[2]. For the generation immediately succeeding that of the Apostles, as the distinguished Hen. Valesius[n] has justly observed, extends as far as to the times of Marcus Antoninus; as it was under that emperor that Polycarp, the disciple of John the Apostle,
[58] (now more than a hundred years old,) obtained the crown of martyrdom, that is to say, according to the Roman Martyrology, on the twenty-sixth of January, A.D. 167. But Justin addressed both his Apologies to Antoninus Pius[o], who died in the year 161 of the Christian era; and under the same emperor shed his blood for the Christian religion, as the same Valesius[p] maintains. All, however, are agreed that that holy man met death for the faith of Christ before the year 167. Hence in his Epistle to Diognetus, Justin calls himself "a disciple of the Apostles[3]." Now this most ancient father and glorious martyr freely throughout his writings professed and strenuously maintained, both against Jews and Gentiles, the doctrine of the pre-existence of the Son before the foundation of the world, and of the creation of the universe through Him, and that as the common and received view of the Church in his time. It will be enough here to adduce two passages; in the Apology, which in the editions of his works is called the first, having spoken of God the Father, he goes on to speak thus concerning the Son[q]; "His Son, who alone is properly called Son, the Word, who, before all created things, was both in being with Him, and begotten [of Him],—when in the beginning He created and set in order all things through Him," &c. In his Dialogue

[2] primam apostolorum διαδοχήν.

[3] ἀποστόλων μαθητήν.

[l] He presented his first Apology to Antoninus Pius about the year 140. Cave in Just. Mart.—BOWYER.

[m] About the year 164.—BOWYER.

[n] In his notes on Eusebius, p. 34. [ii. 23.]

[o] [His first Apology was presented to Antoninus Pius A.D. 140; his second, some years afterwards, to Marcus Antoninus.—LARDNER.—B.]

[p] Notes on Eusebius, pp. 66, 67. [iv. 16.]

[q] ὁ δὲ υἱὸς ἐκείνου, ὁ μόνος λεγόμενος κυρίως υἱὸς, ὁ λόγος πρὸ τῶν ποιημάτων καὶ συνὼν, καὶ γεννώμενος, ὅτε τὴν ἀρχὴν δι' αὐτοῦ πάντα ἔκτισε καὶ ἐκόσμησε, κ.τ.λ.—p. 44. [Apol. ii. 6. p. 92. See the rest of the passage below, iii. 2. 1.]

with Trypho he thus writes[s]; "But this His offspring[1], that was in very deed put forth from the Father, was in being with the Father before any created things, and Him the Father addresses;" that is, in the words which he had previously quoted, "Let us make man," &c.

JUSTIN M.

[1] γέννημα.

[59]

9. Tatian[t], the disciple of Justin, in his Oration against the Greeks, in setting forth the opinion held in common by the Christians of his time, concerning the Son of God, says[u]; "We know that He was the Beginning[2] of the world." And a little afterwards[x]; "For the heavenly Word, having come forth a Spirit from the Father, and a Word from out of the 21
Intellectual Power, in imitation[3] of the Father that begat Him, made man an image of His immortality." And again, after a few intervening words; "The Word, then, before the formation of man, becomes the creator of the angels."

TATIAN.

[2] τὴν ἀρχήν.

[3] κατὰ τὴν μίμησιν.

10. Athenagoras the Athenian, almost contemporary with Justin[y], a very learned philosopher, and a distinguished ornament of the Christian profession, in his Apology[4] for the Christians, which he addressed to Marcus Aurelius Antoninus and his colleague in the empire, putting forth the confession of Christians concerning the most holy Trinity, after having spoken of God the Father, subjoins[z]; "By whom, the universe was made through His Word, and set in order, and is now held together." He also, a little after, calls the Son "the first offspring[5] of the Father, as having come forth [from Him] to be the idea and energy of all things."

ATHENAGORAS.

[4] Legatione.

[5] γέννημα.

[60]

11. Lastly, Irenæus[a] (who in his youth was an attentive[6] hearer of Polycarp, and is therefore justly said by Eusebius[b] to have reached[7] to the first succession after the Apostles)

IRENÆUS.

[6] diligens.

[7] contigisse, κατειληφέναι.

[s] ἀλλὰ τοῦτο τὸ τῷ ὄντι ἀπὸ τοῦ Πατρὸς προβληθὲν γέννημα πρὸ πάντων τῶν ποιημάτων συνῆν τῷ Πατρὶ, καὶ τούτῳ ὁ Πατὴρ προσομιλεῖ.—p. 285. [Ibid., § 62. p. 159.]

[t] Flourished about the year 172. Cave in Tat.—BOWYER. [He wrote about the year 165.—LARDNER.—B.]

[u] τοῦτον ἴσμεν τοῦ κόσμου τὴν ἀρχήν. p. 145. ad calcem Just. Martyr. Par. 1615. [§ 5. p. 247.]

[x] λόγος γὰρ ὁ ἐπουράνιος, Πνεῦμα γεγονὼς ἀπὸ τοῦ Πατρὸς, καὶ λόγος ἐκ τῆς λογικῆς δυνάμεως, κατὰ τὴν τοῦ γεννήσαντος αὐτὸν Πατρὸς μίμησιν εἰκόνα τῆς ἀθανασίας τὸν ἄνθρωπον ἐποίησε. . . . ὁ μὲν οὖν λόγος πρὸ τῆς τῶν ἀνδρῶν κατασκευῆς ἀγγέλων δημιουργὸς γίνεται.—p. 146. [§ 7. p. 249.]

[y] He flourished about the year 177. Cave in. Athen.—BOWYER.

[z] ὑφ' οὗ γεγένηται τὸ πᾶν διὰ τοῦ αὐτοῦ λόγου, καὶ διακεκόσμηται, καὶ συγκρατεῖται. . . . πρῶτον γέννημα τοῦ Πατρὸς, ὡς [τῶν ὑλικῶν] συμπάντων. . . . ἰδέα καὶ ἐνέργεια εἶναι προελθών.—Ad calcem Just. Mart. Par. 1615. p. 10. [§ 10. p. 286.]

[a] Born A.D. 97, wrote his treatise adv. Hæreses A.D. 175. Cave.—BOWYER.

[b] Hist. Eccles. v. 20.

ON THE PRE-EXISTENCE OF THE SON.

has these words concerning the Word, or the Son of God[c]; "Nor yet can any one of those things, which were constituted, and are [now] in subjection, be compared to the Word of God, through whom all things were made, who is our Lord Jesus Christ. For that, whether they be angels or archangels, or thrones or dominions, they were both constituted and created by Him, who is God over all, through His Word; John has thus declared. For after he had said, concerning the Word of God, that 'He was in the Father,' he added, 'all things were made by Him, and without Him was not any thing made.'" Again[d]; "For these things did the Son, who is the Word of God, prepare beforehand[1] from the beginning; the Father standing in no need of angels in order to effect the creation, and to form man, for whom also the creation was made."

[1] præstruebat.

That the other fathers of the first three centuries taught[2] the self-same doctrine concerning our Saviour, all are well aware who are acquainted with their writings; let those who are not versed in them rely on my assurance, until with their own eyes they shall have seen the testimonies of those writers themselves, which declare far greater things than these respecting the Son of God, which I have to quote in the following books. Thus far, then, respecting the preexistence of the Son.

[2] tradidisse.

[c] Sed nec quidquam ex his, quæ constituta sunt, et in subjectione sunt, comparabitur Verbo Dei, per quem facta sunt omnia, qui est Dominus noster Jesus Christus. Quoniam enim sive angeli, sive archangeli, sive throni, sive dominationes, ab eo, qui super omnes est Deus, et constituta sunt et facta per Verbum ejus, Joannes quidem sic significavit. Cum enim dixisset de Verbo Dei, quoniam *erat in Patre*, adjecit, *Omnia per eum facta sunt, et sine eo factum est nihil.*—Lib. iii. cap. 8. [p. 183.]

[d] Idem iv. 17. [cap. 7. p. 236.]

BOOK II.

ON THE CONSUBSTANTIALITY OF THE SON. 25
[69]

CHAPTER I.

THE SUBJECT PROPOSED. THE WORD ὁμοούσιος, "OF ONE SUBSTANCE[a]," EXPLAINED AT LENGTH. THE NICENE FATHERS CLEARED FROM THE SUSPICION OF EMPLOYING NEW AND STRANGE LANGUAGE[1] IN USING THIS WORD TO EXPRESS THE TRUE GODHEAD OF THE SON. THE OPPOSITION[2] BETWEEN THE COUNCIL OF ANTIOCH AGAINST PAUL OF SAMOSATA, AND THE COUNCIL OF NICE AGAINST ARIUS, RECONCILED. PROOF THAT THE TERM ὁμοούσιος WAS NOT DERIVED FROM HERETICS. A BRIEF REVIEW OF THE HEADS OF THE ARGUMENTS BY WHICH THE ANTE-NICENE DOCTORS CONFIRMED "THE CONSUBSTANTIALITY."

[1] καινοφωνία.
[2] ἀντιλογία.

1. ON the question of the Consubstantiality of the Son of God we shall dwell longer, since it is the hinge on which the whole controversy between the Catholics and the Arians turns. On this subject, then, we propose, for very copious illustration and confirmation, the following Proposition.

PROPOSITION.

It was the settled and unanimous opinion[3] of the Catholic Doctors, who flourished in the first three centuries, that the Son of God was of one substance[4], or consubstantial with God the Father; that is, that He was not of any created or mutable essence, but of altogether the same divine and unchangeable nature with His Father; and, therefore, very God of very God.

[3] constans concorsque sententia.
[4] ὁμοούσιος sive consubstantialis.

Before, however, we proceed to the proof of the proposition, it will be necessary to premise some observations on the true meaning and ancient use of the word ὁμοούσιος, "of one substance," which was placed by the Nicene fathers [70]

[a] [The Greek word ὁμοούσιος has been translated by the English words "consubstantial," "of the same substance, or essence," (when Bp. Bull had used *ejusdem substantiæ*, or *essentiæ*,) and "of one substance." The last has been preferred, as being that to which we are accustomed in the Nicene Creed.]

in their Creed. The followers of Arius in old time spoke in a way so strangely tragical about that term, that at length not a few, even amongst the Catholics, wearied out by their importunate clamours, in their love of peace began to disapprove of the word, as we learn from Hilary, in his book On the Synods, and from other writers. That impious and restless faction pretended, at one time, that the phrase *ὁμοούσιος* favoured Sabellianism; at another, by reasoning altogether opposite, that it set up a division of the divine essence; and, lastly, what was mere trifling, that it introduced a substance prior both to the Father and the Son, of which afterwards the Father and the Son were equally partakers. I shall clearly shew, however, that this contest about words[1] was raised by them without any just grounds.

[1] λογομαχία.

26 2. By approved Greek writers, that is styled *ὁμοούσιον,* "consubstantial," which is of the same substance, essence, or nature with some other[b]; a sense which the very etymology of the word carries on the face of it: Porphyry, On Abstinence from Animal Food, book i. n. 19, says; "Since the souls of animals are *ὁμοούσιοι,* of the same essence[2] with ours." The anonymous author of the celebrated Opinions respecting the Soul, published with the *Philocalia* of Origen, quotes a passage of Aristotle, wherein he says; "All the stars are *ὁμοούσια,* of the same essence or nature[3]." In the same sense Irenæus frequently uses this word in explaining the doctrines of the Valentinians; for instance, (in book i. chap. 1[c],) he says that those heretics taught that, "whatsoever is spiritual could not by any means have been formed[4] by Achamoth, since it was *ὁμοούσιον,* of the same essence[5] with her." And presently afterwards he says; "In the first place [they [71] say that] she (Achamoth) out of living substance formed the parent and king of all things, both of those things which are of the same essence with him, (*τῶν τὲ ὁμοουσίων αὐτῷ,*) and of those which were engendered of passion and matter." Again in the same chapter after some interval; that[d] "Hylicus was in image very like unto God, but not of the same essence with

[2] ejusdem essentiæ.

[3] ejusdem essentiæ sive naturæ.

[4] informari.

[5] ejusdem essentiæ.

[b] [But see the concluding words of the extract from St. Basil, p. 62.]

[c] [The words of Irenæus are, ἀλλὰ τὸ πνευματικὸν μὴ δεδυνῆσθαι αὐτῇ (s. αὐτὴν) μορφῶσαι, ἐπειδὴ ὁμοούσιον ἦν αὐτῇ.]—p. 22. [c. 5. p. 23.]

[d] p. 24. [§ 5. p. 27.]

HOMOOUSION.

Him, (παραπλήσιον μὲν, ἀλλ' οὐχ ὁμοούσιον τῷ θεῷ.)" And after a few intervening words; "Not even the Demiurge knew of the offspring[1] of the mother Achamoth, which she brought forth through the contemplation of those angels by whom the Saviour is surrounded, in that it was a spiritual offspring of the same essence with its mother, (ὁμοούσιον ὑπάρχον τῇ μητρὶ πνευματικόν.)" The same word, used in the same sense by the Gnostics, is also found in the extracts from Theodotus, at the end of the works of Clement of Alexandria[e]. And here, (to mention it by the way,) I am quite of opinion that these heretics accommodated this word, which was at that time in use among the Catholics in speaking of the most Holy Trinity, to their Æons, as they did many others. And this view receives no slight confirmation from the circumstance, that the author of a book entitled *Ποιμάνδρης*, a very early Christian writer[f], and (whatever else his madness may have been) far enough removed from the mad dreams of the Gnostics, expressly called the Word, or Son of God, *ὁμοούσιος*, "of one substance" with the Father, as we shall afterwards shew. But to return from our digression. The author of the treatise which bears the title of Questions of the Greeks to the Christians, published amongst the works of Justin, thus writes concerning the soul[g]; "We say that the reasonable soul is a spirit endued with thinking powers, vital and possessing the power of self-motion; with which, we say, that both the angels and the demons are consubstantial[2]." Where the [72] word *ὁμοουσίους* is joined with a genitive case, as in the extracts from Theodotus; though it more frequently governs the dative case. Agapius in Photius (*Bibliothec. Cod.* clxxix.) is said to have taught amongst other impious doctrines, "that the soul is consubstantial with God[3]." Afterwards in the same place Photius says concerning this same Agapius[h]; "With shameless irreverence he descants of the sun and the moon as of divine things, and proclaims them to be consubstantial with God." Lastly, Theodoret, in his dialogue "ἀσύγχυτος,"

[1] partum, κύημα.

[2] ἧς ὁμοουσίους εἶναι φαμὲν τοὺς ἀγγέλους καὶ τοὺς δαίμονας.

[3] τὴν ψυχὴν ὁμοούσιον εἶναι τῷ Θεῷ.

[e] p. 796, 797. [c. 42. p. 979. and c. 50. p. 981.]

[f] [Who seems to have flourished about the year 120. Cave in Herm.—BOWYER.—[The editor of the works of Dionysius of Alexandria, preface, p. xxxvii., contends that this writer was not a Christian, but flourished in the reign of Ptolemy Philadelphus.—B.]

[g] p. 203. [p. 538.]

[h] ἥλιον δὲ καὶ σελήνην ἀναισχύντως θεολογεῖ, καὶ ὁμοούσια κηρύττει Θεῷ. —[Phot. Bibl. c. 179.]

ON THE CONSUBSTANTIALITY OF THE SON.

adduces a passage from Apollinaris, where he says[i]; "Men are of the same substance (*ὁμοούσιοι*) with brutes, as touching their irrational body; but of another substance (*ἑτερούσιοι*) so far as they are rational."

3. That this was the very sense in which the bishops at Nice called the Son "of one substance[1]" with the Father, will be manifest to all men who are fair minded and not of a temper thoroughly contentious, from the very terms of the Nicene Creed[j]. For after saying that the Son of God is "begotten of the Father, only-begotten," the fathers immediately add the words, "that is, of the substance[2] of the Father;" and then they shew the meaning of that expression in the words which follow; "God of God[3], Light of Light, very God of very God, begotten, not made." Lastly, they subjoin *ὁμοούσιον τῷ πατρὶ*, "of one
[73]
substance with the Father," as if it comprised all that had been before said of the Son. Again, at the end of the Creed they shew plainly enough what they meant to be understood by the word *ὁμοούσιος*, when they anathematize the Arians, "who assert that the Son of God is of another substance or essence[4], or that He was created, or is capable of change or alteration[5]." It is evident, then, that the Nicene bishops called the Son of God "of one substance" with the Father, in a sense opposed to the blasphemies of the Arians; that is to say, that He is not of any essence that is created, or other than that[6] of the Father, or changeable; but altogether of the same divine and immutable nature as His Father. In this way entirely the word *ὁμοούσιος* was interpreted by those Catholic doctors, who (it is reasonable to suppose) best understood the mind and view of the Nicene fathers. For thus speaks the great Athanasius, when disputing against those Arians, who falsely pretended that they embraced the Nicene Creed in all other respects, and only shrunk with dread from the term *ὁμοούσιος*, as new and dangerous[k]: "Now if even after all this—even after both the testimony of the bishops of former times, and the subscription of their own fathers, they pretend (as if in ignorance)

[1] ὁμοούσιος.

[2] ἐκ τῆς οὐσίας.

[3] Θεὸν ἐκ Θεοῦ, κ.τ.λ.

[4] ἐξ ἑτέρας ὑποστάσεως ἢ οὐσίας, κ.τ.λ.

[5] τρεπτὸν ἢ ἀλλοιωτόν.

[6] alienæ.

[i] οἱ ἄνθρωποι τοῖς ἀλόγοις ζώοις ὁμοούσιοι κατὰ τὸ σῶμα τὸ ἄλογον· ἑτερούσιοι δὲ, καθὸ λογικοί.

[j] [See the Greek of the Creed above, p. 13.]

[k] εἰ δὲ καὶ μετὰ τοσαῦτα, μετὰ καὶ τὴν μαρτυρίαν τῶν ἀρχαίων ἐπισκόπων, καὶ μετὰ τὴν ὑπογραφὴν τῶν ἰδίων πατέρων, προσποιοῦνται, ὡς ἀγνοοῦντες, τὴν λέξιν φοβεῖσθαι τοῦ ὁμοουσίου, εἰπάτω-

to dread the word *ὁμοούσιος*, let them in simplicity and truth confess and believe that the Son is Son by nature; and let them also anathematize (as the council enjoined) such as say that the Son of God was made or created[1]; or that He was made out of what existed not; or that there was a time when He was not; and that He is liable to change and alteration, and is of another substance[2]; and thus let them flee from the Arian heresy; and we have full confidence that in sincerely anathematizing these things they do therein[3] confess that the Son is 'of the substance of the Father,' and 'of one substance' with Him[4]. For on this account it was that the fathers, after having asserted that the Son is 'of one substance,' immediately added, 'Those who say that the Son is made or created, or that He was made out of what existed not, or that there was a time when He was not, the Catholic Church anathematizes;' in order that they may make it known hereby, that this is what the expression *ὁμοούσιος*, 'of one substance,' signifies; and the force of the word *ὁμοούσιος* is ascertained from [the assertion that] the Son is 'neither created nor made;' and that whosoever says that He is 'of one substance,' does not believe the Word to be a creature; and whosoever anathematizes the before-mentioned propositions, does at the same time[5] believe the Son to be 'of one substance' with the Father; and whosoever says that He is 'of one substance,' acknowledges the Son of God to be the real and true [Son,] and whosoever calls Him the real [Son,] understands that saying, 'I and the Father are one.'"

BOOK II. CHAP. I. § 2—5.

HOMOOUSION.

27

1 κτίσμα ἢ ποίημα.

2 ἐξ ἑτέρας ὑποστάσεως.

3 εὐθύς. q. d. ipso facto.

4 ἐκ τῆς οὐσίας καὶ ὁμοούσιον εἶναι τὸν υἱὸν τῷ Πατρί.

[74]

5 ἅμα.

5. In the same manner Hilary also, in his treatise On Synods against the Arians[1], says; "Is any one displeased [75]

σαν καὶ φρονείτωσαν ἁπλούστερον μὲν καὶ ἀληθῶς τὸν υἱὸν, φύσει υἱὸν, ἀναθεματισάτωσαν δὲ, ὡς παρήγγειλεν ἡ σύνοδος, τοὺς λέγοντας κτίσμα ἢ ποίημα, ἢ ἐξ οὐκ ὄντων, ἢ ἦν ποτε ὅτε οὐκ ἦν ὁ υἱὸς τοῦ Θεοῦ· καὶ ὅτι τρεπτὸς καὶ ἀλλοιωτός ἐστι, καὶ ἐξ ἑτέρας ὑποστάσεως· καὶ οὕτως φευγέτωσαν ἀπὸ τῆς Ἀρειανῆς αἱρέσεως, καὶ θαρροῦμεν, ὅτι γνησίως ταῦτα ἀναθεματίζοντες ὁμολογοῦσιν εὐθὺς, ἐκ τῆς οὐσίας καὶ ὁμοούσιον εἶναι τὸν υἱὸν τῷ Πατρί. διὰ τοῦτο γὰρ καὶ οἱ πατέρες εἰρηκότες ὁμοούσιον εἶναι τὸν υἱὸν ἐπήγαγον εὐθὺς, Τοὺς δὲ λέγοντας κτίσμα, ἢ ποίημα, ἢ ἐξ οὐκ ὄντων, ἢ ἦν ποτε ὅτε οὐκ ἦν, ἀναθεματίζει ἡ καθολικὴ ἐκκλησία· ἵνα διὰ τούτων γνωρίσωσιν, ὅτι ταῦτα σημαίνει τὸ ὁμοούσιον· καὶ ἡ τοῦ ὁμοουσίου δύναμις γινώσκεται ἐκ τοῦ μὴ εἶναι κτίσμα ἢ ποίημα τὸν υἱόν· καὶ ὅτι ὁ λέγων ὁμοούσιον οὐ φρονεῖ κτίσμα εἶναι τὸν λόγον· καὶ ὁ ἀναθεματίζων τὰ προειρημένα ὁμοούσιον ἅμα φρονεῖ εἶναι τὸν υἱὸν τῷ Πατρί· καὶ ὁ ὁμοούσιον λέγων, γνήσιον καὶ ἀληθινὸν λέγει τὸν υἱὸν τοῦ Θεοῦ· καὶ ὁ γνήσιον λέγων νοεῖ τὸ, Ἐγὼ καὶ ὁ Πατὴρ ἕν ἐσμεν.—In Epist. ad African. Episcop., vol. i. p. 940. edit. Paris. 1627. [§ 9. vol. i. p. 898.]

1 Displicet, inquit, cuiquam in sy-

ON THE CONSUBSTANTIALITY OF THE SON.

that the term homoousion ['of one substance'] was adopted in the Nicene council? If so, he must necessarily be pleased that the Arians refused to admit it. For they refused to admit the homoousion, that it might be said of God the Son, not that He is begotten of the substance of God the Father, but that He was formed out of nothing, after the manner of created beings. It is nothing new that I am saying; the faithlessness of the Arians is published in many works, and witnesses against itself. If on account of the irreligion of those who denied [the homoousion], the meaning put on it by those who confessed it at that time was religious, I ask why at this day it is sought to do away with that which at that time it was religious to adopt, because it was irreligious to refuse to admit it. If it was religious to adopt it, why has an appointment of religion come to be matter of accusation, which religiously extinguished irreligion by the very means by which irreligion was caused? Let us see then what the Nicene council laid down[1] in confessing the homoousion, that is the [article] 'of one substance:' not surely to bring to the birth that heresy which is conceived of an erroneous notion of the homoousion. They will not, I imagine, say this, that the Father and the Son divided by partition one anterior substance so as to form their own substance." Then after reciting the Nicene Creed, he thus proceeds; "Surely in these words the most holy council of religious men is not introducing a prior substance, one knows not what, such as to have been divided into two; but the Son begotten of the substance of the Father. And do we at all deny it? or [if we do] what else do we confess?

[1] "had in view." ed. Ben.

nodo Nicæna homoousipn esse susceptum? hoc si cui displicet, necesse est placeat, quod ab Arianis est negatum. Negatum enim idcirco est homoousion, ne ex substantia Dei Patris Deus Filius natus, sed secundum creaturas ex nihilo conditus prædicaretur. Nihil novum loquimur: pluribus edita literis ipsa Arianorum perfidia sibi testis est. Si propter negantium impietatem pia tum fuit intelligentia confitentium, quæro cur hodie convellatur, quod tum pie susceptum est, quia impie negabatur? Si pie susceptum est, cur venit constitutio pietatis in crimen, quæ impietatem pie per ea ipsa, quibus impiabatur, extinxit? Videamus igitur, quid Nicæna synodus statuerit, [ed. Benedict. l. studuerit,] homoousion, id est, unius substantiæ, confitendo: non utique hæresim parturire, quæ de homoousii vitiosa opinione concipitur. Non, opinor, illud loquentur, quod unam anteriorem substantiam Pater et Filius in substantiam suam partiendo diviserint. . . . Non hic sanctissima religiosorum virorum synodus, nescio quam priorem, quæ in duos divisa sit, substantiam introducit; sed Filium natum de substantia Patris. Numquid et nos negamus? aut quid aliud confitemur? Et post cæteras

BOOK II. CHAP. I. § 5, 6.

HOMOOUSION.

[76]

Further, after setting forth those other statements of our common faith, it says, 'begotten, not made; of one substance with the Father,' which they express in Greek by the word ὁμοούσιος. What opening is there here for an erroneous meaning? The Son is declared to be begotten of the substance of the Father, not made, lest the begetting of the Godhead be accounted a handy-work of creation. And therefore it is, 'of one substance,' not as though He subsist singly and alone, but to express that [the Son], being begotten of the substance of God, hath not His subsistence from any other; nor yet that He subsists in any difference of [a] diverse substance. Or will it be said that our faith is not this, that His subsistence is not from any other [than the Father,] and that it is not a dissimilar subsistence? Or does the homoousion here witness to any thing other than that there is one essence of the two, and that no way dissimilar, according to natural propagation, because the essence of the Son is not from any other [than the Father]: and inasmuch as it is not from any other, it will be correct to believe that both are of one essence; because the Son hath the substance which was begotten from no other original than from the nature of the Father."

6. The great Basil, in his three hundredth Epistle[m], arguing against such as embraced the Nicene Creed in all other particulars save that they were unwilling to admit the expression "of one substance[1]," after other things, which will be brought forward hereafter in a more suitable place, thus writes[n]; "And forasmuch as there were still at that time some who affirmed that the Son was brought into being out of what existed not,

[1] ὁμοούσιος.

communis fidei expositiones ait, *Natum, non factum, unius substantiæ cum Patre*, quod Græce dicunt ὁμοούσιον. Quæ hic vitiosæ intelligentiæ occasio est? natus esse de substantia Patris Filius, non factus, prædicatur; ne nativitas divinitatis factura sit creationis. Idcirco autem unius substantiæ; non ut unus subsistat, aut solus, sed ut ex substantia Dei natus non aliunde subsistat; neque ut in aliqua dissidentis substantiæ diversitate subsistat. Aut numquid non hæc fides nostra est, ut non aliunde subsistat, neque quod indissimilis subsistat? Aut aliud hic testatur homoousion, quam ut una atque indissimilis duum sit secundum naturæ propaginem [ed. Benedict. l. progeniem] essentia, quia essentia Filii non sit aliunde; quæ quia aliunde non est, unius recte esse ambo credentur essentiæ; quia substantiam nativitatis Filius non habeat nisi de paternæ auctoritate naturæ?—pp. 241, 242. ed. Basil. 1570. [§ 83. p. 1197.]

m [Ep. lii. 2.]

n καὶ ἐπειδὴ ἐξ οὐκ ὄντων εἰς τὸ εἶναι παρῆχθαι τὸν υἱὸν ἔτι τότε ἦσαν οἱ λέγοντες, ἵνα καὶ ταύτην ἐκτέμωσι τὴν

ON THE CONSUBSTANTIALITY OF THE SON.

to cut off this impiety also [the fathers of Nicæa] used in addition the words 'of one substance;' for the union of the Son with the Father is without time or interval[1]. The preceding words, indeed, sufficiently prove that this was their meaning; for after they had said 'light of light,' and that the Son was 'begotten of the substance of the Father, not made,' they introduced after this the words 'of one substance;' shewing, as by an example, that whatever definition of light one would give in the case of the Father, the same will apply also in the case of the Son; inasmuch as true light compared with true light (as respects the mere notion of light) will allow of no difference. Since, therefore,
[77] the Father is light, without original, and the Son is light, begotten; and both of them are severally light, [the fathers] justly used the term 'of one substance,' in order to set forth the equal dignity of their nature: for not those things which are near akin[2] to one another, are said to be 'of one substance,' as some have conceived; but when both the cause, and that which has its being from the cause, are of the same nature, they are [in that case] said to be of one substance."

1 ἀδιάστατος, "uninterrupted."

28

2 ἀδελφα.

7. Moreover, that this is the true meaning of the expression "of one substance," the semi-Arians themselves at length admitted, in the council of Antioch, [held] under the emperor Jovian; instructed, it would seem, by Meletius, who presided in that council; for that he was a true Catholic is abundantly certain from Basil's statement in his fifty-second, fifty-third, and following Epistles[o], and in his three hundred and twenty-
[78] fifth[p] to Epiphanius. For they in their synodical letter to the excellent emperor have these statements respecting the Nicene council[q]; "Whereas also that which seems to some to be a

ἀσέβειαν, τὸ ὁμοούσιον προσειρήκασιν. ἄχρονος γὰρ καὶ ἀδιάστατος ἡ τοῦ υἱοῦ πρὸς τὸν Πατέρα συνάφεια. δηλοῖ δὲ καὶ τὰ προλαβόντα ῥήματα, ταύτην εἶναι τῶν ἀνδρῶν τὴν διάνοιαν. εἴποντες γὰρ φῶς ἐκ φωτὸς, καὶ ἐκ τῆς οὐσίας τοῦ Πατρὸς τὸν υἱὸν γεγεννῆσθαι, οὐχὶ δὲ πεποιῆσθαι, ἐπήγαγον τούτοις τὸ ὁμοούσιον· παραδεικνύντες, ὅτι ὅνπερ ἄν τις ἀποδῷ φωτὸς λόγον ἐπὶ Πατρὸς, οὗτος ἁρμόσει καὶ ἐπὶ υἱοῦ. φῶς γὰρ ἀληθινὸν, πρὸς φῶς ἀληθινὸν, κατ' αὐτὴν τοῦ φωτὸς τὴν ἔννοιαν, οὐδεμίαν ἕξει παραλλαγήν. ἐπεὶ οὖν ἐστιν ἄναρχον φῶς ὁ Πατὴρ, γεννητὸν δὲ φῶς ὁ υἱὸς, φῶς δὲ καὶ φῶς ἑκάτερος, ὁμοούσιον εἶπαν δικαίως, ἵνα τὸ τῆς φύσεως ὁμότιμον παραστήσωσιν. οὐ γὰρ τὰ ἀδελφὰ ἀλλήλοις ὁμοούσια λέγεται, ὅπερ τινὲς ὑπειλήφασιν· ἀλλ' ὅταν καὶ τὸ αἴτιον, καὶ τὸ ἐκ τοῦ αἰτίου τὴν ὕπαρξιν ἔχον, τῆς αὐτῆς ὑπάρχῃ φύσεως, ὁμοούσια λέγεται.—vol. iii. p. 292. edit. Paris. 1638. [vol. iii. p. 145.]

o [Ep. lxix., xxv.]

p [Ep. cclviii.]

q ὁπότε καὶ τὸ δοκοῦν ἐν αὐτῇ τισὶ

HOMOOUSION.

[new and] strange term in it, we mean that "of one substance," hath received a safe interpretation among the fathers, intimating that the Son was begotten of the substance of the Father, and that in substance He is like unto the Father: and the term substance is not taken [by the fathers of the council] as if there were any idea of passion[1] with respect to that ineffable generation, or according to a certain Greek use of the word; but for the purpose of overthrowing the impious doctrine, which was presumptuously ventured on by Arius, of the Son being out of what existed not." I apprehend that by this time all sufficiently understand what is the legitimate sense of the expression "of one substance," as it stands in the Nicene Creed.

[1] *πάθους τινός.*

8. But further, that this word was not first invented by the Nicene fathers, nor yet used by them in a new sense in the question about the Godhead of the Son (as many have thought), but that it had been passed on from the generations which preceded to those which followed, is expressly testified by Eusebius in his Epistle to his own diocese of Cæsarea. His words are as follows[r]; "We were aware that some learned and distinguished bishops and writers [even] among the ancients made use of the term, 'Of one substance,' in treating of the Godhead of the Father and the Son." There is [79]
no doubt that Eusebius had access to many monuments of primitive antiquity, which are not now extant any where, but have long ago perished, from which he could have most fully established this assertion of his; for even we (notwithstanding the great and deplorable wreck of ancient writers) are not without testimonies such as may sufficiently prove it. Tertullian, at the beginning of his treatise against Praxeas[s], expressly says that the Father, the Son, and the Holy Ghost are "of one substance;" and affirms[2] that this is moreover contained "in the rule of faith" and "the mystery

[2] unius substantiæ.

ξένον ὄνομα, τὸ τοῦ ὁμοουσίου φαμὲν, ἀσφαλοῦς τετύχηκε παρὰ τοῖς πατράσιν ἑρμηνείας, σημαινούσης ὅτι ἐκ τῆς οὐσίας τοῦ Πατρὸς ὁ υἱὸς ἐγεννήθη, καὶ ὅτι ὅμοιος κατ' οὐσίαν τῷ Πατρί· οὔτε δὲ ὡς πάθους τινὸς περὶ τὴν ἄρρητον γέννησιν ἐπινοουμένου, οὔτε κατά τινα χρῆσιν ἑλληνικὴν λαμβάνεται [τοῖς πατράσι] τὸ ὄνομα τῆς οὐσίας· εἰς ἀνατροπὴν δὲ τοῦ ἐξ οὐκ ὄντων περὶ τοῦ υἱοῦ ἀσεβῶς τολμηθέντος 'Αρείῳ.—Apud Socrat. H. E. iii. 25; et Sozom. H. E. vi. 4.

r [ἐπεὶ καὶ] τῶν παλαιῶν τινὰς λογίους καὶ ἐπιφανεῖς ἐπισκόπους καὶ συγγραφέας ἔγνωμεν, ἐπὶ τῆς τοῦ Πατρὸς καὶ υἱοῦ θεολογίας τῷ τοῦ ὁμοουσίου συγχρησαμένους ὀνόματι.—Apud Socrat. H. E. i. 8. [p. 25.]

s [See below, ch. vii. § 6, where the words of Tertullian are quoted.]

ON THE CONSUBSTANTIALITY OF THE SON.

of the dispensation[1]," which was observed and kept by the Catholics. But what, I pray you, does the Latin expression *unius substantiæ* denote, but the same as the Greek *ὁμοούσιος*? nor have I any doubt that Tertullian, as he almost every where studiously imitates the Greek ecclesiastical writers (as learned men are well aware[t],) so here also translated the word *ὁμοούσιος*—which he had found used with respect to the most holy Trinity, in writers of that class, of earlier date than himself—by the words of his mother tongue, *unius substantiæ*. Rufinus (On the Adulteration of the Works of
29 Origen) testifies that this word was often met with in the writings of Origen; when[2] he says[u], "Is it possible that he could have forgotten himself in the same portion[3] of the same book, sometimes (as we have said) in the very next chapter? For example; after he has declared the Father and the Son to be of one substance, (which in Greek is expressed by *ὁμοούσιος*,) could he possibly, in the very next chapters, pronounce Him to be of another substance and created, whom he had just before asserted to be begotten[4] of the
[80] very nature of God the Father?" Pamphilus adduces an instance [of his use of it] in his Apology[v], where he sets before us the following words of Origen, out of his Commentary on the Epistle to the Hebrews; "These illustrations most plainly shew, that the Son hath a communion[5] of substance with the Father. For an effluence[6] seems to be consubstantial (*ὁμοούσιος*,) i. e. of one substance with that body from which it is either an effluence or vapour." Athanasius, in his treatise On the Views[7] of Dionysius of Alexandria, in opposition to the Arians, states that this Dionysius, (who was a disciple of Origen,) in an Epistle to his namesake Dionysius of Rome, said that Christ was "of one substance" with God, *ὁμοούσιος τῷ Θεῷ*[x]; and that Dionysius of Rome

1 sacramento *οἰκονομίας*.
2 dum.
3 opere.
4 natum.
5 communionem.
6 aporrhœa.
7 sententia.

t B. Rhenanus says of Tertullian, that from his constant reading of Greek authors he had imbibed so much of Greek forms of speech, as to be unable to forget them even in writing his Latin.

u Numquid in eodem opere ejusdem libri, interdum, ut diximus, statim in consequenti capitulo oblitus sui esse potuit? V. G. ut qui Patrem et Filium unius substantiæ, quod Græce *ὁμοούσιον* dicitur, designavit, in consequentibus statim capitulis alterius esse substantiæ et creatum poterat dicere eum, quem paulo ante de ipsa natura Dei Patris pronuntiaverat natum?

v Quæ similitudines manifestissime ostendunt, communionem substantiæ esse Filio cum Patre: aporrhœa enim *ὁμοούσιος* videtur, id est, unius substantiæ cum illo corpore, ex quo est vel aporrhœa vel vapor.—[c. 5. p. 33.]

x [Vide Dionysii Opera, p. 90.]

BOOK II. CHAP. I. § 8.

HOMOOUSION.

had required of him to state this in plain terms. Now it is clear, from this statement of Athanasius, that even in the time of these Dionysii the term *ὁμοούσιος* was in frequent use; and that such as rejected[1] it (which was falsely laid to the charge of the Alexandrian Dionysius) incurred the censure of the Church. I am therefore astonished at the ignorance or impudence of Sandius, whichever it be, in saying[y], that even Athanasius was amongst those who acknowledged that the term *ὁμοούσιος* was ultimately[2] fabricated in the Nicene council. Nay, in another passage also, this very Athanasius says expressly, that this word, as it stands in the Nicene Creed, was "approved by the testimony of the bishops of former times," i. e. of those who were anterior to the council of Nice. Look back at the passage which we quoted a little above from Athanasius, out of his letter to the bishops of Africa. But if any doubt the good faith of the great and excellent Athanasius, there is extant at this day an epistle of that very Dionysius of Alexandria against Paul of Samosata, in which he expressly says, that[z] "the Son was declared by the holy fathers to be of one substance with the Father." These [81] words of Dionysius also plainly shew that the holy fathers who preceded him had used the term *ὁμοούσιος* of the Son; and thus they remarkably confirm the testimony of Eusebius, which I just now quoted. In short, from the circumstance that the martyr Pamphilus in his Apology for Origen, (which, as we shall afterwards shew, rightly bears the name of Pamphilus,) contends that Origen expressly said that the Son was "of one substance" with the Father, and therefore was catholic in the article of the Godhead of the Son; from this very circumstance, I say, it is most evident that the word *ὁμοούσιος* was in use among Catholics even prior to the Nicene council, and employed in explaining the doctrine concerning the Godhead of the Son; for this Pamphilus received the crown of martyrdom[a] some years before the council of Nice, in the persecution, that is, under Maximin, as Eusebius, On the Martyrs of Palestine, chap. 7, and Jerome, in his Catalogue, expressly testify. After this, perhaps it may

[1] abhorruisse.

[2] demum.

[y] De Script. Eccles., pp. 39, 40. edit. secund. et pp. 121, 122.

[z] ὁμοούσιον τῷ Πατρὶ εἰρημένον ὑπὸ τῶν ἁγίων πατέρων.—Biblioth. Patr., tom. xi. p. 277. [Opera, p. 214.]

[a] In the year 309. Cave in Pam.—BOWYER.

ON THE CONSUBSTANTIALITY OF THE SON.

be worth while to observe, that the author of the book entitled *Ποιμάνδρης*, and attributed to Mercurius Trismegistus, in the first chapter, expressly says that "the Word of God is of one substance[1] with the Father." It is true that Petavius has proved on solid[2] grounds that the writer was an impostor, that is, not Trismegistus himself, but a Christian falsely assuming his name; yet Petavius also acknowledges[b], that that forger[3] was of very early times, and lived shortly after the Apostles; which is also clearly shewn by testimonies being cited from him by Justin Martyr.

1 ὁμοούσιος. 2 solide. 3 circulatorem.

9. Some persons, however, have thought that there is a very strong presumption against the term ὁμοουσίος ("of one substance") in the fact, that the council of Antioch, which was held against Paul of Samosata about sixty years before the Nicene,
[82] expressly repudiated the term. Theologians, both ancient and modern[c], have been at pains[4] to account for the contradictory language of these councils. In accordance with my design, I shall speak only of the ancients. Hilary, towards the end of his book On the Synods, against the Arians, states that Paul of Samosata confessed that word ὁμοούσιος in a bad sense, and that, on this account, the fathers of the council of Antioch rejected the term. "The Samosatene," he says[d], "did ill when he confessed the homoousion. But did the Arians do better in denying it?" In what sense, however, could the Samosatene have confessed it? Petavius gives the following answer[e]: "He might have admitted the term in the same sense as Sabellius, with whom he coincided in opinion on the doctrine of the Trinity; that is to say, by laying down the substance and essence[5] of the Godhead to be singular, which involved the entire separation of Christ

4 de hac... ἀντιλογίᾳ laborarunt. 5 unicam substantiam . . . et οὐσίαν.

[b] De Trin. i. 2. § 3, 4.

[c] [The editor of the works of Dionysius Alex. (Pref. p. xl. &c.) proves by many arguments that the fathers of Antioch did not by any means repudiate the word ὁμοούσιος.—B. See Dr. Burton's view fully stated in Mr. Faber's Apostolicity of Trinitarianism, vol. ii. p. 302.]

[d] Male, inquit, homoousion Samosatenus confessus est; sed numquid melius Ariani negaverunt?—[Hil. de Synod., § 86. p. 1200.]

[e] Ea ratione potuit admittere, qua Sabellius, cui in Trinitatis dogmate consentaneus erat; uti scilicet unicam substantiam divinitatis et οὐσίαν poneret, a qua plane separandus esset Christus; qui ne ὁμοούσιος Deo constitueretur, in tempore Deus esse cœpisset. Quod enim eodem sensu ὁμοούσιον Verbum esse Samosatenus affirmarit, quo Sabellius, ibidem Hilarius [de Synod., § 81. p. 1196.] ostendit, cum illum dicit ὁμοούσιον esse Filium docuisse, quod in Antiochena synodo Patres usurpari vetuerunt, *quia per hanc unius essentiæ nuncupationem solitarium atque unicum sibi esse Patrem et Filium prædicabat.*—De Trin. iv. 5. 2.

BOOK II. CHAP. I. § 8, 9. HOMOOUSION.

from it; who, that He might not be set down as of one substance with God, must have had His beginning as God in time. For, that the Samosatene asserted the Word to be of one substance in the same sense as Sabellius, is shewn by Hilary in the same passage, when he says, that Paul had taught that the Son is of one substance[1] [with the Father,] a statement which the fathers in the council of Antioch forbad to be used, 'inasmuch as by this use of the term 'of one essence,' he pronounced the Father and the Son to be one only single and solitary Being[2].'" But this, and I say it with all deference to the venerable Hilary, does not seem to me to be by any means likely. For, granting that the Samosatene heretic held precisely the same opinion touching the Son of God as Sabellius, (a position, however, which might with good grounds be questioned,) yet surely Sabellius himself would never have willingly affirmed that the Son is consubstantial (ὁμοούσιος) with the Father, but rather identically-substantial (ταυτοούσιος.) Besides, if the Sabellians before the council of Nice 30
had used the word ὁμοούσιος in order to spread their heresy, it is no way credible, that the fathers of Nice,—who certainly [83]
abhorred the Sabellian, no less than the Arian, heresy,—would have inserted that word in their Creed. Sandius[f], however, confidently maintains "that the followers of Sabellius embraced the term 'of one substance[3],'" that is, of course, before the Nicene council, for if this be not his meaning, his assertion would be nothing to the purpose. Hence in another place he expressly says, that Sabellius himself used the word "of one substance." Let us see by what evidence he proves this assertion of his: "For they," his words are, "who repudiated the term 'of one substance,' affirmed that those who approved of it, were introducing afresh the opinions of Montanus and Sabellius, (observe their agreement in doctrine,) and accordingly they called them blasphemers. Socrat. Eccl. Hist. i. 23, and Sozom. ii. 18." My reply is, that Socrates and Sozomen, in the places cited, do, it is true, relate that after the Nicene council there were great contentions concerning the word ὁμοούσιος amongst the very bishops who subscribed to the Nicene Creed, especially between Eusebius Pamphili and Eustathius of Antioch; the former with his

1 ὁμοούσιος.

2 solitarium atque unicum sibi.

3 homoousion.

f Enucl. Histor. Ecclesiast. i. p. 112.

party charging Eustathius and his party, who asserted the article " of one substance," with Montanism and Sabellianism; the latter, again, objecting against them [that they introduced] the polytheism of the heathens; both sides in the meantime professing their belief to be this[g]; " That the Son of God has a proper subsistence and being; and that there is one God in three persons[1]." For this we have the express testimony of Socrates, and that derived from a careful reading of the tracts and letters which those bishops wrote (in answer) each to the other. It must however be especially observed, that Eusebius and his party no way pretended that
[84] the word *ὁμοούσιος* in itself, or according to its proper signification, went to confirm the heresy of Sabellius, much less that the Nicene fathers wished, by its use, to give the Christian world to taste [the cup of[2]] Sabellianism; but that he merely said this, that Eustathius and his party, who embraced the term " of one substance," wished to introduce Sabellianism; that is, so interpreted the word as to make it altogether to favour the Sabellian heresy. Indeed it is expressly said by Socrates[h], that Eusebius, in the very letter in which he accused Eustathius of Sabellian error in his use of the word *ὁμοούσιος*, openly professed that " he himself did not transgress the Creed of Nicæa." Whether Eusebius charged Eustathius justly with Sabellianism, there is no need for us to enquire anxiously. Certainly, however, Marcellus, who was the teacher of Eustathius, maintained pure[3] Sabellianism in his writings, as is perfectly clear from the books of Eusebius, which he composed against him. Therefore Hilary, (in his book to Constantius,) and Basil the Great, (in his letters 52, 74, and 78[i],) and others, expressly class Marcellus amongst heretics. The circumstance of his being, at least for a considerable time, in very warm favour[4] with the great Athanasius, must, I think, altogether be ascribed to his cunning and hypocrisy, and to the zeal and ardour which he displayed against the Arians. With regard to Eustathius himself, (al-

1 *ὑποστάσεσιν.*

2 propinare.

3 purum putum.

4 in flagranti gratia.

g *ἐνυπόστατόν τε καὶ ἐνυπάρχοντα τὸν υἱὸν εἶναι τοῦ Θεοῦ, ἕνα τε Θεὸν ἐν τρισὶν ὑποστάσεσιν εἶναι.* I am persuaded that Eustathius did not use the very word *ὑποστάσεσι*: but some other term which Socrates considered equivalent to it.

h [*Εὐσέβιος μὲν, τὴν ἐν Νικαίᾳ πίστιν οὔ φησι παραβαίνειν· διαβάλλει δὲ Εὐστάθιον ὡς τὴν Σαβελλίου δόξαν εἰσάγοντα.*—Socrat. E. H. i. 23.]

i [Ep. lxix., cclxiii., and cxxv.]

though I should be unwilling without due grounds at all to detract from the reputation or estimation of a man who was held in much esteem by very many Catholics, and who was also ennobled by the friendship of the great Athanasius,) still I candidly confess that I do not know how it could have come to pass, that the bishops assembled at Antioch, although they may have been—the greater part of them—Arians, singled him out from all those who asserted the article "of one substance," for the charge of "holding rather the opinions of Sabellius, than those which the council of Nice decreed;" and [85]
on that account deposed him from the see of Antioch, (which Socrates witnesses to from the relation of others, although he expresses, on very slender grounds indeed, his own doubts of their trustworthiness, i. 24,) unless he had himself given them at least some handle and occasion for a charge of such a nature. What is to be said to the fact, that Cyrus, bishop of Berœa, who, (according to the relation of George of Laodicæa, the Arian, in the same passage of Socrates,) was the man who accused Eustathius[k] of Sabellianism before the council, was a Catholic, and was afterwards himself deposed by the Arians on account of his maintaining the Catholic doctrine, as Athanasius testifies in his letter To those who were living in Solitude? George indeed, says, that this Cyrus also was deposed for his Sabellian doctrine; but by Sabellian doctrine the heretic in that place had no other idea than the doctrine "of one substance," as Valesius has correctly observed[l]; and this observation easily reconciles the apparent discrepancy[1] in the statement of George, which perplexed Socrates. But how does all this make for the purpose of Sandius? What sort of conclusion, I ask, is this? Eusebius Pamphili accused Eustathius of Antioch, of so interpreting the expression "of one substance," which was correctly understood by 31
the Nicene fathers, as to subserve the introduction into the Church of the heresy of Sabellius; therefore the followers of

[1] ἐναντιοφάνεια.

[k] I am quite of opinion that Eustathius was an over-pertinacious maintainer of the one hypostasis (μία ὑπόστασις) in the Godhead; at the same time that perhaps he meant by the term hypostasis nothing else than essence or substance (οὐσίαν): on which account also the party, which after him were called Eustathians, were shunned by other catholics as Sabellians: and thence followed a great schism at Antioch. See Petavius, de Trinit. iv. 4. 10, &c.

[l] See the note of Valesius on Socrates, p. 14. [i. 24. p. 58.]

[86] Sabellius, before the council of Nice, employed and embraced the very expression "of one substance." The incidental observation of Sandius, on the agreement of Montanus and Sabellius in their doctrine respecting the most Holy Trinity, we will consider by and by, in a more suitable place. I therefore say again, that it seems to me by no means probable that the Sabellians ever used the expression "of one substance" of their own accord and willingly; although, after the word had been sanctioned by the authority of the Nicene council, they endeavoured to drag it (as it were) by force[1] into the service of their own heresy. For the expression "of one substance" in itself is so far from agreeing with the Sabellian heresy, that it is plainly repugnant to it; as was excellently observed by the great Basil (Epistle 300) in these words[m]; "This expression corrects also the evil of Sabellius; for it takes away the identity of the personal subsistence[2], and introduces the idea of the persons as complete; since a thing is not itself 'of one substance' with itself, but one thing with another." I therefore conclude that Paul of Samosata, as agreeing with Sabellius on the doctrine of the Trinity, did not use the words "of one substance" for the purpose of expressing his heresy: and that the fathers assembled at Antioch did not on that account reject it.

[1] obtorto quasi collo trahere.

[2] τὴν ταυτότητα τῆς ὑποστάσεως.

10. No one could have understood this question better than the great Athanasius; for he was himself present at the council of Nice, where, when they were most carefully examining all points respecting the article "of one substance," this main objection (concerning the definition of the fathers in the council of Antioch) must without any doubt have been among the first to be discussed. He declares in his book, On the Synods of Ariminum and Seleucia, that Paul of Samosata did not acknowledge the article "of one substance," but rather, out of that term, which had been employed by the Catholics in explaining the doctrine of the Divinity of the Son, contrived a sophism, for the purpose of overthrowing that doctrine; and that it was for this reason that the fathers at Antioch decided that the word should be suppressed[3]. We

[3] supprimendam.

[m] αὕτη δὲ ἡ φωνὴ καὶ τὸ τοῦ Σαβελλίου κακὸν ἐπανορθοῦται· ἀναιρεῖ γὰρ τὴν ταυτότητα τῆς ὑποστάσεως, καὶ εἰσάγει τελείαν τῶν προσώπων τὴν ἔννοιαν· οὐ γὰρ αὐτό τί ἐστιν ἑαυτῷ ὁμοούσιον, ἀλλ' ἕτερον ἑτέρῳ.—[Ep. lii. 3. vol. iii. p. 146.]

will quote his own words, which most clearly explain this whole subject, but only in Latin, contrary to my custom, because the extract is a long one[n]. Athanasius then, in that work, after shewing, that, prior to the synod of Antioch, the phrase "of one substance" had received the sanction of Dionysius, bishop of Rome, and of a council of bishops assembled under him at Rome to consider the case of Dionysius of Alexandria, and had further been acknowledged also by that Dionysius of Alexandria himself, afterwards proceeds to treat fully of the discrepancy between the councils of Antioch and Nice[o]; "If, then, any one blames[1] the Nicene bishops as having spoken contrary to what their predecessors had decreed, he may also with (equal) justice[2] blame the seventy (bishops)" who were assembled at Antioch against Paul of Samosata, as not "having kept to the statements of their predecessors; for such were the two Dionysii and the (other) bishops, who were assembled on that occasion at Rome. But it is not right to blame either these or those; for they all cared for the things of Christ[3], and all directed their zeal against the heretics. One party, indeed, condemned the Samosatene, and the other the Arian, heresy; but both these and those defined rightly and well according to the matter before them. And as the blessed Apostle, in his Epistle to the Romans, said, 'the law is spiritual, the law is holy; and the commandment holy and just and good;' and yet a little after added, 'for what the law could not do, in that it was weak,' &c. . . . and yet no one would charge the saint, on this account, with writing what was inconsistent and contradictory, but would rather admire him as writing

[1] culpat.

[2] εἰκότως pari jure.

[3] ἐπρέσβευον τὰ Χριστοῦ quæ Christi sunt curavere.

Rom. vii. 12.

Rom. viii. 3.

[n] [The Greek is here supplied, see the next note.]

[o] εἴπερ οὖν μέμφεταί τις τοῖς ἐν Νικαίᾳ συνελθοῦσιν, ὡς εἰρηκόσι παρὰ τὰ δόξαντα τοῖς πρὸ αὐτῶν, [The old reading was ὡς εἰρηκόσι πάντα τὰ δόξαντα τοῖς πρὸ αὐτῶν, which Bp. Bull, not without cause, seems to have corrected to ὡς μὴ εἰρηκόσι, κ.τ.λ. The Benedictine reading however is better, ὡς εἰρηκόσι παρὰ τὰ δόξαντα.—B. This has been followed in the translation. Some of the words added in the Latin version of this extract given by Bull, are retained in parentheses.] ὁ αὐτὸς μέμψαιτ' ἂν εἰκότως καὶ τοῖς ἑβδομήκοντα, ὅτι μὴ τὰ τῶν πρὸ αὐτῶν ἐφύλαξαν· πρὸ αὐτῶν γὰρ ἦσαν οἱ Διονύσιοι, καὶ οἱ ἐν Ῥώμῃ τὸ τηνικαῦτα συνελθόντες ἐπίσκοποι. ἀλλ' οὔτε τούτους, οὔτε ἐκείνους ὅσιον αἰτιάσασθαι· πάντες γὰρ ἐπρέσβευον τὰ Χριστοῦ, καὶ πάντες σπουδὴν ἐσχήκασι κατὰ τῶν αἱρετικῶν· καὶ οἱ μὲν τὸν Σαμοσατέα, οἱ δὲ τὴν Ἀρειανὴν αἵρεσιν κατέκριναν. ὀρθῶς δὲ καὶ οὗτοι κἀκεῖνοι, καὶ καλῶς πρὸς τὴν ὑποκειμένην ὑπόθεσιν γεγράφασι. καὶ ὥσπερ ὁ μακάριος ἀπόστολος Ῥωμαίοις μὲν ἐπιστέλλων, ἔλεγεν, ὁ νόμος πνευματικός ἐστιν· καὶ ὁ νόμος ἅγιος· καί, ἡ ἐντολὴ ἁγία, καὶ δικαία, καὶ ἀγαθή· καὶ μετ' ὀλίγον, τὸ γὰρ ἀδύνατον τοῦ νόμου ἐν ᾧ ἠσθένει· . . καὶ οὐκ ἄν τις αἰτιάσαιτο τὸν ἅγιον ὡς ἐναντία καὶ μαχόμενα γράφοντα, ἀλλὰ

ON THE CONSUBSTANTIALITY OF THE SON.

unto each suitably to the occasion, &c. . . .; so also, if the fathers of the two councils used different[1] expressions in speaking of the term 'of one substance,' still we ought not
[88] for that reason by any means to dissent from them, but to search out their meaning and view[2]; by doing which we shall certainly discover that both councils agree in opinion. For they who deposed the Samosatene, apprehending[3] 'One substance' in a corporeal sense;—Paul (that is) wishing to sophisticate, and saying, 'If Christ did not of man become God, then is He of one substance with the Father; whence it necessarily follows, that there are three substances, one which is prior[4], and the other two which have their origin from it:'—on this account with good reason, guarding against sophism such as this on the part of Paul, they said that Christ was not 'of one substance;' for the Son is not so related to the Father as he imagined. They, however, who anathematized the Arian heresy, having perceived the craft of Paul, and having considered that the expression 'of one substance' has not this meaning, when applied to things incorporeal, and especially to God; knowing, moreover, that the Word is not a creature, but an offspring of the substance[5] [of the Father,] and that the substance of the Father is the origin, root and
32 fountain of the Son; and He was the very true[6] likeness of Him that begat; not as of separate growth, as we are, is He parted from the Father: but as of Him[7], a Son, He exists undivided; as the radiance is to the light; and having likewise before their eyes the illustrations of Dionysius, that of the fountain for instance, and (what else is contained in) his Apology

[1] diversimode.
[2] διανοίαν mentem ac sententiam.
[3] ἐκλαμβάνοντες.
[4] προηγουμένην.
[5] γέννημα ἐκ τῆς οὐσίας.
[6] αὐτοαληθὴς, verum undecumque.
[7] ἐκ αὐτοῦ.

καὶ μᾶλλον θαυμάσειεν ἁρμοζόντως πρὸς ἑκάστους ἐπιστέλλοντα, κ.τ.λ., . . . οὕτως εἰ ἀμφοτέρων τῶν συνόδων οἱ πατέρες διαφόρως ἐμνημόνευσαν περὶ τοῦ ὁμοουσίου, οὐ χρὴ πάντως ἡμᾶς διαφέρεσθαι πρὸς αὐτοὺς, ἀλλὰ τὴν διάνοιαν αὐτῶν ἐρευνᾷν, καὶ πάντως εὑρήσομεν ἀμφοτέρων τῶν συνόδων τὴν ὁμόνοιαν. οἱ μὲν γὰρ τὸν Σαμοσατέα καθελόντες, σωματικῶς ἐκλαμβάνοντες τὸ ὁμοούσιον, τοῦ Παύλου σοφίζεσθαί τε θέλοντος καὶ λέγοντος, εἰ μὴ ἐξ ἀνθρώπου γέγονεν ὁ Χριστὸς Θεὸς, οὐκοῦν ὁμοούσιός ἐστι τῷ πατρὶ, καὶ ἀνάγκη τρεῖς οὐσίας εἶναι, μίαν μὲν προηγουμένην, τὰς δὲ δύο ἐξ ἐκείνης. διὰ τοῦτ' εἰκότως εὐλαβηθέντες τὸ τοιοῦτο σόφισμα τοῦ Σαμοσατέως, εἰρήκασι, μὴ εἶναι τὸν Χριστὸν ὁμοούσιον. οὐκ ἔστι γὰρ οὕτως ὁ υἱὸς πρὸς τὸν πατέρα, ὡς ἐκεῖνος ἐνόει. οἱ δὲ τὴν 'Αρειανὴν αἵρεσιν ἀναθεματίσαντες, θεωρήσαντες τὴν πανουργίαν τοῦ Παύλου, καὶ λογισάμενοι μὴ οὕτως καὶ ἐπὶ τῶν ἀσωμάτων, καὶ μάλιστα ἐπὶ Θεοῦ τὸ ὁμοούσιον σημαίνεσθαι, γινώσκοντές τε μὴ κτίσμα, ἀλλ' ἐκ τῆς οὐσίας γέννημα εἶναι τὸν λόγον, καὶ τὴν οὐσίαν τοῦ πατρὸς ἀρχὴν, καὶ ῥίζαν, καὶ πηγὴν εἶναι τοῦ υἱοῦ· καὶ αὐτοαληθὴς ὁμοιότης ἦν τοῦ γεννήσαντος, οὐχ ὡς ἑτεροφυὴς, ὥσπὲρ ἡμεῖς ἐσμεν, χωριζόμενός ἐστι τοῦ πατρὸς, ἀλλ' ὡς ἐξ αὐτοῦ υἱὸς ἀδιαίρετος ὑπάρχει, ὡς ἔστι τὸ ἀπαύγασμα πρὸς τὸ φῶς· ἔχοντες δὲ καὶ τὰ περὶ Διονύσιον παρα-

[89]

for the words 'of one substance,' and especially[1] that saying of the Saviour, expressive of unity[2], 'I and the Father are one,' and, 'he that hath seen Me hath seen My Father also;' on these grounds they also, with good reason, were led to declare[3] that the Son is 'of one substance.'" He then after a few words goes on to say; "For since the Samosatene held that the Son was not before Mary, but received from her the beginning of His being, on this account the assembled bishops condemned the man as a heretic and deposed him; but touching the Godhead of the Son, writing in simple fashion, they did not busy themselves about the exact meaning of the expression 'of one substance;' but, as they apprehended[4] the 'One substance,' so did they speak of it; for they were only intent on overthrowing what the Samosatene had devised, and on setting forth that the Son was before all things, and that He did not become God from being man, but being God, He put on the form of a servant; and being the Word, He became flesh, as St. John said. And thus was the blasphemy of Paul dealt with. But when the party of Eusebius and Arius taught that the Son was indeed before all time, yet that He was made, and was one of the creatures; and as to the expression, 'Of God,' did not believe it in the sense that He was the true Son of the Father, but affirmed that to be 'of God' held good of Him in the same sense as of the creatures; and, as to the oneness of likeness of the Son to the Father, did not confess that it is in respect of essence[5] or nature, that the Son is like the Father, but is on account of the agreement of doctrines and of teaching; nay

[1] πρὸ τούτων imprimis.

[2] unitricem, ἑνοειδῆ.

[3] inducti sunt ut dicerent.

[4] ἐξειλήφασι.

[5] οὐσίας essentia.

δείγματα, τὴν πηγὴν, καὶ τὴν περὶ τοῦ ὁμοουσίου ἀπολογίαν· πρὸ δὲ τούτων τὴν τοῦ Σωτῆρος ἑνοειδῆ φωνήν· ἐγὼ καὶ ὁ πατὴρ ἕν ἐσμεν· καὶ, ὁ ἑωρακὼς ἐμὲ, ἑώρακε τὸν πατέρα· τούτου ἕνεκεν εἰκότως εἰρήκασι καὶ αὐτοὶ ὁμοούσιον τὸν υἱὸν . . . ἐπειδὴ γὰρ ὁ Σαμοσατεὺς ἐφρόνει μὴ εἶναι πρὸ Μαρίας τὸν υἱὸν, ἀλλ' ἀπ' αὐτῆς ἀρχὴν ἐσχηκέναι τοῦ εἶναι, τούτου ἕνεκεν οἱ τότε συνελθόντες, καθεῖλον μὲν αὐτὸν καὶ αἱρετικὸν ἀπέφηναν· περὶ δὲ τῆς τοῦ υἱοῦ θεότητος ἁπλούστερον γράφοντες, οὐ κατεγένοντο περὶ τὴν τοῦ ὁμοουσίου ἀκρίβειαν, ἀλλ' οὕτως ὡς ἐξειλήφασι περὶ τοῦ ὁμοουσίου εἰρήκασι· τὴν φροντίδα γὰρ εἶχον πᾶσαν, ὅπερ ἐπενόησεν ὁ Σαμοσατεὺς, ἀνελεῖν, καὶ δεῖξαι, πρὸ πάντων εἶναι τὸν υἱὸν, καὶ ὅτι οὐκ ἐξ ἀνθρώπων γέγονε Θεὸς, ἀλλὰ Θεὸς ὢν, ἐνεδύσατο δούλου μορφήν· καὶ λόγος ὢν, γέγονε σάρξ, ὡς εἶπεν Ἰωάννης· καὶ οὕτω μὲν κατὰ τῆς βλασφημίας Παύλου πέπρακται. ἐπειδὴ δὲ οἱ περὶ Εὐσέβιον καὶ Ἄρειον, πρὸ χρόνων μὲν εἶναι τὸν υἱὸν ἔλεγον, πεποιῆσθαι μέντοι, καὶ ἕνα τῶν κτισμάτων αὐτὸν ἐδίδασκον, καὶ τὸ, ἐκ τοῦ Θεοῦ, οὐχ ὡς υἱὸν ἐκ πατρὸς γνήσιον, ἐπίστευον, ἀλλ' ὡς τὰ κτίσματα, οὕτω καὶ ἐπ' αὐτοῦ τὸ ἐκ τοῦ Θεοῦ εἶναι διαβεβαιοῦντο, τήν τε ὁμοιώσεως ἑνότητα τοῦ υἱοῦ πρὸς τὸν πατέρα, οὐκ ἔλεγον κατὰ τὴν οὐσίαν, οὔδε κατὰ τὴν φύσιν, ὡς ἔστιν υἱὸς ὅμοιος πατρὶ, ἀλλὰ διὰ τὴν συμφωνίαν τῶν δογμάτων καὶ τῆς διδα-

and also severed off, and made entirely alien the substance of the Son from the Father, devising for Him another origin of being, and bringing Him down to the number of the creatures: on this account the bishops who assembled at Nice, having perceived the craftiness of those who held this opinion, and having brought together[1] the sense out of the Scriptures, used the phrase 'of one substance' to express it more
[90] clearly[2], in order that by this the truth and genuineness of His Sonship might be known, and that created beings[3] might have nothing in common with Him. For the precision of this term both detects their hypocrisy, if they use the formula 'of God,' and also excludes all their plausible arguments, whereby they seduce[4] the simple-minded. At any rate, they are able to put a sophistical construction upon, and to change the meaning of all other words as they please; this phrase only, as detecting their heresy, they dread; which very phrase the fathers set down as a bulwark against all their impious speculations." Thus far the great Athanasius.

11. He is, moreover, supported in his views by the great Basil, in his three hundredth Epistle; where, having spoken of the publication[5] of the Nicene Creed, he subjoins the following words[q]; "Of this the other portions indeed are altogether incapable of being assailed by calumny; but the word *ὁμοούσιος*, having been used in a wrong sense by some, there are persons who have not yet accepted it. These one might with justice blame, and yet again, on second thoughts, they might be deemed excusable; for, although a refusal to follow the fathers and to consider the word adopted by them, as of more authority than one's own

[1] *συναγάγοντες.*

[2] *λευκότερον ἔγραψαν.*

[3] *γενητά.*

[4] *ὑφαρπάζουσι.*

[5] de præconio F. N. promulgato.

σκαλίας, ἀλλὰ γὰρ καὶ ἀπεσχοίνιζον καὶ ἀπεξενοῦντο παντελῶς τὴν οὐσίαν τοῦ υἱοῦ ἀπὸ τοῦ πατρὸς, ἑτέραν ἀρχὴν αὐτῷ τοῦ εἶναι ἐπινοοῦντες, καὶ εἰς τὰ κτίσματα καταφέροντες αὐτόν· τούτου χάριν οἱ ἐν Νικαίᾳ συνελθόντες, θεωρήσαντες τὴν πανουργίαν τῶν οὕτω φρονούντων, καὶ συνάγαγοντες ἐκ τῶν γραφῶν τὴν διάνοιαν, λευκότερον γράφοντες, εἰρήκασι τὸ ὁμοούσιον· ἵνα καὶ τὸ γνήσιον ἀληθῶς ἐκ τούτου γνωσθῇ τοῦ υἱοῦ, καὶ μηδὲν κοινὸν ἔχῃ πρὸς τοῦτον τὰ γενητά· ἡ γὰρ τῆς λέξεως ταύτης ἀκρίβεια, τήν τε ὑπόκρισιν αὐτῶν, ἐὰν λέγωσι τὸ ἐκ τοῦ Θεοῦ ῥητὸν, διελέγχει, καὶ πάσας αὐτῶν τὰς πιθανότητας, ἐν αἷς ὑφαρπάζουσι τοὺς ἀκεραίους, ἐκβάλλει. πάντα γοῦν δυνάμενοι σοφίζεσθαι καὶ μεταποιεῖν, ὡς θέλουσι, ταύτην μόνην τὴν λέξιν, ὡς διελέγχουσαν αὐτῶν τὴν αἵρεσιν, δεδίασιν· ἣν οἱ πατέρες, ὥσπὲρ ἐπιτείχισμα κατὰ πάσης ἀσεβοῦς ἐπινοίας αὐτῶν, ἔγραφον.—Athan., tom. i. pp. 919, 920. edit. Paris. 1627. [§ 45. vol. i. p. 758.]

[q] οὗ τὰ μὲν ἄλλα παντάπασιν ἐστὶν ἀσυκοφάντητα, τὴν δὲ τοῦ ὁμοουσίου φωνὴν, κακῶς παρά τινων ἐκληφθεῖσαν, εἰσί τινες οἱ μήπω παραδεξάμενοι. οὓς καὶ μέμψαιτ' ἄν τις δικαίως, καὶ πάλιν μέν τοι συγγνώμης αὐτοὺς ἀξιώσειεν. τὸ μὲν γὰρ πατράσι μὴ ἀκολουθεῖν, καὶ

opinion, be deserving of blame, as fraught with wilfulness; BOOK II.
still on the other hand, the suspecting it, in consequence of CHAP. I. § 10—12.
its having had an ill name given it[1] by others, seems in some HOMOOUSION.
measure to exonerate them from that blame. For, in truth, [1] διαβληθεῖσαν.
they who were assembled in the matter of Paul of Samosata,
did give an ill name[2] to this word, as not conveying a good [2] διέβαλον.
meaning[3]; for they said that the term *ὁμοούσιος*, 'of one [3] οὐκ εὔσημον.
substance,' suggests the idea of a substance and the things
which are formed from it; so as that the substance being
divided into parts, gives the appellation 'of one substance'
to the things into which it is divided. And this notion
has some force[r] in the case of metal, and the pieces of
money made from it; but in the instance of God the
Father and God the Son, there is not contemplated any
substance elder than or overlying[4] both; for to think or [4] πρεσβύτερα ἢ ὑπερκειμένη.
assert this were something beyond impiety." You perceive that in these words Basil expressly testifies, that
the word *ὁμοούσιος* was rejected by the fathers of Antioch [91]
only so far as it seemed to denote a certain divine sub- 33
stance anterior to the Father and the Son, which was subsequently divided into the Father and the Son. Now it
is most clear, that neither Paul of Samosata nor Sabellius
confessed the doctrine "of one substance" in this sense.
It therefore follows, that the assertion of Athanasius is
quite true, that Paul framed an argument for impugning
the divinity of Christ out of the word *ὁμοούσιος*, which he
was aware was in use among Catholics, (and possibly so ex- [92]
plained by some of them, as to give occasion to its being
spoken ill of,) and that the fathers, accordingly, determined
on the suppression of it altogether.

12. And this view of the case receives no little confirmation from the history of the Nicene council. It is, I mean,

τὴν ἐκείνων φωνὴν κυριωτέραν τίθεσθαι τῆς ἑαυτῶν γνώμης, ἐγκλήματος ἄξιον, ὡς αὐθαδείας γέμον· τὸ δὲ πάλιν ὑφ' ἑτέρων διαβληθεῖσαν αὐτὴν ὕποπτον ἔχειν, τοῦτό πως δοκεῖ τοῦ ἐγκλήματος αὐτοὺς μετρίως ἐλευθεροῦν. καὶ γὰρ τῷ ὄντι οἱ ἐπὶ Παύλῳ τῷ Σαμοσατεῖ συνελθόντες διέβαλον τὴν λέξιν, ὡς οὐκ εὔσημον. ἔφασαν γὰρ ἐκεῖνοι, τὴν τοῦ ὁμοουσίου φωνὴν παριστᾷν ἔννοιαν οὐσίας τε καὶ τῶν ἀπ' αὐτῆς, ὥστε καταμερισθεῖσαν τὴν οὐσίαν παρέχειν τοῦ ὁμοουσίου τὴν προσηγορίαν τοῖς εἰς ἃ διῃρέθη. τοῦτο δὲ ἐπὶ χαλκοῦ μὲν καὶ τῶν ἀπ' αὐτοῦ νομισμάτων ἔχει τινὰ λόγον τὸ διανόημα· ἐπὶ δὲ Θεοῦ πατρὸς, καὶ Θεοῦ υἱοῦ, οὐκ οὐσία πρεσβυτέρα οὐδ' ὑπερκειμένη ἀμφοῖν θεωρεῖται· ἀσεβείας γὰρ ἐπέκεινα τοῦτο καὶ νοῆσαι καὶ φθέγξασθαι.—Op. Basilii, tom. iii. p. 292. [Ep. lii. 1. p. 145.]

[r] Hoc quidem verissimum est, &c., is the Latin translation.

ON THE CONSUBSTANTIALITY OF THE SON.

altogether probable, that the word *ὁμοούσιος* was rejected by the fathers of Antioch for the very same reason, for which it was also disliked by certain catholic bishops at the council of Nice, that is to say, at first, before the other bishops and Constantine himself explained the word more distinctly. Now what was that reason? Was it because the word in question favoured the opinions of the Samosatene or Sabellius; or that those two heretics had employed it in explaining their heresy? Nothing is further from the truth. The actual reason was, because, on the contrary, the word appeared to some to imply that partition of the divine essence, which I just now mentioned; this is expressly declared by Eusebius Pamphili, in his letter to his diocese of Cæsarea, respecting the Nicene council, in the following words[s]; "After they had dictated this formula," (i. e. the formula of faith now called the Nicene Creed,) "we did not pass over without examination their expressions, 'of the substance of the Father,' and 'of one substance with the Father.' In consequence many questions and answers arose on these points, and the meaning of the terms was tested by discussion; and in particular it was admitted by them, that the expression 'of the substance,' was intended to signify that the Son is indeed of the Father, but yet does not exist as a part of the Father. And as to these points it seemed to us also
[93] right to assent to the meaning." Previously, in the same letter, Eusebius had said that Constantine himself satisfied some of the bishops who raised a question about the expression, "of one substance," by these words[t]; that "he did not use the words 'of one substance' with reference to what takes place in the case of bodies[1], nor yet that the Son subsisted[2], either by way of[3] division or any kind of abscission from the Father; inasmuch as it was not possible that the immaterial, intel-

[1] *κατὰ τὰ τῶν σωμάτων πάθη.*
[2] *ὑποστῆναι.*
[3] *κατὰ.*

[s] *καὶ δὴ ταύτης τῆς γραφῆς ὑπ' αὐτῶν ὑπαγορευθείσης, ὅπως εἴρηται αὐτοῖς τὸ ἐκ τῆς οὐσίας τοῦ Πατρὸς, καὶ τὸ τῷ Πατρὶ ὁμοούσιον, οὐκ ἀνεξέταστον αὐτοῖς καταλιμπάνομεν. ἐπερωτήσεις τοιγαροῦν καὶ ἀποκρίσεις ἐντεῦθεν ἀνεκινοῦντο, ἐβασάνιζέν τε ὁ λόγος τὴν διάνοιαν τῶν εἰρημένων· καὶ δὴ καὶ τὸ ἐκ τῆς οὐσίας ὡμολόγητο πρὸς αὐτῶν δηλωτικὸν εἶναι τοῦ ἐκ μὲν τοῦ πατρὸς εἶναι, οὐ μὴν ὡς μέρος ὑπάρχειν τοῦ Πατρός. ταῦτα δὲ καὶ ἡμῖν ἐδόκει καλῶς ἔχειν συγκατατίθεσθαι τῇ διανοίᾳ [τῆς εὐσεβοῦς διδασκαλίας, κ.τ.λ.]*—Apud Socrat. Eccl. Hist. i. 8. [p. 24.]

[t] *ὅτι μὴ κατὰ τὰ τῶν σωμάτων πάθη λέγοι τὸ ὁμοούσιον, οὔτε οὖν κατὰ διαίρεσιν, οὔτε κατά τινα ἀποτομὴν ἐκ τοῦ Πατρὸς ὑποστῆναι. μήτε γὰρ δύνασθαι τὴν ἄϋλον, καὶ νοερὰν, καὶ ἀσώματον φύσιν σωματικόν τι πάθος ὑφίστασθαι· θείοις δὲ καὶ ἀπορρήτοις ῥήμασι προσήκει τὰ τοιαῦτα νοεῖν.*—[Ibid.]

BOOK II. CHAP. I. § 12.

HOMOOUSION.

lectual, and incorporeal nature should be the subject of any corporeal affection; but of divine and mysterious terms it is fit that we conceive in like manner," [i. e. in divine and mysterious thoughts.] Lastly, before the time of Paul of Samosata, Sabellius also had himself denied the generation of the Son, into a distinct Person, of God the Father Himself, i. e. His being "of one substance," for the same reason, namely, that there would thence follow a division, and a cutting asunder, as it were, of the Divine Substance; as Alexander informs us, not obscurely, in a letter to his namesake, the bishop of Constantinople, given in Theodoret; where he says that the Son[u] "was begotten, not out of what is not[1], but of the Father who Is; not after the likeness of [material] bodies, by cuttings off, or by streamings off, which imply division, as Sabellius fancies." These words of Alexander admit plainly of a twofold meaning. Either, first, that Sabellius himself supposed that the Son was begotten of God the Father, after the manner of [material] bodies, by a cutting into or partition of the Father's substance; or secondly, that that heretic thought that such a partition of the Father's substance necessarily resulted from the view of the Catholics, who taught that the Son was so begotten of the very substance of the Father as to be a distinct Person[2] from the Father, and that on that account he rejected that catholic doctrine. The former of these senses is altogether absurd, since it is known to every one that Sabellius taught that God is one Person only[3]; and that he recognised no real distinction of Persons in the Divine Essence, much less a partition thereof. It remains, then, that we must certainly take the words in the other sense. And indeed the earliest forerunners of Sabellius, whose heresy is stated and refuted by Justin Martyr, (in his Dialogue with Trypho,) opposed a distinction of Persons in the Godhead by the same argument, as we shall afterwards shew[x], where we treat of the doctrine of Justin. Nay, it is certain that all the heretics who have ever denied a distinct subsistence of the Son of God in the Divine Essence, (whether

[1] οὐκ ἐκ τοῦ μὴ ὄντος.

[94]

[2] hypostasis.

[3] μονοπρόσωπος.

[u] γεννηθέντα οὐκ ἐκ τοῦ μὴ ὄντος, ἀλλ' ἐκ τοῦ ὄντος Πατρὸς, οὐ κατὰ τὰς τῶν σωμάτων ὁμοιότητας, ταῖς τομαῖς ἢ ταῖς ἐκ διαιρέσεων ἀπορροίαις, ὥσπερ Σαβελλίῳ δοκεῖ.—Eccl. Hist. i. 4. p. 17. edit. Valesii. [p. 18.]

[x] See chap. iv. sect. 4. of this Book.

they were Sabellians, followers of the Samosatene, or, lastly,
Arians,) have invariably placed the chief support of their
cause on this very sophism. And I have no doubt that the
Nicene fathers wished to counteract this wrong conception
of the doctrine of the "consubstantiality" of the Son, when
(after saying that the Son is "begotten of the substance of
the Father") they subjoined immediately, "God of God, light
34 of light." For by these words they signify that the Son of
God is so begotten of God the Father, God of God, as light
[95] is kindled of another light; not by a partition or diminution
of the Father's essence, but by a simple communication, such
as (if any illustration of so great a mystery may be derived
from things material) is the communication of light from
another light, without any division or diminution of it.

13. And thus after carefully weighing every thing, we are led to the decided opinion, that the following is the most simple way of reconciling this apparent contradiction[1] between the councils of Antioch and Nice. The Catholics before the time of Paul of Samosata, and the council convened at Antioch against him, were accustomed to say, in discoursing of the Godhead of the Father and the Son, that the Son is "of one substance" with the Father; as is abundantly proved by the testimonies of the ancient authors prior to the council of Antioch, which we have alleged before. Paul, however, in striving by every means to overthrow the received doctrine of the divinity of the Son, employed a sophistical argument, derived from a wrong understanding of the meaning of the expression "of one substance:" as thus: If the Son be of one substance with the Father, as you (Catholics) say, it will follow, that the Divine Substance is, as it were, severed into two parts, whereof one constitutes the Father, and the other the Son; and thus that there existed a certain Divine Substance, anterior to the Father and the Son, which afterwards was distributed into those two. The fathers of the council of Antioch with good reason abhorred this interpretation of the word; and therefore, not caring much about words in a question of such moment, they were content to suppress the term itself in silence, in order to cut off all occasion for the cavils of the heretics, provided only that the thing was agreed on, i. e. the true divinity of the Son. When,

[1] ἐναντιοφανείας.

HOMOOUSION.

[96]

however, the Arians afterwards denied the thing itself, which is really represented in the word, that is to say, the true divinity of the Son, and adduced (as is probable) the definition of the fathers of Antioch to screen their heresy, the bishops assembled at Nice with good reason formally recalled (as from exile[1]), and inserted in their Creed, this most fitting expression, which, as they were aware, had been received and approved by holy fathers prior to the council of Antioch, and which Catholics had then had taken from them, simply on account of the absurd cavils of the impious Samosatene; such an explanation being added in the Creed itself, as no one but an heretic could reject. This will be sufficient before fair judges to vindicate the venerable fathers of Nice for adding the word *ὁμοούσιος* to their Creed; an additional reason, however, is given by Athanasius, in the fore-cited passage, and that with great truth; to the effect that the most holy fathers were by a kind of necessity, driven to place that word in their confession of faith, (although it nowhere occurs in the Scriptures, and even had, on somewhat slight grounds, been rejected by some of their predecessors,) driven that is to say, by reason of the "unprincipled cunning[2]" of the Arians, such as can hardly be believed, and such as all good men must simply detest, or (to use another expression of Athanasius[y]) "the wickedness[3] and evil artifice of their impiety." For those eminent masters of pretence and dissimulation did not reject any one form of speech, which the Catholics had adopted and used, either out of Scripture or from tradition, with the sole exception of the word *ὁμοούσιος*; as being a word of which the precision and exactness precluded all attempt at equivocation. When they were asked whether they acknowledged that the Son was begotten of the Father Himself[4]? they used to assent, understanding, as is plain, the Son to be of God in such sense as all creatures are of God, that is, have the beginning of their existence from Him. When the Catholics enquired of them whether they confessed that the Son of God was God, they forthwith answered, Most certainly. Nay more, they used of their own accord openly to declare[5] that the Son of God is true God[6]. But in what sense? Forsooth being made true

[1] quasi postliminio.

[2] τὴν πανουργίαν.

[3] τὴν κακουργίαν καὶ τὴν τῆς ἀσεβείας κακοτεχνίαν.

[4] ex ipso Patre.

[5] ultro prædicabant.

[6] ἀληθινὸν Θεόν.

[y] [Epist. ad Afric. § 7. vol. i. p. 93.]

[97]

[God], He is true [God]; that is, He is true God who was truly made God[z]. Lastly, when they were charged by the Catholics with asserting that the Son of God is a creature, they would repel the charge not without some indignation: with the secret reservation of its being in this sense, that the Son of God is not a creature, as all other creatures are; they being created by God mediately through the Word[1], not immediately, as the Word Himself. The word *ὁμοούσιος*, "of one substance," was the only expression which they could not in any way reconcile with their heresy. Read by all means what Athanasius has written on this subject, in his letter to the African bishops, given by Theodoret, (Eccl. Hist. i. 8;) where this is especially to be observed, that Athanasius asserts that the Nicene fathers had designed to construct the confession of their faith from passages of Scripture exclusively; and that they would have carried this into effect, had they not been diverted from their purpose by the impious and abominable cunning of the Arians in perverting and wresting the words of the sacred oracles, of which they had full proof before their eyes. As to the observation of Athanasius, that the expression *ὁμοούσιος*, "of one substance," was the one word upon which the Arians could not put any false colour, it is remarkably confirmed by Ambrose, (in his treatise On the Divinity of the Son, c. 4,) in these words[a]: "In short, even now they might (so far as the word is concerned) use the phrase *ὁμοούσιος*, as they have all others also, if they knew how to pervert it to another meaning by putting a distorted sense on it; but perceiving themselves to be shut up by this word, they wished that no mention at all
35 should be made of it [in the Creed."] And, in fact, the complete truth of this declaration of Athanasius and Ambrose is abundantly attested by the various and manifold confessions of the Arians, (as they are recorded by Athanasius himself in his treatise On the Councils of Ariminum and Seleucia, and by Hilary in his work On the Councils against the Arians, and

[1] δία τοῦ λόγου.

[z] *γενόμενος ἀληθινὸς, ἀληθινός ἐστιν.* i. e. Verus est Deus, qui vere factus est Deus.

[a] Denique et nunc possent *ὁμοούσιον*, sicut et cætera, verbo tenus nominare, si haberent quomodo illud ad aliam intelligentiam scævo sensu perverterent. Sed cum viderent, se in hoc verbo concludi, nullam omnino hujus mentionem fieri voluerunt.—[Several critics deny that this work is by Ambrose. Vol. ii. Append., p. 351.—B.]

HOMOOUSION.

by other writers;) inasmuch as in these confessions the word ὁμοούσιος, "of one substance," is uniformly omitted, although well-nigh all the other statements[1] of the Catholics concerning the Son of God are found in them. So that the Arian fanatics, in burning with such excessive fury against that word, seem to me to act like mad dogs, that snarl at the iron chains by which they are confined, and attempt in vain to break them with their teeth. [98]

[1] præconia.

14. For the rest; we are by no means to listen to Stephen Curcellæus[b], who could affirm without a blush, that "the insertion of the word ὁμοούσιος into the confession of faith by the Nicene bishops, as a watchword of orthodoxy, after it had been excluded from it as heretical by the council of Antioch sixty years before, happened through an oversight, in that the bishops who met at Nice had heard nothing of the decree of Antioch; and that afterwards when it came to their knowledge, after the council was dissolved, it was no longer open[2] to them to make any alteration." For what man that is in his senses, and (to use an expression of Curcellæus') that has not been possessed by a spirit of dizziness, would think it likely, that out of three hundred and eighteen bishops, of whom some (as we have before seen from Eusebius) were remarkable for learning, and others also venerable from their advanced age, there should not be one who knew what had been decreed in a very celebrated council, of which the remembrance was yet fresh. But even supposing we were to allow as a concession to Curcellæus, that all the rest of the prelates were so ignorant of the history of the Church, it was at any rate quite impossible that Eusebius, bishop of Cæsarea, should have been unacquainted with this fact; seeing that he was a man, beyond all controversy, most thoroughly acquainted with ecclesiastical matters. What is to be said to the fact that Athanasius, who, as it has been said before, was himself present and taking a part in the Nicene council, expressly testifies, in the passage above quoted, that the fathers assembled at Nice thoroughly understood the craft [99]
of Paul[3], that is, of Paul of Samosata, in procuring by his sophistry, among the bishops at Antioch, the throwing aside of a most apt expression, which had been of old in use among

[2] integrum.

[3] τὴν πανουργίαν τοῦ Παύλου.

[b] Quatern. Dissertat., Dissert. i. p. 138. [§ 71. p. 852. Op., ed. 1675.]

ON THE CONSUBSTANTIALITY OF THE SON.

the Catholic doctors; and that, in consequence, they had recalled it again into the use of the Church. Nothing could have been said more express than this against the fabrication[1] of Curcellæus.

[1] figmentum.

15. But before we bring to a close our enquiry respecting the word "of one substance," we must once more briefly meet a statement of Sandius, who in the first book[a] of his "Ecclesiastical History laid open[2]," maintains, that the word ὁμοούσιος was first fabricated by heretics, that is to say, by the Valentinians and other Gnostics; from whom the phrase was afterwards taken up by Montanus, Theodotus, Sabellius, Paul of Samosata, and the Manichees; and alleges that this is witnessed to by Irenæus, Clement of Alexandria, and others. I ask him what his meaning is, when he says that this word was first fabricated by the Valentinians and other Gnostics. Does he mean this, that the Gnostics were the first to devise the Greek word, and to bring it into use? I suppose he was not so utterly foolish as this. At any rate, as has been already shewn, the heathen writers among the Greeks used the very same word. Or did he mean that the Gnostics used that word respecting some of their Æons? We allow that they did; and no more than this is attested by Irenæus and other Catholic writers[b]. But what of that? Surely these same Gnostics also applied to their Æons the words λόγος, σωτήρ, παράκλητος, and very many others which were in use among the Catholics in speaking of the divine Persons. Are we then, on this account, to say, that the Gnostics were the first to invent them? and are the words, on this ground, to be excluded from use in the Church?
[100] Certainly not. The remark of Tertullian is to the purpose, (against Praxeas, chap. 8[c];) "The truth does not refrain from the use of a word, because heresy also uses it. Nay, heresy has rather borrowed it from the truth, to frame it into her own counterfeit." Lastly, was this what he meant, that the Gnostics were the first to teach that the Word, or Son of God, was

[2] Historiæ Ecclesiasticæ enucleatæ.

[a] p. 122.

[b] See above, § 2.

[c] Non ideo, inquit, non utatur et veritas vocabulo [isto (sc. προβολὴν) et re et censu ejus,] quia et hæresis [utitur, imo hæresis] potius ex veritate accepit, quod ad mendacium suum strueret. [p. 504. The Latin is given in full; the words in brackets were omitted by Bp. Bull, and "utatur" altered to "utitur;" the words "utitur, imo hæresis" have been restored in the translation, to complete the sense.]

BOOK II. CHAP. I. § 14, 15.

HOMOOUSION.

of one substance with God the Father? He must surely
allow, either that this was his meaning in the passage I have
cited, or that his observations were not at all to the point.
Now, this is entirely false; neither Irenæus, nor any one of
the ancient writers makes such a statement. On the contrary,
it is most certain that the Gnostics (I mean, the Cerinthians,
Valentinians, &c.) entirely denied the consubstantiality of
the Logos, i. e. of the Word, or Son of God; and were on
that account condemned by the Catholics who wrote against
them, as guilty of heresy. Indeed they separated the Logos
so far from the essence of the most high God, the Father
of all, that that Æon was totally ignorant of that his first
parent; as we learn from Irenæus, Tertullian, and others.
So they also denied the coeternity[1] of the Word, affirming
that Silence preceded the Word; and that, consequently,
there was a time when the Word did not exist at all; and
from this cause also they were vehemently opposed by the
most ancient Catholic doctors of the Church. In a word, the
heresy, which was afterwards called the Arian, had the Gnostics for its first authors and parents; as we shall most clearly
prove in a subsequent portion of the work[d]. Of Sabellius
and Paul of Samosata, I have already said what may suffice.
With regard to Montanus, by what argument will Sandius
prove that he was heretical on the article of the most holy
Trinity? His authorities are Socrates, i. 23, and Sozomen,
ii. 18. They associate Montanus with Sabellius, as thinking
alike on the doctrine of the most holy Trinity. But let us [101]
hear what the excellent Valesius[e] has observed on the passage in Socrates; "It is not clear," he says, "why Socrates
joins Montanus and Sabellius together; for we have the 36
testimony of Epiphanius, (On the Heresy of the Montanists,)
and of Theodoret, (in his third book On the Fables of the
Heretics,) that Montanus himself made no innovation in
the doctrine of the Trinity, but adhered to the faith of the
Catholic Church; some of his followers, however, did away
with the distinction of persons, with Sabellius, as Theodoret in the passage cited above expressly writes[f], 'Certain

[1] τὸ συναΐδιον.

[d] See book iii. 1. § 15, 16.

[e] Notes on Socrat., p. 14. [p. 57.]

[f] τινὲς δὲ αὐτῶν τὰς τρεῖς ὑποστάσεις τῆς θεότητος Σαβελλίῳ παραπλησίως ἠρνήσαντο, τὸν αὐτὸν εἶναι λέγοντες καὶ πατέρα, καὶ υἱὸν, καὶ ἅγιον πνεῦμα.—Theodoret. Hæret. Fab. iii. 2. vol. iv. p. 227.

ON THE CONSUBSTANTIALITY OF THE SON.

of them, almost in the same way as Sabellius, denied the three Persons of the Godhead, alleging that the Father, the Son, and the Holy Ghost are the same person[1].'" To the observations of Valesius I will add this also; Tertullian in his treatise against Praxeas, (a work which was certainly written by him after he had become a Montanist,) most strenuously assailed the heresy which Sabellius embraced; for[2] Praxeas entertained the very same opinions as Sabellius afterwards [did.] It is, therefore, more than certain, that neither Montanus himself, nor his earliest followers, entertained the same views as Sabellius on the doctrine of the Trinity. If Sandius had understood this, he might easily have corrected his many mistakes in the first book of his *Hist. Eccl. Enucl.*, in which he treats of Montanus and his heresy. But what, I ask, is the meaning of Sandius, in enumerating Theodotus among the upholders of the word "of one substance." Does he mean Theodotus the Tanner, who in the time of Pope Victor taught that Christ was a mere man[3]? But what ancient writer, nay what human being, before Sandius, maintained that Theodotus ever dreamt of the consubstantiality of
[102] the Son? Then, with respect to the Manichees, Augustine indeed states, (as Sandius afterwards quotes him, when he is treating of those heretics,) that they acknowledged the Father, the Son, and the Holy Ghost to be of a nature not unequal. Be it so. But what then? Sandius may sooner draw water from a pumice-stone, than hammer out of these facts any thing to suit his purpose! Meanwhile, it is no great merit in the Manichees to confess that the three Persons of the Godhead are of a nature not unequal; for (according to Sandius' own statement) they thought that angels also, and the souls of men had their existence of the divine substance. And thus far of the word ὁμοούσιος, "of one substance." Let us now deal with the thing itself.

16. We affirm that it was the concordant and uniform view of the Catholic doctors, who flourished in the first three centuries, that the Son of God is, in the aforesaid sense, of one substance with God the Father; that is, that He is not of any created or mutable essence, but of altogether the same divine and unchangeable nature with His Father; and therefore is true God. The ancient writers, indeed, teach[4]

[1] τὸν αὐτὸν εἶναι.

[2] scilicet.

[3] ψιλὸν ἄνθρωπον.

[4] tradunt.

BOOK II. CHAP. I. § 15, 16.

HOMOOUSION.

this doctrine in many different ways. 1. They teach the doctrine "of one substance," so often as they affirm that the Son of God is put forth and begotten, not only by the Father[1], but of Him. For that is a most certain axiom, Τὸ ἐκ Θεοῦ γεννηθὲν, Θεός ἐστι[g], "What is begotten of God, is God." 2. They teach the same, so often as they declare that the Son is the true, genuine, proper, and natural Son of God the Father. 3. The very same do they declare by the similes with which they are accustomed, as best they may, to illustrate the generation of the Son. They say that the Son is begotten of[2] the Father, as a tree proceeds out of the root, a stream out of the fountain, a ray out of the sun. But the root and the tree, the fountain and the stream, the light in the disc of the sun and that in the ray, are clearly of the same nature; so are the Father and the Son of altogether the same substance. But you will find no simile, in which the fathers take more [103] delight, than in that of light out of light, as when fire is kindled of[3] fire, or the beam put forth[4] out of the sun. Hence the Nicene prelates in their creed inserted that expression φῶς ἐκ φωτὸς, "Light of Light," in illustration of the article "of one substance." 4. They most openly confirm the doctrine "of one substance," when (as they all do) they except the Son of God from the number of created beings, and expressly deny that He is a creature; for there is nothing midway between God and a creature. 5. They affirm the same, so often as they ascribe to the Son of God attributes which belong to the true God only. 6. Lastly, they teach this very truth, so often as they explicitly pronounce the Son of God to be not only God, but true God also, God by nature, one God with the Father. In most of the fathers all these arguments for the consubstantiality may be found; whilst most of them occur in all. But let us now hear them speak for themselves.

[1] a Patre, sed ex ipso, "out of Himself."

[2] generari ex.

[3] ex.

[4] porrigitur.

[g] [Irenæus, i. 8. 5. p. 41.]

37

CHAPTER II.

THE DOCTRINE OF THE AUTHOR OF THE EPISTLE ASCRIBED TO BARNABAS, OF HERMAS, OR THE SHEPHERD, AND OF THE MARTYR IGNATIUS, CONCERNING THE TRUE DIVINITY OF THE SON, SET FORTH.

ON THE CONSUBSTANTIALITY OF THE SON.

I WILL begin with the apostolic writers. The author of the Epistle which bears the name of Barnabas, in the passages which we have cited before[h] in proof of the pre-existence of the Son of God, remarkably declares His true Godhead also. For therein he calls the Son of God "Lord of the whole earth;" and that antecedently (as they express it) to that dispensation[1], which He vouchsafed to undertake for our salvation; he says also, that the glory of Jesus is so great, that "through Him and for Him are all things[2]:" that is, by Him, as the efficient cause, all things are made, and to Him[3], as their end, all
[104] things are referred; which certainly cannot, without blasphemy, be said of any creature. To this may be added a remarkable passage in the sixth section of the same Epistle; where he teaches that the Lord, who foreknew all things, for this reason said that He would take away from His people their heart of stone, and would put into them a new heart of flesh; "because[i] He was about to be manifested in the flesh, and to dwell in us; for the habitation of our heart, my brethren, is a holy temple to the Lord;" where he is speaking expressly of the Lord, who manifested Himself in the flesh, or the nature of man, that is, of the Son of God; and declares that He is the Lord, who hath His dwelling in the hearts of the saints, as in temples consecrated unto God. Now these expressions so clearly set forth the divine majesty and omnipresence of the Son, as to require no explanation from me; and there are several other passages of the like import, which you may read throughout the same Epistle.

2. Hermas, a writer whose antiquity and authority we have

[1] œconomiam.

[2] per ipsum et propter ipsum.

[3] in ipsum.

h i. 2. 2. [p. 36.]

i ὅτι ἔμελλεν ἐν σαρκὶ φανεροῦσθαι, καὶ ἐν ἡμῖν κατοικεῖν. ναὸς γὰρ ἅγιος, ἀδελφοί μου, τῷ Κυρίῳ τὸ κατοικητήριον ἡμῶν τῆς καρδίας.—p. 222. [p. 19.]

already[k] abundantly established, delivers most plainly the same doctrine. For besides teaching, in the ninth Similitude, (as was shewn above,) that the Son of God was in being before any creature, and was present with His Father, and that as His counsellor[1], at the creation of all things, (statements which, with all men of sound mind, suffice to declare the true divinity of the Son; for who can suppose that the counsellor of God is not Himself God?) in the same Similitude also, a little after, he expressly attributes to the Son of God the upholding of the whole world, and of all the creatures that are in the world, (a truly divine work,) and immensity, which in like manner belongs to [105]
the true God alone. His words are; "The name of the Son of God is great and immeasurable; and the whole world is sustained by Him[l]." And afterwards; "Every creature of God is sustained by His Son;" wherein also he most explicitly distinguishes the Son of God from every creature of God. Hermas also expressly denies that the Son of God is put in the place or condition of a servant. There is a proof of this in his third book, Simil. v., where upon Hermas' enquiring[m], "Why is the Son of God, in this similitude, put in the place of a servant?" the Shepherd returns answer; "The Son of God is not put in the condition of a servant, but in great power and rule." Now the expressions, "to be put in the condition of a servant," and "to be a creature," are equivalent; forasmuch as every creature stands in the relation of a servant to God, the supreme Lord of all. And rightly doth the author of a treatise, entitled An Exposition of Faith, (ἔκθεσις πίστεως,) ascribed to Justin, say[n]; "For if any thing is among the number of things existing, its nature is either created or uncreated. Now that nature which is uncreate is sovereign and free from all necessity; whilst

[1] σύμβουλος.

[k] See book i. 2. 3. [p. 38.]

[l] Nomen Filii Dei magnum et immensum est, et totus ab eo sustentatur orbis. . . . Omnis Dei creatura per Filium ejus sustentatur.—[§ 14. p. 119.]

[m] Quare Filius Dei in similitudine hac servili loco ponitur? respondet Pastor: In servili conditione non ponitur Filius Dei, sed in magna potestate et imperio.—[§ 5, 6. p. 107.]

[n] εἴ τι γάρ ἐστιν ἐν τοῖς οὖσιν, ἢ ἄκτιστος φύσις ἐστὶν, ἢ κτιστή. ἀλλ' ἡ μὲν ἄκτιστος, δεσποτικὴ καὶ πάσης ἀνάγκης ἐλευθέρα· ἡ δὲ, δουλικὴ καὶ νόμοις δεσποτικοῖς ἑπομένη. καὶ ἡ μὲν κατ' ἐξουσίαν ἃ ἂν βούλεται, καὶ ποιοῦσα, καὶ δυναμένη· ἡ δὲ τὴν διακονίαν μόνην, ἣν παρ' αὐτῆς τῆς Θεότητος εἴληφε, καὶ δυναμένη, καὶ ποιοῦσα.—p. 374. [§ 4. p. 422.]

ON THE CONSUBSTANTIALITY OF THE SON.

the other is servile and subject to the laws of a master. And the former, with full power, doeth, and can do, whatever it will; the latter only can do, and only doeth, that service which it hath received from the Godhead Itself." Whence the holy Apostle himself also, in his Epistle to the Philippians, ii. 6, 7, (which single passage, if rightly considered, is enough
38 to refute all the heresies against the Person of our Lord
[106] Jesus Christ,) opposes "the form of a servant" (μορφὴν δούλου) to "the form of God" (μορφὴν Θεοῦ): by the form of a servant understanding (not that condition of wretchedness, which the Lord endured for our salvation, when He was beaten with scourges, spitted upon, and at last nailed to the cross, for of that, as a further degree of humiliation, he afterwards in the same passage speaks distinctly; but) that very nature of man, in likeness of which Christ is said (in the words immediately following, which are manifestly added by way of explanation[1]) to have been made: for of a truth every man, of what condition soever he be, nay, every creature, when compared with God, holds altogether the relation of a servant.

3. Petavius himself adduced this remarkable passage of Hermas, in support of the true Godhead of Christ; although the Jesuit is, in consequence, charged by the author of the *Irenicum Irenicorum* with a want of good faith[2]. It is thus he addresses him[o]; "But if it had been your wish, not to deceive, but to inform others, you ought here, Petavius, to have added what power, and what dominion that was, of which the Shepherd spoke; not, it is plain, of a power and a dominion equal to the Father's, but of a power delivered to Him by the Father after His death, and a dominion over His own people, whom in like manner the Father had given Him, and over whom Christ Himself placed teachers[3][p]. And on this account he says that Christ both is, and is introduced, not as a servant, but as the Lord of His people." But in this instance, O nameless one[4], the charge recoils on yourself; for had you not wished to deceive, rather than to inform others, you ought here to have added what is necessarily connected

[1] ἐξηγητικῶς.

[2] sublestæ fidei.

[3] doctores.

[4] anonyme.

[o] Irenic. Iren., p. 20.

[p] [The words of Hermas following those last quoted are; Ei dixi, Quomodo, inquam, domine? Non intelligo. Quoniam, inquit, eis quos Filio suo tradidit, Filius ejus nuntios præposuit ad conservandos singulos.—§ 6.]

BOOK II. CHAP. II. § 2, 3.

HERMAS.

with the words which you have alleged, and thus presented to your reader the text of Hermas entire. The matter stands thus: in this fifth Similitude the Shepherd had represented Christ our Saviour under a twofold condition[1], as Son of God, and as servant of God. For this is his own explicit [107] interpretation of the parable of the Son and the servant[q]; "The Son," he says, "is the Holy Spirit; but the servant is the Son of God." For as is plain, the Son of God whom he calls the Holy Spirit, is one and the same as the Son of God whom he had in the similitude represented as a servant. By both he certainly means our Saviour, whom he designates both as Son of God, and as a servant; but in a different view in each case. He calls Christ the Son of God, because of that Holy Spirit, that is, the divine nature[2], or the Word, (as was observed above[r],) which was united to the man Christ in one person, by a most intimate and ineffable connexion. On the other hand he introduces that same Christ as the servant of God, in respect of that body, (as the Shepherd soon after speaks,) or that human nature, which the Son of God put on, and in which in very deed He assumed the form of a servant. Nor is it unusual with our Shepherd, by reason of Christ's twofold nature, to attribute to Him, in the same similitude, a twofold condition also. In the ninth, for instance, he had represented Christ under the figure alike of an ancient rock, inasmuch as He is Son of God, being before all creatures with the Father; and of a new gate, inasmuch as in these last days He the same [Person] became man, and appeared [on earth]; as we have also shewn before. Hermas, however, not yet understanding this, and being unable to comprehend in what way He, who is the Son of God, is also the servant of God, asks this question of his Shepherd; "Why is the Son of God in this similitude put in the place of a servant[s]?" In answer to this question, the Shepherd does indeed say those words which the author of the *Irenicum* just now quoted, of all power being given to Christ by the Father, &c.; but this does not make up the full answer of the Shep- [108]

[1] σχέσις.

[2] τὴν θείαν φύσιν.

[q] Filius autem, inquit, Spiritus sanctus est: servus vero ille Filius Dei.—[§ 5. p. 107.]

[r] Vid. i. 2. 5. [p. 46.]

[s] Quare Filius Dei in similitudine hac servili loco ponitur? [§ 5. p. 107.]

herd; since, shortly after, other statements are subjoined by him, which contain a more full and distinct solution of the question put to him, and which are not so much in accordance with the wish and the view of this anonymous author. The Shepherd, as is plain, again distinguishes between the Holy Spirit, or the divine nature[1] in Christ, and the body, or human nature of Christ; and states in express terms that the condition of a servant, in which the Son of God had been represented in the similitude, is to be referred solely to the flesh, or that human nature. For, after he had said respecting this Holy Spirit, that "It was first of all infused into the body, in which God would dwell[2];" he adds presently afterwards; "This body, therefore, into which the Holy Spirit was brought, served that Spirit, walking in modesty, uprightly and purely, nor ever at all defiled that Spirit. Seeing, then, that the body had at all times been obedient to the Holy Spirit, and had laboured righteously and chastely with It, nor had given way at any time, that wearied body lived indeed the life of a servant, but being mightily approved together with that Holy Spirit was received by God[t]." In these words it is quite clear, that the Shepherd is speaking of the body, or the human nature of Christ; and that it is of that body alone that he affirms that it lived the life of a servant; and that after, and by reason of, that life of a servant finished on earth, being approved together with the Holy Spirit, or Word, in which it subsisted[3], it was received by God, that is to say, was raised to the right hand of the Divine Majesty in the highest. Hence [it seems, that] the Shepherd had shadowed forth the exaltation of the man Christ in the similitude, by
39 the figure of the servant whom the Lord of the farm, that
is, God the Father, by reason of the good service which He
[109] had performed, willed to make fellow-heir with His own Son.

[1] τὴν θείαν φύσιν.

[2] in quo habitaret Deus.

[3] in quo subsisteret.

[t] Qui infusus est omnium primus in corpore, in quo habitaret Deus, ... Hoc ergo corpus, in quod inductus est Spiritus Sanctus, servivit illi Spiritui, recte in modestia ambulans et caste, neque omnino maculavit Spiritum illum. Cum igitur corpus illud paruisset omni tempore Spiritui Sancto, recte atque caste laborasset cum eo, nec succubuisset in omni tempore, fatigatum corpus illud serviliter conversatum est, sed fortiter cum Spiritu Sancto comprobatum, Deo receptum est.—An allusion is here evidently made to the words of Paul, ἐδικαιώθη ἐν πνεύματι, "justified in the Spirit;" and ἀνελήφθη ἐν δόξῃ, "received up into glory," 1 Tim. iii. 16. See a similar passage of Justin, observed on iii. 2. 2.

For by the servant he means the body, or human nature of Christ; and by the Son, the divine nature in Christ, as we have more than once intimated to the reader. The servant, therefore, became fellow-heir with the Son, at the time when the body, or human nature of Christ, after His resurrection, was set on the right hand of God, and was made associate and partaker, as far as it was capable of it, of the same glory and honour which the Son of God (or the Word) possessed with His Father even before the foundation of this world. The same was the meaning of the author of the so-called Epistle of Barnabas, who was undoubtedly contemporary with Hermas, when, in the eleventh chapter, after citing the words of Christ by the prophet, "Jacob[u] is to be praised above all[1] the earth," he after his manner thus interprets it[v]; "By this He means the vessel of His Spirit," (that is, of His divinity,) which He was about to glorify." Any one who shall have carefully perused the fifth Similitude of Hermas, will at once perceive that I have here given the true meaning of the Shepherd. And from all these proofs it is now most clear, that according to the doctrine of the Shepherd, the Son of God, as Son of God and as God, in no wise hath, nor ever had, even in respect of God the Father, the relation of a servant; and that in no other way, than on account of the dispensation of His incarnation[2], which He voluntarily undertook, was He at any time the servant of God; which is the very point we had to prove. But of a truth, in this case, the words with which the author of the *Irenicum*[x] twitted Petavius may very fairly be turned against himself; "These and other statements of the same kind are made by our author concerning the Son; which are widely different from what thou, hiding thy name, representest unto us."

[1] super παρὰ.

[2] incarnationis dispensationem.

4. I am ashamed and grieved to state what the author of the *Irenicum* and Sandius have adduced, in support of their [110] heresy, in opposition to these testimonies of Hermas so clear and express for the Catholic doctrine; but, lest I should seem to shrink[3] from meeting them, I will notwithstanding bring

[3] tergiversari.

[u] [Bp. Bull's words are; Jacob laudabilis super omnem terram. The original is; καὶ ἦν ἡ γῆ τοῦ Ἰακὼβ ἐπαινουμένη παρὰ πᾶσαν τὴν γῆν, and the passage probably refers to Zeph. iii. 19; though it is not identical with the LXX version.]

[v] τοῦτο λέγει τὸ σκεῦος τοῦ Πνεύματος αὐτοῦ ὃ δοξάζει.—p. 235. [p. 38.]

[x] Iren. Irenic., p. 21.

them forward. In the first place, then, they both[y] allege as an objection the words of the Shepherd in book ii., (which is especially entitled the Shepherd,) Mand. 1[z]; "Believe that there is one God, who [created and] constituted all things, and caused them to be, who is able to comprehend all things, and is not comprehended of any." But what the sophists would extract from these words in furtherance of their cause, I cannot even divine: unless indeed they imagine that it is impossible for any one, who acknowledges a Trinity of divine Persons of one substance[1], to believe that there is one God. But if this is what they think, they are greatly deceived; seeing that at this day all Catholics believe both. And the primitive Catholic Church professed the same also in her rule of faith, as Tertullian testifies at the opening of his book against Praxeas, where he says[a], "We believe in one only God indeed, but yet under this dispensation, which we call 'economy,' that there is of this one only God, the Son also, His Word, who proceeded from Him," &c. And a little after; "One is all, in that[2] all are of one, by unity, that is, of substance; and nevertheless the mystery of the economy is guarded, which distributes the unity into a Trinity, placing in their order three [Persons,] the Father, the Son, and the Holy Ghost." The author of the *Irenicum,* however, and Sandius plainly appear to have entertained the same notions as those "unwise and simple men[3]," whom Tertullian presently after mentions in the same place[b], who, "forasmuch as the rule of faith itself transfers [them] from the many gods of the world, unto one only and true God, not understanding that He must be be-

[1] ὁμοουσίων.

[2] dum.

[3] imprudentes et idiotæ.

[y] Irenic., p. 19; Sand. Enucl. Hist. Eccl., p. 55.

[z] Crede quoniam unus est Deus, qui omnia constituit et fecit, ut essent omnia, omnium capax, et qui a nemine capitur.—[p. 85. The Greek is; πρῶτον πάντων πίστευσον ὅτι εἷς ἐστὶν ὁ Θεὸς, ὁ τὰ πάντα κτίσας καὶ καταρτίσας καὶ ποιήσας ἐκ τοῦ μὴ ὄντος εἰς τὸ εἶναι τὰ πάντα. Bp. Bull follows Irenæus, who quotes the words of Hermas, iv. 20, 2. p. 253.—B.]

[a] Nos unicum quidem Deum credimus, sub hac tamen dispensatione, quam οἰκονομίαν dicimus, ut unici Dei sit et Filius, Sermo ipsius, qui ex ipso processerit, [per quem omnia facta sunt et sine quo factum est nihil.] . . . . [Quasi non sic quoque] unus sit [est Bull,] omnia, dum ex uno omnia, per substantiæ scilicet unitatem: et nihilominus custodiatur οἰκονομίας sacramentum, quæ unitatem in Trinitatem disponit, tres dirigens, Patrem, [et] Filium, et Spiritum Sanctum.—[2. p. 501.]

[b] Quoniam et ipsa regula fidei a pluribus Diis sæculi ad unicum et verum Deum transfert, non intelligentes unicum quidem, sed cum sua οἰκονομίᾳ esse credendum, expavescunt ad οἰκονομίαν. Numerum et dispositionem

BOOK II. CHAP. II. § 4, 5.

HERMAS.

lieved to be indeed one only, but yet with His own [proper] economy[1], are startled at that economy. They assume that number and mutual relation[2] in the Trinity is a division of the unity: whereas the unity, deriving the Trinity out of itself, is not destroyed, but rather ministered unto, by it." Yet [111] whatever these modern dogmatisers may think, it is at any rate clear, and certain, that our Hermas, who wrote in the apostolic age, was not ignorant of that most sacred economy. For, we may observe, his Shepherd did himself believe, and taught others to believe, that there is one God, in such sense as at the same time to confess, that the Father of all things hath His Son, who was in being with Him before all creatures; and who was also present with Him in the framing of all things as His counsellor and fellow-worker; who, even as His Father, is infinite, and sustains the universe by His almighty word[3]; who, lastly, in Himself and in His own nature hath no way the relation of a servant to God the Father; as has been shewn from the very words of Hermas himself, which have been already quoted.

1 οἰκονομίᾳ.

2 dispositionem.

3 "the word of His power."

5. The passages, however, which the author of the *Irenicum* adduces besides out of Hermas, against the Catholics, are indeed astonishing[c]; "What is to be said to the fact," says he, 'that it evidently appears from his (Hermas') fifth Similitude, that he either acknowledged the Son of God as man only, or at least believed Him to be much inferior to the Father, nay and to the Holy Spirit. For in the passage which has been quoted he introduces the Son not only as the servant of the Father, but also as the servant of the Holy Ghost, and obedient to Him. His words are[d]; 'And on this account the body of Christ, that is, of the Son of God, into which the Holy Spirit had been infused, was subservient to this Spirit,'" &c. And here I am myself well-nigh stupified at the stupidity of the heretic. For first, were we to grant him, that by the Holy Spirit, in this passage of Hermas, the third Person of the Godhead ought certainly to be understood, what will the unhappy man gain thence in support of his impious and desperate [112]

Trinitatis divisionem præsumunt unitatis: quando unitas ex semetipsa derivans Trinitatem non destruatur ab illa, sed administretur.—[p. 6.]

c Irenic., p. 21.

d Et propterea corpus Christi, seu Filii Dei, cui infusus erat Spiritus Sanctus, huic Spiritui servivit, &c.

ON THE CONSUBSTANTIALITY OF THE SON.

40

cause? Surely nothing whatever! For can any one be found so blind as not at once to see, that Hermas is there expressly speaking only of the body, or human nature, of Christ? And what wonder is it, if this, being a creature, be said to be subservient to the Holy Spirit, who is God? But, secondly, I have already at some length and most clearly proved, that Hermas, in this passage, under the designation of the Holy Spirit, understood the Word, or divine nature in Christ, which is most properly called the Son of God. This is so obvious from the tenour of the whole parable, that it is strange that Petavius himself did not perceive it. That very learned man was, I suppose, misled by the circumstance that Hermas, soon afterwards in the same passage, says that the Holy Spirit dwells in our bodies likewise. But in that place it must either be said, that the Shepherd abruptly passed to another signification of the Holy Spirit; or it must be understood (as I should rather think) in the sense in which every true Christian is said to be a sacred dwelling-place and temple of the whole most holy Trinity. [It is] at any rate [true that] the Word, who is joined[1] to the man Christ Jesus "by a communion supreme and not to be surpassed," (*ἄκρᾳ καὶ ἀνυπερβλήτῳ κοινωνίᾳ*,) as Origen somewhere[e] expresses the hypostatic union, as He Is every where by His influence and power, so does He fix for Himself a place and an habitation, by a peculiar mode of presence, in the hearts of the godly[f]. Hence Ignatius in his Epistle to the Ephesians[g], speaking of the Son of God, exhorts the saints in this manner; "Let us then do all things as having Him dwelling in us, that we may be His temples, and that He may be within us, [who is] our God." And, above, Barnabas called our heart a habitation (*κατοικητήριον*), and a temple (*ναὸν*) of the Son of God. Thus also Justin Martyr says[h], that God the Father has firmly fixed within our hearts the
[113] holy and incomprehensible Word, whom He had sent down from heaven to men. And indeed even from this it is evident that those most ancient doctors of the Church believed

[1] adhæret.

e [Contra Celsum, vi. 48. p. 670.]

f See Apocalypse iii. 20, and John xiv. 23. (Add Ephes. iii. 17.—GRABE.)

g [§ 15. p. 15. Vid. infr., p. 114.]

h [*αὐτὸς ἀπ' οὐρανῶν τὴν ἀλήθειαν καὶ τὸν λόγον τὸν ἅγιον καὶ ἀπερινόητον ἀνθρώποις ἐνίδρυσε, καὶ ἐγκατεστήριξε ταῖς καρδίαις αὐτῶν.*]—Epist. ad Diognet., p. 493. [§ 7. p. 237.]

BOOK II. CHAP. II. § 5, 6.

the Son of God to be true God, and that in the very highest sense [1].

HERMAS.

Of Hermas I shall say no more, after I have informed the reader, that even Petavius, who is in other cases, at least on this question, a most unfair critic of the fathers, expressly allows [i] that this Hermas "was never accused by any," that is by any ancient catholic writer, "of heresy or false doctrine, specially [2] concerning the Trinity:" which is indeed most true and worthy of remark. As to what that modern and most trifling writer, Sandius, further objects to him, that he taught that "the Holy Spirit converses with man, not when He wills, but when God wills," any one will clearly see that it is utterly frivolous, who weighs carefully the actual words of Hermas on that subject; (book ii. Mand. 12 [k].) For he will perceive that the words, "not when he wills," refer, not to the Holy Spirit Himself, but to the man to whom the Holy Spirit speaks.

[1] ipsissimum Deum.

[2] maxime.

IGNATIUS.

6. After Hermas we have next to speak of Ignatius. In his genuine Epistles, edited by Isaac Vossius [l], (and these alone, I may once for all inform my reader, I shall employ in this work,) he throughout declares the true divinity of the Son of God in the clearest terms. His Epistle to the Smyrneans begins with these words [m]; "I glorify Jesus Christ, the God who has given unto you such wisdom." In the salutation of the Epistle to the Ephesians [n], he styles them predestined and chosen, "by the will of the Father and of Jesus Christ, our God." And in the Epistle itself he writes [o]; "There is nothing hidden from the Lord [3], but even our secret things are nigh unto Him. Let us, therefore, do all things as having Him dwelling within us, that we may be His temples, [114]

[3] τὸν Κύριον.

[i] Præf. in tom. ii. Dogm. Theol., c. 2. § 6.

[k] [§ 1. p. 100. Spiritus, qui desursum est, quietus est et humilis—et nemini respondet interrogatus, nec singulis respondet: neque cum vult homini loquitur Spiritus Dei, sed tunc loquitur cum vult Deus.]

[l] A.D. 1646.

[m] *δοξάζω Ἰησοῦν Χριστὸν τὸν Θεὸν, τὸν οὕτως ὑμᾶς σοφίσαντα.*—p. 1. [p. 33.]

[n] *ἐν θελήματι τοῦ Πατρὸς καὶ Ἰησοῦ Χριστοῦ τοῦ Θεοῦ ἡμῶν.*—p. 16. [p. 11.]

[o] *οὐδὲν λανθάνει τὸν Κύριον, ἀλλὰ καὶ τὰ κρυπτὰ ἡμῶν ἐγγὺς αὐτῷ ἐστίν. πάντα οὖν ποιῶμεν, ὡς αὐτοῦ ἐν ἡμῖν κατοικοῦντος, ἵνα ὦμεν αὐτοῦ ναοὶ, καὶ αὐτὸς ᾖ ἐν ἡμῖν Θεὸς ἡμῶν· ὅπερ καὶ ἔστιν καὶ φανήσεται πρὸ προσώπου ἡμῶν, ἐξ ὧν δικαίως ἀγαπῶμεν αὐτόν.*—p. 26. [§ 15. p. 15.]

and that He may be within us, [who is] our God; which indeed is so, and will be manifested before our face, wherefore we justly love Him." That Ignatius in this passage is speaking of Christ, there can be no doubt, not merely from the word *Κύριος* (Lord), by which he always designates Christ, but also from the whole context of his discourse, which treats only of Jesus the Saviour. Again, in his Epistle to the Romans[p]; "Permit me to be an imitator of the suffering of my God." But there is a most remarkable passage in the Epistle to the Ephesians; where Ignatius thus speaks of Christ[q]; "There is one Physician, both fleshly and spiritual; made and not made[1]; having become God incarnate," *ἐν σαρκὶ γενόμενος Θεὸς*, (instead of which Athanasius, Theodoret, and Gelasius have *ἐν ἀνθρώπῳ Θεὸς*, "God in man," which comes to the same thing,) "true life in death," *ἐν θανάτῳ ζωὴ ἀληθινὴ*, (for so, not *ἐν ἀθανάτῳ*, "in the immortal," ought it to be read, as Athanasius, Theodoret, and Gelasius agree in reading, and as the sense certainly requires,) "both of Mary and of God."
[115] Here we rightly translate *γεννητὸς καὶ ἀγέννητος*, "made and not made," as did Gelasius, since the sense requires it, and it is very well known that by the Greeks the words *γενητὸς* and *γεννητὸς* were used promiscuously; although the Catholic writers of the Church for the most part, especially such as lived after the third century, distinguished more accurately between them, in the question of the divinity of the Son. Theodoret, indeed, (Dial. i.,) reads *γεννητὸς ἐξ ἀγεννήτου*[2], ("begotten of the unbegotten;") the reading, however, which I have followed, is confirmed not merely by the Greek MS. of the Medicean library, and by the ancient
41 Latin version of Ussher, but also by Athanasius, On the Synods, and Gelasius[r], On the two Natures; and it is also absolutely required by the manifest antithesis, which is carried on throughout the passage, between the two natures of Christ and the attributes peculiar to each, "fleshly and

[1] [or "begotten and not begotten," (scil.) after the flesh; but see what follows.]

[2] Instead of *γεννητὸς καὶ ἀγέννητος*.

[p] ἐπιτρέψατέ μοι μιμητὴν εἶναι [τοῦ] πάθους τοῦ Θεοῦ μου.—p. 60. [§ 6. p. 29.]

[q] εἷς ἰατρός ἐστιν, σαρκικός τε καὶ πνευματικὸς, γεννητὸς καὶ ἀγέννητος, ἐν σαρκὶ γενόμενος Θεὸς, ἐν θανάτῳ ζωὴ ἀληθινὴ, καὶ ἐκ Μαρίας καὶ ἐκ Θεοῦ.—p. 21. [§ 7. p. 13.]

[r] Tertullian too read the passage in this way. See chap. 7. § 3. of this book.

BOOK II. CHAP. II. § 6. IGNATIUS.

spiritual," &c., which is broken off by the reading of Theodoret. I make no doubt that Theodoret herein followed a copy transcribed by some smatterer, who, thinking that *ἀγέννητον* necessarily meant "unbegotten," that is, one who hath the principle of his being from none but himself, (in which sense the word is applicable to God the Father alone,) presumed to alter *ἀγέννητος* into *ἐξ ἀγεννήτου*. And for the same reason the interpolator of his works has entirely omitted this clause of the sentence in Ignatius, *γεννητὸς καὶ ἀγέννητος*: just as, in the Epistle to the Trallians, he has pronounced accursed all who say that the Son of God is *ἀγέννητος*, (in the sense, namely, in which that is the peculiar property of God the Father,) on those, that is, who make no distinction between the Father and the Son. Hence also, before the passage of Ignatius which we are now considering, he inserts some remarks of his own concerning God the Father, in which he says that He alone is *ἀγέννητος*. If Sandius had understood this, he would never have wearied himself and his reader so uselessly, about the condemnation of the word *ἀγέννητος* by the pseudo-Ignatius, as he does in the first [116]
book of his "Ecclesiastical History laid open," where he treats of Ignatius. The genuine reading of the passage being thus established, every one must perceive that these words of Ignatius are a death-blow to the Arian blasphemy; inasmuch as Christ is herein not only acknowledged as God, truly immortal, in flesh which at one time was mortal, but is also expressly declared to be not-made, that is, uncreate. And so the great Athanasius has admirably expressed the meaning of Ignatius in the following passage, in which he has also accurately distinguished the twofold acceptation of the word *ἀγένητος* or *ἀγέννητος*, as we find it used by the ancients: "We are persuaded," he says[t], "that the blessed Ignatius also wrote correctly, when he designated Him [the Son of God] as generated because of His flesh, for Christ 'was made flesh;' yet withal ingenerate, inasmuch as He is not of the number of things made and generated, but Son from Father. And

[s] p. 71.

[t] πεπείσμεθα ὅτι καὶ ὁ μακάριος Ἰγνάτιος ὀρθῶς ἔγραψε, γενητὸν αὐτὸν λέγων διὰ τὴν σάρκα· ὁ γὰρ Χριστὸς σὰρξ ἐγένετο· ἀγένητον δὲ, ὅτι μὴ τῶν ποιημάτων καὶ γενητῶν ἐστιν, ἀλλ' υἱὸς ἐκ Πατρός. οὐκ ἀγνοοῦμεν δὲ, ὅτι καὶ οἱ εἰρηκότες ἓν τὸ ἀγένητον, τὸν Πατέρα

ON THE CONSUBSTANTIALITY OF THE SON.

we are aware also, that such as have asserted that the ingenerate is One, meaning the Father, wrote this, not as though the Word were generate[1] or made, but because [the Father] has not any who is to Him a cause [of being], and rather Himself is Father of Wisdom, and by Wisdom hath made all things which are generated[2] [u]." We shall, however, adduce more out of Ignatius afterwards, in the third book[x], concerning the Co-eternity[3] of the Son.

[117] 7. And now we must have a few words with the author of the *Irenicum* and Sandius. The remarkable passage of Ignatius, which I have quoted, had been also brought forward by Petavius, out of Theodoret and Athanasius, with some others in addition out of Theodoret only. But what does the author of the *Irenicum*[y] say in reply to them? listen, and you will be surprised at his effrontery! "The passages," he says, "which Petavius has quoted from Theodoret, and which he supposes to be quite[4] genuine, may be understood of the man Christ only, as born through the Spirit of God." Is it indeed so? in that case, say I, any words may be made to mean any thing. And so the author of the *Irenicum* himself, not venturing to abide by this answer, devises another most suited to his desperate cause! His words are; "The passages alleged out of Theodoret are not of force to shew that the profession of a twofold nature in Christ was derived from the tradition of Christ and the Apostles. For even allowing this profession to have existed at that time also, why may it not have been a tradition from some false Christ or false apostle, and not necessarily[5] a tradition of Christ and the Apostles; just like some other strange[6] and even absurd notions of Ignatius or of other ancient writers, which even Petavius himself does not admit?" With what knot are you to hold this Proteus? With what argument to bind such an opponent? He affirms that Justin first originated the notion of the divine nature of Jesus Christ; we prove against him,

[1] genitum (hoc est factum.)
[2] omnia genita (hoc est, quæ facta sunt.)
[3] τῷ συναϊδίῳ.
[4] maxime.
[5] mox.
[6] incommodæ.

λέγοντες, οὐχ ὡς γενητοῦ καὶ ποιήματος ὄντος τοῦ λόγου οὕτως ἔγραψαν, ἀλλ' ὅτι μὴ ἔχει τὸν αἴτιον, καὶ μᾶλλον αὐτὸς Πατὴρ μέν ἐστι τῆς σοφίας, τὰ δὲ γενητὰ πάντα ἐν σοφίᾳ πεποίηκε.—De Synod. Arim. et Seleuc., tom. i. p. 922. [vol. i. p. 761. § 47.]

[u] [Concerning the words γενητὸς and γεννητὸς, compare Suicer on the words ἀγένητος and γενητός. Huet. Origen.ii. 2. 2. § 23. Waterland, Works, vol. iii. pp. 239, 260.—B.]

[x] [See book iii. chap. 1.]

[y] Irenic., p. 27.

that Ignatius, who was earlier than Justin, nay even contemporary with the Apostles, held the same opinion. He next miserably wrests the words of Ignatius! and at last, distrusting this his own interpretation, comes to such a pitch of madness as not to shrink from asserting that it is by no means [118] improbable, that even Ignatius himself was deceived by some false apostle! I suppose, if at last we were to adduce as a witness some Apostle in person[1], we should effect nothing with him. Indeed experience has by this time shewn, that persons of this party toss about [as worthless] the very writings of the Apostles, (which certainly speaks no less clearly of the divinity of Christ than do the remains of the fathers;) and by their glosses, so strangely alien from the evident meaning of the words, pervert and misinterpret them, at the same time that they omit no contrivance or labour whereby to 42
depreciate their trustworthiness and authority. If these heretics would at length openly make profession of their unbelief, and publicly aver that the doctrine of the divine nature of Jesus Christ, which has been delivered by the Apostles and all the Doctors of the Church, is in their opinion repugnant to sound reason; (in their opinion, I say, mere weak men as they are, that crawl upon the ground, and are unable to explain perfectly the nature of even the little worm, "who is their brother," much less to comprehend in the narrow limits of their minds the infinite essence of the most high and holy God, and of the effluence[2] of His mind!) and [would say] that on that account they call into question the whole of the Christian religion, (confirmed though it be by miracles so many and so great, and, further, fully approving itself to us by its own innate light and authority, in all those points which do not go beyond our powers of comprehension, especially in those which relate to virtue and morality;) [were they to do this,] they would exhibit, I think, not much greater impiety, and certainly far more candour and ingenuousness! But, says the author of the *Irenicum*, Ignatius entertained some notions not only strange[3] but even palpably absurd, which you yourselves even do not admit. Where, I ask, doth he state them? Produce a passage, thou nameless one, out of the genuine Epistles of Ignatius, and we will at once yield you the victory. Certainly no

[1] ipsissimum.

[2] ἀποῤῥοίας.

[3] incommodas.

ON THE CONSUBSTANTIALITY OF THE SON.

one of all those adversaries who have been most opposed to Polycarp's Collection[z] [of those Epistles], neither Blondel, nor Salmasius, nor Daillé, nor Daillé's recent anonymous
[119] champion[1], have yet produced any thing of this kind out of that collection, but what very learned men, Ussher, Vossius, Hammond, and Pearson, have clearly proved to have been blamed without cause. Besides, if we were to allow that Ignatius in certain more minute points had turned aside a little from the doctrine of the Apostles, can it, on that account, seem probable to any one that he was thus shamefully mistaken in so momentous an article of the Christian faith? Is there any one, that would even harbour a suspicion, that he, who had conversed so familiarly with the true Apostles of Jesus Christ, and whom the tradition of all antiquity has declared to have been a martyr for the apostolic faith, was deceived by some false apostle in a primary doctrine of Christianity?

[1] Larroque, see above, i. 2. 7.

——— Credat Judæus Apella,
Non ego ———

8. I now come to Sandius, who in book i. of his *Hist. Eccl. Enucl.*, in treating on Ignatius[a], is altogether silent[2] on the testimonies which we have adduced out of the genuine Epistles of Ignatius in favour of the Catholic doctrine; whilst from the interpolated Epistles of Ignatius, as well as from those which have been falsely ascribed to him, he brings forward several passages, and endeavours by them to establish the blasphemies of Arius. One would suppose that he had never seen the editions of Ignatius by Ussher and Vossius, nor ever read what these same learned men, and Hammond and Pearson, have written concerning the Epistles of Ignatius. And yet he mentions Ussher's edition in this same place; and elsewhere, I mean in his book on the Ecclesiastical Writers, where also he treats of Ignatius, he mentions the editions both of Vossius and Ussher; and we cannot doubt that he was even at that time acquainted with Hammond's Dissertations, and still more with Pearson's *Vindiciæ*,
[120] which latter was published in the year 1672, that is, four

[2] prorsus dissimulat.

[z] [i. e. the collection of the Epistles of St. Ignatius, sent by St. Polycarp to the Philippians, with his own Letter still extant.]

[a] p. 70.

years previous to the second edition of his *Hist. Eccl. Enucl.* For the sake of such of my readers as are not familiar with ecclesiastical antiquity, I will add a brief and fair statement of the whole subject. Besides the Epistles bearing the name of Ignatius, which are extant only in Latin, and which at this day all critics, whether Roman Catholics or belonging to ourselves, unanimously reject, there are twelve Greek Epistles, of which seven are mentioned by Eusebius[b], but not the remaining five. The seven mentioned by him are; 1. That to the Ephesians; 2. To the Magnesians; 3. To the Trallians; 4. To the Romans; 5. To the Philadelphians; 6. To the Smyrneans; 7. To Polycarp, bishop of Smyrna. The other five are; 1. That to Maria Cassobolita; 2. To the people of Tarsus; 3. To the people of Antioch; 4. To Hero, the deacon; 5. To the Philippians. Further, of the seven Epistles which were known to Eusebius, the Greek editions are of two classes; one which has been long extant, the other that which was first edited by Isaac Vossius from the Medicean MS. Of the five Epistles on which Eusebius is silent, the very learned Pearson thus most truly writes[c]; "A distinction seems to be correctly drawn between those seven Epistles which are mentioned by Eusebius, and which the rest of the most ancient fathers frequently quote, and five others, which were not acknowledged by any Greek writer, until after several centuries, and on that account are, with good reason, either called in question, or even entirely rejected: and that, not only because it is unlikely, that if they had been extant in his time, they could have been unknown to Eusebius, or could have been passed over by him, if he had known them; but also from the circumstance that, both in style[1], they appear to be very different from those enumerated by Eusebius; and, in subject matter, are more in harmony with the doctrine, the institutions, and the customs of the later Church, and resemble the Ignatian Epistles mentioned by Eusebius only through imitation and that excessively affected." As to Sandius' assertion[d], "that the style of the five Epistles," which were unknown to Eusebius, "so agrees with the former undoubted Epistles, that it is

[1] modus loquendi.

[121]

[b] [Euseb. E. H., lib. iii. c. 36.]

[c] In Prooemio ad Vind. Epist. S. Ignat., c. 4.

[d] De Script. Eccles., p. 18.

ON THE CONSUBSTANTIALITY OF THE SON.

absurd to doubt of Ignatius being their author," it was recklessly made, as his way is. Certainly if by the former undoubted Epistles he means the seven mentioned by Eusebius, as they were published[1] prior to the edition of Vossius, it is certainly true that there is a very great similarity of style between them and the other five. And what wonder? It was the judgment of Ussher[e] (and the thing speaks for itself) that it was the same forger "who interpolated[2] the genuine Epistles of Ignatius, and increased them by adding as many more[f]." Let any one, however, compare the seven Epistles, when the interpolated passages are taken out[3], as edited by Vossius, with the remaining five, and he will certainly admit, if he is able to judge of the case, that there is a very wide difference between the two, in respect both of style and of doctrine. In this one particular alone is there an apparent resemblance; in that the impostor, who patched together the five Epistles, employs sundry forms of construction, and expressions which are in familiar use in the genuine Ignatius;' but these too are so studiously affected by the forger, and so thrust in out of place[4], that from this evidence alone the imposture may be detected[5]. In the same place Sandius further argues in this way; "Origen, in his sixth Homily on St. Luke, quotes some words from the Epistle to the Philippians," (one, that is, of the five which we reject,) "from which its genuineness[6] is evident." But here the sophist writes with his usual shamelessness. The words of Origen
[122] (in his sixth Homily[g] on Luke) concerning Ignatius and his Epistle, are as follows; "I find it well[7] remarked in a letter of a certain martyr,—I mean Ignatius, who was bishop of Antioch next after Peter, and who, in a persecution, fought with beasts at Rome,—that 'the virginity of Mary was unknown to the prince of this world.'" Not a word is here said about the Epistle to the Philippians; whilst in that written to the Ephesians, (one of Eusebius' seven,) we now read as follows[h]; ἔλαθε τὸν ἄρχοντα τοῦ αἰῶνος τούτου ἡ παρθενία Μαρίας, "the virginity of Mary was unknown to the prince of this

1 vulgatæ.
43
2 incrustavit.
3 defæcatas.
4 importune.
5 sorex prodatur.
6 auctoritas.
7 eleganter.

e Proleg. ad Epist. Ignat., c. 5.

f [Ussher rejected the Epistle to Polycarp, thus making the number of the spurious and genuine equal.]

g Eleganter in cujusdam martyris Epistola scriptum reperi, Ignatium dico, episcopum Antiochiæ post Petrum secundum, qui in persecutione Romæ pugnavit ad bestias, *Principem sæculi hujus latuit virginitas Mariæ.*—[vol. iii. p. 938.]

h [19. p. 16.]

world." Granted, that this sentence is repeated by the impostor who aped Ignatius in the spurious Epistle to the Philippians, what follows? In order, however, that the imposture of the author of this Epistle to the Philippians may be more clearly seen, even out of Origen himself, we must observe that the passage of Ignatius, which he cites, is indeed found, word for word, in the Epistle to the Ephesians, thus, "the virginity of Mary was unknown to the prince of this world;" whereas in the Epistle to the Philippians it has been altered, a ridiculous apostrophe being made to the devil, thus[i]; "For many things are hidden from thee; the virginity of Mary, the strange birth," &c. But for the present leaving Sandius, a writer who deserves the detestation of all lovers of truth and fairness, let us return to the right reverend Pearson, who further sets forth his own judgment, and that of other very learned men, concerning the seven Epistles, known to Eusebius, as they existed in the Greek text prior to the edition of Vossius. His words are; "It has been correctly observed by very many persons, that even the seven most ancient and most genuine Epistles, in the Greek edition of that period," (i. e. before the edition of Vossius,) "were interpolated and corrupted; and this is plain from the passages adduced by the ancient fathers, which in that edition either do not appear, or are not correctly given, as well as from many other pas- [123]
sages, which agree neither with antiquity, nor with the sentiments of Ignatius, and are inserted in a way that does not harmonize with the general tenour of the Epistles." The worthy prelate has also, throughout his very lucid work, proved on sure grounds, and to the satisfaction of all learned men, who are not biassed by excessive party-spirit, the genuineness of the seven Epistles of Ignatius, enumerated by Eusebius, as they have been edited by Vossius. Now if, out of these seven Epistles, (as they were published after the Medicean MS.,) agreeing as they do with the quotations made from them by Athanasius, Theodoret, Gelasius, and others of the ancients, Sandius can produce one single iota, which is repugnant to the Nicene creed, we will no longer refuse to admit, that Ignatius, an apostolic bishop, and most celebrated martyr, de-

[i] πολλὰ γάρ σε λανθάνει· ἡ παρθενία Μαρίας, ὁ παράδοξος τοκέτος, κ.τ.λ.—[8. p. 115.]

serves to be classed with the forerunners of the impious heresy of Arius. This, however, we are perfectly certain that he never[1] will be able to do. We are not therefore by any means to account Ignatius an Arian, but Sandius, rather, an egregious calumniator of a most holy father. It must also in the meantime be observed, that even in the spurious and interpolated Epistles of Ignatius, (such as Sandius employs,) very many things are found diametrically opposed to the Arian heresy; and that the passages which have been brought forward by Sandius out of these same Epistles, will for the most part easily admit of a catholic construction; this it would not have been difficult (had we now leisure for it) to demonstrate. But enough of Ignatius[k]. And thus far have we heard the venerable triumvirate of apostolic writers confirming by their witness the creed of Nicæa.

[1] ante Græcas calendas.

48

CHAPTER III.

[132]

CLEMENT OF ROME AND POLYCARP INCIDENTALLY VINDICATED FROM THE ASPERSIONS OF THE AUTHOR OF THE IRENICUM, AND OF SANDIUS.

1. Of the writers of the apostolic age, besides those whose views we set forth in the preceding chapter, there remain in all two others, Clement[1] of Rome and Polycarp. I have
[133] not mentioned them, hitherto, amongst the witnesses of the catholic tradition in the apostolic age, both because very few genuine remains of them are extant at this day, and because, even in those which exist, they touch sparingly and with less clearness on the doctrine of the divinity of the Son, as being intent upon other subjects. Since, however, the author of the *Irenicum* and Sandius have laid hold of this very circumstance as a handle for making false charges against them, (the one dragging forward these most holy fathers by force and against their will[2], into a sanctioning of the Socinian blasphemy, the other of the Arian,) I have thought it best, in

[2] obtorto quasi collo protrahente.

[k] [For other testimonies to the Nicene faith from the genuine Epistles of St. Ignatius, see Grabe's notes on this chapter in the Appendix.]

[1] Clement succeeded to the Roman see in the year 64 or 65, and occupied it to the year 81 or 83. Cave in Clem. —Bowyer.

passing, to say a few words in opposition to their fallacies. I will first treat of Clement.

CLEM. R.

2. Both the author of the *Irenicum* and Sandius (on the suggestion of Petavius [1]) observe, that Photius long ago suspected him of heresy against the divinity of Christ. Photius, it would seem, in treating of Clement and his Epistles, after mentioning certain other things in his first Epistle as deserving of censure, remarks this also [m]; "That in calling our Lord Jesus Christ a high-priest and defender [2] [n], he does not employ concerning Him those expressions which are of a higher character and suitable to God; not however that he any where openly utters blasphemy against Him in these respects." But Photius, who is too severe a critic of the ancients, must himself bear the disgrace of his own rashness; and let no one blame me for expressing myself freely respecting a comparatively recent patriarch of Constantinople [o], who, wantonly and without any cause, brings under the suspicion of heresy a Roman patriarch appointed by the Apostles themselves. Those persons, indeed, have always appeared to me very absurd, who, upon reading an epistle or short treatise of an [134]
ancient writer, (and that perhaps the only undoubted relic of the author which has been preserved,) and finding there some doctrine of the Christian faith either altogether untouched, or not explained with sufficient clearness, (because the author, as his subject requires, is intent on some other point,) at once suspect him of some heresy or other. It is, however, enough for our purpose, that Clement nowhere in his Epistle, (on Photius' own admission,) blasphemes our Lord Christ.

3. Leaving Photius, then, I come to the author of the *Irenicum,* who thus argues against the received catholic doctrine [3], from the first Epistle of Clement [p]; "It is certain that Clement, upon examination, will be found to speak continually in such wise as to leave [4] and attribute to the Father a superiority [5] over Christ, by calling Him on all occasions Almighty God, the One God, the Crea-

[1] Petavio monitore.

[2] προστάτην.

[3] traditionem.

[4] relinquat.

[5] prærogativam præ Christo.

[m] ὅτι ἀρχιερέα καὶ προστάτην τὸν Κύριον ἡμῶν Ἰησοῦν Χριστὸν ἐξονομάζων, οὐδὲ τὰς θεοπρεπεῖς καὶ ὑψηλοτέρας ἀφῆκε περὶ αὐτοῦ φωνάς· οὐ μὴν οὐδ' ἀπαρακαλύπτως αὐτὸν οὐδαμῆ ἐν τούτοις βλασφημεῖ.—Cod. cxxvi.

[n] [Photius refers to S. Clem. ad Cor. i. § 36, 58; pp. 168, 181.]

[o] Elected patriarch in the year 858. Cave on Photius.—BOWYER.

[p] Irenicum, pp. 23, 24.

ON THE CONSUBSTANTIALITY OF THE SON.

tor of all things, and God, &c. Whereas, on the other hand, he describes Christ, (as I have also remarked of Hermas,) in such a manner only as to seem scarcely[1] to have acknowledged in Him any nature other than the human." What he here alleges concerning the pre-eminence[2] of the Father being so religiously observed by Clement, does not excite in me the very slightest difficulty; inasmuch as I well know, and recollect, that the Apostle Paul also did the same, (though to my mind it is beyond all controversy, that he both believed and taught the true Godhead of the Son,) and that the same expressions were employed respecting God the Father by all the fathers, even by the Nicene fathers themselves, and by those who wrote subsequently to that council. The reason for this, indeed, we shall clearly explain below, in the fourth book, On the Subordination of the Son, &c. And now to those words of the anonymous writer, in which he says that Clement, as also Hermas, "describes Christ in such a manner only, as that he scarcely seems to have acknowledged in Him any nature
[135] other than the human," I reply, that what he says of Hermas is a glaring[3] falsehood, as I have already most clearly proved. And as regards Clement, the heretic was cautious in adding that word "scarcely;" for it would have been too great effrontery to have said, that nothing could be found in the Epistle of Clement, to indicate that there was in Christ any other than a human nature. Of this kind, for instance, is the passage in which, describing the magnificent gifts (τὰ μεγαλεῖα τῶν δωρεῶν), which were of old bestowed by God on the family of
49 Abraham on account of his faith, the author says[q]; "From him [came] our Lord Jesus Christ, according to the flesh;" where by the limitation, "according to the flesh," it is plainly intimated, that there was in Christ another nature besides the human, or that flesh which He derived from Abraham. Besides, it is very unlikely that Clement should have entertained notions of Christ so mean and low, as to regard Him as a mere man[4], when he dignifies Him with titles so exalted. For he styles Christ[r], "The effulgence of the Majesty of God (ἀπαύγασμα τῆς μεγαλωσύνης τοῦ Θεοῦ);" and soon after teaches us, that the superiority of Christ over all

[1] vix.

[2] ἐξοχῇ.

[3] splendidum.

[4] ψιλὸν ἄνθρωπο.

[q] ἐξ αὐτοῦ ὁ Κύριος Ἰησοῦς τὸ κατὰ σάρκα.—p. 72. [§ 32. p. 166.]

[r] p. 82. [§ 36. p. 168.]

the angels consists in this, that they are ministers (*λειτουργοὶ*), that is, servants of God, the Lord of all creatures; whilst He is not a servant, but the Son of God. Here, however, Clement agreed in expression with the author of the Epistle to the Hebrews, and indeed the learned Junius discovered in many passages such a resemblance, both of thought and expression, between that Epistle and this of Clement, that (following Jerome and other ancient writers) he imagined that the same person was the author of both. Now he must be blinder than a mole, who does not perceive that by the words *ἀπαύγασμα τῆς δόξης τοῦ Πατρὸς*, "the effulgence of the Father's glory," Heb. i. 3, is meant that divine nature and majesty of the Son, in which, before the world was[1], He existed with God the Father, in which He [136] Himself made the worlds[2], and in which also, by His own almighty power, He even now upholds and governs the fabric of the universe.

4. Elsewhere[s], in the same Epistle, Clement had also called our Saviour, "The sceptre of the Majesty of God;" (*τὸ σκῆπτρον τῆς μεγαλωσύνης τοῦ Θεοῦ.*) Now if this passage be brought forward entire, and the scope and context of the author be considered, it will sufficiently shew what the view of this apostolic writer was concerning Christ. In it he is exhorting the Corinthians to humility or lowliness[3] of mind, from the amazing example of Christ, in these words[t]; "The sceptre of the Majesty of God[u], our Lord Jesus Christ, came not in the pomp of pride and arrogancy, though He might have so come, but with lowliness of mind[4]." I consider it certain, that Clement in these words meant to express the divine nature and majesty of the Saviour, in which He subsisted before His birth of the most blessed Virgin. Nor is there room for doubt on this point, when it is observed, that Clement calls Christ "the sceptre of the Majesty of God," in that state in which He existed before His coming into the world. For if Christ were not the sceptre of God's Majesty prior to His advent

[1] ante sæcula.

[2] sæcula ipsa condidit.

[3] modestiam.

[4] *ταπεινοφρονῶν.*

[s] p. 36. [§ 16. p. 156.]

[t] *τὸ σκῆπτρον τῆς μεγαλωσύνης τοῦ Θεοῦ, ὁ Κύριος ἡμῶν Χριστὸς Ἰησοῦς, οὐκ ἦλθεν ἐν κόμπῳ ἀλαζονείας, οὐδὲ ὑπερηφανίας, καίπερ δυνάμενος· ἀλλὰ ταπεινοφρονῶν· κ.τ.λ.*—[Ibid.]

[u] i. e. the power of God, (1 Cor. i. 24,) by a metonymy of the sign for the thing signified.

among men, of what nature, I ask, will be that condescension[1] of His, which Clement so greatly celebrates; in that, during the period of His advent, He did not demean Himself as the sceptre of the Majesty of God? Besides, Clement in this passage proposes Christ as an example of infinite [137] condescension, which, in our own small measure, we may and ought to imitate indeed, (just as we should the perfect holiness of God, Matt. v. 48; 1 Pet. i. 15, 16,) though we shall never be able to equal it. For thus, after quoting the words of Isaiah and David, predicting the humiliation of Christ, the holy man goes on to say[v]; "Ye see, beloved, what that pattern is which has been vouchsafed to us. For if the Lord was so lowly in mind, what shall we do, who have come beneath the yoke of His grace?" Where, however, is that infinite disparity, if you conceive Christ to be merely and simply man[2]? This passage of Clement is clearly parallel to that of St. Paul to the Philippians, ii. 6, &c.: for whereas there it is, "being in the form of God," here it is, "the sceptre of God's Majesty;" and whereas there it is, "He thought it not robbery to be equal with God," here it is, "He came not in the pomp of pride and arrogance, though He might have so come." And even as Paul commends[3] the infinite condescension of Christ from this circumstance, that, being in the form of God, He made no display of His equality[4] in honour with God, (for this is what is signified by the words "He thought it not robbery[5] to be equal with God,") so Clement teaches, that Christ, though in very deed the sceptre of the Majesty of God, still concealed His greatness when He came [to sojourn] among men; i.e. a stress should be laid upon the words, "although He might have so come:" (*καίπερ δυνάμενος*.) Lastly, Paul's expression, "He made Himself of no reputation," (*ἐκένωσεν ἑαυτὸν*,) is evidently tantamount to that of Clement, "He was lowly in mind," (*ἐταπεινοφρόνησε*.) If the reader wants an interpreter to open more clearly the meaning both of Paul and Clement, let him by all means [138] consult the noble passage of Justin, which we shall adduce below, out of his Epistle to Diognetus, chap. iv. § 7 of this book.

[1] *συγκατάβασις.*

[2] purum putum hominem.

[3] commendat.

[4] suam cum Deo *ἰσοτιμίαν*.

[5] *οὐχ ἁρπαγμὸν ἡγήσατο.*

[v] *ὁρᾶτε, ἄνδρες ἀγαπητοὶ, τίς ὁ ὑπογραμμὸς ὁ δεδομένος ἡμῖν. εἰ γὰρ ὁ Κύριος οὕτως ἐταπεινοφρόνησεν, τί ποιήσομεν ἡμεῖς, οἱ ὑπὸ τὸν ζυγὸν τῆς χάριτος αὐτοῦ [δι' αὐτοῦ] ἐλθόντες.*—p. 40. [§ 16. p. 157.]

5. But there is extant another Epistle under the name of Clement in a mutilated condition, which, Eusebius says[x], "was not known equally with the former one." Without doubt, the first Epistle of Clement, whether you look to the abundance of[1] matters treated of in it, or to its vigorous style, is far superior to the second; and accordingly, as it deserved, was held in greater esteem, and was more frequently quoted by the doctors of the Church. From this circumstance it was that Jerome and Ruffinus, in this instance not very happy interpreters of Eusebius, have stated, that the second Epistle was absolutely rejected and disallowed by the ancients as altogether spurious. But it has been truly said by an excellent man, "Reliance ought to be placed on the author, not on the interpreters." But that this Epistle was called in question by some persons, even in ancient times, seems to me to have arisen from the fact that the first alone, for the reasons I have mentioned, was judged worthy of being read in the public assemblies of the Church; whilst the other, not being thus honoured, was by degrees neglected, as if it were not really the writing of Clement. On this account also other Epistles of his (for it is, in my opinion, beyond doubt, that the holy man wrote others also) have been utterly lost[2]. At any rate the second Epistle, as it is called, was circulated in Clement's name before the time of Eusebius; it was addressed to the Corinthians; like the first, it was engaged in refuting their error concerning the resurrection of the body; expressions and phrases familiarly used by Clement occur throughout it; and in short there is in it nothing strange or unworthy of Clement, so as to warrant us in suspecting it to be the forgery of an impostor. An additional argument in its favour may be found in the fact, that both the Epistles [139] of Clement are equally received in the Apostolic Canons, (in the last canon,) and are acknowledged by Epiphanius and others. Now, in the very beginning of this second Epistle we read[y]; "Brethren, we ought so to think of Jesus Christ as of God." And afterwards; "It behoves us not to en-

[1] copiam.

[2] interciderunt.

[x] οὐχ ὁμοίως τῇ προτέρᾳ γνώριμος.—Eccl. Hist. iii. 38.

[y] ἀδελφοί, οὕτως δεῖ ἡμᾶς [l. ὑμᾶς] φρονεῖν περὶ Ἰησοῦ Χριστοῦ, ὡς περὶ Θεοῦ, [ὡς περὶ κριτοῦ ζώντων καὶ νεκρῶν] .... καὶ οὐ δεῖ ἡμᾶς μικρὰ φρονεῖν περὶ τῆς σωτηρίας ἡμῶν· ἐν τῷ γὰρ φρονεῖν ἡμᾶς μικρὰ περὶ αὐτοῦ, μικρὰ καὶ ἐλπίζομεν λαβεῖν.—[§ 1. p. 185.]

tertain low views of our salvation[1]; for whilst we think little of Him, little have we to hope to receive [of Him]." No doubt the allusion here is to the heresy of Cerinthus, which was not unknown either to Clement or the Corinthians. It is, however, especially to be observed, that Clement herein instructs us, that we ought not only to call Christ God, (which neither the Arians nor the Socinians refuse to do,) but to think of Him in very truth as God; that is to say, we must conceive that idea of Christ in our minds, as of Him who is God, not a mere creature; and that they who think otherwise of Christ endanger their salvation. There is a remarkable passage concerning the twofold nature of Christ, in the ninth chapter[z] of the same Epistle, (according to the division of the last Oxford edition, and, as I hear, of Cotelerius' also,) in which the author, in treating of the resurrection of the body, writes thus; "Jesus Christ the Lord, who saved us, being at first spirit, became flesh, and thus called us. In like manner we also shall receive our reward in this flesh." He here calls the divine nature of Christ, in which He subsisted before His assuming flesh, spirit (*πνεῦμα*); as do also
[140] his contemporaries, the author of the Epistle ascribed to Barnabas, Hermas, Ignatius, and the divinely inspired writers of the New Testament, as I have already shewn[a]. Besides these passages it may be mentioned, (by way of addition[2],) that Basil (in his work, On the Holy Spirit, c. 29) brings forward a remarkable testimony of Clement of Rome, on the doctrine of the most Holy Trinity. The passage of Basil stands thus[b]; "But Clement also, in more primitive style, says, 'God liveth, and the Lord Jesus Christ, and the Holy Ghost;'" where there is no doubt that Clement said "God liveth" in the same sense in which in Scripture God is called "the living God;" that is, in contrast with the idols, and dead and feigned gods of the heathen. He declares, therefore, that God the Father, and Jesus Christ, (that is to say, in so far forth as He is spirit, subsisting even before His assumption of our flesh, nay[3] from everlasting,) and the

[1] *σωτηρίας.*

[2] mantissæ loco.

[3] adeoque.

[z] [ὡς] (ὁ Ἰησοῦς) Χριστὸς ὁ Κύριος, ὁ σώσας ἡμᾶς, ὢν μὲν τὸ πρῶτον Πνεῦμα, ἐγένετο σάρξ, καὶ οὕτως ἡμᾶς ἐκάλεσεν· οὕτως καὶ ἡμεῖς ἐν ταύτῃ τῇ σαρκὶ ἀποληψόμεθα τὸν μισθόν.—[p. 188.]

[a] [Book i. chap. 2. § 5.]

[b] ἀλλὰ καὶ ὁ Κλήμης ἀρχαϊκώτερον· Ζῇ, φησὶν, ὁ Θεὸς, καὶ ὁ Κύριος Ἰησοῦς Χριστὸς, καὶ τὸ Πνεῦμα τὸ ἅγιον.—tom. ii. p. 358. edit. Paris. 1637. [vol. iii. p. 61. § 72.]

Holy Ghost, are that living and true God, whom alone, renouncing idols, we ought to worship and adore. Now I am well aware that these words of Clement are nowhere to be found either in the first[c] Epistle to the Corinthians, or in that fragment of the second which is extant: whether they occurred in that part of it which is lost, I know not. But the credit due to the great and excellent Basil plainly requires us to believe that Clement, that very early father, somewhere wrote to that effect[1].

6. I now come to Sandius, who brings the charge of Arianism against the holy Clement of Rome[d], out of the books of the Constitutions. One would think that the man, after having made shipwreck of faith and a good conscience, had lost all shame too. [141] For all the reformed divines agree in saying, that those Constitutions are not the work of Clement, nor is it denied at this day by the more learned among the Roman Catholics, indeed the facts of the case speak for themselves[e]. And who can endure a man, who, whilst boasting that he has brought out the very kernel[2] of ecclesiastical history, obtrudes such wares upon his reader? Meanwhile most, if not all[3], the passages, which he has adduced out of the Constitutions, as making in favour of the Arians, can without difficulty be accounted for[4], on the ground that they are said by the author in reference to that pre-eminence[5] of the Father, which He has as the fountain of Deity, and that he wished to distinguish the Son from the Father, in opposition to that heresy which Sabellius embraced; as will at once be plain on examining the passages themselves. There is, indeed, one statement objected against the author of the Constitutions by Sandius, which admits of no defence; it is to this effect, that "the Son of God was created out of[6] (or from) nothing, and once did not exist." But I do not remember ever having read this in the books of the Constitutions; nor do I think

[1] talia scripsisse.

[2] nucleus.

[3] pleraque omnia.

[4] excusari.

[5] ἐξοχήν.

[6] ex (vel de) nihilo.

[c] [See, however, the passages cited by Grabe from Ep. i. 46, in his annotations *ad locum*.—B.]

[d] Enucl. Hist. Eccl. i. p. 67.

[e] The eight books of the Constitutions, which were written at about the same period as the Canons, (i. e. towards the close of the second century,) appear to have been originally compiled out of the various instructions (διδασκαλίαι) and rules (διατάξεις) which apostolic men of that time used to issue. It is most clearly certain that these Constitutions, which had been seriously corrupted by heretics in the time of Epiphanius, are very different from those which previously existed; as might easily have happened in consequence of additions, mutilations, and interpolations. Cave in Clem.—BOWYER.

ON THE CONSUBSTANTIALITY OF THE SON.

that any such thing is any where to be found therein. At any rate the author expressly teaches the contrary in the forty-first chapter of book vii., which very chapter is enumerated by Sandius amongst those, in which [he says] Clement Arianizes. For setting forth there the profession of faith which had to be made by the candidate for baptism, he thus explains the belief concerning God the Father[f]; "I believe, and am
[142] baptized, into One Unbegotten, Only True God Almighty, the Father of Christ, the Creator and Maker[1] of all things." You see here that God is distinctly said to be the Father of Christ, not His Creator or Maker, whilst of all the creatures He is distinctly called the Creator and the Maker. Then, afterwards, the author thus paraphrases the article on the only-begotten Son of God[g]; "And in the Lord Jesus Christ, His only-begotten Son, ... begotten, not created, by whom all things were made." Words, which by no clever charm[2], (except such as would deserve to be laughed at, rather than refuted,) can be made to agree with the Arian doctrine. Again, in book vi. chap. 11, he teaches that the faith of the Apostles was that by which we believe[h], that "there is one God, the Father of one Son, not more; of one Paraclete through Christ; the Maker of all other orders; one Creator[3]; Maker, through Christ, of the various creatures." In this place, also, he clearly excepts the Holy Spirit from the class of things created by God. To these passages may be added the frequent occurrence, whenever this author recites the liturgy of the ancient Church, of this form of doxology[i]; "With whom[4] (that is, the Son) to Thee (God the Father) be glory, honour, praise, glorification[5], and thanksgiving; and to the Holy Ghost, for ever and ever, Amen." It is so in book viii. chap. 38; whilst in the fifteenth chapter of the same book, near the end, the same doxology is expressed in these words[j]; "To Thee (the Father) be glory, praise, majesty,

[1] conditorem et opificem.

[2] σοφῷ φαρμάκῳ.

[3] unum mundi architectum.

[4] μεθ' οὗ.

[5] δοξολογία.

[f] πιστεύω καὶ βαπτίζομαι εἰς ἕνα ἀγέννητον μόνον ἀληθινὸν Θεὸν παντοκράτορα, τὸν πατέρα τοῦ Χριστοῦ, κτιστὴν καὶ δημιουργὸν τῶν ἁπάντων.—[Apost. Const. vii. 42. p. 447.]

[g] καὶ εἰς τὸν Κύριον Ἰησοῦν τὸν Χριστὸν, τὸν μονογενῆ αὐτοῦ υἱὸν, . . . γεννηθέντα, οὐ κτισθέντα, δι' οὗ τὰ πάντα ἐγένετο, [κ.τ.λ.—Ibid.]

[h] [καταγγέλλομεν] ἕνα Θεὸν, ἑνὸς υἱοῦ πατέρα, οὐ πλειόνων· ἑνὸς παρακλήτου διὰ Χριστοῦ· τῶν ἄλλων ταγμάτων ποιητήν· ἕνα δημιουργόν· διαφόρου κτίσεως διὰ Χριστοῦ ποιητήν.—[Ibid. vi. 11. p. 383.]

[i] μεθ' οὗ σοι δόξα, τιμὴ, αἶνος, δοξολογία, εὐχαριστία, καὶ τῷ ἁγίῳ Πνεύματι εἰς τοὺς αἰῶνας, ἀμήν.—[Ibid. viii. 38. p. 503.]

[j] σοὶ δόξα, αἶνος, μεγαλοπρέπεια, σέβας, προσκύνησις· καὶ τῷ σῷ παιδὶ Ἰησοῦ τῷ Χριστῷ σου, τῷ Κυρίῳ ἡμῶν, καὶ

worship, and adoration; also to Thy child Jesus, Thy Christ, our Lord, and God, and King; and to the Holy Ghost, both now, and ever, and world without end. Amen." See also, chapp. 16, 18, 20—22, 29, 39, 41, of the same book. [143] Now in this ascription of glory, the same honour, the same glory and majesty, is evidently given to the Father, the Son, and the Holy Ghost, conjointly. But on this point there is an excellent remark of the *Pneumatomachi* in Basil[k]; "We maintain that connumeration[1] (to be reckoned together) is suitable to such as are equal in honour; but subnumeration[2] (to be reckoned after) to such as differ so as to be inferior[3]." Hence the Arians never willingly used this form of doxology, but changed the μεθ' οὗ (with Whom), into δι' οὗ, or ἐν ᾧ (through Whom, or, in Whom), with the design, of course, of intimating, that in nature the Son is inferior to, and therefore alien from the Father[4]. On the other hand[5], several, even of the Catholics, prior to the Council of Nice, (as also the author of the Constitutions in other places,) employed the phrase δι' οὗ (through Whom), and others again combined the two δι' οὗ and μεθ' οὗ; understanding, that is, that it is through the Son that the glory of the Father is manifested, and that all the glory of the Son redounds to the Father, as the fountain of deity: and that the Son, nevertheless, ought to be adored together with the Father, as a partaker of the same divine nature and majesty. To speak more plainly, the ancient Catholics, when they glorified the Father through the Son, meant to express the subordination of the Son, in that He is the Son, and the pre-eminence[6] of the Father in that He is the Father; and on the other hand, by worshipping the Son with the Father, theymeant to express His consubstantiality, and His subsistence[7] with the Father in the same divine essence and nature. That the Arians however altogether disliked the expression μεθ' οὗ, and ac- [144] cordingly, whenever they were in power, changed that received formula of doxology in the public Liturgies into δι' οὗ, is testified by ecclesiastical history[l]. Nay, Philostorgius

1 συναρίθμησιν.
2 ὑπαρίθμησιν.
3 πρὸς τὸ χεῖρον παρηλλαγμένοις.
4 adeoque alienum.
5 alioqui.
6 Patris ἐξοχήν.
7 subsistentiam.

Θεῷ, καὶ βασιλεῖ· καὶ τῷ ἁγίῳ πνεύματι, νῦν, καὶ ἀεὶ, καὶ εἰς τοὺς αἰῶνας τῶν αἰώνων, ἀμήν.

k ἡμεῖς τοῖς μὲν ὁμοτίμοις φαμὲν τὴν συναρίθμησιν πρέπειν· τοῖς δὲ πρὸς τὸ χεῖρον παρηλλαγμένοις τὴν ὑπαρίθμησιν.—Lib. de Spirit., c.17. [§ 42. p. 36.]

l See Socrates ii. 21. and Sozomen iii. 8; and Valesius' notes on both.

ON THE CONSUBSTANTIALITY OF THE SON.

himself, the Arian historian, iii. 13, states that Flavian of Antioch, an upholder of the Nicene Creed, having collected a multitude of monks[m], "first raised the acclamation, Glory to the Father, and to the Son, and to the Holy Ghost; for that of those before him some, indeed, said, Glory to the Father, through the Son, in the Holy Ghost; (and that this was the form of acclamation most in use;) but that others said, Glory to the Father, in the Son, and in the Holy Ghost." This assertion, however, is altogether false, that Flavian was the first to introduce into use in the Church the form of doxology, 'Glory be to the Father, and to the Son,' (or, with
52 the Son,) 'and to the Holy Ghost,' the expressions, 'through the Son,' or 'in the Son,' having alone been in use before him. For in the ancient formulæ of prayers which obtained in the Church prior to [the time of] Flavian, and even of the Nicene Council, the same doxology was in use, as is evident from the Constitutions. We shall afterwards[n] shew, that the same doxology is found in the writings of certain of the ante-Nicene Fathers, and in particular of Clement of Alexandria (who moreover paraphrases that formula in such a way as no Arian could digest[1]). Lastly, the fact that the words *μεθ' οὗ* (with Whom), were approved and employed by writers even of the apostolic age, will appear presently,
[145] when we come to treat of Polycarp. In the meantime, you may learn from this, how unpalatable the words *μεθ' οὗ*, (with Whom,) and the form, "Glory be to the Father, and to the Son," &c. were to the Arians. I return to Sandius, who attempts to prove, out of the books of the Recognitions also, that Clement was an Arian. But that these Recognitions are the work of Clement, no one who is in his right mind will seriously affirm; they have accordingly been disallowed and rejected[o], as spurious and certainly forged

[1] concoquere.

[m] *πρῶτον ἀναβοῆσαι, Δόξα πατρὶ, καὶ υἱῷ, καὶ ἁγίῳ πνεύματι. τῶν γὰρ πρὸ αὐτοῦ, τοὺς μὲν, Δόξα πατρὶ δι' υἱοῦ ἐν ἁγίῳ πνεύματι λέγειν· καὶ ταύτην μᾶλλον τὴν ἐκφώνησιν ἐπιπολάζειν· τοὺς δὲ, Δόξα πατρὶ ἐν υἱῷ καὶ ἁγίῳ πνεύματι.*—[Philost. E. H., iii. 13. p. 495.]

[n] Cap. 6. § 4.

[o] The books (of the Recognitions) are spurious (*pseudepigraphi*) and apocryphal, composed in the second century by a learned and eloquent man, who was however more of a philosopher and philologist than a theologian, and by no means skilled in the invention and arrangement of fictitious narratives. Cotelerius, Judicium de libris Recogn. [Patr. Apost., tom. i. 490.]—BOWYER.

by most, if not all[1], the learned, both of our own and the papal communion. And thus far concerning Clement of Rome.

[1] plerisque omnibus.

POLYCARP.

7. I now proceed to Polycarp[p]. Of him Sandius[q] only observes in a summary way, that "In his Epistle to the Philippians, he frequently distinguishes Christ from God." The author of the Irenicum, however, urges this at greater length, and wrests him to the support even of the Socinian heresy. He writes to this effect[r]; "Nothing of his (Polycarp's) writings has been left to us, except his Epistle to the Philippians, and a few fragments preserved by Eusebius. But the Epistle to the Philippians contains nothing whatever to prove the divinity of Christ; nay, Christ is not only always distinguished from the Almighty, or supreme, God, (who is also called the God of our Lord Jesus Christ,) but is continually introduced, (as in the previously-mentioned[2] Epistle of Clement of Rome,) merely as a man, and as one who has come in the flesh, having been constituted, that is, the servant[3] of all, and at length raised up [from the dead] and exalted by God, and Who [now] is our Lord and High-Priest for ever, in Whom therefore, all men ought to believe, &c." Let us, then, first consider about the Epistle of Polycarp; and to begin; What though we granted to our anonymous [objector], that that Epistle "contains nothing to prove the divinity of Christ?" it certainly would not therefore by any means follow, that Polycarp did not acknowledge the divinity of Christ. For is it necessary that one who believes that Christ is God, should profess that belief of his as often as he writes any letter? Ridiculous! How many lengthy epistles may you read of ecclesiastical writers, who from their hearts believed the divinity of the Son, in which notwithstanding you will not find even the least word[4] to prove the divinity of Christ. Take, for example, the epistle of Cyprian to Antonianus, the fifty-second in Pamelius' edition; it is a pretty long one, yet Cyprian doth not make any express statement in it respecting Christ as God; nay, he throughout "distinguishes Christ from God." Suppose now, that this alone

[2] superiori.

[146]

[3] minister.

[4] ne γρὺ quidem.

[p] Polycarp, a disciple of the apostle John, was appointed bishop of Smyrna by him, about the year 94. Cave in Polycarp.—BOWYER.

[q] Enucl. Hist. Eccles., i. p. 75.

[r] [p. 28.]

had been extant of all Cyprian's letters: might not the spirit of that most blessed martyr with justice complain of very grave injury done to him, by the man who should thence conclude that Cyprian did not acknowledge the divinity of Christ? Most certainly he might. For from many other writings of the same Cyprian still extant, we gather assuredly that he most thoroughly held the divinity of Christ. So likewise of Polycarp; Irenæus testifies (in an epistle to Florinus, in Eusebius' Eccles. History, v. 20,) that beside his Epistle to the Philippians, he wrote others, both to the neighbouring Churches, and also to certain of the brethren, from which the purity of his doctrine might be gathered. What if in these he declared more explicitly
[147] his faith in the divinity of Christ? Indeed Jerome actually enumerates Polycarp amongst the ancient and apostolic writers, who by their works refuted the heresy against the divinity of Christ, which Ebion was the first to maintain of the Jewish, and Theodotus of Byzantium of the Gentile Christians. His words, against Helvidius, are as follows[s]; "Can I not bring forward against you the entire series of ancient authors, Ignatius, Polycarp, Irenæus, Justin Martyr, with many other apostolic and eloquent men, who wrote volumes full of wisdom against Ebion and Theodotus of Byzantium (and Valentinus[t]), who held these same opinions? If you had ever read these, you would be a wiser man." And it is extremely probable, that out of the other epistles
53 of Polycarp, now lost, were taken those five fragments by no means to be despised, which Feuardentius first published (at the end of his notes on Irenæus, l. iii. c. 31.) from a MS. in very ancient characters; as they are quoted in it by Victor, bishop of Capua, eleven hundred years ago. Now in the third of these fragments the following words of Polycarp

[s] Numquid non possum tibi totam veterum scriptorum seriem commovere, Ignatium, Polycarpum, Irenæum, Justinum Martyrem, multosque alios apostolicos et eloquentes viros, qui adversus Ebionem et Theodotum Byzantinum (et Valentinum) hæc eadem sentientes plena sapientiæ volumina conscripserunt? quæ si legisses aliquando, plus saperes.—Chap. ix. [§ 17. vol. ii. p. 225.]

[t] Marianus Victor observes that this [i. e. the reference to Valentinus] is wanting in most copies; indeed the thing speaks for itself, that the name of Valentinus was inserted into the text by some sciolist; for it is plain, that the heresy of Ebion and Theodotus was widely different from the views of Valentinus concerning Christ.

BOOK II. CHAP. III. § 7, 8. POLYCARP.

occur[u]; "John who was settled at Ephesus, where, being Gentiles, they[1] were ignorant of the law, began his Gospel with the cause of our redemption; which cause is apparent from this, that God willed His own Son to become incarnate for our salvation. Luke, on the other hand, commences with the priesthood of Zacharias, that by the miracle of his son's nativity, and by the office of so great a preacher, he [148] might manifest to the Gentiles the divinity of Christ." In this passage the very holy man most distinctly avows and acknowledges a Son of God, who was such before He was made man, and who afterwards became incarnate, in other words, was made man, for the salvation of mankind, at the time and in the manner that God the Father willed; and further he expressly teaches, that John meant to describe a Son of God of this kind, in the beginning of his Gospel. He affirms, moreover, that Luke's purpose also at the commencement of his Gospel was, to proclaim to the Gentiles, by the wonderful birth of the forerunner of Christ, and by his preaching, the divinity of Christ Himself.

[1] qui.

8. But, secondly, there are some things even in Polycarp's Epistle to the Philippians which imply (and that not obscurely) the divinity of Christ. Of this kind is that very passage referred to by the author of the *Irenicum*, the words of which in the Latin version (for the Greek of that part is not extant) are as follows[x]; "The God and Father of our Lord Jesus Christ, and the everlasting High-Priest Himself, the Son of God, Jesus Christ, build you up in faith and truth, and in all meekness and freedom from wrath, in patience also, and long-suffering, and endurance, and chastity, and grant unto you a lot and portion amongst His saints," &c. In these words Polycarp invokes Christ, the Son of God, along with God the Father, as the Giver of grace in this life, and of glory in a future life. Now that an invocation of this

[u] Joannes ad Ephesum constitutus, qui legem tanquam ex gentibus ignorabant, a causa nostræ redemptionis evangelii sumpsit exordium; quæ causa ex eo apparet, quod Filium suum Deus pro nostra salute voluit incarnari. Lucas vero a Zachariæ sacerdotio incipit, ut ejus filii miraculo nativitatis, et tanti prædicatoris officio, divinitatem Christi gentibus declararet.—[p. 205, ed. Coteler.]

[x] Deus autem et Pater Domini nostri Jesu Christi, et ipse sempiternus Pontifex, Dei Filius Jesus Christus, ædificet vos in fide et veritate, et in omni mansuetudine et sine iracundia, et in patientia, et longanimitate, et tolerantia, et castitate; et det vobis sortem et partem inter sanctos suos, &c. —Page 23. [p. 191.]

ON THE CONSUBSTANTIALITY OF THE SON.

kind is suited to God alone, and not befitting to any creature, (however the Arians and the Socinians may fret against it[1],) Holy Scripture, right reason, and the unanimous opinion of the ancient catholic doctors agree in teaching us. Especially clear[y], again, are the words of Polycarp, concerning Christ as the Overseer and the Judge of all men; [149] "For we are before the eyes of our Lord and God, and must all stand before the judgment-seat of Christ and give account every one for himself. Thus then let us serve Him with fear and all reverence, as He hath Himself commanded, and the Apostles, who preached the gospel unto us, and the prophets, who foretold the coming of our Lord." In this passage Polycarp either is speaking concerning Christ alone, calling Him both God and Lord, (as indeed he seems to be speaking of a single Person,) or, at any rate, he joins with God the Father Christ His Son, as equally the universal Overseer, *παντεπόπτης*, unto whose eyes all things are subjected: as also the universal Judge, *παντοδικαστὴς*, at whose tribunal all men, without exception, will have to stand: and by this argument he exhorts the faithful to serve the same Lord Jesus with fear and all reverence. And the sense of this passage of Polycarp is made clear by a parallel passage of the blessed Ignatius, in his Epistle to the Ephesians, "There is nothing hidden from the Lord," &c., which we adduced in the preceding chapter[z].

9. But let us at length pass to the fragments of Polycarp, which are preserved by Eusebius. Amongst them is especially memorable that prayer of Polycarp[a], now on the point of suffering martyrdom, preserved in Eusebius' Eccl. Hist. iv. 15; it concludes with this remarkable doxology[b]; "Wherefore also for all things I praise Thee, I bless Thee, I glorify Thee, through the eternal High-Priest, Jesus Christ,
[150] Thy beloved Son, through whom, unto Thee, with Himself,

[1] obganniant.

[y] ἀπέναντι γὰρ τῶν τοῦ Κυρίου καὶ Θεοῦ ἐσμὲν ὀφθαλμῶν, καὶ πάντας δεῖ παραστῆναι τῷ βήματι τοῦ Χριστοῦ, καὶ ἕκαστον ὑπὲρ ἑαυτοῦ λόγον δοῦναι. οὕτως οὖν δουλεύσωμεν αὐτῷ μετὰ φόβου καὶ πάσης εὐλαβείας, καθὼς αὐτὸς ἐνετείλατο, καὶ οἱ εὐαγγελισάμενοι ἡμᾶς ἀπόστολοι, καὶ οἱ προφῆται, οἱ προκηρύξαντες τὴν ἔλευσιν τοῦ Κυρίου ἡμῶν.—§ 6. p. 188.]

[z] [c. ii. § 6. p. 95.]

[a] He suffered A.D. 175. Cave. Bowyer.

[b] διὰ τοῦτο καὶ περὶ πάντων σὲ αἰνῶ, σὲ εὐλογῶ, σὲ δοξάζω διὰ τοῦ αἰωνίου ἀρχιερέως Ἰησοῦ Χριστοῦ, τοῦ ἀγαπητοῦ σοῦ παιδός· δι' οὗ σοι σὺν αὐτῷ ἐν πνεύματι ἁγίῳ δόξα καὶ νῦν καὶ εἰς τοὺς μέλλοντας αἰῶνας· Ἀμήν.—[Euseb. E. H., iv. 15, Mart. Polyc., § 14. Patr. Ap. ii. 201.]

in the Holy Ghost, be glory both now and for ever. Amen." You perceive that here God the Father is glorified not only through, but also together with the Son, one and the same glory being attributed to them both "in the Holy Ghost." And I have already in this chapter in part shewn, how altogether opposed is this form of doxology to the heresy of those who deny the true divinity of Christ. Indeed Petavius himself had alleged this passage, in proof of the doctrine of the most holy Trinity. But what answer does the author of the *Irenicum* make to him? "With respect," he says[c], "to the short prayer[1] ascribed to Polycarp, and which Petavius adduces in confirmation of his [opinion concerning the] Trinity[2], it is more to the prejudice than to the support of his cause: inasmuch as in it he manifestly calls the Father of Jesus Christ alone the true God and Creator of all things, and invokes Him through the Son, whom he merely names High-Priest. I ask, therefore, what does this mode of speech indicate, nay, what can it indicate, other than that Polycarp
held and regarded (as in his Epistle also) the Father alone 54
to be the supreme God?" In these words, I think, that the man's craft is worthy to be noted first, in that he wishes to suggest to his reader a suspicion that this prayer of Polycarp is not really his, but only "ascribed" to him. Yet certainly there is scarcely any fragment of primitive antiquity, preserved by Eusebius, which is worthy of more credit than this last prayer of the dying Polycarp. It is extracted from an Epistle written by the brethren of Smyrna, who had been eye-witnesses of the suffering of the blessed Polycarp, to the
Church at Philomelium, on their request to be put in posses- [151]
sion of all the particulars of the martyrdom of that most holy man. Of this Epistle no man of learning up to this time has entertained a doubt, nor is it possible for any one hereafter to do so with any reason, inasmuch as even before Eusebius' time it was read among the public acts of the martyrs, and breathes throughout the spirit of the first Christians, that is, their purity of doctrine, their piety and their simplicity. Respecting these acts of Polycarp and of the martyrs of Gaul, hear the judgment of the great Joseph Scaliger[d]; "So affected," he says, "is the mind of the pious reader by their

[1] precatiunculum.

[2] pro Trinitatis suæ confirmatione.

[c] Page 29.

[d] Animadvers. in Eusebii Chron. num. 2183.

perusal, as never to leave them with feelings of satiety; and that this is indeed the case, every one may perceive in proportion to his intelligence and his measure of inward sense[1]. For my own part, I certainly have never met with any thing in ecclesiastical history, from the reading of which I rise more moved, even to such an extent as to seem to be no longer master of myself[2]."

10. But this most illustrious monument of the faith of Polycarp has greatly vexed the author of the *Irenicum*, notwithstanding his pretences to the contrary. I scarcely know how he had the effrontery to assert that this prayer "told more against than in favour of Petavius," when he argued from it in defence of [the doctrine of] the most sacred Trinity. Nay, he says it is manifest that Polycarp in this prayer calls the Father of Jesus Christ alone the true God and Creator of all things; and invokes Him through the Son, calling the latter only High-Priest; and, in fact, he so speaks as that he seems to have acknowledged the Father only to be the supreme God. But here the heretic only serves up to our disgust, for the tenth time, the self-same dish[3]. We confess, we freely confess, that the Father alone is, in one point of view[4], the supreme God; I mean, in that He Himself is (as Athanasius expresses it) "the fountain of Deity," (πηγὴ θεότητος,) that is, He alone is God of Himself[5], from whom the Son and the Holy Ghost receive their [152] Godhead; and on this account also it is, that the appellation of "the true God" is frequently assigned, in a peculiar sense[6], to the Father, both in the Holy Scriptures and in the writings of the ancients, especially when the divine Persons are mentioned together. Notwithstanding, at the same time we, with the fathers of Nice, do also firmly maintain that the Son is "Light of Light, God of God," and consequently "very God of very God." And the anonymous author might on like ground have alleged their confession of faith in opposition to the doctrine concerning the divinity of the Son and concerning the most holy Trinity; for thus do they begin their creed; "We believe in one God, the Father Almighty, the Maker of all things, visible and invisible." It is, however, worth while here to put before the reader the words of Polycarp in the opening of his prayer, which ap-

[1] conscientiæ modo.
[2] non amplius meus.
[3] cramben decies recoctam.
[4] aliquo respectu.
[5] a seipso.
[6] proprie.

peared to the author of the *Irenicum* to be so very favourable to his heresy: they are as follows[e]; "[O Lord God,] the Father of Thy beloved and blessed Son Jesus Christ, through whom we have received the knowledge of Thee; God of angels, and powers, and of the whole creation," &c. Now I affirm that utter darkness must envelope the mind of that man who does not perceive that in these words the death-blow is struck at Socinianism, and at Arianism too. For Polycarp here teaches that God is the Father of His blessed Son, but the God (that is, the Creator) of angels, and powers, and of the whole creation; so as thereby most clearly to distinguish and most widely to separate the blessed Son of God from angels, and powers, and the whole order of created beings; and, consequently, to take Him out of the class[1] of creatures, and to teach that God is in quite a different relation[2] to His blessed Son, from that in which He stands to the angels and the host of other created beings. Added to this, the epithet *εὐλογητὸς*, (blessed,) applied by Polycarp in this passage to the Son of God, was by the [153]
ancient Jews employed in a peculiar application[3] in the celebration of the divine name; for (as the learned are well aware) ברוך השם, "blessed be the Name," was the accustomed formulary in their doxologies. And they have been imitated by the writers of the New Testament, whenever they wished to speak in terms of special reverence of the divine Persons, and to celebrate more clearly their supreme glory and majesty. Compare Mark xiv. 61; Luke i. 68; Rom. i. 25; ix. 5; 2 Cor. xi. 31; Ephes. i. 3; 1 Pet. i. 3, with Genesis ix. 26; xiv. 20; xxiv. 27, &c. That is untrue, therefore, which the anonymous author asserts, that Polycarp here gives merely the appellation of High-Priest to Christ, and therefore it is to no purpose, that he afterwards observes, that the appellation of High-Priest, which is applied to Christ, denotes that He is man. For suppose it be so, what will follow? that Christ is man as well[4] [as God], which we likewise firmly believe. Therefore, supposing that the title of *ἀρχιερεὺς*, (High-Priest,) implies that He is

[1] creaturarum censu.
[2] σχέσιν.
[3] proprie.
[4] etiam hominem.

[e] [Κύριε ὁ Θεὸς . . .] ὁ τοῦ ἀγαπητοῦ καὶ εὐλογητοῦ παιδός σου Ἰησοῦ Χριστοῦ πατὴρ, δι' οὗ τὴν περὶ σὲ ἐπίγνωσιν εἰλήφαμεν· ὁ Θεὸς ἀγγέλων καὶ δυνάμεων καὶ πάσης τῆς κτίσεως· κ.τ.λ.—[§ 14. p. 200.]

Son of man, yet at any rate the designation of ὁ παῖς θεοῦ, ὁ ἀγαπητὸς, ὁ εὐλογητὸς, "the Son of God, the beloved, the blessed," most certainly sounds like something more than man; especially when such a description of the beloved and blessed Son of God is added, as puts that Son into a condition separate from and above that of creatures.

55 11. But the charge which the heretic[f] brings against Petavius is quite amusing[1], namely, that "The prayer of Polycarp, as it is adduced by him, is very different from that which Scultetus brings forward in his *Medulla Theologiæ Patrum*, xi. 1. A grave charge indeed! As if Petavius had not done right in giving the prayer in the precise words in which it was reported by the brethren of Smyrna in their letter extant in Eusebius! What will you say of the fact that[2] Scultetus in the alleged passage does not recite the very words of Polycarp's prayer, but only summarily gives the sense of it? From this, however, and many other indications, you will be right in conjecturing that this anonymous writer, for the most part, did not derive the ancient [154] testimonies, which he has heaped together in his *Irenicum*, by his own industry from the original sources, but transcribed them into his own book from Scultetus, Petavius, and others. So that of all creatures[3] he was the most unfit[4] to undertake "to lay before the Christian world, more clearly than had ever been done before, the true monuments of primitive antiquity and of the faith of the first Christians;" which he most foolishly boasts of having done in the imposing[5] title which he prefixes to the third section of his *Norma Reconciliatrix*[g],—his rule of reconciliation,—as he calls it.

[1] festivum.

[2] Quid, quod.

[3] bipedum.

[4] ineptissimum.

[5] splendido.

12. But let us now, at last, consider what may be gathered from the doxology with which Polycarp's prayer concludes, in confirmation of the Godhead of the Son, and therefore of the consubstantiality of the Trinity. We maintain, then, that the embracing of the Three in the same formula and participation of glory, indicates unity of nature and of Godhead, and in that respect the equality of the Persons. For most truly does Athanasius say, in his third oration against the Arians[h],

[f] Irenic., p. 30.

[g] Irenic., p. 13.

[h] ποία γὰρ κοινωνία τῷ κτίσματι πρὸς τὸν κτίστην; ἢ διὰ τί τὸ πεποιημένον συναριθμεῖται τῷ ποιήσαντι.—[Orat. ii. p. 41. vol. i. p. 508.]

in treating of the form of Baptism: "For what fellowship is there between the creature and the Creator? or wherefore is that which is made classed[1] with the Maker?" Well, too, is it said by Gregory Nazianzen, in his thirteenth Oration[i]; "The Trinity is really a Trinity[2], my brethren; a Trinity however is not a numbering up of things unequal; else what hinders but that we should give It the name[3] of decade, century, or myriad, if taken together with so many? for there are many things that may be counted, and more than these; but it is a taking together[4] of things equal, and of the same honour." And indeed, if in the Christians' [155] doxologies the Son and Holy Ghost were joined unto God the Father, not as of one substance with Him, but only as created beings of a higher class, why should not other superior creatures also be numbered together with Them, in their own order, in the same [doxologies]? Why should we not say, Glory be to the Father, and to the Son, and to the Holy Ghost, and to Michael, and to the rest of the archangels and angels? And so, forsooth, that blasphemous formula of the papists would at last have to be accounted legitimate, Praise be to God and to the Virgin Mother of God. But far otherwise was it that the disciples of the Apostles were taught.

[1] συναριθμεῖται.
[2] τριάς.
[3] ὀνομάζειν.
[4] σύλληψις.

13. Let us consider what the author of the *Irenicum* alleges in reply to these considerations. He first takes occasion for cavil from the circumstance that Polycarp in this formula does not say, "with the Holy Ghost," or "and to the Holy Ghost," but "in the Holy Ghost." "Nay but," he says, "the expression 'in the Holy Ghost' does not in itself[5] imply an association into the same fellowship of glory. For in Eph. vi. 18, we are taught to pray in the Spirit, without any intimation of equality between the Spirit and the Father." But what is trifling in a grave matter and openly playing the sophist, if this be not? By the phrase "in the spirit," in the Epistle to the Ephesians, is not meant the Holy Ghost, but our own spirit, assisted in-

[5] adhuc.

[i] τριὰς ὡς ἀληθῶς ἡ τριὰς, ἀδελφοί· τριὰς δὲ οὐ πραγμάτων ἀνίσων ἀπαρίθμησις· ἢ τί κωλύει καὶ δεκάδα, καὶ ἑκατοντάδα, καὶ μυριάδα ὀνομάζειν, μετὰ τοσούτων συντιθεμένην; πολλὰ γὰρ τὰ ἀριθμούμενα, καὶ πλείω τούτων· ἀλλ' ἴσων καὶ ὁμοτίμων σύλληψις. [ἑνούσης τῆς προσηγορίας τὰ ἡνωμένα ἐκ φυσέως καὶ οὐκ ἐώσης σκεδασθῆναι ἀριθμῷ λυομένῳ τὰ μὴ λυόμενα.]—Page 211. ed. Par. 1630. [Orat. xxiii. 10. p. 431.]

ON THE CONSUBSTANTIALITY OF THE SON.

deed by the grace of the Holy Ghost. So that to "pray in the spirit," is the same as the expression "in your heart," that is, with sincere affection of heart, in chap. v. ver. 19. of the same Epistle. But this very thing induces me to suspect that this anonymous author belongs to the number of the Pneumatomachi, [fighters against the Spirit,] who deny not only the divinity, but also the personality, as they express it, of the Holy Ghost. Yet whatever this weak man[1], who is but of yesterday, may think about the Holy Ghost, it is certain that blessed Polycarp, and the Catholics his contemporaries, believed that the Holy Ghost is a Person distinct from the Father and the Son, and at the same time divine, that is to say, a partaker of the same majesty, dominion, and honour with the Father and the Son. Here is a testimony of this, which is above all exception, the confession of the brethren of Smyrna, who at any rate knew very well the mind both of Polycarp and of the Catholic Church of that time. For thus do they conclude their letter respecting the martyrdom of Polycarp[j]: "Our prayer for you, brethren, is that ye may be strong, walking in the word of Jesus Christ, which is according to His gospel; with whom be glory and honour to God both Father and Holy Ghost, for the salvation of the elect saints[2]." In these words divine glory and honour is expressly attributed to the Holy Ghost, together with the Father and the Son; nor is the Son more clearly distinguished from the Father than the Holy Ghost is from both. Altogether parallel to this is the doxology of the companions of Ignatius, towards the conclusion of the Acts of the Martyrdom of that saint[k]: "Glorifying in his (Ignatius') venerable and sacred memory, our Lord Jesus Christ, through whom and with whom to the Father be glory and power, with the Holy

[1] homuncio.

[156]

[2] τῶν ἁγίων ἐκλεκτῶν.

[j] ἐρρῶσθαι ὑμᾶς εὐχόμεθα, ἀδελφοὶ, στοιχοῦντας τῷ κατὰ τὸ εὐαγγέλιον λόγῳ, Ἰησοῦ Χριστοῦ· μεθ' οὗ δόξα τῷ Θεῷ καὶ πατρὶ καὶ ἁγίῳ πνεύματι, ἐπὶ σωτηρίᾳ τῇ τῶν ἁγίων ἐκλεκτῶν. κ.τ.λ. See Valesius' notes on Euseb., p. 73. [p. 171.]

[k] [The Latin of this passage given by Bp. Bull is, "Glorificantes in ipsius (Ignatii) venerabili et sancta memoria Dominum nostrum Jesum Christum: per quem et cum quo Patri gloria et potentia cum Spiritu Sancto in sancta ecclesia in sæcula sæculorum. Amen." The concluding words of the Greek original, ὑμνοῦντες τὸν Θεὸν, τὸν δοτῆρα τῶν ἀγαθῶν, καὶ μακαρίσαντες τὸν ἅγιον . . . . ἐν Χριστῷ Ἰησοῦ τῷ κυρίῳ ἡμῶν, δι' οὗ καὶ μεθ' οὗ τῷ πατρὶ ἡ δόξα καὶ τὸ κράτος σὺν τῷ ἁγίῳ πνεύματι εἰς αἰῶνας. ἀμήν. § 7. Patr. Ap. ii. 161.]

Ghost, in the holy Church, for ever and ever. Amen." Wherein also you will observe by the way that both phrases "through whom" and "with whom" are employed respecting the Son, just as in the prayer of Polycarp; the reason of which I have mentioned above. However, it appears to me that the ancients in their doxologies used not only the forms "with the Holy Ghost," or "and to the Holy Ghost," but also sometimes "in the Holy Ghost," for the very purpose of signifying that the Holy Ghost, insomuch as He proceedeth[1] [157] from the Father and the Son, or from the Father through the Son, constitutes the communion and unity of them both; and thus is as it were the bond of the most holy Trinity, as indeed He is expressly called by some of the ancients[l]. This is more distinctly expressed in that very ancient formula: "Glory be to the Father and to the Son in the unity of the Holy Ghost." Accordingly a very early writer, Athenagoras, (in his[m] Apology[2] for the Christians,) calls the Father and the Son one ἑνότητι Πνεύματος, "by the unity of the Spirit." Synesius, in his hymns, elegantly expresses this mystery in more than one passage; for instance, in his third hymn, he thus addresses the Holy Ghost:

POLYCARP. 56

[1] quatenus procedit.

[2] legatio.

> Ὅρος εἶ φυσέων,
> Thou art the boundary of the natures;
> Τᾶς τικτοίσας,
> Of the begetting [nature,]
> Καὶ τικτομένας,
> And of the begotten.

and in his fourth hymn after celebrating the praises of God the Father and the Son, he proceeds to sing:

> Μεσάταν ἀρχὰν,
> The intervening principle;
> Ἁγίαν πνοιὰν,
> The Holy Spirit;
> Κέντρον γενέτου,
> Centre of the Father,
> Κέντρον δὲ κόρου,
> And centre of the Son.

14. I return, however, to the author of the *Irenicum*, who

[l] See Petav. de Trin. vii. 12. 8.
[m] P. 10. [§ 10. p. 287. B. The passage is quoted at length, ii. 4. 9.]

ON THE CONSUBSTANTIALITY OF THE SON.

thus proceeds with his cavils: "Besides, the earlier writers, when they praised the Son together with the Father and the Holy Ghost, nevertheless did not (as is now being fully shewn in this place, and will afterwards be shewn in the case of Justin Martyr and others) either lay down, or believe, that either the Son or the Holy Ghost is equal with the Father: nay, they did not even venture to designate the Holy Ghost, God." My answer is this; What these earlier writers thought concerning the equality of the Persons, (I mean of the Father and of
[158] the Son,) we shall shew at length in our fourth book; where it will be made clear, that those earlier writers laid down no other inequality between the Persons of the Father and of the Son, than was recognised by the fathers who flourished after the council of Nice, by Catholics of the present day, and further, by the very schoolmen themselves. Meanwhile, this is certain, that the fathers of the first three centuries without exception, taught, that the Son is of the same nature with the Father, and therefore is very God; and that it was under no other conception [of Him] that they glorified Him together with God the Father. We have already proved this in the case of the author of the Epistle attributed to Barnabas, of Hermas, Ignatius, and Clement of Rome; we are now shewing the same respecting Polycarp, and, finally, shall shew it of Justin Martyr and all the other fathers who preceded the council of Nice, one by one, in the course of this book. With respect to the Holy Ghost, we shall in this work incidentally shew that the same earlier fathers confessed His consubstantiality also, and by consequence, His divinity; nay, that by some of them the Holy Ghost is expressly called God.

15. At last the heretic essays to explain how it is that we are bound to offer divine worship to Christ, notwithstanding that He is in His own nature a mere man. "In truth," he says, "both angels and men are bound to adore the man Christ, and to worship and to glorify Him with and next to[1] God, according to the divine prediction, Jer. xxx. 9; Ezek. xxxiv. 23, 24, yet only as the servant and the ambassador of God, and made Lord[2]. Compare Phil. ii. 9—11; Acts ii. 36." To which I reply; Christ is proposed for our worship in the Scriptures, not only as the servant and ambassador of God, who afterwards was made Lord, but as the Son of God, begotten of the Father before the worlds, who out of His infinite

[1] juxtim cum.

[2] Dominumque factum.

love to the human race, having taken upon Himself that office of ambassador to man, earned for Himself, as it were by a new title, that divine honour should be paid to Him by men; in other words, by a new and amazing act of kindness He bound [159]
men to worship and to serve Him. At any rate, in that passage to the Philippians, (which the anonymous author and his crew[1] especially put forward[2],) it is shewn that He, who after His death is declared to have been very highly exalted by God, did also before He assumed the form of a servant, that is, (as Paul interprets himself,) before He was made man, exist in the form of God, and was equal with God. The interpretations by which both Arians and Socinians endeavour to elude the force of that passage are manifestly absurd, as any one will easily perceive who carefully weighs the context of the whole passage. So also in the Epistle to the Hebrews i. 2, 3, He, who, after "He had by Himself purged our sins, sat down at the right hand of the majesty in the highest," the same is declared to be the Son of God, "through whom the worlds were made, and the brightness of the Father's glory, upholding all things by the word of His power." We do not, however, deny that the human nature of Christ, so far forth as it was capable[3], came into a participation of glory and honour with the Divine Person of the Son of God. Certainly[4] this is what Paul plainly teaches as does the author of the Epistle, called that of Barnabas, when he says, that Christ willed "the vessel of His spirit to be glorified," as we have observed already[n]. And Hermas means no other when (in the passage which we also quoted above[o]) he says, 57
that "the servant," that is, the man Christ, "by reason of the good service which He had performed, was made co-heir with the Son of God." This passage of Hermas also completely overthrows the notion of the anonymous writer. For in it there is made a most manifest distinction between that divine honour which Christ, as Son of God, (that is, according to Hermas' own interpretation,) existing before all creatures, had previously with the Father, and that honour which was given to Christ, the servant, that is, the man "who [160]
became obedient to death, even the death of the cross," as a reward after His death. Meanwhile the human nature of Christ, being exalted after death, has become a partaker of

[1] gregales.
[2] venditant.
[3] pro suo captu.
[4] scilicet.

[n] Chap. 2. § 3. of this book, p. 91. [o] [Ibid. p. 90.]

ON THE CONSUBSTANTIALITY OF THE SON.

[1] per se.
[2] in personam terminetur, non in naturam.
[3] tendat in Creatorem.

the divine dominion and honour, not of itself[1], but by reason of the person of the Word, by which it is sustained, and to which it is united; so that that honour properly has its object in the person and not in the nature[2]; and accordingly it is plain, that when the manhood of Christ is worshipped, the creature is not in such wise worshipped, but that the act [of worship] properly tends to the Creator[3], Who has joined a created nature unto Himself in unity of person. This subject is well explained by the truly great Athanasius, in an Epistle to the Bishop Adelphius, against the Arians, in these words[o]: "It is not a creature that we worship, God forbid! for to the heathen and the Arians does such error belong; but it is the Lord of the creation, incarnate, the Word of God, whom we worship; for although the flesh taken by itself is a portion of created things, yet it has been made the body of God. And neither do we worship such a body as this by itself parting it from the Word, nor wishing to worship the Word do we separate it from the flesh[4]; but knowing, as we said before, what is written, 'the Word was made flesh,' Him we acknowledge to be God, even when He has come to be in the flesh." And afterwards in the same Epistle[p] he says, "Let them," that is, let the Arians, "know, that when we worship the Lord in the flesh, we do not worship[5] a creature[p], but the Creator, who hath clothed Himself in the created body." Lastly, he concludes his epistle with these words[q], which are especially worthy of being observed: "The faith of the Catholic Church knoweth the Word of God as Maker and Creator of all things; and we know that 'in the beginning was the Word, and the Word was with God;' and Him, having become man also for our salvation, do we worship: not as if He had come to be in the body

[4] *μακρύνομεν.*

[5] *οὐ κτίσματι προσκυνοῦμεν.*

[o] *οὐ κτίσμα προσκυνοῦμεν, μὴ γένοιτο. ἐθνικῶν γὰρ καὶ Ἀρειανῶν ἡ τοιαύτη πλάνη· ἀλλὰ τὸν Κύριον τῆς κτίσεως σαρκωθέντα τὸν τοῦ Θεοῦ λόγον προσκυνοῦμεν. εἰ γὰρ καὶ ἡ σὰρξ αὐτὴ καθ' ἑαυτὴν μέρος ἐστὶ τῶν κτισμάτων, ἀλλὰ Θεοῦ γέγονε σῶμα· καὶ οὔτε τὸ τοιοῦτον σῶμα καθ' ἑαυτὸ διαιροῦντες ἀπὸ τοῦ λόγου προσκυνοῦμεν, οὔτε τὸν λόγον προσκυνῆσαι θέλοντες μακρύνομεν αὐτὸν ἀπὸ τῆς σαρκός· ἀλλ' εἰδότες, καθὰ προείπομεν, τὸ, ὁ λόγος σὰρξ ἐγένετο, τοῦτον καὶ ἐν σαρκὶ γενόμενον ἐπιγινώσκομεν Θεόν.*—Tom. i. p. 157. [vol. i. p. 912. § 3.]

[p] *γινωσκέτωσαν ὅτι τὸν Κύριον ἐν σαρκὶ προσκυνοῦντες οὐ κτίσματι προσκυνοῦμεν, ἀλλὰ τὸν κτίστην ἐνδυσάμενον τὸ κτιστὸν σῶμα.*—Pp. 161, 162. [p. 916. This (*κτίσματι*) is the reading of the Benedictine editor even, following all others: but it should be corrected to *κτίσμα τι*.—B.]

[q] *ἡ πίστις τῆς καθολικῆς ἐκκλησίας κτίστην οἶδε τὸν τοῦ Θεοῦ λόγον καὶ δημιουργὸν τῶν ἁπάντων· καὶ οἴδαμεν ὅτι ἐν ἀρχῇ μὲν ἦν ὁ λόγος, καὶ ὁ λόγος ἦν πρὸς τὸν Θεόν. γενόμενον δὲ αὐτὸν καὶ ἄνθρωπον διὰ τὴν ἡμετέραν σωτηρίαν προσκυνοῦμεν, οὐχ' ὡς ἴσον ἐν ἴσῳ γενό-*

POLYCARP.

as one of two equal things may be in another[1], but as a Master having taken to Himself the form of a servant, and as Maker and Creator, having come to be in a creature, that in it having set all things free, He might bring near[2] the world unto the Father, and make at peace all things, both those that are in heaven and those that are on earth. For thus do we both acknowledge His Godhead which He has from the Father, and we worship His presence in the flesh, even though the Arian madmen burst with rage[3].

16. I return to Polycarp and the brethren of Smyrna. It is evident that they glorified Christ together with God the Father, not as a servant who afterwards was made Lord, but [162] as the "beloved and blessed Son," the only-begotten of the Father; as will easily be seen by any one who reads the Epistle of the Smyrneans. And that by these titles the divine nature, glory, and majesty of the Son of God are expressed, we have already shewn in part from the consent of the ancient Church, and shall elsewhere demonstrate more fully. But the Smyrneans also, in assigning a reason, why, at the same time that they adored[4] Christ, a man, and that crucified, they yet did not worship[5] the martyrs, the followers of the sufferings[6] of Christ, thus speak[7] distinctly concerning Christ[8]; "For Him indeed we worship as being the Son of God," (not as a mere man;) presently after, respecting the martyrs they add, (and O that the papists would mark their words,) "The martyrs however we love, as is their due[8], as disciples and followers[9] of the Lord, for their affection[10] to their own King and Master, an affection which cannot be surpassed." Besides, these same Smyrneans, as we have seen, ascribe divine honour unto the Holy Ghost also, together with God the Father. But, I ask, on what ground? Is it as having been made Lord? Let the author of the *Irenicum* tell us, when and how the Holy Ghost from being a servant was made Lord?

1 οὐχ' ὡς ἶσον ἐν ἴσῳ γενόμενον τῷ σώματι.

2 προσαγάγῃ.

3 διαρρηγνύωσιν.

4 adorarent.

5 colerent.

6 imitantes passionem.

7 respondent.

8 ἀξίως.

9 μιμητάς.

10 εὐνοίας.

μενον τῷ σώματι, ἀλλ' ὡς δεσπότην προσλαβόντα τὴν τοῦ δούλου μορφὴν, καὶ δημιουργὸν καὶ κτίστην ἐν κτίσματι γενόμενον· ἵν' ἐν αὐτῷ τὰ πάντα ἐλευθερώσας τὸν κόσμον προσαγάγῃ τῷ Πατρὶ, καὶ εἰρηνοποιήσῃ τὰ πάντα, τὰ ἐν οὐρανοῖς καὶ τὰ ἐπὶ τῆς γῆς. οὕτω γὰρ καὶ τὴν πατρικὴν αὐτοῦ θεότητα ἐπιγινώσκομεν, καὶ τὴν ἔνσαρκον αὐτοῦ παρουσίαν προσκυνοῦμεν, κᾂν 'Αρειομανῖται διαρρηγνύωσιν ἑαυτούς.—pp. 161, 162. [p. 916.]

8 τοῦτον μὲν γὰρ υἱὸν ὄντα τοῦ Θεοῦ προσκυνοῦμεν. . . . τοὺς δὲ μάρτυρας ὡς μαθητὰς καὶ μιμητὰς τοῦ Κυρίου ἀγαπῶμεν ἀξίως, ἕνεκα εὐνοίας ἀνυπερβλήτου τῆς εἰς τὸν ἴδιον βασιλέα καὶ διδάσκαλον. [§ 17. Patr. Ap. ii. 202.]

Or is it, as being a created spirit, more excellent than the other spirits, or angels? But all admit that divine worship is not due to any created being, *per se*, be he never so exalted. Besides, the sacred Scriptures every where[t] most clearly teach, that the Holy Ghost subsists in God Himself, and that His mind and all His secret things are intimately known and perceived by Him, that He is every where present, &c.;
[163] nor have they any where delivered one iota to lead you to suspect that He is placed in the rank of created beings. Hence the greatest and more sagacious portion of those who contend against the Holy Spirit[1] have at all times thought it better roundly to deny the personality itself of the Holy
58 Ghost, and to assert that He is nothing else than the influence[2] and power of God the Father Himself, and not distinguished from Him, than to affirm that He is a creature, against so many and such clear testimonies of Scripture. But they also are as nothing: for in the Scriptures the Holy Ghost is not less clearly distinguished from the Father than is the Son Himself, (an assertion which, if that were the matter in hand, might very easily be proved;) and the whole Catholic Church has ever believed and taught that the Holy Ghost is a person distinct from the Father. It remains, therefore, that we confess that the ancient Christians worshipped the Holy Ghost under this conception, that He is the Spirit of God, subsisting in God Himself, and consequently Himself God; but yet personally[3] distinct from God, whose Spirit He is. Now if this be true, as indeed it is most true, it will follow that these same ancients either worshipped the Son as being in His nature God[4], or regarded Him as inferior to the Holy Ghost; for, without doubt, it is a greater prerogative of honour to be worshipped as being in nature God, than as one that has been made God and Lord. But that the Son is inferior to the Holy Ghost was never dreamt of amongst Catholics; seeing that[5] in the Scriptures the Holy Ghost is said to be sent by the Son, and to have received from Him what He hath of His own[6]; and in all the doxologies of the ancients, wherein the divine Persons are enumerated in their order, the Son has assigned to Him the second, (δευτέ-

[1] Pneumatomachorum.

[2] virtutem.

[3] persona.

[4] natura Deum.

[5] scilicet.

[6] sua ab eodem Filio.

[t] See especially 1 Cor. ii. 10, 11.

ραν,) whilst the Holy Ghost has the third place or rank, (*τρίτην χώραν ἢ τάξιν,*) to use the words of Justin[u]. BOOK II. CHAP. III. § 16, 17. POLYCARP.

17. This [last consideration] is indeed a most irrefragable argument for the divinity of Christ; and so the ancients judged. For thus Novatian, or the author of the Book on the Trinity amongst the works of Tertullian, writes, chap. 24[v]; "If Christ be only man, how is it that He says that the Comforter shall take of His[1] what He is about to declare[2] [unto men[x]]? For the Comforter does not receive any thing from man, but [rather] the Comforter communicates knowledge to man; neither does the Comforter learn from man the things that shall come to pass, but [rather] the Comforter instructs man respecting what shall come to pass. It follows, therefore, either that the Comforter did not receive from Christ, a [mere] man, what He has to declare, since it will never be in the power of man to give any thing to the Comforter, from whom it behoves man himself to receive, and [in that case] Christ in this passage misleads and deceives by saying that the Comforter shall receive from Him, a [mere] man, what He has to declare; or [this is the alternative, that] He does not mislead us, (as neither indeed does He deceive us,) and the Comforter did receive from Christ that which He has to declare. But if [it be so, that] He did receive from Christ what He has to declare, then it follows at once that Christ is greater than the Comforter, since the Comforter would not receive from Christ if He were not less than Christ: but the Comforter [being] less than Christ, does from this very fact prove Christ also to be God, from whom He received what He declares. So THAT IT IS A GREAT TESTIMONY TO THE DIVINITY OF CHRIST, that the [164]

[1] de suo.

[2] quæ nuntiaturus sit.

u [Apol. i. § 16. pp. 60, 61.]

v Si homo tantummodo Christus, quomodo Paracletum dicit de suo esse sumpturum, quæ nuntiaturus sit? neque enim Paracletus ab homine quicquam accipit, sed homini scientiam Paracletus porrigit; nec futura ab homine Paracletus discit, sed de futuris hominem Paracletus instruit. Ergo aut non accepit Paracletus a Christo homine quod nuntiet, quoniam Paracleto homo nihil poterit dare, a quo ipse homo debet accipere, et fallit in præsenti loco Christus et decipit, cum Paracletum a se homine accepturum, quæ nuntiet, dicit; aut non nos fallit, sicut nec fallit, et accepit Paracletus a Christo, quæ nuntiet. Sed si a Christo accepit quæ nuntiet, major ergo jam Paracleto Christus est; quoniam nec Paracletus a Christo acciperet, nisi minor Christo esset; minor autem Christo Paracletus, Christum etiam Deum esse hoc ipso probat, a quo accepit quæ nuntiat. UT TESTIMONIUM CHRISTI DIVINITATIS GRANDE SIT, dum minor Christo Paracletus repertus ab illo sumit quæ cæteris tradit.—[Pag. 722.]

x [John xvi. 14. ἐκ τοῦ ἐμοῦ λήψεται καὶ ἀναγγελεῖ ὑμῖν. "He shall receive of Mine, and shall tell it unto you."]

ON THE CONSUBSTANTIALITY OF THE SON.

Comforter being found to be less than Christ, takes from Him what He delivers unto all else." With regard to what he here says of the Holy Ghost being less than the Son, it is to be understood exactly in the same way as we shall explain the subordination of the Son with reference to the Father, in the fourth book; that is to say, in such sense as that the Holy Ghost be said to be less than the Son, not in respect of nature, but of origin; inasmuch as He is derived from the Father through the Son, as Tertullian says in his treatise against Praxeas, chap. 4[y]; and, accordingly, receives all that He has[1] from the Father through the Son, agreeably to the declaration of Novatian[z]. Tertullian, again, in the same book,
[165] (chap. 8[a],) more clearly explains this subordination of the Holy Ghost in the following words; "For the Spirit is third from God and His Son, just as the fruit out of the tree is third from the root, or as the stream out of the river is third from the fountain, or the point out of the ray is third from the sun. NOTHING, HOWEVER, IS ALIEN FROM THAT ORIGINAL SOURCE WHENCE IT DERIVES ITS OWN PROPERTIES. In like manner the Trinity, flowing down from the Father through intertwined and connected steps, does not at all dis-

[1] sua omnia.

[y] [Page 502.]

[z] To the same purpose the author of the Constitutions (vi. 11.) says; "There is one God, the Father of one Son, of one Paraclete through Christ; *ἑνὸς υἱοῦ Πατέρα, [οὐ πλειόνων·] ἑνὸς Παρακλήτου διὰ Χριστοῦ.* Gregory Nyssen (in his epistle to Ablabius, tom. ii. p. 459, [vol. iii. p. 27.]) thus declares how from the same principle, i. e. from God the Father, both the Son and Holy Ghost have their origin in manner diverse; "For the One is from the First immediately, the other from the First through that which is immediately [from Him];" *τὸ μὲν γὰρ προσεχῶς ἐκ τοῦ πρώτου, τὸ δὲ διὰ τοῦ προσεχῶς ἐκ τοῦ πρώτου.* Cyril (book i. on the Adoration &c.) has the words: "The Spirit poured forth from the Father, through the Son;" *ἐκ πατρὸς δι' υἱοῦ προχεόμενον πνεῦμα.* vol. i. [p. 9.] See moreover his Letter to the Empresses, [*καὶ γάρ ἐστιν ἐκ πατρὸς φυσικῶς, προχεόμενον δι' υἱοῦ τῇ κτίσει.* "for He is naturally from the Father being poured forth to the creation through the Son," vi. p. 44.] Damascene (book i. on the Orthodox Faith, chap. 18. [cap. 12. vol. i. p. 148.]) says: "And [He is] the Spirit of the Son also, not as proceeding from Him, but as through Him, from the Father;" *καὶ υἱοῦ δὲ πνεῦμα, οὐχ' ὡς ἐξ αὐτοῦ, ἀλλ' ὡς δι' αὐτοῦ, ἐκ τοῦ Πατρὸς ἐκπορευόμενον.* Hilary, (lib. xii. [§ ult. p. 444] on the Trinity,) prays thus; "Preserve untainted, I beseech Thee, this religion of my faith, that what I professed in the creed of my regeneration, ... I may always hold fast; viz., that I may worship Thee who art our Father; and together with Thee Thy Son; and likewise may attain unto Thy Holy Spirit, who is from Thee, through Thine Only-begotten." Conserva hanc, oro, fidei meæ incontaminatam religionem, ut quod in religionis meæ symbolo...professus sum, semper obtineam, Patrem scilicet te nostrum, Filium tuum una tecum adorem, Sanctum Spiritum tuum, qui ex te per unigenitum tuum est, promerear.

[a] Tertius enim est Spiritus a Deo et Filio, sicut tertius a radice fructus ex frutice, et tertius a fonte rivus ex flumine, et tertius a sole apex ex radio. NIHIL TAMEN A MATRICE ALIENATUR, A QUA PROPRIETATES SUAS DUCIT; ita Trinitas per consertos et connexos gradus a Patre decurrens et monarchiæ nihil obstrepit, et *οἰκονομίας* statum protegit.—[P. 504.]

turb the monarchy, [and yet] guards the state of the economy[b]." In these words he declares the Holy Ghost to be third in reference to[1] the Father and the Son, in such sense as at the same time to profess distinctly that He is of the same essence and nature with the Father and the Son, and in no degree alien from the divinity of the Father. If, however, any one should suspect that the ante-Nicene fathers alone employed this reasoning, let him know that the most approved doctors of the Church, who flourished after the council of Nice, also established the Godhead of the Son by the selfsame argument; which I could have abundantly proved, if the nature of my design had permitted a digression of this kind. Let it suffice here to adduce the testimonies of two fathers who beyond all controversy held most firmly to the Nicene
Creed. Athanasius, in his second Oration against the Arians, 59
says[c]; "But to the disciples, shewing His divinity and His
majesty, and no longer [allowing them to think] that He [166]
was inferior to, but intimating that He was greater than, and equal to[d] the Spirit, He gave the Spirit, and said, 'Receive ye the Holy Ghost,' and 'I send Him,' and 'He shall glorify Me.'" Augustine (in his fifteenth book on the Trinity, c. 26,) says[e]; "How is it possible that He is not God who gives the Holy Spirit? Nay, rather, how great a God is He who giveth God!" Thus much, then, concerning Polycarp's short prayer and the form of blessing[2] of the brethren of Smyrna, which I have on this account followed out more fully, that all may perceive how ancient and clearly apostolic is that form of doxology which is used even at the present day in the Catholic Church, "Glory be to the Father, and to the Son, and to the Holy Ghost:" and what a firm and fixed monument and bulwark of the apostolic tradition concerning the consubstantial Trinity it presents against all the attacks[3] of heretics.

18. As concerns Polycarp, however, I will subjoin by way

[1] a.

[2] εὐλογία.

[3] machinas.

[b] [See above, p. 92.]

[c] τοῖς δὲ μαθηταῖς τὴν θεότητα καὶ τὴν μεγαλειότητα δεικνὺς ἑαυτοῦ, οὐκέτι δὲ ἐλάττονα τοῦ πνεύματος ἑαυτὸν, ἀλλὰ (μείζονα καὶ) ἴσον (ὄντα) σημαίνων, ἐδίδου μὲν τὸ πνεῦμα, καὶ ἔλεγεν, Λάβετε τὸ πνεῦμα ἅγιον· καὶ, Ἐγὼ αὐτὸ ἀποστέλλω· κᾀκεῖνος ἐμὲ δοξάσει.—[Orat. i. 50. vol. i. p. 454.]

[d] Greater, in respect of causation (κατ' αἰτίαν); equal, in respect of nature (κατὰ φύσιν.) [The words μείζονα καὶ, "greater than, and" are omitted in the Benedictine edition.—B.]

[e] Quomodo Deus non est, qui dat Spiritum Sanctum? imo quantus Deus est, qui dat Deum?—[Vol. viii. p. 999.]

ON THE CONSUBSTANTIALITY OF THE SON.

[1] mantissæ loco.

[2] abhorruerit.

of addition[1] two considerations besides, from which it will become still more manifest, how much he shrunk from[2] both the Samosatene and the Arian views respecting the Son of God. First then, if you would know what was the belief of Polycarp respecting the Son of God, consult Irenæus. He, in his youth, was a most attentive hearer of this apostolic bishop, and even in old age retained his discourses firmly fixed in his memory; (those especially in which he set forth what he had himself heard from the Apostles concerning the Lord Jesus;) Irenæus, moreover, was able to refute the

[3] vigentes.

heresies which prevailed[3] in his own time, by the analogy

[167] of the faith which was held by Polycarp, even calling God to witness to the truth of the tradition, as he testifies himself in the fragment of an Epistle to Florinus, which is extant in Eusebius, (Eccles. Hist. v. 20;) so that it is most unlikely to be true, nay, is absolutely incredible, either that Irenæus should have been ignorant of Polycarp's sentiments respecting the primary doctrine of Christianity, or that (knowing them) he should willingly depart from them even by a

[4] vel latum unguem.

hair's breadth[4]. Now I would venture to affirm, that no one of the upholders of the Nicene faith (Athanasius himself not excepted) has any where put forward statements more exalted respecting the Son of God, or more express against the Arian blasphemy, than those which Irenæus has made in his writings respecting that very Son of God. This one point I except, that Irenæus does not use the word *ὁμοούσιος* itself. Any one who shall attentively read what will be adduced in this and the next book out of Irenæus will say that I have not made this statement at random. The second consideration, from which one may with certainty gather the belief and opinion of Polycarp concerning the Son of God, is this; Eusebius testifies that Polycarp in his Epistle to the Philippians recommended to them Ignatius' Epistles as most worthy of being read, and[f] "as containing faith, and patience, and all edification, that pertaineth unto our Lord." Polycarp then by his testimony expressed his approval of the whole doctrine of the Epistles of Ignatius. Now in the seven Epistles of Ignatius, which were edited by Vossius,

[f] περιέχουσι πίστιν καὶ ὑπομονὴν, καὶ πᾶσαν οἰκοδομὴν, τὴν εἰς τὸν Κύριον ἡμῶν ἀνήκουσαν.—Eccles. Hist. iii. 36.

(and which, as no sound-minded person will deny, are the same with Polycarp's collection of them, known to Eusebius,) the true divinity of our Saviour is again and again taught in the clearest terms, as I have already shewn.

And thus far have we set forth the faith and opinion of those doctors of the Church, who were taught immediately[1] by the Apostles themselves, on the doctrine that the Son is of one substance [with the Father.]

[1] viva voce.

CHAPTER IV.

65 [178]

CONTAINING AN EXPOSITION OF THE VIEWS OF JUSTIN MARTYR, ATHENAGORAS, TATIAN, AND THEOPHILUS OF ANTIOCH; WITH AN INCIDENTAL DECLARATION OF THE FAITH OF CHRISTIANS RESPECTING THE HOLY TRINITY, IN THE AGE OF LUCIAN, OUT OF LUCIAN HIMSELF.

JUSTIN M.

1. JUSTIN MARTYR must be placed in the class next after the Apostolic writers, if not actually enumerated with them; and his works are almost all replete with so many and so clear testimonies to the consubstantiality of the Son, that I cannot but feel indignant when I read the calumnies, with which certain presumptuous writers of this day[2] have essayed to stain[3] the memory of that most holy father and martyr, as [179] though he agreed in opinion with the impious Arians.

[2] neoterici.

[3] conspurcarunt.

In the Apology, which is called the second, (although it is really the first[g],) Justin censures those[h] who deny "that the Father of all things has a Son, who, being also the first-born Word of God, is also God." Here he plainly infers that the Son, equally with the Father, is really God, from the fact that He came forth from, and was generated of God the Father Himself, as His Word and First-born. In a similar way in his dialogue with Trypho[i], he reproves the blindness of the Jews, for denying that Christ "is God, [being the] Son of the only and unbegotten and ineffable

[g] He wrote his first apology about the year 140. Cave.—BOWYER.

[h] *ὅτι ἐστὶν υἱὸς τῷ Πατρὶ τῶν ὅλων· ὃς καὶ λόγος πρωτότοκος ὢν τοῦ Θεοῦ καὶ Θεὸς ὑπάρχει.*—p. 96. [Apol. i. 63. p. 81.]

[i] *εἶναι Θεὸν, τοῦ μόνου καὶ ἀγεννήτου καὶ ἀρρήτου Θεοῦ υἱόν.*—p. 355. [§ 126. p. 219.]

ON THE CONSUBSTANTIALITY OF THE SON.

God." And shortly afterwards in the same book, he pronounces[k] Christ to be "Lord and God, being[1] the Son of God."

[1] ὑπάρχοντα. [2] germanum.

2. Justin, accordingly, every where declares Christ to be the true, genuine, real[2] and properly-so-called Son of God; which the Arians never did or could have acknowledged from their heart. Thus, in the first (or rather the second) Apology[l], "And His Son, who alone is properly called Son." In the second Apology[m], according to the common editions, he says: "The Son of God, who is called Jesus, even if He
[3] κοινῶς. had been man only in a sense common to all[3], would yet on account of His wisdom have been worthy to be called the Son
[180] of God, for all writers call God 'the Father of men and gods;' but if further we say that He, the Word of God,
[4] ἰδίως. was generated of God IN A PECULIAR WAY[4], beyond the generation common to all, as we said before, let this be common to us and you." A little afterwards[n] in the same work he says; "Jesus Christ alone has been in a peculiar
[5] ἰδίως. way[5] generated [as] Son unto God, being His Word and First-born and Power." Lastly, in his Dialogue with Trypho[o], he calls Christ "the Only-begotten unto the Father of
[6] ἰδίως. all, in a peculiar way[6] generated of Him, [as His] Word and Power, and afterwards made man through the Virgin." Athanasius has admirably expressed the meaning of Justin in these passages, as well as that of Holy Scripture when it calls Christ the proper and only-begotten Son of God, in these few words[p]; "For that which is naturally begotten of any one, and not taken to one's-self from without, nature recognises as a son, and this is the signification of the name [son."] See Petavius, On the Trinity, ii. 10, throughout.

[k] Κύριον καὶ Θεὸν, Θεοῦ υἱὸν ὑπάρχοντα.—p. 357. [§ 128. p. 221.]

[l] ὁ δὲ υἱὸς ἐκείνου, ὁ μόνος λεγόμενος κυρίως υἱός.—p. 44. [Apol. ii. 6. p. 92.]

[m] υἱὸς δὲ Θεοῦ, ὁ Ἰησοῦς λεγόμενος, εἰ καὶ κοινῶς μόνον ἄνθρωπος, διὰ σοφίαν ἄξιος υἱὸς Θεοῦ λέγεσθαι· Πατέρα γὰρ ἀνδρῶν τε θεῶν τε πάντες συγγραφεῖς τὸν Θεὸν καλοῦσιν. εἰ δὲ καὶ ἰδίως παρὰ τὴν κοινὴν γένεσιν γεγενῆσθαι αὐτὸν ἐκ Θεοῦ λέγομεν λόγον Θεοῦ, ὡς προέφημεν, κοινὸν τοῦτο ἔστω ὑμῖν.—p. 67. [Apol. i. 22. p. 57.]

[n] Ἰησοῦς Χριστὸς μόνος ἰδίως υἱὸς τῷ Θεῷ γεγένηται, λόγος αὐτοῦ ὑπάρχων καὶ πρωτότοκος καὶ δύναμις.—p. 68. [23. p. 57.]

[o] μονογενὴς [γὰρ ὅτι ἦν] τῷ Πατρὶ τῶν ὅλων, [οὗτὸς] ἰδίως ἐξ αὐτοῦ λόγος καὶ δύναμις γεγενημένος, καὶ ὕστερον ἄνθρωπος διὰ τῆς παρθένου γενόμενος. p. 332. [§ 105. p. 200.]

[p] τὸ γὰρ ἔκ τινος φύσει γεννώμενον, καὶ μὴ ἔξωθεν ἐπικτώμενον, υἱὸν οἶδεν ἡ φύσις, καὶ τοῦτο τοῦ ὀνόματός ἐστι τὸ σημαινόμενον.—De Decret. Nicæn. Synod. [§ 10. vol. i. p. 217.]

BOOK II. CHAP. IV. § 1—3.

JUSTIN M.

3. Besides this, Justin throughout explains the divine generation of the Son in such a manner, and illustrates it by such similes, that it is very clear that he himself entirely acknowledged His consubstantiality. There is a passage in [181] his Dialogue with Trypho especially remarkable, where he declares the mode of the generation of the Son in these words[q]; "[It has been shewn] that this power, which the word of prophecy calls both God, (as has been in like manner shewn at length,) and angel, is not, like the light of the sun, numbered[1] [as another] merely in name, but is also numerically another thing; and in what was said before I examined the reason in few words, when I said that this power was generated from the Father by His power and 66 counsel; yet not by way of abscission, as though the essence of the Father was divided off, even as all other things being severed and cut, are not the same as they were before they were cut; and I took as an example the fires which are lit as from a fire, which we see are other, and yet that fire from which many may be lit is in no way diminished, but remains the same." In these words Justin expressly teaches that the Son is indeed "numerically another thing," (*ἀριθμῷ ἕτερόν τι,*) another, that is, than the Father in number, or (in other words) in person[2], but by no means different from Him in nature; inasmuch as He was begotten[3] of the very essence of God the Father, and therefore is His Son, consubstantial with Him. For having attempted up to a certain point to unfold the mode of the generation of the Son, he says the [182] Son is begotten of the Father "not by way of abscission, as if the Father's essence were divided off," (*οὐ κατ' ἀποτομὴν, ὡς ἀπομεριζομένης τῆς τοῦ Πατρὸς οὐσίας.*) To what purpose, however, would this assertion be, if the Son in His generation have nothing in common with the substance of the Father? In the next place the simile by which Justin here

[1] ἀριθμεῖται.

[2] numero seu persona alium a Patre.

[3] progenitus.

[q] [ἀποδέδεικται] ὅτι δύναμις αὕτη, ἣν καὶ Θεὸν καλεῖ ὁ προφητικὸς λόγος, [ὡς] διὰ πολλῶν ὡσαύτως ἀποδέδεικται, καὶ ἄγγελον, οὐχ' ὡς τὸ τοῦ ἡλίου φῶς ὀνόματι μόνον ἀριθμεῖται, ἀλλὰ καὶ ἀριθμῷ ἕτερόν τι ἐστὶ, καὶ ἐν τοῖς προειρημένοις διὰ βραχέων τὸν λόγον ἐξήτασα, εἰπὼν τὴν δύναμιν ταύτην γεγενῆσθαι ἀπὸ τοῦ Πατρὸς, δυνάμει καὶ βουλῇ αὐτοῦ· ἀλλ' οὐ κατ' ἀποτομὴν, ὡς ἀπομεριζομένης τῆς τοῦ Πατρὸς οὐσίας, ὁποῖα τὰ ἄλλα πάντα μεριζόμενα καὶ τεμνόμενα οὐ τὰ αὐτά ἐστιν ἃ καὶ πρὶν τμηθῆναι· καὶ παραδείγματος χάριν παρειλήφειν τὰ ὡς ἀπὸ πυρὸς ἀναπτόμενα πυρὰ, [ἃ] ἕτερα ὁρῶμεν, οὐδὲν ἐλαττουμένου ἐκείνου, ἐξ οὗ ἀναφθῆναι πολλὰ δύνανται, ἀλλὰ ταὐτοῦ μένοντος.—p. 358. [§ 128. p. 221.]

illustrates the Catholic doctrine, manifestly confirms the consubstantiality of the Son. For he says that the Son is begotten of the Father, just as fire is kindled of fire. But who will refuse to allow that the fire which is kindled of another fire is of the self-same nature and substance as it? as Justin himself elsewhere in the same Dialogue, in shadowing forth by the same metaphor the mode of the generation of the Son, had distinctly reminded his reader. These are his words[r]; "Just as, in the case of fire, we see another produced, that from which the kindling was made being not diminished, but remaining the same as it was; whilst that which has been kindled of it, itself also is seen to exist, without having diminished that of which it was kindled." When he says here that what is kindled of fire itself, is itself fire also, he clearly means to imply that, in an analogous way[1], the Son of God, who is begotten of God Himself, is also God in the most absolute sense[2]. So bright is the light which shines forth from these passages, that Petavius, (the very same who accused Justin of Arianism,) after quoting them in part, subjoins these remarks[s]; "What can be added to this profession of the faith and of the Trinity? or what has been set forth more express, more significant, or more effectual, in the assembly of the fathers at Nice itself, or after it? For the formula which was there
[183] settled, God of God, Light of Light, very God of very God, was anticipated so long before by this sentiment of Justin: from which the consubstantiality[3] also is established, that is, the communion and identity of substance without any partition.

[1] pari ratione.
[2] Deum ipsissimum.
[3] τὸ ὁμούσιον.

4. We must, however, carefully observe, that Justin, in the first passage which we adduced in the preceding paragraph out of his Dialogue with Trypho, (and which occurs in the 358th page of the work itself,) is professedly impugning the heresy of those who were at that time teaching very nearly[4] the same as was afterwards maintained by Sabellius; namely, that[t] "The Power which came forth[5] from the Father of all things, and appeared to Moses or Jacob or Abra-

[4] fere.
[5] provenientem.

r ὁποῖον ἐπὶ πυρὸς ὁρῶμεν ἄλλο γινόμενον, οὐκ ἐλαττουμένου ἐκείνου ἐξ οὗ ἡ ἄναψις γέγονεν, ἀλλὰ τοῦ αὐτοῦ μένοντος, καὶ τὸ ἐξ αὐτοῦ ἀναφθὲν, καὶ αὐτὸ ὂν φαίνεται, οὐκ ἐλαττῶσαν ἐκεῖνο ἐξ οὗ ἀνήφθη.—p. 284. [§ 61. p. 58.]

s Præfat. in tom. ii. Theolog. Dogmat., c. 3. n. 1.

t [The Greek words are: γινώσκω τινας . . φάσκειν τὴν δύναμιν τὴν παρὰ τοῦ πατρὸς τῶν ὅλων φανεῖσαν τῷ Μωϋσεῖ ἢ τῷ Ἀβραὰμ ἢ τῷ Ἰακὼβ ἄγγελον

ham, is called an angel when He goes forth unto mankind, inasmuch as through Him the Father's commands are announced unto them; but [He is called] Glory, when at any time He is manifested in an incomprehensible splendour[1]; and again, [He is called] Man and Human being[2], when He is beheld in such forms as the Father wills; and He is called the Word, inasmuch as He conveys to men the communications that are from the Father[3]. But that that Power is indivisible and inseparable from the Father, in the same manner as they say that the light of the sun upon the earth is indivisible and inseparable from the sun which is in the heaven; and when that sets, the light is carried away along with it; in such wise [they say that] the Father, when He wills, causes His power to go forth from Himself, and, when He wills, He withdraws it back into Himself." Now these heretics, as it appears, strove to confirm their heresy by an argument derived from the confession of the Catholics, who were in the habit of teaching[4] that the Son is of the same essence with God the Father. From that, as it would seem, they framed this sophism; Either the Son is the same with the Father, and not personally distinct from Him, or we must say that the divine essence is divided into two parts, of which one constitutes the Person of
the Father, the other that of the Son. This we gather from [184]
this passage of Justin, by the following very[5] evident reasoning. There were no Catholics who asserted that the divine essence is divided; indeed Justin utterly rejects that notion as blasphemous: neither did the heretics against whom he is arguing assert it, but on the contrary, they laid down that the nature of God is unipersonal[6], with the very view of escaping from such a partition of the divine essence. It 67
remains, therefore, that those forerunners of Sabellius loaded

[1] φαντασίᾳ (Lat. visione.)

[2] ἄνδρα καὶ ἄνθρωπον.

[3] τὰς παρὰ τοῦ Π. ὁμιλίας.

[4] docerent.

[5] satis.

[6] μονοπρόσωπον.

καλεῖσθαι ἐν τῇ πρὸς ἀνθρώπους προόδῳ, ἐπειδὴ δι' αὐτῆς τὰ παρὰ τοῦ πατρὸς τοῖς ἀνθρώποις ἀγγέλλεται· δόξαν δὲ, ἐπειδὴ ἐν ἀχωρήτῳ ποτὲ φαντασίᾳ φαίνεται· ἄνδρα δέ ποτε καὶ ἄνθρωπον καλεῖσθαι, ἐπειδὴ ἐν μορφαῖς τοιαύταις σχηματιζόμενος φαίνεται, αἷσπερ βούλεται ὁ πατήρ· καὶ λόγον καλοῦσιν, ἐπειδὴ καὶ τὰς παρὰ τοῦ πατρὸς ὁμιλίας φέρει τοῖς ἀνθρώποις· ἄτμητον δὲ καὶ ἀχώριστον τοῦ πατρὸς ταύτην τὴν δύναμιν ὑπάρχειν, ὅνπερ τρόπον τὸ τοῦ ἡλίου φασὶ φῶς ἐπὶ γῆς εἶναι ἄτμητον καὶ ἀχώριστον ὄντος τοῦ ἡλίου ἐν τῷ οὐρανῷ· καὶ, ὅταν δυσῇ, συναποφέρεται τὸ φῶς· οὕτως ὁ πατὴρ, ὅταν βούληται, λέγουσι, δύναμιν αὐτοῦ προπηδᾶν ποιεῖν· καὶ, ὅταν βούληται, πάλιν ἀναστέλλει εἰς ἑαυτόν. The Latin version only is given by Bp. Bull; it has been followed in part in the translation.—§ 128. p. 221.]

ON THE CONSUBSTANTIALITY OF THE SON.

the Catholic doctrine that the Son is begotten of the substance of the Father, so as to be a distinct Person from the Father, with the weight of this invidious consequence[1], namely, that it would follow from it that the divine substance is, as it were, cut asunder and divided into two parts. Nothing is more certain. Now to meet this piece of sophistry, Justin does not deny that the Son is produced of[2] the substance of the Father; nay, he rather regards that as an undoubted truth; but he shews that the Son is generated of the Father Himself, and that in such a manner as to be a distinct Person from the Father; not by a cutting off from the Father's essence, (according to the cavils of the heretics,) but by a simple communication of essence[3]; such, almost, as is between fire, which, without any loss or diminution of itself, produces other fire, and the fire itself [thus] produced. This mode of explanation is also employed by Tatian, the disciple of Justin, (in his Oration against the Greeks,) in the following words[u]; "He was generated, however, by division[x], not by abscission. For that which is cut off is separated from the original, but that which is divided in voluntarily taking its part in the economy, does not impoverish Him from whom it is taken. For as from a single torch many fires are kindled, yet the light of the first torch is not diminished by reason of the many being kindled from it, so also the Word, [or Reason,] proceeding forth from the Power of the Father, did not cause Him who generated It to be without Word[4] [or Reason."] Now from all that has been said the result is clearly
[185] this, that the doctrine relating to the consubstantiality of the Son, that is, His being produced of the very essence and substance of God the Father, was, in the time of Justin, the received, fixed, settled, and established doctrine in the Ca-

[1] *πόρισμα.*

[2] ex.

[3] essentiæ.

[4] *ἄλογον*, without *λόγος*.

[u] *γέγονε δὲ κατὰ μερισμὸν, οὐ κατ' ἀποκοπήν· τὸ γὰρ ἀποτμηθὲν τοῦ πρώτου κεχώρισται· τὸ δὲ μερισθὲν οἰκονομίας τὴν αἵρεσιν προσλαβὸν οὐκ ἐνδεᾶ τὸν ὅθεν εἴληπται πεποίηκεν. ὥσπερ γὰρ ἀπὸ μιᾶς δαδὸς ἐνάπτεται μὲν πυρὰ πολλὰ, τῆς δὲ πρώτης δαδὸς διὰ τὴν ἔξαψιν τῶν πολλῶν δαδῶν οὐκ ἐλαττοῦται τὸ φῶς, οὕτω καὶ ὁ λόγος προελθὼν ἐκ τῆς τοῦ Πατρὸς δυνάμεως οὐκ ἄλογον πεποίηκε τὸν γεγεννηκότα.*—p. 145. [§ 5. p. 247, 248.]

[x] [*κατὰ μερισμόν.* Bp. Bull translates the words "participatione sive communicatione," by participation, or, in other words, by communication. It has been thought better to adopt the same English term as in the translations from Justin: though the word *μερισμὸς* is obviously used by Tatian in a different sense, as appears by its being opposed to *κατ' ἀποκοπήν*. Bishop Kaye translated it by "division." See his Just. Martyr, p. 162. ed. 1836.]

tholic Church: and that the heretics of those days opposed this doctrine by the very same cavils as were afterwards employed by the Arians and other heretics; and, lastly, that the Catholics of Justin's age refuted[1] that sophistry with precisely the same answer as the Catholic doctors used in silencing the Arians, after the controversy had been raised by Arius touching the doctrine "of One Substance." I would have you by all means call to mind what we said above in this book, chap. i. §§ 10, 11, 12.

5. Moreover, this same Justin, in his Dialogue with Trypho[y], shews at great length that Christ, in the Scriptures of the Old Testament, is called "God" and "Lord," "the Lord of hosts[2]," "the God of Israel;" that it was He who appeared to Abraham, Moses, and the patriarchs, whom they worshipped as their God, and who is by the Holy Ghost dignified[3] with the four-lettered name[z]. Further, those things which are spoken in these same Scriptures, and especially in the Psalms, of the supreme Lord and God of all things, these he proves to belong to Christ. Thus, for instance, after quoting that passage of David, Psalm xlv. 6, "Thy throne, O God, is for ever and ever," &c., he applies it to Christ, agreeing herein with the author of the Epistle to the Hebrews, and the most ancient Jewish teachers; and thence concludes that our [186] Saviour, *καὶ προσκυνητὸν, καὶ Θεὸν*, "both is to be worshipped and is God." That conceit had never entered into the mind of Justin, (nor indeed of any among the ancient Catholics,) by which Erasmus, and after him Grotius, seeks to evade the sense of the Psalmist's words,—both of them, I know not by what fate, born to disturb[4] all the more remarkable passages of Scripture which make for the divinity of the Son, whilst at the same time themselves appear to have acknowledged that doctrine. For Erasmus says[a], "It may be read[5]," and Grotius insists that "It ought to be read[6]," not, "O God, Thy throne is for ever and ever," but, "God Himself is Thy throne for ever and ever;" that is to say, God will uphold Thy throne for ever. What argument (unhappily[7]) could have induced these learned men to try to bring darkness over this clear testi-

[1] diluisse.
[2] Dominum virtutum.
[3] honestatur.
[4] convellenda.
[5] legi posse.
[6] legi debere.
[7] malum.

[y] p. 286, 287, [§ 63. p. 160.]

[z] ['Nomine tetragrammato;' that is, יהוה, or Jehovah.]

[a] In Not. ad Epist. ad Heb. i. 8.

mony against the Jews and judaizing Christians? "The Greek expression," says Erasmus, "is capable of two constructions[1] [b]." Be it so. Still the meaning and object of the author of the Epistle to the Hebrews is certain and clear, from the second and third verses, in which he calls Christ the Son of God, through[2] whom the worlds were made, the Brightness of the Father's Glory, the Express Image of His Essence[3], who upholdeth all things by the word of His power[4]. This divine glory and majesty of Christ, and His infinite pre-eminence above all angels and the highest orders of created beings, (in opposition, that is, to the Gnostics and other heretics, who commonly made their Æons and angels and powers equal to the Son of God[c], which ought to be particularly observed, otherwise the comparison made with so much pains, between Christ [who is] God, and the angels, who are creatures, would seem altogether without point[5],) is what the inspired author wished to prove in the following verses, down to the end of the chapter. If, however, the passage quoted from
[187] the Psalmist (verses 8, 9) be understood according to the interpretation of Erasmus and Grotius, how, I ask, does it make for the purpose of the author of the Epistle? And what man of sound mind doubts but that, in the verses immediately following, (i.e. the tenth, eleventh, and twelfth,) the author meant to shew, out of the same Psalmist, that Christ is that Lord who in the beginning laid the foundation of the earth, and with His own hands formed the heaven, who also, when the whole fabric of this world fails, will continue to eternity the same unchangeable God? Again, suppose that the words admit of two constructions, yet certainly the authority of the ancients ought to have turned the nicely-balanced scale. For Justin does not stand alone on this point; he is encompassed as it were by the whole host of the holy fathers, who all
68 with one consent take ὁ Θεὸς (God) in this passage as a vocative[d], as it is frequently employed by the LXX in the Psalms, and it is besides a familiar usage in Greek, especially in Attic Greek, to put the nominative case for the vocative. The more ancient Jews also (however the modern rabbis may trifle) interpreted this passage of the Psalmist just as we Christians do;

1 anceps.
2 per.
3 characterem essentiæ.
4 verbo suo potenti.
5 frigida.

b Vid. Poli. Syn. Crit. in Heb. i. 8. —BOWYER.

c Cf. Coloss. ii. 8—10, 18, 19.

d [Vid. Luc. xviii. 13.]

BOOK II. CHAP. IV. § 5, 6.

JUSTIN M.

Aquila, at any rate, according to the testimony of Jerome, rendered the original אלהים by the vocative Θεέ. And what Origen[e] relates is worthy to be remarked, that he once pressed a Jew, who was esteemed a wise man amongst his people, closely with this testimony; and that he, being unable to escape from the difficulty, answered as became a Jew, that is to say, that these words, "Thy throne, O God, is for ever and ever, a sceptre of righteousness[1] is the sceptre of Thy kingdom," referred to the God of the universe; whilst the passage, "Thou hast loved righteousness, and hated iniquity," &c., referred to the Messiah. That learned Jew, you see, though fully prepared and ready to escape by any other way whatever, never even dreamt of the conceit of Erasmus and Grotius, that God is the throne of the Messiah. At the same time we accept from Grotius his concession, that "for ὁ Θεὸς the Hebrew is אלהים; a name which is wont to be applied both to angels and judges, when more than one; but when it is applied to one only, as here, it belongs to God alone, because it is then an elliptical expression or אלהי אלהים God of gods." This however is a digression. I return to Justin. [188]

[1] directionis.

6. There is another passage of our author well worthy of notice; it occurs later in the same dialogue[f]. Trypho here interprets the testimony of Isaiah, "There shall come forth a Branch out of the root of Jesse, and the Spirit of God shall rest upon Him," of Christ, as indeed he was bound to do, and then puts this question to Justin on the subject of that testimony; "You both affirm that He was previously in being as God, and also affirm that according to the counsel and will[2] of God, having been made flesh, He was born man through the Virgin; how [then] can He be proved to have been previously in being who is being fulfilled through the powers of the Holy Spirit, which the word enumerates through Isaiah, as though He were wanting in these?" To this question Justin replies thus[g]; "Your enquiry is most sensible and intelli-

[2] de consilio et voluntate.

[e] Contr. Cels. i. p. 43. [§ 56. p. 371.]

[f] καὶ Θεὸν αὐτὸν προυπάρχοντα λέγεις, καὶ κατὰ τὴν βουλὴν τοῦ Θεοῦ σαρκοποιηθέντα αὐτὸν λέγεις διὰ τῆς παρθένου γεγενῆσθαι ἄνθρωπον, πῶς δύναται ἀποδειχθῆναι προυπάρχων, ὅστις διὰ τῶν δυνάμεων τοῦ πνεύματος τοῦ ἁγίου, ἃς καταριθμεῖ ὁ λόγος διὰ Ἡσαίου, πληροῦται, ὡς ἐνδεὴς τούτων ὑπάρχων.—p. 314. [§ 87. p. 184.]

[g] νουνεχέστατα μὲν καὶ συνετώτατα ἠρώτησας· ἀληθῶς γὰρ ἀπόρημα δοκεῖ εἶναι· ἀλλ' ἵνα ἴδῃς καὶ τὸν περὶ τούτων λόγον, ἄκουε ὧν λέγω. ταύτας τὰς κατη-

gent; for, in truth, there does appear to be a difficulty[1]. Hear, however, what I have to say, in order that you may see the account to be given of these points also. With respect to these powers of the Holy Spirit which are enumerated, the word says that they have come upon Him, not as implying that He was wanting in them, but that they were about to make their rest on Him, that is, to terminate in Him, so that no longer, as in the days of old, were prophets to arise in your nation. Which you may see even with your own eyes, for after Him hath no prophet at all arisen amongst
[189] you." I own that Justin's interpretation of the prophet's words is a strange one; for it is obvious to all that they are to be explained as referring to the man Christ, enriched, beyond all others, with the gifts of the Holy Ghost. At the same time it is clear from this place that Justin held that this was to be taken as a certain and settled point, that the Son of God, as being [Himself] very God, is, in His own nature, most complete and perfect, wanting in nothing, and having no need at any time even of the gifts of the Holy Ghost Himself. For Trypho's argument is plainly this; He that is very God[2] cannot possibly be wanting in any thing; but Christ, according to the testimony of Isaiah, was wanting in the gifts of the Holy Ghost; therefore Christ is not very God, as you, Justin, maintain. Justin admits the major premiss, but denies the minor, and that on good grounds; for the dispute between himself and Trypho was concerning Christ as God; although, as I have already said, he interprets the passage of Isaiah incorrectly. If, on the other hand, Justin had held the same view as Arius, he might most easily and without any trouble have replied to Trypho, that there is nothing absurd in laying down that the Son of God was wanting in the grace of God; and was capable of improvement[3], inasmuch as He is a creature, and made God by adoption. Certainly Arius did not hesitate to say openly that the Son of God was liable to change and alteration, and

[1] ἀπόρημα.

[2] verus Deus.

[3] et in melius proficere potuisse.

ριθμημένας τοῦ πνεύματος δυνάμεις, οὐχ' ὡς ἐνδεοῦς αὐτοῦ τούτων ὄντος, φησὶν ὁ λόγος ἐπεληλυθέναι ἐπ' αὐτὸν, ἀλλ' ὡς ἐπ' ἐκεῖνον ἀνάπαυσιν μελλουσῶν ποιεῖσθαι, τουτέστιν, ἐπ' αὐτοῦ πέρας ποιεῖσθαι, τοῦ μηκέτι ἐν τῷ γένει ὑμῶν κατὰ τὸ παλαιὸν ἔθος προφήτας γενήσεσθαι. ὅπερ καὶ ὄψει ὑμῖν ἰδεῖν ἐστι· μετ' ἐκεῖνον γὰρ οὐδεὶς ὅλως προφήτης παρ' ὑμῖν γεγένηται.—[Ibid.]

BOOK II. CHAP. IV. § 6, 7.

JUSTIN M.

was, by reason of[1] the freedom of His will, capable of virtue and vice; as is manifest from the epistle of Alexander addressed to his brethren, catholic bishops[2] throughout the world[h], and from the synodical letter of the Nicene fathers, [190] and lastly, from the Nicene Creed itself. If, however, Justin had made this reply, he would have completely overthrown his own previous argument; inasmuch as in that he is wholly intent on proving, that our Saviour is very God, and to be worshipped.

[1] pro.
[2] co-episcopos.

7. In another place also, I mean in the Hortatory Address to the Greeks[i], Justin observes, that He who appeared to Moses in the bush, (whom he uniformly declares to have been the Son of God,) speaks of Himself as the "I am," (τὸν ὄντα), and then he expressly remarks, that this designation "belongs to the ever-existing God," (τῷ ἀεὶ ὄντι Θεῷ προσήκειν). We shall adduce the passage entire in a more fitting 69
place, that is, in the following book, concerning the co-eternity of the Son. To this we must add a very illustrious passage of Justin, contained in his admirable epistle to Diognetus. That this epistle is a genuine work of our author, is not doubted (so far as I am aware) by any learned man of the present day; hence Scultetus classes it amongst those writings which are by common consent attributed to Justin. The objection raised by Sandius[k], that Bellarmine did not even enumerate this epistle in the list of Justin's works, is altogether frivolous; forasmuch as it is plain that Bellarmine followed Robert Stephens' edition of the works of Justin, printed at Paris in the year 1551, in which the Address to the Greeks, and the Epistle to Diognetus are omitted. Afterwards, however, in the year 1592, these works were edited separately by Robert Stephens' son, Henry, accompanied with a Latin version of his own and copious annotations. Hence the Address to the Greeks too, as it was wanting in Robert Stephens' edition, is also omitted in Bellarmine's catalogue. Its genuineness, however, will not be doubted of by any one who shall read it atten- [191]
tively, and compare it with Justin Martyr's other writings. But with respect to the epistle to Diognetus, Frederick

[h] Vide Socrat. H. E., i. 6, and 9.

[i] pp. 19, 20. [§ 21. p. 22. quoted at length iii. 2. 2.]

[k] De Script. Eccl., p. 20.

ON THE CONSUBSTANTIALITY OF THE SON.

Sylburg[1] has justly remarked, that, when compared with his other works, it will be found to breathe the spirit of Justin, and to have many points in common with the rest of his writings. But what need is there to say much? Sandius himself in another place (*Enucl. Hist. Eccl.* p. 76,) recognises this epistle as the genuine work of Justin. Let us now recite the very full testimony which we undertook to produce out of this epistle. It is as follows[m]: "The Almighty and all-creating and invisible God Himself hath Himself from heaven established[n] the Truth and the holy and incomprehensible Word amongst men; and hath fixed It in their hearts; not, as one might suppose, by sending unto men A MINISTER—either angel, or prince, or any one of those who order things on earth, or any of those to whom hath been entrusted the administration of things in heaven; but THE VERY FRAMER AND CREATOR of the universe Himself; by Whom He founded the heavens, by Whom He shut in the sea within its proper bounds; Whose mysteries all the elements do faithfully observe; from Whom [the sun] hath[o] received to observe the due measures of the course of the day; Whom the moon obeys when He bids her shine by night; Whom the stars obey as they follow the course of the moon; by Whom all things have been arranged, and determined, and placed in due subjection, the heavens and all that is in the heavens, the earth and all that is in the earth, the sea and all that is in the sea, fire, air, and the abyss; all that is in the heights above, all that is in the depths beneath, and all

[1] In a note to page 501. v. 43. of the works of Justin.

[m] αὐτὸς ὁ παντοκράτωρ καὶ παντοκτίστης καὶ ἀόρατος Θεὸς, αὐτὸς ἀπ' οὐρανῶν τὴν ἀλήθειαν καὶ τὸν λόγον τὸν ἅγιον καὶ ἀπερινόητον ἀνθρώποις ἐνίδρυται, καὶ ἐγκατεστήριξε ταῖς καρδίαις αὐτῶν· οὐ καθάπερ ἄν τις εἰκάσειεν, ἀνθρώποις ὑπηρέτην τινὰ πέμψας, ἢ ἄγγελον, ἢ ἄρχοντα, ἤ τινὰ τῶν διεπόντων τὰ ἐπίγεια, ἤ τινὰ τῶν πεπιστευμένων τὰς ἐν οὐρανοῖς διοικήσεις· ἀλλ' αὐτὸν τὸν τεχνίτην καὶ δημιουργὸν τῶν ὅλων· ᾧ τοὺς οὐρανοὺς ἔκτισεν· ᾧ τὴν θάλασσαν ἰδίοις ὅροις ἐνέκλεισεν. οὗ τὰ μυστήρια πιστῶς πάντα φυλάσσει τὰ στοιχεῖα· παρ' οὗ τὰ μέτρα τῶν τῆς ἡμέρας δρόμων εἴληφε φυλάσσειν· ᾧ πειθαρχεῖ σελήνη, νυκτὶ φαίνειν κελεύοντι· ᾧ πειθαρχεῖ τὰ ἄστρα, τῷ τῆς σελήνης ἀκολουθοῦντα δρόμῳ· ᾧ πάντα διατέτακται καὶ διώρισται καὶ ὑποτέτακται, οὐρανοὶ καὶ τὰ ἐν οὐρανοῖς· γῆ καὶ τὰ ἐν τῇ γῇ· θάλασσα καὶ τὰ ἐν τῇ θαλάσσῃ· πῦρ, ἀὴρ, ἄβυσσος. τὰ ἐν ὕψεσι, τὰ ἐν βάθεσι, τὰ ἐν τῷ μεταξύ· τοῦτον πρὸς αὐτοὺς ἀπέστειλεν· ἆρά γε, ὡς ἀνθρώπων ἄν τις λογίσαιτο, ἐπὶ τυραννίδι, καὶ φόβῳ, καὶ καταπλήξει; οὔ μενοῦν· ἀλλ' ἐν ἐπιεικείᾳ (καὶ) πραΰτητι, ὡς βασιλεὺς πέμπων υἱὸν βασιλέα ἔπεμψεν· ὡς Θεὸν ἔπεμψεν· ὡς πρὸς ἀνθρώπους ἔπεμψεν· ὡς σώζων ἔπεμψεν· κ.τ.λ. —Justin, Epist. ad Diog., p. 498. [§ 7. p. 237.]

[n] ἐνίδρυται, otherwise read ἐνίδρυσε.

[o] Stephens remarks, that the word ἥλιος (the sun) is wanting before εἴληφε, or after φυλάσσειν. Perhaps, however, instead of εἴληφε φυλάσσειν, (hath received to observe,) we ought to read ἥλιος φυλάσσει, (the sun observes.)

that is in the region that lies between. This One sent He unto them. Was it then, as any one of men might suppose, for despotic sway, and fear, and terror? In no wise; but rather, in clemency and meekness; even as a King sending His Son, a King, He sent Him; as God[p] He sent Him; as unto men He sent Him; as willing to save He sent Him." A [192]
passage most worthy of all attention, as admirably describing the profound mystery of the redemption of man, and as also affording the means of setting right[1] all the passages in which the holy writer may seem to speak with too little [193]
honour of the Son of God. So far, however, as relates to our present purpose, what could have been said more distinct than this in defence of the true divinity of the Son against the blasphemy of Arius? Justin expressly denies that the Word, or Son of God, is a minister (ὑπηρέτην), or creature, (for these two words are equivalent, as I have several times observed, and as, indeed, is of itself evident enough;) calling Him incomprehensible and the very Framer and Creator of all things, on whose will depends, and by whose power is upheld the whole fabric of the universe, whether of heaven or of earth; and to whom all creatures, of what rank soever, 70
are in subjection and obedience, as unto their Author, their God, and their Lord. He says also that He was sent into this world as a King by a King, as God by God; that is in effect, the Son, a King, [sent] by the Father, a King; the Son, God, [sent] by the Father, God[q]. I have observed above[r], that the passage of S. Paul to the Philippians, ii. 6, &c., and a parallel passage[2] in Clement's epistle to the Corinthians, receive very clear light from this passage of Justin Martyr, as they in turn throw light on it; whether I made that assertion rashly[3] or not, the intelligent[4] reader will now be able to judge. What is said by Paul concerning Christ before His humiliation[5], that He then subsisted "in the form of God," and by Clement, that He was "the sceptre of the Majesty of God," this Justin so sets forth, as to say that Christ in that state was "not a minister of God,"

[1] medelam.

[2] ei geminum.

[3] temere.

[4] cordatus.

[5] κένωσιν, lit. 'emptying of Himself.'

[p] That is to say, who is beneficent and kindly in His nature, and full of love to mankind. See Clement of Alexandria, Pædag. p. 109. [p. 131.] p. 113, [135.] and compare 1 John iv. 8. ["God is love."]

[q] [There is more on this passage in Bp. Bull's reply to G. Clerke, § 20.—B.]

[r] See of this book ch. 3. § 4.

ON THE CONSUBSTANTIALITY OF THE SON.

(inasmuch as He had not yet assumed the form of a servant, or in other words, a created nature,) but "the Lord and Creator of the universe Himself." What Paul says, that Christ afterwards "took the form of a servant, and was made man;" the same is [in effect] said by Justin, when he declares that the Word, or Son of God, being sent from heaven,
[194] "was placed amongst men." Lastly, what Paul teaches, that Christ, when He came into the world, "did not make a display of[1] His equality with God the Father, but emptied Himself;" what Clement also says, that "Christ came not in the boasting of pride and arrogancy, although it was in His power [so to have come], but in humility;" the same is meant by Justin, when he adds that the Word and Son of God was not sent into the world by the Father "in despotic sway, and fear, and terror:" that is, not with a display of the dreadful majesty of His Godhead[2], but "with clemency and meekness, as one who was sent unto men." Certainly no more apt comparison of passages can be imagined.

[1] non venditasse.

[2] tremendæ suæ majestatis divinæ.

8. I will conclude my citations out of Justin with a passage taken from his second Apology, so-called, in which the holy martyr explicitly acknowledges a perfect Trinity of divine Persons, who ought conjointly to be adored with the same religious worship, and who alone, to the exclusion of all created beings, are worthy of that kind of adoration. For in this passage Justin replies to the heathen, who accused the Christians of atheism for repudiating the worship of idols, that they are not atheists, forasmuch as, though they do despise and set at nought the gods of the Gentiles, falsely so called and accounted, yet they do most religiously worship and reverence One true[3] God, in three distinct Persons[4]. His words are these[s]: "We confess, indeed, that in respect of such supposed gods we are atheists, but not in respect of the most true God, the Father of righteousness and temperance and all other virtues, in Whom is no admixture of evil. But we worship and adore both Him, and His Son, Who came from Him, (and hath taught us

[3] unum et verum.

[4] tribus personis distinctum.

[s] καὶ ὁμολογοῦμεν τῶν τοιούτων νομιζομένων θεῶν ἄθεοι εἶναι· ἀλλ' οὐχὶ τοῦ ἀληθεστάτου, καὶ Πατρὸς δικαιοσύνης καὶ σωφροσύνης καὶ τῶν ἄλλων ἀρετῶν, ἀνεπιμίκτου τε κακίας Θεοῦ· ἀλλ' ἐκεῖνόν τε, καὶ τὸν παρ' αὐτοῦ υἱὸν ἐλθοντα, καὶ διδάξαντα ἡμᾶς ταῦτα καὶ τὸν τῶν ἄλλων ἑπομένων καὶ ἐξομοιουμένων ἀγαθῶν ἀγγέλων στρατὸν, πνεῦμά τε τὸ προφητικὸν σεβόμεθα καὶ προσκυνοῦμεν, λόγῳ καὶ ἀληθείᾳ τιμῶντες. — p. 56. [Apol. i. 6. p. 47.]

BOOK II. CHAP. IV. § 7, 8.

JUSTIN M.

[respecting][t] these things and [respecting] the host of the other good angels, who follow Him and are made like unto Him,) and the prophetic[1] Spirit, honouring Them in reason[2] and truth." From this passage, indeed, Bellarmine endeavours to establish the religious adoration of angels; which inference of his, (if it be valid,) will entirely subvert the argument which I have derived from this place, in favour of the true divinity of the Son and the Holy Ghost. That is to say, Bellarmine, after the words, *διδάξαντα ἡμᾶς ταῦτα*, ("Who hath taught us [respecting] these things,") inserts a stop[3], and reads; "But we worship and adore both Him and His Son, who came from Him, and hath taught us these things, and the host of the other good angels, who follow Him and are like unto Him, and the Holy Ghost," &c. But Scultetus[u] kindled with just indignation[4], meets him with this severe and acute reply: "But what reason," he says, "does he adduce for this little note of punctuation, devised in the Roman Lycæum? He adduces none; therefore we reject the sophistical comma[5] of Perionius. Justin uniformly teaches, that the Son hath revealed all things, and even God Himself, to us; in this passage he adds, that by Him we have also been instructed concerning the ministry of angels. Was then this to be dissevered from its context by the jesuitical clause[6], that so by the suffrage of Justin also the superstitious worship of angels might be established? You did not perceive, sycophant, that if your little stop were admitted, the Holy Ghost would (contrary to the uniform tenor of Justin's views[7]) be made inferior to the angels, inasmuch as He would have to be worshipped only in the fourth place. Had you turned over a single page, you would have seen the clouds which obscure the present passage, dispelled by the very clear light of another place[x], where he teaches, that the Father is worshipped by Christians in the first place, the Son in the second, and the Holy Ghost in the third; not that the angels are worshipped in the place next to the Son, nor even in the fourth place, nor in the fifth. You should have consulted the Dialogue with Trypho, as it is entitled,

[195]

[196]

[1] sanctum, Lat. vers.

[2] ratione, Lat. vers.

[3] distinctionis notam.

[4] ardore.

[5] incisum.

[6] articulo Jesuitico.

[7] perpetuum Justini sensum.

[t] [In translating this passage Bp. Bull's rendering has necessarily been adhered to.]

[u] Medulla Patrum, in the compendium of Justin Martyr's doctrine, chap. 18.

[x] [See § 13. pp. 60, 61.]

ON THE CONSUBSTANTIALITY OF THE SON.

and you would have found it proved from the divine worship[1] paid to Him, that the Angel who appeared to Lot was the Son of God; which proof would have had no force, on the supposition of worship[2] being paid to angelic creatures." To this you may add, what indeed ought to be especially noticed, that in those very words of Justin, from which
71 Bellarmine wished to educe[3] the adoration of angels, angels are expressly called following or attendant[4] spirits[z] (*τοὺς ἑπομένους*), (he calls them ministers, (*ὑπηρέτας*), in the passage just now adduced from the epistle to Diognetus, wherein also he excepts from the number and rank of ministers, the Son of God, as he does both the Son and the Holy Ghost, in this passage,) whence it follows that they are in no wise to be worshipped[5]. But, you will ask, with what view is the mention of our being taught respecting the ministry of the good angels by the Son of God, parenthetically inserted when he is speaking of the Son? My reply is, that the parenthesis has reference (and I wish the reader to note this carefully) to what had immediately preceded in the same passage of Justin; Justin had asserted that Socrates was put to death by wicked men, at the instigation of the devil, as being an atheist and an impious man, because he maintained that we are to worship the One true God alone, putting away the idols of the Gentiles as demons, that is, as evil spirits, enemies to God; then he adds, that precisely the same had happened
[197] to Christians. His words are[a]: "And in like manner in our case do they effect the same; for not only among the Greeks were these things proved [against them], by a word, through Socrates, but among barbarians also, by the Word Himself, having assumed a [bodily] form, and become man, and been called Jesus Christ. In Whom believing, we declare that the demons, who did such things, not only are not upright beings[b], but are evil and unholy spirits, who in

1 cultu adorationis.
2 adoratio.
3 exsculpere.
4 sequentes sive famulantes.
5 adorandos.

z That is, a metaphorical expression derived from the servants (pedissequi, "lackeys,") who are accustomed to follow their masters.

a *καὶ ὁμοίως ἐφ' ἡμῶν τὸ αὐτὸ ἐνεργοῦσιν· οὐ γὰρ μόνον Ἕλλησι διὰ Σωκράτους ὑπὸ λόγου ἠλέγχθη ταῦτα, ἀλλὰ καὶ ἐν βαρβάροις ὑπ' αὐτοῦ τοῦ λόγου μορφωθέντος καὶ ἀνθρώπου γενομένου, καὶ Ἰησοῦ Χριστοῦ κληθέντος. ᾧ πεισθέντες ἡμεῖς τοὺς ταῦτα πράξαντας δαίμονας οὐ μόνον μὴ ὀρθοὺς εἶναι φαμὲν, ἀλλὰ κακοὺς καὶ ἀνοσίους δαίμονας, οἳ οὐδὲ τοῖς ἀρετὴν ποθοῦσιν ἀνθρώποις τὰς πράξεις ὁμοίας ἔχουσι.*—[Ibid.]

b Grabe in his Adversaria reads *θεούς*. BOWYER.

BOOK II. CHAP. IV. § 8. JUSTIN M.

their actions are not even like such men as are seeking after virtue." Now, after he had said that by the faith of Christ we had been instructed to shun the worship of wicked angels, he most appositely adds immediately after, in the parenthesis we are speaking of, that by the same Christ we have also been instructed concerning other, that is, good, angels, as concerning spirits, who along with ourselves do service to God, and consequently are not by any means to be worshipped; so that the words in the parenthesis are altogether to be construed and expounded to this effect; "Who hath taught us these things, namely, what had gone before, about not worshipping the wicked angels, and also about the host of holy angels, which do service to God and imitate His goodness." The sum of the matter is this; We have been instructed by Christ as well respecting wicked as good angels; of the wicked [we have been taught] that they are evil spirits and rebels against God, and therefore worthy rather of execration than of adoration; of the good, that they are spirits which serve and obey God, and after their own poor measure imitate His goodness; and so not even they are to be worshipped[c]. This passage, consequently, is [198]
so far from making at all in favour of Bellarmine and the Papists, that, on the contrary, it furnishes an invincible argument against the religious worship of angels; and most clearly shews, that, according to the mind of the primitive Christians, a worship[1] of that kind ought not to be paid either to angels or to any order of beings who serve and wait upon God, (that is to say, to any order of created beings,) but unto the most Holy Trinity alone, Who created all things, and

[1] cultus.

[c] Justin, however, in the words which have thus far been explained, [by Bp. Bull in the text,] rather means that Christ manifested, or more clearly revealed, to the angels, as well as to men, the justice and the other attributes of God the Father; as I have said in my notes on this passage of Justin, p. 11. of my edition, and proved from parallel words out of Irenæus. GRABE. [The Benedictine editor rejects both these interpretations—Bull's and Grabe's—and strongly contends that Justin's words speak of the worship of angels. Bull has more on this point in his answer to G. Clerke, § 20.—B.] [Le Nourry and others agree with Bp. Bull; Cave and Waterland with Grabe; Bp. Kaye (On Justin Martyr, p. 52. note 7,) construes the clause as Bellarmine does, and suggests that the heavenly host are mentioned subordinately, and that the words καὶ τὸν ... στρατὸν are equivalent to μετὰ τοῦ ... στρατοῦ, Justin having in his mind the glorified state of Christ, surrounded by the host of heaven; and he quotes, in confirmation of this view, passages from Justin. Others, who adopt the mode of construction which Bull mentions as Bellarmine's, shew that it does not involve the assertion that the angels were worshipped with the worship given to God.]

ON THE CONSUBSTANTIALITY OF THE SON.

unto Whom all things are subject, the Father, Son, and Holy Ghost; a statement which entirely overthrows the inventions of the Arians also, and of all other anti-trinitarians. For the rest, those passages of Justin, which some have imagined to be inconsistent with these, we shall afterwards consider in our own fourth book, on the subordination of the Son to the Father. I fear however that I may there omit one passage objected by Sandius, that, I mean, in which Justin is said to have taught, that the Son of God is "a created angel!" Let the reader, however, be assured that such a passage is no where found in the writings of Justin; but that Sandius, shamelessly, as his way is, has falsely attributed it to the most holy martyr. I now pass on from Justin to other fathers.

9. Athenagoras[d], in his Apology[1] for the Christians, most explicitly acknowledges the community of nature and essence which exists between the Father and the Son; for, with the view of explaining to the heathen philosophers, who
[199] that Son of God is, whom the Christians worship, he says[e]: "But the Son of God is the Word[2] of the Father, in idea and in operation. For by Him[3] and through Him were all things made, the Father and the Son being One; and, the Son being in the Father, and the Father in the Son, by the unity and power of the Spirit[f]: the Son of God is the mind and Word[4] of God." What Arian ever spoke thus of the Son of God? He says, that the Father and the Son are one; and that not only by an agreement of will[5], as the Arians con-
72 tended; but by a mutual περιχώρησις, "*circumincessione*," as the schoolmen express it, so that the Son is in the Father and the Father in the Son. He says, that the Son is the very Mind and Word of God the Father; in what sense this is to be understood we shall explain afterwards[g]; meanwhile it is certain that it cannot in any sense be reconciled with the Arian doctrine. Nor must we overlook the fact that Athenagoras, in treating of the work of creation, which in the Scriptures

[1] Legatione.
[2] λόγος ἐν ἰδέᾳ καὶ ἐνεργείᾳ.
[3] πρὸς αὐτοῦ.
[4] νοῦς καὶ λόγος.
[5] consensu.

[d] Athenagoras flourished about the year 177. Cave.—BOWYER.

[e] ἀλλ' ἔστιν ὁ υἱὸς τοῦ Θεοῦ λόγος τοῦ πατρὸς ἐν ἰδέᾳ καὶ ἐνεργείᾳ. πρὸς αὐτοῦ γὰρ καὶ δι' αὐτοῦ πάντα ἐγένετο, ἑνὸς ὄντος τοῦ πατρὸς καὶ τοῦ υἱοῦ· ὄντος δὲ τοῦ υἱοῦ ἐν πατρὶ, καὶ πατρὸς ἐν υἱῷ, ἑνότητι καὶ δυνάμει πνεύματος, νοῦς καὶ λόγος τοῦ πατρὸς ὁ υἱὸς τοῦ Θεοῦ.—p. 10. ad calcem Just. Mart. edit. Paris. 1615. [§ 10. p. 286, 287.]

[f] [The words are so understood by Bp. Bull, ii. 3, 14.]

[g] Book III. 5. § 4—6.

is attributed to the Son of God, teaches, that the universe was created, not only δι' αὐτοῦ, "through" the Son, which the Arians were willing to allow, (understanding, of course, 'through Him' to mean, through Him as an instrument, which of itself has no power to do any thing,) but also πρὸς αὐτοῦ[h], "by Him," that is, as, conjoined with the Father, the primary efficient cause; and that with the addition of [200]
this reason, that the Father and the Son are one[1], in essence, that is to say, and nature, and consequently in power[2] and operation; which is diametrically opposed to the Arian heresy. Presently after, however, in the same passage, Athenagoras distinctly denies, that the Son in the beginning came forth from the Father to create all things "as made," (ὡς γενόμενον) or created by God, [a denial] which aims a deadly blow[3] at the Arian blasphemy. We shall hereafter bring forward the passage entire, in our third book[i]. A few words after he makes a full confession of the consubstantial[4] Trinity, in these words[k]; "Who then would not think it strange, to hear us called atheists, who speak of God the Father and God the Son, and the Holy Ghost, shewing both Their power in unity and Their distinction in order?" Parallel to this is the exposition of the view of Christians touching the most holy Trinity, which he advances elsewhere in the same[l] book, conceived in the following terms: "We speak of God, and the Son His Word, and the Holy Ghost, being one[5] indeed in power, the Father, the Son, and the Spirit[6]: in that the Son is the Mind, Word, Wisdom, of the Father, and the Spirit an effluence[7], as light from fire." Where he very plainly enough infers that the Father, the Son, and the Holy Ghost are one God, from this, that there is one only foun-

[1] unum sint.
[2] virtute.
[3] jugulum ipsum petit.
[4] τῆς ὁμοουσίου τριάδος.
[5] ἑνούμενα.
[6] Spiritum Sanctum. Bull.
[7] ἀπόρροια.

[h] ["I dislike this reading very much. For it is not (as the learned Bull thought) equivalent to ὑπ' αὐτοῦ: nor can any instance be brought forward in which all things are said to have been created πρὸς τοῦ λόγου, instead of, what is very often used, ὑπὸ τοῦ λόγου. If, however, we read πρὸς αὐτὸν, a very good meaning will come out, that is to say, that all things were created 'after' the Word, that is, after the pattern delineated in the Word; 'omnia secundum Verbum, sive secundum exemplar in Verbo descriptum creata esse.'" Edit. Benedict.—B.]

[i] Chap. v. 2.

[k] τίς οὖν οὐκ ἂν ἀπορήσαι, λέγοντας Θεὸν πατέρα καὶ υἱὸν Θεὸν καὶ πνεῦμα ἅγιον, δεικνύντας αὐτῶν καὶ τὴν ἐν τῇ ἑνώσει δύναμιν, καὶ τὴν ἐν τῇ τάξει διαίρεσιν, ἀκούσας ἀθέους καλουμένους.—p. 11. [p. 287.]

[l] Θεὸν φαμὲν, καὶ υἱὸν τὸν λόγον αὐτοῦ, καὶ πνεῦμα ἅγιον, ἑνούμενα μὲν κατὰ δύναμιν, τὸν πατέρα, τὸν υἱὸν, τὸ πνευμα· ὅτι νοῦς, λόγος, σοφία υἱὸς τοῦ πατρὸς, καὶ ἀπόρροια, ὡς φῶς ἀπὸ πυρὸς, τὸ πνεῦμα.—p. 27. [§ 24. p. 302.]

tain of Deity, namely the Father, from whose essence[1] the Son and the Holy Ghost are derived, and that in such wise, as that the Son is the λόγος, [Word or Wisdom,] from everlasting existing and springing out of the very mind of the Father, (for that this was Athenagoras' meaning we shall 201 clearly prove hereafter,) and that the Holy Ghost also flows forth and emanates from God the Father Himself[2], (through the Son, that is to say, as we have shewn above,) as light proceeds from fire. In passing you may observe, how completely Athenagoras acknowledged the consubstantiality of the Holy Ghost, equally with that of the Son. This divine philosopher, however, immediately[3] proceeds in the same passage to mention the angels, whom he styles *ἑτέρας δυνάμεις*, "powers, other and different from" the Father, the Son, and the Holy Ghost; inasmuch as they are very far[4] removed from that uncreated nature in which the Father, the Son, and the Holy Ghost have their subsistence. On this account he soon after expressly says, that the angels were "made" by God (*γενομένους*). As for those passages which Petavius, Sandius, and others have produced out of Athenagoras as favourable to Arianism, we shall afterwards (in the third book[m] on the co-eternity of the Son) shew, that they have been alleged by them to no purpose. And indeed, respecting the other Fathers of the first three centuries, I once for all inform my reader, that whatever passages alleged out of them by sophists in support of Arianism, I have passed over in this book, these I have carefully weighed elsewhere, either in that third book, or in the fourth, on the subordination of the Son, and, if I mistake not, have given a clear account of them. And thus much concerning Athenagoras.

[1] ex cujus essentia.

[2] ex ipso Deo Patre.

[3] ἀμέσως.

[4] longissime.

10. We have already[n] heard TATIAN declaring, that the Son is begotten of God the Father, *οὐ κατ' ἀποκοπήν*, "not by an abscission," *ἀλλὰ κατὰ μερισμόν*, "but by a participation[5]," or communication of the Father's essence, just as one fire is lighted from another; now this, as we at the time shewed, clearly shews the consubstantiality of the Son. [202] THEOPHILUS of Antioch[o] in his books addressed to Autoly-

[5] [or "division," see above, p. 140.]

[m] Chapter v. throughout.

[n] See the fourth section of this chapter, [p. 140.]

[o] Theophilus was promoted to the Bishopric of Antioch, circa an. 168. Cave.—BOWYER.

cus, which alone out of his numerous writings are extant at this day, has some passages which remarkably confirm the catholic doctrine. Thus in the second book[p]; "The Word being God, and[1] born of God," (Θεὸς ὢν ὁ λόγος, καὶ ἐκ Θεοῦ πεφυκώς:) in which words he infers that the Son is God, from the circumstance that He is born of God Himself[q]; that is, according to the rule which I have elsewhere[r] given from Irenæus[s]; "Whatsoever is begotten of God, is God," (τὸ ἐκ Θεοῦ γεννηθὲν Θεός ἐστι.) Theophilus had shortly before informed us, that by the Son of God we must doubtless understand "the Word, which exists perpetually laid up in the heart of God," (τὸν λόγον, τὸν ὄντα διαπαντὸς ἐνδιάθετον ἐν καρδίᾳ Θεοῦ,) manifestly implying, that the Son has an eternal subsistence in the very essence of God the Father. That Theophilus also recognised the entire most Holy Trinity, is clear from those words of his in which he teaches, that the three days, which preceded the creation of the sun and the moon, were types "of the Trinity, that is, of God, and of His Word, and of His Wisdom," (τῆς τριάδος, τοῦ Θεοῦ, καὶ τοῦ λόγου αὐτοῦ, καὶ τῆς σοφίας αὐτοῦ[t].) It is true that Petavius, who seems to have read the writings of the primitive fathers for the very purpose of finding or making blemishes[2] and errors in them, endeavours from these very words of Theophilus to construct a charge against that excellent father. His words are these[u]: "Theophilus' explanation of the Trinity is widely different from what the Christian confession of It allows; seeing that he calls those three days, which, at
the beginning of the world, preceded the production of the [203]
sun and of the moon, a figure 'of the Trinity, that is, of God, 73
and of His Word, and of His Wisdom.' He makes no mention there of the Spirit, Whom he appears to have confounded with the Word; for we have before shewn that he called the same Being the Word and Spirit of God, and truly [His] Wisdom." Now to this I reply, that, as well on account of Their common nature, as of Their common deri-

[1] utpote, "as being." Bull.

[2] nævos.

[p] Θεὸς ὢν ὁ λόγος, καὶ ἐκ Θεοῦ πεφυκώς.—p. 100. [§ 22. p. 365.]

[q] [The Latin version of Bp. Bull is Deus existens sermo, *utpote* ex Deo progenitus; this particular portion of his argument is grounded on that translation.]

[r] [p. 102.]

[s] Lib. i. p. 39. GRABE. [I. 8. 5. p. 41.]

[t] p. 94 [§ 15. p. 360.]

[u] Petav. de Trin. i. 3. 6.

ON THE CONSUBSTANTIALITY OF THE SON.

[1] ab eadem πηγῇ Θεότητος.

vation from one and the same fountain of Godhead[1], the ancients used to make the names also of the second and the third Persons [of the Trinity] common. Hence, as the name "Spirit of God," which more frequently marks the third divine Person, is (as I have shewn already[y]) sometimes applied by them to the second Person; so the name Wisdom, though it is used for the most part to denote the second Person, is occasionally employed to designate the third. And, besides Theophilus, we shall elsewhere[z] have to observe that this was done also by Irenæus and Origen; and yet these holy fathers must not on that account be regarded as confounding the second and the third Persons of the Trinity; forasmuch as it is most manifest from their writings, and that from those very passages in which they interchange the names of either [Person,] that they did themselves account the Son and the Holy Ghost to be Persons really distinct from each other. And with respect to Theophilus, every one must see that his words are of themselves sufficient for their own vindication? For how it is to be supposed that he confounded the Holy Ghost, the third Person of the Godhead, with the Word, when he expressly confesses *τὴν τριάδα*, the Trinity? What? Can the Father and the Son, without the Spirit, or a third Person distinct from both, constitute a Trinity? It is clear, therefore, that Theophilus confused the names only, not the Persons, of the Son and the Holy Ghost. But concerning Theophilus of Antioch, this is enough at present.

LUCIAN.

[204] 11. And here I entreat the reader to allow me to turn aside for a moment from the remains of the holy fathers to the writings of a heathen. The author of the dialogue, ascribed to Lucian, which is entitled Philopatris, toward the conclusion[a] by way of ridicule introduces a Christian catechising a heathen, (whom, on that account, he somewhere in the Dialogue expressly calls a catechumen,) and amongst other subjects explaining to him the mystery of the most Holy Trinity. Upon the heathen asking the Christian, "By whom then shall I swear?" Triephon, who sustains the part of the Christian, replies[b], "'By the God who reigns on high,

[y] [i. 2. 5. p. 48.]

[z] See c. v. § 7. of this book, and iv. 3—11.

[a] [Vol. iii. p. 596. ed. Hemsterhus.]

[b] Ὑψιμέδοντα Θεὸν, μέγαν, ἄμβροτον, οὐρανίωνα,
υἱὸν πατρὸς, πνεῦμα ἐκ πατρὸς ἐκπορευό-

great, immortal, celestial, the Son of the Father, the Spirit Who proceeds from the Father, One of Three[1], and Three of One[2]: believe These to be Jove, and esteem Him God." To which the heathen after some other matters thus retorts[3]; "I know not what thou sayest; One Three, Three One[d]!" Truly he must have bad sight, who does not perceive, that in these words is most clearly taught a Trinity of one substance[4], or one God subsisting in three Persons. And there is no doubt but that the author derived this from the system of teaching[5] of the Christians of his own age. Now if this Dialogue was written by Lucian, he flourished under Marcus Antoninus, (as the great I. Gerard Vossius has most clearly proved,) that is about the year of our Lord 170, a little after the time of Justin; so that he was contemporary with Tatian and Athenagoras, whose doctrine we have just been explaining. But James Micyllus in his Introduction[6] says, there is ground for doubt, whether this Dialogue be Lucian's; since, though in its matter it be not unlike his characteristic genius and wit, yet its style, and indeed its general construction, are quite unlike the rest of Lucian's [205] writings; and some other learned men besides have followed this opinion of Micyllus. That writer, however, adds as follows; "Whoever," he says, "was the author of this Dialogue, it seems to have been his special object to offer congratulation to the Emperor Trajan on a victory obtained in the east, in opposition to those persons who at that period forboded dangers and ruin either to Rome herself, or to some other place (for he only calls it their country[7]): these from the first he calls sophists, but at last he describes them in such a way, that he almost seems to mean the Christians. For this is the bearing of what he says at the end about Persian pride, Susa, and the whole region of Arabia. For all these were at that time conquered by Trajan and reduced beneath the power of Rome, as may be seen in Dion, Eutropius, and the other historians of that period." Now, if this view of the case be a true one, we may then easily gather hence, what the faith of the Christians was, touching the

[1] ἓν ἐκ τριῶν.
[2] τρία ἐξ ἑνός.
[3] regerit.
[4] ὁμοούσιον.
[5] disciplina.
[6] in Argumento.
[7] patriam.

μενον, ἓν ἐκ τριῶν, καὶ ἐξ ἑνὸς τρία· ταῦτα νόμιζε Ζῆνα, τὸν δὲ ἥγου Θεόν. —[Ibid.]

[d] Οὐκ οἶδα τί λέγεις· ἓν τρία, τρία ἕν.

[e] De Histor. Græc. ii. 15.

ON THE CONSUBSTANTIALITY OF THE SON.

most Holy Trinity, even in the reign of Trajan, long before the age of Lucian. I should, however, rather believe that the allusion at the end of the Dialogue is to a victory over the Persians gained by Marcus Antoninus, in whose reign, as we have already said, Lucian flourished. For thus Sextus Aurelius Victor[f] writes of him: "Under his conduct, the Persians, though at first victorious, at last yielded up the palm." Just so the author of the Dialogue likewise, towards the conclusion, introduces one Cleolaus, hurrying and panting to bring these joyful tidings, *Πέπτωκεν ὀφρὺς ἡ πάλαι βοωμένη Περσῶν, καὶ Σοῦσα, κλεινὸν ἄστυ*: "The long vaunted pride of the Persians is fallen; and Susa, that noted city!" There is, however, a further, and that no obscure, indication
[206] of the age of Marcus Antoninus, in the circumstance, that in this Dialogue certain persons are remarked on, who lamented the very heavy and unwonted calamities, with which the Roman state was then afflicted, and foreboded in consequence still worse evils. Now hear what Aurelius Victor in his
74 Epitome says respecting the commencement of this emperor's reign. His words are; "Marcus Antoninus reigned 18 years. He was a man endowed with all virtues and a heavenly cast of mind, and was stationed as a living outwork against the miseries of the state. For had he not been born for those times, surely all parts of the Roman empire must have fallen, as with one crash. For nowhere was there any repose from arms. Throughout the entire east, Illyricum, Italy, and Gaul, wars were raging. There were earthquakes, with destruction of cities; rivers overflowed their banks, pestilences were frequent, and a sort of locusts infested the lands; so

[f] Ejus ductu Persæ, cum primum superavissent, ad extremum triumpho cessere.—In libro de Cæsaribus in M. Aurel. Antonino. [Marcus Antoninus did not go in person to the Eastern wars. The antecedent, to which the words of the historian as quoted in the text refer, is undoubtedly his colleague Lucius Verus, to whom the command was entrusted: "Lucium Verum in societatem potentiæ accepit. Ejus ductu Persæ, cum primum superavissent, ad extremum triumpho cessere, Rege Vologesæ."—Aur. Victor. de Cæsaribus. 16. p. 260. ed. Schott.]

[g] M. Antonius, inquit, imperavit annos 18. Iste virtutum omnium cœlestisque ingenii extitit, ærumnisque publicis quasi defensor objectus est. Etenim nisi ad illa tempora natus esset, profecto quasi uno lapsu ruissent omnia status Romani. Quippe ab armis nusquam quies erat; perque omnem orientem, Illyricum, Italiam, Galliamque bella fervebant; terræ-motus non sine interitu civitatum, inundationes fluminum, lues crebræ, locustarum species agris infestæ; prorsus ut prope nihil, quo summis angoribus atteri mortales solent, dici seu cogitari queat, quod non illo imperante sævierit.—[Ibid.]

that one may almost say, that no one thing, which is wont to afflict mankind with the heaviest suffering, can be mentioned or conceived of, which did not rage during this emperor's reign." The dialogue in question therefore was written, either by Lucian himself (as I am inclined to think), or at any rate by a contemporary of Lucian; and that is just as suitable for our present purpose. Let us now hear what Sandius advances in opposition to this testimony; his words are, "I should say for my part[h], that Tryphon" (he ought to have called him Triephon, or Triepho) "represents that class of men, concerning whom we read in Clement of Rome, (Constitutions vi. 25,) Ignatius to the Trallians, Tarsians and Philippians, and also in Justin, against Trypho, who are earlier than Lucian." The fact is, he has himself no scruple in saying, devising, inventing any thing, if only it ministers anyhow to his impious cause. For any one may perceive, that the author of the Dialogue is not exhibiting for ridicule merely a particular and obscure sect of Christians, but the Christian religion itself! Besides, the heretics, who [207]
are mentioned in the Pseudo-Clement, in the interpolated Ignatius, and in Justin, affirmed the Son to be Him who is God over all things, that is to say, God the Father Himself. Whereas, in this brief confession of the Trinity, "the God who reigns on high," that is, the Father, is first mentioned as the fountain of Godhead; then the Son of the Father is subjoined, as a Person distinct from that supreme God and Parent of all; nevertheless He, with the Holy Ghost, is represented as so intimately conjoined in nature with God the Father, as that the Three constitute but One God, and yet in very deed continue Three; a doctrine which is, and ever has been, held by Catholics; but which differs entirely from the opinions of those heretics of whom Sandius was dreaming. Furthermore Critias, the counterfeit catechumen, derides this doctrine as incomprehensible[1]; "I do not understand," says he, "what thou affirmest; One, Three; and Three, One!" But the heretics alluded to by Sandius, avouched an opinion wherein is nothing incomprehensible; for they made God unipersonal (*μονοπρόσωπον*), that is, one only and singular Person[2]; called merely, according to His

[1] ἀκατάληπτον.

[2] unam et singularem Personam.

[h] Enucl. Histor. Eccl. i. p. 88.

ON THE CONSUBSTANTIALITY OF THE SON.

[1] φάσις.

threefold aspect[1] (so to say) sometimes the Father, sometimes the Son, and sometimes again the Holy Ghost. Lastly, Critias, afterwards in the same Dialogue, (taught, you will observe, by Tricphon,) scoffingly swears by the Son after this manner: "By the Son, Him who is of the Father, this shall in no wise be;" *Νὴ τὸν υἱὸν τὸν ἐκ Πατρὸς, οὐ τοῦτο γενήσεται.* Now the Catholics acknowledged the Son to be

[2] ἐκ.

Him who is of[2] the Father; not so those heretics whose opinion Sandius pretends is set forth in this dialogue. The whole point admits of no doubt. From the profane author I return to the holy doctors of the Church.

77
[212]

CHAPTER V.

SETTING FORTH THE DOCTRINE OF IRENÆUS CONCERNING THE SON OF GOD, MOST PLAINLY CONFIRMATORY OF THE NICENE CREED.

1. Let us now carefully attend to what that holy bishop and martyr, Irenæus[i], both learned of his apostolic instructor, Polycarp, and himself taught to others, concerning the true divinity of the Son of God. I have already pledged[k] myself to adduce marked testimonies out of this writer against the Arians; whether I have, in this present chapter, fulfilled my promise, let the reader whose mind is not altogether prejudiced, judge. In his third book, chap. 6[l], Irenæus is wholly occupied in proving this point; that "Neither the Lord, nor the Holy Ghost, nor the Apostles, ever gave to him who was not God, the name of God definitely and absolutely, if he were not very God. Nor called any one Lord in his own person, but Him, who is Lord of all, God the Father and His Son." He soon after quotes that testimony out of the forty-fifth

[i] He was born A.D. 97, and wrote his work Adv. Hæreses, A.D. 175. Cave.—Bowyer.

[k] [p. 134.]

[l] Neque Dominus, neque Spiritus S. neque apostoli, eum qui non esset Deus, definitive et absolute Deum nominassent aliquando, nisi esset verus Deus; neque Dominum appellassent aliquem ex sua persona, nisi qui dominatur omnium, Deum Patrem et Filium ejus, &c.—Chap. 3. § 18. Grabe. [p. 167.]

BOOK II. CHAP. V. § 1, 2. IRENÆUS.

Psalm, cited also by Justin[i], "Thy throne, O God, is for ever," &c.; and thus comments on it[j]; "The Spirit hath signified both under the appellation of God, as well Him who is anointed, the Son, as Him who anoints, i. e. the Father." From which we construct an argument to this effect; Whosoever in the Scriptures is absolutely and definitely called God, is God in very deed; but the Son, equally with the Father, is in the Scriptures absolutely and definitely called God; therefore the Son, equally with the Father, is God in very deed. The premises are Irenæus's; therefore also is the [213] conclusion which necessarily follows from them. He subsequently remarks that[k], "when the Scripture names those [as gods] that are not gods, it does not set them forth as gods altogether[1], but with some addition and intimation by which they are set forth as not being gods."

[1] in totum.

2. To this must be joined a passage in book iv. chap. 11[l]. "For our Lord and Master," he says, "in the answer which He made to the Sadducees, (who say that there is no resurrection, and thereby dishonour God and detract from the law,) both shewed the resurrection, and also revealed God; declaring to them; 'Ye do err, not knowing the Scriptures nor the power of God. For,' He said, 'as touching the resurrection of the dead, have ye not read that which was spoken by God, saying, I am the God of Abraham, and the God of Isaac, and the God of Jacob?' And added, 'He is not the God of the dead, but of the living: for all live unto Him.' By these words He has made it clear that He, who spake unto Moses out of the bush, and manifested Himself to be God the Father, He is the God of the living. For who

[i] [See chap. 4. § 5. of this book.]

[j] Utrosque Dei appellatione significavit Spiritus, et eum qui ungitur Filium, et eum qui ungit, id est, Patrem. —[Ibid.]

[k] Cum eos, qui non sunt dii, nominat, non in totum scriptura ostendit illos deos, sed cum aliquo additamento et significatione, per quam ostenduntur non esse dii.—[§ 3. p. 181.]

[l] Dominus enim noster, et Magister in ea responsione, quam habuit ad Sadducæos, qui dicunt resurrectionem non esse, et propter hoc inhonorantes Deum atque legi detrahentes, et resurrectionem ostendit, et Deum manifestavit, dicens eis, *Erratis nescientes Scripturas, neque virtutem Dei. De resurrectione*, inquit, *mortuorum non legistis quid dictum est a Deo dicente, Ego sum Deus Abraham, et Deus Isaac, et Deus Jacob?* et adjecit, *Non est Deus mortuorum, sed viventium; omnes enim ei vivunt.* Per hæc utique manifestum fecit, quoniam is qui de rubo locutus est Moysi, et manifestavit se esse Deum Patrem, hic est viventium Deus. Quis enim est vivorum Deus, nisi qui est super omnia Deus, super quem alius non est Deus? . . . .

is the God of the living, but He who is God over all[1] [m], over whom there is no other God?" And a little afterwards; "He, therefore, who was worshipped by the prophets as the living God, He is the God of the living, and His Word, who also spake unto Moses, who also refuted the Sadducees, who also was the Giver of the resurrection." Then after a short space he thus concludes: "Christ, therefore, Himself with the Father is the God of the living, who spake unto Moses, and was manifested also to the fathers." What can be more plain than this? I mean that, according to Irenæus, He who spoke
[214] to Moses out of the bush and revealed Himself to the patriarchs, is the living God, the God of the living, God over all, and over whom there is no other god: but, according to the same Irenæus, it was Christ Himself with the Father, who spake unto Moses and was manifested to the fathers. Now what follows from these things? What, but that Christ Himself with the Father is the living God, the God of the living, God over all, and over whom there is no other God; which is also affirmed by Irenæus in so many words[2].

[1] super omnia.

[2] in terminis.

3. This is more fully confirmed by the fact, that Irenæus also, iii. 18[n], cites the testimony of the Apostle (Romans ix. 5) in the same words, and in the same sense, as Catholics of the present time receive them. For, with the view of proving against the heretics, "that Jesus was not one, and Christ another, but one and the same;" after other things he thus adduces that passage of Paul[n]: "And again, writing to the Romans concerning Israel, he says; 'Whose are the fathers, and of whom according to the flesh [is] Christ, who is God
78 over all, blessed for ever.'" Erasmus, however, (whom some others have followed,) has endeavoured to render uncertain even this irrefragable evidence for the true divinity of the Son; for he has devised three constructions of these words, of which one only acknowledges the Godhead of the Son. The very ancient father Irenæus, however, recognised none other

Qui igitur a prophetis adorabatur Deus vivus, hic est vivorum Deus, et Verbum ejus, qui et locutus est Moysi, qui et Sadducæos redarguit, qui et resurrectionem donavit. . . . . Ipse igitur Christus cum Patre vivorum est Deus, qui locutus est Moysi, qui et Patribus manifestatus est.—[cap. v. 2. p. 232.]

[m] [The words 'super omnia' are rejected by the Benedictine editor.—B.]

[n] Neque alium [quidem] Jesum, alterum [autem] Christum [suspicaremur] fuisse, sed unum et eundem [sciremus] esse ... et iterum ad Romanos scribens de Israel, dicit; *Quorum Patres, et ex quibus Christus secundum carnem, qui est Deus super omnes benedictus in sæcula.*—[cap. xvi. 3. p. 205.]

BOOK II. CHAP. V. § 2—4. IRENÆUS.

than the received reading and construction. And with Irenæus agree Tertullian in his Treatise against Praxeas, c. xiii. [p. 507.], &c.; xv. [p. 509.] Novatian on the Trinity, c. xiii. and xxx.[o]; Cyprian, Testimonies against the Jews, book ii.[p], (although Erasmus stated the contrary, being misled by a faulty copy of Cyprian); Origen on Romans ix. 5[q]; Athanasius, Orations ii. and v. against the Arians, and in his work on the Common Essence[r]; Gregory Nyssen against Eunomius, book x.[s]; Marius Victorinus against Arius, book i.[t]; Hilary, books iv. and viii.[u]; Ambrose, on the Holy Spirit, book i. c. 3[v]; and on the Faith, book iv. c. 6[w]; Augustin on the Trinity, book ii. c. 13[x], also against Faustus, book xii. c. 3 and 6[y]; Cyril, in book i. of the *Thesaurus*[z]; Idacius against Varimadus[a], book i.; Cassian on the Incarnation, book iii., near the beginning[b]; Gregory the Great in his Eighth Homily on Ezekiel[c]; Isidore of Seville in his book on Difference, num. 2[d]; and almost all the other fathers, "who" (as Petavius[e] says) "convict Erasmus of unthinking rashness, in that he hesitated not to declare; 'They who contend that from this passage there is evident proof that Christ is expressly called God, appear either to place little reliance on other testimonies of Scripture, or not to give the Arians credit for any ability, or to consider with little attention the words[1] of the Apostle.'" This, as Petavius adds, is a false and shameless assertion of his, for which he was reproved even by Beza. But I return to Irenæus. [215]

[1] sermonem.

4. There is a very illustrious passage of his, in book iv. c. 8, in which he says[f]; "God maketh all things in measure and order, and nothing is not measured with Him, because nothing

[See Wisd. xi. 20.]

[o] [pp. 715, and 729.]

[p] [c. vi. p. 286.]

[q] [Vol. iv. p. 612. To these Antenicene testimonies add Hippolytus, (cont. Noet. 2. vol. ii. p. 7, &c., 6. p. 10.) Dionysius of Alexandria, (p. 246. and 248; Epist. Syn. Concil. Antioch.) —B.]

[r] [Athanas. Orat. i. 11. vol. i. p. 415; Orat. iv. 1. p. 617; Epist. ii. ad Serap. ii. p. 684; Epist. ad Epict. 10. p. 908; De communi essentia, 27. vol. ii. p. 16.]

[s] [Vol. ii. p. 693.]

[t] [Ap. Bibl. Patr. Max. Lugd. 1677, t. iv. p. 258.]

[u] [De Trin. iv. § 39. p. 850; viii. § 37. p. 970.]

[v] [§ 46. t. ii. p. 609.]

[w] [c. xi. § 133. t. ii. p. 546.]

[x] [§ 23. t. viii. p. 785.]

[y] [t. viii. pp. 228, 229.]

[z] [t. v. p. 20.]

[a] [Bibl. Patr. Max., t. v. p. 728.]

[b] [c. 1. p. 984.]

[c] [Lib. i. Hom. 8. § 3. tom. i. p. 1236.]

[d] [De different. Spirit., § 2. p. 185.]

[e] De Trin. ii. 9. 2.

[f] Omnia, inquit, mensura et ordine Deus facit, et nihil non mensum apud eum, quoniam nec incompositum [ἅπαντα μέτρῳ καὶ τάξει ὁ Θεὸς ποιεῖ, καὶ οὐδὲν ἄμετρον παρ' αὐτοῦ, ὅτι μηδὲν ἀνα-

ON THE CONSUBSTANTIALITY OF THE SON.

[1] ἀναρίθμητον, incompositum. [2] capit. [3] quantus quantus sit.

is unnumbered[1], and [he spoke] well, who said, that the immeasurable Father Himself is measured in the Son. For the Son is the measure of the Father, since He also contains[2] Him." What can be clearer than this? He teaches that the Son is commensurate with the immeasurable Father, and that He contains and comprehends Him wholly, how great soever He be[3]; consequently that the Son is equal to the Father in all things, with this single exception, that He is from the Father. For with Irenæus, to contain the greatness of the
[216] Father is the same as to be equal to the Father, as is evident from another passage in his works (i. 1,) where he relates the fable of Valentinus, namely, that Bythus (Depth) begat Nus (Mind)[g], "similar and equal to him, who had put him forth, and alone containing the greatness of his father." It is, moreover, to be observed, that this is not a single testimony, nor that of Irenæus alone, but that it declares the mind of another catholic writer, earlier than he, or, at all events, his contemporary, whose words he here quotes. But see how the author of the Irenicum endeavours to evade this invincible testimony of Irenæus. He replies forsooth[h]; "Irenæus does not here speak of every measure, by which the Son may measure the Father; but either of that measure of which he had just been treating, namely, the Son's fulfilling, perfecting, and comprehending such things in the law, as had hitherto been measured and determined with the Father[4]; or, if he speaks of any other measure besides, that of knowledge for instance, he means that it is perfect of its kind, but not therefore[5] absolutely supreme." To this I answer: In the first place, what the heretic says in reply concerning the fulfilment, perfection, and comprehension of the law by[6] Christ, is mere sophistry. For those words of the passage on which our proof rests, namely, "the immeasurable Father Himself is measured in the Son," &c., are not immediately connected with what Irenæus had stated respecting the law, at the beginning of the chapter. I mean, he there affirms, that the ancient ritual law had had its own time measured and defined by God, so, that is, that it should begin

[4] apud Patrem. [5] mox. [6] per.

ρίθμητον.] Et bene qui dixit, ipsum immensum Patrem in Filio mensuratum. Mensura enim Patris Filius, quoniam et capit eum."—[c. iv. 2. p. 231.]

[g] ὁμοιόν τε καὶ ἴσον τῷ προβαλόντι, καὶ μόνον χωροῦντα τὸ μέγεθος τοῦ Πατρός.—[p. 5.]

[h] Irenic. p. 46.

with Moses and terminate with John [the Baptist.] And then passing from the particular to the universal, he incidentally teaches, that God made all things whatsoever in measure and order, and that there is nothing that is not measured with God[1]. Whilst, however, he is thinking on these things, as if his mind was by a sudden flight uplifted, (a transition, which [217]
is by no means uncommon on other occasions in writers of this character,) the Saint perceives that God so loves measure and proportion, that not even to Himself would He choose to have measure lacking, whereby His own infinitude and immensity should be, as it were, circumscribed and contained. And this he confirms by this remarkable and excellent saying of a certain catholic writer; "The immeasurable Father Himself is measured in the Son," &c. But soon recollecting himself, and, as it were, quitting that sublime flight, he returns to his subject, shewing that the entire dispensation of the Old Testament[2] was temporal. Any one will easily see that this is a correct analysis of the chapter, who reads it with any attention whatever[3]. Besides, who is so foolish as seriously to suppose that the words, "the immeasurable Father Himself is measured in the Son," &c., merely mean this; that God willed that the ritual law of Moses should have its own definite time, and that, as it commenced with Moses, so at length being fulfilled through Christ, it should cease and be abolished? For in this passage Irenæus is evidently treating, not of the moral law, which is perpetual and everlasting; but of what is called the ceremonial law, even of that which[1] "began with Moses," and "in due course terminated in John," and of that "giving of the law[4]," which "was to come to an end, at the revelation of the New Testament." Secondly, as to the other interpretation of the anonymous writer, Irenæus expressly speaks not of a measure which is perfect in its own kind, whatever that be, but of a supreme[5] and adequate measure, such an one, that is, wherein the im- 79
measurable Father Himself, how immeasurable soever He be, may be measured. There is certainly a marked emphasis on the word *ipsum*, (Himself); so that the sentence, *ipsum im-*

[1] apud Deum.

[2] totam V. Test. administrationem.

[3] non oscitanter.

[4] et de legisdatione.

[5] summa.

1 [Irenæus' words are; Lex] a Moyse inchoavit, ... consequenter in Joanne desivit; . . . [Hierusalem adimplens tempora sua legisdationis] finem oportuit habere, manifestato Novo Testamento.—[iv. 2. p. 231.]

ON THE CONSUBSTANTIALITY OF THE SON.

[218]

mensum Patrem in Filio mensuratum, &c., ("the immeasurable Father *Himself* is measured in the Son,") can have no other meaning than that the Father, in so far as He is immeasurable, i.e. in so far as He cannot be contained by any creature, is yet comprehended by the Son. Gregory Thaumaturgus has given the sense of the passage, and I am inclined to think he had the passage itself in his view, in his panegyric oration on Origen, at the place where he says, that God the Father by His Son, "goes forth and surrounds[1]" Himself; an expression, which he presently explains by saying, that the Son enjoys "that power [which is] in all respects equal to the Father's;" (τῇ ἴσῃ πάντῃ δυνάμει τῇ αὐτοῦ.) We shall give the entire passage afterwards[j]. Thirdly, the sophist's endeavour to elude the force of this passage of Irenæus by means of that other, not far from the beginning of the fifth book, is altogether vain. For Irenæus does not there say, that man contains the greatness of the Father, or that the immeasurable Father Himself is measured in him; and again, in another passage, (book iv. chapter 37), he clearly explains in what manner a pious man is said up to a certain point[2] to contain the Father. His words are[k]; "For the prophets signified beforehand, that God should be seen by men, as the Lord also says, 'Blessed are the pure in heart, for they shall see God.' But in respect of His greatness and His wonderful glory, no man shall see God and live; for the Father is incomprehensible[3]; in respect, however, of His love and mercy, and because He can do all things[4], He does grant even this to such as love Him, that is, to see God." Here Irenæus expressly asserts, that the pure in heart do not see God, or comprehend Him in respect of His greatness and wonderful glory, since in this respect God is incomprehensible, that is to say, by [mere] man or any other creature; (on which account also he had said in the same passage, a little before, that God[1] "in His greatness is unknown to all those, who have

[1] ἐκπεριϊέναι.

[2] aliquatenus.

[3] incapabilis.

[4] et quod omnia possit.

[j] Chap. 12. § 4.

[k] Præsignificabant enim prophetæ quoniam videbitur Deus ab hominibus, quemadmodum et Dominus ait, *Beati mundo corde, quoniam ipsi Deum videbunt.* Sed secundum magnitudinem quidem ejus, et mirabilem gloriam, *nemo videbit Deum et vivet;* incapabilis enim Pater; secundum autem dilectionem et humanitatem, et quod omnia possit, etiam hoc concedit iis qui se diligunt, id est, videre Deum.—p. 370. [c. xx. 5. p. 254.]

[1] Secundum magnitudinem ignotus est omnibus his qui ab eo facti sunt.—[Ibid.]

been made by Him;") yet in the passage of which we are treating, he clearly teaches, that the Son of God comprehends His Father even according to His greatness; viz., in such a manner, as that the immeasurable Father Himself is measured in His Son. On a subject evident to all men there is no need to say more.

5. It would be well nigh endless, were I to adduce all the passages of Irenæus, which go to confirm the consubstantiality of the Son. I shall therefore be satisfied when I have added to the testimonies of the blessed martyr already brought forward one or two more, which quite give a death blow to the Arian heresy. In book ii. c. 43. he represses and beats down the monstrous pride of the Valentinians, who arrogated to themselves a sort of omniscience, by drawing a most excellent comparison between a [mere] man and the Son of God: his words are these[m]: "But further, if any one be unable to discover the cause of all the things which are sought after, let him reflect that man is infinitely inferior to God, and [is a being] that has received grace [only] in part, and that is not yet equal, or like unto his Maker, and that cannot possess acquaintance with[1], and power of reflecting upon all things as God does. For in proportion as he, who is a creature of to-day, and has received a beginning of created existence, is inferior to Him, who is not made and who is always the same,—just in the same proportion is he inferior to His Maker in knowledge, and in [the capacity of] investigating[2] the causes of all things. FOR THOU ART NOT UNCREATED, O MAN; NOR WAST THOU ALWAYS COEXISTENT WITH GOD, LIKE HIS OWN WORD; but on account of His eminent goodness, now receiving a beginning of created existence, thou art gradually learning from the Word the dispensations of God, who made thee. Keep therefore the place[3] of thy knowledge, and [219]

[1] experientiam.

[2] ad investigandum.

[3] ordinem.

[m] Si autem et aliquis non invenerit causam omnium quæ requiruntur, cogitet quia homo est in infinitum minor Deo, et qui ex parte acceperit gratiam, et qui nondum æqualis vel similis sit factori, et qui omnium experientiam et cogitationem habere non possit ut Deus: sed in quantum minor est ab eo qui factus non est, et qui semper idem est, ille qui hodie factus est et initium facturæ accepit, in tantum secundum scientiam, et ad investigandum causas omnium, minorem esse eo qui fecit. NON ENIM INFECTUS ES, O HOMO, NEQUE SEMPER COEXISTEBAS DEO, SICUT PROPRIUM EJUS VERBUM; sed propter eminentem bonitatem ejus, nunc initium facturæ accipiens, sensim discis a Verbo dispositiones Dei, qui te fecit. Ordinem ego serva tuæ scientiæ, et ne ut bonorum ignarus supertranscendas ipsum Deum.—[c. xxv. 3. p. 153.]

ON THE CONSUBSTANTIALITY OF THE SON.

do not, as one ignorant of what is good, seek to transcend God Himself[n]." These words shine forth with so clear a light, that they require not any commentary whatever or inference of mine. There is, however, another passage parallel to this, book iii. c. 8, in which Irenæus in like manner institutes a
[220] comparison between the Word, or Son of God, and the creatures; it is as follows[o]; "None of all the things, which were created[1] and are in subjection, must be compared to the Word of God, through whom all things were made, who is our Lord Jesus Christ. For whether they be angels or archangels, or thrones, or dominions, that they were created[2] and made by Him, who is God over all, through His Word, John for his part has thus intimated: in that, when he had said concerning the Word of God, that He was in the Father, he added, 'All things were made by[3] Him, and without Him was not any thing made.' David also, after he had enumerated His praises—all the things severally[4] which we have mentioned,—both the heavens and all the powers thereof,—added, 'For He commanded, and they were created; He spake, and they were made.' Whom then did He command? His Word surely, through whom, he says, 'the heavens were established, and all the host of them by the Spirit of His mouth.' But that He made all things freely and after His own will, David says again, 'Whatsoever things He would, them did our God make in the heavens above, and in the earth also.' But the things which were created[5], are different from Him who created them, and the things which were made, different from Him who made them.

[1] constituta.

[2] constituta.

[3] per.

[4] nominatim.

Ps. cxlviii. 5.

Ps. xxxiii. 6.

Ps. cxxxv. 5.

[5] constituta.

[n] [See these words quoted again in iii. 2. 4.—B.]

[o] Sed nec quidquam, ex his quæ constituta sunt, et in subjectione sunt, comparabitur Verbo Dei, per quem facta sunt omnia, qui est Dominus noster Jesus Christus. Quoniam enim sive angeli, sive archangeli, sive throni, sive dominationes, ab eo, qui super omnes est Deus, et constituta sunt et facta per Verbum ejus, Joannes quidem sic significavit. Cum enim dixisset de Verbo Dei, quoniam erat in Patre, adjecit, *Omnia per eum facta sunt, et sine eo factum est nihil.* David quoque, cum laudationes enumerasset, nominatim universa quæcumque diximus, et cœlos, et omnes virtutes eorum, adjecit, *Quoniam ipse præcepit, et creata sunt; ipse dixit, et facta sunt.* Cui ergo præcepit? Verbo scilicet, per quod, inquit, *Cœli firmati sunt, et Spiritu oris ejus omnis virtus eorum.* Quoniam autem ipse omnia fecit libere, et quemadmodum voluit, ait iterum David, *Deus autem noster in cœlis sursum, et in terra, omnia, quæcumque voluit, fecit.* Altera autem sunt quæ constituta sunt ab eo qui constituit, et quæ facta sunt ab eo qui fecit. Ipse enim infectus, et sine initio, et sine fine, et nullius indigens, ipse sibi sufficiens, et adhuc reliquis omnibus, ut sint, hoc ipsum præstans: quæ vero ab eo sunt facta, initium

BOOK II. CHAP. V. § 5.

IRENÆUS.

For He Himself is uncreated, without either beginning or
end, wanting nothing, Himself sufficient unto Himself, and,
besides, bestowing on all others this very gift of being[1];
but the things which have been made by Him have had
a beginning; but whatever things have had a beginning,
are capable of dissolution, and have been made subject, and
stand in need of Him Who made them; it is [therefore]
absolutely necessary that they should have a different appel- 80
lation, even amongst those who possess but a slight power of
discrimination in such subjects; so that He who made all
things is, TOGETHER WITH HIS WORD, justly called God and
Lord alone; but those things which are made, are thereby[2]
incapable of sharing this same appellation; nor ought they in [221]
justice to assume that name which belongs to the Creator."
In this passage Irenæus plainly teaches, that the Word, or
Son of God, is separated by an interval so infinite from all
things which are created, made, and placed in subjection,
(though they be creatures of the highest order, whether, that
is to say, they be angels or archangels, or thrones, or dominions,)
that they are not worthy in any way to come into
comparison with Him, even for this very reason that they
are created, made, and placed in subjection. He teaches,
that the Son of God also is, just as His Father, uncreate
and eternal, wanting nothing, self-sufficient, and furthermore
conferring on all creatures the gift of being. He moreover
expressly declares, that the Word, or Son of God, inasmuch
as both He Himself is uncreated, and all things were
made through Him, ought to be admitted to partake of the
Divine Name together with His Father; whilst as respects all
other beings, which have been created and made, it is altogether
by a misapplication and an improper use of the word[3]
that we give to them the appellation, Lord, or God, which
belongs peculiarly to the Creator. In fine, he asserts all this
with so great earnestness, as to declare that those who cannot
in this manner distinguish and discriminate an uncreated

[1] et adhuc reliquis omnibus, ut sint hoc ipsum præstans.

[2] jam.

[3] abusive atque improprie omnino.

sumpserunt; quæcumque autem initium sumpserunt, et dissolutionem possunt percipere, et subjecta sunt, et indigent ejus qui se fecit; necesse est omnino, uti differens vocabulum habeant, apud eos etiam, qui vel modicum sensum in discernendo talia habent; ita ut is quidem, qui omnia fecerit, CUM VERBO SUO, juste dicatur Deus et Dominus solus; quæ autem facta sunt, non jam ejusdem vocabuli participabilia esse, neque juste id vocabulum sumere debere, quod est Creatoris.—[p. 183.]

nature from created things, are absolutely devoid of common sense. I question, indeed, whether any thing more effectual than this against the Arian blasphemy was ever uttered or advanced by any one of the Catholic doctors, who wrote after the council of Nice.

6. Yet not even this passage of Irenæus could escape the criticism of Petavius; for from the circumstance that this excellent father, after he had quoted the words of the Psalmist, "For He commanded and they were created," &c.; added "Whom then did He command? His Word surely;" the Jesuit infers[p], that a subordinate operation and ministerial function[1] [only] in the creation of the universe, is attributed by him to the Son of God, such as he intimates in book iv. chap. 17[q]. But who can fail to feel the want of fairness and candour here exhibited by Petavius? How easy [222] was it for him, to give a sound interpretation to Irenæus's words from the very context itself! As thus[2]; God gave commandment to His Word for the creation of the world, not as a master to a servant, (for Irenæus, in the very same passage, distinctly excepts the Son of God from the class of those things which are created, and made, and put in subjection,) but as the Father to the Son, of the same uncreated nature as Himself, and a partner of the divine dominion and power. God, moreover, gave commandment to His Son that the world should be made, in other words, He willed that the world should be created by His Word, the will of the Word Himself concurring thereunto. Accordingly, Petavius himself in another place, as if forgetful of his own declaration[3], acknowledges that Irenæus's statements in this passage are catholic, and that some ancient writers, who lived after the Nicene Council, and were most energetic opponents of the Arian heresy, used the same way of speaking without giving any offence. For in his work, on the Trinity, book ii.[r], he writes thus; "There are some writers, who have used the same way of speaking, without any offence whatever, taking the words ('Let us make man,' &c., Genesis i. 26) to imply a command and precept of the Father. For so Irenæus says,

[1] ὑπουργίαν quandam et ministri functionem.

[2] scilicet.

[3] sui oblitus.

[p] Petavius *de Trinit.* I. 3. 7. See also Sandius, *Enucleat. Hist. Eccles.* i. p. 91.

[q] [c. 7. 4. p. 236.]

[r] c. 7. n. 7.

BOOK II. CHAP. V. § 5, 6.

IRENÆUS.

that the Word is uncreated and eternal, and that God gave unto Him commandment to create all things. And elsewhere[s], that man was created, 'the Father willing and commanding, the Son executing and creating.' Basil[t] also speaks both of the Lord as commanding (προστάσσοντα), and of the Word as accomplishing the creation (δημιουργοῦντα λόγον); so Cyril again, in the twenty-ninth Book of his *Thesaurus*[u]; [223]
and Athanasius, in his treatise on the decrees of the Council of Nice[v], explains the words of the thirty-second Psalm, 'He commanded, and they were created,' in such a manner, as to understand that the Father gave command to the Son. Marius Victor likewise, in his first book on the Creation of the World, thus speaks; 'Which, when the Almighty Son filled with His Father's mind created at the commandment of God.' The author, moreover, of a treatise on the Incarnation which is extant in the fourth volume of Augustine's works[w], says, that the Son ministered to the Father in all the work of creation[1], inasmuch as through Him all things were made. To the same effect are the words of Prosper in his commentary on the one hundred and forty-eighth Psalm[x]. 'He commanded and they were created;' 'for what God speaks, He says unto His Word, and the Word, through whom all things were made, accomplishes the command of Him who speaks.'" Thus, it seems, Petavius himself has given the very best reply to himself! But whereas in the passage of which we are treating, Irenæus says, that God Himself made all things with entire freedom, proving his assertion by David's words, "our God hath made all things whatsoever He would, in the heavens above and in the earth;" on this the author of the Irenicum proceeds to argue as follows[y]; "As much as to say, the Word indeed made all things, according to the mandate of the Father; but God Himself made freely whatsoever He would; an opposition which indicates that the Father is spoken of as greater than the Son." If, however,

[1] in omni conditione.

[s] Patre volente ac jubente, Filio vero exsequente et efficiente. Iren. iv. 75. [The Greek words are; τοῦ μὲν Πατρὸς εὐδοκοῦντος καὶ κελεύοντος, τοῦ δὲ υἱοῦ πράσσοντος καὶ δημιουργοῦντος. c. 38. 3. p. 285.—B.]

[t] Basil. lib. de Spirit. S., c. 16. [vol. iii. p. 32.]

[u] [tom. v. p. 254.]

[v] [§ 9. vol. i. p. 216.] See also Athanasius Orat. contr. Gentes., tom. i. p. 51. [§ 46. vol. i. p. 45.]

[w] [Lib. i. c. 1. tom. viii. Append. p. 51.]

[x] [Quod enim Deus dicit, Verbo dicit; et Verbum per quod facta sunt omnia, mandatum dicentis exequitur. P. 529. Op. Prosp. Aquit. Par. 1711.]

[y] P. 46.

ON THE CONSUBSTANTIALITY OF THE SON.

[224] 81

this heretic had ever read Irenæus with attention, it is certain, that he would have refrained entirely from so silly a cavilling; for doubtless, when Irenæus asserts, that God the Father made all things of His own uncontrolled will, through His Word or Son, he is opposing the Gnostics, who taught that the world was made by inferior powers, and that independently of the mind[1] and will of the Most High God. Against them the holy bishop, everywhere in his writings, affirms and proves these two points; First, that this world was in no wise created by inferior powers, alien from the essence and nature of the Most High God; but was made by the Most High God Himself, through "His own offspring[2]," and through "His own hands[3]," (to use the very words[z] of Irenæus,) that is to say, through the Son and the Holy Ghost. Secondly, that this world was not fashioned by any powers "cut off from the mind[4] of God," (as he expresses himself in a passage, which we shall quote by and by from his first Book, ch. 19[a],) that is to say, which acted independently of His mind and will, but that it was produced by God Himself, through the Son and the Holy Spirit, advisedly and with absolute freedom[5]. I repeat it, he either cannot have read the writings of Irenæus at all, or at best but carelessly and superficially, who does not perceive that this is the very mind[6] and view of that most excellent father.

7. With respect to the other passage, (in book iv. chap. 17[b],) at which Petavius carps, and in which Irenæus seems to attribute to the Son, as also to the Holy Ghost, the function of a minister in the creation of the world, I reply, that Irenæus does not there mean, (as the Arians would have it,) a minister extraneous[7] to the Father, but of one substance[8] and of the selfsame nature[9] with Him; or rather he merely meant, that God the Father accomplished that work of creation through the Son and the Holy Ghost, which the heretics used to attribute to ministering angels or inferior powers. Hear Irenæus's own words[c]; "For the Son, who is the Word of God," he says, "was preparing [10] these things from the beginning; for the Father stood in no need of angels to effect the creation, and to form man, for whose sake also the creation

1 præter sententiam.
2 suam progeniem.
3 suas manus.
4 sententia.
5 consulto et liberrime.
6 ipsissimam mentem.
7 extraneum.
8 ὁμοούσιον.
9 connaturalem.
10 præstruebat.

z [See iv. 20. 1; and v. 1 and 28.]
a [c. 22. p. 98; see next page.]
b [c. 7, 4. p. 236.]
c Hæc enim Filius, inquit, qui est Verbum Dei, ab initio præstruebat, non indigente Patre angelis, uti faceret conditionem, et formaret hominem, propter quem et conditio fiebat; neque rursus indigente ministerio ad fabricationem eorum quæ facta sunt ad disposi-

BOOK II. CHAP. V. § 6, 7.

IRENÆUS.

[225]

was made; nor yet did He lack ministering power for the formation of those things which were made for the disposing of those matters which concerned man[1], but possessed an ample and ineffable ministering power; seeing that to Him there ministereth in all things, His own progeny and image[2], that is, the Son and the Holy Ghost, His Word and Wisdom, to whom all the angels are subservient and subjected." As much as to say; The Father of all things had no need of ministering agents to effect the creation, whether angels, or other inferior powers, separated from His own essence and nature, as ye, heretics, have rashly and even impiously imagined; inasmuch as both for this and for all things, His own progeny was fully sufficient, which was of Him and in Him, namely, the Son and the Holy Ghost, who are so far from being servants that they have in very deed all creatures, and even the angels themselves, ministering, serving, and subject unto Them. O! how far is all this from Arianism! To set the subject, however, in a clearer light I will add to this a few other passages of Irenæus. In book i. chapter 19[d], near the beginning, he thus speaks concerning the creation of all things through the Son and the Holy Ghost; "'All things were made through Him, and without Him was not any thing made.' From 'all things,' nothing is excepted; but through Him did the Father make all things, whether visible or invisible, perceptible or intelligible[3], whether temporal for some special purpose[4], or everlasting and without end[5], not through angels or any powers cut off from His mind[6]; for the God of all stands in need of nothing; but through His Word and His Spirit making, ordaining, governing, and giving being to all things." He teaches the same doctrine in book ii. chap. 55, towards the end, in the following words[e]; "There is One only God the

[226]

[1] quæ secundum hominem erant.

[2] progenies et figuratio sua.

[3] sive sensibilia sive intelligibilia, i.e. "cognisant by the senses or by the mind."

[4] propter quandam dispositionem.

[5] sempiterna et æonia (αἰώνια.)

[6] abscissos ab ejus sententia.

tionem eorum negotiorum, quæ secundum hominem erant, sed habente copiosum et inenarrabile ministerium. Ministrat enim ei ad omnia sua progenies et figuratio sua, id est, Filius et Spiritus Sanctus, Verbum et Sapientia; quibus serviunt et subjecti sunt omnes angeli.—[Ibid.]

[d] *Omnia per ipsum facta sunt, et sine ipso factum est nihil.* Ex omnibus autem nihil subtractum est; sed omnia per ipsum fecit Pater, sive visibilia, sive invisibilia, sive sensibilia, sive intelligibilia, sive temporalia propter quandam dispositionem, sive sempiterna et æonia, non per angelos, neque per virtutes aliquas abscissas ab ejus sententia; nihil enim indiget omnium Deus; sed et per Verbum et Spiritum suum omnia faciens et disponens et gubernans, et omnibus esse præstans.—[c. 22. p. 98.]

[e] Solus unus Deus Fabricator, hic, qui est super omnem principalitatem et potestatem et dominationem et virtutem; hic Pater, hic Deus, hic Con-

ON THE CONSUBSTANTIALITY OF THE SON.

Creator; even He, who is above all principality, and power, and dominion, and might; He is the Father, the God, the Founder, the Maker, the Creator, who made these things by HIS OWN SELF, that is to say, by His Word and His Wisdom,—the heaven and the earth and the seas, and all things which are therein." A passage parallel to this we have in book iv. chap. 37, near the beginning[f]; "The angels, then, neither formed us, nor fashioned us; nor were angels able to make the image of God; nor any other [being] except the Word of God, nor any power far removed from the Father of the universe. For God had no need of these, to make those things which He had fore-ordained within Himself to be made, as if He Himself had not hands of His own. For there is ever present with Him His Word and His Wisdom, the Son and the Spirit, through whom and in whom[1] He made all things freely and spontaneously; unto whom also He speaks, when he says, 'Let us make man in Our own image and likeness;' HE HIMSELF RECEIVING FROM HIMSELF the substance of the creatures, and the pattern of what was made, and the figure of the embellishments which are in the world!" In these passages Irenæus asserts such an identity of essence[2] (saving always the distinction of persons) between the Father, the Son, and the Holy Ghost, (whom with Theophilus of Antioch and others, he designates under the name of Wisdom,) as to say, that the Father, in creating the world through the Son and the Holy Ghost, made it through His own self[3]. From all these places, however, it at length becomes most evident, that Irenæus entirely abhorred the Arian dogma, and altogether held that faith which was afterwards set forth by the Fathers of Nicæa.

[1] per quos et in quibus.

[2] οὐσίας ταυτότητα.

[3] per semetipsum.

8. The objection, which is made against the venerable writer by the author of the Irenicum, by Sandius and others,
[227] that he attributes to the Son of God, even as God, an igno-

ditor, hic Factor, hic Fabricator, qui fecit ea per SEMETIPSUM, hoc est, per Verbum et per Sapientiam suam, cœlum et terram et maria, et omnia quæ in eis sunt.—[c. 30, 9. p. 163.]

[f] Non ergo, inquit, angeli fecerunt nos, nec nos plasmaverunt, nec angeli potuerunt imaginem facere Dei, nec alius quis præter Verbum Domini, nec virtus longe absistens a Patre universorum. Nec enim indigebat horum Deus ad faciendum quæ ipse apud se præfinierat fieri, quasi ipse suas non haberet manus. Adest enim ei semper Verbum et Sapientia, Filius et Spiritus, per quos et in quibus omnia libere et sponte fecit, ad quos et loquitur, dicens, *Faciamus hominem ad imaginem et similitudinem nostram;* IPSE A SEMETIPSO substantiam creaturarum, et exemplum factorum, et figuram in mundo ornamentorum accipiens.—[c. 20. p. 253.]

rance of the day and hour of the final judgment, we shall easily prove to be a mere senseless cavil. In book ii. chap. 49[g], indeed, he thus writes; "For if any one were to search out the cause, wherefore the Father, communicating with the Son 82
in all things, has [yet] been declared by our Lord alone to know the hour and the day, he will not find a reason more fitting, or more becoming, or less dangerous, than this in this present time, (since the Lord is our only true teacher,) that we may through Him learn that the Father is over all things. For 'My Father,' He says, 'is greater than I;' for this cause, therefore, does our Lord declare the Father to be pre-eminent in respect to knowledge also[1], that we also, in so far as we are in the fashion of this world, may yield up to God perfect knowledge and such enquiries [as this]; and may not perchance in seeking to investigate the transcendent greatness of the Father, fall into so great peril as to enquire, whether there be another God higher than God[2]." I admit that these words do, at the first glance, seem to attribute ignorance to the Son of God, even in that He is, most properly [speaking], the Son of God. If, however, these sophists had found leisure to read the whole of that chapter of Irenæus, they would easily have seen, that the holy father's mind and view was quite otherwise. For in that very chapter he had a little before written concerning Christ our Lord to this effect[h]; "For albeit the Spirit of the Saviour, which is in Him, 'searcheth all things, even the deep things of God;' still in our case[3], there are diversities of gifts, and diversities of administrations, and diversities of operations; and we, who

[1] secundum agnitionem præpositus.

[2] an super Deum alter sit Deus.

[3] quantum ad nos.

[g] Etenim si quis exquirat causam, propter quam in omnibus Pater communicans Filio solus scire horam et diem a Domino manifestatus est, neque aptabilem magis, neque decentiorem, nec sine periculo alteram quam hanc inveniat in præsenti, (quoniam enim solus verax Magister est Dominus,) ut discamus per ipsum, super omnia esse Patrem. Etenim *Pater*, ait, *major me est;* et secundum agnitionem itaque præpositus esse Pater annuntiatus est a Domino nostro ad hoc, ut et nos, in quantum in figura hujus mundi sumus, perfectam scientiam et tales quæstiones concedamus Deo; et ne forte quærentes altitudinem Patris investigare in tantum periculum incidamus, uti quæramus, an super Deum alter sit Deus.—[c. 28, 8. p. 158.]

[h] Etsi enim *Spiritus* Salvatoris, qui in eo est, *scrutatur omnia, et altitudines Dei;* sed quantum ad nos, *divisiones gratiarum sunt, et divisiones ministeriorum, divisiones operationum,* et nos super terram, quemadmodum et Paulus ait, *ex parte quidem cognoscimus, et ex parte prophetamus.* Sicut igitur ex parte cognoscimus, sic et de universis quæstionibus concedere oportet ei, qui ex parte nobis præstat gratiam.—[Ibid.]

are upon the earth, 'know' (as St. Paul says) 'in part, and prophecy in part.' As, therefore, our knowledge is [but] partial, so we ought also in all questions whatsoever to
[228] yield unto Him, who bestows on us [this] grace in part." Here by the Spirit of the Saviour is clearly meant His divine nature. For so in other places also, along with other ancient writers, whom I have mentioned above, he calls the Godhead of Christ, Spirit; for instance in v. 1[1], "If He [merely] appeared to be man, when He was not man, neither did He remain that which He really was, the Spirit of God[1];" and shortly afterwards he says in the same place; "At last the Word of the Father and the Spirit of God, having united Himself[2] to the ancient substance of Adam's creation, made a living and perfect man." It is, therefore, manifest, that Irenæus attributed ignorance to Christ only as man; whilst to His Spirit, that is to say, His Godhead, he allowed the most absolute omniscience. For surely it will not appear absurd to any one of a sound mind [to say] that the divine Wisdom impressed its effects on the human mind of Christ according to times[3]; and that Christ, in that He was man, "increased [made advance] in wisdom," (as it is expressly asserted in Luke ii. 52,) and, consequently, for the time of His mission[4] [on earth], when He had no need of such knowledge, might have been ignorant of the day of the general judgment; although the reformed are strangely attacked by the Papists for this opinion, and especially by Feuardentius, who uses the very foulest language, and on this very passage of Irenæus, calls us "the modern Gnostics, who differ not a hair's breadth from the ancient;" and "a generation of vipers," being himself the most virulent viper of all. But to return to Irenæus. This is certain, that the holy doctor, wherever else he speaks of the Son of God, ascribes to Him, as Son, the most perfect knowledge both of the nature and will of His Father. Furthermore he, throughout his work, charges the Gnostics with impiety, for making the Wisdom and the Only-begotten of the Father[5] subject to the affections of ignorance. Especially clear

[1] neque Dei Spiritus remanebat.

[2] unitus.

[3] pro temporum ratione.

[4] pro tempore suæ ἀποστολῆς.

[5] Sophiam et Monogenen Patris.

[1] Si hominis tantum speciem præbebat, cum homo non esset, sane neque id quod vere erat, hoc est Dei Spiritus, remanebat; . . . In fine Verbum Patris et Spiritus Dei adunitus antiquæ substantiæ plasmationis Adæ, viventem et perfectum effecit hominem. [Εἰ δὲ μὴ ὢν ἄνθρωπος ἐφαίνετο ἄνθρωπος, οὔτε ὃ ἦν ἐπ' ἀληθείας ἔμεινε, πνεῦμα Θεοῦ.—p. 53.]

are his words concerning Wisdom, ii. 25[k], at the very opening; "But how is it not a vain thing that they say, that even His Wisdom was in ignorance, diminution, and passion? For these things are alien from Wisdom, and contrary to her; they are no affections of hers; for wheresoever there is want of foresight and an ignorance of what is useful, there is not Wisdom. Let them not therefore any longer give the name of Wisdom to a passible æon; but let them relinquish either its name or its passions." Now can any one suppose that Irenæus would have objected to these heretics their ascribing to their fictitious Wisdom the affection of ignorance, if he had himself attributed to the true Wisdom, that is, to the Son of God, the very same imperfection? Besides, it is Irenæus whom we have heard declare, that the immeasurable Father is measured in the Son; that the Son contains and embraces the Father. Is it credible that he who wrote thus should have himself supposed that the Son of God was in any respect ignorant of the will of the Father? In short, if any one is doubtful in this point, let him read over again the words of Irenæus[l] which we have already quoted in this chapter, § 5. For there, in instituting a comparison between man and the Son of God, he attacks the omniscience which the Valentinians impiously arrogated to themselves, on this ground, that no man, no created being, "is equal to, or like the Creator, nor has been for ever co-existent with God, as His own proper Word has." It is therefore certain, that Irenæus did allow a most absolute omniscience to the proper Word of God the Father, as equal to, and eternally co-existent with Him[m].

9. But inasmuch as some writers, with whom Sandius leagues himself, charge Irenæus also with this, that he nowhere in his writings acknowledges the divinity of the Holy Ghost, I have thought it well in this place, in passing, to vindicate the most holy martyr from this calumny likewise.

[k] Quomodo autem non vanum est, quod etiam Sophiam ejus dicunt in ignorantia, et in deminoratione, et in passione fuisse? Hæc enim aliena sunt a Sophia et contraria, sed nec affectiones ejus sunt; ubi enim est improvidentia et ignorantia utilitatis, ibi Sophia non est. Non jam igitur Sophiam passum æonem vocent; sed aut vocabulum ejus aut passiones prætermittant.—[c. 18. p. 140.]

[l] [c. 25, 3. p. 153.]

[m] [See Bp. Bull's Reply to G. Clerke [28], where he speaks more at length concerning this passage of Irenæus. —B.]

I shall therefore shew, briefly indeed, but most clearly, that Irenæus believed that the Holy Ghost is, 1. A Person distinct from the Father and the Son, not a mere unsubsisting energy of the Father[h]; 2. A divine Person, that is to say, of the same nature and essence with God the Father
83 and the Son. The former proposition is sufficiently proved from the following passages, not to mention very many others. In book iv. chap. 14[i], he thus speaks concerning the Son; "Receiving testimony from all, that He is truly man and that He is truly God, from the Father, from the Spirit, from the angels," &c.; where the Father is manifestly one witness, and the Holy Ghost another, and both distinct from the Son, to whom they bore witness. He refers, it is plain, to the baptism of Christ, in which all the three Persons of the most Holy Trinity distinctly shewed themselves at the same time, the Father in the voice which sounded from heaven, the Holy Ghost in the dove which descended from above, the Son in human flesh. Shortly after, in this same passage, he says again; "There is one God the Father, and one Word, the Son, and one Spirit." Here "one," and "one," and "one," necessarily make three Persons; and it is likewise clear that the Holy Ghost is by Irenæus called one in the same sense as the Son also is called one; but the Son, as all allow, was held by Irenæus to be a Person distinct from the Father. But most explicit is the passage from the 37th chapter of the same book, the whole of which I have quoted above; I will however again cite a portion of it[k]; "For there is ever present with Him (the Father) His Word and His Wisdom, the Son and the Spirit, through whom and in whom He made all things freely and spontaneously; to whom also He speaks, when He says, 'Let us
[231] make man in Our own image and likeness.'" Observe, both
the Son and the Holy Ghost were ever, i. e., from eternity[1], present with the Father; yet neither of them was the Father

[1] ab æterno.

[h] Non meram Patris ἐνέργειαν ἀνυπόστατον, [i.e. not a mere energy of the Father, without a distinct personality or subsistence.]

[i] Ab omnibus accipiens testimonium, quoniam vere homo et quoniam vere Deus, a Patre, a Spiritu, ab angelis, &c. . . . Unus Deus Pater, et unum Verbum, Filius, et unus Spiritus, &c. —[c. 6, 7. p. 235.]

[k] Adest enim, inquit, ei (Patri) semper Verbum et sapientia, Filius et Spiritus, per quos et in quibus omnia libere et sponte fecit, ad quos et loquitur dicens, *Faciamus hominem ad imaginem et similitudinem nostram.*—[c. 20. p. 253. See above, p. 174.]

Himself; and if in the words, "Let us make man," &c., the Father addressed not only the Son but the Holy Ghost likewise, then the Holy Ghost, equally with the Son, is a Person distinct from the Father. Besides, from this passage the divinity also of the Holy Ghost is certainly inferred; for He is said to have existed from eternity with the Father and the Son; nothing however is eternal, at least in the judgment of Irenæus, except God. Next, He is associated with the Father and the Son in the work of creation; the work of creation however, according to Irenæus, (and indeed according to all of sound mind,) is the peculiar attribute of God alone. For in book iii. chap. 8, (a passage which we have already adduced[1],) he teaches that He who makes and creates other things, is so distinguished from what is made and created, that He who creates is Himself uncreated, eternal, self-sufficient; whilst they on the other hand have a beginning of existence, are susceptible of dissolution, depend upon their Creator, and do service, and are subject to Him. Whence also, in the same passage, from the fact that God the Father created all things through His word or Son, he infers that the Son Himself is, equally with the Father, uncreated, eternal, and Lord of all. But in other places also Irenæus expressly asserts the divinity of the Holy Ghost. Thus in a passage also quoted already, in book iv. chap. 17[1], the Son and the Holy Ghost are called the very offspring and image[2] of God the Father; and that for the purpose of distinguishing them from ministering angels, created by[3] God the Father through[4] the Son and the Holy Ghost, which are all in consequence declared to do service and to be subject to the Son and to the Holy Ghost, equally as to God the Father, that is, as to their Creator. But beyond all exception is that passage of Irenæus in book v. chap. 12, wherein he teaches that the Holy Spirit differs from that breath[5], or spirit, whereby Adam was made a living soul, inasmuch as the Holy Spirit, being uncreated, is the Creator and God of all things, whereas that breath was created. The passage is most worthy of being quoted entire; "The breath of life," he says[m], "which also makes man a living being, is one thing,

[1] [p. 168.]

[2] ipsa progenies et figuratio.

[3] a.

[4] per.

[5] afflatus.

[232]

[1] [c. 7, 4. p. 236. See above, p. 172.]

[m] Aliud est, inquit, afflatus vitæ, qui et animalem efficit hominem; et aliud Spiritus vivificans, qui et spiritalem

ON THE CONSUBSTANTIALITY OF THE SON.

and the life-giving Spirit, which also makes him spiritual, is another thing; and on this account Isaiah[1] says; 'Thus saith the Lord, that created the heaven and fixed it, that made firm the earth, and all that is in it; that giveth breath to the people that are upon it, and [the] Spirit to them that tread thereon;' declaring that breath is bestowed in common upon all the people that are on the earth; but the Spirit peculiarly to such as tread under foot earthly desires. Wherefore Isaiah[2] himself says again, distinguishing the things we have spoken of, 'For the Spirit shall go forth from Me, and I have made every breath;' reckoning the Spirit indeed to be peculiarly in God[3], who in these last times hath shed It forth on the human race through the adoption of sons; but the breath in common on the creation, declaring it also to be a created being. Now that which is created is a different thing from Him who created it; the breath accordingly is temporal, but the Spirit is eternal[n]." We do not now trouble ourselves with this awkward interpretation of the prophet's words, for we are not consulting Irenæus as at all times the happiest expositor of Holy Scripture, but as a most trustworthy witness of the apostolic tradition, at any rate so far as concerns a primary point of Christian doctrine. Nor is it our present concern to enquire how valid the Scripture testimonies are by which he has established catholic doctrine, (although generally even in this respect he

1 [Isaiah xlii. 5.]

2 [Isaiah lvii. 16.]

3 in Deo deputans.

efficit eum. Et propter hoc Esaias ait, *Sic dicit Dominus, qui fecit cœlum, et fixit illud; qui firmavit terram, et quæ in ea sunt; et dedit afflatum populo, qui super eam est, et Spiritum his, qui calcant illam;* afflatum quidem communiter omni, qui super terram est, populo dicens datum; Spiritum autem proprie his, qui inculcant terrenas concupiscentias. Propter quod rursus ipse Esaias distinguens quæ prædicta sunt ait, *Spiritus enim a me exiet, et afflatum omnem ego feci.* Spiritum quidem proprie in Deo deputans, quem in novissimis temporibus effudit per adoptionem filiorum in genus humanum; afflatum autem communiter in conditionem, et facturam ostendens illum; aliud autem est, quod factum est, ab eo qui fecit; afflatus igitur temporalis, spiritus autem sempiternus. [ἕτερόν ἐστι πνοὴ ζωῆς, ἣ καὶ ψυχικὸν ἀπεργαζυμένη τὸν ἄνθρωπον· καὶ ἕτερον πνεῦμα ζωοποιοῦν, τὸ καὶ πνευματικὸν αὐτὸν ἀποτελοῦν. καὶ διὰ τοῦτο Ἠσαΐας φησίν· οὕτω λέγει Κύριος ὁ ποιήσας τὸν οὐρανὸν, καὶ στερεώσας αὐτὸν, ὁ πήξας τὴν γῆν, καὶ τὰ ἐν αὐτῇ· καὶ διδοὺς πνοὴν τῷ λαῷ τῷ ἐπ' αὐτῆς, καὶ πνεῦμα τοῖς πατοῦσιν αὐτήν· τὴν μὲν πνοὴν παντὶ κοινῶς τῷ ἐπὶ γῆς λαῷ φήσας δεδόσθαι· τὸ δὲ πνεῦμα ἰδίως καταπατοῦσι τὰς γεώδεις ἐπιθυμίας· διὸ καὶ πάλιν ὁ αὐτὸς Ἠσαΐας διαστέλλων τὰ προειρημένα φησί· πνεῦμα γὰρ παρ' ἐμοῦ ἐξελεύσεται, καὶ πνοὴν πᾶσαν ἐγὼ ἐποίησα, τὸ πνεῦμα ἰδίως ἐπὶ τυῦ Θεοῦ τάξας τοῦ ἐκχέοντος αὐτὸ . . . διὰ τῆς υἱοθεσίας ἐπὶ τὴν ἀνθρωπότητα· τὴν δὲ πνοὴν κοινῶς ἐπὶ τῆς κτίσεως, καὶ ποίημα ἀναγορεύσας αὐτήν· ἕτερον δέ ἐστι τὸ ποιηθὲν τοῦ ποιήσαντος. ἡ οὖν πνοὴ πρόσκαιρος, τὸ δὲ πνεῦμα ἀένναον.—c. 7, 4. p. 306.]

n See also Tertullian adv. Marcion. ii. 4. almost throughout.

has remarkably approved himself to all men of learning and piety,) but rather what he held to be catholic doctrine. In this place therefore, I say, Irenæus manifestly declares, that the Holy Ghost is both God and Creator. For, as Petavius has very well remarked, the phrase, the Spirit being reckoned to be in God (*in Deo deputari*), which in Greek would be ἐν Θεῷ, or εἰς Θεὸν λογίζεσθαι, means the same as to be reckoned to be God (*Deum deputari*)[o]; just as when he immediately adds[p], "declaring the breath [to belong] in common to the creation, and to be created," what he says is the same as, that it is held to be created and made. Then he clearly asserts, that what is made, that is to say, the breath, is different from the Spirit, that is, from Him who made it; and that the latter is eternal, whilst the former is but temporal. According to Irenæus, therefore, the Holy Ghost is neither a thing created, nor made, but is God, proceeding forth from God[1], and the Creator, and Eternal. And thus much at present is enough concerning Irenæus.

BOOK II. CHAP. V. § 9, 1.

IRENÆUS. [233]

[1] Deus ex Deo exiens.

87 [239]

CHAPTER VI.

CONTAINING EXCEEDINGLY CLEAR TESTIMONIES OUT OF ST. CLEMENT OF ALEXANDRIA, CONCERNING THE TRUE AND SUPREME DIVINITY OF THE SON; AND, FURTHER, CONCERNING THE CONSUBSTANTIALITY OF THE WHOLE MOST HOLY TRINITY.

CLEM. AL.

1. I NOW proceed to St. Clement of Alexandria, the contemporary[q] of Irenæus, and the genuine disciple of the celebrated Pantænus, who, as Photius, [Bibliotheca] cod. 118, relates on the testimony of others, had for his masters those who had seen the Apostles; nay, and who had also himself been a hearer of some of them. Of him even Petavius[r] allows, that he adapted the Christian doctrine concerning the Word and Son of God to the views of Plato, for the most part without being at all suspected of error; and that [240]

[o] The Greek in John Damascene is, τὸ πνεῦμα ἰδίως ἐπὶ τοῦ Θεοῦ τάξας, τὴν δὲ πνοὴν κοινῶς ἐπὶ τῆς κτίσεως, καὶ ποίημα ἀναγορεύσας αὐτήν. The last words confirm the explanation of the most learned Bp. Bull.—GRABE.

[p] [Thus understood by Petavius; Afflatum in conditionem, et facturam ostendens.]

[q] Clement flourished from the year 192. Cave.—BOWYER.

[r] De Trinitate, i. 4. 1.

ON THE CONSUBSTANTIALITY OF THE SON.

his statements relating to the Son of God are correct, and in harmony with the catholic faith. In the same passage, however, and almost with the same breath, (that none of the ancients might slip through his hands without being branded by him with the stigma of error on this article,) he finds fault with certain things, even in Clement, as savouring, forsooth, of the character of the doctrine of Plato and Arius; of these we shall treat in their proper place. But I am beyond measure surprised at Peter Daniel Huet, a very learned, and, (so far as one can judge from his writings,) an extremely candid man; in that, when Bellarmine defends Origen on the ground that the opinions of his tutor Clement, and of his pupils Dionysius of Alexandria, and Gregory Thaumaturgus were sound and orthodox on the mystery of the most holy Trinity, Huet in his Origeniana makes this reply[s]; "Nothing, certainly, could he have said more prejudicial to the cause of Origen; for not one of the three entertained very[1] pure and sound views respecting the Trinity. For whilst Clement separates the substance of the Son from that of the Father, in such a way as to make it inferior; Dionysius of Alexandria affirmed that the Son was a creature[2] of the Father, and dissimilar to Him, and 'uttered expressions altogether unsuited to the Spirit,' saith Basil (Epist. xli.)[t], who also animadverts on Gregory Thaumaturgus, for having openly declared the Son to be a created being." By and by we shall have to speak of the illustrious pair of Origen's
[241] pupils, as well as of Origen himself. At present our enquiry relates to Origen's teacher, Clement. I have, certainly, with no small diligence, examined all the genuine writings of Clement of Alexandria which are now extant, and that with the especial view of ascertaining his sentiments on this article [of the faith.] The result of this examination is my conviction, that of the catholic doctors who preceded the Nicene Council, and even of those who succeeded it, no one has inculcated the true Godhead of the Son more clearly, distinctly, and significantly than the Clement of whom we are treating. In truth this writer's pages are full on both sides with this doctrine. Accordingly Ruffinus (on the corruption

[1] satis.

[2] ποίημα.

[s] Huet. Origeniana. ii. 2. quæst. 2. n. 10. [p. 122.]

[t] ἀφῆκε φωνὰς ἥκιστα πρεπούσας τῷ πνεύματι. [Ep. ix. § 2. t. iii. p. 91.]

BOOK II. CHAP. VI. § 1, 2.

CLEM. AL.

of the books of Origen) wrote thus of Clement[u]; "Clement, a presbyter of Alexandria and catechist[1] of that Church, in almost every one of his books declares the glory and eternity of the Trinity to be one and the same." Out of this so great store we will select some of the more marked passages.

[1] magister.

2. Not far from the opening of his *Protrepticon*, or Exhortation to the Gentiles, Clement cites[x] that notable passage of Paul, out of his Epistle to Titus, ii. 11—13: "The grace of God, that bringeth salvation, hath appeared[2] unto all men, teaching us that, denying ungodliness and worldly lusts, we should live soberly, righteously, and godly in this present world; looking for that blessed hope, and the glorious appearing[3] of the great God and our Saviour Jesus Christ:" and understands by the designation of 'the great God,' in this passage, our Saviour Christ to be meant; subjoining these most beautiful words; "This is the new song, the Epiphany[4], which hath now shone forth amongst us, of that Word, who was in the beginning, and who was before; and now of late hath He appeared, the Saviour who was before; He who is in Him that is hath appeared, in that the Word, who was with God, by whom all things were made, hath appeared our Instructor; the Word, who at the first gave unto us life, when He had moulded us as Creator; manifesting Himself as our Instructor, hath taught us good life, that [242]
afterwards, as God, He might bestow upon us eternal life." 88
Here Clement recognises our Saviour Christ as eternal, "existing," that is, "in the beginning and before [the beginning];" as consubstantial with the Father, as being "Him that is in Him that is," that is to say, subsisting in the very essence of God the Father; and, lastly, as "God, the Giver of the present life and of everlasting life." In the same book he exhorts the Gentiles to believe in the Son, in these[y]

[2] ἐπεφάνη.

[3] ἐπιφάνειαν.

[4] ἐπιφάνεια.

[u] Clemens Alexandrinus presbyter et magister illius ecclesiæ, in omnibus pene libris suis, Trinitatis gloriam atque æternitatem unam eandemque designat. [p. 50.]

[x] τοῦτό ἐστι τὸ ᾆσμα τὸ καινὸν, ἡ ἐπιφάνεια, ἡ νῦν ἐκλάμψασα ἐν ἡμῖν τοῦ ἐν ἀρχῇ ὄντος καὶ προόντος λόγου. ἐπεφάνη δὲ ἔναγχος ὁ προὼν σωτήρ· ἐπεφάνη ὁ ἐν τῷ ὄντι ὢν, ὅτι ὁ λόγος, ὃς ἦν πρὸς τὸν Θεὸν, διδάσκαλος ἐπεφάνη, ᾧ τὰ πάντα δεδημιούργηται. λόγος, ὁ καὶ τὸ ζῆν ἐν ἀρχῇ μετὰ τοῦ πλάσαι παρασχὼν ὡς δημιουργὸς, τὸ εὖ ζῆν ἐδίδαξεν, ἐπιφανεὶς ὡς διδάσκαλος, ἵνα τὸ ἀεὶ ζῆν ὕστερον ὡς Θεὸς χορηγήσῃ.—p. 6. [p. 7.]

[y] πίστευσον, ἄνθρωπε, ἀνθρώπῳ καὶ Θεῷ· πίστευσον, ἄνθρωπε, τῷ παθόντι, καὶ προσκυνουμένῳ Θεῷ ζῶντι· πιστεύσατε, οἱ δοῦλοι, τῷ νεκρῷ· πάντες ἄνθρωποι πιστεύσατε μόνῳ τῷ πάντων ἀνθρώπων Θεῷ.—p. 66. [p. 84.]

ON THE CONSUBSTANTIALITY OF THE SON.

words; (in the translation of which Hervetus[z], as is usual with him, blunders[1] miserably; the passage ought to be turned thus;) "Believe, O man, in [Him who is] man and God; believe in Him that suffered and is worshipped, the living God; ye slaves, believe in Him, who was dead; all ye men believe in Him, who is the only God of all men." In these words he pronounces Christ to be God as well as man, the living God who is worshipped, (which is a manifest circumlocution for the true God,) and [who is] in short, the only God of all men.

[1] hallucinatur.

3. What again can be more noble than those words which we read in the same book, in the next page but one? there
[243] Clement calls our Saviour[a], "The divine Word, who truly is the most manifest God, made equal to the Lord of all; because He was His Son, and [because] the Word was in God[b]." He employs words so emphatic that he seems to have used his utmost endeavour to express fully the supreme Godhead of the Saviour. He calls Christ the divine Word, very God, very God most manifest[2], equal to God the Father; and he subjoins this as a reason, that He is the Son of God, that is, true Son born of Himself; and that He is the Word, subsisting in God Himself. Again, in his Pædagogus, i. 5, near the end, after observing that the greatness of the Son of God is declared by Isaiah, namely, in these words, "Wonderful, Counsellor, the mighty God, the everlasting Father, the Prince of Peace," he immediately subjoins[c]; "O the mighty God! O the perfect Child! the Son in the Father, and the Father in the Son." Afterwards in the sixth chapter of the same book he speaks of the Son as[d] "the perfect Word, born[3] of the perfect Father," that is to say, the Son corresponds to His Father, of whom He was begotten[4], in every kind of perfection. The reader would find it worth while to weigh attentively this entire passage in Clement's own book.

[2] Verum Deum manifestissimum.

[Isaiah ix. 6.]

[3] φυντα.

[4] natus.

[z] [Hervetus (Gentianus), Canon of Rheims, is the author of the Latin translation, which Potter has retained in his edition of Clement's works.]

[a] ὁ θεῖος λόγος ὁ φανερώτατος ὄντως Θεὸς, ὁ τῷ δεσπότῃ τῶν ὅλων ἐξισωθείς· ὅτι ἦν υἱὸς αὐτοῦ, καὶ ὁ λόγος ἦν ἐν τῷ Θεῷ.—p. 68. [p. 86.]

[b] [See these words again quoted in Book iv. 2. 4. B.—Bp. Bull translated these words, (ὁ φανερώτατος ὄντως Θεὸς,) "qui est manifestissime verus Deus," "who is most manifestly the true God;" (as did also Dr. Burton in his Testimonies to the Divinity of Christ, p. 148.)]

[c] ὦ τοῦ μεγάλου Θεοῦ· ὦ τοῦ τελείου παιδίου· υἱὸς ἐν πατρὶ, καὶ πατὴρ ἐν υἱῷ.—p. 91. [p. 112.]

[d] τὸν λόγον τέλειον, ἐκ τελείου φύντα τοῦ πατρός.—p. 92. [p. 113.]

After a considerable interval, he in the same chapter utters a full and perfect confession of the most holy Trinity in these words[e]; "One, first, is the Father of all things; and one also is the Word of all things; and the Holy Ghost is one and the same in every place." Observe, how to each several Person of the Holy Trinity he attributes divine energy, such [244]
as to pervade all things[1]; the first Person being the Father of all things[2], the second being in like manner the Word of all things[2], and, lastly, the third being present every where and in all. Furthermore, in the seventh chapter of the same book, he thus speaks concerning Christ the Instructor (*Pædagogus*)[f]; "But our Instructor is the holy God Jesus, the Word who is the Guide of the entire human race; Himself, the God who loveth man, is our Instructor."

4. Also throughout the eighth chapter of the same book, he is taken up in proving that all the attributes of God the Father, (those, I mean, which are absolute[g],) are common to Him with the Son, by reason of the divine nature which belongs to both alike, and that whatsoever is predicated of the Father is also applicable to the Son. The whole chapter indeed deserves to be read, but it may be enough for me to point out a few passages to the reader. He proves that Christ hates no man, but rather desires the salvation of all, by the following argument[h]; "If therefore the Word hates any thing, He wishes that it should not exist; there is, however, nothing of which God doth not afford the cause of its existing; nothing therefore is hated of God, nay, nor yet of the Word; for Both are One[3], [that is,] God." Then, after treating fully out of the Scriptures concerning the primary attributes of God, that is to say, goodness and justice, and after shewing that they equally belong to the Father and the Son, he

[1] rerum universitatem.

[2] universorum.

[3] ἕν.

[e] εἷς μὲν ὁ τῶν ὅλων Πατήρ· εἷς δὲ καὶ ὁ τῶν ὅλων Λόγος· καὶ τὸ Πνεῦμα τὸ ἅγιον ἓν, καὶ τὸ αὐτὸ πανταχοῦ. [Bp. Bull translated these words, "et Spiritus Sanctus unus, qui et ipse est ubique," "and the Holy Ghost one, who Himself also is every where," and it will be seen argues from that translation.]—p. 120. [p. 123.]

[f] ὁ δὲ ἡμέτερος παιδαγωγὸς ἅγιος Θεὸς Ἰησοῦς, ὁ πάσης τῆς ἀνθρωπότητος καθηγεμὼν λόγος· αὐτὸς ὁ φιλάνθρωπος Θεός ἐστι παιδαγωγός.—p. 109. [p. 131.]

[g] [Because some are relative, e.g. to be the Father of our Lord Jesus Christ, &c.]

[h] εἴ τι ἄρα μισεῖ ὁ λόγος, βούλεται αὐτὸ μὴ εἶναι· οὐδὲν δὲ ἔστιν, οὗ μὴ τὴν αἰτίαν τοῦ εἶναι ὁ Θεὸς παρέχεται· οὐδὲν ἄρα μισεῖται ὑπὸ τοῦ Θεοῦ· ἀλλ' οὐδὲ ὑπὸ τοῦ λόγου· ἓν γὰρ ἄμφω, ὁ Θεός.—p. 113. [p. 135.]

ON THE CONSUBSTANTIALITY OF THE SON.

thus at length concludes[i]; "So that in very truth[1] it is evident that the God of all is one only, good, just, the Creator, the Son in the Father, to whom be glory for ever and ever. Amen."
[245] 89 And here the reader who has any sense whatever will not need any one to suggest it in order to perceive, that the Son, in the Father, and with the Father, is declared to be God of all, who alone is good, and just, and the Creator of all things, and to whom accordingly should be ascribed glory for evermore. Again he makes use of these very magnificent expressions concerning the Son of God[k]; "For he that hath THE ALMIGHTY GOD THE WORD[2], is in need of nothing, and never is at any time without supply of that which He wants; for the Word is a possession that needeth nothing, and the cause of all abundance[l]." Lastly, at the end of his Pædagogus, he thus prays to the Word or Son of God, together with the Father[m]; "Be Thou merciful to Thy children, O Instructor, Thou, O Father, charioteer of Israel, Son and Father, Both One, O Lord;" and soon afterwards pours forth praises to the most holy Trinity in the following form: "Let us give thanks," he says, "to the alone Father and Son, Son and Father, the Son our Instructor and Teacher, together with the Holy Ghost also; all things to the One; in whom are all things; through whom[3] all things are one; through[4] whom is eternity[5]; whose members all are; whose glory are the ages[n6]; all things to the Good, all things to the Lovely, all things to the Wise; all things to the Righteous; to Him be glory both now and unto all ages.
[246] Amen." That man is blind in mid-day light, who does not

[1] ταῖς ἀληθείαις.

[2] θεὸν λόγον ἔχων.

[3] δι' ὅν.

[4] δι' ὅν.

[5] τὸ ἀεί.

[6] αἰῶνες.

[i] ὡς εἶναι ταῖς ἀληθείαις καταφανὲς τὸ τῶν συμπάντων Θεὸν ἕνα μόνον εἶναι, ἀγαθὸν, δίκαιον, δημιουργὸν, υἱὸν ἐν πατρὶ, ᾧ ἡ δόξα εἰς τοὺς αἰῶνας τῶν αἰώνων, Ἀμήν.—p. 119. [p. 142.]

[k] ἀνενδεὴς γὰρ ὁ τὸν παντοκράτορα Θεὸν λόγον ἔχων, καὶ οὐδενὸς, ὧν χρῄζει, ἀπορεῖ ποτε· κτῆσις γὰρ ὁ λόγος ἀνενδεὴς, καὶ εὐπορίας ἁπάσης αἴτιος.—Pædagog. iii. 7. p. 236, 237. [p. 277.]

[l] [Bp. Bull quotes this passage of Clement again in his answer to G. Clerke, § 8.—B.]

[m] ἵλαθι τοῖς σοῖς, παιδαγωγὲ, παιδίοις, πατὴρ, ἡνίοχε Ἰσραὴλ, υἱὲ καὶ πατὴρ, ἓν ἄμφω, Κύριε. . . . τῷ μόνῳ πατρὶ καὶ υἱῷ, υἱῷ καὶ πατρὶ, παιδαγωγῷ καὶ διδασκάλῳ υἱῷ σὺν καὶ τῷ ἁγίῳ πνεύματι· πάντα τῷ ἑνί· ἐν ᾧ τὰ πάντα· δι' ὃν τὰ πάντα ἕν· δι' ὃν τὸ ἀεί· οὗ μέλη πάντες· οὗ δόξα, αἰῶνες· πάντα τῷ ἀγαθῷ, πάντα τῷ καλῷ, πάντα τῷ σοφῷ, τῷ δικαίῳ τὰ πάντα· ᾧ ἡ δόξα καὶ νῦν καὶ εἰς τοὺς αἰῶνας, Ἀμήν.—p. 266. [p. 311.]

[n] [*Cujus sunt gloria et sæcula*, 'whose are the glory and the ages,' is Bp. Bull's version of this clause; on this GRABE observes; "I think it should rather be translated *cujus gloria sunt sæcula*; whose glory are the celestial spirits, or the angels. For which signification of the word αἰῶνες, see what I have noted on Irenæus, p. 9. numb. 2." (p. 32. Var. Annot. in edit. Benedict.)]

clearly see that in this doxology is contained a full and perfect acknowledgment of the Trinity of one substance, that is to say, of one God subsisting in three Persons, the Father, the Son, and the Holy Ghost.

5. But that I may not appear to have altogether neglected the books of the Stromata, I shall here adduce one or two passages out of them. In the fourth book he thus speaks concerning Christ[o]; "Thus the Lord draws near unto the righteous, and nothing is hid from Him of our thoughts, and of the reasonings which we entertain[p]; the Lord Jesus, I mean, who, according to His almighty will, is the inspector[1] of our hearts." These words need no comment. In the seventh book, in treating of the divinity of the Word, or Son of God, every where present, and having a care for all things, even the least, he illustrates it with this most apposite and elegant similitude[q]; "For even as the sun not only enlightens the heaven and the whole world, shining both on land and sea; but also sends its light through windows and the little crevice into the innermost recesses of the house; so the Word, shed abroad everywhere, looks upon the most minute portions of the actions of life." There are, indeed, many more passages from Clement, which I might have added to these; but one who is not satisfied with these, nothing will satisfy. [247]

[1] *ἐπίσκοπον.*

6. Let us now see what Petavius and the other over-critical censurers of the holy Fathers, (not to call them by a worse name,) have brought forward out of Clement, in opposition to these so clear and express statements, in order to prove that he was infected in some degree with the taint of Arianism. The first passage which Petavius[r] alleges is from the seventh book of the Stromata, in which Clement writes thus concerning the Son of God[s]: "Most perfect, indeed, and most holy, and most lordly, and most commanding, and most royal, and most beneficent is the nature of

[o] *οὕτως ἐγγίζει τοῖς δικαίοις ὁ Κύριος, καὶ οὐδὲν λέληθεν αὐτὸν τῶν ἐννοιῶν καὶ τῶν διαλογισμῶν ὧν ποιούμεθα· τὸν Κύριον Ἰησοῦν λέγω, τὸν τῷ παντοκρατορικῷ θελήματι ἐπίσκοπον τῆς καρδίας ἡμῶν.*—p. 517. [p. 611.]

[p] [The words *ἐγγίζει* (*ἐγγύς ἐστι* in S. Clement of Rome) *τοῖς δικαίοις ὁ Κύριος, καὶ οὐδὲν λέληθεν αὐτὸν τῶν ἐννοιῶν καὶ τῶν διαλογισμῶν ὧν ποιούμεθα*, are taken from Clement of Rome, c. 21.—B.]

[q] *ὅνπερ γὰρ τρόπον ὁ ἥλιος οὐ μόνον τὸν οὐρανὸν καὶ τὸν ὅλον κόσμον φωτίζει, γῆν τε καὶ θάλασσαν ἐπιλάμπων, ἀλλὰ καὶ διὰ θυρίδων καὶ μικρᾶς ὀπῆς πρὸς τοὺς μυχαιτάτους οἴκους ἀποστέλλει τὴν αὐγήν· οὕτως ὁ λόγος πάντῃ κεχυμένος καὶ τὰ σμικρότατα τῶν τοῦ βίου πράξεων ἐπιβλέπει.*—p. 711. [p. 840.]

[r] De Trin. i. 4. 1. p. 702.

[s] *τελειωτάτη δὴ, καὶ ἁγιωτάτη, καὶ κυριωτάτη, καὶ ἡγεμονικωτάτη, καὶ βασιλικωτάτη, καὶ εὐεργετικωτάτη ἡ υἱοῦ*

ON THE CONSUBSTANTIALITY OF THE SON.

the Son, which is most closely conjoined[1] with the alone Almighty." For thus I conceive the word *προσεχεστάτη* [in the last clause] should be translated; in the sense in which things which are most near to, and conjoined with, any thing, and immediate cause[2], are called *προσεχῆ* by philosophers[t]. Petavius makes this remark, however, on the passage: "He says the nature of the Son is most near[3] to Almighty God; which savours of the spirit of the Platonic and the Arian dogmas. But the nature of the Son is not most near to, but identical with the Father." And I suppose Huet had this
[248] passage, cited by Petavius, in view, when he declared "that it was laid down by Clement that the substance of the Son is inferior to that of the Father." The answer, how-
90 ever, is easy. In this passage the divine nature of the Son is viewed by Clement not absolutely, but relatively, or personally, as they express it, [i. e.] so far forth as it constitutes the Person[4] of the Son; for[5] the word *φύσις*, as also the word *οὐσία*, is sometimes used by ancient writers to signify Person. (See chap. ix. sect. 11, of this book.) So that Clement is to be regarded as having meant nothing else than that the Son is most intimately conjoined with His Father. And what harm, I ask, is there in this? At any rate Gregory Nyssen in his Epistle to Ablabius, without incurring any blame, designated the Son as "that[u] which is *προσεχῶς*, most nearly, continuously, or (in other words) immediately [derived] from[6] the first [cause]," that is, from God the Father. But even if you were to understand Clement in this passage to attribute the first place to the Father, and the second to the Son—what is there new in this? Indeed that there is a certain eminency[7] appertaining to the Father, inasmuch as He is the fountain of Deity and the principle of the Son[8], the Scriptures throughout testify, and the fathers acknowledge with one consent, both ante-Nicene and Nicene, and those also who wrote subsequently to that council; as we shall afterwards shew in its proper place[x]. It is certain, however, that Clement did not at all mean that the substance of the Son is inferior to that

[1] conjunctissima.
[2] conjuncta cum re et causa immediata.
[3] citimam esse.
[4] Filii *ὑπόστασιν*.
[5] scilicet.
[6] *ἐκ*.
[7] *ἐξοχὴν* quandam.
[8] Principium Filii.

φύσις, ἣ τῷ μόνῳ παντοκράτορι προσεχεστάτη.—[p. 831.]

[t] [See the answer to Gilb. Clerke, § 19.]

[u] *τὸ προσεχῶς ἐκ τοῦ πρώτου*, id quod proxime, continenter, sive immediate est ex primo.—Oper., tom. ii. p. 459. [vol. iii. p. 27. See above, p. 232, note z.]

[x] [Book iv.]

of the Father. The many passages which we have already adduced, in which he (if any ancient writer whatever) most openly acknowledges the consubstantiality of the Son and His true divinity, are inconsistent with this notion; indeed, the context of this passage itself is inconsistent with it. For in the words which immediately follow, Clement speaks with exceeding honour[1] (as Petavius himself observes) concerning the Son of God, attributing to Him these primary attributes of Deity, indivisibility, unchangeableness, eternity, omniscience, and omnipresence. But especially is it to be remarked, that in the self-same passage, the Son is designated by Clement, as being "entirely the mind[2], entirely the light of the Father;" which words certainly do plainly declare the common nature of the Father and the Son[y]. [249]

[1] perquam honorifice.

[2] ὅλος νοῦς, ὅλος φῶς πατρῷον.

7. Furthermore, Petavius alleges the following words of Clement, occurring after a short interval, in the same book[z]; "Nor could the Lord of all be ever restrained by another, especially in ministering to[3] the will of His good and almighty Father:" but what darkness has this very learned man here made in a clear sky! Let every lover of truth peruse the words of Clement which precede and follow, and he will wonder, I am sure, what has here come into Petavius's mind. Throughout the passsage Clement is intent upon shewing that Christ is the common Saviour, and promotes the salvation of all men, so far as in Him lies, saving always the liberty of the human will. Now he says that no creature is able to hinder Christ in bringing about the salvation of mankind, since He is Lord of all; moreover that the Father, who is also together with the Son the Lord of all, wills not to hinder Him; inasmuch as in this work the Son is fulfilling the Father's will. Clement asserts the same, (and the expression is approved of by Petavius himself,) when he calls[a] the Son "the true Comrade[4] with the good-will of God towards man." Lastly Petavius alleges a passage of Clement, Strom. iv.[b]: "God, then,

[3] καὶ μάλιστα ἐξυπηρετῶν.

[4] συναγωνιστὴν γνήσιον.

[y] [See this passage of Clement again quoted and defended in Bp. Bull's Reply to G. Clerke, § 24.—B.]

[z] οὔθ' ὑφ' ἑτέρου κωλυθείη ποτ' ἂν ὁ πάντων Κύριος, καὶ μάλιστα ἐξυπηρετῶν τῷ τοῦ ἀγαθοῦ καὶ παντοκράτορος θελήματι Πατρός.—p. 703. [p. 832.]

[a] τῆς τοῦ Θεοῦ φιλανθρωπίας συναγωνιστὴς γνήσιος.—Pædagog. i. 8. p. 114. [p. 136.]

[b] ὁ μὲν οὖν Θεὸς ἀναπόδεικτος ὢν οὐκ ἔστιν ἐπιστημονικός· ὁ δὲ υἱὸς σο-

ON THE CONSUBSTANTIALITY OF THE SON.

as not being within the range of demonstration[1], is not within that of knowledge[2]; but the Son is wisdom, and knowledge, and truth, and whatsoever else is akin to this; and especially also admits both of demonstration and explication[3]." It is, however, manifest, that Clement in these words meant nothing else than that God the Father can-
[250] not by any be found out[4] and known immediately and by Himself[5], but is revealed by[6] the Son, who, as the Word of God made flesh, hath revealed both Himself and His Father to men, according to their capacity. Now if this be Arianism, I fear that the Apostle John himself, will at last be called an Arian; for, in his Gospel, i. 18, he has written thus, "No man hath seen God at any time; the Son, who is in the bosom of the Father, He hath revealed Him." Nay more, in the same passage, in the very next words, Clement with a single stroke, as it were, gives a death-blow to all the Arian blasphemies, when he says of Christ, that He is an infinite circle, comprehending within Himself alone all the virtues and powers of the Godhead, immense, and, in fine, eternal, having neither beginning nor end of being[7]. We shall quote the passage afterwards in the third book. You see how frivolous are the points which Petavius has alleged against our Clement.

8. Others also have censured him for having somewhere[c] called the Son of God "the first created Wisdom[8][d]." But this likewise is altogether to no purpose. For in that passage of Clement it is evident that the word κτιστὸς (created) means the same as γεννητὸς (begotten); as also in
[251] Latin the word *creare* (to create), is put for *gignere* (to beget); as '*Sulmone creatos*,' i. e., '*progenitos*.' Certainly from what has been already brought forward out of his own writings, it is clearer than noon-day that Clement did not believe the Son of God to be a creature. I shall here subjoin the words of that great man Hen. Valesius; "At all

1 ἀναπόδεικτος.
2 οὐκ ἐπιστημονικὸς.
3 ἀπόδειξιν ἔχει καὶ διέξοδον.
4 cognosci.
5 per se.
6 per.
7 existendi.
8 πρωτόκτιστον σοφίαν.

φία τε ἐστὶ, καὶ ἐπιστήμη, καὶ ἀλήθεια, καὶ ὅσα ἄλλα τούτῳ συγγενῆ, καὶ δὴ καὶ ἀπόδειξιν ἔχει καὶ διέξοδον.—p. 537. [p. 635.]

c Strom. v. p. 591. [699.]

d No doubt he had in view that passage in Proverbs viii. 22; where Wisdom says; Κύριος ἔκτισέ με ἀρχὴν ὁδῶν αὐτοῦ εἰς ἔργα αὐτοῦ, "The Lord created me in the beginning of His ways, before His works of old (LXX);" as Clement cites these very words in his Hortatory Address, and explains them of the Word, or Son of God.—p. 52. B. C.—[p. 67.]—GRABE.

events the ancient theologians," he says[e], "and especially those who wrote before the time of the council of Nice, understood by the word *κτίζειν*, not only the act of creation which takes place out of nothing, but generally all production, as well that which is eternal as that which takes place in time." In precisely the same way must that passage be expounded which Clement cites from the Apocryphal books of Peter, in his Stromata vi.[f] "For God is in truth one, who made the Beginning of all things, meaning His first-begotten Son." That is, it was usual with the Greeks, as it seems, (whom we also imitate in our English,) to say *ποιεῖν τέκνα, facere liberos* for *liberos generare;* and thus does the author of this last passage explain himself by immediately subjoining, "meaning His first-begotten Son[1]."

[1] μηνύων τὸν πρωτόγονον υἱόν.

9. Lastly Sandius[g] reproaches Clement with a work which was formerly extant but is now lost, entitled *Hypotyposes,* in which, according to the testimony of Photius, cod. 109, there were many germs of Arian heresy[2], especially in that he numbered the Son of God amongst created beings. But this is nothing worth[3], and is unbecoming a man who has undertaken to give us the very kernel[4] of ancient ecclesiastical history. For learned men of the present day (and amongst them Petavius himself) allow that those blasphemous statements [252] [in the Hypotyposes] were by no means Clement's own, but foisted on him by some impostor; and this judgment of theirs is abundantly confirmed out of Photius himself; since Photius in the same place declares that in these books of Hypotyposes it is taught, that matter is eternal; that ideas are introduced[5] as it were by determinate decrees; that souls pass from body to body; that many worlds existed previous to Adam; that Eve came forth from Adam not in the way the sacred Scriptures relate, but in some unclean way; that angels had connexion with women and raised up children of them: moreover, that there were two Words of the Father, of which the lesser was seen by men, nay, not even that. How contrary all these statements are to the teaching of

[2] perfidiæ.

[3] nauci.

[4] nucleus.

[5] induci.

[e] In his notes on Eusebius, p. 8. [i. 2. p. 9.]

[f] εἷς γὰρ τῷ ὄντι ἐστὶν ὁ Θεὸς, ὃς ἀρχὴν τῶν ἁπάντων ἐποίησεν, μηνύων τὸν πρωτόγονον υἱόν.—p. 644. [p. 769.]

[g] Sandius de Script. Eccl., p. 24; and Enucl. Hist. Eccles. i. p. 94.

ON THE CONSUBSTANTIALITY OF THE SON.

Clement, as expressed in his genuine and undoubted writings, it is needless to say. Added to which the same Photius, who otherwise was easily led to entertain the worst suspicions of Clement, as being the preceptor of Origen, intimates plainly enough that he did not at all believe these statements to be really Clement's, in that he shortly afterwards adds[h], "and a thousand other blasphemies and follies does he utter, either himself, or some other person assuming his name." Lastly, Photius himself, cod. 110, when treating of the three books of the Pædagogus and the Exhortation to the Gentiles, which all allow to be genuine works of Clement, observes that, whether you look to doctrine or style, these works are very unlike the Hypotyposes; his words are[i]; "These discourses have no resemblance to the Hypotyposes, for they are both altogether free from their foolish
[253] and blasphemous opinions, and the style is flowery, and elevated to a becoming dignity, combined with sweetness, and the manifold learning is befitting." For my own part I have no doubt that it was mainly these books of the Hypotyposes that Ruffinus had in view, (and perhaps also the eighth book of the Stromata in the corrupted state in which it appeared in some of the copies of his time, as Photius has also noticed in the place cited before, cod. 110,) and that it was these which he was comparing with all the other undoubted writings of Clement, in which the catholic doctrine of the most blessed Trinity is uniformly maintained, when he used the words (in part cited by me before) concerning him[k], "Clement also, presbyter of Alexandria, and catechist[1] of that Church, in nearly all his books speaks of the glory and eternity of the Trinity, as one and the same; and yet sometimes we find certain chapters in his books in

[1] magister.

[h] *καὶ ἀλλὰ δὲ μυρία βλασφημεῖ καὶ φλυαρεῖ, εἴτε αὐτὸς, εἴτέ τις ἕτερος τὸ αὐτοῦ πρόσωπον ὑποκριθείς.*—[Phot. cod. 109.]

[i] *οὐδὲν δὲ ὅμοιον ἔχουσι πρὸς τὰς ὑποτυπώσεις οὗτοι οἱ λόγοι. τῶν τε γὰρ ματαιῶν καὶ βλασφήμων ἀπηλλαγμένοι δοξῶν καθεστήκασι, καὶ ἡ φράσις ἀνθηρὰ, καὶ εἰς ὄγκον ἠρμένη σύμμετρον μετὰ τοῦ ἡδέως, καὶ ἡ πολυμάθεια ἐμπρέπουσα.*—[Phot. cod. 110.]

[k] Clemens quoque Alexandrinus presbyter, et magister ecclesiæ illius, in omnibus pene libris suis Trinitatis gloriam atque æternitatem unam eandemque designat; et interdum invenimus aliqua in libris ejus capitula, in quibus Filium Dei creaturam dicit. Numquin credibile est de tanto viro, tam in omnibus catholico, tam erudito, ut vel sibi contraria senserit, vel ea, quæ de Deo non dicam credere, sed vel audire quidem impium est, scripta reliquerit?—Ruffinus de adult., lib. Origen.—[p. 50.]

which he calls the Son of God a creature. But is it credible respecting so great a man, who was so catholic in all points, and so learned, that he either held self-contradictory opinions, or left behind him in writing statements which it were impiety, I will not say to believe respecting God, but even to listen to?" And thus far concerning St. Clement of Alexandria.

CHAPTER VII.

[93 [256]

THE DOCTRINE OF TERTULLIAN CONCERNING THE CONSUBSTANTIALITY OF THE SON IS SHEWN TO COINCIDE ALTOGETHER WITH THE NICENE CREED.

TERTULLIAN.

1. WE have now come to Tertullian[1]. Although this writer has been supposed by some to have denied the eternity of the Son,—by such, that is, as either have been unable, or have not cared to investigate the meaning of an obscure author, for I shall hereafter shew that Tertullian, however he may in some places have expressed himself, did in reality acknowledge the eternal existence also of the second Person of the most holy Trinity,—still has he every where uniformly and in the most express terms confessed the consubstantiality of the Son. Read only his single work against Praxeas, in which he treats fully and professedly of the most holy Trinity; he there asserts the consubstantiality of the Son so frequently and so plainly, that you would suppose the author had written after the time of the Nicene council. We shall exhibit to the reader some of the more striking passages both out of this book and out of other writings of Tertullian. In the twenty-first chapter of his Apology, he says[m]: "We have been taught concerning Him as concerning one put forth[1] from God, and by [that] putting forth[2] generated[3], and consequently called the Son of God and God, from UNITY OF SUBSTANCE, for God also is a Spirit." Here he plainly infers that the Son is of one substance with the Father, that is to say, is ὁμοούσιος (consubstantial) with Him, from

[1] prolatum.
[2] prolatione.
[3] generatum.

[1] Tertullian embraced the Christian religion about the year 185. Cave.—BOWYER.

[m] Hunc ex Deo prolatum didicimus, et prolatione generatum, et idcirco Filium Dei et Deum dictum, ex UNITATE SUBSTANTIÆ: nam et Deus Spiritus.—[p. 19.]

ON THE CONSUBSTANTIALITY OF THE SON.

the circumstance that He has been generated of the Father[1]. His meaning is the same, when, in his book against Praxeas, chap. 7, he thus writes concerning the Son of God[n]; "He is the First-begotten, as begotten before all things; and the Only-begotten, as alone begotten of God, in a way peculiar to Himself[2], from the [very] womb of His heart."

2. Let us, however, consider the similes, by which Tertullian has attempted, up to a certain point, to explain the generation of the Son; [for] these manifestly prove His being
[257] of one substance [with the Father.] In the Apology, after the words already quoted, these also follow[o]; "And when a ray of light stretches forth from the sun, [it is] a portion from the whole, but the sun will be in the ray, because it is a ray of the sun, and the substance is not separated, but extended: so is Spirit from Spirit, and GOD FROM GOD, AS LIGHT kindled FROM LIGHT: the original source of matter[3] remains entire and unimpaired, although you borrow thence many derivations of [scil. possessing its] qualities[4]; so also what has proceeded from God is God and the Son of God, and Both are One: so also [is] Spirit from Spirit, and GOD FROM GOD: [This] has made a second[5] in mode[6], not in number; in gradation, not in state[7]; and It has not gone away from, but has gone forth from Its original source." Here you have the very words of the Nicene Creed and a meaning also exactly the same. There is also a remarkable[8] passage in the book against Praxeas, chap. 8[p]; "This," says he, "will be the putting forth[9] of [scil. taught by] the truth, the guard of the Unity; whereby we say, that the Son was put forth from the Father, but not separated. For God put forth the Word, as the root the plant, and the fountain the stream, and the sun the ray. For these forms[10] also are put-

[1] ex Patre.
[2] proprie.
[3] materiæ matrix.
[4] traduces qualitatum.
[5] alterum.
[6] modulo.
[7] gradu non statu.
[8] illustris.
[9] προβολὴ, probola.
[10] species.

[n] Primogenitus, ut ante omnia genitus; et unigenitus, ut solus ex Deo genitus, proprie de vulva cordis ipsius.—[p. 503.]

[o] Et cum radius ex sole porrigitur, portio ex summa, sed sol erit in radio, quia solis est radius, nec separatur substantia, sed extenditur: ita de Spiritu Spiritus, et DE DEO DEUS, UT LUMEN DE LUMINE accensum: manet integra et indefecta materiæ matrix, etsi plures inde traduces qualitatum mutueris; ita et quod de Deo profectum est, Deus est et Dei Filius, et unus ambo; ita et de Spiritu Spiritus, et DE DEO DEUS: modulo alterum, non numero, gradu, non statu fecit; et a matrice non recessit, sed excessit.—Apol. c. 21. [p. 19.]

[p] Hæc erit probola veritatis, custos unitatis, qua prolatum dicimus Filium a Patre, sed non separatum. Protulit enim Deus Sermonem, . . . sicut radix fruticem, et fons fluvium, et sol radium. Nam et istæ species probolæ sunt EARUM SUBSTANTIARUM, ex quibus prodeunt.—[p. 504.]

tings forth[1] OF THOSE SUBSTANCES, out of which they come forth." Parallel to this is another passage of the same book, chap. 13[q]; "I shall follow the Apostle," he says, "so that, if the Father and the Son are to be mentioned together[2], I shall call the Father God, and name Jesus Christ Lord. But when Christ is [mentioned] alone, I shall be able to call Him God, as the same Apostle says, 'Of whom is Christ, who is over all, God blessed for ever.' For a ray of the sun also, [spoken of] by itself, I should call sun; but if I were speaking of the sun, of which it is a ray, I should not forthwith call the ray also sun. For although I make not two suns, still I should reckon both the sun and its ray to be as much two things, and two forms[3] of ONE UNDIVIDED SUBSTANCE, as God and His Word, as the Father and the Son." In these [258]
words he affirms, that Christ is called by the Apostle, "God over all, blessed for ever," and distinctly teaches that the Father and the Son are of one, and that an undivided, substance[4]. So also in his third book against Marcion, chap. 6[r], he expressly declares, that "Christ is both the Spirit and THE SUBSTANCE of the Creator," and that "such as knew[5] not the Father, could not know[6] the Son, by reason of His being OF THE SAME SUBSTANCE[7]." This, indeed, was the invariable teaching of Tertullian, as he testifies himself, in his treatise 94
against Praxeas, chap. 4, where he says[s], "I derive not the Son from any other source, but from THE SUBSTANCE OF THE FATHER." So also in the twelfth chapter of the same book[t], "Still," he says, "I every where hold one substance in three coherent [Persons]."

1 προβολαί, probolæ.
2 pariter.
Rom. ix. 5.
3 species.
4 unius et indivisæ substantiæ.
5 agnoverint.
6 agnoscere.
7 per ejusdem substantiæ conditionem.

3. Hence also in his Treatise "On the Flesh of Christ," [in] distinguishing the twofold nature in Christ, the divine

q Apostolum sequar, ut si pariter nominandi fuerint Pater et Filius, Deum Patrem appellem, et Jesum Christum Dominum nominem. Solum autem Christum potero Deum dicere, sicut idem apostolus, *Ex quibus Christus, qui est*, inquit, *Deus super omnia benedictus in ævum omne.* Nam et radium solis seorsum solem vocabo; solem autem nominans, cujus est radius, non statim et radium solem appellabo. Nam etsi soles duos non faciam, tamen et solem et radium ejus tam duas res et duas SPECIES UNIUS INDIVISÆ SUBSTANTIÆ numerabo, quam Deum et Sermonem ejus, quam Patrem et Filium.—[p. 507.]

r [Non negans enim filium] et Spiritum et SUBSTANTIAM Creatoris esse [Christum ejus], eos qui Patrem non agnoverint, nec Filium agnoscere potuisse, per EJUSDEM SUBSTANTIÆ conditionem [concedas necesse est.]—[p. 400.]

s Filium non aliunde deduco, sed de SUBSTANTIA PATRIS.—[p. 502.]

t Cæterum ubique teneo unam substantiam in tribus cohærentibus.—[p. 506.]

and the human, in opposition to those who denied the reality of the Flesh of Christ, Tertullian also expressly teaches that the same Christ, in respect of His more excellent nature, is truly God, and of[1] the substance of God; and also, in regard of His other nature, is in like manner[2] truly man, and has truly taken unto Himself the substance of man; and, moreover, declares that in the former nature He was not born, that is to say was uncreate or not made; in the latter, was born and made. These are his own express statements in the fifth chapter of the forementioned treatise[u]; "Thus His being classed under each substance[3] exhibited Him as man and God; on the one hand born, on the other not born[4]; on the one hand fleshly, on the other spiritual; on the one hand weak, on the other of surpassing strength[5]; on the one hand dying, on the other living; which peculiar properties of these conditions, the divine and the human, are distinguished[6] by the equal reality of each nature, by the same certainty[7] [of the existence] both of the Spirit and
[259] of the flesh." In this passage a countryman of ours interprets the words "not born" thus, "that is, [not born] of a human mother;" but altogether wrongly; for by parity of reasoning, Christ might, even as man, be said to be not born, i. e., [not born] of a human father. I am, however, quite persuaded that Tertullian (who gained much[8] from [the study of] the Greek ecclesiastical writers) here had in view, and in great measure transcribed, the celebrated passage of Ignatius, out of his Epistle to the Ephesians, which we have before quoted[x]: "There is one Physician," &c. For Ignatius's expression in that place, γεννητὸς καὶ ἀγέννητος, is rendered by Tertullian *natus et non natus* ("born and not born"); so also Ignatius's σαρκικὸς καὶ πνευματικὸς is in Tertullian *hinc carneus inde spiritalis* ("on the one hand fleshly, on the other spiritual"); what Ignatius expressed by ἐν σαρκὶ or ἐν ἀνθρώπῳ Θεὸς, ("God in flesh," or "in man,") that Tertullian expresses by *et Deus et homo* ("both God and man"); and lastly, what Ignatius expressed by ἐν θανάτῳ ζωὴ, ("life

1 ex.
2 pariter.
3 utriusque substantiæ census.
4 non natum.
5 præfortem.
6 dispuncta est.
7 fide.
8 multum profecit.

u Ita utriusque substantiæ census hominem et Deum exhibuit; hinc natum, inde non natum; hinc carneum, inde spiritalem; hinc infirmum, inde præfortem; hinc morientem, inde viventem. Quæ proprietas conditionum, divinæ et humanæ, æqua utique naturæ utriusque veritate dispuncta est, eadem fide et spiritus et carnis.—[p. 310.]

x See chap. 2. § 6 of this Book, [p. 96.]

TERTULLIAN.

in death,") that Tertullian expressed by *hinc moriens, inde vivens* (" on the one hand dying, on the other living"); so that Tertullian seems to have translated the Greek text of Ignatius almost *verbatim* into Latin. And, indeed, several considerations induce me to believe, that in this place Tertullian used the words of another, (I mean, of Ignatius,) not his own. First, it might justly be thought very strange, if Tertullian had by mere chance fallen upon so many of the very words of Ignatius, and that just as they were arranged by him in continuous antithesis. Secondly, Tertullian, when he uses his own mode of expression, uniformly speaks of the Father alone, as not born (*non natum*); understanding that alone to be properly called 'not born,' which has not sprung from any original. But, doubtless, Ignatius's expression *ἀγέννητος*, had to be rendered with verbal precision *non natus;* and Tertullian perceived, from the antithesis, that nothing else was meant by Ignatius than that Christ, in that He is God, is uncreate; and this he himself also acknowledged. And to this we must also add the fact, that that sentence of Ignatius in his Epistle to the Ephesians seems to have been regarded as a remark- [260]
able saying, and of great use against heretics who taught blasphemous doctrines respecting the Person of Christ; so that it became of very frequent use[1] amongst the doctors of the Church. Accordingly Athanasius, Gelasius, and Theodoret have all employed it. Hence too, (I may observe in passing,) there is a clear refutation of the sophistical argument of Daillé against the Epistles of Ignatius derived from the silence of Tertullian; "Tertullian," he says, "remarks, that the Marcionites were 'premature abortions'[2], in that they called Christ a phantom; and this he proves from the Apostle John. But Ignatius censures their doctrine, so that, if Tertullian had had any knowledge of him, he would have added his testimony to that of John." To this it is replied by that right reverend and most learned prelate of ours, Bp. Pearson[y], that in the extant writings of Tertullian, he has never quoted, in the exact words, any passage from any ecclesiastical author, with the mention of his name; and this I think is most true. And I add this, that nevertheless in the passage cited, Tertullian has adopted the

[1] celebrem.

[2] præcoquos et abortivos.

[y] Vind. Epist. Ignat. Part I. c. xi. p. 102.

ON THE CONSUBSTANTIALITY OF THE SON.

thoughts of Ignatius, and to a great extent his very words, suppressing all mention of his name; and that against those who maintained that Christ was a phantom, the same whom Ignatius also impugned. I leave this to the judgment of the learned, and myself return to the course of my subject.

4. In harmony with all this is the fact, that Tertullian, in more than one place, explicitly declares that the Son, in that He is God, is of like honour[1] with God the Father, and equal to Him. Presently we shall hear his own words[2] asserting, that all the three Persons of the Godhead, the Father, the Son, and the Holy Ghost, as they are of one substance, so are they also OF ONE STATE[3], AND OF ONE POWER. And as respects the Son, he confesses, in his book against Praxeas, chap. 17, that all the names and attributes of the Father belong also to the Son, so far forth as He is the Son of God.
[261] His words are[z]; "The names of the Father—God Almighty, the Most High, the Lord of Hosts, the King of Israel, He that Is—inasmuch as[4] the Scriptures so teach, these we say belonged also to the Son, and that in these the Son has come, and in these has ever acted, and thus manifested them in Himself unto men. 'All things,' He says, 'that the Father hath[5], are Mine.' Then why not His names also? When therefore you read Almighty God, and Most High, and God of Hosts, and King of Israel, and He that Is, consider whether the Son also be not indicated by these, who IN HIS OWN RIGHT is God Almighty, in that He is the Word of God Almighty." There is a still more explicit passage in his treatise against Marcion, iv. 25[a]; "'All things,' (He saith,) 'are delivered unto Me of the Father.' Thou mayest believe Him, if He be the Christ of the Creator, to whom all things belong[6]; since [in that case] the Creator hath [but] delivered all things to Him who is not less than Himself—to the SON:—all things [I say] which He created by Him, i. e.

[1] ἰσότιμον.
[2] ipsum.
[3] unius status.
[4] quatenus.
[5] omnia Patris. [John xvi. 15.]
[6] si Creatoris est Christus, cujus omnia.

[z] Nomina Patris, Deus omnipotens, Altissimus, Dominus virtutum, Rex Israelis, Qui est, quatenus ita Scripturæ docent, hæc dicimus et in Filium competiisse, et in his Filium venisse, et in his semper egisse, et sic ea in se hominibus manifestasse. *Omnia,* inquit, *Patris mea sunt.* Cur non et nomina? Cum ergo legis Deum omnipotentem, et Altissimum, et Deum virtutum, et Regem Israelis, et Qui est, vide ne per hæc Filius etiam demonstretur, SUO JURE Deus omnipotens, qua Sermo Dei omnipotentis.—[p. 510.]

[a] *Omnia sibi tradita* dicit *a Patre.* Credas, si Creatoris est Christus, cujus omnia, (; ed. Par. 1674.) quia NON MINORI se tradidit omnia FILIO Creator, quæ per eum condidit, per Sermonem scilicet suum.—[p. 440.]

TERTULLIAN.

by His own Word." You may add to these passages the express words of Tertullian in his treatise on the Resurrection of the Flesh, chap. 6[b]; "For the Word also is God, who being[1] in the form[2] of God, thought it not robbery TO BE EQUAL with God;" and also those in the seventh chapter of his treatise against Praxeas[c]; "Thenceforth making Him EQUAL WITH Himself, from whom by proceeding, He became His Son;" and also those words of the same Tertullian in the twenty-second chapter of the same work[d]; "In saying 'I and My Father are One[3],' He shews that they are Two[4], whom He MAKES EQUAL[5] and joins together."

[1] constitutus, [ὑπάρχων.]
[2] effigie.
[3] unum.
[4] duos.
[5] æquat.

5. And by these statements should be explained those expressions which occur in the writings of Tertullian, in which he says, that the Son stands in the same relation to the Father as "a part[6]" to "the sum[7]," or whole, from which it is taken, and, as it were, plucked off[8]. That is to say, metaphorical expressions of this sort ought not to be pressed too closely[9], but to be interpreted with candour, in a fair and good sense, with attention, that is, to the mind and views of the author, as they are elsewhere explained with greater clearness and in unmetaphorical language[10]. In some respects the analogy holds good; in others, however, it is unsuitable[11]. In the following respects it corresponds; 1. In that, as a part does not, alone and of itself, constitute the whole, so the Son also is not the whole of that which is God[12], but, besides the Son, other Persons[13] also subsist in the divine essence, namely the Father and the Holy Ghost. 2. In that, as a part is taken out of the sum or whole, and the whole is naturally prior to its portions or parts, so the Son also is derived from the substance of the Father, and the Father, as Father, is, as it were, naturally prior to the Son. The analogy however fails in the following respects; 1. We understand by "a portion" that which is divided and separated from the whole: the Son, however, is, and ever was, undivided from the Father. And this Tertullian uniformly and on all occasions affirms. Thus in a passage already adduced out of his

[6] portio.
[7] summam.
[8] decerpitur.
[9] non ad vivum resecanda.
[262]
[10] propriis verbis.
[11] disconveniens.
[12] non est omne id quod est Deus.
[13] aliæ ὑποστάσεις.

[b] Et Sermo enim Deus, qui in effigie Dei constitutus non rapinam existimavit PARIARI Deo.—[p. 328, 329.]

[c] Exinde eum PAREM sibi faciens, de quo procedendo filius factus est.—[p. 503.]

[d] *Unum sumus*, dicens, *Ego et Pater*, ostendit duos esse, quos ÆQUAT et jungit.—[p. 513.]

ON THE CONSUBSTANTIALITY OF THE SON.

treatise against Praxeas, chap. 8[e]: "The Son, we say, was put forth from the Father, but not separated from [Him]; and chap. 9[f]: "Keep in mind on all occasions, that I profess this rule [of faith], by which I testify, that the Father, the Son, and the Spirit are inseparable[1] from each other;" and chap. 19[g]; "We have likewise shewn that in Scripture two Gods are spoken of, and Lords two; and yet, that they may not be offended at this assertion, we explained how that they are not said to be two, in that they are Gods, nor yet in that they are Lords; but two, in that they are Father and Son: and this not by separation of substance[2], but from their mutual relation[3]; since we declare the Son to be indivisible and inseparable[4] from the Father." 2. A part is less than the whole from which it is taken; the Son, however, is in all respects, (excepting that He is the Son,) like, and equal to[5] the Father, and has and possesses all that the Father has. This also Tertullian plainly teaches in the several passages which we have just now adduced[h]. To these may be added an expression in book iii. chap. 6[i] of his treatise against Marcion, where, after saying, that the
[263] Son is a portion out of the fulness of the divine essence, he soon after expressly adds, that that portion is "co-sharer of the fulness[6]." When, however, Tertullian, in his treatise against Praxeas, chap. 14[k], compares together the Father and the Son by an analogy derived from the sun, (that is, as he expresses it, from the "sum itself of the substance," which is in the heavens, the excessive brightness whereof cannot be looked on, and its ray, whose brightness is endurable, "tempered as it is by its being only a portion[7],") it must be understood (unless you are disposed to charge Tertullian with the grossest contradiction) of that economy[1] which the Son of

[1] inseparatos.
[2] non ex separatione substantiæ.
[3] sed ex dispositione.
[4] inseparatum.
[5] par et æqualis.
[6] plenitudinis consortem.
[7] pro temperatura portionis.

e Prolatum dicimus Filium a Patre, sed non separatum.—[p. 504.]

f Hanc me regulam professum, qua inseparatos ab alterutro Patrem et Filium et Spiritum testor, tene ubique. —[Ibid.]

g Ostendimus etiam duos Deos in Scriptura relatos et duos Dominos; et tamen ne de isto scandalizentur, rationem reddidimus, qua Dei non duo dicantur, nec Domini, sed qua Pater et Filius, duo; et hoc non ex separatione substantiæ, sed ex dispositione, quum individuum et inseparatum Filium a Patre pronuntiamus.—[p. 511.]

h See also iv. 2. 5.

i [p. 400.]

k [Tertullian's words are; "Sicut nec solem nobis contemplari licet, quantum ad ipsam substantiæ summam, quæ est in cœlis, radium autem ejus toleramus oculis pro temperatura portionis, quæ in terras inde porrigitur." p. 508.]

1 These words of Tertullian may also be referred to that condescension of the Son, wherein from the [time of]

God, out of His great love to the human race, voluntarily undertook; by which, that is to say, ever since the fall of the first man, He condescended[1], and made Himself, so far as might be[2], visible to holy men in every age, and in the fulness of time became man, and held familiar intercourse with mankind. Nay, I shall hereafter, in the fourth book, most evidently shew, that this was indeed the very mind and view of Tertullian and of the rest of the fathers, in those passages in which they prove that He who appeared to the patriarchs, was not God the Father Himself, but His Son—on this ground, that the Father is invisible, and cannot be inclosed in space; whereas the Son is visible, and is found to have a local presence[3].

[1] se demisit.
[2] utcunque.
[3] et in loco reperiatur.

6. But why dwell on this? Tertullian throughout his writings explicitly confesses the entire Trinity of one substance and of one majesty[4]. Thus in the second chapter of his treatise against Praxeas, having recited the rule of faith[5], he thus proceeds[m]; "But keeping that prescription inviolate[n], still some opportunity must be given for reviewing [the statements of the heretics], with a view to the instruction and protection of certain persons; were it only that it may not seem that each perversion is condemned without examination, and prejudged; especially that [perversion,] which supposes itself to possess the pure truth, in thinking that one cannot believe in one only God in any other way, than by saying, that the Father, the Son, and the Holy Ghost are the very same Person. As if in this way also One were not All, in that All are of One, by unity, that is, of substance, whilst nevertheless the mystery of the economy is guarded, which

[4] ὁμοούσιον et ὁμότιμον.
[5] regulam fidei.

[264]

creation itself He stooped and accommodated Himself to the things created; on this point see iii. 9. § 10, 11.

[m] Sed salva ista præscriptione, utique tamen propter instructionem et munitionem quorundam, dandus est etiam retractatibus locus; vel ne videatur unaquæque perversitas non examinata, sed præjudicata damnari; maxime hæc, quæ se existimat meram veritatem possidere, dum unicum Deum non alias putat credendum, quam si ipsum eundemque et Patrem et Filium et Spiritum S. dicat. Quasi non sic quoque unus sit omnia, dum ex uno omnia, per substantiæ scil. unitatem, et nihilominus custodiatur οἰκονομίας sacramentum, quæ unitatem in Trinitatem disponit, tres dirigens, Patrem, Filium et Spiritum S.; tres autem non statu, sed gradu; nec substantia, sed forma; nec potestate, sed specie; UNIUS AUTEM SUBSTANTIÆ, ET UNIUS STATUS, ET UNIUS POTESTATIS; quia unus Deus, ex quo et gradus isti, et formæ, et species, in nomine Patris et Filii et Spiritus S. deputantur.—[p. 501.]

[n] [That is, the principle by which a position that is contrary to the creed is thereby determined to be false, without further examination.]

ON THE CONSUBSTANTIALITY OF THE SON.

distributes the Unity into a Trinity, placing in their order three [Persons], the Father, the Son, and the Holy Ghost; three, however, not in condition[1], but in degree; not in substance, but in form; not in power, but in aspect[2] o: YET OF ONE SUBSTANCE, AND OF ONE CONDITION[3], AND OF ONE POWER;
96 inasmuch as it is one God, from whom these degrees, and forms, and aspects[4] are reckoned, under the name of the Father, and of the Son, and of the Holy Ghost." Where, if I mistake not, by the word *gradus* (degree) he would have us understand that order, whereby the Father exists of Himself, the Son goes forth[5] immediately from the Father, and the Holy Ghost proceeds[6] from the Father through the Son; so that the Father is rightly designated the first, the Son the second, and the Holy Ghost the third Person of the Godhead. And by the expressions *formæ* (forms) and *species* (aspects), he seems to have meant to indicate the different modes of subsistence[7], whereby the Father, the Son, and the Holy Ghost subsist in the same divine nature. Be that however as it may, it is manifest that in these words all the three Persons of the Godhead are laid down to be of one substance and one dignity[8]. And to this should be added another passage of the same treatise, chap. 13; where he says p; "We do indeed distinguish[9] two, the Father and the Son, and again Three, with the Holy Ghost, according to the principle of the [divine] economy, which introduces[10] number, in order that the Father may not (as you perversely infer) be Himself believed to have been born and to have suffered, which it is not lawful to believe, forasmuch as it hath not been so handed down[11]. Still never do we utter from
[265] our mouth [the words] two Gods, or two Lords, not as if it were not true that the Father is God, and the Son is God, and the Holy Ghost is God, and each is God; but forasmuch as in earlier times there were two Gods and two Lords

[1] statu.
[2] specie.
[3] status.
[4] species.
[5] prodeat.
[6] procedat.
[7] diversos τρόπους ὑπάρξεως.
[8] ὁμοουσίους et ὁμοτίμους.
[9] definimus.
[10] facit.
[11] traditum.

o [The word *species* is inadequately represented by "aspect;" see the use of it in the passages quoted above, from this Treatise, p. 194, note p, and p. 195, note q.]

p Duos quidem definimus, Patrem et Filium, et jam tres cum Spiritu S. secundum rationem Œconomiæ, quæ facit numerum, ne (ut vestra perversitas infert) Pater ipse credatur natus et passus, quod non licet credi, quoniam non ita traditum est. Duos tamen Deos et duos Dominos nunquam ex ore nostro proferimus; non quasi non et Pater Deus, et Filius Deus, et Spiritus S. Deus, et Deus unusquisque; sed quoniam retro et duo Dii et duo Domini prædicabantur, ut, ubi venisset Christus, et Deus agnosceretur, et Dominus vocaretur, quia Filius Dei et Domini.—[p. 507.]

spoken of, in order that, when Christ came, He might both be recognised as God, and be called Lord, being the Son of [Him who is] God and Lord." Where, by the way, you may observe that Tertullian expressly pronounces the Holy Ghost also to be God, equally with the Father and the Son. This I remark in opposition to an inconsiderate assertion of Erasmus [q], to the effect, that for a considerable time, that is, until the times of Hilary, the ancient writers never ventured to give the name of God to the Holy Ghost. I might, if that were now the question, refute this allegation of Erasmus at great length; but the reader, if he please, can consult Petavius on the Trinity, iii. 7. 1, &c. I return to my subject, only adding to the passages which have been already cited one quotation more from Tertullian, which may be found in his tract *de Pudicitia*, c. 21, where he expressly acknowledges [r] "The Trinity of THE ONE GODHEAD, the Father, the Son, and the Holy Ghost."

7. Before, however, we pass from Tertullian to other ecclesiastical writers, we must detain the reader a short time, whilst we refute a strange notion [1] of Sandius. He says it is plain that Tertullian, prior to his falling into the heresy of Montanus, entertained the same opinions as those of Arius, concerning the Father, the Son, and the Holy Ghost. And then on this most idle assumption he argues thus; "Hence, if any thing is found in the writings of Tertullian in favour of the doctrine of consubstantiality, the Arians have much more right to detract from his authority by alleging his Montanism [as an objection to it]," (that is, he means to say, than the Catholics, who employ that argument for the purpose of correcting certain statements of Tertullian respecting the Son of God, which appear to them unsound), "as though he had only at last, on adopting the views of Montanus, begun to believe in a consubstantial Trinity." But on this point this most frivolous person is convicted of error by the following very evident arguments. First, it is certain that the Catholic doctors who preceded both Montanus and Tertullian, whose writings have come down to us, did universally hold the consubstantiality of the Son, as also of the Holy Ghost,—it is certain, I say, [266]

[1] commentum.

[q] In his preface to Hilary.

[r] Trinitas UNIUS DIVINITATIS, Pater, et Filius, et Spiritus Sanctus.—[p. 574.]

ON THE CONSUBSTANTIALITY OF THE SON.

from the very clear testimonies which I have already quoted from them one by one. Tertullian, therefore, first learnt the doctrine of the consubstantial Trinity from the Catholic Church, in whose communion he remained for a considerable time, and not "at last[1]" from Montanus, to whose party he afterwards fell away. Again, in all the works of Tertullian, both those which he wrote previously to, as well as those which he wrote after, his defection to the heresy of Montanus, statements are found which most plainly establish the doctrine of the Trinity of one substance, as all are well aware who have studied his writings, and as the passages which have already been adduced fully evidence. Furthermore, Tertullian himself, after he became a Montanist, although he makes a very ridiculous boast, that he had been more assured concerning the mystery of the holy Trinity, as also concerning the other heads of the Christian religion which appertain to the rule of faith, by the spirit of Montanus, than he had previously been through the letter of Scripture and the tradition of the Church, still expressly allows that he had ever held the self-same belief and view concerning the Father, the Son, and the Holy Ghost. His words in the second chapter of his treatise against Praxeas are clear[s]; "We indeed," he says, "have ever believed, and much more now,—as being better instructed by the Paraclete, who is the bringer down[2] of all truth,—do we believe, that there is indeed one only[3] God, but yet under this dispensation, which we call the economy, that of the one only God, there be also the Son His Word, who came forth from Him," &c.
[267] Then having recited the rule of faith, he affirms that the Trinity of one substance is therein taught. Now that by the Paraclete, Tertullian meant the Paraclete of Montanus, (to whose guidance, after having deserted the Church, he had now surrendered himself,) the learned are agreed, and the thing speaks for itself. In conclusion I would have the reader at this place to turn again to what has been already said concerning Montanus in the first chapter, § 15, of this book [pp. 83, 84.]

1 demum.

2 deductorem.

3 unicum.

s Nos vero et semper, et nunc magis, ut instructiores per Paracletum, deductorem scilicet omnis veritatis, unicum quidem Deum credimus, sub hac tamen dispensatione, quam οἰκονομίαν dicimus, ut unici Dei sit et Filius Sermo ejus, qui ex ipso processerit, &c.—[p. 501.]

8. But the reader should observe the wonderful acquaintance of Sandius with the writings of the ancients, which he has undertaken to criticise. To prove his hypothesis he makes use of this argument, that those doctrines which savour of Arianism, are mainly to be discovered in those 97
works of Tertullian, "which Jerome does not enumerate amongst those which he wrote in defence of Montanus[1], yea, which he must necessarily have written before he lapsed into Montanism, such as are his treatises against Praxeas and Hermogenes." But, in the first place, we have shewn above[t] that in his book against Praxeas the consubstantiality of the Son, which is opposed enough to the Arian heresy, is taught most frequently and most explicitly. Secondly, so far is it from being necessary, that it is manifestly untrue, that Tertullian wrote his treatise against Praxeas before he lapsed into Montanism. For Tertullian himself expressly professes, and that in this very treatise against Praxeas, that even at the time he was writing, he was already dissevered from "the carnal[2]," as he called them, that is from the catholics, and had joined himself to the party of Montanus. For not far from the [268]
opening of his treatise, he thus writes[u]: "For when the bishop of Rome was on the point of acknowledging the prophecies of Montanus, Prisca, and Maximilla, and in consequence of that acknowledgment was introducing peace among the Churches of Asia and Phrygia, this very same man (Praxeas), by false representations about the prophets themselves and their assemblies, and by upholding the example of his predecessors as an authority[3], induced him both to recall the letter of peace[4]

[1] pro Montano.

[2] psychicis.

[3] præcessorum auctoritates.

[4] literas pacis.

[t] To the very many testimonies of Tertullian which have already been quoted in this chapter from the treatise against Praxeas, in support of the consubstantiality of the Son, I add a passage, out of the same treatise, c. 25. [p. 515], concerning the Holy Trinity, which is especially worthy of attention: "Thus the connection of the Father in the Son, and of the Son in the Comforter, produces three [Persons] coherent one to another. These three [Persons] (*tres*) are one thing (*unum*), not one Person (*unus*); as it is said, I and My Father are one (*unum*); with respect to unity of substance, not singularity of number." (Ita connexus Patris in Filio, et Filii in Paracleto, tres efficit cohærentes, alterum ex altero. Qui tres unum sint, non unus; quomodo dictum est, *Ego et Pater unum sumus*; ad substantiæ unitatem, non ad numeri singularitatem.) Compare also what is adduced in the following chapter, 8. § 4.—GRABE.

[u] Nam idem (Praxeas) tunc episcopum Romanum agnoscentem jam prophetias Montani, Priscæ, Maximillæ, et ex ea agnitione pacem ecclesiis Asiæ et Phrygiæ inferentem, falsa de ipsis prophetis et ecclesiis eorum adseverando, et præcessorum ejus auctoritates defendendo, coegit et literas pacis revocare jam emissas, et a

ON THE CONSUBSTANTIALITY OF THE SON.

which he had already issued, and to desist from his intention of recognising the gifts[1]. Thus did Praxeas manage at Rome two affairs of the devil; he thrust out prophecy, and brought in heresy; he put the Paraclete to flight, and crucified the Father." Tertullian, you observe, was so incensed with Praxeas, as to say, that he had herein been managing the devil's business, in advising the bishop of Rome to repudiate Montanus with his followers, and their prophecies. Tertullian, then, was not only at that time a Montanist, but zealot for that sect. And in the same treatise you may read shortly after[x]; "And the recognition and defence of the Paraclete dissevered us also from the carnally-minded." As to the allegation that Jerome does not enumerate the treatise against Praxeas amongst the works which Tertullian wrote in defence of Montanus[2], my answer is, that a clear distinction must be made between those works which Tertullian, when already a Montanist, wrote specifically in defence of Montanus against the Church, and those which he composed, as a Montanist indeed, yet not in defence of Montanus against the Church, but rather in defence of the common doctrines of the Church and of Montanus, in opposition to other heretics. In the former list Jerome puts the treatises *de Pudicitia, de Jejuniis, de Monogamia, de Ecstasi;* we have given the clearest proofs, that the treatise against Praxeas belongs to the latter class. This, however, is enough for the present concerning Tertullian.

1 recipiendorum charismatum.

2 pro Montano.

98
[269]

CHAPTER VIII.

THE NICENE CREED, ON THE ARTICLE OF THE CONSUBSTANTIALITY OF THE SON, CONFIRMED BY THE TESTIMONIES OF THE PRESBYTER CAIUS, AND OF THE CELEBRATED BISHOP AND MARTYR ST. HIPPOLYTUS.

CAIUS.

1. I NOW come to those ecclesiastical writers who lived nearest to the age of Tertullian. There was extant in the time of

proposito recipiendorum charismatum concessare. Ita duo negotia Diaboli Praxeas Romæ procuravit; prophetiam expulit, et hæresim intulit; Paracletum fugavit, et Patrem crucifixit.—[p. 501.]

x Et nos quidem agnitio Paracleti atque defensio disjunxit a psychicis.—[Ibid.]

BOOK II. CHAP. VIII. § 1, 2.

CAIUS.

Photius a work entitled, *περὶ τοῦ Παντὸς*, (On the Universe,) which some persons very absurdly attributed to Josephus the Jew, others to Justin Martyr, and some again to Irenæus, Photius[y] also reports. Photius, however, correctly followed the view of those who handed down a tradition that the work was really written by the presbyter Caius,—who was the author of a celebrated treatise called the Labyrinth, and flourished[z] chiefly in the time of Zephyrinus, bishop of Rome,—as Caius himself at the end of the Labyrinth has left it on record, that he was the author[a] of a book on the Nature of the Universe. However, how consistently in all respects with the catholic doctrine this author wrote concerning the true Godhead of Christ, Photius informs us in the following terms[b]; "However, respecting the Divinity of Christ our true God, he treats most accurately[1], both declaring the appellation itself to belong to Christ, and describing irreprehensibly His ineffable generation from the Father." But Caius certainly would not [270] have been regarded, at least in the judgment and under the criticism of Photius, as treating most accurately[2] and irreprehensibly of the true Divinity of our Saviour, and of His ineffable generation, if any thing had fallen from him which would make for the Arians, or would be inconsistent, even in appearance, with the consubstantiality of the Son. It is therefore on most just grounds that we class this writer amongst those who assert and maintain the catholic faith of Nicæa.

1 ὡς ἔγγιστα θεολογεῖ.

2 aptissime.

HIPPOLYTUS.

2. After the presbyter Caius we must place next[3] St. Hippolytus the martyr[c], and bishop of Portus, (as we learn from Anastasius the librarian), who flourished during the reign of the Emperor Alexander, the son of Mammea, i. e., about the

3 succenturiandus.

[y] In his Bibliotheca, cod. 48.

[z] Caius flourished about the year 210. Cave.—BOWYER.

[a] Caius wrote a work 'On the Nature of the Universe,' (Περὶ τῆς τοῦ παντὸς οὐσίας,) as he has himself left on record, at the conclusion of his book entitled 'the Labyrinth', as transcribed by Photius. Whether, however, that work is the same as that which bears the title, Περὶ τοῦ παντὸς, 'On the Universe,' and is commonly appended to the writings of Hippolytus, is uncertain. Cave.—BOWYER. [See Routh, Reliq. Sacr. ii. p. 31.—B.]

[b] περὶ μέν τοι Χριστοῦ τοῦ ἀληθινοῦ Θεοῦ ἡμῶν ὡς ἔγγιστα θεολογεῖ, κλῆσίν τε αὐτὴν ἀναφθεγγόμενος Χριστοῦ, καὶ τὴν ἐκ Πατρὸς ἄφραστον γέννησιν ἀμέμπτως ἀναγράφων.—[Biblioth. cod. 48.]

[c] [Jerome and Theodoret mention Hippolytus as a martyr; and it has been supposed, that he suffered either in the Decian persecution in 250, or in that of Maximus in 235. According to either of these dates we may safely follow Lardner, in considering him to have flourished about the year 220. Dr. Burton, Test., vol. i. 244.]

ON THE CONSUBSTANTIALITY OF THE SON.

year of Christ 220. He in his *Opuscula*, written against Beron and Helix[d], which are found in the *Collectanea* of Anastasius, accurately distinguishes the twofold nature in Christ, and shews that His divine nature is absolutely the same as that which is in the Father. For he says, that[e] "Christ both is, and is conceived to be, as well infinite[1] God as circumscribed[2] man, possessing perfectly the perfect substance[3] of each." To the same author belongs the following noble[4] confession touching the natures of Christ, the divine and the human, than which none more express or significant was ever put forth by any one, even after the Nicene council. "For the Godhead[5]," he says[f], "as it was before His incarnation, is also after His incarnation, by nature infinite, incomprehensible, impassible, incapable of being compounded, unchangeable, unalterable, self-powerful, and in a word, having a substantial existence[6], alone a good of infinite power." Nor will any one
[271] wonder that Hippolytus should have put forth these so clear and magnificent statements concerning the Son of God, if he recollects that he was, as the ancients have handed down, the disciple of Clement of Alexandria, who treated most accurately[7] of the divinity of Christ, the true God; as we have shewn above.

[1] ἄπειρον. [2] περιγραπτόν. [3] οὐσίαν. [4] illustris. [5] τὸ Θεῖον. [6] ὑφεστὸς οὐσιῶδες. [7] ὡς ἔγγιστα θεολογεῖ.

3. And as these testimonies are so clear and express, Sandius could discern no other way of evading them, than by boldly pronouncing[g], as is forsooth his practice, that "the treatises on the Divinity and the Incarnation, against Beron and Helix, Serm I. in the *Collectanea* of Anastasius, are not works of Hippolytus." But let us see by what reasoning he defends this his authoritative decision, in opposition to the judgment of that ancient and great librarian, who was es-
99 pecially versed, as his office implied, in the MSS. of the earlier Fathers; "Neither Eusebius," he says, "nor Jerome have mentioned any treatise of that kind." As if, forsooth, Eusebius and Jerome had made particular mention

[d] Hippolytus, Sermon I. in Anastasius's Collectanea, p. 210.

[e] Θεὸν ἄπειρον ὁμοῦ, καὶ περιγραπτὸν ἄνθρωπον ὄντα τε καὶ νοούμενον, τὴν οὐσίαν ἑκατέρου τελείως τελείαν ἔχοντα. —[vol. i. p. 226.]

[f] τὸ γὰρ θεῖον, ὡς ἦν πρὸ σαρκώσεως, ἔστι καὶ μετὰ σάρκωσιν κατὰ φύσιν ἄπειρον, ἄσχετον, ἀπαθὲς, ἀσύγκριτον, ἀναλλοίωτον, ἄτρεπτον, αὐτόσθενες, καὶ τὸ πᾶν εἰπεῖν, ὑφεστὸς οὐσιῶδες, μόνον ἀπειροσθενὲς ἀγαθόν. — [Hippolytus, Serm. I. apud Anastas. in Collect. p. 211.]

[g] De Script. Eccl., p. 27.

of all the writings of all the ancient doctors. Nay further, Eusebius expressly declares, that he had not by any means given a full catalogue of the works of Hippolytus, as, after enumerating certain of his writings, he adds[l]; "and you will find very many others, and those preserved by several persons." And Jerome added very few writings of Hippolytus to Eusebius's catalogue. Indeed with no less semblance of truth might Sandius have contended that Hippolytus never was bishop of any church, seeing that both Eusebius and Jerome were wholly ignorant of the place of which he was bishop, and we learned it at last from Anastasius. [272]
Here too is another trifling argument of his; "The author of those *Excerpta*[m] must necessarily have been either a Sabellian or a Eutychian, because of these words of his: Ὃ ταυτόν ἐστι τῷ Πατρὶ, γενόμενος ταυτὸν τῇ σαρκὶ διὰ τὴν κένωσιν, 'in which He is the same with the Father, having become the same with the flesh through His emptying of Himself[1].' But both forms of expression are heretical in the judgment of Ignatius in his Epistle to the Trallians, when he says that heretics teach[n] ταυτὸν εἶναι πατέρα, καὶ υἱὸν, καὶ πνεῦμα ἅγιον, 'that the Father, and the Son, and the Holy Ghost are the same,' and afterwards[o] οὐδὲ γὰρ ταυτὸν Θεὸς καὶ ἄνθρωπος, 'for neither is God and man the same.' For if ταυτὸν be said to denote identity of subsistence[2], it is most clearly Sabellianism; if it mean unity of essence and nature, it is palpable Eutychianism." To this I reply, that ταυτὸν in the former clause of the passage, [i. e. of the quotation from Hippolytus,] does certainly denote unity of essence or nature, and not identity of subsistence; which latter sense alone the Pseudo-Ignatius[3], whom Sandius quotes, attacked. Still it must not on this account be conceded, that the phrase ταυτὸν τῇ σαρκί ("the same with the flesh") establishes Eutychianism. In order that you may perceive more clearly the insufferable ignorance or dishonesty, whichever it be, of the objector, see here, reader, the passage of Hippolytus entire[p]: "The Word or Son of God," he says, "under-

[1] [Cf. Phil. ii. 7. ἐκένωσεν ἑαυτόν.]

[2] subsistentiæ, i. e. hypostasis, or person.

[3] spurius ille Ignatius.

πλεῖστά τε ἄλλα καὶ παρὰ πολλοῖς εὕροις ἂν σωζόμενα.—[Hist. Eccles. vi. 22.]

[m] [The treatises of Hippolytus just spoken of.]

[n] [S. Ignat. Interp. Ep. ad Trall., c. vi. p. 62.]

[o] [Ibid., c. ix. p. 64.]

[p] τροπὴν οὐχ ὑπέμεινεν, μηδ' ἐνὶ παντελῶς, ὃ ταυτόν (ταυτό ed. Cotel.) ἐστι

ON THE CONSUBSTANTIALITY OF THE SON.

went no change, not in any one point, in which He is the same with the Father, having become the same with the flesh[1] through His emptying of Himself. But just as He was when apart from flesh, so did He continue, free from all circumscription." You see that Hippolytus does not here affirm, but expressly denies, that the Word or Son of God, after His Incarnation, became in any respect whatever the same with the flesh. Surely nothing could have been said more expressly opposed to the madness of Eutyches. But
[273] Sandius still presses the point; "It is, moreover," he says, "abundantly clear that the author was a Sabellian, from his words in Anastasius, in which he attributes to the Son the quality of being ἀγέννητος[2]; for Ignatius, in the passage referred to[q], writes, that the heretics (the followers of Simon, who were the precursors of Sabellius) thought that Christ was ἀγέννητος." Surely the sophist is here in sport, and wishing to make sport of his reader through the palpable double-meaning of the word ἀγεννησία. I have already shewn that the words ἀγένητος and ἀγέννητος are used indiscriminately by ecclesiastical writers, especially those who were prior to the council of Nice; so that ἀγέννητος, as well as ἀγένητος, indicated that which is uncreate or not made; in which sense the true Ignatius expressly declared that the Son is ἀγέννητος. See what we have already said in chapter ii. § 6. of this book, [pp. 96, 97.] Anastasius, therefore, has correctly, though barbarously[3], translated ἀγεννησία, the word used by Hippolytus, by *infactio*. I am sorry to have so often to remind the reader of such trite and well-known points.

4. More specious is the objection of those who attempt to prove that these *Excerpta* are not the writings of Hippolytus, on the ground that they contain a clear refutation of the heresy of Eutyches, who lived long after Hippolytus. Possevin, after[4] Canisius, replies to them in his Apparatus[r], by saying that "the error" respecting the mixture[5] of the natures in Christ, "against which Hippolytus is disputing, was not for the first time[6] originated and introduced by Apollinaris

[1] ταυτὸν τῇ σαρκί.
[2] ἀγεννησίαν.
[3] barbare.
[4] ex.
[5] de permixtione.
[6] demum.

τῷ Πατρὶ, γενόμενος ταυτὸν τῇ σαρκὶ διὰ τὴν κένωσιν· ἀλλ' ὥσπερ ἦν δίχα σαρκὸς, πάσης ἔξω περιγραφῆς μεμένηκε. —Anastas. in Collect., p. 210. [vol. i. p. 226.]

[q] [Ibid., c. vi. p. 62.]

[r] [p. 763. ed. 1608. Cf. Canisii Lect. Antiq., tom. i. p. 11. ed. 1725.]

and Eutyches, but was very much earlier, since Justin Martyr makes mention of it in his Exposition of the Faith." Perhaps Canisius and Possevin were wrong, in attributing the Exposition of the Faith to Justin Martyr; still it is very certain from other sources, that the error respecting the mixture of the natures in Christ was earlier than Apollinaris and Eutyches; and moreover, that it was opposed by doctors of the Church who lived before Hippolytus. I might make good this statement by many testimonies, but I shall be content with a single passage out of Tertullian; in his treatise against Praxeas, which is of unquestioned genuineness, chap. 27[8], [274]
he thus speaks concerning the Incarnation of the Word; "This we must enquire into, how the Word became flesh, whether [by] having been as it were transformed in flesh[1], or having put on flesh? Surely, having put on [flesh.] For the rest, we must needs believe God to be unchangeable, and incapable of form[2], as being eternal. But transformation is a destruction of that which previously existed[3]; for whatsoever is transformed into something else, ceases to be that which it had been, and begins to be what it was not. But God neither ceases to be [what He is,] nor can He be any thing else [than He is.] But the Word is God, and the Word of the Lord abideth for ever, by continuing, that is, in His own form. Now if He admit not of being transformed, it follows, that He be in this sense understood to have been made flesh, when He comes to be in the flesh, and is manifested, and is seen, and is handled by means of the flesh; inasmuch as the other points also require to be thus 100
understood. For if the Word has been made flesh by a transformation and change[4] of substance, it follows at once that Jesus will be one substance out of two substances, a kind of mixture[5] [made up] of flesh and spirit, just like

[1] transfiguratus in carne.

[2] informabilem.

[3] interemptio pristini.

[4] demutatione.

[5] mixtura quædam.

[8] De hoc quærendum, quomodo Sermo caro sit factus, utrumne quasi transfiguratus in carne, an indutus carnem? Imo indutus. Cæterum Deum immutabilem et informabilem credi necesse est, ut æternum. Transfiguratio autem interemptio est pristini; omne enim quodcumque transfiguratur in aliud, desinit esse quod fuerat, et incipit esse quod non erat; Deus autem neque desinit esse, neque aliud potest esse. Sermo autem, Deus; et Sermo Domini manet in ævum, perseverando scilicet in sua forma. Quem si non capit transfigurari, consequens est, ut sic caro factus intelligatur, dum fit in carne et manifestatur, et videtur, et contrectatur per carnem: quia et cætera sic accipi exigunt. Si enim Sermo ex transfiguratione et demutatione substantiæ caro factus est, una jam erit substantia Jesus ex duabus, ex carne et spiritu mixtura quædam, ut electrum ex auro et argento; et incipit nec

ON THE CONSUBSTANTIALITY OF THE SON.

electrum [made up] of gold and silver; and there begins to be neither gold, that is to say, Spirit, nor silver, that is, flesh; the one being changed by the other, and a third substance[1] produced. Jesus, therefore, will neither be God; for He who is made flesh has ceased to be the Word; nor will He be flesh, that is, Man; inasmuch as He who was the Word is not properly Flesh. Consequently, [being made up] of both, He is neither; [but rather] He is a third substance very different from either. But now we find Him expressly set forth as both God and Man . . . clearly in all respects[2] the Son of God, and the Son of Man, as being God and Man, without doubt according to each substance differing in what is peculiar to itself[3], because the Word is nothing else but God, and the Flesh nothing else but Man.
[275] Thus does the Apostle also teach concerning His twofold substance; 'Who was made,' says he, 'of the seed of David[4];' here He will be Man and Son of Man: 'Who was declared to be the Son of God, according to the Spirit;' here He will be God, and the Word of God, the Son. We see the twofold state, which is not confounded, but joined in one Person, Jesus, God and Man." These are the words of Tertullian, who was earlier than Hippolytus, than which nothing was ever said more express or effectual against the heresy of Eutyches. Yet, who would not regard that man as an egregious sophist, who should conclude from this that the treatise against Praxeas was not Tertullian's, but the work of an author who wrote subsequently to the time of Eutyches? But forsooth as in the world, so in the Church, the same play is ever acted over again, and the heresies which a later age calls new, are in truth nothing but ancient errors revived, and recalled from the shades.

[1] tertium quid.

[2] usquequaque.

[3] in sua proprietate.

[4] [Rom. i. 3.]

aurum esse, id est, spiritus, neque argentum, id est, caro, dum alterum altero mutatur, et tertium quid efficitur. Neque ergo Deus erit Jesus; Sermo enim desiit esse, qui caro factus est: neque caro, id est, homo; caro enim non proprie est, qui Sermo fuit. Ita ex utroque neutrum est; aliud longe tertium est, quam utrumque. Sed enim invenimus illum directo et Deum et hominem expositum . . . . certe usquequaque Filium Dei et Filium hominis, cum Deum et hominem, sine dubio secundum utramque substantiam in sua proprietate distantem; quia neque Sermo aliud quam Deus, neque caro aliud quam homo. Sic et apostolus de utraque ejus substantia docet; *Qui factus est*, inquit, *ex semine David;* hic erit homo et filius hominis: *qui definitus est Filius Dei secundum Spiritum;* hic erit Deus et Sermo Dei, Filius. Videmus duplicem statum, non confusum, sed conjunctum in una persona, Deum et hominem Jesum.—[p. 516.]

BOOK II. CHAP. VIII. § 4, 5.

HIPPOLYTUS.

5. But what does the author of the Irenicum[u] mean, by rejecting these fragments of Hippolytus as "very recently brought forward[1]?" Is Anastasius himself very recent, who flourished eight hundred years ago? yet in his *Collectanea*, these *Excerpta* are extant, and are brought forward as (beyond controversy) the genuine works of Hippolytus. Or does he suspect that those *Collectanea*, which Sirmond edited in the year 1620, are not the production of Anastasius the librarian? And yet Anastasius himself, in the preface to his undoubted work, the Ecclesiastical History, or *Chronographia tripartita*, expressly professes himself to be the author of those *Collectanea*, and mentions (as P. Labbé has observed) some of the tracts which he had translated into Latin and inserted in that collection. As to this anonymous writer's further objection, that certain statements are found in those *Excerpta* touching the eternity of the Son, which are inconsistent with the doctrine of Hippolytus in his undoubted work against the heresy of Noetus, I shall clearly shew how frivolous it is, when I come to the third book, on the coeternity of the [276] Son. It is also to no purpose that he adduces out of this same treatise against Noetus the following passage, as inconsistent with the theology of the *Excerpta*[x]: "For neither was the Word without flesh, and of Himself, perfect Son, whilst yet He was the perfect WORD, [being] the Only-begotten: neither could the flesh apart from the Word subsist of itself, forasmuch as it had its *ὑπόστασις* in the Word, (that is to say, it subsisted in the Word)." For surely Hippolytus was not so insane as to say (what our anonymous author would have him say) that aught of intrinsic perfection really accrued to the Word, or Only-begotten, from His assuming flesh; nay, he plainly teaches the contrary. For, in the first place, he expressly declares, that our Lord was the perfect Word, and Only-begotten, previous to His incarnation. And then he clearly teaches, that so far was the Word or Only-begotten from being bettered by[2] the human flesh,

[1] recentissime producta.

[2] melioratum ex.

[u] p. 67.

[x] [The Greek is, *οὔτε γὰρ ἄσαρκος καὶ καθ' ἑαυτὸν ὁ λόγος τέλειος ἦν υἱὸς, καὶ τοι τέλειος λόγος ὢν μονογενὴς, οὐθ' ἡ σὰρξ καθ' ἑαυτὴν δίχα τοῦ λόγου ὑποστάναι ἠδύνατο, διὰ τὸ ἐν λόγῳ τὴν σύστασιν ἔχειν.* vol. ii. p. 17. Both Bp. Bull and the author of the Irenicum, from want of care, substitute in the Latin *ὑπόστασιν* for *σύστασιν*.—B. The words added in the Latin version are enclosed in parentheses.]

that that flesh owes its very subsistence to the Word. What then, you will say, did Hippolytus mean, by saying that the Word and Only-begotten was not, without flesh, a perfect Son? I reply, his meaning manifestly was, that, previous to the Incarnation, the Word had not, so to speak, fulfilled every kind of sonship[1]; or in other words, was not, as yet, the Son of God, in every way in which the Father willed Him to be. What I mean[2] is this; the ancients attributed to our Lord a threefold nativity and sonship. The first is that whereby, as the Logos, He was from eternity born of[3] the mind of the Father. From this nativity there has existed[4] a perfect Divine Person; nor has any thing subsequently been added[5] to Him; but the remaining nativities have been rather συγκαταβάσεις, or condescensions of the Son of God. For[6] the second
[277] nativity is that by which the Word came forth in operation[7] from God the Father, (with whom He had been, when as yet there was nothing in being besides God, and consequently from eternity,) and proceeded forth from His womb, as it were, and lowered Himself[8] for the creation of the universe. The third and last nativity took place at that time, when the same Word became flesh, and descending from the bosom of the Father into the womb of the most blessed Virgin, was born Man of her, through the overshadowing of the Holy Ghost. This was that extreme condescension of the Word, (eternally to be adored by us men, aye, and by the very angels,) on the completion of which He became the perfect Son of God, that is, as I have already said, He fulfilled every kind of sonship; inasmuch as the other sonships, which regard the human nature of Christ, depend upon this, and follow from it[9]. This we shall explain more at length in the third book, concerning the coeternity of the Son; in the meantime this is to be observed, that among the passages, which the author of the
101 *Irenicum* has adduced from Hippolytus's book against Noetus, as contrary to the Catholic, i. e., the Nicene faith, there are some which singularly confirm that very faith. Such is the following passage; "When I say that He is another," (that is, the Son from the Father,) "I do not say that there are two Gods, but [I say that He is another,] as light from light, and water from a fountain, or a ray from the sun. For the Power from the Whole is one[10]; the Whole, however, is the

[1] filiationis genere defunctum.
[2] scilicet.
[3] ex.
[4] ex hac nativitate extitit.
[5] accessit.
[6] nempe.
[7] κατ' ἐνέργειαν.
[8] seque demisit.
[9] ex hac dependent, atque ex ipsa consequuntur.
[10] δύναμις μία ἡ ἐκ τοῦ παντός.

Father, the Power from whom is the Word. But this [Word] is the mind or sense[1], which, going forth into the world, was manifested to be the Son of God[y]. All things therefore, were (made[2]) through Him, but He Himself alone is (begotten[3]) of[4] the Father." In this passage he proves that the Father and the Son, though distinct in Person, are yet one God, by this argument, that the Son is not God of Himself[5], but God of[6] God, and that He comes forth from[7] the Father, as light from[7] light, and water from[7] the fountain, and the ray from[8] the sun; at the same time he most distinctly excepts the Son from the number of things made by God, in that He declares Him alone to be begotten from God the Father Himself, [statements] which entirely agree with the Nicene Confession. Nor ought it to cause the slightest difficulty to any one, that in the same passage Hippolytus calls the Father the Whole[9], and the Son the Power from the Whole[10]. For the Father is rightly designated the Whole, inasmuch as He is the fountain of Godhead (*πηγὴ Θεότητος*), seeing that the Godhead which is in the Son and in

[278]

1 *νοῦς* mens sive sensus.

2 facta, Lat. V.

3 genitus, Lat. V.

4 *ἐξ.*

5 a seipso.

6 de.

7 ex.

8 a.

9 totum.

10 virtutem ex toto.

y In the Greek text, which has been lost through the lapse of time, the reading no doubt was, *Ὁ προελθὼν εἰς τὸν κόσμον ἐφανερώθη ὁ παῖς τοῦ Θεοῦ.* For this same writer's words, in his interpretation of the second Psalm, are to a similar effect, which I quote from Theodoret, in p. 103. col. 1. init. [i. e. of Grabe's folio edition of Bp. Bull's works; see Append. on this passage.] *Ὁ προελθὼν εἰς τὸν κόσμον Θεὸς καὶ ἄνθρωπος ἐφανερώθη.* [The entire passage is given by Fabricius, (who first published this work in Greek,) thus; (Bibl. Græc.) vol. ii. p. 13. *Ἕτερον δὲ λέγων οὐ δύο θεοὺς λέγω, ἀλλ' ὡς φῶς ἐκ φωτὸς, ἢ ὡς ὕδωρ ἐκ πηγῆς, ἢ ὡς ἀκτῖνα ἀπὸ ἡλίου. Δύναμις γὰρ μία ἡ ἐκ τοῦ παντὸς, τὸ δὲ πᾶν Πατὴρ, ἐξ οὗ δύναμις λόγος. οὗτος δὲ νοῦς, ὃς προβὰς ἐν κόσμῳ ἐδείκνυτο παῖς Θεοῦ. Πάντα τοίνυν δι' αὐτοῦ, αὐτὸς δὲ μόνος ἐκ Πατρός.*—B. The Latin version in Bp. Bull is; Cum alium dico, non duos Deos dico, sed tanquam lumen ex lumine, et aquam ex fonte, aut radium a sole; una enim virtus ex toto; totum vero Pater, ex quo virtus, Verbum; hoc vero mens sive sensus, qui, prodiens in mundum, ostensus est Puer Dei. Omnia igitur per eum facta sunt; ipse solus ex Patre genitus.] But that it was usual also for Hippolytus to call Christ *τὸν παῖδα τοῦ Θεοῦ*, the Child, or rather the Son, of God, (puerum sive potius filium,) is evident from his treatise called 'Demonstratio de Christo et Antichristo,' inserted in the last Auctarium of the Bibliotheca Patrum of Combefis, Paris, 1672. For there, not far from the beginning, [3. vol. i. p. 5,] he propounds this question: "You enquire how, in old time, the Word of God, Himself again the Child of God, who of old indeed was the Word, made a revelation to the blessed prophets?" (*Πῶς ἂν πάλαι τοῖς μακαρίοις προφήταις ἀπεκάλυψεν ὁ τοῦ Θεοῦ λόγος, αὐτὸς πάλιν ὁ τοῦ Θεοῦ παῖς, ὁ πάλαι μὲν λόγος, τυχεῖν ἐπιζητεῖς.*) And after a short interval, *εἷς γὰρ καὶ ὁ τοῦ Θεοῦ παῖς, κ.τ.λ.*; "For the Child of God also is one," &c., &c. Compare also his expression in section 61, cited p. 104. col. 2. [ed. fol. see Appendix. "Christ the child of God, *παῖδα Θεοῦ*, both God and man."] Hippolytus and some other of the ancient fathers gave this appellation to Christ from Isaiah xlii. 1, and other passages; where God says of Him; *'Ιδοὺ ὁ παῖς μου·* although *παῖς* there means servant. This however is by the way.—GRABE.

ON THE CONSUBSTANTIALITY OF THE SON.

the Holy Ghost is the Father's, because it is derived from the Father. In like manner the statements are especially catholic, which the sophist soon afterwards produces from the same work of Hippolytus; I mean these; "The Father commands, the Word performs; and the Son is manifested, through whom the Father is believed on. The economy of agreement is gathered up into One God[1]; for God is One; for He who commands [is] Father, He who obeys [is] Son, that which teaches
[279] wisdom [is] Holy Ghost. The Father who is above all, the Son through all, and the Holy Ghost in all[z]." Here, as you see, Hippolytus plainly teaches, that the Father, the Son, and the Holy Ghost are one God, and attributes to each Person of the Trinity omnipresence, and divine power such as to pervade all things; and in saying of the Father that He commands, and of the Son that He obeys, he has other orthodox fathers agreeing with him, and using similar expressions, not only such as lived before, but also such as flourished after the Nicene Council. Refer by all means to what we have before said on Irenæus, in chap. v. § 6. of this book, [pp. 170, 171.] In like manner what he says of the Father, that He is in a peculiar sense over[2] all things, is altogether to be referred to that pre-eminence[3] of the Father, as the Father, which all catholics acknowledge. But why need I say more? The very title of the book against Noetus sufficiently shews, how utterly vain is the attempt of the author of the *Irenicum* to build up from it the Arian blasphemy; for the book is thus entitled: "A Homily respecting God, Three and One[4], and the mystery of the Incarnation, against the heresy of Noetus[a]." But, certainly, no Arian can, without sophistry and deceit, acknowledge that God is Three and One[5]. And thus much concerning St. Hippolytus.

[1] συνάγεται εἰς ἕνα Θεόν.

[2] super.

[3] ἐξοχὴν illam.

[4] trino et uno.

[5] trinum et unum.

[z] [The Greek is, Πατὴρ ἐντέλλεται, λόγος ἀποτελεῖ, υἱὸς δὲ δείκνυται δι' οὗ πατὴρ πιστεύεται. Οἰκονομία συμφωνίας συνάγεται εἰς ἕνα Θεὸν, εἷς γάρ ἐστιν ὁ Θεός· ὁ γὰρ κελεύων πατὴρ, ὁ δὲ ὑπακούων υἱὸς, τὸ δὲ συνέτιζον ἅγιον πνεῦμα. Ὁ ὢν πατὴρ ἐπὶ πάντων, ὁ δὲ υἱὸς διὰ πάντων, τὸ δὲ ἅγιον πνεῦμα ἐν πᾶσιν. Vol. ii. p. 15, 16.—B. The Latin as given by Bp. Bull is Pater mandat, Verbum perficit; Filius autem ostenditur, per quem Pater creditur. Œconomia consensionis redigitur ad unum Deum. Unus enim est Deus, qui mandat Pater, qui obedit Filius, qui docet scientiam Spiritus Sanctus. Pater, qui est super omnia, Filius per omnia, Spiritus Sanctus in omnibus. The Greek has been followed in the translation.]

[a] [Homilia de Deo Trino et uno et de mysterio Incarnationis contra hæresim Noeti.]

CHAPTER IX.

WHEREIN IT IS SHEWN FULLY AND CLEARLY THAT THE DOCTRINE OF ORIGEN, CONCERNING THE TRUE DIVINITY OF THE SON OF GOD WAS ALTOGETHER CATHOLIC, AND PERFECTLY CONSONANT WITH THE NICENE CREED, ESPECIALLY FROM HIS WORK AGAINST CELSUS, WHICH IS UNDOUBTEDLY GENUINE, AND MOST FREE FROM CORRUPTION, AND WHICH WAS COMPOSED BY HIM WHEN IN ADVANCED AGE, AND WITH MOST EXACT CARE AND ATTENTION. 105 [286]

1. NEXT after Hippolytus should come his rival[1], who also, in that rivalry, proved to be far his superior, I mean Origen[b]. It is astonishing how much theologians, both of ancient and modern times, have been divided into parties, and how very keenly they have contended, about the doctrine of this celebrated[2] man. To treat only of the ancients, in conformity with my design; of these, some praise and extol Origen to the skies, others anathematize him as the worst of heresiarchs, nay, as the fountain and spring of almost all heresies, especially of those which relate to the Church's faith concerning the most Holy Trinity. As respects the catholic doctors, however, who were nearer to the time of Origen, the larger, and by far the more weighty[3] portion are ranged on his side[4]. Alexander of Jerusalem, Theoctistus of Cæsarea, Dionysius of Alexandria, Firmilian of Cæsarea, Gregory Thaumaturgus, and Athenodorus, contemporaries of Origen, always held him in the highest estimation; whilst the whole of Palestine, Arabia, Phœnicia and Achaia defended his cause against Demetrius of Alexandria. Afterwards Pamphilus the Martyr, and Eusebius of Cæsarea, in an Apology containing six books, whereof one only is extant, maintained the same cause. Again, Photius informs us, Cod. 118, that several other men of great name in the times of Eusebius, had written Apologies for Origen. Moreover, the great Athanasius, in his treatise concerning the Decrees of the Council of Nice, commended Origen as a strenuous supporter of the Catholic faith, against the heresy which was afterwards called Arian. [287]

[1] æmulus.
[2] πολυθρύλλητος.
[3] longe potior.
[4] ipsi adstipulati sunt.

[b] He was born in the year 186. Cave.—BOWYER.

With these must be classed Didymus of Alexandria, (a celebrated man, whom Jerome often boasts of having had for his teacher,) who published an apologetic discourse for Origen, and Titus, bishop of Bostra, and the noble pair of Gregories, of Nazianzum and of Nyssa, with John of Jerusalem, who is on this account assailed with continual reproaches by Epiphanius and Jerome. Methodius too, who wrote long before the rise of the Arian controversy, though he was at first a most determined adversary of Origen, after a time laid aside his enmity, and in the end was not ashamed to profess himself one of his admirers. Finally, Ruffinus (who, whatever a later[1] age may have thought of him, is called by Cassian, in his seventh book on the Incarnation[c], "a Christian philosopher, holding no contemptible place among the doctors of the Church," and whose sanctity was at one time commended in the highest terms, even by Jerome himself, as appears from his fifth Epistle[d] to Florentius) was a very earnest champion on the side of Origen; to say nothing of the numberless monks, scattered throughout Egypt, who engaged in the warmest conflicts with Theophilus of Alexandria, in his cause.

[1] sequior, implying inferiority.

2. In this so great difference of opinion among men so great, it were to be wished, that of the innumerable writings which this unwearied author[2] composed, a greater number had come down to us entire and uncorrupted, from which we, who do not belong to either party[3], might have been able to judge for ourselves with more certainty about his doctrine. But, alas, some of Origen's works were corrupted and interpolated, even in his own lifetime, by worthless and idle[4] men, and some writings no way his own[5], but altogether spurious, were published under his very celebrated name, as he himself com-
[288] 106 plained in a letter[e] to certain persons in Alexandria. So that you may easily conjecture with how much greater boldness those dishonest men[6] would perpetrate such forgeries after his death. It is certain that by far the greatest portion of the works of Origen have now entirely perished; whilst those which still remain, with the exception of his Treatise against

[2] chalcenterus ille.
[3] neutri parti addicti.
[4] maleferiatis.
[5] aliena prorsus.
[6] tenebriones.

c Christianæ philosophiæ vir, haud contemnenda ecclesiasticorum doctorum portio.—[c. 27. p. 1125.]

d [Epist. iv. 2. vol. i. p. 14.—B.]

e Extant in Ruffinus, de Adulter. libb. Origen. [pp. 51, 52.]

Celsus, and certain extracts from his writings, called Philocalia, were extant only in Latin, and that much interpolated and altered by translators[1], as is certain from positive evidence, until the famous Daniel Huet recently published in Greek several of his exegetical works from the MSS.; and on this account, that very learned man has deserved well of all lovers of antiquity, as will be acknowledged by every one who is not influenced by ill-will. Yet Huet[f] himself declares, that he thinks it probable, "that all the works of Origen, which fortune has transmitted to us, have been corrupted, and those especially which, besides the errors of copyists and the adulterations of heretics, have also suffered from the mistakes and dishonesty of translators." Unless I am mistaken, he ought to have excepted the books against Celsus; for no one, to my knowledge, has hitherto suspected that they have suffered any other injury worth notice, beyond the errors of transcribers[2], from which none of the works of the ancients are altogether free.

[1] interpretibus.

[2] librariorum σφάλματα.

3. But if all the writings of Origen were now extant, and that in a pure and uncorrupted state, they still would not all be of equal service for shewing his true and genuine opinions; inasmuch as the purport[3] of the various compositions of a voluminous author would be different. For some of his works were written privately[g] to friends, which he never expected to see the light; in these he discussed subjects freely [289] and almost sceptically, and generally propounded not so much his own fixed and definite views, as either the reasonings of others, or little difficulties[4] and slight doubts of his own, for the clearer elucidation of the truth. Others he himself published, either against unbelievers, or in opposition to heretics, or, lastly, for the instruction of Christians in general[5]; in which, proceeding along the beaten and safe road, he studiously taught the doctrine received in the Catholic Church. Then again, some he dictated[6] hastily, others he wrought out with more diligent care. And, lastly, some things (to use the

[3] ratio.

[4] scrupulos quosdam.

[5] Christianam plebem.

[6] dictitavit.

[f] Origenian. p. 233.

[g] Respecting these, Jerome, Epist. lxv. ad Pamm. et Ocean. [Ep. lxxxiv. 10. vol. i. p. 527,] testifies that Origen, in a letter written by him to Fabian, expressed regret for having written such things; and threw back upon Ambrose [his contemporary and friend] the charge of inconsiderateness in having made public what he had sent out in private.

ON THE CONSUBSTANTIALITY OF THE SON.

words of Huet) Adamantius, now grown old, revised when his genius was somewhat tempered by age; others he poured out with the profusion which puts itself forth in the heat of youth. Concerning these works Jerome beautifully said in the Prologue to his Commentaries[h] on Luke, that in some of his treatises Origen was "like a boy playing at dice; that the works of his middle life are different from the serious productions of his advanced age." Now it cannot be denied, that the expression of Origen's judgment[1] on Catholic doctrine ought to be derived chiefly from those works which he himself designed for publication, which he wrote thoughtfully and attentively, and which, lastly, he composed in advanced life, and after he had been instructed by long practice and experience. Of this sort, as all are agreed, are his eight books against Celsus the Epicurean; inasmuch as in them he defends the common doctrine of Christians against a very well armed[2] enemy of our religion; these were wrought out with the utmost care on the part of the author, and with the greatest learning, and that when he was now more than sixty years of age, as is expressly declared by Eusebius, (Eccl. Hist. vi. 36.) Accordingly it will be from these books chiefly that I shall allege my testimonies to shew the catho-
[290] licity of Origen on this article [of the faith]; adding only a few passages out of his other writings, such as are supplied me by catholic doctors who lived nearer to the age of Origen, and so best knew how to distinguish his genuine writings from what were spurious. From all this I trust that the intelligent reader will at length clearly perceive, how wildly[3] Petavius raved[4] against Origen, when he was not ashamed to write thus of a most holy and learned father, as even his enemies allow him to have been[i]; "As to Origen, it is certain," he says, "that he entertained impious and absurd opinions concerning the Son and the Holy Ghost;" and again[k], a little after, "Origen, as he preceded Arius in time, so was he his equal in impiety; nay, he taught him his impious doctrine." And throughout his work he constantly casts asper-

[1] suffragium.

[2] instructissimum.

[3] impotenter.

[4] debacchatus.

[h] Quasi puerum talis ludere; alia esse virilia ejus, et alia senectutis seria. —[vol. vii. p. 247.]

[i] De Origene, inquit, constat, eum de Filio ac Spiritu Sancto impie absurdeque sensisse.—De Trin. i. 12. 9.

[k] Origenes ut ætate Arium antecessit, sic impietate par, imo impii dogmatis auctor illi fuit.—Ibid. § 10.

sions such as these on Origen. Perhaps the Jesuit thought that his religion bound him thus to malign the venerable father, because, forsooth, Origen and the Origenists, together with their doctrines, were condemned and anathematized in the fifth [general] council[l]. But there have not been wanting illustrious men of the Church of Rome, (I mean John Picus of Mirandula, James Merlin of Victurnia, Desiderius Erasmus of Rotterdam, Sixtus of Siena, Claudius Espencæus, Gilbert Genebrard, and Peter Halloix,) who, having no fear 107
for themselves from the anathemas of the fifth council, have had the courage not merely to mention Origen without reproaches, but even to take his part openly and avowedly. No doubt they judged rightly, that it was not so much Origen himself, or his genuine opinions[1], that were anathematized, as those very pernicious dogmas concerning a Trinity [291]
of different substance[2], and an imaginary[3] resurrection of the body, which were contained in the adulterated writings of Origen, or which certain Origenists, as they are called, used to advance under the sanction of his great name. It is true that the council condemned, along with these, paradoxical speculations concerning the pre-existence of souls, the animated nature of the stars and of the elements, &c., which were really Origen's own; but these were condemned only as false and very absurd, not as heretical, unless there were in addition an inflexible obstinacy of mind, and that contempt of catholic opinion, which, as it was quite alien from Origen himself, so did it display itself to excess in most of the Origenists. But let us now approach the subject itself.

[1] placita.
[2] de Trinitate ἑτερουσίῳ.
[3] phantastica.

4. In his books against Celsus, Origen[m] so frequently declares the nature of the Word and Son of God to be truly divine, that is to say, uncreate, infinite, incomprehensible, and unchangeable, that were I disposed to adduce all the statements which bear on this subject, I should be obliged to transcribe a great part of his treatise. I shall, therefore, bring forward only some more select passages out of that work. In the first book, treating of the Magi, who came from the East to Judea, to see the King, whom the unwonted

Or rather in another synod held at Constantinople prior to the fifth council. See the notes of Valesius on Evagrius, p. 111. [iv. 38. note 6.]

[m] Written about the year 247. Cave. —BOWYER.

ON THE CONSUBSTANTIALITY OF THE SON.

appearance of the star pointed out, he thus speaks[n]; ["They came] bringing gifts, which they offered as symbols to One, who was, so to say, a compound[1] of God and mortal man; the gold as to a King, the myrrh as to One who was to die, and the frankincense as to God." Here, in the Person of Christ, he recognises both mortal man and the immortal God, to whom is due divine honour, which used formerly to be exhibited [292] by the offering of frankincense. A passage exactly corresponding to this occurs in the same book a few pages after; where, when Celsus jests at the blood of Jesus shed upon the cross, and says, "that it was not such blood as the blessed gods are wont to have," Origen thus answers him[o]: "We, believing Jesus Himself, when He says of the Godhead which is in Him, 'I am the way, and the truth, and the life,' and whatever else there is to the like effect; and, on the other hand, when He thus speaks[2] of the fact of His being in a human body, 'Now ye seek to kill Me, a man that hath told you the truth,' we say that He became something compounded[3]." Afterwards he says that Christ had[p] "something more divine[4] within the manhood which was seen, which was He that is properly[5] the Son of God, God the Word, the Power of God, and the Wisdom of God." And then after some considerable interval, he designates Christ as[q] "God, who appeared in human body for the benefiting of our race."

[1] *συνθέτῳ τινί.*

[2] John viii. 40.

[3] *σύνθετόν τι.*

[4] *θειότερόν τι.*

[5] *ὁ κυρίως υἱός.*

5. In the second book, citing Gen. i. 26, "Let us make man in our image and after our likeness;" and that passage of David, Ps. cxlviii. 5, "He spake and they were made, He commanded and they were created;" he collects, that it was the Son and Word of God unto whom the Father thus spake and gave commandment, by the following argument[r];

[n] *φέροντες μὲν δῶρα, ἃ (ἵν' οὕτως ὀνομάσω) συνθέτῳ τινὶ ἐκ Θεοῦ καὶ ἀνθρώπου θνητοῦ προσήνεγκαν σύμβολα μὲν, ὡς βασιλεῖ τὸν χρυσὸν, ὡς δὲ τεθνηξομένῳ τὴν σμύρναν, ὡς δὲ Θεῷ τὸν λιβανωτόν.*—p. 46. ed. Cantab. 1658. [§ 60. vol. i. p. 375.]

[o] *ἡμεῖς δ' αὐτῷ πιστεύοντες Ἰησοῦ, περὶ μὲν τῆς ἐν αὐτῷ θειότητος λέγοντι, Ἐγώ εἰμι ἡ ὁδὸς, καὶ ἡ ἀλήθεια καὶ ἡ ζωὴ, καὶ εἴ τι τούτοις παραπλήσιον· περὶ δὲ τοῦ, ὅτι ἐν ἀνθρωπίνῳ σώματι ἦν, ταῦτα φάσκοντι, Νῦν δὲ ζητεῖτέ με ἀποκτεῖναι, ἄνθρωπον ὅστις τὴν ἀλήθειαν ὑμῖν λελάληκα· σύνθετόν τι χρῆμά φαμεν αὐτὸν γεγονέναι.*—[§ 66. p. 380-81.]

[p] *θειότερόν τι ἐν τῷ βλεπομένῳ ἀνθρώπῳ, ὅπερ ἦν ὁ κυρίως υἱὸς Θεοῦ, Θεὸς λόγος, Θεοῦ δύναμις, καὶ Θεοῦ σοφία.*—p. 52.

[q] *[κατ' ἐπαγγελίαν τοῦ] Θεὸν [εἶναι], ἐν ἀνθρωπίνῳ φανέντα σώματι ἐπ' εὐεργεσίᾳ τοῦ γένους ἡμῶν.*—[§ 68. p. 383.]

[r] *εἰ γὰρ ἐνετείλατο ὁ Θεὸς, καὶ ἐκτίσθη τὰ δημιουργήματα, τίς ἂν, κατὰ τ'*

"For if God commanded, and the creatures were made, who
must He be, who, according to the mind[1] of the prophetic
Spirit, was able to execute so great a commandment of the
Father, other than He who is, so to call Him, His living[2] Word [293]
and the Truth?" In these words he most explicitly distinguishes the Son of God from all created things; and moreover clearly teaches, that the work of creation, which had
been committed to that Son of God by His Father, was so
great, (as being peculiarly that of divine omnipotence,) as that
it could not any way have been accomplished but by Him,
who is the very Word of God the Father, and the Truth.
Now all who have any eyes[3] perceive, how far removed this
reasoning is from the mind of the infatuated Arians, in their
misapplication of these passages of Scripture, and how exactly it accords with the sentiments of the Catholics, who
vindicate the Godhead of the Son from the work of creation.
In the same place Origen teaches that the Godhead of the
Word of God was by no means so circumscribed by the Incarnation, as not to exist any where external to the body
and soul of Jesus, but that It is, and has ever been, every
where present[4]. Lest, however, any one should apply this to
sanction the heresy of Cerinthus, he presently adds[s]; "We
say this, not as separating the Son of God from Jesus; for
after the Incarnation[5] the body and the soul of Jesus have
become in the highest degree one with the Word of God."
Now could any one set forth, in more catholic terms than 108
Origen has done in these passages, the twofold nature of
Christ and the hypostatic union of these two natures? Presently afterwards he calls the body of Christ[t] "that which
is truly the temple of God the Word and Wisdom and [294]
Truth," which the Jews despised, whilst they venerated more
than enough the material[6] temple of God.

[1] κατὰ τὸ ἀρέσκον.

[2] ἔμψυχος.

[3] oculati omnes.

[4] φθάνοντα πανταχοῦ.

[5] μετὰ τὴν οἰκονομίαν.

[6] lapideum.

6. In the third book, on Celsus objecting to the Christians, "that they believe Jesus, consisting of a mortal body,
to be God, and imagine that they act piously in so doing,"

ἀρέσκον τῷ προφητικῷ πνεύματι, (juxta mentem prophetici Spiritus,) εἴη ὁ τὴν τηλικαύτην τοῦ πατρὸς ἐντολὴν ἐκπληρῶσαι δυνηθεὶς ἢ ὁ (ἵν' οὕτως ὀνομάσω) ἔμψυχος λόγος καὶ ἀλήθεια τυγχάνων.—p. 63. [§ 9. p. 393.]

[s] ταῦτα δέ φαμεν οὐ χωρίζοντες τὸν υἱὸν τοῦ Θεοῦ ἀπὸ τοῦ Ἰησοῦ· ἓν γὰρ μάλιστα μετὰ τὴν οἰκονομίαν γεγένηται πρὸς τὸν λόγον τοῦ Θεοῦ ἡ ψυχὴ καὶ τὸ σῶμα Ἰησοῦ.—p. 64. [p. 394.]

[t] τὸν ἀληθῶς ναὸν Θεοῦ τοῦ λόγου καὶ τῆς σοφίας καὶ τῆς ἀληθείας.—[§ 10. p. 394.]

ON THE CONSUBSTANTIALITY OF THE SON.

Origen meets him with this reply[u]; "Let those who bring this charge against us know, that He, who, we believe and are persuaded, was God and the Son of God from the beginning, is also the very Word[1], and the very Wisdom, and the very Truth: whilst of His mortal body and the human soul within it, we say that it has by its—not communion only, but—union also and intimate commingling[2] with Him, received the greatest [gifts], and by partaking of His divinity has passed[3] into God." Now (if I have any insight [into it]) the manifest sense of this reply is as follows; Does this trouble you, O ye philosophers, that we Christians call our Saviour Christ God, though He consist of a mortal body? Nay, snarl as ye will[4], we still affirm that He is, in the truest sense, very God[5]; that is to say, very Word[x], very Truth, very Wisdom; nay, is so far forth God, that we scruple not to say, that His human nature even, through its union with the divine, has been in a certain manner deified. In this passage we ought to note the expressions *αὐτολόγος, αὐτοαλήθεια,* which are thoroughly
[295] roughly Platonic. For Plato called that which is truly and in itself[6] good, *αὐτοαγαθὸν,* applying that epithet to the true and most high God alone, from whom he widely separated the Logos. Origen, however, as though correcting the philosophy of Plato by the Christian, declares that the Logos also, or Son of God, has just claims to be called very Wisdom, very Truth, and by consequence very Goodness[7]. But there is not any ground for our Lutheran brethren, who maintain a kind of ubiquity of the human nature in Christ, to suppose that there is any support for their cause from these words of Origen. For in the passage which we just now adduced out of the second book, Origen plainly teaches, that the Word is so conjoined with the human nature of Christ, as to exist even externally to the soul and body of Jesus; and that the attribute of ubiquity[8] pertains to the Godhead alone. Moreover, in this very passage, not long after the words quoted,

1 ὁ αὐτολόγος, ἡ αὐτοσοφία, ἡ αὐτοαλήθεια.
2 ἑνώσει καὶ ἀνακράσει.
3 εἰς Θεὸν μεταβεβηκέναι.
4 ringamini licet.
5 ipsissimum Deum.
6 per se.
7 αὐτοαγαθόν.
8 τὸ ubique esse.

u ἴστωσαν οἱ ἐγκαλοῦντες, ὅτι ὃν μὲν νομίζομεν καὶ πεπείσμεθα ἀρχῆθεν εἶναι Θεὸν καὶ υἱὸν Θεοῦ, οὗτος ὁ αὐτολόγος ἐστὶ, καὶ ἡ αὐτοσοφία, καὶ ἡ αὐτοαλήθεια· τὸ δὲ θνητὸν αὐτοῦ σῶμα, καὶ τὴν ἀνθρωπίνην ἐν αὐτῷ ψυχὴν, τῇ πρὸς ἐκεῖνον οὐ μόνον κοινωνίᾳ, ἀλλὰ καὶ ἑνώσει καὶ ἀνακράσει, τὰ μέγιστά φαμεν προσειληφέναι, καὶ τῆς ἐκείνου θειότητος κεκοινωνηκότα εἰς Θεὸν μεταβεβηκέναι.—p. 135, 136. [§ 41. p. 473-74.]

x [Ipsam Rationem, &c., equivalent to Origen's ὁ αὐτολόγος, κ.τ.λ.]

Origen himself distinctly explains what he had said of the commixture[1] of the human nature in Christ with the divine, in such a way as to declare that he had no other meaning than this, that the glorified flesh of Jesus, by a change of its qualities, was made such as to be fitted to dwell in the highest heaven[2], retaining nothing of that infirmity of the flesh which was born with it[3]. If you have leisure, peruse what follows in Origen; I return from this digression to my subject.

[1] de permixtione. [2] in summo æthere. [3] congenitæ.

7. In the fourth book, Celsus the Epicurean is introduced disputing against the doctrine of the Christians respecting the coming down upon earth of the Son of God and His Incarnation, in the following manner; "God is good, beautiful, happy, of the best and fairest form; were He to descend to the condition of man[4], He must undergo a change; but the change will be from good to evil, from beautiful to base, from happy to unhappy, from the best to the worst. Who would wish to be thus changed? It is true that a [296] change and transformation of this kind is incident to mortal man; but it befits an immortal being, that he continue ever to exist in the same state. God, therefore, could never become the subject of such a change." Now if Origen had entertained the same view concerning the Son of God which Arius subsequently did, how easily might he have overthrown the very foundation of this argument—by saying, I mean, in one word, that neither he himself nor the catholic Christians of his time believed the Son of God to be in very deed the unchangeable God; but simply held Him to be a creature of a nature different from the divine, and altogether capable of change. Far otherwise, however, and without doing any violence at all to[5] the hypothesis of catholics, concerning the truly divine and unchangeable nature of the Son of God, does Origen reply, in the following words[y]: "Now I conceive that I shall have returned a sufficient answer to this, if I set forth that descending[6] of God unto the condition of man[7] which is spoken of in the Scriptures; for which He has no need of change, as Celsus supposes that we maintain, nor of passing from good to evil, or from beautiful to base,

[4] πρὸς τὰ ἀνθρώπινα. [5] salvâ omnino. [6] κατάβασιν. [7] πρὸς τὰ ἀνθρώπινα.

[y] δοκεῖ δή μοι πρὸς ταῦτα λέγεσθαι τὰ δέοντα, διηγησαμένῳ τὴν ἐν ταῖς γραφαῖς λεγομένην κατάβασιν Θεοῦ πρὸς τὰ ἀνθρώπινα· εἰς ἣν οὐ μεταβολῆς αὐτῷ δεῖ, ὡς Κέλσος ἡμᾶς οἴεται λέγειν, οὔτε τροπῆς, τῆς ἐξ ἀγαθοῦ εἰς κακὸν, ἢ ἐκ καλοῦ εἰς αἰσχρὸν, ἢ ἐξ εὐδαιμονίας εἰς κακοδαιμονίαν, ἢ ἐκ τοῦ ἀρίστου εἰς

or from happy to unhappy, or from the best to the worst;
for, remaining unchangeable in His essence, He condescends
to the circumstances of men[1] by His providence and dispensation. Yea, and we allege also the divine Scriptures, which
declare that God is unchangeable, both in the words, 'But
Thou art the same[2];' and, 'I change not[3];' whilst the gods
of Epicurus, being compounded of atoms, and [consequently],
so far as depends on their constitution, capable of dissolution[4], have enough to do to shake off[5] the atoms that cause
corruption from themselves; nay, the god of the Stoics also,
as being corporeal, has sometimes the whole substance [turned
into] mind[6], when the conflagration happens; and sometimes
becomes [only] a part of the same, when a re-arrangement
happens. For these [philosophers] could not even clear our
natural conception[7] of God, as [of a Being] every way incorruptible, simple, uncompounded and indivisible. That how-
109 ever which came down unto men, was in the form of God,
and out of loving-kindness unto man He emptied Himself[8],
in order that He might be comprehensible by men; but yet
[297] certainly there was no change from good[q] to evil in Him," &c.
&c. Shortly afterwards Adamantius subjoins these words[r];
"Now if Celsus thinks that the immortal God, the Word,
in having assumed a mortal body and a human soul, un-
dergoes change and transformation, let him learn that the
Word, remaining Word[9] still in His essence, is not affected
by any[10] of those things by which the body and the soul are
affected; but condescending at a particular time to that

[1] τοῖς ἀνθρωπίνοις πράγμασιν.
[2] [Ps. cii. 27.]
[3] [Mal. iii. 6.]
[4] τὸ ὅσον ἐπὶ τῇ συστάσει ἀνάλυτοι.
[5] πραγματεύονται ἀποσείεσθαι.
[6] ἡγεμονικὸν.
[7] τρανῶσαι τὴν φυσικὴν ἔννοιαν.
[8] ἐκένωσεν ἑαυτὸν. [Phil. ii. 6.]
[9] λόγος.
[10] οὐδὲν πάσχει.

τὸ πονηρότατον. μενων γὰρ τῇ οὐσίᾳ ἄτρεπτος, συγκαταβαίνει τῇ προνοίᾳ καὶ τῇ οἰκονομίᾳ τοῖς ἀνθρωπίνοις πράγμασιν. ἡμεῖς μὲν οὖν καὶ τὰ θεῖα γράμματα παρίσταμεν, ἄτρεπτον λέγοντα τὸν Θεὸν, ἔν τε τῷ, Σὺ δὲ ὁ αὐτὸς εἶ· καὶ ἐν τῷ, Οὐκ ἠλλοίωμαι· οἱ δὲ τοῦ Ἐπικούρου θεοὶ, σύνθετοι ἐξ ἀτόμων τυγχάνοντες, καὶ τὸ ὅσον ἐπὶ τῇ συστάσει ἀνάλυτοι, (ex atomis constantes hoc ipso dissolvi possent; Bened.) πραγματεύονται τὰς φθοροποιοὺς ἀτόμους ἀποσείεσθαι· ἀλλὰ καὶ ὁ τῶν Στωϊκῶν θεὸς, ἅτε σῶμα τυγχάνων, ὁτὲ μὲν ἡγεμονικὸν ἔχει τὴν ὅλην οὐσίαν, ὅταν ἡ ἐκπύρωσις ᾖ· ὁτὲ δὲ ἐπὶ μέρους γίνεται αὐτῆς, ὅταν ᾖ διακόσμησις. οὐδὲ γὰρ δεδύνηνται οὗτοι τρανῶσαι τὴν φυσικὴν τοῦ Θεοῦ ἔννοιαν, ὡς πάντῃ ἀφθάρτου, καὶ ἁπλοῦ, καὶ ἀσυνθέτου, καὶ ἀδιαιρέτου. τὸ δὲ καταβεβηκὸς εἰς ἀνθρώπους ἐν μορφῇ Θεοῦ ὑπῆρχε, καὶ διὰ φιλανθρωπίαν ἑαυτὸν ἐκένωσεν, ἵνα χωρηθῆναι ὑπ' ἀνθρώπων δυνηθῇ. οὐ δήπου δ' ἐξ ἀγαθῶν [Forte ἀγαθοῦ, ut paulo ante. GRABE. Ita ed. Bened.—B.] εἰς κακὸν γέγονεν αὐτῷ μεταβολή· κ.λ.—p. 169, 170. [§ 14. p. 510.]

[q] ἐξ ἀγαθῶν εἰς κακὸν, κ.τ.λ.: instead of ἐξ ἀγαθῶν, Grabe conjectured ἐξ ἀγαθοῦ, as it occurs in the context. [This is the reading in the Benedictine edition.—B.]

[r] εἰ δὲ καὶ σῶμα θνητὸν καὶ ψυχὴν ἀνθρωπίνην ἀναλαβὼν ὁ ἀθάνατος Θεὸς λόγος δοκεῖ τῷ Κέλσῳ ἀλλάττεσθαι καὶ μεταπλάττεσθαι, μανθανέτω ὅτι ὁ λόγος τῇ οὐσίᾳ μένων λόγος οὐδὲν μὲν πάσχει ὧν πάσχει τὸ σῶμα ἢ ἡ ψυχή· συγκαταβαίνων δ' ἐσθ' ὅτε τῷ μὴ δυναμένῳ αὐτοῦ

which cannot look upon His brilliancy[1], and the splendour of His Godhead, becomes as it were flesh, being spoken of after a bodily fashion[2]." Let any intelligent person say, whether these are the words of one who "surpassed Arius in impiety, and even originated for him his blasphemous dogma." For surely in this passage Origen clearly teaches, that the Word, or Son of God, is the immortal God, unchangeable in His substance, and, so far as He subsists in the form of God, equally with the Father, of a nature every way incorruptible, simple, uncompounded and indivisible. A little after, when about to answer another objection which Celsus had urged, akin to the former, he thus begins[s]: "A reply might be made to this by distinguishing between the nature of the Divine Word, who is God, and the soul of Jesus." Here you see it is expressly said that the nature itself of the Word is God, or in other words, that the Word is by nature God. A passage similar to this is quoted in the Catena of Balthasar Corderius, on John i. 1, in which the Son of God is called by Origen, "The Maker[3] of the universe, being in essence God the Word[t]." What Arian, however, would have said, that the Son is in His own very essence and substance God? Surely this is the very point which the Nicene Fathers decreed in opposition to Arius, namely, that the Son of God is of one substance with God.

[298]

[1] τὰς μαρμαρυγὰς.

[2] σωματικῶς λαλούμενος.

[3] ὁ δημιουργὸς.

8. In his fifth book, in giving a reason why Christians worship the Son of God, but not the sun, the moon, or the stars, he says[u], "It were not, then, reasonable that those, who have been taught to ascend in nobleness of nature[4] above all created beings[5], ... who are in training to attain to the bright and unfading Wisdom, or have even already attained to it, being, as it is, a radiance from Light eternal, should be so far overpowered by the sensible[6] brightness of the sun and the moon and the stars, as, because of their

[299]

[4] μεγαλοφυῶς ὑπεραναβαίνειν.

[5] πάντα τὰ δημιουργήματα.

[6] αἰσθητὸν.

τὰς μαρμαρυγὰς καὶ τὴν λαμπρότητα τῆς θειότητος βλέπειν, οἱονεὶ σὰρξ γίνεται, σωματικῶς λαλούμενος.—[p. 511.]

[s] πρὸς τοῦτο λέγοιτ' ἂν πῇ μὲν περὶ τῆς τοῦ θείου λόγου φύσεως, ὄντος Θεοῦ· πῇ δὲ περὶ τῆς Ἰησοῦ ψυχῆς.—p. 171. [18. p. 512.]

[t] ὁ δημιουργὸς τοῦ παντὸς, . . . τυγχάνων Θεὸς λόγος κατ' οὐσίαν.—[p. 7. ed. Antw. 1620.]

[u] οὐ τοίνυν ἦν εὔλογον τοὺς διδαχθέντας μεγαλοφυῶς ὑπεραναβαίνειν πάντα τὰ δημιουργήματα . . . ἀσκοῦντας ἔχειν τὴν λαμπρὰν καὶ ἀμάραντον σοφίαν, ἢ καὶ ἀνειληφότας αὐτὴν οὖσαν ἀπαύγασμα φωτὸς ἀϊδίου, καταπλαγῆναι τὸ αἰσθητὸν ἡλίου καὶ σελήνης, καὶ ἄστρων φῶς ἐπὶ τοσοῦτον, ὥστε διὰ τὸ αἰσθητὸν φῶς

ON THE CONSUBSTANTIALITY OF THE SON.

[1] *νοητὸν.*

sensible light, to suppose themselves to be in some inferior position, and to offer them adoration, seeing that they themselves have so great a light perceptible by thought[1], the Light of knowledge, and the true Light, and the Light of the world, and the Light of men." Here Origen expressly says, that the Wisdom, or Son of God, is that true Light, the Light of the world, the radiance of the eternal Light, which Christians, neglecting the sun and the moon and the other luminaries of heaven, do on this account worship, because they have been taught nobly to ascend above all created things in their worship. From this it is most manifest, that Origen by no means dreamt, with Arius, that the Son of God is to be classed among created beings (*τὰ δημιουργήματα*). This point he sets forth still more plainly a little afterwards, in these words[x]: "And just as those, who worship the sun, and moon, and stars, because their light is sensible and celestial, would not worship a spark of fire or a lamp on the earth, seeing, as they do, the incomparable superiority of the luminaries which they deem worthy to be worshipped, above the light of sparks and lamps; so likewise they who have perceived how God is Light, and have comprehended how the Son of
110 God is the 'true Light, which lighteneth every man that
[300] cometh into the world,' and who understand also in what sense He says, 'I am the Light of the world,' would not act reasonably in worshipping what, in comparison with that Light, which is God, is as it were a little spark of the true Light, in the sun, the moon, or the stars. And we speak thus concerning the sun, and moon, and stars, not as at all dishonouring such vast works of God, nor, like Anaxagoras, saying that the sun, and moon, and stars are heated masses; but as

ἐκείνων νομίσαι ἑαυτοὺς κάτω που εἶναι, ἔχοντας τηλικοῦτον νοητὸν γνώσεως φῶς, καὶ φῶς ἀληθινὸν, καὶ φῶς τοῦ κόσμου, καὶ φῶς τῶν ἀνθρώπων, κᾀκείνοις προσκυνῆσαι.—p. 237. [10. p. 584.]

[x] *καὶ ὥσπερ οἱ διὰ τὸ φῶς αἰσθητὸν καὶ οὐράνιον εἶναι προσκυνοῦντες ἥλιον, καὶ σελήνην, καὶ ἄστρα, οὐκ ἂν προσκυνήσαιεν σπινθῆρα πυρὸς, ἢ λύχνον ἐπὶ γῆς, ὁρῶντες τὴν ἀσύγκριτον ὑπεροχὴν τῶν νομιζομένων ἀξίων προσκυνεῖσθαι παρὰ τὸ τῶν σπινθήρων καὶ τῶν λύχνων φῶς· οὕτως οἱ νοήσαντες, πῶς ὁ Θεὸς φῶς ἐστι, καταλαβόντες δὲ, πῶς ὁ υἱὸς τοῦ Θεοῦ φῶς ἀληθινόν ἐστιν, ὃ φωτίζει πάντα ἄνθρωπον ἐρχόμενον εἰς τὸν κόσμον, συνιέντες δὲ καὶ πῶς οὗτός φησι τὸ, Ἐγώ εἰμι τὸ φῶς τοῦ κόσμου· οὐκ ἂν εὐλόγως προσκυνήσαιεν τὸν οἱονεὶ βραχὺν σπινθῆρα, ὡς πρὸς φῶς τὸν Θεὸν, ἀληθινοῦ φωτὸς, ἐν ἡλίῳ, καὶ σελήνῃ, καὶ ἄστροις. καὶ οὐκ ἀτιμάζοντές γε τὰ τηλικαῦτα τοῦ Θεοῦ δημιουργήματα, οὐδ' Ἀναξαγορίως μύδρον διάπυρον λέγοντες εἶναι τὸν ἥλιον, καὶ σελήνην, καὶ ἀστέρας, τοιαῦτά φαμεν περὶ ἡλίου,*

BOOK II. CHAP. IX. § 8. ORIGEN.

having some perception of the divine nature of God, which transcends with ineffable superiority, and besides also of that of His only-begotten Son, who transcends all else." What, I ask, could be said more express than this to set forth the true Godhead of the Son? For here Origen explicitly teaches, that the Son, with the Father, is that true Light, which is God, in comparison of which the very light of the sun is as a little spark; and, further, distinctly attributes to the Son, equally as to the Father, "a Divinity excelling with ineffable superiority, which immeasurably surpasses all created beings[1]." [301]
Lastly, from this he again draws the conclusion, that God the Father and His only-begotten Son alone, (in the unity, that is to say, of the Holy Ghost, which Origen himself elsewhere acknowledges,) are to be honoured with divine worship; setting at nought, so far as adoration is concerned, the sun, moon, and other luminaries of heaven. In the same passage, after a few words, he says, that God the Father, of His goodness, condescends unto men, not locally (τοπικῶς), as being infinite and not included in space, but by way of providence (προνοητικῶς); whilst the Son of God is present with His disciples at all times, and not simply during His sojourn amongst men; and although, out of His infinite love to the human race, He vouchsafed to dwell locally also with us, in the human nature which He assumed, still is He altogether present every where (πανταχοῦ)[2]. Having laid down these positions, he proceeds to argue thus for the worship of God the Father alone, and of His only-begotten Son, in opposition to the adoration of the heavenly bodies[3] [y]; "Seeing that He who has filled heaven and earth, and has said, 'Do not I fill heaven and earth? saith the Lord,' is with us and near unto us, (for I believe Him, when He says, 'I am a God

[1] [see note x.]

[2] omnino πανταχοῦ præsentem.

[3] luminum.

καὶ σελήνης, καὶ ἀστέρων· ἀλλ' αἰσθανόμενοί γε τῆς ἀφάτῳ ὑπεροχῇ ὑπερεχούσης θειότητος τοῦ Θεοῦ, ἔτι δὲ καὶ τοῦ μονογενοῦς αὐτοῦ ὑπερέχοντος τὰ λοιπά.—[11. p. 585. Bp. Bull translated the concluding words, "Dei et Filii ejus unigeniti inenarrabili præstantia præcellentem divinitatem, quæ cætera omnia longe post se relinquit," "the Divinity of God and His only-begotten Son excelling with ineffable superiority which leaves all other things far behind."]

[y] ἄτοπον δ' ἐστὶ, τοῦ πληρώσαντος τὸν οὐρανὸν καὶ τὴν γῆν, καὶ εἰπόντος, Οὐχὶ τὸν οὐρανὸν καὶ τὴν γῆν ἐγὼ πληρῶ; λέγει Κύριος, ὄντος μεθ' ἡμῶν, καὶ πλησίον ἡμῖν τυγχάνοντος, (πιστεύω γὰρ αὐτῷ λέγοντι, Θεὸς ἐγγίζων ἐγώ εἰμι, καὶ οὐ Θεὸς πόρρωθεν, λέγει Κύριος,) ζητεῖν εὔχεσθαι τῷ μὴ φθάνοντι ἐπὶ τὰ σύμπαντα ἡλίῳ, ἢ σελήνῃ, ἤ τινι τῶν ἀστέρων.—p. 239. [12. p. 586.]

near at hand, and not a God afar off, saith the Lord,') it is absurd to seek to pray to the sun, which is not present to all things, or to the moon, or to any of the stars."

9. In the sixth book, he proves the absolutely divine and
[302] uncreated nature of the Son in these words, which are clearer than any light[z]; "For no one can worthily know Him who is ingenerate[1] and the first-born of all generated[2] nature, as [can] the Father who begat Him, nor [can any one know] the Father as [can] the living Word, [Who is] both His Wisdom and Truth." In these words, I say, Origen, as if he had himself even now been sitting in the assembly of the fathers at Nice, distinctly pronounces, in opposition to Arius, that the Son of God is neither made[3] nor created, (for the word *ἀγένητος* (ingenerate) embraces both these within its compass;) moreover he distinctly teaches, that the Father and the Son are alike reciprocally comprehensible by each other, but absolutely incomprehensible by all creatures. Sandius, however, in order to evade the force of this remarkable passage, pretends that the text of Origen in this place has been interpolated and corrupted: "Petavius," he says, "proves, on the Trinity, book i. chap. 3, n. 5 and 6," (or rather, chap. iv. n. 6 and 7,) "that the passage of Origen, in which, in his sixth book against Celsus, he calls the Son *ἀγένητον*, 'ingenerate,' is interpolated, on the ground that Epiphanius, 'On the heresy of Origen,' censures him for having called the Son, in his Commentary on the [first] Psalm, 'a generated God[4].'" But Petavius does not there say, much less does he prove, that this passage of Origen is interpolated; nor if the Jesuit had so said, would his criticism have been worth much; for all the Greek MSS. which have been discovered any where[a], agree with the printed copies in this place; and the tenor[5] of the passage is altogether in accordance with the
[303] uniform teaching of these books against Celsus, in which Origen throughout expressly excepts the Son of God from the class of created beings[6], as is clear from the testimonies
111 which we have already adduced. And as to the objection which

[1] ἀγένητον, qui factus non est.
[2] γενητῆς. factæ.
[3] οὐδὲ ποιητὸν, οὐδὲ κτιστὸν.
[4] γενητὸν. Deum.
[5] sententia.
[6] τῶν δημιουργημάτων.

[z] οὔτε γὰρ τὸν ἀγένητον καὶ πάσης γενητῆς φύσεως πρωτότοκον κατ' ἀξίαν εἰδέναι τις δύναται, ὡς ὁ γεννήσας αὐτὸν Πατὴρ, οὔτε τὸν Πατέρα, ὡς ὁ ἔμψυχος λόγος, καὶ σοφία αὐτοῦ, καὶ ἀλήθεια.—p. 287. [17. p. 643.]

[a] [In the Benedictine edition it is mentioned that the reading *τὸν γεννητὸν* occurs in one MS. alone, the second English one.]

BOOK II. CHAP. IX. § 8, 9.

ORIGEN.

Petavius brings from Epiphanius, that Origen in his Commentary on the first Psalm had called the Son of God γεννητὸν Θεὸν (a generated God), Sandius could not have been ignorant, that the great Huet had given a luminous reply to it in his Origeniana ii. p. 43[b]. "Origen," he says, "in calling the Son γεννητὸν Θεὸν, should be taken to mean, 'one that has a principle of His being and an origin of existence[1].' It is common, indeed, to the Son with created beings to have a principle and origin of His being; but the mode[2] of emanation and going forth from that principle is quite different; for the Son goes forth by an eternal generation; created beings go forth by creation in time. . . . . And thus the Son may be called ἀγένητος, one who has not His being from any other, that is, as a work, or a thing made, or as a thing created; and also γεννητὸς, one who has His being from another, that is, as a thing begotten and a Son. Thus Origen, who is charged with having called the Son γεννητὸς Θεὸς, ... yet in his sixth book against Celsus calls the Son ἀγένητος." A little afterwards Huet subjoins these words; "When he (Origen) called the Son γεννητὸς, he meant to say, that He has a principle of His being: Jerome, on the contrary, interpreted [him as meaning] that the Son was made. For he loved thus to interpret the words of Origen in the worse sense. In the same way Epiphanius says, that he would approve the use of the word γεννητὸς in others, but that he condemned it in Origen." Much more may be read on this subject in Huet, in the same place. I return to the books of Origen against Celsus. In this same sixth book, when Celsus says, that God is not even comprehensible by reason, Origen replies[c]: "I make a distinction as [304]

[1] qui principium sui habet et existendi initium.

[2] ratio.

[b] Origenes, inquit, cum Filium appellat γεννητὸν Θεὸν, sic accipe, *qui principium sui habet et existendi initium.* Filio quidem commune est cum creatis rebus sui principium ac originem habere; emanandi autem ex illo principio ac prodeundi ratio plane diversa est; prodit enim Filius per generationem æternam; prodeunt creatæ res per temporariam creationem. . . . Atque ita Filius dici potest ἀγένητος, qui ab alio non habet ut sit, nempe tanquam opus seu res facta, vel tanquam res creata; et γεννητὸς, qui ab alio habet ut sit, nempe tanquam res genita et Filius. Sic Origenes, qui γεννητὸν Θεὸν appellasse Filium insimulatur . . . Filium tamen ἀγένητον vocat lib. vi. contra Cels. . . . Cum Filium dixit (Origenes) γεννητὸν, id sibi voluit, *habere ipsum sui principium;* contra Hieronymus exposuit, *esse factum.* Nempe sic verba Origenis in pessimum sensum trahere amabat. Ita Epiphanius vocis γεννητὸς usum in aliis probaturum se dicit, in Origene damnare.—[Lib. ii. Quæst. ii. § 23.]

[c] διαστέλλωμαι τὸ σημαινόμενον, καὶ

ON THE CONSUBSTANTIALITY OF THE SON.

[1] ἐνδιαθέτῳ.
[2] προφορικῷ.
[3] ἐφικτὸς.

to what is meant, and say, if [it be meant, comprehensible] by reason (λόγος) that is in us, whether abiding in [the mind[1],] or also put forth [in sound[2],] we will also say that God is not comprehensible[3] by reason (λόγος), but if [we use the expression λόγος] having in mind, 'the Word (*Λόγος*) was in the beginning, and the Word was with God, and the Word was God,' then we declare that by this *Λόγος* God is comprehensible." As much as to say, God cannot be comprehended except by God, nor what is infinite except by what is infinite; from which it follows that the Word (*ὁ Λόγος*), inasmuch as He is able to comprehend God, is Himself God, which also Origen, together with John the Evangelist, affirms in express terms. Every one then must perceive how diametrically opposed this declaration of Origen is to the blasphemy of Arius. For Arius, in a work entitled Thalia, (as Athanasius states, in his work on the Synods[e],) said, "It is not possible for the Son to trace out[4] the Father, Who He is by Himself, for the Son Himself does not know His own substance." A passage precisely similar follows, in the same book [against Celsus vi.], after some interval[f]; "And who else is able to save the soul of man, and to bring it to God who is over all, but God the Word? who being in the beginning with God, on account of those who have been joined unto the flesh, and have become the very same as flesh, became flesh, in order that He may be comprehended by those who were unable to behold Him, in that He was [the] Word[5], and was with God, and was God." Lastly, Origen, soon after, in the same passage, calls the Son, equally with the Father, great and incomprehensible; and moreover affirms that the Father had made the only-begotten Son a partner even of His own greatness. We shall quote the passage entire in a more suitable place hereafter.

[4] ἐξιχνιάσαι.

[5] λόγος.

[305]

φημι, εἰ μὲν λόγῳ τῷ ἐν ἡμῖν, εἴτε ἐνδιαθέτῳ, εἴτε καὶ προφορικῷ, καὶ ἡμεῖς φήσομεν, ὅτι οὐκ ἔστιν ἐφικτὸς τῷ λόγῳ ὁ Θεός· εἰ δὲ νοήσαντες τὸ, Ἐν ἀρχῇ ἦν ὁ λόγος, καὶ ὁ λόγος ἦν πρὸς τὸν Θεὸν, καὶ Θεὸς ἦν ὁ λόγος, ἀποφαινόμεθα, ὅτι τούτῳ τῷ λόγῳ ἐφικτός ἐστιν ὁ Θεός.—p. 320. [65. p. 682.]

[e] ἀδύνατα γὰρ αὐτῷ (ἀδύνατον υἱῷ, Bull) τὸν Πατέρα ἐξιχνιάσαι, ὅς ἐστιν ἐφ' ἑαυτοῦ· αὐτὸς γὰρ ὁ υἱὸς τὴν ἑαυτοῦ οὐσίαν οὐκ οἶδεν.—[15. vol. i. p. 729.]

[f] τίς δ' ἄλλος σῶσαι καὶ προσαγαγεῖν τῷ ἐπὶ πᾶσι Θεῷ δύναται τὴν τοῦ ἀνθρώπου ψυχὴν, ἢ ὁ Θεὸς λόγος; ὅστις ἐν ἀρχῇ πρὸς τὸν Θεὸν ὢν, διὰ τοὺς κολληθέντας τῇ σαρκὶ καὶ γενομένους ὅπερ σὰρξ, ἐγένετο σὰρξ, ἵνα χωρηθῇ ὑπὸ τῶν μὴ δυναμένων αὐτὸν βλέπειν καθὸ λόγος ἦν, καὶ πρὸς Θεὸν ἦν, καὶ Θεὸς ἦν.—[68. p. 684.]

10. You see, reader, how repeatedly and most openly Origen asserts the true Divinity of the Son, in his books against Celsus, which are universally allowed to be the most genuine, pure, and uncorrupted of all his writings. Who now would suspect that out of these very writings any thing could be gathered, to shew that Origen was favourable to the Arian blasphemy? And yet Petavius[g] alleges against Origen, as savouring of Arianism, a passage out of his sixth book against Celsus, in which he wrote, that[h] "the Son of God, the Word, was the immediate Creator[1], and, as it were, the actual framer[2] of the world; whilst the Father of the Word was primarily[3] Creator, by reason of His having given commandment to His Son, the Word, to make the world." I have, however, already shewn how these words are to be understood, in chap. v. § 6. [p. 171.] of this book, in treating of the doctrine of Irenæus, to which I refer the reader. It is, indeed, so far from being an Arian tenet, that all things were created by the Father issuing, as it were, His mandate as the Supreme Maker, through the Son performing the Father's commandment and will, that even catholic doctors, who lived after the council of Nice, and [306] who were the keenest opponents of the Arian heresy, did not hesitate to affirm it throughout their writings, as we shewed in the same place out of Petavius himself. To the writers there adduced, I would here add one other, Hilary; who, in his fourth book on the Trinity, treating of the words in Genesis i., "Let us make man in our image," &c. speaks thus[i], "By that which is said, 'Let us make man,' [it appears, that] the origin is from Him, from whom the Word also hath His beginning[4]; but in that 'God made man after the image of God,' He also is signified through whom the work [of creation] is accomplished." Then again a little after; "In that it is said, 'Let us make,' both the commanding and the execution are made[5] equal." And again, presently after, concerning Wisdom, or the Son of God, rejoicing with

1 τὸν προσεχῶς δημιουργόν.
2 αὐτουργόν.
3 πρώτως.
4 cœpit.
5 exæquatur; scil. He who commands and He who executes are made equal.

g De Trinit. i. 4. 5.

h τὸν μὲν προσεχῶς δημιουργὸν εἶναι τὸν υἱὸν τοῦ Θεοῦ λόγον, καὶ ὡσπερεὶ αὐτουργὸν τοῦ κόσμου· τὸν δὲ Πατέρα τοῦ λόγου, τῷ προστεταχέναι τῷ υἱῷ ἑαυτοῦ λόγῳ ποιῆσαι τὸν κόσμον, εἶναι πρώτως δημιουργόν.—p. 317. [60. p. 678.]

i Per id quod dictum est, *Faciamus hominem*, ex eo origo est, ex quo cœpit et Sermo; in eo vero quod Deus ad imaginem Dei fecit, significatur etiam is, per quem consummatur operatio.... In eo quod dicitur, *Faciamus*, et jussio

ON THE CONSUBSTANTIALITY OF THE SON.

His Father in the works of creation, he has these words: "Wisdom hath taught [us] the cause of Her rejoicing; She was rejoicing because of the Father's joy, who joyed in the completion of the world and in the children of men. For it is written, 'And God saw that they were good.' She [Wisdom] is glad that Her works, wrought through Herself at His command, are well-pleasing to the Father." These last words of Hilary express fully the meaning of the passage in Origen at which Petavius cavils. This is further to be observed, that Origen expressly softened down his assertion, lest it should seem harsh to any one, by the adverb ὡσπερεὶ, 'as it were.' "The Son," his words are, "is the immediate Creator of the world, since He was[1], *as it were*, Himself the actual framer of it;" by which caution he meant, without doubt, to meet the error of those who refused to admit the undivided operation of the Father and the Son in the same work of creation. But what is to be the end of this bold and reckless temper of scholastic theologians in passing their censure on the statements of the ancients? Certainly, if
[307] he, who has said that the Father, as the Father, is the primary Creator of the world, who made the universe through His Son, is to be accounted an Arian, scarcely will Paul himself be pure from the stain of Arianism; seeing that in his first Epistle to the Corinthians, viii. 6, he thus treats of the shares[2], so to say, which the Father and the Son had respectively in the creation and renewal of all things: "To us there is one God, the Father, of whom[3] are all things, and we in Him; and one Lord Jesus Christ, through whom[4] are all things, and we through Him." For it is evident that the expression ἐξ οὗ, 'of whom,' denotes the primary cause. Hence also, Theodore Beza makes this annotation on the passage: "Whensoever the Father is distinguished from the Son, origination is attributed to the former." All these statements, I mean, are to be referred altogether to that subordination of the Son, by which He is subjected to the Father "as His Author," (I here again use the very words of Hilary,) of

[1] qui velut per se ipse fabricarit. Lat. Vers.

[2] partibus.

[3] ἐξ οὗ.

[4] δι' οὗ.

exæquatur, et factum. . . . Causam lætitiæ suæ Sapientia docuit; lætatur ob lætitiam Patris, in perfectione mundi et in filiis hominum lætantis. Scriptum est enim, *Et vidit Deus quia bona sunt.* Placere Patri opera sua gaudet, PER SE EX PRÆCEPTO EJUS EFFECTA.—p. 39, 40. [§ 20, 21. p. 839, 840.]

which we shall treat more at length in the fourth book. But what is to be said of this, that in the Nicene Creed itself we are commanded to believe, first, "In one God the Father Almighty, Maker of all things, visible and invisible:" secondly, "in one Lord Jesus Christ, &c., by[1] whom all things were made?" I suppose, that if the Nicene Fathers had not been assembled in an œcumenical council, which it is an act of impiety to contradict, they would hardly have escaped the severe censure of the Jesuit Petavius, for these expressions. To sum up the whole subject in few words; Whosoever affirms, that God the Father, as the fountain of Godhead, and, therefore, the origin of all the divine operations, created the world from Himself[2] through His Son, and that He is in consequence the primary Maker of all things, he surely is no way to be charged with Arian heresy, unless indeed we be ready to fasten the charge of Arianism on all the ancient fathers of the Church, and even on the divinely inspired writers themselves. But this would certainly be characteristic of Arian blasphemy, if any one should teach, that the Father created all things through the Son, as through an instrument extraneous to Himself, or as [308]
through some power created before all other things, and alien from His own essence,—an impiety which never entered the mind of Origen even in a dream, as is evident from the passages we have adduced above.

11. But there are some other statements in these very books against Celsus, which even Huet notes as wrong, and marks with condemnation[3]; the principal of which we shall discuss. In the first place, Huet[j] adduces, as very difficult of explanation, these words of Origen[k]: "But if any one from these words shall be distracted with fear, that we are deserting to those, who deny that the Father and the Son are two hypostases[4], let him give heed to that saying, 'And of all them that believed the heart and the soul was one,' in order that he may understand those words, 'I and My Father are one.'" And again[l], "We therefore worship the Father of the Truth, and

[1] per.

[2] a seipso.

[3] atro calculo notat, et veru transfigit.

[4] *δύο ὑποστάσεις.*

[j] Origeniana ii. 32. [Quæst. 2. 3.]

[k] *εἰ δέ τις ἐκ τούτων περισπασθήσεται, μή πη αὐτομολοῦμεν πρὸς τοὺς ἀναιροῦντας δύο εἶναι ὑποστάσεις πατέρα καὶ υἱὸν, ἐπιστησάτω τῷ, Ἦν δὲ πάντων τῶν πιστευσάντων ἡ καρδία καὶ ἡ ψυχὴ μία, ἵνα θεωρήσῃ τὸ, ἐγὼ καὶ ὁ πατὴρ ἕν ἐσμεν.*—Lib. viii. contr. Cels., p. 386. [12. p. 750.]

[l] *θρησκεύομεν οὖν τὸν πατέρα τῆς*

ON THE CONSUBSTANTIALITY OF THE SON.

the Son [who is] the Truth, being two things in hypostasis[1],
but One in unanimity, and agreement, and identity of will."
Upon these passages the learned writer observes thus; "He
says that 'the Father and the Son are two[2] in hypostasis,
one in agreement and unanimity.' But *ὑπόστασις* in early
times was ordinarily used for *οὐσία* (substance) by heathen
and Christian writers. Jerome, in his 57th Epistle to Damasus
says, 'The whole school of secular literature knoweth of no
[309] other sense of *ὑπόστασις* than that of *οὐσία*[l].' In this sense
the Nicene fathers understood it, in this sense did those of
Sardica; in this sense also is it probable that Origen understood it." I reply first: The words *ὑπόστασις* and *οὐσία*
were variously employed in early times, at least by Christians.
I mean that *ὑπόστασις* was sometimes taken by them for
what we call *οὐσία* (substance), and, *vice versa*, the word
οὐσία for that which we call *ὑπόστασις* (person): sometimes
ὑπόστασις was used by the ancients, even by those who preceded the council of Nice, for that which we at this day
designate *person* or subsistence. That the word *ὑποστάσις*
is occasionally[3] used by the ancients to signify that which
we call *οὐσία* is not only confessed but contended for by
Huet; although (candidly to confess the truth) I do not
113 remember that I ever found the word thus used by any
catholic writer, in treating of the most Holy Trinity, before
the Nicene council, or for some time after it. It is however
most certain that the word *οὐσία* was sometimes taken by
these very writers, for what we call *ὑπόστασις*. Thus Pierius,
martyr and presbyter, the teacher of the martyr Pamphilus,
though his views concerning the Father and the Son were
catholic, yet made the statement, (as is related by Photius[m],)
that the Father and the Son are two *οὐσίαι* and *φύσεις*,
meaning by the words *ousia* and nature[4], *hypostasis*; as is
evident, Photius likewise says, from what precedes and
follows. We have observed above[n], that the word *φύσις*
was used by Clement of Alexandria in this sense, though,
like the term *οὐσία*, it has in other cases[5] a wider appli-

1 δύο τῇ ὑποστάσει πράγματα.

2 duo.

3 quandoque.

4 usiæ et naturæ.

5 alioqui.

ἀληθείας, καὶ τὸν υἱὸν τὴν ἀλήθειαν, ὄντα δύο τῇ ὑποστάσει πράγματα, ἓν δὲ τῇ ὁμονοίᾳ, καὶ τῇ συμφωνίᾳ καὶ τῇ ταυτότητι τοῦ βουλήματος.—[p. 751.]

l Tota secularium literarum schola nihil aliud ὑπόστασιν nisi οὐσίαν novit. [Epist. xv. vol. i. p. 39.]

m Biblioth. Cod. 119. [See Routh. Reliq. Sacr., vol. iii. p. 212.—B.; see the whole passage quoted below, 13. 1.]

n [ch. vi. § 6. p. 118.]

cation. And that this word was taken in the same sense by Gregory Nyssen, Epiphanius, and even by Athanasius himself, is shewn by Petavius, de Trin. iv. 1. n. 2, 3. Lastly, (which bears more nearly on our subject,) it is certain from many instances that the word ὑπόστασις was at times used by the primitive doctors of the Church, even those who preceded the council of Nice, to signify a *subsistence*[1], or a single thing subsisting *per se*, which in things endued with intelligence is the same as person. [310] Tertullian, in his treatise against Praxeas, wishing to assert the personal subsistence[2] of the Son in opposition to those who denied that He was a distinct Person from the Father, affirms of the Son of God, that He is "a substance" and "a substantive thing." Thus, in the seventh chapter[o]: "Do you then, (you ask,) grant that the Word is a certain substance[3], constructed by the Spirit and the communication of Wisdom[4]? Certainly I do. For you are unwilling to hold Him to be substantive in reality[5], by having a substance of His owr[6], so as that He may be regarded as a thing and a person[7], and so, being constituted second to God [the Father], be able to make two[8], Father and Son, God and the Word. For, you will say, what is a word, but a voice and sound of the mouth, or (as grammarians teach) air struck against[9], intelligible on being heard, but, for the rest, a sort of void and empty[10] and incorporeal thing? I, on the contrary, contend, that nothing empty and void could have come forth from God, seeing that it is not put forth from that which is empty and void; nor could that be devoid of substance, which has proceeded from so great a substance," &c. Again, in the 26th chapter, treating of the distinction between the Father and the Son, he speaks to this effect; "[But if He be] God of God, as a substantive thing, [He] will

1 subsistentia.
2 subsistentiam.
3 aliquam substantiam.
4 Spiritu et Sophiæ traditione.
5 substantivum in re.
6 per substantiæ proprietatem.
7 persona quadam.
8 duos.
9 offensus.
10 vacuum et inane.

o Ergo, inquis, das aliquam substantiam esse Sermonem, Spiritu et sophiæ traditione constructam? plane. Non vis enim eum substantivum habere in re, per substantiæ proprietatem, ut res et persona quædam videri possit, et ita capiat secundus a Deo constitutus duos efficere, Patrem et Filium, Deum et Sermonem. Quid est enim, dices, sermo, nisi vox et sonus oris, et (sicut grammatici tradunt) aer offensus, intelligibis auditu, cæterum vacuum nescio quid, et inane, et incorporale? At ego nihil dico de Deo inane et vacuum prodire potuisse, ut non de inani et vacuo prolatum; nec carere substantia, quod de tanta substantia processit, &c. . . . [Quod si] Deus Dei tanquam substantiva res, non erit ipse Deus; sed hactenus Deus, quia ex ipsius Dei substantia, qua et substantiva res est, &c.—[p. 503, 504.]

not be God [the Father] Himself; but thus far God, because [He is] of the substance of God Himself, whereby also He is a substantive thing." He goes on to say, that wisdom and providence are not "substantive things" or "substances," that is, hypostases (ὑποστάσεις). For this form of expression Tertullian, the known imitator of the Greeks, seems altogether to have derived from the Greek Fathers, translating the Greek word ὑπόστασις by the Latin *substantia* and *res substantiva;* though the Latins had, besides[1], a word of their own, even in the time of Tertullian, for expressing a subsistence in the divine essence, namely, the word *persona*,
[311] which is sometimes used by Tertullian himself in the same treatise. Hippolytus, who was next to Tertullian in date, and earlier than Origen, in a passage which has been already quoted[p] by us, says that the flesh or human nature in Christ does not subsist by itself, but has its subsistence (τὴν ὑπόστασιν) in the Word, that is to say, subsists in the Word. Dionysius of Alexandria, a disciple of Origen, in his answer to the fourth question of Paul of Samosata, speaks thus of the three persons of the Holy Trinity[q]; "The two hypostases (that is, of the Father and of the Son) are inseparable[r], and also the insubsisting[2] Spirit of the Father, which was in the Son." And it seems to me that by this passage of Dionysius of Alexandria the opinion of his namesake and contemporary, Dionysius of Rome, is by all means to be explained; for the latter in his Epistle against the Sabellians, [preserved] in Athanasius[s], after refuting them, proceeds to confute those who separated the Godhead "into three divided hypostases[3]." Petavius, indeed, on the (Trinity, iv. 1. 5) would have it that the word ὑπόστασις in this passage was used in a more general signification for οὐσία: led to this, I suppose, by the consideration, that Dionysius professes his dissent from those, who divided the Godhead into three hypostases. But this is nothing to the point: for Dionysius does not blame those against whom he argues

[1] alioqui.

[2] ἐνυπόστατον.

[3] εἰς τρεῖς μεμερισμένας ὑποστάσεις.

[p] See 8. § 5. of this book [p. 213, where I observed that Hippolytus wrote σύστασις, not ὑπόστασις.—B.]

[q] αἱ δύο ὑποστάσεις ἀχώριστοι, καὶ τὸ ἐνυπόστατον τοῦ πατρὸς πνεῦμα, ὃ ἦν ἐν τῷ υἱῷ.—[p. 230.]

[r] See Theodoret, E. H. i. 4.

[s] εἰς τρεῖς μεμερισμένας ὑποστάσεις. Athanasius de Syn. Nic. Decretis, p. 275. edit. Paris. 1627. [vol. i. p. 231. and in Routh's Rel. Sacr., vol. iii. p. 179, &c.; see the passage quoted below, cap. xi. § 1.]

simply for making three hypostases in the Godhead, but on this account only, that they thought that those three hypostases were *divided* (μεμερισμένας). And afterwards in the same passage he expresses this more fully, when he [312] says again, "that the same heretics divided the Godhead[t] into three hypostases, foreign to, and altogether separate from, each other." Very ill, therefore, has Petavius translated the Greek of Dionysius into Latin, as *distinctas hypostases,* (distinct hypostases). Against these heretics, Dionysius in the next place proceeds to lay down, that[u] "the divine Word is made one[1] with the God of the universe, and that the Holy Ghost reposes[2] in God and hath His dwelling in Him;" that is to say, that the Three Divine Persons are intimately and mutually conjoined with Each Other by an 114 inexplicable kind of circumincession[3], and that They reciprocally, as it were, enter into Each Other, so that One cannot in any wise be separated from Another; but on this point we shall say more hereafter. The reader may see this passage from Dionysius quoted entire in chap. xi. § 1 of this book. When, therefore, Dionysius of Rome denies that there are in the Godhead three divided and separate hypostases, he clearly meant the same as the other Dionysius, when he affirms that the Father and the Son are two hypostases by no means separate [from each other], and that the Holy Ghost also is an hypostasis subsisting in the Son Himself, and, consequently, not disjoined either from the Son or from the Father. It is plain that both alike confessed a distinction of hypostases in the Godhead; both alike denied a division or separation of hypostases. There is, however, another passage of Dionysius of Alexandria, which throws the clearest light on this subject; it is quoted by Basil the Great, in his treatise concerning the Holy Spirit, chap. 29[w], where he introduces Dionysius arguing to this effect, in his Apology against the Sabellians, near the middle, "If, because [313] hypostases are Three, they say that they are divided, Three

[1] ἡνῶσθαι.

[2] ἐμφιλοχωρεῖν.

[3] inexplicabilem quandam περιχώρησιν. [see book iv. 4. 14.]

[t] εἰς τρεῖς ὑποστάσεις ξένας, ἀλλήλων παντάπασι κεχωρισμένας, [διαιροῦντας τὴν ἁγίαν μονάδα.] Ibid.

[u] ἡνῶσθαι γὰρ ἀνάγκη τῷ θεῷ τῶν ὅλων τὸν θεῖον λόγον· ἐμφιλοχωρεῖν δὲ τῷ θεῷ καὶ ἐνδιαιτᾶσθαι δὲ τὸ ἅγιον πνεῦμα.—Ibid.

[w] εἰ τῷ τρεῖς εἶναι τὰς ὑποστάσεις, μεμερισμένας εἶναι λέγουσι, τρεῖς εἰσι, κἂν μὴ θέλωσιν, ἢ τὴν θείαν τριάδα παντελῶς ἀνελέτωσαν.—Opera Basilii, tom. ii. p. 358. edit. Paris. 1637. [Vol. iii. p. 61. Op. Dionys., p. 98, 99.]

there are, (though they would not have it so,) or else let them entirely do away with the divine Trinity." From these words it is clearly gathered, that amongst the catholics of the age of Dionysius it was a fixed and settled point, that there are three hypostases in the Godhead[1]; and that the Sabellians thought that it followed from that position, that there were three divided hypostases, as being unable to conceive of three distinct Persons subsisting in the divine essence without division. This consequence, however, both the Dionysii entirely reject in the passages which have been adduced. To proceed. The six bishops, contemporaries of the two Dionysii, who wrote an epistle[x] to Paul of Samosata, from the council of Antioch, deny in it, in opposition to Paul and Sabellius, that the Son of God is "the unsubsisting[2] knowledge" of the Father; and in the same place they call the Son of God Himself "the living and insubsisting energy[3]" of God the Father. Who then can doubt, that these bishops meant that the Son also was a distinct hypostasis[4] from the Father? Especially since Dionysius of Alexandria, in the same age, used the terms τὴν ὑπόστασιν and τὸ ἐνυπόστατον as having the same meaning, as is evident from the passage above quoted. Alexander, bishop of Alexandria, in an epistle to Alexander, bishop of Constantinople, written before the council of Nice[y], seems to have taken the word in the same sense, by writing to this effect on the words of the Evangelist, John i. 1; "For he set forth His (the Son's) peculiar hypostasis[5], when he said, 'In the beginning was the Word, and the Word was with God.'" And, if trust
[314] is to be placed in the great Basil rather than in the modern Jesuït, Petavius, the Nicene fathers understood the word in the same sense, that is, according to the ancient use of it in the Church, when in their creed they anathematized those, who said that the Son was of "another hypostasis or substance[6]" than the Father. For Basil, in his 78th epistle, stating how Marcellus of Ancyra and some other abettors of the

1 in divinis.

2 ἐπιστήμην ἀνυπόστατον.

3 ἐνέργειαν ζῶσαν καὶ ἐνυπόστατον.

4 ὑπόστασιν.

5 ἰδιότροπον ὑπόστασιν.

6 or "essence." ἐξ ἑτέρας ὑποστάσεως ἢ οὐσίας.

x Bibl. Patr., tom. xi. [Routh. Rel. Sacr., vol. ii. p. 469.—B. [The passage is this: δι' οὗ ὁ πατὴρ πάντα πεποίηκεν, οὐχ ὡς δι' ὀργάνου, οὐδ' ὡς δι' ἐπιστήμης ἀνυποστάτου, γεννήσαντος μὲν τοῦ πατρὸς τὸν υἱὸν ὡς ζῶσαν ἐνέργειαν, καὶ ἐνυπόστατον, ἐνεργοῦντα τὰ πάντα ἐν πᾶσιν.]

y τὴν γὰρ ἰδιότροπον αὐτοῦ ὑπόστασιν ἐδήλωσεν, εἰπὼν, Ἐν ἀρχῇ ἦν ὁ λόγος, καὶ ὁ λόγος ἦν πρὸς τὸν Θεόν, κ.λ.—In Theodoret. E. H. i. 4. [p. 12.]

Sabellian heresy, had sought support from these words of the Nicene council, denies that the words *οὐσία* and *ὑπόστασις* were used by the fathers as parallel[1] and as signifying the same. He proves this by the following argument[z]; "For if the words had expressed one and the same idea, what need was there of both? but it is evident that, inasmuch as there were some who denied that [the Son] is of the *οὐσία* of the Father, and others who said, not only that He was not of the *οὐσία* of the Father, but that He was of some other *ὑπόστασις*, they thus renounced both opinions as alien from the mind of the Church." I should wish here, however, by the way, to examine briefly the chief arguments, by which Petavius[a] has endeavoured to overthrow this view of the great Basil; "First," he says, "it is quite certain, that the fathers added this clause of the Creed in opposition to the dogma of Arius alone." I might have asked Petavius, whence it is so certain? Surely it is most certain, that the [Nicene] fathers in their Creed, although they intended primarily to impugn the dogma of Arius, do yet in some places touch on the heresies of others. For instance, when they define that all things were made by the Son, they do [315]
not aim a blow at the Arians, who never denied this, but at the Ebionites, Artemonites, Samosatenes, and other heretics of the same stamp. But suppose we allow that that clause was added by the Fathers in opposition to the dogma of the Arians alone, (which I think to be most true,) what follows? "The Arians," says Petavius, "did not teach that the Son derived His origin from another person[2] than that of the Father." Neither, I answer, did any one of the Arians teach that the Son derived His origin of[3] another substance, if we would speak strictly and exactly. But, as all the Arians 115
denied that the Son was born of[4] the substance of the Father, so some denied, that He was in any way born of[5] the Father Himself, or of the hypostasis of the Father. That is, there were two main classes of Arian fanatics; the one acknowledged, indeed, that the Son was born[6] in a manner

1 ἐκ παραλλήλου.

2 ab aliâ personâ.

3 ex aliâ substantiâ.

4 natum e.

5 natum ex.

6 natum.

z εἰ γὰρ μίαν καὶ τὴν αὐτὴν ἐδήλουν ἔννοιαν αἱ φωναὶ, τίς χρεία ἦν ἑκατέρων; ἀλλὰ δῆλον ὅτι, ὡς τῶν μὲν ἀρνουμένων τὸ ἐκ τῆς οὐσίας εἶναι τοῦ πατρὸς, τῶν δὲ λεγόντων, οὔτε ἐκ τῆς οὐσίας, ἀλλ' ἐξ ἄλλης τινὸς ὑποστάσεως, οὕτως ἀμφότερα ὡς ἀλλότρια τοῦ ἐκκλησιαστικοῦ φρονήματος ἀπηγόρευσαν.—[Ep. cxxv. 1. vol. iii. p. 215.]

a De Trin. iv. 1. 6.

peculiar [to Himself] of the Hypostasis of the Father Itself,—not, as the other creatures, made out of nothing,—but yet denied that the Son was begotten[1] of the substance of the Father, regarding Him only as a kind of power[2] of the Father, not an effluence[3] of the Father's substance; the other class, in order to avoid admitting that the Son was begotten in a manner peculiar [to Himself] of the Father Himself, affirmed in round terms, that He, as the other creatures, was made simply out of nothing[4]. The former class were called Semiarians, and their opinion is best explained in few words by Petavius[b] himself in another place, out of their own Confession, in Epiphanius, Hæres. lxxiii. n. 2. &c., in the following terms; "In this," he says, "they bring forward many things very like the Catholic doctrine; especially in that they deny that the Son is a creature, on the ground that He is a true Son, and produced by a true generation, and not by that figurative one, whereby created beings are said to be begotten by[5] God; on the contrary, that [the
[316] Father] is truly a Father, whom they confess also to have begotten the Son, of Himself[6], and that before all thought, and all reckonings, and times, and ages. These expressions are plausible in appearance, and approach very near to the Catholic Confession. But there is yet that wanting in them, wherein consists the strength and chief point[7] of the faith, in that they do not acknowledge that the Son was begotten by the Father of His substance[8], but of the likeness of the Father[9], namely, by His generative energy[10]; since they affirm that the Father has various modes of acting[11], one creative[12], another generative, whereby He produces the Son. Then they lay it down, that there is not the same essence in Both, but two mutually like each other." The Nicene fathers, therefore, strike a blow at both these parties of the Arians, in the words, "of another hypostasis or substance[13];" that is to say, both at those who denied that the Son was in any wise born[14] of the Person of the Father, or of the Father Himself, and affirmed that He was made out of nothing; as also at those who, while they confessed that the Son was born[15] in a manner peculiar [to Himself] of the Father Himself, did yet deny altogether that He was be-

1 progenitum.
2 virtutem aliquam.
3 ἀπόρροιαν.
4 ex non existentibus.
5 genitæ a.
6 genuisse ex sese.
7 caput.
8 ἐκ τῆς οὐσίας.
9 ἐκ τῆς ὁμοιότητος τοῦ Πατρὸς.
10 ἐνεργείᾳ γεννητικῇ.
11 actiones.
12 κτιστικὴν.
13 ἐξ ἄλλης ὑποστάσεως ἢ οὐσίας.
14 natum.
15 natum.

b De Trin. i. 10. 7.

gotten of the substance of the Father, and that He was in consequence of one substance[1] with the Father. To put the question beyond all controversy, the Confession of the Arians, which was presented to the Emperor Constans, by the hands of Maris, Theodorus, and Mark, and is recited by Athanasius, in his work on the Synods of Ariminum and Seleucia, concludes with these words[c]; "Those, however, who say that the Son is out of what existed not, or of another hypostasis, and not of God, and that there ever was a time, when He was not, the Catholic Church regards as aliens." The same thing is evident from the [317]
Confession sent into Italy, by the hands[2] of Eudoxius, Martyrius, and others, and from the Sirmian Confession, which follow in the same place in Athanasius. Now you see here, that those Arians denied that the Son was created, or made, out of nothing, and acknowledged that the Son was born[3] *ἐξ ὑποστάσεως*, of the hypostasis of God the Father, in other words, of[4] God Himself; whilst it is yet most certain that these same heretics never acknowledged, and never would have acknowledged that the Son was begotten *ἐξ οὐσίας*, of the substance of the Father. Rightly, therefore, and learnedly did Basil distinguish between the words *ὑπόστασις* and *οὐσία*, in the Nicene Creed; and quite inconsiderately does the Jesuit Petavius carp at that observation of the great doctor. And as to the argument adduced by Basil—that the Nicene fathers would not have employed those words together in so short a creed, had the meaning of both been the same—Petavius's reply to it is easily refuted. "If," he says, "there were force in that reasoning of Basil, neither would this be free from objection, that in the same creed, after the fathers had pronounced an anathema against such as held, that 'there was a time when the Son was not,' they immediately add what has the same meaning, 'and that before He was begotten He was not;' and again, 'that He was made out of what existed not[5].'" But I deny that the words, "He was not before He was begotten," have entirely the same signification as the preceding clause, "there was a time

[1] ὁμοούσιον.

[2] per.

[3] natum.

[4] ex.

[5] nullis substantibus.

[c] *τοὺς δὲ λέγοντας ἐξ οὐκ ὄντων τὸν υἱὸν, ἢ ἐξ ἑτέρας ὑποστάσεως, καὶ μὴ ἐκ τοῦ Θεοῦ, καὶ (ὅτι) ἦν χρόνος ποτὲ (ἢ αἰὼν), ὅτε οὐκ ἦν, ἀλλοτρίους οἶδεν ἡ καθολικὴ ἐκκλησία.*—tom. i. p. 895. [§ 25. vol. i. p. 738.]

when He was not." For the former sentence attributes, indefinitely, a beginning to the existence of the Son; the second determines the very point[1], so to speak, of that beginning. There is indeed a sense latent[2] in the latter words, which has escaped the acuteness even of Petavius; what that is, however, we shall explain at large, in a more suitable place, hereafter[d]. Neither is it true, that in the following words, "that He was made out of what existed not," there is
[318] again a mere repetition. For among the crowd of Arians, there were some (as Petavius himself has observed in another place) whom Theodoret (lib. iv. de Hær.) says were afterwards called Psathyriani, who, as they said that the Father had ever existed, so [they said] that the Son had been ever created by Him; for that with God to beget is nothing else than to create. They did not assert, that there was a time when the Son was not; yet they maintained that the Son was made out of what existed not. Further also, Gelasius of Cyzicus, in his Acts of the Council of Nice, (part ii. c. 12,) represents Hosius as making reply, by the command and decree of the whole council, and declaring a Trinity of hypostases[3]; which the fathers afterwards make profession of through Leontius the bishop, (ibid., c. 21.) Accordingly Anastasius Sinaita stated that the Nicene fathers had defined, that[e] "there are three Hypostases, or Persons[4], in the Holy and Consubstantial Trinity." The authority of these writers, however, Petavius set at nought, relying, forsooth, on those arguments by which he groundlessly
116 boasts that he has refuted the opinion of Basil. Yet certainly Eusebius of Cæsarea, (who was present at the council of Nice, and than whom no one knew better the ancient use of the word *ὑπόστασις* in the Church,) in his Letter to Eustathius of Antioch, acknowledged, (according to Socrates[f],) "that the Son of God is substantive[5] and subsisting[6], and that there is one God in three hypostases." And in this sense (I conceive) the word *ὑπόστασις* would have

[1] punctum.
[2] latet.
[3] *τριάδα ὑποστάσεων.*
[4] *ὑποστάσεις, ἤτοι πρόσωπα.*
[5] *ἐνυπόστατον.*
[6] *ἐνυπάρχοντα.*

[d] Book iii. 9. 2, &c.

[e] *τρεῖς εἶναι ὑποστάσεις, ἤτοι πρόσωπα, ἐπὶ τῆς ἁγίας καὶ ὁμοουσίου τριάδος·* Anastasius in 'Οδηγ. c. 21. [c. 20. ed. Ingolstadt, 1606. Anastasius Sinaita was bishop of Antioch in the sixth century. This work, however, is considered by Cave to have been made up out of the works of Anastasius and other writers.—B.]

[f] *ἐνυπόστατόν τε καὶ ἐνυπάρχοντα τὸν υἱὸν εἶναι τοῦ Θεοῦ, ἕνα τε Θεὸν ἐν τρισὶν ὑποστάσεσιν εἶναι [ὁμολογοῦντες].*—E. H. i. 23.

continued to be used without offence, had not the Arians abused it to propagate their own heresy, taking it, in a more general signification, for nature and substance, and teaching that the Father and the Son are two hypostases, [319] that is [two] diverse natures or substances, mutually differing from each other. For it was against them that the catholic doctors affirmed in the council of Sardica, that there is one hypostasis[1] of the Father and of the Son. The words of the fathers of Sardica, on this subject, in their Synodical Letter[g], preserved by Theodoret, are worthy to be transcribed here[h]: "The party of the heretics obstinately maintains, that the hypostases of the Father, and of the Son, and of the Holy Ghost are different[2], and are separate from each other; we, however, have received and been taught and hold this, the catholic and apostolic tradition and faith and confession, that there is one hypostasis, which the heretics themselves call substance[3], of the Father, and of the Son, and of the Holy Ghost." Here these Fathers expressly inform us, that they called the Father, the Son, and the Holy Ghost one hypostasis[4], only in that sense in which the heretics took the word hypostasis as equivalent to substance[5]; intimating, as is plain, that they were not ignorant of another sense of the word, received among the ancient catholic doctors of the Church, by whom, that is, it was used to signify person or subsistence,—and that they would willingly have embraced [320] it, and, in accordance with that acceptation of the word, would have acknowledged that there are three persons, or subsistences[6], in the Godhead. From this cause, however, it is certain that there arose that sad division[7], which afterwards disturbed the Churches of the East, and of the West also, touching one or three hypostases in the Godhead[8]; whilst some, that is, chose to conform to the language of the fathers of the council of Sardica, and others retained the ancient use and meaning of the word. And this

[1] μίαν ὑπόστασιν.
[2] διαφόρους.
[3] οὐσίαν.
[4] μίαν ὑπόστασιν.
[5] οὐσία.
[6] subsistentias.
[7] discidium.
[8] divinis.

[g] Or rather in an appendix to their Letter, which was added by some of them, under protest from the rest of the bishops. See Athanasius, Epist. Synod. ad Antiochenses, p. 576. ed. Paris. [§ 5. vol. i. p. 772.]

[h] τὸ τῶν αἱρετικῶν σύστημα φιλονεικεῖ, διαφόρους εἶναι τὰς ὑποστάσεις τοῦ Πατρὸς καὶ τοῦ υἱοῦ καὶ τοῦ ἁγίου πνεύματος, καὶ εἶναι κεχωρισμένας· ἡμεῖς δὲ ταύτην παρειλήφαμεν καὶ δεδιδάγμεθα, καὶ ταύτην ἔχομεν τὴν καθολικὴν καὶ ἀποστολικὴν παράδοσιν καὶ πίστιν καὶ ὁμολογίαν, μίαν εἶναι ὑπόστασιν, ἣν αὐτοὶ οἱ αἱρετικοὶ οὐσίαν προσαγορεύουσι, τοῦ Πατρὸς καὶ τοῦ υἱοῦ καὶ τοῦ ἁγίου πνεύματος.—E. H. ii. 8. [p. 81.]

use the first council of Constantinople at length ratified by its authority, in its Synodical Letter, found in the Ecclesiastical History of Theodoret, v. 9. The Arians, however, at length determined to throw out from their creeds the word *ὑπόστασις* as well as *οὐσία*. For in the Confession which was drawn up at Constantinople by Acacius, Eudoxius, and others, who, on being condemned by the decree of the council of Seleucia, betook themselves to the emperor, towards the end they define to this effect[k]: "But as for the word substance (*οὐσια*), which was set down by the fathers in simplicity[1], but being unknown to the people caused offence, inasmuch as the Scriptures do not contain it, it has seemed good to us that it be taken away. . . . For not even ought the word hypostasis (*ὑπόστασις*) to be used touching the Father, the Son, and the Holy Ghost; but we say that the Son is like unto the Father[2], &c." By this decree those Arians completely rescinded their former Confessions, in which they had declared that the Son was begotten, though not of the substance[3] yet nevertheless, of the hypostasis[4] of God the Father.

[1] ἀπλούστερον.
[2] ὅμοιον τῷ Πατρί.
[3] ἐξ οὐσίας.
[4] ἐξ ὑποστάσεως.

Secondly, after premising this very lengthy, yet not use-
[321] less, general dissertation, touching the ancient use in the Church of the terms *οὐσία* and *ὑπόστασις*, I now, at last, return to Origen. It is certain, that the word *ὑπόστασις* is throughout employed by Origen to signify either subsistence, or a single and individual thing subsisting *per se*, which in beings endued with understanding is the same as what we now call person. Nay I do not remember, that I have anywhere found the word taken by him in any other sense, when he is speaking of the Trinity; whence a great man, Hugo Grotius, (in his Notes on John i. 2, and on the Epistle to the Hebrews i. 3,) affirms, that Origen was the first to transfer the term in this sense from the Platonists to the use of the Church—which however I do not believe to be true. As regards the passage, which is noted by Huet, nothing is more evident than that Origen there affirms that the Father and

[k] τὸ δὲ ὄνομα τῆς οὐσίας, ὅπερ ἁπλούστερον ὑπὸ τῶν πατέρων ἐτέθη, ἀγνοούμενον δὲ τοῖς λαοῖς, σκάνδαλον ἔφερε, διότι μηδὲ αἱ γραφαὶ τοῦτο περιέχουσιν, ἤρεσε περιαιρεθῆναι. . . . καὶ γὰρ οὐδὲ ὀφείλει ὑπόστασις περὶ πατρὸς, καὶ υἱοῦ, καὶ ἁγίου πνεύματος ὀνομάζεσθαι. ὅμοιον δὲ λέγομεν τῷ πατρὶ τὸν υἱόν.—Athanasius de Synod. Arim. et Seleuc., tom. i. p. 906. [§ 30. vol. i. p. 747.]

the Son are two in hypostasis[1], in the same sense in which the heretics, whom he is glancing at in that place, denied it? And who were they? beyond all doubt the Noetians and others, who taught that God was unipersonal[2], and acknowledged only one hypostasis, i. e. one person, in the Godhead. And as to that further objection of Huet, that Origen, when
he said that the Father and the Son are one in unanimity 117
and agreement, apparently rejected all other unity, it is certainly of little weight. For he who in a given passage mentions only a unity of agreement between the Father and the Son, is not straightway to be regarded as having been entirely ignorant of any other unity. Then again, Origen in a thousand other passages has acknowledged the Father and the Son to be of one substance[3], if you look to the thing which is signified by the expression; full often, too, has he in express terms confessed the consubstantiality[4], according to the quotations of Pamphilus the martyr and the testimony of Ruffinus. The same I shall clearly shew in the proper place concerning Novatian, or whoever is the author of the treatise on the Trinity, amongst the works of Tertullian, whom Huet notes on account of a similar expression.
Moreover, Origen, in his first tome on John, says of the [322]
Valentinians and other heretics of the same kind[5][l]: "They use that passage, 'My heart hath poured forth a good Word,' [Ps. xlv. 1.] supposing, that the Son of God is an emanation of the Father, as it were in syllables; and accordingly, if we strictly enquire of them, they do not allow an hypostasis to Him, neither do they clearly[6] declare His substance." Here Huet allows, that *ὑπόστασις* is indeed distinguished from *οὐσία*; he says however that it does not mean *person* but *subsistence*. But I ask, what difference is made by the ancients, when they are speaking of the Trinity, between person and subsistence? As Petavius[m] has rightly observed, they certainly took "*subsistence* for a concrete noun, as it is called, and confounded it with *person*." Supposing then, next, that in that passage of Origen, to which Huet objects, the word *ὑπόστασις* be, accordingly, taken for subsistence, so that the Father and the Son

1 τῇ ὑποστάσει.
2 μονοπρόσωπον.
3 ὁμοούσιους.
4 τὸ ὁμοούσιον.
5 ejusdem farinæ.
6 σαφηνίζουσιν.

l χρῶνται τῷ, Ἐξηρεύξατο ἡ καρδία μου λόγον ἀγαθὸν, οἰόμενοι προφορὰν πατρικὴν, οἱονεὶ ἐν συλλαβαῖς κειμένην εἶναι τὸν υἱὸν τοῦ Θεοῦ, καὶ κατὰ τοῦτο ὑπόστασιν αὐτῷ, εἰ ἀκριβῶς αὐτῶν πυνθανοίμεθα, οὐ διδόασιν, οὐδὲ οὐσίαν αὐτοῦ σαφηνίζουσιν.—[23. vol. iv. p. 25.]

m Petav. de Trin. iv. 3. 6.

ON THE CONSUBSTANTIALITY OF THE SON.

be declared to be two in subsistence; can any catholic find fault with this? nay, is not he a heretic rather who denies it? But Huet assaults him more keenly: "Why do we attempt," says he, "to set up a defence for Origen, when he himself betrays his own cause, in his second tome on John, where, impugning a certain person[n] as 'teaching, that there subsists not any peculiar substance[1] of the Holy Ghost other[2] than the Father and the Son,' he shortly after adds, 'we however, who are persuaded, that there are three hypo-
[323] stases, the Father, the Son, and the Holy Ghost,' &c. By these words he shews, that he dissents from one who asserts that there is only one substance[3] in the Trinity, and that he admits [that there are] three hypostases, that is three substances. For if the word *ὑποστάσεις* here signified *ἰδιότητες*, i. e. persons, he would fail altogether to express his dissent from him who thought that the Trinity was of one substance[4]." But, I maintain, nothing else can be collected from this passage, than that the adversary against whom Origen is there arguing, understood by the word *οὐσία* hypostasis or person, which we have already proved that many others, even catholics, did. For it is plain that the opponent, against whom Origen is there arguing, was, in reality, of the school of Noetus, who maintained that the Holy Ghost differs in no respect at all from the Father and the Son, but "is the same thing[5] as the Father," as Origen himself states in the same passage. In reply to him, Origen in this place shews, that in Matt. xii. 32, there is, without any controversy, a distinction set forth between the Holy Ghost and the Son; whence he concludes, that the Holy Ghost, as also the Son, differs in person[6] from the Father; and then adds, that both he himself and other catholics believe that the Father, the Son, and the Holy Ghost are three *ὑπόστασεις*, three subsistences[7]. Indeed the word *ὑπόστασις* almost uniformly[8] in Origen signifies either subsistence in the abstract, or a single and individual thing subsisting by itself, which, as I have repeatedly said, is equivalent, in the case of those beings which are endowed with life and

1 οὐσίαν.
2 ἑτέραν παρὰ.
3 οὐσίαν.
4 οὐσίας.
5 τὸ αὐτὸ εἶναι τῷ Πατρί.
6 personâ differre.
7 τρεῖς ὑποστάσεις.
8 fere constanter.

n . . . δογματίζων, μηδὲ οὐσίαν τινὰ ἰδίαν ὑφεστάναι τοῦ ἁγίου πνεύματος, ἑτέραν παρὰ τὸν πατέρα καὶ τὸν υἱὸν, . . . ἡμεῖς μέντοιγε τρεῖς ὑποστάσεις πειθόμενοι τυγχάνειν, τὸν πατέρα, καὶ τὸν υἱὸν, καὶ τὸ ἅγιον πνεῦμα, κ.λ.—[6. p. 61.]

BOOK II. CHAP. IX. § 11.

ORIGEN.

understanding, to person. But why do we detain the reader
with these disputes[1]? There is a passage extant in the Greek
Commentaries of Origen, edited by Huet himself, which most
clearly establishes our interpretation of Origen's meaning. In
the twelfth tome on John, p. 186 of Huet's edition, Origen
mentions certain persons (some of the Noetians that is),
who, from certain passages of Scripture, wrongly understood, [324]
thought that it was shewn, that[o] "the Son did not differ
numerically[2] from the Father, but that being Both one, not
only in substance but also in subject[3], they were called
Father and Son, in respect of certain different ways of viewing them[4], but not in respect of hypostasis[5]." To whom he
makes this reply[p]: "We must say to them, first of all, that
the Son is other than the Father, and that it is necessary
that the Son be the Son of a Father, and the Father be
the Father of a Son." Here substance and hypostasis[6]
are clearly distinguished, exactly in the same way as they
are by us at this day; and the view of Origen and other
catholics is accurately distinguished from that of the Noe- 118
tians. The catholics taught that the Father and the Son are
indeed one in substance, that is, that they are *ὁμοούσιοι*, (of
one substance or consubstantial,) but two in hypostasis and
in subject; whilst the heretics contended, on the other hand,
that the Father and the Son are one, not only in substance
but also in hypostasis, and that they are merely distinguished
according to our different notions or conceptions, and called
at one time in one respect, Father; and at another time and
in another respect, Son. Nothing surely is more manifest
than this. I have treated of the ancient ecclesiastical signification of the word *ὑπόστασις*, when used of the Godhead[7], at greater length perhaps than was called for by the objection that was put forward; yet the intelligent reader will not, I trust, take it amiss, when he considers how entirely[8], not only the mass of theologians, but also men of the greatest learning are in error on this point[q].

[1] hisce ambagibus.

[2] *τῷ ἀριθμῷ διαφέρειν*, i. e., personally.

[3] *ὑποκειμένῳ.*

[4] *ἐπινοίας.*

[5] *κατα ὑπόστασιν.*

[6] *οὐσία* et *ὑπόστασις.*

[7] in divinis.

[8] totâ viâ.

[o] . . . *μὴ διαφέρειν τῷ ἀριθμῷ τὸν υἱὸν τοῦ πατρὸς, ἀλλ' ἓν, οὐ μόνον οὐσίᾳ, ἀλλὰ καὶ ὑποκειμένῳ τυγχάνοντας ἀμφοτέρους, κατά τινας ἐπινοίας διαφόρους, οὐ κατὰ ὑπόστασιν, λέγεσθαι πατέρα καὶ υἱόν.*—[tom. x. 21. p. 199.]

[p] *λεκτέον πρὸς αὐτοὺς πρῶτον μὲν, . . . ἕτερον εἶναι τὸν υἱὸν παρὰ τὸν πατέρα, καὶ ὅτι ἀνάγκη τὸν υἱὸν πατρὸς εἶναι υἱὸν, καὶ τὸν πατέρα υἱοῦ πατέρα.*—[Ibid.]

[q] [See also the notes on the Orige-

ON THE CONSUBSTANTIALITY OF THE SON.

[325]

12. There follows another objection of Huet, taken from these words of Origen, against Celsus[r], book viii.: "But suppose it to be the case, that, as may be expected in a numerous body of persons who believe and admit of difference of opinion, that some from their precipitancy put forth the view that our Saviour is the God[s] who is over all[1]; still we do not say any such thing, who believe Him when He says, 'The Father, who hath sent Me, is greater than I.'" Upon which Huet[t] makes these observations: "There were some who affirmed that Christ is God over all[2], and that in a true and orthodox sense. Now this statement certainly relates to the divine, not to the human nature of Christ. Origen, on the contrary, denies that our Saviour is God over all, which he proves from this, that He is less than the Father, who is God over all. He takes away, therefore, from the divine nature of Christ, that supreme Godhead over all things, and assigns it to the Father; and in consequence he makes the Son inferior to the Father in a certain kind of greatness[3], and that as God to God, not as man to God." But, in the first place, the very learned commentator is (if he will permit me to say it) in very grave error in supposing that it was in a true and orthodox sense, that they against whom Origen's strictures are here directed, affirmed, that the Son is God over all; for Origen expressly speaks of a certain few among the Christians, who differed in what they alleged from the remaining very numerous body of believers, that is to say, from the Catholic Church of Christ. Moreover, if you
[326] read what precedes and follows this passage of Origen, you will find that the objections which Celsus there brings against the Christians, are taken entirely from the inventions of the heretics. Now who were they, who, in a heterodox sense, and departing from the common consent of Christians, affirmed that our Saviour is the God over all Himself? I apprehend

[1] τὸν [μέγιστον, ed. Ben.] ἐπὶ πᾶσι Θεὸν, ille universorum Deum. Vers. Lat.

[2] universorum Deum.

[3] μεγέθει τινί.

niana of Huet, in the Benedictine edition, ad loc.—B.]

[r] ἔστω δέ, τινας ὡς ἐν πλήθει πιστευόντων, καὶ δεχομένων διαφωνίαν, διὰ τὴν προπέτειαν ὑποτίθεσθαι, τὸν σωτῆρα εἶναι τὸν [μέγιστον, ed. Ben.] ἐπὶ πᾶσι Θεόν· ἀλλ' οὔτι γε ἡμεῖς τοιοῦτον, οἱ πειθόμενοι αὐτῷ λέγοντι, Ὁ Πατὴρ, ὁ πέμψας με, μείζων μου ἐστί.—p. 387. [14. p. 752.]

[s] [In the Benedictine edition we read τὸν μέγιστον ἐπὶ πᾶσι Θεὸν, "the greatest God over all," from which it more plainly appears, what was the dogma of the heretics, whom Origen censures, and how perverse is the argument of Huet.—B.]

[t] Origenian. ii. p. 34. [Quæst. 2. 7. p. 121.]

that those heretics are intended, who in the time of Origen were known by the name of Noetians, who taught that the Son is God the Father Himself, whom the catholics of that age used to call, by way of distinction[1], ὁ ἐπὶ πᾶσι Θεὸς, 'God over all[2].' At any rate Justin, in what is called his Second Apology, notices the impious madness of certain heretics of that class, known in his day by a different name, in language not dissimilar, in the following passage[u]: "For they who assert that the Son is the Father, are convicted both of being ignorant of the Father, and of not knowing that the Father of all hath a Son, who being also the first-born Word of God is also God." In these words he not only distinguishes the Son from the Father of all, and denies, in opposition to the heretics, that He is God the Father Himself, but also confesses that the Son, equally with the Father, is in very deed God, as being begotten of God the Father Himself. Perhaps however, in the passage under review, Origen is assailing the Marcionites and other monstrous forms of heresy[3], who taught that our Saviour is not the Son of that God who framed the world, but is His Lord, and superior to Him, and on that ground the God over all. Certainly it is evident that he is treating of them both in what precedes and follows. Secondly, what Origen asserts in the passage cited, that the Son, even in that He is God, (that is, God of God,) is less than the Father, (which Huet censures,) is quite catholic, and maintained [327]
even by the fathers who most keenly impugned the Arian heresy after the council of Nice, as I shall afterwards shew in the fourth book[x], where I shall also most clearly prove that Origen in his books against Celsus, whilst he laid down that God the Father was in respect of causation[4] greater than the Son, still acknowledged the Father and the Son to be altogether alike and equal in respect of nature[5].

1 διακριτικῶς.
2 universorum Deus. Ver. Lat.
3 et alia id genus hominum monstra.
4 κατ' αἰτίαν.
5 κατὰ φύσιν.

13. In the third place, Huet censures a passage in the fifth book of the treatise against Celsus, where Origen writes thus[y]: "When our Lord and Saviour was once addressed

u οἱ γὰρ τὸν υἱὸν πατέρα φάσκοντες εἶναι, ἐλέγχονται μήτε τὸν πατέρα ἐπιστάμενοι, μήθ' ὅτι ἐστὶν υἱὸς τῷ πατρὶ τῶν ὅλων γινώσκοντες· ὃς καὶ λόγος πρωτότοκος ὢν τοῦ Θεοῦ, καὶ Θεὸς ὑπάρχει.—p. 96. [Apol. i. 63. p. 81.]

x See iv. 2. 6.

y ὁ σωτὴρ ἡμῶν καὶ κύριος, ἀκούσας

with, 'Good Master,' He referred the man who thus spoke, to His Father, saying, 'Why[1] callest thou Me good? There is none good but One, that is God the Father.' Now if the well-beloved Son of the Father said this with good reason, as being the image of the goodness of God, would not the sun with much greater reason say to those who worship it, Why dost thou worship me? for, thou shalt worship the Lord
119 thy God," &c. Upon these words the learned commentator observes thus[z]: "He takes away that goodness which belongs[2] to God the Father, from Christ, not merely so far as He is Man, but even so far as He is the image of the goodness of God, that is to say so far as He is God." As if Christ forsooth were not, even as Man, in a peculiar way the image of the goodness of God! But who can believe that Origen was so dull of understanding[3], as not to perceive that
[328] that text of the Evangelist relates entirely to the economy[4] of Christ, which He took on Him when He assumed human nature. Nay, Origen in the same passage expressly intimates, that he introduces Christ speaking thus as an example[5], which Christ Himself (that is) whilst conversing among men, was willing to exhibit to men. But even if we were to allow that Origen is there speaking of Christ so far as He is God, yet surely the Son is rightly called the image, the adequate and perfect image, I mean, of the Father's goodness; and yet so far as He is the image of the Father, He is not the Father Himself,—that is to say, so far as He has His goodness, as also the other attributes of the divine nature, and even the divine nature itself, by derivation from the Father, as from a fountain[6], and so possesses Godhead *in secundo signo originis* (in the second degree of origin, as the schoolmen say), the first place[7] might in that way of viewing it be attributed, not incorrectly, to the Father. It is, however, very certain, (if Origen's meaning and opinions are to be judged of out of his treatise against Celsus,) that what Huet gathers from these words is altogether alien from the meaning of Origen him-

[1] [Matt. xix.16,17.]

[2] convenit.

[3] stupidi ingenii.

[4] οἰκονομίαν.

[5] παράδειγμα.

[6] ex paterno fonte.

[7] primas.

ποτὲ, Διδάσκαλε ἀγαθὲ, ἀναπέμπων τὸν λέγοντα τοῦτο ἐπὶ τὸν ἑαυτοῦ Πατέρα, φησὶ, Τί με λέγεις ἀγαθόν; οὐδεὶς ἀγαθὸς εἰ μὴ εἷς, ὁ Θεὸς ὁ Πατήρ. εἴπερ δὲ τοῦτ' εὐλόγως, ὡς εἰκὼν τῆς ἀγαθότητος τοῦ Θεοῦ τυγχάνων, εἴρηκεν ὁ υἱὸς τῆς ἀγάπης τοῦ Πατρὸς, πῶς οὐχὶ εὐλογώτερον ἂν τοῖς προσκυνοῦσιν εἶπεν ἥλιος, Τί με προσκυνεῖς; κύριον γὰρ τὸν Θεόν σου προσκυνήσεις; κ.λ.—p. 238. [ii. p. 585-86.]

[z] Origenian. ii. p. 39. [Quæst. 2. 15. p. 126.]

self, that Origen, I mean, altogether took away from Christ that goodness which belongs to God the Father, and supposed, (as Huet himself presently says in the same place,) that the Son is but "a minute portion and a kind of an imperfect breath[a]" of the Father's goodness. For seeing that in the passages which we have quoted above Origen clearly teaches that the Son, equally with the Father, is very God, uncreate, immortal, unchangeable, impassible, immeasurable, omnipresent, and every way happy and perfect; how was it possible that he should in the very same work take away from the Son, in that He is God, the goodness which belongs to the Father? But we have also already heard Adamantius[1] (book iii.[b] against Celsus) say, that the Son of God is "the very" (or most absolute) "Word, and the very Wisdom, and the very Truth." Why then should not the Son be called very or most absolute Goodness, not a minute portion and kind of imperfect breath of some higher goodness[2]? seeing that the same holds good[3] of all the divine attributes. Thus, in book v.[c] against Celsus, from which this charge is taken, Origen a second time calls the Son, "the very Word, and the very Wisdom, and the very Righteousness." And if any one wishes for a lucid commentary on these passages of Origen, let him turn to the great Athanasius, in his Oration against the Gentiles[d], where he thus writes respecting the Son of God: "He is the Power and Wisdom and Word of the Father; and these He is, not in the way of participation, nor do these accrue to Him from without[4], as in the case of those who partake of Him, and are made wise through Him, and in Him are endued with power and reason; on the contrary, He is very Wisdom, very Word, and the very own Power of the Father, very Light, very Truth, very Righteousness, very Virtue, and also the Impress[5], and the Radiance, and the Image, and

[329]

1 i. e. Origen.

2 bonitatis alicujus superioris.

3 ratio par est.

4 ἔξωθεν.

5 χαρακτὴρ. [Heb. i. 3.]

a [particulam et auram quandam imperfectam.—cf. Hor. Sat. ii. 2. 75, divinæ particulam auræ.]

b [41. p. 473-4; see above, p. 224.]

c τὸν αὐτολόγον, καὶ τὴν αὐτοσοφίαν, καὶ τὴν αὐτοδικαιοσύνην.—p. 258. [39. p. 608.]

d δύναμίς ἐστι τοῦ πατρὸς, καὶ σοφία, καὶ λόγος, οὐ κατὰ μετοχὴν ταῦτα ὢν, οὐδὲ ἔξωθεν ἐπιγινομένων τούτων αὐτῷ κατὰ τοὺς αὐτοῦ μετέχοντας, καὶ σοφιζομένους δι' αὐτοῦ, καὶ δυνατοὺς καὶ λογικοὺς ἐν αὐτῷ γινομένους· ἀλλ' αὐτοσοφία, αὐτολόγος, αὐτοδύναμις ἰδία τοῦ πατρός ἐστιν, αὐτοφῶς, αὐτοαλήθεια, αὐτοδικαιοσύνη, αὐτοαρετὴ, καὶ μὲν καὶ χαρακτὴρ, καὶ ἀπαύγασμα, καὶ εἰκών· καὶ συνελόντι φράσαι, καρπὸς παντέλειος τοῦ πατρὸς ὑπάρχει, καὶ μόνος ἐστὶν υἱὸς, εἰκὼν ἀπαράλλακτος τοῦ πατρός.—tom. i. p. 51. [§ 46. vol. i. p. 46.]

ON THE CONSUBSTANTIALITY OF THE SON.

(in a word) the all-perfect Fruit[1] of the Father; and He alone is Son, an undeviating[2] Image of the Father."

14. I still press on the track of the most learned Huet, who having professed that he would lay aside irrelevances[3] and search out the very innermost recesses of the doctrine of Origen, observes[e], that "Origen believed that the Son
[330] emanated[4] from the substance of God, even as light from the sun, and, therefore, that He is of the same substance as the Father, forasmuch as light is of the same substance as the sun; and on the other hand, that he separated[5] the Son from the substance and Godhead of the Father, forasmuch as light when it has gone forth from the sun by way of effluence[6], may be said to be separated and removed from the sun; moreover that the Son is inferior to the Father, forasmuch as the sun is more noble than light, and superior in dignity." Huet had before concluded, from Origen's use of the same simile[f], that "the Trinity was divided by Origen into parts, and was distinguished by certain gradations, as it were, of essence and Godhead." But this (I would say it with all respect for this most distinguished man) is not to "search out the innermost recesses of Origen's doctrine," so much as to peep into and to suspect things of which Origen himself never even dreamed. I admit that Origen, even in his books against Celsus, illustrates the generation of the Son from the Father by the similitude of a ray or brightness thrown out from the sun or other luminous body. But what of that? Did not all the catholic fathers, both those who wrote before and those who wrote after the council of Nice, employ the same simile? Did not the Nicene fathers themselves, and that in their very Creed, say that God the Son was sprung[7] of God the Father, as Light of Light? Lastly, what is to become of the inspired author of the Epistle to the
120 Hebrews, who was not afraid to call the Son of God[8] "the brightness of the Father's glory?" Certainly two at least
[331] of the inferences[9] which Huet draws from this comparison and fixes on Origen, are altogether foreign from his meaning. The first is, that the Son is severed and separated from the Father, as a portion of the divine essence from the

[1] καρπὸς. [2] ἀπαράλλακτος. [3] ambages. [4] manasse. [5] segregasse. [6] effluvium. [7] nasci. [8] Heb. i. 8. [9] porismata.

[e] Origenian. ii. p. 44. [Quæst. 2, 24. p. 132.]

[f] Ibidem. p. 37. [Quæst. 2. 12. p. 123.]

whole, and that consequently the essence of God is cut into parts. But can any one believe that such foolish[1] blasphemy could have entered the mind of Origen, who certainly was no unlearned man? And how often in his writings has Adamantius[2] expressly repudiated that blasphemy! Thus (to omit a thousand other passages) how does he, in his fourth book against Celsus[g], (in a passage which we have before in this chapter adduced entire,) deride the Epicureans and Stoics for being unable "to clear our natural conception of God, as a Being every way incorruptible, and simple, and uncompounded, and indivisible?" He immediately adds, that the Son of God subsists in the form of God, that is, in the divine essence, and is accordingly Himself also equally with the Father Himself unchangeable. Nothing, however, is more expressly opposed to this imagination [of Huet] than the words of Origen, which Pamphilus, in his Apology[h], quotes from his second book on John, to this effect; "Therefore the only-begotten God[3], our Saviour, who alone is generated[4] from the Father, is Son by nature not by adoption. He is sprung[5] of the very mind of the Father, as the will [is] of[6] the mind. For the divine nature, that is to say [the nature] of the unbegotten Father, is not divisible, that we should suppose the Son was begotten either by division or diminution of His substance." See § 19 of this chapter, near the end. As to the other inference of Huet, that Origen made the Son inferior to the Father, we shall hereafter shew most plainly in its proper place, that Origen never made the Son unequal to the Father in essence, but only in respect of origin, so far, that is, as the Father is [332] the author and principle[7] of the Son. In short, Origen and other catholic fathers, when they employed the simile of the sun and the ray, of light and radiance, intended only to intimate these points, nor did any thing else enter into their mind; 1. That the Father is the fountain of Godhead[8], as the sun is the fountain of the radiance which is sent forth

BOOK II. CHAP. IX. § 13, 14.

ORIGEN.

1 insulsam.

2 i. e. Origen.

3 unigenitus ergo Deus.

4 solus a P. generatus.

5 natus.

6 ex.

7 principium.

8 πηγὴν θεότητος.

g p. 169. [14. p. 510. see above p. 226.]

h Unigenitus ergo Deus Salvator noster, solus a Patre generatus, natura et non adoptione Filius est. Natus est autem ex ipsa Patris mente, sicut voluntas ex mente. Non enim divisibilis est divina natura, id est, ingeniti Patris, ut putemus vel divisione, vel imminutione substantiæ ejus Filium esse progenitum.—[cap. 5. p. 34.]

ON THE CONSUBSTANTIALITY OF THE SON.

from it. 2. That the Son is of the same nature and substance as the Father; seeing that He is begotten of the very essence of the Father, as light proceeds from light. 3. That the Son no way exists divided or separated from His Father; just as the ray is not disjoined from the sun, nor radiance from light. 4. Lastly, that the Son is sprung[1] from the Father without alteration or diminution of the divine essence. And certainly that illustration wonderfully assists these conceptions of our mind, concerning the adorable generation of the Son of God; on which account it was also employed by the Nicene fathers in their very Confession of Faith.

[1] nasci.

15. There remains the fifth and last accusation which Huet[1] brings against Origen, out of his books against Celsus; to the effect, that he taught that "the Father ought to be adored with more humble supplication than the Son." That this was the genuine opinion of Origen he gathers principally from two passages out of these books. One is found in the fifth book[j], where Origen speaks thus: "All supplication and prayer, and intercession and thanksgiving ought to be offered up unto the God who is over all, through Him who is above all angels, the High-Priest, the living Word and God. Moreover the Word Himself also we will supplicate, and unto Him intercede and give thanks, and pray also, provided we are able to understand in the case of prayer, the strict meaning
[333] of the word, and its metaphorical application." Upon which Huet observes, "He enjoins that prayer, in the proper acceptation of the word[2], be offered up to God the Father, but to the Son in an improper and metaphorical sense[3]; to the former, as unto the supreme God, the giver of all good things; to the latter, as unto a Mediator, to present our prayers unto God." You may read the other passage in the eighth book[k]; "Therefore do we worship the one God, and His one Son, and Word, and Image, by supplications and entreaties to the utmost of our power, offering unto the God of

[2] proprie.
[3] impropriam et καταχρηστικήν.

[1] Origenian. ii. p. 48. [Quæst. 2, 29. p. 136.]

[j] πᾶσαν μὲν γὰρ δέησιν καὶ προσευχὴν, καὶ ἔντευξιν, καὶ εὐχαριστίαν ἀναπεμπτέον τῷ ἐπὶ πᾶσι Θεῷ διὰ τοῦ ἐπὶ πάντων ἀγγέλων ἀρχιερέως, ἐμψύχου λόγου καὶ Θεοῦ. δεησόμεθα δὲ καὶ αὐτοῦ τοῦ λόγου, καὶ ἐντευξόμεθα αὐτῷ, καὶ εὐχαριστήσομεν, καὶ προσευξόμεθα δὲ, ἐὰν δυνώμεθα κατακούειν τῆς περὶ προσευχῆς κυριολεξίας, καὶ καταχρήσεως.—p. 233. [4. p. 580.]

[k] διὸ τὸν ἕνα Θεὸν, καὶ τὸν ἕνα υἱὸν αὐτοῦ, καὶ λόγον, καὶ εἰκόνα, ταῖς κατὰ τὸ δυνατὸν ἡμῖν ἱκεσίαις καὶ ἀξιώσεσι σέβομεν, προσάγοντες τῷ Θεῷ τῶν ὅλων

all, our prayers, through His Only-begotten, to whom we first offer them, beseeching Him, who is the propitiation for our sins, that He would, as a High-Priest, present our prayers and our sacrifices and our intercessions unto the God over all[1]." I wonder that these passages of Origen should cause the slightest difficulty to that learned man, in which (to confess the truth) I have myself[2] always thought that the catholic doctrine touching the person and the office of our Saviour was not ill set forth. But to the subject. Christ our Lord may be regarded in a two-fold point
of view, as He is God, and as He is God-Man[3], or Mediator [334]
between God and man. If you look at our Saviour under the latter character[4], it is certain from many places of Scripture and the consent of all Christians, that all the worship which we offer to God must be presented unto Him through
Christ the Mediator, and moreover that all the worship and 121
honour, which we offer to Christ, altogether redounds (as Paul expresses it, Phil. ii. 11) "unto the glory of God the Father." But that Christ is the Mediator between God and men in respect of both natures, (whatsoever some of the papists[k] object to the contrary,) the ancient catholic fathers, with the Holy Scriptures, have unanimously[5] taught. And it is manifest that Origen, in each of the passages which have been quoted, had this character[6] of our Jesus especially in view; for in both of them he speaks of Christ as thé High-Priest who intercedes for us with God the Father, and who offered Himself as a propitiation for our sins. If, however, we regard Christ as God, without respect to His mediatorial office, we may again consider Him under a two-fold aspect. For He is regarded either absolutely as God, or relatively as God of God, in other words as the Son of God. If we consider the Word under the former view, Origen in many places explicitly confesses, that by reason of the ineffably transcendent Godhead which He possesses in common with the Father, the very same divine worship which we offer unto the Father is altogether due to Him: that is to say, that

[1] τῷ ἐπὶ πᾶσι Θεῷ.

[2] egomet.

[3] Θεάνθρωπος.

[4] σχέσει.

[5] uno ore.

[6] σχέσιν.

τὰς εὐχὰς διὰ τοῦ μονογενοῦς αὐτοῦ· ᾧ πρῶτον προσφέρομεν αὐτὰς, ἀξιοῦντες αὐτὸν, ἱλασμὸν ὄντα περὶ τῶν ἁμαρτιῶν ἡμῶν, προσαγαγεῖν ὡς ἀρχιερέα τὰς εὐχὰς, καὶ τὰς θυσίας, καὶ τὰς ἐντεύξεις ἡμῶν τῷ ἐπὶ πᾶσι Θεῷ.—p. 386. [13. p. 751.]

[k] [E. g. S. Thom. Aquin. Summa Theol., par. iii. q. 26. art. 2.]

in our mind and thoughts[1], by which alone we (properly speaking) worship[2] God, we ought to ascribe unto the Son all those same perfections of the divine nature, which we attribute to the Father. Read over again the passages which we have already quoted in this chapter, § 8. But if, on the other hand, we regard the Son relatively, as He is the Son, and derives His origin from God the Father, then again it is cer-
[335] tain, that all the worship and veneration which we offer to Him, redounds to the Father, and is ultimately referred to Him, as the fountain of Godhead[k]. Origen seems to have had this also in view in the latter passage cited by Huet, in which, after the words which have been already quoted, the following are immediately subjoined[l]; "In[3] God therefore is our faith, through His Son, who confirms it in us: and Celsus cannot charge us with any insubordination[4] in regard of the Son of God; yea and we do indeed venerate the Father whilst we admire[5] His Son, [who is His] Word, and Wisdom, and Truth, and Righteousness, and whatsoever we have learned the Son of God to be; thus also [we venerate the Father, in admiring] Him who is begotten of such a Father." That this doctrine is sound and catholic is known to all who have even a moderate acquaintance with the writings of the ancient doctors. What is to be said to the fact, that this pre-eminence[6] of the Father is even at this day recognised in all the Liturgies of the Catholic Church? For both in doxologies we give glory to God the Father in "the first rank," (ἐν πρώτῃ τάξει,) as Justin expresses it, and unto Him do we direct most of[7] our prayers. On this point the remarks of Petavius (on the Trinity, iii. 7, 15) are indeed worthy to be observed, when, in replying to Crellius respecting the Holy Ghost, he says, "In vain doth Crellius frame a false charge on the fact, that in the Church public prayers are usually not addressed to the Holy Ghost; since, in accordance with ancient usage, they are for the most part[8] referred to the Father. And thus we find it decreed in the twenty-third

[1] conceptione.
[2] colimus.
[3] περὶ.
[4] στάσιν.
[5] θαυμάζοντες.
[6] ἐξοχὴ.
[7] plerasque.
[8] pleræque.

[k] See our observations on the doxologies of the primitive Church, above, c. 3. § 6. [p. 112.]

[l] περὶ τὸν Θεὸν οὖν ἡ πίστις ἡμῶν, διὰ τοῦ ταύτην βεβαιοῦντος ἐν ἡμῖν υἱοῦ αὐτοῦ. καὶ οὐδεμίαν ἡμῶν ἔχει δεῖξαι στάσιν περὶ τὸν υἱὸν τοῦ Θεοῦ ὁ Κέλσος· καὶ σέβομέν γε τὸν Πατέρα, θαυμάζοντες αὐτοῦ τὸν υἱὸν, λόγον, καὶ σοφίαν, καὶ ἀλήθειαν, καὶ δικαιοσύνην, καὶ πάντα ἅπερ εἶναι μεμαθήκαμεν τὸν υἱὸν τοῦ Θεοῦ· οὕτω δὴ καὶ τὸν γεννηθέντα ἀπὸ τοιούτου Πατρός.—[Orig. ubi supr. 13. p. 751. On the word στάσιν, comp. § 11. p. 750.]

canon of the third council of Carthage[1]; 'when standing at the altar, let prayer be always directed to the Father.' Doubtless, because as at that time the Body of Christ, or the Man Christ is offered up, and the memorial of His ancient [336] and bloody sacrifice is celebrated, it is right that all should be referred unto the Father, as Author and Principle[2]; in order that we may imitate our great High-Priest, the Lord Christ, who both was wont to refer all His words and actions to the honour of the Father, and especially in that last sacrifice 'gave Himself for us, an offering and a sacrifice[3] unto God for a sweet-smelling savour.' Nor does it follow from this, either that Christ is not God, or that the Holy Ghost [is not God]; this only follows, that there is a supreme Principle of Both[4], from whom as They are distinct in what is peculiar[5] to each Person, so are They not different in nature and substance."

1 [A.D. 397.]
2 principium.
3 hostiam.
Eph. v. 2.
4 summum utriusque principium.
5 proprietatibus.

16. Hitherto we have been defending those passages which the very learned writers Petavius and Huet have censured in the books of Origen against Celsus. But, besides these, Jerome in old time,—giving way too much to his hatred of Origen, or rather of the translator of Origen, Ruffinus, and thence being fond of wresting every word and saying of his to the very worst sense,—noted many other expressions also concerning the Son of God in other works of Origen, as being absurd and impious, which are all easily refuted out of the single treatise against Celsus; we will touch on the most important of them. In his fifty-ninth letter, to Avitus[m], in enumerating the errors of the treatise περὶ ἀρχῶν, Jerome declares that Origen, in the first volume of that work, wrote to this effect; that "God the Father, being invisible by nature, is not seen even by the Son;" and, in the second[n] volume, thus; "It remains that God be invisible; but if He is by nature invisible, He will not be visible even to the Saviour." Likewise, in his sixty-first letter, to Pammachus, chap. 3, he brings forward and condemns the [337] following words of Origen out of his work περὶ ἀρχῶν[o]; "For as it is incongruous to say, that the Son can see the

[m] Deum Patrem, per naturam invisibilem, etiam a Filio non videri.—[Ep. CXXIV. 2. vol. i. p. 911.]

[n] Restat ut invisibilis sit Deus. Si autem invisibilis per naturam est, neque Salvatori visibilis erit.—[§ 6. p. 916.]

[o] Sicut enim incongruum est dicere,

ON THE CONSUBSTANTIALITY OF THE SON.

Father, so is it unsuitable to suppose that the Holy Ghost can see the Son." And Epiphanius (Hæres. lxiv. c. 4, and *in Ancorat.* c. 63) lays down this as the foremost and chief among the errors of Origen. But let us hear Origen him-
122 self, out of his undoubted work against Celsus, clearly unfolding his own view respecting the knowledge, by which the Father and the Son mutually know each other, in these words[q]; "But our Saviour and Lord also, the Word of God, putting before us the greatness of the knowledge of the Father,—how that worthily, in a pre-eminent sense[1], He is comprehended and known by Himself alone [i. e. by the Son alone], and in a secondary sense by those who have their reason enlightened by Him who is Himself the Word and God,—says, 'No man knoweth the Son save the Father, neither knoweth any man the Father save the Son, and he to whomsoever the Son shall reveal Him.' For no one can worthily know Him who is uncreate[2] and the first-born[3] of all created[4] nature, as the Father who begat Him, neither can any one [know] the Father, as the living Word, who is also His Wisdom and Truth." Nothing was ever stated
[338] in stricter accordance with catholic doctrine. Moreover we have before[r] heard Origen say, that "the Father is comprehensible (ἐφικτὸν) by His Word," or Son. With respect, indeed, to the passages which have been adduced from his books περὶ ἀρχῶν, I might have replied, that of all the writings of Origen, these have been the most corrupted and interpolated, and that this has been shewn by many arguments by Ruffinus[s]. But in this case we have no need of such a reply, since the very words of Origen, as they are brought forward entire by Ruffinus[t], who explains both the drift of

[1] προηγουμένως.

[2] ἀγένητον.

[3] πρωτότοκον.

[4] γενητῆς.

quod possit Filius videre Patrem, ita inconveniens est opinari, quod Spiritus S. possit videre Filium.—[Vol. ii. p. 413, for this work is not placed among the Epistles in the Benedictine edition.—B.]

[q] ἀλλὰ καὶ ὁ σωτὴρ ἡμῶν καὶ Κύριος, λόγος τοῦ Θεοῦ, τὸ μέγεθος παριστὰς τῆς γνώσεως τοῦ Πατρὸς, ὅτι κατ' ἀξίαν προηγουμένως αὐτῷ μόνῳ λαμβάνεται καὶ γιγνώσκεται, δευτέρως δὲ τοῖς ἐλλαμπομένοις τὸ ἡγεμονικὸν ὑπ' αὐτοῦ τοῦ λόγου καὶ Θεοῦ, φησὶν, Οὐδεὶς ἐπιγινώσκει [ἔγνω ed. Ben.] τὸν υἱὸν εἰ μὴ ὁ Πατὴρ, οὐδὲ τὸν Πατέρα εἰ μὴ ὁ υἱὸς, καὶ ᾧ ἂν ὁ υἱὸς ἀποκαλύψῃ. οὔτε γὰρ τὸν ἀγένητον καὶ πάσης γενητῆς φύσεως πρωτότοκον κατ' ἀξίαν εἰδέναι τις δύναται, ὡς ὁ γεννήσας αὐτὸν Πατὴρ, οὔτε τὸν Πατέρα ὡς ὁ ἔμψυχος λόγος, καὶ σοφία αὐτοῦ καὶ ἀλήθεια.—Lib. vi. p. 286. [17. p. 643.]

[r] See § 9 of this chapter, [p. 232.]

[s] See Ruffinus' Prolegomena to the treatise περὶ ἀρχῶν.

[t] See Ruffinus' Invectivæ, amongst the works of Jerome, tom. ix. p. 139. [vol. ii. p. 598.]

the author and the context of his discourse, are abundantly sufficient for their own vindication. The case stood thus; Origen, in his first book περὶ ἀρχῶν, had mooted a question in opposition to those who say that God is corporeal and represent Him with human limbs and form[1]; which the heresy of the Valentinians and Anthropomorphites particularly asserted. Origen, in maintaining the faith of the Church against these heretics, had proved from reason[2] that God is without a body of any sort[3], and consequently is also invisible[4]. Then, the order of the question challenging him to it, he subjoins these words[u]; "These assertions however may be thought to possess less authority by those who in matters pertaining to God[5] wish to be instructed out of the Holy Scriptures, and desire also to have it proved to them from those [Scriptures], how the nature of God surpasses[6] the nature of bodies. Consider then whether the Apostle also does not assert this same thing, when he speaks of Christ, saying, 'Who is the image of the invisible God, the first-born of every creature.' For the nature of God is not, as some suppose, visible to some[7], and invisible to others; for the Apostle did not say 'the image of God [who is] in- [339]
visible to men,' or 'invisible to sinners,' but pronounces most decidedly[8] of the nature of God itself[9], saying, 'the image of the invisible God.' And John also in his Gospel, in saying, 'No one hath seen God at any time,' manifestly declares to all who are capable of understanding, that there is no nature to which God is visible; not as though He were such as to be by nature indeed visible, and to escape and surpass the power of sight of created beings as being too frail, but because it is naturally impossible that He be seen. But if you ask me, what I think concerning the Only-begotten

1 habitu.
2 rationibus.
3 omni genere incorporeum.
4 invisibilem.
5 de rebus divinis.
6 supereminet.
7 alicui.
8 valde constanter.
9 de ipsa natura Dei.

u Verum istæ assertiones minus fortassis auctoritatis habere videantur apud eos, qui ex S. Scripturis de rebus divinis institui volunt, et etiam sibi inde approbari quærunt, quomodo natura Dei supereminet corporum naturam. Vide ergo si non etiam apostolus hoc idem ait, cum de Christo loquitur, dicens, *Qui est imago invisibilis Dei, primogenitus omnis creaturæ.* Non enim, ut quidam putant, natura Dei alicui visibilis est, et aliis invisibilis; non enim dixit apostolus, *imago invisibilis Dei hominibus,* aut *invisibilis peccatoribus,* sed valde constanter pronunciat de ipsa natura Dei dicens, *imago invisibilis Dei.* Sed et Joannes in evangelio dicens, *Deum nemo vidit unquam,* manifeste declarat omnibus, qui intelligere possunt, quia nulla natura est, cui visibilis sit Deus; non quasi qui visibilis quidem sit per naturam, et velut fragilioris creaturæ evadat atque excedat aspectum; sed quoniam naturaliter videri impossibile est. Quod si requiras a me, quid etiam de ipso Uni-

ON THE CONSUBSTANTIALITY OF THE SON.

Himself also, let it not be at once judged by you either impious or absurd, if I say, that the nature of God, which is naturally invisible, is not visible even to Him; for I will add a reason in due course[1]. It is one thing to see, another to know[2]; to be seen and to see are properties of bodies, to be known and to know of intellectual nature. Whatsoever, therefore, is a property of bodies, this is not to be believed either of the Father or of the Son. But that which pertains to the nature of the Deity, this, it is certain, holds between the Father and the Son. Lastly, even He Himself in the Gospel said not, 'No one hath seen the Father, save the Son; nor the Son, save the Father;' but He said, 'No one knoweth the Son save the Father, neither knoweth any one the Father, save the Son.' From this it is manifestly intimated, that whatsoever [in what takes place] between[3] corporeal natures is expressed by the terms to be seen or to see, this [in what takes place] between[4] the Father and the Son is expressed by the terms to be known or to know[5], through the power of knowledge[6], not through the weakness of any visible nature. Since therefore, in speaking of an incorporeal and invisible nature, it cannot in strictness be said, that it either sees or is seen, in consequence neither is the Father in the Gospel said to be seen by the Son, nor the Son by the Father, but to be known." Who does not at once admit with Ruffinus, that Origen in these words says nothing about
[340] a comparison between the Father and the Son, but is enquiring about the very nature of Deity[7], whether the term visible[8] seem in any way suitable to it? For Origen does not deny, rather he teaches plainly enough, that the Father is perceived[9] by the Son, equally as the Son by the Father,

[1] consequenter.
[2] cognoscere.
[3] inter.
[4] inter.
[5] cognosci et cognoscere.
[6] scientia.
[7] de ipsa Deitatis natura.
[8] visibilitatis vocabulum.
[9] percipi.

genito sentiam, si ne ipsi quidem visibilem dicam naturam Dei, quæ naturaliter invisibilis est, ne tibi statim vel impium videatur esse, vel absurdum; rationem quippe dabimus consequenter. Aliud est videre, aliud cognoscere; videri et videre corporum res est; cognosci et cognoscere intellectualis naturæ est. Quicquid ergo proprium corporum est, hoc nec de Patre est nec de Filio sentiendum. Quod vero ad naturam pertinet Deitatis, hoc inter Patrem et Filium constat. Denique etiam ipse in evangelio non dixit, quia *nemo vidit Patrem nisi Filius, neque Filium nisi Pater;* sed ait, *Nemo novit Filium nisi Pater, neque Patrem quis novit nisi Filius.* Ex quo manifeste indicatur, quod quicquid inter naturas corporeas videri et videre dicitur, hoc inter Patrem et Filium cognoscere dicitur et cognosci, per virtutem scientiæ, non per visibilitatis fragilitatem. Quia igitur de incorporea natura et invisibili nec videre proprie dicitur nec videri; idcirco neque Pater a Filio, neque Filius a Patre videri in evangelio dicitur, sed cognosci.—[1. 8. vol. i. p. 52.]

that is, most perfectly; all he says is, that One is perceived by the Other, "not through the weakness of any visible nature, but through the power of knowledge." What does Jerome, however, say to this? Hear and judge for yourself. In his Apology against Ruffinus, book ii.[x], he speaks to this effect; "On the first book περὶ ἀρχῶν, in which Origen has with sacrilegious tongue blasphemously asserted, that the Son does not see the Father, you offer reasons also, as if in the person of the writer; and you translate the explanation[1] of Didymus, in which with useless labour he attempts to defend another's error, that Origen forsooth spoke well, but we—simple mortals and dull old-fashioned folk—cannot understand either his wisdom, or yours who have translated him." But why does he not prove, that the words of Origen do not admit[2] of that explanation of Didymus, (who certainly was a man of great name in the Church, and once the teacher of Jerome himself,) or that Ruffinus did not faithfully quote and translate them? I suppose, because he could not. It was, we know, usual for Jerome (as might be expected from his great rhetorical power) either simply to pass over in silence such arguments as pressed him, or to evade their force by jest and satire. Certainly the words of Origen, as they are alleged by Jerome himself, sufficiently indicate that the reply of Ruffinus, and of Didymus before him, is most true. For he says, that Origen wrote, that "God the Father, being invisible by nature, is not seen by the Son;" and again, "If God is by nature invisible, He is not visible even to the Saviour." From this, I say, it is no uncertain inference, that Origen for this reason asserted [341] of the Father, that He could not be seen by the Son, not because the Son, as though of weaker vision[3], were unable to see the Father, who, otherwise, of His own nature might have been seen by competent faculties; but because God is in Himself and of His very nature invisible; that is, incorporeal, and cannot become an object of sight[4]; and that

[1] σχόλιον.

[2] respuere.

[3] aspectus.

[4] neque sub aspectum cadat.

[x] In primo libro περὶ ἀρχῶν ubi Origenes lingua sacrilega blasphemavit, quod Filius Patrem non videat, tu etiam causas reddis, quasi ex per sona ejus qui scripsit; et Didymi interpretaris σχόλιον, in quo ille casso labore conatur alienum errorem defendere; quod Origenes quidem bene dixerit, sed nos simplices homines et cicures Enniani nec illius sapientiam, nec tuam, qui interpretatus es, intelligere possumus.—tom. ii. p. 511. [§ 11. vol. ii. p. 502.]

ON THE CONSUBSTANTIALITY OF THE SON.

in this sense Origen declared the Father and the Son to be alike invisible to Each Other. Frankly to confess the truth, Jerome, in thus accusing Origen, has so manifestly betrayed a temper devoid of candour, and carried away by passion, that he seems to have deprived himself of all credit, in respect of the rest of his charges. Any one will at once acknowledge this, who will not think it too much trouble to compare "The Invectives[1]" (as the treatise is called) of Ruffinus, with Jerome's "Apology against Ruffinus[2]."

[1] Invectivæ.
[2] Hieronymi adv. Ruffinum Apologia.

17. Again, in the same letter to Avitus, Jerome attributes to Origen the following impious assertion also; "that the Son when compared with the Father is not Truth; but among us He is seen [as] imaged[3] Truth[y]." Others of the ancients fasten on him a still more atrocious blasphemy, namely, that "the Son in comparison with the Father is falsehood." Who however, in his sound senses, can suppose that Origen was so mad as this? at any rate we have already shewn that Origen, both in his treatise against Celsus and elsewhere, taught in express terms, that the Son of God is "very Truth[4], (αὐτοαλήθεια)." But to this charge[5] an answer seems to gleam out from the very charge itself, as it is stated in Greek by an anonymous vindicator of Origen, in Photius, cod. 117. Here amongst the points which used to be censured in Origen, he places this last[z], "That the Image of God, in respect of Him of whom He is an image, so far forth as He is an image, is not the Truth." Now if
[342] this proposition be duly weighed, it will be found to be sound and catholic. For it is most certain, that the Son, so far forth as He is the Image of the Father, is not the Truth, that is to say, is not the Father Himself, of whom He is the Image. For this, you will observe, appears to have been said by Origen, in opposition to the Noetians, who asserted that the Person of the Father, and of the Son, was the same. In his sixth book against Celsus, however, Origen expressly

[3] imaginariam.
[4] ipsissimam veritatem.
[5] objectio.

[y] Filium [qui sit imago invisibilis Patris] comparatum Patri non esse veritatem; apud nos autem [qui Dei omnipotentis non possumus recipere veritatem] imaginariam veritatem videri, [ut majestas ac magnitudo majoris quodammodo circumscripta sentiatur in Filio.—ibid.]

[z] ὅτι ἡ εἰκὼν τοῦ Θεοῦ, ὡς πρὸς ἐκεῖνον, οὗ ἐστιν εἰκὼν, καθ' ὃ εἰκὼν, οὐκ ἔστιν ἀλήθεια.—[Phot. cod. 117. See Ruffinus' translation in the work περὶ ἀρχῶν, I. 2. 6. p. 56, which does not at all agree with the Greek as here quoted.—B.]

teaches that the Son of God is the true, living, and most perfect Image of His Father, answering to the Father Himself throughout[1], even in His greatness[2]; we shall afterwards adduce the passage entire[a].

18. Lastly, Jerome, in his letter to Avitus, attributes to Origen the following blasphemy also[b]; "that God the Father is Light incomprehensible; that Christ in comparison with the Father is a very small luminary[3]." And yet we have seen above, that Origen in more than one passage in his treatise against Celsus, expressly taught that the Father and the Son are alike incomprehensible. This charge, however, appears to be derived from those passages, in which Origen states, that, "In the Father is no darkness at all; but the Son shineth[4] in darkness[c]." Origen himself, however, has clearly explained his own meaning and drift in these passages, in the following words in his fourth volume on John, thus[d]; "But let no man suppose that, in saying this, we are acting with impiety[5] towards the Christ of God; for in the sense in which the Father alone hath immortality, seeing that our Lord, out of loving-kindness towards men, took upon Him the death [which He endured] on our behalf, in this sense is it true of the Father alone, that in Him is no [343]
darkness at all, forasmuch as Christ, out of His beneficence towards mankind, took our darknesses upon Himself."

19. Thus have we at last clearly shewn that the doctrine of Origen's books against Celsus, in the article touching the Son of God, is orthodox and catholic; and, further, to the impious sayings which Jerome and others have attributed to this distinguished teacher, we have opposed assertions plainly contrary, taken out of the same work, of which the genuineness is undoubted. Further, whosoever wishes to acquaint himself with the catholic testimonies which are found in the rest of Origen's writings, should con-

[1] per omnia.
[2] etiam magnitudine.
[3] perparvum splendorem.
[4] lucere.
[5] ἀσεβοῦντας.

[a] [(Book iv. 2. 6.) Cf. Huet's Origeniana, II. 2. 16. p. 126, and the notes on it in the Benedictine edition.—B.]

[b] Deum Patrem esse lumen incomprehensibile; Christum collatione Patris splendorem esse perparvum.—[Ibid.]

[c] In Patre nullas esse tenebras; Filium vero in tenebris lucere. [This is perhaps taken from the work περὶ ἀρχῶν, I. 2. 8. p. 56.—B.]

[d] μηδεὶς δ' ἡμᾶς ὑπολαμβανέτω ταῦτα λέγειν ἀσεβοῦντας εἰς τὸν Χριστὸν τοῦ Θεοῦ. ᾧ γὰρ λόγῳ ὁ Πατὴρ μόνος ἔχει ἀθανασίαν, τοῦ Κυρίου ἡμῶν διὰ φιλανθρωπίαν θάνατον τὸν ὑπὲρ ἡμῶν ἀνειληφότος, τούτῳ ὁ Πατὴρ ἔχει μόνος τὸ, σκοτία ἐν αὐτῷ οὐκ ἔστιν οὐδεμία, τοῦ Χριστοῦ διὰ τὴν πρὸς ἀνθρώπους εὐεργεσίαν ἐφ' αὐτὸν τὰς ἡμῶν σκοτίας ἀναδεδεγμένου.—vol. iv. in Joan. edit. Huet., p. 73. [tom. ii. 21. p. 79.]

ON THE CONSUBSTANTIALITY OF THE SON.

sult the Apology of Pamphilus the martyr in defence of Origen, which is extant amongst the works of Jerome[e]; that this was the genuine work of Pamphilus we shall by and by clearly prove, in opposition to Jerome. It may suffice for
124 us to recite in this place a few choicer passages out of that Apology. From his first book περὶ ἀρχῶν[f] Pamphilus quotes these words of Origen[g]; "There is, therefore, no nature, which does not admit of evil, except the nature of God, which is the fountain of all. And Christ is Wisdom, and wisdom, it is plain, cannot admit of folly; and He is Righteousness, but
[344] righteousness certainly will never admit of unrighteousness; He is also the Word or Reason, which, it is plain, cannot be made irrational; but He is also Light, and it is certain that light is not comprehended by darkness. In like manner also the nature of the Holy Ghost which is holy, admits not of pollution; seeing that It is naturally or essentially[1] holy. If any other nature, however, be holy, it hath this its sanctification, by receiving[2], or being inspired by, the Holy Ghost, possessing it, not of its own nature, but as an accident; and on this account being an accident it may cease to be attached to it[3]." Here, Origen expressly teaches that sinlessness[4], or the being incapable of admitting evil, belongs only to the nature of God; and, at the same time, he no less expressly declares, that neither the Son, nor the Holy Ghost, can admit of evil; certainly[5] therefore Origen thought, that both the Son and the Holy Ghost subsist in the divine nature; which I would have those persons to observe, who think that Origen reckoned the Holy Ghost at any rate amongst created beings. But afterwards also in the same passage he clearly

[1] substantialiter.

[2] assumptione.

[3] decidere potest.

[4] ἀναμάρτησιν.

[5] omnino.

[e] Tom. ix. edit. Marian. Victor. Paris. 1623. [And in the Benedictine edition of the works of Origen, vol. iv.—B.]

[f] [c. 8, 3. p. 77.]

[g] Nulla ergo natura est, quæ non recipiat malum, excepta Dei natura, quæ fons omnium est. Et Christus sapientia est; et sapientia utique stultitiam recipere non potest. Et justitia est; justitia autem nunquam profecto injustitiam capiet. Et Verbum est vel ratio, quæ utique irrationabilis effici non potest. Sed et lux est; et lucem certum est quod tenebræ non comprehendant. Similiter autem et natura Spiritus Sancti, quæ sancta est, non recipit pollutionem; naturaliter enim vel substantialiter sancta est. Si qua autem alia natura sancta est, ex assumptione hoc, vel inspiratione Spiritus Sancti habet ut sanctificetur, non ex sua natura hoc possidens, sed accidens; propter quod et decidere potest quod accidit.—p. 120. [c. 4. p. 27.] The Benedictine edition reads, 'fons bonorum omnium est et Christi. Sapientia enim est,' &c., "is the fountain of all good things and of Christ. For He is Wisdom," &c.—B. All the editions and MSS. of Pamphilus' Apology have the text as Bp. Bull gives it, except that some read Christi for Christus: the correction of the Benedictine editor is made from the Lat. Vers. of the book *de Principiis* itself.]

BOOK II. CHAP. IX. § 19. ORIGEN.

recognises the unchangeableness[1] and eternity of the whole most holy Trinity in the following words[h]; "If the Holy Ghost knows the Father through the Son's revealing Him, it follows that He has passed from a state of ignorance to one of knowledge; but this, as is plain, is alike impious and absurd, to confess the Holy Ghost, and yet to attribute ignorance to Him. For it is not the case, that having been something else before He was the Holy Ghost, He came to be the Holy Ghost by way of advancement[2], so as that any one may presume to say that at that time indeed, whilst as yet He was not the Holy Ghost, He knew not the Father, but that after He received [that] knowledge He also became the Holy Ghost. For had this been so, never certainly would the Holy Ghost Himself also be accounted to be in the unity of the Trinity, that is, of God the Father who is unchangeable, and of His Son, except because He Himself also ever was the [345] Holy Ghost." Of the Son of God, moreover, Origen writes thus, in his first book on the Epistle to the Romans[i], as quoted by Pamphilus; "Some one perhaps may make a question whether the Son is Love, chiefly for this reason, that John has referred this word to God the Father, saying, 'for God is Love.' (1 John iv. 8.) But on the other hand we will adduce also out of that same epistle of his that which he says, 'Beloved, let us love one another, for Love is of God.' (1 John iv. 7.) He therefore, who said, 'for God is Love,' does himself again teach that Love is of God; which Love I believe to be no other than His only-begotten Son, who, as He is God of God begotten, so is

[1] inconvertibilitatem.

[2] per profectum.

[h] Si revelante Filio cognoscit Patrem Spiritus Sanctus, ergo ex ignorantia ad scientiam venit; quod utique et impium pariter et stultum est, Spiritum S. confiteri, et ignorantiam ei adscribere. Non enim cum aliud aliquid esset antequam Spiritus Sanctus, per profectum venit in hoc, ut esset Spiritus Sanctus, ut quis audeat dicere, quia tunc quidem, cum nondum esset Spiritus Sanctus, ignorabat Patrem, postea vero quam recepit scientiam, etiam Spiritus Sanctus effectus est. Quod si esset, nunquam utique in unitate Trinitatis, id est, Dei Patris inconvertibilis, et Filii ejus, etiam ipse Spiritus S. haberetur, nisi quia et ipse semper erat Spiritus Sanctus.—[De Princip. I. 3, 4. p. 62.]

[i] Quærat fortassis aliquis, si Filius charitas est, præcipue propter hoc quod Joannes ad Deum Patrem retulit hanc vocem, dicens, *quia Deus charitas est.* Sed rursum ex ipsa ejus Epistola proferemus et illud quod ait, *Charissimi, diligamus invicem, quoniam charitas ex Deo est.* Qui ergo dixit, *quia Deus charitas est,* ipse iterum charitatem docet esse ex Deo; quam charitatem credo non esse alium nisi unigenitum Filium ejus, sicut Deum ex Deo, ita charitatem ex charitate progenitum.—p. 122. [c. 5. p. 33. These words do not occur any where in the Commentaries on the Epistle to the Romans, as they have come down to us in the translation of Ruffinus. See the note on I. 5. p. 466, (of the Bened. edition of the commentary on Romans).—B.]

ON THE CONSUBSTANTIALITY OF THE SON.

He Love of Love. . . . The only-begotten[k] Son our Saviour, who alone was born[1] of the Father, is alone Son by nature and not by adoption." Pamphilus presently afterwards cites the following from Origen's Commentary on the Epistle to the Hebrews[l]: "We ought, however, to know that Holy Scripture, framing a mode [of expression] for itself[2], by means of certain ineffable and secret and recondite things—endeavours to intimate [truths] to men, and to suggest to them subtle understanding. For instance, in introducing the word vapour, it is on this account that it has taken it [into use] from corporeal things, that we may be able, in some measure at least, to conceive how Christ, who is Wisdom, after the likeness of the vapour which proceeds from any corporeal substance, does thus also Himself arise as a kind of vapour out of[3] the power of God Himself. So Wisdom also, proceeding from Him, is generated of the very substance of God; thus, nevertheless, is She also said, after the similitude of
[346] a corporeal effluence[4], to be 'a certain pure and undefiled effluence of the glory of the Almighty[5];' both which similitudes do most manifestly shew that there is a communion of substance between the Father and the Son. For an effluence seems to be consubstantial, that is, of one substance with that body, from which it is an effluence or vapour." Lastly, the most blessed martyr adduces the following passage also of Origen[m]: "For care should be taken, that one run not into the absurd fables of those who imagine to themselves a kind of emanations[6], so as to cut the divine nature into

1 natus.
2 quemdam modum sibi faciens.
3 de.
4 corporalis aporrhœæ.
5 [See Wisd. vii. 25.]
6 prolationes quasdam.

[k] Unigenitus Filius Salvator noster, qui solus ex Patre natus est, solus natura et non adoptione Filius est. [These words, according to Pamphilus, are taken from book v. on John.—B. Of this fragments only have come down to us: the words are quoted by Bp. Bull as part of the extract from the commentary on Romans.]

[l] Oportet autem scire nos, quia per ineffabilia quædam et secreta ac recondita quemdam modum sibi faciens Scriptura sancta conatur hominibus indicare et intellectum suggerere subtilem. Vaporis enim nomen inducens, hoc ideo de rebus corporalibus assumpsit, ut vel ex parte aliqua intelligere possimus, quomodo Christus, qui est sapientia, secundum similitudinem ejus vaporis, qui de substantia aliqua corporea procedit, sic etiam ipse ut quidam vapor exoritur de virtute ipsius Dei; sic et sapientia, ex eo procedens, ex ipsa substantia Dei generatur. Sic nihilominus et secundum similitudinem corporalis aporrhœæ esse dicitur aporrhœa gloriæ omnipotentis pura quædam et sincera. Quæ utræque similitudines manifestissime ostendunt, communionem substantiæ esse Filio cum Patre. Aporrhœa enim ὁμοούσιος videtur, id est, unius substantiæ cum illo corpore, ex quo est vel aporrhœa vel vapor.—[Ibid.]

[m] Observandum namque est, ne quis incurrat in illas absurdas fabulas eorum, qui prolationes quasdam sibi ipsis depingunt; ut divinam naturam in partes vocent, (puto legendum *secent*, Bull,) et Deum Patrem, quantum in se est,

BOOK II. CHAP. IX. § 19, 20.

ORIGEN.

parts, and, so far as lies in them, to divide God the Father; whereas to entertain such an idea, even in a slight degree, respecting a nature which is incorporeal, is [a mark] not only of extreme impiety, but also of the last degree of folly; nor, is it at all congruous even as a matter of conception[1], that a substantial division of an incorporeal nature should be imaginable. Rather, therefore, as will proceeds from mind, and yet neither cuts off any portion of the mind, nor is separated or divided from it, in some such way is it to be supposed that the Father begot the Son, that is to say, as His own image; so that, as He is Himself invisible by nature, so has He begotten an Image which is also invisible. For the Son is the Word, and therefore nothing [of a nature] subject to sense is to be conceived of in Him. He is Wisdom, and in Wisdom nothing corporeal is to be surmised. He is, moreover, 'the true Light, which lighteneth every man that cometh into this world,' but He has nothing in common with the light of this sun."

[1] vel ad intelligentiam consequens.

John i. 9.

20. Now who can fail to see that by these passages of Origen, which Pamphilus has adduced, the catholic faith respecting the Son of God, and further respecting the consubstantial Trinity, is most plainly established? Some, however, attempt to invalidate the authority of these testimonies under this pretence, that the alleged passages were [347] 125
nowhere to be found entire in the Greek Apology, be it of Pamphilus or Eusebius; but were invented and added by Ruffinus in his Latin translation. The whole ground[2] of this opinion is the fact, that Jerome objects against Ruffinus that the Greek Apology of Eusebius (for he would not have it to be the work of Pamphilus) did in fact defend the Arian creed, and shewed that Origen was of that same

[2] prora et puppis.

dividant; cum hoc de incorporea natura vel leviter suspicari non solum extremæ impietatis sit, verum etiam ultimæ insipientiæ; nec omnino vel ad intelligentiam consequens, ut incorporeæ naturæ substantialis divisio possit intelligi. Magis ergo sicut voluntas procedit e mente, et neque partem aliquam mentis secat, neque ab ea separatur aut dividitur, tali quadam specie putandus est Pater Filium genuisse, imaginem scil. suam; ut sicut ipse est invisibilis per naturam, ita imaginem quoque invisibilem genuerit. Verbum enim est Filius, et ideo nihil in eo sensibile intelligendum est. Sapientia est, et in sapientia nihil corporeum suspicandum est. *Lumen est verum, quod illuminat omnem hominem venientem in hunc mundum;* sed nihil habet commune ad solis hujus lumen. —[Pamph. Apol. p. 34, from the treatise περὶ ἀρχῶν, I. 2—6. p. 55.]

ON THE CONSUBSTANTIALITY OF THE SON.

belief. For thus he writes in his Apology against Ruffinus, ii. 4[n]; "The learned Eusebius, throughout six volumes, is engaged in nothing else than in shewing that Origen was of his own faith, that is, of the Arian faithlessness." From this Sandius[o] concludes that the Apology which was published by Ruffinus in Latin, under the name of that of Pamphilus, "either was not [the production] of Eusebius," (or Pamphilus,) "or was so translated by Ruffinus into Latin, that not a single line was left as it originally stood[1]; or lastly, if any portion was left by Ruffinus as it originally stood, it must afterwards have been cut out even from his version." It may however be proved by the strongest arguments, that on this point Jerome is not to be trusted; for, in the first place, Photius, cod. 118, testifies that he had himself read in the Greek the six books of Pamphilus the Martyr and Eusebius in defence of Origen; in which that severe critic does not mark any traces of Arian heresy, although at other times in the writings of others he is constantly accustomed to animadvert on all the slightest points which bear even the appearance of Arianism. Again, this same Photius, cod. 117[p], in mentioning a certain ancient anonymous author, who likewise wrote a Defence[2] of Origen, says, that that author in his Apology contended for Origen and his opinions on the authority both of other more ancient writers, and especially of Pamphilus the Martyr and Eusebius of Cæsarea.
[348] Photius' words are, "But more than on all the others does he lean[3] on Pamphilus the Martyr and on Eusebius." So that it appears to me to be beyond doubt, that this anonymous writer pursued the very same method of defending Origen as Pamphilus and Eusebius. But was the Apologist an Arian? Any thing rather; for Photius himself, who in another place attributes to him most of the errors of Origen, expressly says, that "concerning the Holy Trinity he maintains none of the erroneous doctrines[4]." How then does the

[1] genuina.

[2] Apologiam.

[3] ἐπερείδεται.

[4] οὐδὲν τῶν ἐσφαλμένων λέγει.

n Vir doctissimus Eusebius, per sex volumina nihil aliud agit, nisi ut Origenem suæ ostendat fidei, id est, Arianæ perfidiæ.—[§ 16. vol. II. p. 507.]

o De Script. Eccles., p. 47.

p [ἀνεγνώσθη βίβλιον ὑπὲρ Ὠριγένους, ... ἐν τόμοις έ. ἀνεπίγραφον δὲ τὴν ὀνομασίαν ἐτύγχανε τοῦ συντεταχότος .... ὁ δὲ τοῦ συγγράμματος πατὴρ μάρτυρας ὑπὲρ Ὠριγένους τε καὶ τῶν αὐτοῦ δογμάτων . . . προκομιζει] . . . μᾶλλον δὲ τῶν ἄλλων ἁπάντων Παμφίλῳ τε τῷ μάρτυρι ἐπερείδεται, καὶ τῷ Εὐσεβίῳ. . . περὶ [μέντοι] τῆς ἁγίας τριάδος οὐδὲν τῶν ἐσφαλμένων λέγει. . . φησὶ δὲ, καὶ περὶ τοῦ Ὠριγένους, μηδὲν αὐτὸν κατὰ δόξαν ἐσφάλθαι περὶ τῆς τριάδος.—Phot. Bibl. cod. 117.

[anonymous] author defend Origen? "And he also declares," says Photius, "respecting Origen, that he entertained no erroneous opinion[1] concerning the Holy Trinity." Photius afterwards states, that this writer had proved that the fifteen points[2] which were objected to Origen, (of which the first three, the thirteenth, and the last, related to the article of the Trinity[q],) "were [mere] calumnies[3], deriving his proofs out of the writings of (Origen) himself." The very same principle and method is observed in the Apology, which was published by Ruffinus under the name of Pamphilus. From these facts the following, at least, certainly results; that an ancient Greek writer, who, even in the opinion of Photius, was catholic on the article of the holy Trinity, adduced out of the actual[4] writings of Origen, as they were then extant in Greek, testimonies which shewed that Origen also[5] was catholic on that same article [of faith], and that that writer did this after the example of the martyr Pamphilus and Eusebius, and following in their footsteps. Lastly, we have evidently proved elsewhere, that Eusebius himself never embraced the heresy, which was afterwards called Arian; he could not therefore have defended the Arian impiety in Origen, either alone, or in conjunction with Pamphilus,—for the Apology was their joint work, as we shall afterwards[r] shew. But Pamphilus and [349] Eusebius in that Apology, adduced, I conceive[6], some testimonies from Origen, in which were intermixed little words[7] and phrases which in the time of Jerome were offensive to catholic ears, as having been employed by the Arians at that time to propagate their heresy: and these passages, I imagine, Ruffinus for that very reason cut out from his version, being content to translate such passages of Origen quoted by Pamphilus, as taught the catholic doctrine in terms unequivocally catholic. And Ruffinus himself seems to intimate this, when in the conclusion[8] [attached] to his translation, and addressed to Macarius, he declares, that[s] he had "translated into the Latin tongue the Apology of the holy martyr Pamphilus, according to his ability, or AS THE CASE REQUIRED." For the

1 μηδὲν κατὰ δόξαν ἐσφάλθαι.

2 capite.

3 διαβολὰς.

4 ipsis.

5 pariter.

6 videntur.

7 voculæ.

8 epilogo.

q [ἔστι δὲ, ἃ λέγει μάτην αὐτοῦ κατηγορηθῆναι,] διαβολὰς εἶναι, ἐκ τῶν αὐτοῦ ἐκείνου συγγραμμάτων ποιούμενον τοὺς ἐλέγχους.—[Ibid.]

r See ch. 13. § 3, of this book.

s Apologeticum sancti martyris Pamphili, ... prout potuimus, vel RES POPOSCIT, Latino sermone digessimus.—[p. 48; see below, p. 274.]

ON THE CONSUBSTANTIALITY OF THE SON.

rest I am persuaded, that Ruffinus inserted no testimony of Origen in his version, which was not contained in so many words in the Apology of Pamphilus and Eusebius; and that, whatever he may have omitted, he added nothing of his own. For near the beginning of his preface to the Apology of Pamphilus, Ruffinus himself solemnly avows to Macarius, that he had, in reply to Macarius' enquiries, set forth in that work[t], "not his own opinion" concerning Origen, "but that of the holy martyr Pamphilus;" and had defended Origen "in the words of another," and not in his own; and that Ruffinus was a man who endeavoured after[1] sincere piety, there are many circumstances to shew, however much the subtle[2] arts of Jerome may have made him an object of dislike to the Romans. Afterwards in the same passage he appeals against[3] his adversaries to the tremendous judgments of God on this very point, in these words; "But since we shall have to appear before the judgment-seat of God, let none refuse to know that which is true, lest peradventure they should offend through ignorance; rather, considering that to wound the consciences of weak brethren by false accusations is to sin against Christ, let them, on this account, not lend their ear to accusers, nor learn what the faith of one is from the report of another, especially when there is full opportunity before them to ascertain it, and when there is the confession of his own mouth to shew, what or how each man believes. Let the tenor of this short treatise declare what are indeed the sentiments[4] of Origen on each particular point[u]." It is true that in translating most of the works of Origen, Ruffinus added much of his own; but so often as he has used this liberty he has himself[x] expressly informed his

[1] studiosum.

[2] vafræ.

[3] provocat.

[4] qualiter sentiat Origenes in singulis.

[t] [Quamvis non meam de eo] sententiam, sed sancti martyris Pamphili [sciscitatus sis et librum ejus . . . transferri tibi poposceris in Latinum: tamen non dubito futuros quosdam, qui et in eo læsos se putent, si nos aliquid pro eo vel] alieno sermone [dicamus.] —p. 19.]

[u] Sed quoniam ad judicium Dei venturi sumus, non refugiant scire quod verum est, ne forte ignorantes delinquant; sed considerantes quia falsis criminationibus percutere fratrum infirmorum conscientias, in Christum peccare est, ideo non accommodent criminatoribus aurem suam, nec ab alio discant alterius fidem, maxime cum coram experiri sit copia, et oris sui confessio, quid vel qualiter unusquisque credit, ostendat. Qualiter ergo sentiat Origenes in singulis, tenor libelli hujus edoceat.—[In the Benedictine edition the reading is, Qualiter ergo Origenes de singulis capitulis sanctarum Scripturarum senserit, &c., i. e. "What indeed were the sentiments of Origen on the several points of the Holy Scriptures," &c.]

[x] See Ruffinus' preface to the treatise περὶ ἀρχῶν, and his Peroration to

reader, as became an honest man and one who loves the truth. Nay, what is to be said to the fact, that[1] Jerome himself, who in any other case would on no account have forgiven Ruffinus so clear an act of fraud, has not marked even one single passage of Origen quoted in the Apology, be it of Pamphilus or Eusebius, as having been rendered by Ruffinus into Latin in any other sense than that in which it occurred, whether in that Apology or in Origen himself.

[1] Quid? quod, &c.

21. Who then would not be surprised that Jerome should bring these objections against Ruffinus respecting this very version of his? "There are," he says[y], "to be found in it many scandals[2] and most open blasphemies. Eusebius, or rather Pamphilus, (as you will have it,) in that volume declares that the Son is the servant of the Father[3]; that the Holy Ghost is not of the same substance with the Father and the Son; that the souls of men fell[4] from heaven," &c. Now although Pamphilus is indeed introduced in the Apology translated by Ruffinus, as defending Origen for having believed the pre-existence of souls, yet still that blasphemy about the Holy Ghost is no where found in that work. But you will say, Ruffinus expunged it from his books[5] on being reminded of it by Jerome. How then does it come to pass, that [351] there is not now extant a single copy of the work in which that blasphemy is to be found? For copies of Ruffinus' translation had been very widely dispersed before Jerome brought forward that objection. Surely it is not likely, that Ruffinus, whom the arts of Jerome had brought into contempt at Rome, could either have suppressed or corrected[6] all those earlier copies? Then again, Ruffinus, in his Conclusion to Pamphilus' Apology, as he himself first published it, thus addresses Macarius, (as we are also informed by Jerome[z];) "In respect to these things, which in the foregoing treatise we have set forth according to our ability, or as the case required, in the Latin tongue, following the Apology of the

[2] scandala.

[3] Patris ministrum.

[4] lapsas esse.

[5] codicibus.

[6] emendare.

the Comment. of Origen on the Epistle to the Romans.

[y] In illo scandala reperiuntur et apertissimæ blasphemiæ. Dicit Eusebius, imo, ut tu vis, Pamphilus in isto volumine, Filium Patris ministrum; Spiritum S. non de eadem Patris Filiique substantia; animas hominum lapsas esse de cœlo, &c.—Apol. advers. Ruffin. II. 4. [§ 15. vol. ii. p. 506.]

[z] In his quæ in superiori libro, secundum Apologeticum sancti martyris Pamphili, quem pro Origene Græco sermone edidit, prout potuimus vel res poposcit, Latino sermone digessimus,

ON THE CONSUBSTANTIALITY OF THE SON.

holy martyr Pamphilus, which he published in Greek in vindication of Origen, there is this of which I wish you, my dear Macarius, to be reminded, that you may know that this which we have set forth above out of his works, is that rule of faith which ought to be embraced, and held fast. For it is evidently proved that a catholic sense pervades them all." Now it is manifestly impossible that Ruffinus, who without any doubt was catholic in the article of the Holy Trinity, should have deliberately asserted, that it was clearly proved that there was a catholic sense contained in so open a blasphemy, and this in that very treatise addressed to Macarius, in which he religiously[a] avouches his belief, "that the Holy Trinity is coeternal, and of one nature, and of one power and substance;" and denounces an anathema on the man who should teach the contrary. Or was Ruffinus so dull as not of himself to detect, without a prompter, so gross a blasphemy in his own translation? Certainly not; what then must we say? I trust the candid reader will here permit me to throw out a conjecture. Pamphilus towards the end of his Apo-
[352] logy, as translated by Ruffinus[1], when defending, or, at any rate, excusing, the error of Origen respecting the pre-existence of souls, and disputing against such as maintained the propagation of souls, describes two classes of these latter; the first, that of those, who, whilst they held that the souls of men were derived by propagation[2], nevertheless maintained that the first soul was of the substance of God; the other, that of those, who asserted, that that first soul was made by God out of nothing. Against the former Pamphilus reasons thus[b]; "Now as respects those, who hold that souls come from propagation and that they are sown together with the seed of the body, if indeed, (as certain of themselves are wont to affirm,) they maintain that soul is nothing else than the in-breathing of the Spirit of God, that, namely, which at the beginning of the creation of the world God is said

[1] Apologiæ a Ruffino versæ.

[2] ex traduce.

illud est quod te, desideriorum vir Macari, admonitum esse volo, ut scias hanc quidem fidei regulam, quam de libris ejus supra exposuimus, esse, quæ et amplectenda sit, et tenenda. In omnibus enim his catholicum inesse sensum evidenter probatur.—[Ibid., p. 48.]

[a] See Ruffinus's preface to Macarius. [Pamph. Apol., p. 17.]

[b] Jam vero illi, qui ex traduce animas venire affirmant, et simùl cum corporali eas semine seminari, siquidem, ut quidam ipsorum affirmare solent, non aliud dicunt animum esse quam insufflationem Spiritus Dei, illam

to have breathed into Adam, asserting that this is of the BOOK II.
very substance of God; how shall not these too be believed CHAP. IX. § 21.
some how to be making this assertion in opposition to the ORIGEN.
rule of Scripture and the analogy of the faith[1], [namely,] [1] rationem
that it is the substance of God which sins?" These words, I pietatis.
have little doubt, were the foundation of Jerome's calumnious charge[2] against Pamphilus. For, along with many of the [2] calumniam.
ancients, Jerome held that the breath of life, which God is
said to have breathed into the first man, was the Holy Spirit
Himself[3] infused into that same man, together with his soul[4]. [3] ipsum.
Thus in his Commentary on chap. iv. of the Epistle to the [4] anima.
Ephesians, on the words, "Grieve not the Holy Spirit where- ch. iv. 30.
by ye have been sealed in the day of redemption," he has this
note[c]; "For we were sealed with the Holy Spirit of God,
that both our spirit and soul may have the impress of God's
seal[5], and that we may again receive that image and likeness, [5] signaculum.
after which, in the beginning, we were created. This seal 127
of the Holy Spirit, according to the language of our Saviour, is sealed by the impress of God." Here he makes that
image and likeness of God, after which man was formed at [353]
his very creation, to be the seal of the Holy Spirit; and this
he appears to have done simply from believing that the
breath of life, which God is said to have breathed into the
first man when He formed him, was the Holy Spirit. This is
more clearly expressed by Tertullian in his Treatise on Baptism, chap. v., where he speaks thus of the regeneration of
man which is wrought by[6] baptism[d]; "Thus man is restored [6] per.
to God, after His likeness, who in time past had been made
after God's image, &c. For he receives again that Spirit of
God, which at that time he had received from His in-breathing[7], but afterwards had lost by sin." Pamphilus, then, [7] adflatu.
or the author of the Apology, (understanding, as it appears,

scil. quam initio facturæ mundi Deus dicitur insufflasse in Adam, de ipsa Dei esse eam substantia profitentes; quomodo non et isti videbuntur quodammodo hæc præter Scripturæ regulam et rationem pietatis asserere, quod substantia Dei est quæ peccat?—p. 127. [c. 9. p. 43.]

[c] Signati autem sumus Spiritu Dei Sancto, ut et spiritus noster et anima imprimantur signaculo Dei, et illam recipiamus imaginem et similitudinem, ad quam in exordio conditi sumus. Hoc signaculum Sancti Spiritus, juxta eloquium Salvatoris, Deo imprimente signatur.—[Vol. vii. p. 632.]

[d] Ita restituitur homo Deo ad similitudinem ejus, qui retro ad imaginem Dei fuerat, &c. Recipit enim illum Dei Spiritum, quem tunc de adflatu ejus acceperat, sed post amisera per delictum.—[p. 226.]

ON THE CONSUBSTANTIALITY OF THE SON.

by in-breathing, as did the opponents whom he is refuting, nothing else than the soul of man itself,) denied that the in-breathing of the Spirit of God was of the very substance of God; and from this it seems to have arisen that Jerome accused him, as though he had taught that the Spirit of God, the Third Person of the Godhead, was not of the substance of God, and was, consequently, a servant of God or a creature. If, however, any one does not like this conjecture of mine, he must, I think, of necessity maintain that Ruffinus' version of the Apology of Pamphilus was corrupted by his opponents and Jerome's partizans; and that Jerome laid hold of that accusation from some corrupted copy. It is indeed certain, that Ruffinus himself complains of some wrong of this kind done to his translation of Origen's work περὶ ἀρχῶν, appealing to God who knows the hearts, to avenge the wrong. For he writes thus in the first book of his Invectives against Jerome [e]; "They should have adduced my very words, just as I had translated. But now hear what they do, and see whether there be any precedent or example
[354] for their flagitious conduct. In the passage where it was written, 'But if you demand of me what I think concerning the Only-begotten Himself, let it not at once be thought by you either impious or absurd, if I say that the nature of God, who is naturally invisible, is not visible even to Him: for we will give you a reason in due course[1].' Now instead of what we wrote, 'We will in due course give you a reason,' they substituted, 'Let it not at once be thought by you either impious or absurd, that as the Son sees not the Father, so neither does the Holy Ghost see the Son.' Now if he[2] who was sent from the monastery to Rome, as being most expert in calumny, had committed such an offence in the courts, or in the affairs of the world, every one knows what

[1] consequenter.

[2] [Eusebius of Cremona.]

[e] Ipsa, sicut transtuleram, mea verba posuissent. Sed nunc ausculta, quid faciant; et flagitii eorum require, si ullum præcessit, exemplum. In eo loco, ubi scriptum erat, 'Quod si requiris a me, quid etiam de ipso Unigenito sentiam, si ne ipse [ipsi ed. Ben.] quidem visibilem dicam naturam Dei, qui naturaliter invisibilis est, non tibi statim vel impium videatur esse, vel absurdum: rationem quippe dabimus consequenter;' pro eo quod nos scripsimus, *rationem quippe dabimus consequenter,*' illi scripserunt, 'Non tibi statim impium vel absurdum videatur esse; *quia sicut Filius Patrem non videt, ita nec Spiritus S. videt Filium.*' Hoc si in foro positus vel negotiis sæcularibus commisisset ille, qui de monasterio Romam, quasi calumniandi peritissimus, missus est, norunt omnes, quid consequeretur ex legibus publicis ejusmodi criminis reus. Nunc vero quia sæcularem vitam reliquit, et a

BOOK II. CHAP. IX. § 21, 22.

ORIGEN.

[punishment] a person convicted on a charge of this kind would have incurred from the public laws. But now that he has relinquished a secular life, and has turned himself from the chicanery of public pleading to a monastery, and has attached himself to a distinguished teacher[1], he learns from him a second time, instead of moderation, fury and madness; instead of quietness, to excite commotion; instead of peace, to kindle war; instead of concord, to awaken dissension; to be perfidious for the faith, and a falsifier for truth." Presently after in the same book he gives this account concerning the falsifier: "when he was reading out," he says, "a forged passage of this kind at Milan, and I declared that what he read was forged; on being asked from whom he had procured his copy, he replied that a lady[2] had given it to him: I said of her, 'Whosoever she be, I say nothing; but I leave her to her own consciousness and that of God.'" And this must suffice at present concerning Pamphilus' Apology for Origen.

[1] [Jerome.]

[2] matronem [Marcella.]

22. To bring this chapter to a close at last; in the course of a very attentive consideration of those passages of Origen, which have been adduced above, I come to this conclusion; that this father, who has been attacked by the censures of so many divines, both ancient and modern, in respect of [355] the article of the divinity of the Son and even of the Holy Trinity, was yet really catholic; although in his mode of explaining this article, he sometimes expressed himself otherwise than Catholics of the present day are wont to do; but this is common to him with nearly all the fathers who lived before the council of Nice. Further—inasmuch as I have very carefully studied the works of Origen, and have accurately weighed his history as the ancients have narrated it, —I may be permitted freely to record my judgment of his theology in general, without offence to any one. He was

tergiversatione illa actuum publicorum ad monasterium conversus est, et adhæsit magistro nobili, ab ipso edocetur iterum pro modestia furere, insanire; pro quiete seditiones movere; pro pace movere bellum; pro concordia movere dissidia; perfidus esse pro fide, pro veritate falsarius. . . . Cum falsam, inquit, hujusmodi sententiam apud Mediolanum recitaret, et a me, quæ exigebat, falsa esse dicerentur, interrogatus a quo accepisset exemplaria, respondit, Matronam quandam sibi dedisse; de qua ego, Quæcunque illa est, nihil dico; sed sui eam et Dei conscientiæ derelinquo.—Inter opera Hieron., tom. ix. p. 140. [vol. ii. p. 600.]

indeed a man, as all agree, of remarkable piety, but of a too inquisitive and almost wanton genius. His piety and religious reverence restrained him from making any innovation on the rule of faith, (of which a great part is the doctrine of the most Holy Trinity;) but on other points, which might be made matter of discussion without trenching on the rule of faith, yielding too much to his natural disposition, he put forward not a few opinions differing very widely from the views more commonly entertained by the teachers who were his contemporaries. To this class I refer his paradoxes concerning the pre-existence of the soul, the stars being animated, an infinity of worlds, and the like. But even on these subjects he observed the modesty which becomes a pious person, in that he propounded them not in a dogmatic and positive manner, but as though he were diligently enquiring into the truth on points which had not yet been expressly defined by the judgment of the Church. On this the reader should by all means consult the Apology of Pamphilus near the beginning[f].

23. This judgment of mine concerning Origen, is confirmed by many other considerations, besides the testimonies which have been already adduced in this chapter. In the first place, the defenders of Origen, who were all catholic on
128 the article concerning the Holy Trinity, at the same time
[356] that they did not deny other heterodox sentiments, which were attributed to him, such for instance as those which we have just mentioned, but either excused or even defended them, still strenuously maintained, that in respect of the Trinity, Origen's own views agreed with those of all Catholics. It was on this ground, as we have just shewn, that Pamphilus the Martyr and that anonymous apologist mentioned by Photius, defended Origen; and that Didymus of Alexandria, a man eminent for piety and erudition, and a most resolute supporter of the Nicene Creed, adopted the same course in his defence of Origen, is testified by Jerome himself, who, in his Apology against Ruffinus, thus addresses Ruffinus himself[g]: "What answer, he asks, will you make

[f] See likewise, Huet's Origeniana: ii. p. 189. [lib. ii. Quæst. 14. c. 3. § 11, 12. p. 255.]

[g] Quid respondebis pro Didymo, qui certe in Trinitate catholicus est, cujus etiam nos de Spiritu Sancto li-

on behalf of Didymus, who at any rate is orthodox on the docrine of the Trinity, and whose treatise on the Holy Ghost I myself have translated into Latin? He certainly could not have agreed to those things which heretics have added to the works of Origen; and on those very books of Principles[1], which you have translated, he wrote short commentaries, in which he did not deny that what is written, is written by Origen, but [asserted] that we simple folk could not understand what he said, and endeavours to persuade us in what sense they should be taken so as to have a good meaning. This, however, refers only to his statements respecting the Son and the Holy Ghost; as regards other doctrines both Eusebius and Didymus do most openly give in to the tenets of Origen, and maintain that statements which all the churches reprobate, are catholic and religious." The words of Socrates, in his Ecclesiastical History, iv. 26, about Basil the Great and Gregory of Nazianzum, are also worthy of observation[h]: "And yet," he says, "when the Arians appealed[2] to the books of Origen in confirmation, as they thought, of their own doctrine, these confuted them, and shewed that they did not understand the meaning of Origen." [357] In the second place, the earlier adversaries and the chief opponents of Origen, who on other points attacked him with the greatest vehemence, and with too much severity, were almost entirely silent respecting any heresy of his on the doctrine of the Trinity. Indeed, Socrates, Hist. Eccl. vi. 13, in treating of the leading accusers of Origen, viz., Methodius, Eustathius, Apollinaris, and Theophilus, (whom speaking rather freely he calls "a quaternion[3] of calumniators,") makes this observation respecting them[i]; "But I affirm that even additional evidence in favour of[4] Origen re-

BOOK II. CHAP. IX. § 22, 23. ORIGEN.

[1] περὶ ἀρχῶν.

[2] τῶν Ἀρειανῶν καλούντων.

[3] κακολόγων τετρακτὺν.

[4] εἰς σύστασιν.

brum in Latinam linguam vertimus? certe hic in iis, quæ ab hæreticis in Origenis operibus addita sunt, consentire non potuit; et in ipsis περὶ ἀρχῶν, quos tu interpretatus es, libris breves dictavit commentariolos, quibus non negaret ab Origene scripta quæ scripta sunt, sed nos simplices homines non posse intelligere quæ dicuntur; et quo sensu in bonam partem accipi debeant, persuadere conatur. Hoc duntaxat de Filio et Spiritu Sancto; cæterum in aliis dogmatibus et Eusebius et Didymus apertissime in Origenis scita concedunt, et, quod omnes ecclesiæ reprobant, catholice et pie dictum esse defendunt.—Tom. iii. p. 512. [§ 16. vol. ii. p. 507.]

[h] καίτοι, τῶν Ἀρειανῶν τὰ Ὠριγένους βιβλία εἰς μαρτυρίαν, ὡς ᾤοντο, τοῦ ἰδίου καλούντων δόγματος, αὐτοὶ ἐξήλεγχον, καὶ ἐδείκνυον μὴ νοήσαντας τοῦ Ὠριγένους σύνεσιν.—[Socr. E. H. iv. 26.]

[i] ἐγὼ δέ τι, καὶ πλέον ἐκ τῆς ἐκείνων αἰτιάσεως εἰς σύστασιν Ὠριγένους φημί. οἱ γὰρ κινήσαντες ὅσαπερ ᾤοντο

ON THE CONSUBSTANTIALITY OF THE SON.

sults from their accusations of him. For those who brought up whatever points they thought worthy of blame, and in the course of these did not at all censure him as holding wrong opinions respecting the Holy Trinity, are hereby most clearly shewn to testify to his orthodox piety." Theophilus, indeed, (if we are to trust Jerome,) in the first of those Paschal Letters, which were translated into Latin by Jerome, and are extant at this day both in the *Bibliotheca Magna Patrum*[k], and among the works of Jerome[l], does censure certain errors of Origen on the subject of the Trinity; but these might easily[1] be explained if we had had leisure for it at present. It is certain, however, that Sulpicius Severus, an historian of very great credit, Dial. I. c. 3, in narrating the history of a council, which was convened in his
[358] own times by Theophilus against the writings of Origen, writes to this effect[m]; "Many extracts from his books were read by the bishops, which were certainly opposed to the catholic faith; but the passage which excited the most unfavourable feeling against him, was that, in which it was stated, that the Lord Jesus, even as He had come in the flesh for the redemption of man, had endured the cross for the salvation of man, and had tasted death for the immortality of man, so would He in the same order of suffering redeem the devil also; inasmuch as it was befitting His goodness and piety, that, He who had renewed[2] ruined man, should likewise liberate the fallen angel." Now if it had been evident that Origen's opinions, touching the prime doctrine of Christianity, I mean, the most Holy Trinity, had been as impious as Jerome and others have alleged, surely Theophilus and the bishops of his party, who ransacked every corner of Origen's writings, to find a handle for accusing him, and who seem to have been especially bent upon exciting the

[1] nullo negotio.

[2] reformasset.

μέμψεως ἄξια, δι' ὧν ὡς κακῶς δοξάζοντα περὶ τῆς ἁγίας τριάδος οὐδ' ὅλως ἐμέμψαντο, δείκνυνται περιφανῶς τὴν ὀρθὴν εὐσέβειαν μαρτυροῦντες αὐτῷ.—[Ibid. vi. 13.]

[k] [Tom. v. pp. 843, sqq. Lugd. 1677.]

[l] [Tom. ii. pp. 545, sq.]

[m] Cum ab episcopis excerpta in libris illius multa legerentur, quæ contra catholicam fidem scripta constaret, locus ille vel maximam parabat invidiam, in quo editum legebatur, quia Dominus Jesus, sicut pro redemptione hominis in carne venisset, crucem pro hominis salute perpessus, mortem pro hominis æternitate gustasset, ita esset eodem ordine passionis etiam Diabolum redempturus; quia hoc bonitati illius pietatique congrueret, ut qui perditum hominem reformasset, prolapsum quoque angelum liberaret.—Pag. 548. ed. Lugd. Batavor. 1654.

BOOK II. CHAP. IX. § 23.

ORIGEN.

greatest general ill-will against Origen, (whose authority the factious monks were making an ill use of against the Church,) would have exposed his heresy on this point[1] unreservedly to all; inasmuch as, in that age, this heresy, above all others, was regarded by Catholics (and justly so) with the greatest abhorrence. But they being wary men, knew full well that such an accusation might have been most easily refuted by the defenders of Origen, out of Origen's own unquestioned writings; therefore they passed it by, and laid the stress of their charge against him on other heads, on which he could not be so easily defended. Severus adds in the same passage, that what was objected to Origen at that council was, in his own opinion, an *error*, not a *heresy*, and yet it is certain, that the
Arian doctrine was regarded by Severus as a most pesti- 129
lential heresy; it follows therefore that Origen was in no wise declared guilty of Arianism at that synod. Thirdly,
that is worthy of observation, which Eusebius (in his Eccl. [359]
History, vi. 2, near the end) relates respecting the constancy of Origen in maintaining the orthodox faith, adding these words[n]; "Preserving even from boyhood the rule of the Church, and abominating[2], as he somewhere himself says, using that very word, the doctrines of heresies." Surely no one who is familiar with Ecclesiastical History, can be ignorant that Origen was the foremost[3] and well nigh the only champion of the Church in defence of the catholic faith against whatsoever heresies were springing up in his time. For, as often as, and wheresoever, there arose any heretic, who presumed to impugn the faith received in the Church, recourse was at once had to Origen alone; that he, as another David, might attack with his sling the Goliath who reproached the army of the Lord; nay, he used to present himself of his own accord for contests such as this, (herein again resembling David,) out of the love and zeal which he bore to the truth. Surely no one at any time deserved more than Origen to be called *malleus omnium hæreticorum.* Now the Catholic Church has at all times judged the doctrine concerning the true Divinity of the Son to belong to the un-

[1] præcipue.

[2] βδελυττόμενος.

[3] primarium ac pene unicum.

[n] φυλάττων, ἐξ ἔτι παιδὸς κανόνα ἐκκλησίας, βδελυττόμενός τε, ὥς αὐτῷ ῥήματί φησί που αὐτὸς, τὰς τῶν αἱρέσεων διδασκαλίας.--[Euseb. E. H. vi. 2.]

ON THE CONSUBSTANTIALITY OF THE SON.

changeable rule of faith; nor did Origen entertain any other view; for in his first book, *περὶ ἀρχῶν*, (as quoted by Pamphilus in his Apology,) in making a distinction between doctrines, which are necessary to be known and believed, and those which are not necessary, he puts amongst the necessary these following[o]; "First, that there is one God, who created all things. . . . . Then next, that Jesus Christ was begotten[1] of the Father before every creature . . . that whereas He was God, He became incarnate, and being made man He continued to be what He was, God. . . . Then next, that the Holy Ghost is associated with the Father and the Son, in honour
[360] and dignity[p]." Amongst the doctrines that are not necessary, or in other words, questions which might be debated on either side, [so it be done] temperately and without detriment to the peace of the Church, he enumerates in the same passage, questions concerning the time and mode of the creation of angels, concerning the sun, the moon, and the stars, whether they be animate or inanimate, &c. In the discussion, indeed[2], of questions of this sort, Origen perhaps allowed himself too much freedom; but so far as relates to those other doctrines, he scrupulously refrained from departing a hair's-breadth from the rule of faith which was fixed and established in the Church. Fourthly, Bellarmine's[q] argument (which we have elsewhere touched on incidentally[r]) seems to me to be of great weight, however much the very learned Huet despised it. He proves that Origen was catholic on this article, from the orthodoxy and soundness of the opinions of his teacher Clement, and of his pupils, Dionysius of Alexandria, and Gregory Thaumaturgus, respecting the mystery of the most Holy Trinity. For, as regards Clement, I have already in treating of his belief, most evidently proved, that no one ever acknowledged or declared the catholic doctrine respecting the consubstantial Trinity, more clearly than he. We shall hereafter shew the same as clearly with respect to Dio-

[1] natus.

[2] scilicet.

[o] Primo quod unus est Deus, qui omnia creavit . . . Tum deinde quia Jesus Christus ante omnem creaturam natus ex Patre est. . . . Incarnatus est, cum Deus esset, et homo factus mansit quod erat Deus. . . . Tum deinde honore ac dignitate Patri et Filio sociatum esse Spiritum Sanctum.—[c. 1. p. 20.]

[p] These statements are found in the preface of his book *περὶ ἀρχῶν*.—GRABE.

[q] Bellarminus de Christo I. 10. [vol. i. Op., p. 339.]

[r] Supra c. vi. § 1. [p. 182.]

BOOK II. CHAP. IX. § 23.

ORIGEN.

nysius of Alexandria, and Gregory Thaumaturgus, although the Jesuit Petavius has branded these two very great names, to the disgrace of his own name, with the mark of the Arian impiety. What then? is it likely, that the man who had a master so catholic on this article, and who had disciples so orthodox, who also at all times regarded their master with admiration as the most illustrious doctor of the Church, was himself heretical in that very article? Fifthly, in the next place, the great Athanasius ought to be as good as a thousand witnesses as to the orthodoxy of Origen on this question: and he, in his work On the Decrees of the Nicene council, expressly declares [r], that Origen agreed with the [361]
Nicene fathers respecting the very and eternal Godhead of the Son: his words are these; "Concerning the everlasting co-existence of the Word with the Father, and that He is not of another substance or hypostasis [1], but properly [2] of the substance of the Father, as they in the council said, be it permitted that you hear again from the labour-loving [3] Origen also." In this passage, however, before he quotes the very words of Origen, Athanasius admits, that there are certain things premised by Origen in the passage which he is about to cite first, which are seemingly repugnant to sound doctrine; but these, he says, Origen states as a disputant, not as one who is making an absolute assertion, whilst the words which he himself adduces, contain the truly genuine opinion of Origen; his words are: "For after what he advances as in an exercise of strength [4] against the heretics, he immediately introduces his own views [5], saying thus . . . [s]" He then quotes a famous sentence of Origen respecting the eternity and consubstantiality of the Son; to which he also 130
subjoins a second from another of Origen's works; which passages we reserve for our third book [t]. And indeed, I have not myself the slightest doubt, that that method of discussion which Origen pursued in almost all [6] his writings, that, I mean, by which he was wont first to represent the opinions of the heretics, assuming as it were the person of

[1] οὐσίας ἢ ὑποστάσεως.

[2] ἴδιον.

[3] φιλοπόνου.

[4] τὰ ὡς ἐν γυμνασίᾳ λεγόμενα.

[5] τὰ ἴδια.

[6] fere ubique in.

[r] περὶ δὲ τοῦ ἀϊδίως συνεῖναι τὸν λόγον τῷ πατρὶ, καὶ μὴ ἑτέρας οὐσίας ἢ ὑποστάσεως, ἀλλὰ τῆς τοῦ πατρὸς ἴδιον αὐτὸν εἶναι, ὡς εἰρήκασιν οἱ ἐν τῇ συνόδῳ, ἐξέστω πάλιν ὑμᾶς ἀκοῦσαι καὶ παρὰ τοῦ φιλοπόνου Ὠριγένους.—Opera Athanasii, tom. i. p. 227. [§ 27. vol. i. p. 232.]

[s] μετὰ γοῦν τὰ ὡς ἐν γυμνασίᾳ λεγόμενα πρὸς τοὺς αἱρετικοὺς, εὐθὺς αὐτὸς ἐπιφέρει τὰ ἴδια, λέγων οὕτως.—[Ibid.]

[t] [See book iii. 3. 1.]

[362] the heretics themselves, and afterwards to lay open the catholic doctrine, first gave to unlearned and ill-disposed persons a handle for charging Origen himself with heresy, as though, that is, he had defended those heretical positions in earnest. But Huet [u] says that Origen's view "was not seen through by Athanasius." That learned man, however, will pardon us, if, notwithstanding, we are still persuaded, that Athanasius, a bishop of Alexandria, who lived so near the times of Origen, also of Alexandria, and who was moreover both a most industrious and most clear-sighted student of the works of Origen and of other ancient writers, saw through Origen's opinions much better than any one amongst ourselves, who are but their remote descendants[1], can do. Huet, however, proceeds to say; "I do not deny that Origen used these expressions; but that he used them in the same sense as the council of Nice, that I cannot admit." I answer again; No one could have known the meaning of the Nicene council better than Athanasius, who was himself present at that council. Athanasius however testifies, that Origen altogether agreed in opinion with the Nicene fathers as well respecting the consubstantiality[2] of the Son as His co-eternity[3], and indeed as concerns the eternity of the Son, Huet will not deny that this is true; as to the consubstantiality, however, he declares that he cannot admit it. And yet we have already shewn, clearly and at length, that the Nicene Bishops declared the Son to be of one substance with the Father in no other sense than that, which lays down that the Son is very God equally with the Father, not of any created or mutable essence. And that Origen acknowledged the Son to be of one substance with the Father in this very sense, we have abundantly proved, in this chapter. As to what is called the numerical unity of substance of the Father and the Son, (which Huet in the same place asserts that Origen denied,) I can clearly shew, that Origen acknowledged that unity, so far as any one of the more ancient fathers, and
[363] even Athanasius himself, acknowledged it; that is to say, that Origen believed, that the Father, the Son, and the Holy Ghost, whilst they are in very deed Three Persons, still do not by any means exist as three men, separately and apart

[1] seris nepotibus.

[2] de Filii τῷ ὁμοουσίῳ.

[3] de ipsius τῷ συναϊδίῳ.

[u] Origenian., lib. ii. p. 33. [Quæst. 2, 5. p. 119.]

BOOK II. CHAP. IX. § 23. x. § 1.

ORIGEN.

from each other[1], but that They intimately cohere together and are conjoined One with Another; and thus that they exist One in the Other, and, so to speak, mutually run into and penetrate Each Other, by a certain ineffable *περιχώρησις*, which the schoolmen call *circuminsessio*; from which *περιχώρησις*[2] Petavius[x] contends, that that numerical unity necessarily results; there will, however, be a more suitable place for discussing this subject in another part [of our treatise][y]; meanwhile let us pass on from Origen to other fathers.

1 seorsim et separatim.

2 ex qua . . effici.

CHAPTER X. 131

CONCERNING THE FAITH AND VIEWS OF THE MARTYR CYPRIAN, OF NOVATIAN OR THE AUTHOR OF A TREATISE ON THE TRINITY AMONG THE WORKS OF TERTULLIAN, AND OF THEOGNOSTUS.

CYPRIAN.

1. CONTEMPORARY with Origen was Cyprian[z]; [he was] during his lifetime chief bishop[3] of Africa, a man of the greatest sanctity and of a truly apostolic spirit, and who at last obtained also the crown of a most glorious martyrdom. So pure and sound were both his sentiments and his expressions concerning the Divinity of the Son, that Petavius himself could find nothing whatever in his works to transfix with his mark[4], or, as his way is, to asperse with the spot and stain of Arianism. It may, therefore, suffice to adduce but few testimonies out of this writer. In the second book of his Testimonies against the Jews, addressed to Quirinus[a], he proves most copiously from the Scriptures that Christ is God; attri- [364] buting unto Him all those things, which in the same Scriptures are attributed only to the true and supreme God: Thus, in chap. 5 and 6, he quotes the passage of Isaiah, xlv. 14[b], "For God is in Thee, and there is none other God beside Thee: for Thou art God, and we knew it not, O God of Israel, the Saviour;" that of Baruch also, iii. 35, "This is our God, and none other shall be accounted beside[5] Him;" that

3 primarius episcopus, [the primate.]

4 veru atque obelo suo.

5 absque.

x De Trinitate, iv. 16.

y Book iv. 4. 9; and following.

z He embraced Christianity about the year 246. Cave.—BOWYER.

a [Page 284, &c.]

b Quoniam in te Deus est, et non est Deus alius præter te: tu enim es Deus, et non sciebamus, Deus Israel Salvator, (Isa. xlv. 14); . . . Hic Deus noster, et non deputabitur alius absque

ON THE CONSUBSTANTIALITY OF THE SON.

[1] vacate.

[2] claritatem.

[3] virtutes.

[4] concretus ex utroque genere.

[5] pariter ὁμογενῆ sive ὁμοούσιον.

of David also, Psalm xlvi. 10, "Be still[1], and know that I am God, I will be exalted among the heathen, and I will be exalted in the earth;" that of Paul also, Romans ix. 5, "Who is over all things God blessed for ever;" also that of the Apocalypse i. 8. and xxi. 6, "I am Alpha and Omega, the beginning and the end;" and that of Isaiah, again, xxxv. 4, "Our God will recompense judgment, He will come and save us;" and that of the same Isaiah xlii. 8, "I am the Lord God, that is My Name, My brightness[2] will I not give to another, nor My powers[3] to graven images." Now these and other passages, in which the Supreme God is clearly designated, Cyprian, I say, understands to be said of Christ. To which you may add that, in chap. 10. of the same book[d], he professedly undertakes to prove; "That Christ is both Man and God, made up OF BOTH NATURES[4], that He might be the mediator between us and the Father;" words which plainly imply, that Christ is equally of one nature[5], or of one substance, with God the Father, in that He is God, and with us men, in that He is Man. For the rest, it is certain, that these books of Testimonies, addressed to Quirinus, are the genuine production of Cyprian; since Jerome, Dial. I. against the Pelagians[e], Augustine, book iv. against the two Letters of Pelagius, c. 8 and 10[f], Gennadius, in his Catalogue under Pelagius, and Bede, Retract. on Acts, c. iii., do all in express terms attribute them to Cyprian. The criticism of Erasmus, therefore, is rash, when he declares that in his view it is more probable, that these books are not the
[365] work of Cyprian. And as to the reason which he gives for his criticism, namely, that the author does not display Cyprian's style any where, save in the preface, who would not be surprised that it should have fallen from so great a man? For it was only in the preface that Cyprian could have displayed his style; inasmuch as the entire three books are nothing

illo, (Baruch. iii. 35); . . Vacate et cognoscite, quoniam ego sum Deus. Exaltabor in gentibus, et exaltabor in terra, (Psal. xlvi. 10); . . . Qui est super omnia Deus benedictus in sæcula, (Rom. ix. 5); . . . Ego sum Alpha et Omega, initium et finis, (Apoc. i. 8; xxi. 6); . . . Deus noster judicium retribuet, ipse veniet et salvos faciet nos, (Isa. xxxv. 4); . . . Ego Dominus Deus, hoc mihi nomen est, claritatem meam alii non dabo, neque virtutes meas sculptilibus, (Id. xlii. 8.) [ch. vi., vii., pp. 286, 287. In translating these passages S. Cyprian's version of the texts of Scripture is followed.]

[d] Quod et homo et Deus Christus EX UTROQUE GENERE concretus, ut Mediator esse inter nos et Patrem posset.—[p. 288.]

[e] [§ 32. vol. ii. p. 715.]

[f] [Vol. ix. p. 480, 485.]

else than a collection of testimonies of Scripture, arranged under certain heads, in citing which it was natural that the saint would follow the Latin version of the Scripture, which was received and circulated in Africa in his own time.

2. But in the other writings of Cyprian also, you may every where meet with passages which remarkably set forth the true Divinity of the Son. I will here produce one or two. In his 63rd epistle to Cæcilius, near the beginning[g], he calls Jesus Christ "our Lord and God," as he does a second time also in a subsequent part of the same epistle[h]. There is, however, a marked passage in his treatise On the Vanity of Idols, in which Cyprian thus speaks concerning the Word[1] and Son of God[i]; "As the Dispenser[2] and Master, therefore, of this grace and teaching, the Word[1] and Son of God is sent, who was foretold of by all the prophets in times past as the Enlightener and Teacher of the race of man. This is the Power of God, This His Reason, This His Wisdom and Glory: He descends into the Virgin, and puts on flesh by the co-operation of the Holy Spirit, (or rather, as it should be read, the Holy Spirit puts on flesh,) God is united with[3] man, This is our God, This is the Christ." Here I embrace, as the true reading, *carnem Spiritus sanctus*[4] *induitur*, because most of the oldest MSS. exhibit the passage in this 132
form. Certain sciolists, as I conceive, corrupted the true text [366]
in some of the copies, supposing forsooth, that by the Holy Spirit none other than the Third Person of the Godhead could be meant. We have, however, elsewhere[k] shewn that Each several Person of the Trinity[5], because of the divine and spiritual nature common to the Three, is called the

[1] Sermone.
[2] arbiter.
[3] miscetur cum.
[4] *sancti*, edd.
[5] Unamquamque Trinitatis hypostasim.

[g] Jesus Christus, Dominus et Deus noster.—Page 84. [p. 104.]

[h] Page 86. [p. 109.]

[i] Hujus igitur gratiæ disciplinæque arbiter et magister Sermo et Filius Dei mittitur, qui per prophetas omnes retro illuminator et doctor humani generis prædicabatur. Hic est virtus Dei, hic ratio, hic sapientia ejus et gloria, hic in Virginem illabitur, carnem Spiritu Sancto co-operante induitur, (*leg.* carnem Spiritus Sancti induitur, *Bull.*) Deus cum homine miscetur, hic Deus noster, hic Christus est. —Page 170. [p. 228. The text is here given as it stood in the editions before the Benedictine; the emendation suggested by Bp. Bull, as printed in the Latin, stands thus, carnem Spiritus *Sancti* induitur, on which Dr. Burton's note is, "Read *Sanctus*, the reading which some MSS. exhibit, and which the Benedictine editor has received;" no MS. reads *Sancti*; it may therefore be inferred that the word which Bp. Bull intended in his emendation is *Sanctus*, and this view has been acted on in the translation].

[k] [Book i. 2. 5. p. 52. See also the Benedictine editor's preface to St. Hilary's works, § 57.—B.]

ON THE CONSUBSTANTIALITY OF THE SON.

Spirit, both in the Scriptures and throughout the writings of the ancients; [a fact] which is also noted on this passage in the margin, in some of the MSS., as Pamelius intimates, who, notwithstanding, thought that no alteration ought to be made in the reading, fearing, I suppose, lest the Antitrinitarians should draw their poison out of this place, and allege that Cyprian did not acknowledge the Third Person of the Godhead. Vain fear! inasmuch as it is abundantly clear from many passages of Cyprian, that he believed in the whole consubstantial Trinity, an assertion which we may also with good grounds make with regard to the other fathers, who have used a similar mode of expression. Thus in his letter to Jubaianus, about baptizing heretics, he proves that the baptism of heretics is not valid by this argument[l]; "If any one," he says, "could be baptized among heretics, it follows that he might also obtain remission of sins. If he has obtained remission of sins, [he has also been sanctified and made the temple of God,] I ask, Of what God? If [you say] of the Creator, he could not [be so], for he has not believed in Him: if of Christ, neither could he have been made His temple, who denies that Christ is God. If of the Holy Ghost, seeing that the Three are One (*cum tres unum sint,*) how can the Holy Ghost be at peace with him who is an enemy either of the Son or of the Father?" Here you see that the Holy Ghost is expressly called God, equally with the Father and the Son, as we have already[m] observed was done by Tertullian. You may also, by the way, observe that Cyprian, in this place, certainly has an eye to the passage of John, in his 1st Epistle
[367] v. 7, "And these three are One" (*et hi tres unum sunt*). In his treatise 'On the Unity of the Church,' however, (chap. 4, near the end), he professedly quotes this passage, in these words[n]; "Concerning the Father, the Son, and the Holy

[l] Si, baptizari quis apud hæreticos potuit, utique et remissam peccatorum consequi potuit. Si peccatorum remissam consecutus est, et sanctificatus est, et templum Dei factus est; [si sanctificatus est, si templum Dei factus est,] quæro, cujus Dei? si Creatoris, non potuit, quia in eum non credidit: si Christi, nec hujus fieri potuit templum, qui negat Deum Christum: si Spiritus Sancti, cum tres unum sint, quomodo Spiritus S. placatus esse ei potest, qui aut Filii aut Patris inimicus est.—Page 106. [p. 133. The words within brackets were omitted by Bp. Bull.]

[m] [Page 202.]

[n] [Et iterum de Patre, et Filio, et Spiritu Sancto scriptum est, *Et hi tres unum sunt.*—[Page 195, 196.]

Ghost, it is written, 'And these Three are One[1].'" So also, before Cyprian, Tertullian manifestly alluded to the same passage in his work against Praxeas, c. 25 [o]; "The connection," he says, "of the Father in the Son, and of the Son in the Paraclete produces Three coherent, one from another; and these Three are one [substance] (*unum*), not one [person] (*unus*) [p]." This is to be observed in opposition to those who suspect that these words were introduced into the text of John by the Catholics, after the Arian controversy. To return, however, to the point from which I have digressed a little. Cyprian, in the same epistle to Jubaianus [q], also proves that baptism conferred in the name of Jesus Christ only[2], is of no efficacy, from the circumstance that "He Himself commands the nations to be baptized in the full and united[3] Trinity." Where by "the full and united Trinity" it is manifest that the Three Persons, the Father, the Son, and the Holy Ghost are designated, as all subsisting in one Godhead; and, therefore, that the Holy Ghost, equally with the Son, is united[4] with God the Father in the same fellowship of Divine honour[5].

3. In opposition to these passages of Cyprian, so clear and so express, Sandius [r], in order to persuade the reader that this most blessed martyr favoured the heresy which was afterwards called Arian, brings forward, or rather refers to[6], certain expressions of Cyprian, which may seem to savour of Arianism[7]. Most of them, however, relate to the economy[8] of the Son; as that Christ prayed to the Father to glorify Him, and fulfilled His will even unto the obedience of drinking the cup, and of undergoing death, &c. Others are to [368] be referred to the subordination of the Son, in that He is the Son, to the Father, as to His Principle and Author[9]. On this ground it is, that Cyprian, in his 74th epistle, addressed to Pompeius, declares that the Holy Ghost is less than the Son [s], as he that is sent is less than he that sends

[1] unum.
[2] in solo J.C. nomine.
[3] adunata.
[4] adunari.
[5] in eodem divini honoris consortio.
[6] indicat.
[7] Arianismum sapere.
[8] οἰκονομίαν.
[9] principium atque auctorem suum.

[o] Connexus Patris in Filio, et Filii in Paracleto tres efficit cohærentes, alterum ex altero; qui tres unum sint, non unus [quomodo dictum est, ego et Pater unum sumus; ad substantiæ unitatem non ad numeri singularitatem.—Page 515.]

[p] [See also Tertullian de Baptismo, c. 6. p. 226.—B.]

[q] [Quando] ipse Christus gentes baptizari jubeat in plena et adunata Trinitate.—Page 107. [p. 135.]

[r] Enucl. Hist. Eccles., i. p. 112, 113.

[s] [Page 139. St. Cyprian does not say this; his words are; Qui potest apud hæreticos baptizatus Christum induere, multo magis potest Spiritum

him. The rest are mere calumnies fastened by Sandius
on the holy martyr; as, for instance, when he asserts that
Cyprian taught, "that Christ was created[1] out of the mouth
[1] procreatum. of the Most High." It is true that Cyprian, in the second
book of his Testimonies against the Jews, c. 1, quotes the
words of Solomon, (Prov. viii. 22—30, inclusive,) with the
[2] primogenitum. view of proving, that "Christ is the First-begotten[2], the
Wisdom of God, by whom all things were made[t]." He
then cites a passage from Ecclus. xxiv. in which these words
[Ecclus. xxiv. 3.] occur; "I (Wisdom) came forth out of the mouth of the
Most High, the first-begotten before every creature." But
who would hence infer with Sandius, that Cyprian taught,
[3] procreatum. that Christ was created[3] or made out of the mouth of God,
like the word, that is, of a human being, which has no existence before it be put forth from the mouth, as the Valentinian and other heretics supposed. Nay, in these very
books of Testimonies Cyprian expressly teaches out of the
Scriptures, that the Son of God has neither beginning nor
end of existence, as will be shewn in its proper place[u].
With the like unfairness the sophist cites the following
opinion as if it were Cyprian's; "That Christ did not presume to compare Himself to God, neither is He equal to
Him, but that the Father is greater;" subjoining, "statements which Huet in his Origeniana, book iii. append. n. 12,
allows to savour of Arianism;" and adds, "that is to say,
he thinks it robbery[5], for Christ to be equal with God;
[and] that there is as much difference between Christ and
God, as there is between the Apostles and Christ." The
[369] reader who loves the truth, however, should know, that in
[4] Libellus de Singularitate Clericorum. a short treatise on the Celibacy of the Clergy[4], the following words are indeed found[x]: "If Christ ventured to compare Himself to God, who saith, My Father is greater than
[5] coæquare. I; or if the Apostles ventured to equal[5] themselves to Christ,

Sanctum, quem Christus misit, accipere. Cæterum major erit mittente, qui missus est, ut incipiat foris baptizatus Christum quidem induisse sed Spiritum Sanctum non potuisse percipere: his argument, that on the view he is opposing the Holy Spirit would be greater than the Son—He who is sent than He who sends.]

[t] Christum primogenitum esse, Sapientiam Dei, per quem omnia facta sint .... Ego ex ore Altissimi prodivi primogenita ante omnem creaturam. [p. 284.]

[u] [Book iii. ch. iv.]

[x] Si Christus se ipsum comparare ausus est Deo, qui ait, *Pater major me est;* aut si Apostoli coæquare semetipsos ausi sunt Christo, et nos hodie apostolis æquales facit consimilis fortitudo.—Page 304. [p. clxxix.]

a fortitude like theirs makes us also at the present day equal to Apostles;" but all learned men, at this day, including Huet himself, agree in thinking that this treatise is spurious and supposititious. "That this work is not Cyprian's," such are the words of Huet in the passage cited by Sandius, "is proclaimed by the following barbarous phrases, of a class of which you find none in the pure and polished language of Cyprian; *constitutionarios, repulsorium, vulgaritatis, fluxurarum, probrositas, &c.* Who would say, that Cyprian was the father of monstrosities such as these?" Here is an excellent specimen of the candour of Sandius! Meanwhile, the words quoted, whosesoever they be, easily admit of a sound interpretation, and may be understood of Christ, whilst living upon earth, and fulfilling the economy of our redemption. Nay, that this was the very meaning of the author is apparent from his quoting, after a few intervening sentences, the following words out of the Epistle to the Philippians, chap. ii.[y]; "Let this mind be in you, which was also in Christ Jesus, who being in the form of God thought it not robbery to be equal with God, but emptied Himself[1], and took upon Him the form of a servant." This passage of Paul, thus translated, manifestly intimates that Christ, inasmuch as He was[2] in the form of God, might indeed, without arrogance and without any injury to God His Father, have thought Himself equal to God, and have borne Himself as such: but, notwithstanding, He emptied Himself, &c. Sandius again foully calumniates the saint, in attributing to him presently afterwards this heresy; "That the Word" (in Christ) "was in the stead of a soul;" for it is the unvarying doctrine of Cyprian, as all who are not altogether strangers to his writings are aware, that the Word, or Son of God, took on Him not only flesh, but man[3] and the son of man, that is to say, true and perfect man, consisting of a reasonable soul and a human body.

BOOK II. CHAP. X. § 3, 4. CYPRIAN. 133

[1] exinanivit, [ἐκένωσεν.]

[2] constitutus fuit.

[3] hominem.

[370]

4. But who, that has any love for truth and candour, could patiently endure this most shameless sophist, when he endeavours to prove out of Ruffinus, that Cyprian was an Arian? "Wherefore," these are his words, "Ruffinus, in

[y] Hoc sentite de vobis, quod et in Christo Jesu, qui cum in forma Dei esset constitutus, non rapinam arbitratus est esse se æqualem Deo, sed semetipsum exinanivit, formam servi accipiens.—p. 305. [p. clxxix.]

ON THE CONSUBSTANTIALITY OF THE SON.

his Apology for Origen, says, that 'very many in those parts, (he is speaking of Constantinople,) 'were persuaded that the holy martyr Cyprian was of that belief, which has been set forth, not correctly, by Tertullian in his writings.' Tertullian he certainly honoured with the title of master, and applied himself[1] daily to the study of his writings; and that Tertullian's belief was Arian, we have already stated." A little after he subjoins, "It is clear from the words of Ruffinus which immediately precede, that Arianism and Macedonianism were what Ruffinus and the orientals meant." But with what face could he have referred his reader to the preceding words of Ruffinus? seeing that from them it will be clearer than noon-day, that most dishonestly is Ruffinus alleged to prove that Cyprian's belief was the same as that of Arius. Here, reader, is the passage of Ruffinus entire[z]; "The whole collection[2] of the Epistles of the martyr St. Cyprian," he says, "is usually written in one volume: in this collection, certain heretics who blaspheme against the Holy Ghost, inserted a short treatise of Tertullian on the Trinity, written, so far as regards the truth of our faith, in a way open to blame; and making as many transcripts as they could from these copies, they caused them to be circulated throughout the great city of Constantinople at a low
[371] price, in order that people, attracted by the smallness of the price, might the more readily buy their unknown and latent snares; that by this means the heretics might be able to gain belief for their misbelief[3] from the authority of so great a man. It happened, however, that not long after this had been done[4], certain of our catholic brethren, happening to be there[5], laid open the artifices of the villainy which had been practised, and in some measure recovered such as they could from the entanglement of this error; not-

[1] incubuit.
[2] omne corpus.
[3] fidem perfidiæ suæ.
[4] recenti adhuc facto.
[5] inventi

[z] See Ruffinus' Apology for Origen among the works of Jerome, tom. ix. p. 131. Sancti Cypriani, martyris solet omne Epistolarum corpus in uno codice scribi. Huic corpori hæretici quidam, qui in Spiritum S. blasphemant, Tertulliani libellum de Trinitate reprehensibiliter, quantum ad veritatem fidei nostræ pertinet, scriptum inserentes, et quamplurimos codices de talibus exemplariis conscribentes, per totam Constantinopolim urbem maximam distrahi pretio viliori fecerunt, ut exiguitate pretii homines illecti ignotos et latentes dolos facilius compararent: quo per hoc invenirent hæretici perfidiæ suæ fidem tanti viri auctoritate conquirere. Accidit tamen, ut recenti adhuc facto quidam ex nostris fratribus catholicis inventi admissi sceleris commenta retegerent, et ex parte aliqua, si quos possent, ab erroris hujus laqueis revocarent. Quamplurimis tamen in illis partibus, sanc-

BOOK II. CHAP. X. § 4. CYPRIAN.

withstanding, very many in those parts were persuaded that the holy martyr Cyprian was of that belief, which has been set forth, not correctly, by Tertullian in his writings." By this time any one may clearly see that the heretics at Constantinople were Pneumatomachians, who were endeavouring to persuade others that Cyprian's belief was different from the catholic; and that they went about to prove this not from any genuine work of the martyr, (inasmuch as he has every where written as a Catholic on the doctrine of the Holy Trinity,) but from a treatise of some other writer, which these worthless deceivers had themselves inserted among the works of Cyprian, by an impious fraud which was soon after discovered by the Catholics. And, in truth, no ecclesiastical writer has ever stated that Cyprian wrote a work on the Holy Trinity. Nor indeed do I believe that that treatise which these heretics circulated[1] was Tertullian's throughout, but that it was in many places corrupted by themselves. For Tertullian never held the opinions of the Pneumatomachians, but, even when he had fallen into heresy, constantly believed three Persons of one Godhead, and expressly called the Holy Ghost *God*, as well as the Father and the Son, as is evident from the passages which we have already quoted from him. But the Catholics of that period did not care much about the character and reputation of Tertullian; for, on account of other doctrines of his, he was at that time regarded among all the orthodox as a heretic and an alien from the Church. Of Novatian, too[a], whose treatise on the Trinity (the one, I mean, which is now extant among the works of Tertullian) was thought by Jerome to have been [372] that which was circulated by the heretics, almost the same must be said[b]; for he too held the catholic view on the Trinity, as we shall presently shew. The reader, however, 134 may see further from these and many other indications, what it is that Sandius means by "bringing out the kernel[2] of ecclesiastical history;" namely, to seek out and bring together, from every quarter, exploded and silly stories, and manifest

[1] venditatum.

[2] enucleare.

tum martyrem Cyprianum hujus fidei, quæ a Tertulliano non recte scripta est, fuisse persuasum est. [Epilog. ad Apol. sive de Adult. Lib. Orig., p. 53.]

[a] See Jerome, advers. Ruffin. Apol. ii. 5, sub finem, [§ 19. vol. ii. p. 513.]

[b] [That is, that his work was corrupted by those who circulated it as St. Cyprian's.]

ON THE CONSUBSTANTIALITY OF THE SON. falsehoods, wherewith to gain credit and authority for the condemned heresy of the Arians. And thus far have we laid open the views of Cyprian.

NOVATIAN. 5. Next to Cyprian follows Novatian, or the author of the treatise On the Trinity[c], which we have just mentioned. Of this author Petavius[d] declares, "that he did not speak with sufficient accuracy, nay, that he has made very many[1] absurd statements" respecting the mystery of the Trinity; and Sandius[e], relying, as usual, too much on Petavius's judgment, classes him amongst those who taught the same opinions as Arius, before his time. It will, however, be shewn in its proper place, that these 'inaccurate[2] and absurd statements' ought to be referred either to the economy[3] of the Son, or to that inferiority[4] which the Son has when compared with the Father, regarded as His Author and Principle[5], which [inferiority] has been acknowledged by all Catholics, even since the council of Nice. In the meantime we will prove, by adducing a few, but those very clear testimonies from the author himself, that, whoever he was, he by no means agreed in opinion with Arius on the chief point[6]. To this proof we premise this one observation, that Petavius himself elsewhere[f] acknowledges, in express terms, that those
[373] 'inaccurate and absurd statements,' which the author inserted in his work, "are at variance with the catholic rule, either in the mere mode of expression, or at any rate without trenching on the substance of the mystery[7]." With this brief observation, let us pass on to the subject itself. In the twenty-third chapter[g] the author thus establishes the divinity[8] of Christ; "If Christ be merely man, how is it that He says,
[John xvi. 28.] 'I came forth from God, and am come,' since it is certain that man was made by God, and did not come forth from God? but in a manner in which man did not come forth from God, did the Word of God come forth [from Him];" presently he adds, "[It was] God, therefore, [that] came

[1] pleraque.
[2] minus accurata.
[3] οἰκονομίαν.
[4] minoritatem.
[5] auctorem et principium.
[6] in rei summa.
[7] citra mysterii substantiam.
[8] divinitatem adstruit.

[c] Novatian wrote this treatise "on the Trinity," about the year 257. It is usually printed with the works of Tertullian. Cave.—BOWYER.

[d] De Trinit. i. 5. 5.

[e] Enucl., Hist. Eccl., i. p. 110.

[f] Preface to vol. ii. 5. 3.

[g] Si homo tantummodo Christus, quomodo dicit, *Ego ex Deo prodii, et veni*, cum constet hominem a Deo factum esse, non ex Deo processisse? ex Deo autem homo quomodo non processit, sic Dei Verbum processit. . . . Deus ergo processit ex Deo, dum qui processit Sermo, Deus est, qui processit ex Deo.—[p. 721.]

forth from God, inasmuch as the Word which came forth is God, who came forth from God." What is there said, almost in the Nicene Creed itself, more explicitly opposed to Arius? for the author expressly opposes these two things, *to be made by God*, and *to come forth from God;* and he affirms no less expressly that Christ, in His more excellent nature, was not made; in other words[1] was not[2] created, but proceeded from God Himself, and therefore is God of[3] God. A little afterwards in the same chapter[h], he says again; "If Christ be only man, what is [the meaning of] that which He says, 'I and the Father are One?' For in what sense [is it true that] 'I and the Father are One,' if He be not both God and Son, who on that account may be called One [with the Father], in that He is of Him[4], and in that He is His Son, and in that He is born of Him, seeing that He is found to have proceeded from Him,—through which also He is God." From this passage there is a clear refutation of Petavius's calumny against the author of this treatise, where he alleges that[i] "he explained those words in the tenth of John, 'I and the Father are One,' in a manner almost Arian;" quoting, in confirmation of this censure, those words of his out of the 22nd chapter[k]; "But in that He saith '*One*,' it is with reference to concord, and sameness of sentiment, and to the fellowship itself of love; so that the Father and the Son are with good reason One, through concord, and through love, and through affection." But, I affirm, it is certain from the passage which we just now adduced, that the author altogether understood those words of John as Catholics do, not of concord alone, or consent of will, (as the Arians did,) but also, and primarily, of that communion of substance which exists between the Father and the Son. This indeed the author expresses clearly enough in that very passage which Petavius cites: in that he immediately subjoins these words, (which Petavius against all good [374]

[1] sive.
[2] minime.
[3] ex.
[4] ex ipso.

[h] Si homo tantummodo Christus, quid est quod ait, *Ego et Pater unum sumus?* quomodo enim *Ego et Pater unum sumus*, si non et Deus est et Filius, qui idcirco unum potest dici, dum ex ipso est, et dum Filius ejus est, et dum ex ipso nascitur, dum ex ipso processisse reperitur, per quod et Deus est.—[p. 722.]

[i] Ubi supra.

[k] *Unum* autem quod ait, ad concordiam et eandem sententiam, et ad ipsam charitatis societatem pertinet; ut merito unum sit Pater et Filius per concordiam, et per amorem, et per dilectionem.—[p. 720.]

ON THE CONSUBSTANTIALITY OF THE SON.

faith[1] suppresses[1];) "And since He is of[2] the Father, whatsoever That[3] is, the Son is; the distinction still remaining, that He who is the Son, be not the Father, forasmuch as neither is He the Son, who is the Father." For, without doubt, he is here attacking exclusively the heresy of Sabellius, which declares the Father and the Son to be in such sense One, as altogether to do away with the distinction of Persons. In opposition to this heresy he teaches, that the Father and Son are indeed One, as well by consent of will as by unity of substance also, since the Son is derived from the very fountain of the Father's essence; but that notwithstanding they are altogether Two in subsistence, or (in other words) in person. Certainly the unfairness of the Jesuit Petavius towards the ancient writers is quite intolerable, in thus wresting, as he does throughout, to a foreign and heretical sense, their sound and catholic statements, [and that] in opposition to their own evident mind and view.

[1] haud bonâ fide.
[2] ex.
[3] illud.

6. But I return to our author, in order to adduce but one passage more from him, such as to confirm most clearly the consubstantiality of the Son. It will be found in the eleventh chapter[m], where the author thus speaks of the twofold nature of Christ, the divine and the human: "For Scripture as well proclaims on the one hand that the Christ is God, as it proclaims on the other hand that God is very
[375] man: it sets forth as well Jesus Christ [as] man, as it sets forth the Lord Christ [as] God also. Forasmuch as it does not put before us that He is the Son of God only, but also [that He is the Son] of man; nor does it say that He is [the Son] of man only, but is wont to speak of Him as [the Son] of God also; that so, seeing He is of Both, He may be [proved to be] Both[4], lest, if He were One of the Two[5] only, He could not [be proved to be even] that One[6]. FOR AS NATURE ITSELF HAS TAUGHT[7] THAT HE WHO IS OF

[4] utrumque sit.
[5] alterum.
[6] alterum.
[7] præscripsit.

[1] Et quoniam ex Patre est, quicquid illud est, Filius est; manente tamen distinctione, ut non sit Pater ille qui Filius, quia nec Filius ille qui Pater est.—[Ibid.]

[m] Tam enim Scriptura etiam Deum adnuntiat Christum, quam etiam ipsum hominem adnuntiat Deum; tam hominem descripsit Jesum Christum, quam etiam Deum quoque descripsit Christum Dominum. Quoniam nec Dei tantum illum Filium esse proponit, sed et hominis; nec hominis tantum dicit, sed et Dei referre consuevit; ut dum ex utroque est, utrumque sit, ne, si alterum tantum sit, alterum esse non possit. UT ENIM PRÆSCRIPSIT IPSA NATURA HOMINEM CREDENDUM ESSE, QUI EX HOMINE SIT, ITA EADEM NATURA PRÆSCRIBIT ET DEUM CRE-

NOVATIAN.

MAN, MUST BE BELIEVED TO BE MAN, SO THE SAME NATURE EQUALLY TEACHES THAT HE ALSO MUST BE BELIEVED TO BE GOD, WHO IS OF GOD; lest, if He be not God also, whenas He is of God, He be not man either, albeit He be of man; and so in either one of the two both be endangered, the one being proved to have lost its credibility through the
other." Surely, his mind must be completely in the dark, 135
who does not at once clearly see, that in these words it is most explicitly taught, that Christ is consubstantial with God the Father, in that He is of God, just as He is consubstantial with us men, in that He is of man; and that He is not less very God, than He is very man. For the rest, I will add concerning this author, though it is not required by my argument[1], that he held the catholic doctrine respecting the Holy Ghost also. For in chap. 29, at the very beginning, he teaches that, according to the rule of faith, we must believe not only in the Father and the Son, but also in the Holy Ghost: and in the course of the chapter, he assigns to the Holy Ghost such powers and operations as are in no wise compatible with a created being: and lastly, near the end of the chapter, he expressly attributes to the same Holy Ghost "divine eternity." In what sense, however, he said that the Holy Ghost is less than the Son we have shewn elsewhere[n]. And let it suffice to have said thus much at present concerning this author.

THEOGNOSTUS.

7. We shall number Theognostus of Alexandria with the writers mentioned in this chapter; although the age when
he lived is scarcely ascertained[o]. This one thing we may be [376]
assured of, that he was much earlier than the Nicene council, and later than Origen. It is certain that he was later than Origen, because Photius taunts[2] him as a follower of Origen. But that he lived long before the council of Nice you may gather from the fact, that Athanasius (in his treatise on that passage in the Gospel, "Whosoever shall speak a word against the Son of Man," &c.) enumerates[p] him among "the

[1] ex abundanti.

[2] sugillat.

DENDUM ESSE, QUI EX DEO SIT; ne si non et Deus fuerit, cum ex Deo sit, jam nec homo sit, licet ex homine fuerit, et in alterutro utrumque periclitetur, dum alterum altero fidem perdidisse convincitur.—[p. 713.]

[n] See above, c. 3. § 17. [p. 132.]

[o] Theognostus seems to have flourished about the year 270. Cave.—BOWYER.

[p] Tom. i. p. 971. [Epist. iv. ad Serap. 9. vol. i. p. 702.]

ON THE CONSUBSTANTIALITY OF THE SON.

ancients," (*παλαιοὺς ἄνδρας*); and places his testimony next after that of Origen. The same Athanasius, in his work on the Decrees of the Nicene council[q], calls him "a learned man," (*ἄνδρα λόγιον*,) and in the treatise quoted just before he gives him the appellation of "the admirable," (*τὸν θαυμάσιον*). He was the author of books of the Hypotyposes[1] which have long ago been lost. But out of the second of them Athanasius quotes this illustrious testimony to the consubstantiality[r]; "The substance of the Son is not any one that was brought in[2] from without, nor was it superinduced out of nothing; but it sprang[3] from the substance of the Father, as the radiance[4] of the light, and vapour of water; for neither the radiance, nor the vapour, is the water itself, or the sun itself; nor yet is it any thing alien, but it is an effluence of the Father's substance, yet so that the Father's substance underwent not division. For as the sun remains the same and is not diminished by the rays poured forth by it, so neither did the Father's substance undergo alteration,
[377] in having the Son an image of itself." Surely nothing was ever said, even in the venerable council of the Nicene fathers itself, more expressly opposed to the Arians.

8. And, consequently, that cannot be true which Photius writes, cod. 106, (which yet not only Sandius[s], but the very learned Huet[t] also, places confidence in,) to the effect that this Theognostus taught, and that in the very book which Athanasius cites, the second book of the Hypotyposes, that the Son of God, in the sense in which He is properly the Son of God, is a created being. Nay, Photius himself detracts from his own trustworthiness, when, towards the conclusion of the same chapter, he states that Theognostus said that the Son of God is "not circumscribed in His operation[5]," which certainly cannot be said of any creature. Moreover he soon after admits that this writer, in the seventh book of his Hypotyposes, treated with more reverence[6] both of other subjects,

[1] *τῶν ὑποτυπώσεων.*
[2] *ἐπευρεθεῖσα.*
[3] *ἔφυ.*
[4] *ἀπαύγασμα.*
[5] *τῇ ἐνεργείᾳ μὴ περιγραφόμενον.*
[6] *εὐσεβέστερον.*

[q] Tom. i. p. 274. [§ 25. vol. i. p. 230.]

[r] *οὐκ ἔξωθέν τίς ἐστιν ἐφευρεθεῖσα ἡ τοῦ υἱοῦ οὐσία, οὐδὲ ἐκ μὴ ὄντων ἐπεισήχθη, ἀλλὰ ἐκ τῆς τοῦ πατρὸς οὐσίας ἔφυ, ὡς τοῦ φωτὸς τὸ ἀπαύγασμα, ὡς ὕδατος ἀτμίς· οὔτε γὰρ τὸ ἀπαύγασμα, οὔτε ἡ ἀτμὶς, αὐτὸ τὸ ὕδωρ ἐστὶν, ἢ αὐτὸς ὁ ἥλιος· οὔτε ἀλλότριον, ἀλλὰ ἀπόρροια τῆς τοῦ πατρὸς οὐσίας, οὐ μερισμὸν ὑπομεινάσης τῆς τοῦ πατρὸς οὐσίας. ὡς γὰρ μένων ὁ ἥλιος ὁ αὐτὸς οὐ μειοῦται ταῖς ἐκχεομέναις ὑπ' αὐτοῦ αὐγαῖς, οὕτως οὐδὲ ἡ οὐσία τοῦ Πατρὸς ἀλλοίωσιν ὑπέμεινεν, εἰκόνα ἑαυτῆς ἔχουσα τὸν υἱόν.*—Ibid.

[s] Enucl. H. E., i. p. 109.

[t] Origenian., p. 45. [p. 134.]

"and especially, towards the end of the book, concerning the Son[u]." Certainly, what Theognostus wrote in that place respecting the Son of God must have been very excellent, when Photius himself commended it as expressed with especial reverence[1]. But who can believe, that so great a man, as it is certain Theognostus was, could maintain in the same treatise positions so incompatible? The truth is, Photius, from his very bitter hatred to Origen, was unfair towards this Theognostus also, his follower and defender, and on that account he understood his writings in a bad sense, or rather wished them to be so understood by others. Theognostus, it would appear[2], made that statement as the opinion of others, with whom he was disputing, and not as declaring his own [378]
view. This is gathered, not obscurely, from Photius himself, for, after charging Theognostus with the blasphemy in question, he soon after introduces a supposed person defending that illustrious man, on the ground that he had put forward these statements, "by way of argument, and not as his own opinion," (*ἐν γυμνασίας λόγῳ καὶ οὐ δόξης*). And this Photius does not deny, but only censures a method of disputation of that kind, at least respecting the divine mysteries, and in a written discourse; although I have no doubt that he would have easily forgiven this fault in any other writer who was not an Origenist. The great Athanasius, however, puts the point beyond all controversy; for, after having recited the testimony of Theognostus, which we have quoted above, he immediately adds[x]; "Theognostus then, having prosecuted the above enquiries in the way of argument, afterwards, in laying down his own view, expressed himself thus." It is therefore clear that, in this second book of Hy- 136
potyposes, Theognostus had first put forward the views of the heterodox, and amongst them the opinion of those, who said that the Son of God was a created being: and this in such a way as, to a certain degree, to assume their character, and represent their arguments; that at last, however, he stated his own purely catholic view, which was opposed to theirs, in the words quoted by Athanasius.

[1] pie imprimis dicta.

[2] scilicet.

[u] [*εὐσεβέστερόν πως περί τε τῶν ἄλλων διαλαμβάνει,*] *καὶ μάλιστα πρὸς τῷ τέλει τοῦ λόγου περὶ τοῦ υἱοῦ.*—[Phot. cod. 106.]

[x] *ὁ μὲν οὖν Θεόγνωστος, τὰ πρότερα ὡς ἐν γυμνασίᾳ ἐξετάσας, ὕστερον τὴν ἑαυτοῦ δόξαν τιθεὶς, οὕτως εἴρηκεν.*—[S. Athan., ubi supra.]

ON THE CONSUBSTANTIALITY OF THE SON.

9. That which Photius further objects against Theognostus, namely, that he taught that the Son of God "presides over rational beings only," (*τῶν λογικῶν μόνον ἐπιστατεῖν,*) is easily removed. For it would seem that the holy man by no means meant, that the dominion of the Son is in such wise tied to rational creatures, as that the other creatures are excluded from His rule. Far be it! For how could he have restrained the divine providence and power of the Son of God
[379] from any one of God's creatures, who declared, as Photius himself, as we have seen, admits, that the Son is in no degree whatsoever circumscribed in His power and operation? What follows? Without doubt Theognostus meant the same as his master Origen, who, as Photius (cod. 8) reports, taught[y] "that the Father indeed pervades all things that exist, the Son so far only as rational beings, the Holy Ghost so far only as the saved." And how these statements are to be understood, we learn from Huet in his Origeniana[z]; "These assertions," he says, "if taken thus apart from the context[1], could scarcely escape censure. But if any one will look rather to the meaning of Origen than to his words, he will think otherwise. For although the external operations of the Holy Trinity be one and the same, and whatsoever in things external [to the Godhead] the Father doeth, that the Son also doeth, [and] that the Holy Ghost also doeth; still there are certain things which are usually assigned to the Father, others to the Son, others to the Holy Ghost. As, therefore, to the Father is commonly attributed the creation of the world, although it is [the work] of the Three Persons equally, so does Origen ascribe to the Son, who is Reason[2], the care of all reasonable beings[3], and assigns to the Holy Ghost the bestowing of holiness, according to Romans i. 4, and 2 Thess. ii. 13, although it be owing to the whole Trinity. In 1 Peter i. 2, it is written 'According to the foreknowledge of God the Father, unto sanctification[4] of the Spirit, unto obedience and sprinkling of the blood of Jesus Christ.'" That this was Origen's meaning Huet proves from the clearest testimonies alleged out of his works. To these he also adds an illustrious passage of

1 ἀποτόμως ita sumpta.

2 λόγος.

3 λογικῶν.

4 in sanctificationem.

y διήκειν μὲν τὸν πατέρα διὰ πάντων τῶν ὄντων, τὸν δὲ υἱὸν μέχρι τῶν λογικῶν μόνον [μόνων], τὸ δὲ πνεῦμα μέχρι μόνον [μόνων] τῶν σεσωσμένων.—[Phot. ibid.]

z Lib. ii. p. 46, 47. [Quæst. 2. 28. p. 135.]

[380]

Paschasius the deacon, on the Holy Spirit, book i. c. 9[a], who adopts the sentiment of Origen, and writes thus; "So far as it is found most manifestly in the Holy Scriptures, the Father Himself performs some operations by Himself, others in a special manner by the Son, others by the Holy Ghost, although under the privilege[1] of a power common [to all Three.] That we exist seems properly to be referred to the Father, 'in whom,' as the Apostle says, 'we live, and move, and have our being:' that, moreover, we are capable of reason, and wisdom, and righteousness, is especially attributed to Him, who is Reason, and Wisdom, and Righteousness, i. e., to the Son; and that being called we are regenerated, and being regenerated are renewed, being renewed are sanctified, is evidently ascribed in the divine oracles to the Person of the Holy Ghost." He further adds also a very remarkable testimony of Augustine[b]; "Just as we call the Word of God alone peculiarly[2] by the name of Wisdom, although, in a sense which includes all[3], both the Holy Ghost and the Father Himself be Wisdom; so is the Holy Ghost peculiarly designated by the name of Love[4], although, in a sense which includes all[5], both the Father and the Son be Love." For the rest, the statement which the same learned Huet had before made in the same passage, that Athanasius, in his treatise on Matthew xii. 32, "had condemned[6] both Origen and his disciple Theognostus" on account of these statements, is not true. For Athanasius only reminds us that the statements of both should be considered, and some deeper sense sought for in them. His words are these[c]: "But I, from what I have learned, think that the opinion of each requires some measure[7] of examination and

[1] sub privilegio potentiæ communis.

[2] proprie.

[3] universaliter.

[4] charitatis.

[5] universaliter.

[6] explosisse.

[7] *μετρίας.*

[a] Quantum in Scripturis sanctis manifestissime deprehenditur, alia Pater ipse per se, alia specialiter per Filium, alia per Spiritum Sanctum, licet sub privilegio potentiæ communis, operatur. Quia *sumus*, ad Patrem proprie referri videtur; *in quo*, sicut apostolus dicit, *vivimus, movemur, et sumus.* Quod vero rationis, et sapientiæ, et justitiæ capaces sumus, illi specialiter, qui est ratio et sapientia et justitia, id est, Filio deputatur. Quod autem vocati regeneramur, et regenerati innovamur, innovati sanctificamur, per divina eloquia personæ Spiritus Sancti evidenter adscribiter.—[Bibl. Patr. Colon. 1618. vol. v. part 3. p. 737.]

[b] Sicut unicum Dei Verbum proprie vocamus nomine *sapientiæ*, cum sit universaliter et Spiritus Sanctus, et Pater ipse Sapientia; ita Spiritus S. proprie nuncupatur vocabulo *charitatis*, cum sit universaliter charitas et Pater et Filius.—Lib. xv. de Trinit. cap. 17. [vol. viii. p. 989. § 31.]

[c] *ἐγὼ δὲ ἀφ' ὧν ἔμαθον, νομίζω τὴν ἑκατέρου διάνοιαν μετρίας τινὸς δοκιμασίας ἐπιδεῖσθαι καὶ κατανοήσεως, μὴ ἄρα κεκρυμμένος ἐστί τις ἐν αὐτοῖς τοῖς ὑπὸ αὐτῶν εἰρημένοις βαθύτερος νοῦς.*—Oper. Athanas., tom. i. p. 972. [Epist. iv. ad Serap. 12. vol. i. p. 703.]

ON THE CONSUBSTANTIALITY OF THE SON.

consideration, whether [it may not be[1] that] there is some actual deeper meaning hidden under their statements." This certainly is not to reject Origen and Theognostus on account of these statements. That profounder sense, moreover, Huet has himself drawn out and given to us. And let thus much be said of the doctrine and faith of the holy Theognostus.

[1] μὴ ἄρα.

[381]

141 [389]

CHAPTER XI.

IN WHICH IS SET FORTH THE CONSENT OF THE DIONYSIUS'S OF ROME AND OF ALEXANDRIA WITH THE NICENE FATHERS.

1. Dionysius, bishop of Rome, who, whilst yet a presbyter, had been designated by his namesake, Dionysius of Alexandria, "a learned and admirable man," (λόγιός τε καὶ θαυμάσιος[d],) flourished[e] in the reigns of the emperors Valerian and
[390] Gallienus. In the fragments of this Dionysius there is nothing that incurs the censure of Petavius, as savouring of Arianism; on the contrary he is praised by him, as entertaining thoroughly catholic views regarding the Holy Trinity. Sandius himself too, who has left nothing unturned[2] in antiquity, which might seem to make ever so little in favour of the Arians, very wisely observes a complete silence concerning this writer, both in his work on Ecclesiastical writers, and in his Nucleus of Ecclesiastical History. In order, however, that the reader who loves truth may not be ignorant of so great a vindicator and witness of the catholic faith, we will bring forward his testimony. He wrote a learned epistle against the Sabellians, which is lost; a portion of it, however, of some length, well worth its weight in gold[3], has been preserved by Athanasius; in which there is contained a most complete confession of the Holy Trinity. For after having therein refuted the dogma of Sabellius, Dionysius goes on thus to speak against another heresy, the opposite of the Sabellian[f]; "And I should naturally, in the next place speak also against those who divide,

[2] nihil non ruspatus est.

[3] auro contra non carum.

[d] See Eusebius, H. E., vii. 7. [These are the words of Eusebius, not of Dionysius.—B.]

[e] He held the episcopate of the Roman Church from the year 259 to the year 269. Cave.—Bowyer.

[f] ἑξῆς δ' ἂν εἰκότως λέγοιμι καὶ πρὸς διαιροῦντας, καὶ κατατέμνοντας, καὶ ἀναι-

BOOK II. CHAP. X. § 9. xi. § 1.

DIONYSIUS ROM.

and cut up, and destroy that most sacred doctrine of the
Church of God, the Monarchy, dividing it into three powers
(so to say[1]), and divided hypostases[2], and Godheads three.
For I understand that there are some of the catechists and
teachers of the divine word among you, who are introducing this opinion; who are, so to speak, diametrically opposed
to the opinions of Sabellius. For he blasphemes by asserting that the Son Himself is the Father, and conversely [that
the Father is the Son]; whilst these, in some sort, preach
three Gods, dividing the Holy Unity[3] into three hypostases,
foreign to each other[4] [and] wholly separated. For the Divine Word must needs be one[5] with the God of all; and the
Holy Ghost must needs repose[6] and habitate[7] in God; and
further, thus[8] the Divine Trinity[9] must be gathered up and
brought together into One[10], as into a point[11],—the God (I
mean) of all, the Almighty." These words are so express, [391]
that they need no inference of ours to shew, how extremely
full and simple is the exposition, which they contain, of the
whole doctrine of the Holy Trinity, in opposition to all heresies whatsoever. The same Dionysius, however, shortly after
subjoins the following words against those who affirmed that
the Son of God was a created being[g]; "And no less should
one censure those also who imagine that the Son is a thing
made[12], and consider that the Lord has come into being[13]
just as one of the things that have been really brought into
being[14]; whereas the divine oracles attest for Him a begetting, such as is suitable and becoming, but not any form-
ing and making." He immediately adds these words[h]; "It 142

[1] τινάς. [2] μεμερισμένας ὑποστάσεις. [3] τὴν ἁγίαν μονάδα. [4] ξένας ἀλλήλων. [5] ἡνῶσθαι. [6] ἐμφιλοχωρεῖν. [7] ἐνδιαιτᾶσθαι. [8] ἤδη καί. [9] τὴν θείαν τριάδα. [10] εἰς ἕνα. [11] κορυφήν. [12] ποίημα. [13] γεγονέναι. [14] τῶν ὄντως γενομένων.

ροῦντας τὸ σεμνότατον κήρυγμα τῆς ἐκκλησίας τοῦ Θεοῦ, τὴν μοναρχίαν, εἰς τρεῖς δυνάμεις τινὰς, καὶ μεμερισμένας ὑποστάσεις, καὶ θεότητας τρεῖς· πέπυσμαι γὰρ εἶναί τινας τῶν παρ' ὑμῖν κατηχούντων καὶ διδασκόντων τὸν θεῖον λόγον ταύτης ὑφηγητὰς τῆς φρονήσεως· οἳ κατὰ διάμετρον, ὡς ἔπος εἰπεῖν, ἀντίκεινται τῇ Σαβελλίου γνώμῃ· ὁ μὲν γὰρ βλασφημεῖ, αὐτὸν τὸν υἱὸν εἶναι λέγων τὸν πατέρα, καὶ ἔμπαλιν· οἱ δὲ τρεῖς Θεοὺς τρόπον τινὰ κηρύττουσιν, εἰς τρεῖς ὑποστάσεις ξένας ἀλλήλων παντάπασι κεχωρισμένας διαιροῦντες τὴν ἁγίαν μονάδα. ἡνῶσθαι γὰρ ἀνάγκη τῷ Θεῷ τῶν ὅλων τὸν θεῖον λόγον· ἐμφιλοχωρεῖν δὲ τῷ Θεῷ καὶ ἐνδιαιτᾶσθαι δεῖ τὸ ἅγιον πνεῦμα· ἤδη καὶ τὴν θείαν τριάδα εἰς ἕνα, ὥσπερ εἰς κορυφήν τινα, τὸν Θεὸν τῶν ὅλων τὸν παντοκράτορα λέγω, συγκεφαλαιοῦσθαί τε καὶ συνάγεσθαι πᾶσα ἀνάγκη.—Athanasius, de Decretis Synodi Nicææ, tom. i. p. 275. [§ 26. vol. i. p. 231.]

[g] οὐ μεῖον δ' ἄν τις καταμέμφοιτο καὶ τοὺς ποίημα τὸν υἱὸν εἶναι δοξάζοντας, καὶ γεγονέναι τὸν Κύριον, ὥσπερ ἕν τι τῶν ὄντως γενομένων, νομίζοντας, τῶν θείων λογίων γέννησιν αὐτῷ τὴν ἁρμόττουσαν καὶ πρέπουσαν, ἀλλ' οὐχὶ πλάσιν τινὰ καὶ ποίησιν προσμαρτυρούντων.—[pp. 231, 232.]

[h] βλάσφημον οὖν οὐ τὸ τυχὸν, μέγιστον μὲν οὖν, χειροποίητον τρόπον τινὰ λέγειν τὸν Κύριον.—[Ibid.]

ON THE CONSUBSTANTIALITY OF THE SON.

[392]

is therefore a blasphemy, and no ordinary one, but rather the greatest, to say that the Lord is in any way a handy-work." Finally, after several statements which are well worthy of being read, Dionysius concludes thus[h]; "Neither therefore ought we to break up[1] the wonderful and divine Unity[2] into three Godheads, nor to limit[3] the dignity and exceeding majesty of the Lord by saying that He is created[4]; but we ought to believe in God the Father Almighty, and in Christ Jesus His Son, and in the Holy Ghost; and that the Word is One[5] with the God of all. 'For I,' says He, 'and the Father are One;' and, 'I am in the Father, and the Father in Me.' For in this way both the Divine Trinity, and the holy doctrine[6] of the Monarchy, will be preserved." Who at any time, even after the council of Nice, has written any thing better against the Arian or other heretical opinions touching the Trinity? But of the faith of this Dionysius of Rome, we shall say more in treating of Dionysius of Alexandria, to the elucidation of whose views I now proceed.

[1] καταμερίζειν.
[2] μονάδα.
[3] κωλύειν.
[4] ποιήσει.
[5] ἡνῶσθαι.
[6] κήρυγμα.

DIONYSIUS ALEX.

2. Dionysius[i], Bishop of Alexandria, whom Eusebius, Basil[k], and others call the Great, was, as we have already intimated, both the namesake and the contemporary of Dionysius of Rome; and the histories of both, so far as concerns the subject of which we are treating, are so mutually interwoven, that one cannot be related fully without the other.

[393]

Of this Dionysius, however, the Arians of old time used wonderfully to boast, as if he were their own; and not without cause indeed, if we are to believe the modern Arian, Sandius, though in reality most unreasonably. But let us first hear what Sandius[l] has written of him: "He taught," says he, "that the Son of God is a created being, and made; not in nature one with, but a stranger and alien, in respect of substance, to the Father, just as the husbandman is in relation to the vine, or the shipwright in relation to the ship; for,

[h] οὔτ' οὖν καταμερίζειν χρὴ εἰς τρεῖς θεότητας τὴν θαυμαστὴν καὶ θείαν μονάδα, οὔτε ποιήσει κωλύειν τὸ ἀξίωμα καὶ τὸ ὑπερβάλλον μέγεθος τοῦ Κυρίου· ἀλλὰ πεπιστευκέναι εἰς Θεὸν Πατέρα παντοκράτορα, καὶ εἰς Χριστὸν Ἰησοῦν τὸν υἱὸν αὐτοῦ, καὶ εἰς τὸ ἅγιον πνεῦμα· ἡνῶσθαι δὲ τῷ Θεῷ τῶν ὅλων τὸν λόγον· Ἐγὼ γὰρ, φησὶ, καὶ ὁ Πατὴρ ἕν ἐσμεν· καὶ, Ἐγὼ ἐν τῷ Πατρὶ, καὶ ὁ Πατὴρ ἐν ἐμοί. οὕτω γὰρ ἂν καὶ ἡ θεία τριὰς καὶ τὸ ἅγιον κήρυγμα τῆς μοναρχίας διασώζοιτο.—[Ibid., p. 232.]

[i] Made bishop about the year 232. Cave.—BOWYER.

[k] Eusebius, H. E., lib. vii., at the very beginning; Basil. Epist. Canon. ad Amphiloch. [Ep. 188, vol. iii. p. 269.]

[l] Enucl. Hist. Eccl., l. i. p. 122.

DIONYSIUS ALEX.

he says, existing as a creature[1], He was not before He was made[2]." That you may understand, however, from what masters Sandius learned this, he shortly afterwards adds: "Huet (Origeniana ii. 2. q. 2. § 10, 25) says that Dionysius of Alexandria gave utterance to unworthy and insufferable sentiments respecting the Trinity; for that he said that the Son is a work (ποίημα) of the Father, that is, a creature, and made, and unlike Him, and alien from the Father as to substance, as is the husbandman in relation to the vine; and, forasmuch as He is a creature, He existed not before He was made; and that he also uttered expressions little suited to[3] the Spirit. And in chapter iii. § 6, he states that he was the author of erroneous and absurd notions respecting the Trinity. Accordingly Dionysius Petavius not without reason[4] classes this his namesake also among those who propounded the same doctrine as Arius before his time." At last, he thus concludes: "It was not without ground[5], then, that the Arians, in the very presence of Athanasius, boasted of Dionysius's agreeing with them." These are the statements of Sandius.

3. We, however, on the contrary, hesitate not to assert that the Arians appealed to the views of Dionysius, not only without grounds[6] and falsely, but also most unwisely, and to the ruin of their cause; nay, further, we contend that scarcely any thing occurs in the ecclesiastical history of the events which preceded the council of Nice, which makes [394] more against the Arians than the history of this very Dionysius, if faithfully told. Of that history, therefore, we will give a true and succinct relation. When the Sabellian heresy was daily spreading more and more in Egypt and Pentapolis, whence it had its origin, Dionysius, who was bishop of Alexandria at the time, in writing an epistle against it addressed to Ammonius and Euphranor, in his anxiety to distinguish with extreme accuracy[7] the Persons [of the Godhead,] appeared to lean to the other extreme; that is to say, not merely to distinguish the Divine Persons, by attributing to Each His own property, but also to divide Each from the Other in substance, and thus to deny that the Son was of one substance[8] with the Father. Hereupon, some of the people of Pentapolis accused him of treason against the

[1] tanquam creatura existens.
[2] non erat antequam fieret.
[3] parum convenientes.
[4] non temere.
[5] non immerito.
[6] temere.
[7] accuratius.
[8] ὁμοούσιον.

ON THE CONSUBSTANTIALITY OF THE SON.

faith[1], before the bishop of Rome, who also at that time was called by the same name, Dionysius. A synod of bishops having been convened at Rome in this cause, the bishop of Alexandria was requested by them to make a declaration of his views. He accordingly wrote an apology to the aforementioned bishop of Rome, in which he defended himself from the calumnies which had been brought against him, and in so doing admirably preserved unimpaired[2] the catholic doctrine respecting the consubstantiality, and satisfied the bishop of Rome in all points. St. Athanasius, who was afterwards bishop of the same church of Alexandria, attests the truth of this, both in his Commentary on the councils of Ariminum and Seleucia, and especially in the treatise which he wrote professedly in opposition to the Arians, who used to boast that Dionysius had long before professed
143 the same opinions as themselves. In refuting them, Athanasius informs us, that Dionysius held right views in all points respecting the catholic faith, and that what he had stated ambiguously in any part of his epistle to Ammonius and Euphranor, the same he had more clearly explained both in that epistle itself, and afterwards in some other writings of his, and especially in those, which he addressed to
[395] his namesake, the bishop of Rome, which, as Eusebius and Jerome testify, were contained in four books. Persons, however, who were not aware of these facts, and who had not read what had been written by Athanasius in defence of Dionysius, did not hesitate, even after this, to accuse Dionysius of furnishing weapons to the Arians; for instance, Basil and Gennadius of Marseilles; although Basil[m], having afterwards learnt the facts of the case, as it would seem, made honourable mention of him as an orthodox man. Ruffinus[n] of Aquileia, however, was deceived in supposing that the writings of Dionysius had been tampered with and corrupted by the Arians. For Athanasius, in defending him, alleges no plea of this kind: on the contrary, he intimates that these writings had remained entire and uncorrupted, even as he had written them, so as to exhibit clearly that their author's

[1] læsæ fidei.

[2] sartam tectam.

[m] Basil. ad Amphiloch. de Spirit. S. c. 29. [§ 72. vol. iii. p. 60.]

[n] Ruffin. Apolog. pro Origene. [Sive De Adult. lib. Orig., p. 50.]

opinions were correct. Such is pretty nearly the history as given to us in brief, by Baronius.

DIONYSIUS ALEX.

4. Now in this history, two points particularly call for our observation. First, it is clear from this that Dionysius of Alexandria never really wrote what was objected against him by his accusers of Pentapolis, namely, that the Son of God, in that He is properly[1] the Son of God, is a creature or work: and that at no time did he not[2] acknowledge the same Son of God to be of one substance and nature[3] with the Father. Athanasius proves this, first, from the very title of the work which this Dionysius addressed to Dionysius of Rome. The words of Athanasius are as follows[o]; "First, then, he entitled his epistle, Of Refutation and Defence[4]. And what is this, but that he refutes his slanderers, and defends himself respecting what he had written? shewing that he had not himself written with the meaning that Arius has supposed; but that, when he mentioned what was spoken of the Lord in reference [396] to His human nature, he was not ignorant, that He was the inseparable Word and Wisdom of the Father." And indeed, if Dionysius had ever really held the views which his accusers of Pentapolis objected against him, he would not, (being, as he was, a man of remarkable piety,) have designated his reply to the charges made against him a Refutation and Defence[5], but rather a Confession or a Retractation[6]. For it is certain from his Apology itself, that Dionysius did not in a barefaced way[7] defend the blasphemies laid to his charge; nor if he had done so, would he ever have cleared himself to the satisfaction of Dionysius of Rome, who, as we have already shewn, was a man especially orthodox on the article of the Holy Trinity. Athanasius next proves the same from the circumstance, that Dionysius himself openly complained in his Apology, that his adversaries had not quoted his words fairly, but had maimed and mutilated them, and had framed from them, in this their maimed and mutilated form, certain heretical propositions to lay to his charge.

[1] proprie.

[2] nunquam non.

[3] ὁμοούσιον et ὁμογενῆ.

[4] Ἐλέγχου καὶ Ἀπολογίας (Apology).

[5] apologia.

[6] palinodiam.

[7] γυμνῇ κεφαλῇ.

[o] πρῶτον μὲν οὖν Ἐλέγχου καὶ Ἀπολογίας ἔγραψεν [leg. ἐπεγράψεν, inscripsit, Bull.] ἑαυτοῦ τὴν ἐπιστολήν. τοῦτο δὲ τί ἐστιν, ἢ ὅτι τοὺς μὲν ψευδομένους ἐλέγχει, περὶ δὲ ὧν ἔγραψεν, ἀπολογεῖται; δεικνὺς, ὅτι μὴ, ὡς Ἄρειος ὑπενόησεν, ἔγραψεν αὐτὸς, ἀλλ' ὅτι τῶν ἀνθρωπίνως εἰρημένων περὶ τοῦ Κυρίου μνησθεὶς οὐκ ἠγνόει τοῦτον εἶναι λόγον καὶ σοφίαν ἀδιαίρετον τοῦ Πατρός.—Athanasius, de sententia Dionysii Alex., tom. i. p. 559. [§ 14. vol. i. p. 253.]

ON THE CONSUBSTANTIALITY OF THE SON.

The words of Athanasius, immediately following those which
we have adduced, are express: "In the next place," says
Athanasius[p], "he charges his accusers as not adducing his
statements entire, but mutilating them; and as speaking not
with a good, but an evil conscience, just as they choose; and
he compares them to such as bring calumnious charges
against the Epistles of the blessed Apostle: now a complaint
[1] φαύλης. such as this on his part sets him entirely free from evil[1] sus-
[397] picion." Athanasius lastly shews, point by point, that Dio-
[2] ἀπολογία. nysius had, in his Defence[2], replied to each several objection
brought against him, and had proved himself catholic in all:
this, I repeat, Athanasius clearly shews by adducing the
express words of Dionysius themselves: I cannot, therefore,
sufficiently express my surprise at those learned and orthodox men, who do not cease, even at the present day, to fix
the slanderous charge of Arianism on that immortal ornament
of the Alexandrian Church.

5. To lay the subject more clearly before the reader, we
will here note out of the charges brought against Dionysius
one or two of the principal, upon which the others depend.
His accusers complained that Dionysius, in mentioning the
Father, did not at the same time mention the Son, and on the
other hand, on occasion of mentioning the Son, was silent as
to the name of the Father; inferring from this that he sepa-
[3] elongasse. rated, widely removed[3], and divided the Son from the Father.
144 To this the excellent prelate, as quoted by Athanasius[q], makes
this reply; "Of the names which were mentioned by me, each
[4] τοῦ πλησίον. is inseparable and indivisible from the other[4]. I mentioned
the Father, [but] even before I introduced [the name of]
[5] ἐσήμανα. the Son, I implied[5] Him also in the Father: I introduced
the Son, [and] even if I had not previously mentioned the
Father, He would most certainly have been implied by anti-
[6] προείληπτο. cipation[6] in the Son. I added the Holy Ghost, but at the
[7] ἅμα. [8] πόθεν. same time[7] I associated both Him from whom[8] and Him

[p] ἔπειτα αἰτιᾶται τοὺς κατειπόντας αὐτοῦ, ὡς μὴ ὁλοκλήρους λέγοντας, ἀλλὰ περικόπτοντας αὐτοῦ τὰς λέξεις· καὶ ὡς μὴ καλῇ συνειδήσει, ἀλλὰ πονηρᾷ λαλοῦντας ὡς θέλουσι· τούτους δὲ τούτοις ἀπεικάζει, τοῖς τὰς τοῦ μακαρίου ἀποστόλου διαβάλλουσιν ἐπιστολάς. ἡ δὲ τοιαύτη μέμψις αὐτοῦ πάντως ἀπὸ φαύλης ὑποψίας αὐτὸν ἀπολύει.—[Ibid.]

[q] τῶν ὑπ' ἐμοῦ λεχθέντων ὀνομάτων ἕκαστον ἀχώριστόν ἐστι καὶ ἀδιαίρετον τοῦ πλησίον. Πατέρα εἶπον, καὶ πρὶν ἐπαγάγω τὸν υἱὸν, ἐσήμανα καὶ τοῦτον ἐν τῷ Πατρί· υἱὸν ἐπήγαγον, εἰ καὶ μὴ προειρήκειν τὸν Πατέρα, πάντως ἂν ἐν τῷ υἱῷ προείληπτο. ἅγιον πνεῦμα προ-

BOOK II. CHAP. XI. § 4—6.

DIONYSIUS ALEX.

through whom[1] He came. But these know not that neither is the Father, in that He is Father, separated[2] from the Son, for the name is calculated to introduce [the idea of] the union[3]: neither is the Son removed from the Father, for the designation 'Father' manifests the communion; and in Their hands is the Spirit, which is not capable of being severed[4] either from Him that sends, or Him that conveys Him. How then could I, who use these names, believe that they are parted and wholly severed from each other?"
After a short interval he sums up all this in a few words, by [398]
saying, as Athanasius states[r], "That the Trinity is gathered up into a Unity[5] without being divided or diminished."

[1] διὰ τίνος.
[2] ἀπηλλοτρίωται.
[3] προκαταρκτικὸν τῆς συναφείας.
[4] στέρεσθαι.
[5] εἰς μονάδα. συγκεφαλαιοῦσθαι.

6. His adversaries further urged against Dionysius, that he taught that the Son of God is alien from the substance of the Father; and that the relation of the Father to the Son is like that of the husbandman to the vine, or of a shipbuilder to a vessel. To this the holy man replies in the following words[s]: "But when I had said that some things are conceived of as brought into existence[6] and some as made, of such, as being of less importance, I adduced examples [only] by the way. For I neither said that the plant was . . . . to the husbandman, nor the vessel . . . . to the shipwright[t]. After that I dwelt upon points which are more connected with and cognate [to the subject], and I treated
more fully of what were more real[7] [scil. less metaphorical], [399]
having brought out various additional proofs, which I also communicated to you in another epistle, in which[8] I also shewed that the charge which they bring against me, is a falsehood, that I deny that Christ is of one substance[9] with God: for

[6] γενητὰ, [genita, "begotten," Bull.]
[7] ἀληθεστέρων.
[8] ἐν οἷς.
[9] ὁμοούσιον.

σέθηκα· ἀλλ' ἅμα καὶ πόθεν, καὶ διὰ τίνος ἧκεν, ἐφήρμοσα. οἱ δὲ οὐκ ἴσασιν ὅτι μήτε ἀπηλλοτρίωται Πατὴρ υἱοῦ, ᾗ Πατήρ· προκαταρκτικὸν γάρ ἐστι τῆς συναφείας τὸ ὄνομα· οὔτε υἱὸς ἀπῴκισται τοῦ Πατρός· ἡ γὰρ Πατὴρ προσηγορία δηλοῖ τὴν κοινωνίαν. ἔν τε ταῖς χερσὶν αὐτῶν ἐστι τὸ πνεῦμα, μήτε τοῦ πέμποντος, μήτε τοῦ φέροντος δυνάμενον στέρεσθαι. πῶς οὖν ὁ τούτοις χρώμενος τοῖς ὀνόμασι μεμερίσθαι ταῦτα καὶ ἀφωρίσθαι παντελῶς ἀλλήλων οἴομαι.—Tom. i. p. 561. [§ 17. p. 254.]

[r] P. 562. [§ 19. p. 256.—The words of Dionysius in Athanasius are; οὕτω μὲν ἡμεῖς εἴς τε τὴν τριάδα τὴν μονάδα πλατύνομεν ἀδιαίρετον, καὶ τὴν τριάδα πάλιν ἀμείωτον εἰς τὴν μονάδα συγκεφαλαιούμεθα. See Grabe's annotations in the appendix.]

[s] πλὴν ἐγὼ γενητά τινα καὶ ποιητά τινα φήσας νοεῖσθαι, τῶν μὲν τοιούτων ὡς ἀχρειοτέρων ἐξ ἐπιδρομῆς εἶπον παραδείγματα. ἐπεὶ μήτε τὸ φυτὸν ἔφην τῷ γεωργῷ, μήτε τῷ ναυπηγῷ τὸ σκάφος [Deesse hic quidpiam monet editor Benedict.] εἶτα τοῖς ἱκνουμένοις καὶ προσφυεστέροις ἐνδιέτριψα, καὶ πλέον διεξῆλθον περὶ τῶν ἀληθεστέρων, ποικίλα προσεπεξευρὼν τεκμήρια· ἅπερ καὶ σοὶ δι' ἄλλης ἐπιστολῆς ἔγραψα· ἐν οἷς ἤλεγξα καὶ ὃ προφέρουσιν ἔγκλημα κατ' ἐμοῦ, ψεῦδος ὄν, ὡς οὐ λέγοντος τὸν Χριστὸν ὁμοούσιον εἶναι τῷ Θεῷ. εἰ γὰρ

ON THE CONSUBSTANTIALITY OF THE SON.

although I say that I have not found nor read this word in any place of the Holy Scriptures, still my arguments which immediately follow, of which they make no mention, are not at variance with this belief. For I even put forward[1] as an example, human offspring[2], as clearly being of one nature (homogeneous[3]), asserting that parents undoubtedly[4] are other than their children only in that they are not themselves the children[u]. The letter [itself], indeed, as I said before, I cannot send, owing to present circumstances[5]; had it been otherwise, I would have sent you the very words I then used, or rather a copy of the whole letter; which, if I shall have the means[6], I will [still] do. I know however and recollect, that I added several parallels of things cognate[7]; for I said that a plant, which has come up from a seed or a root, is different from that from which it sprang, and is [at the same time] altogether of the same nature[8] with it[v]: and that a river which flows from a fountain has received another form and name; (for neither is the fountain called a river, nor the river a fountain;) yet that they both have a substantive existence[9]; and that the fountain is as it were the father, and the river is the water from the fountain. These things, however, and such as these, they [say] that they do not see written, but, as it were, pretend to be blind, whilst

1 παρεθέμην.
2 γονὴν.
3 ὁμογενῆ.
4 πάντως.
5 διὰ τὰς περιστάσεις: ob casus temporum.
6 εὐπορήσω.
7 τῶν συγγενῶν.
8 "of like nature." Bp. Bull.
9 ὑπάρχειν.

καὶ τὸ ὄνομα τοῦτό φημι μὴ εὑρηκέναι, μηδ' ἀνεγνωκέναι που τῶν ἁγίων γραφῶν, ἀλλάγε τὰ ἐπιχειρήματά μου τὰ ἑξῆς, ἃ σεσιωπήκασι, τῆς διανοίας ταύτης οὐκ ἀπᾴδει. καὶ γὰρ (καὶ) [om. ed. Ben.] ἀνθρωπείαν γονὴν παρεθέμην, δῆλον ὡς οὖσαν ὁμογενῆ· φήσας πάντως τοὺς γονεῖς μόνον ἑτέρους εἶναι τῶν τέκνων, ὅτι μὴ αὐτοὶ εἶεν τὰ τέκνα. καὶ τὴν μὲν ἐπιστολὴν, ὡς προεῖπον, διὰ τὰς περιστάσεις οὐκ ἔχω προκομίσαι. εἰ δ' οὖν, αὐτά σοι τὰ τότε ῥήματα, μᾶλλον δὲ καὶ πάσης ἂν ἔπεμψα τὸ ἀντίγραφον. ὅπερ ἂν εὐπορήσω, ποιήσω. οἶδα δὲ καὶ μέμνημαι πλείονα προσθεὶς τῶν συγγενῶν ὁμοιώματα. καὶ γὰρ καὶ φυτὸν εἶπον, ἀπὸ σπέρματος ἢ ἀπὸ ῥίζης ἀνελθὸν, ἕτερον εἶναι τοῦ, ὅθεν ἐβλάστησε, καὶ πάντως ἐκεῖνο [ἐκείνῳ ed. Ben.] καθέστηκεν ὁμοιοφυές [ὁμοφυές ed. Ben.] καὶ ποταμὸν ἀπὸ πηγῆς ῥέοντα ἕτερον σχῆμα καὶ ὄνομα μετειληφέναι· μήτε γὰρ τὴν πηγὴν ποταμὸν, μήτε τὸν ποταμὸν πηγὴν λέγεσθαι· καὶ ἀμφότερα ὑπάρχειν, καὶ τὴν μὲν πηγὴν, οἱονεὶ (τὸν) [om. ed. Ben.] Πατέρα εἶναι, τὸν δὲ ποταμὸν εἶναι τὸ ἐκ τῆς πηγῆς ὕδωρ. ἀλλὰ ταῦτα μὲν καὶ τὰ τοιαῦτα μηδὲ ὁρᾷν γεγραμμένα, ἀλλ' οἱονεὶ τυφλώττειν ὑποκρίνονται· τοῖς δὲ δυσὶ ῥηματίοις ἀσυνθέτοις, καθάπερ λίθοις, μακρόθεν ἐπιχειροῦσί με βάλλειν.—Apud Athanasium, tom. i. p. 561. [§ 18. p. 255.]

t [The Benedictine editor intimates that there is something wanting here. —B.]

u [The following clause is omitted by Bp. Bull, ἢ μήτε γονεῖς ἀναγκαῖον ὑπάρχειν εἶναι μήτε τέκνα. "Otherwise, it must needs follow, that there are neither parents nor children." See Grabe's annotations on this passage. —B.]

v [Read ἐκείνῳ, (see Grabe's annotations,) and presently ὁμοφυές.—B. These corrections, which are the readings of the Bened. edition, are followed in the translation: Bp. Bull read ὁμοιφυὲς, *similis naturæ:* this is noticed in the margin.]

DIONYSIUS ALEX.

with the two little words apart from the context[1], as with stones, they try to strike me from a distance." Thus Dionysius; and what can be clearer than this defence? For as it appears, this great man, in the epistle at which his adversaries carped, had endeavoured to illustrate the distinction between the Father and the Son, in opposition to the Sa- 145
bellians, by various similes: some of which related only to the human nature of Christ, created by the Father; as that [401]
of the husbandman in relation to the vine, or that of the shipwright to the vessel; whilst others were adapted also to the Divine nature of the Saviour, received by eternal generation from the Father. On examples of the first kind, as less apt, he had touched but lightly and by the way; whilst on the latter, as being most suitable and applicable, he had dwelt a longer time. Amongst these were several, which eminently confirmed in reality the consubstantiality of the Son, although Dionysius allows that he had not in this place used the term. For he had even adduced as an example human birth, and subjoined these express words; "Parents undoubtedly are other than their children only in this, that they are not themselves their children." By this example both the communion of nature, which subsists between the Father and the Son, and also the distinction of Persons, is manifestly declared. He had added, that the plant which grows up from a seed or a root, is other than[2] that from which it springs, and still is of a nature altogether the same with it; and many other examples of that sort. But the sophists, suppressing the mention of all this, seized a handle for falsely accusing[3] him, from two little words only, which they themselves had put in a wrong connection[4], and drawn to a sense, other than that which Dionysius intended. But why, you will say, did Dionysius employ at all those examples, which are less suitable, and apply only to the human nature of Christ? The great Athanasius gives an excellent reason[x]; "And this form[5] [of reasoning]," he says,
"is in truth persuasive in overthrowing the madness of Sa- [402]
bellius, so that he, who wishes by a short method to convict such men, should not begin from the passages which indi-

[1] ἀσυνθέτοις.

[2] aliud ab.

[3] calumniandi.

[4] a se male compositis.

[5] τύπος.

[x] [καὶ ἔστιν ἀληθῶς τύπος οὗτος πιθανὸς πρὸς ἀνατροπὴν τῆς Σαβελλίου μανίας, ὥστε τὸν βουλόμενον ταχέως διελέγχειν τοὺς τοιούτους, μὴ ἀπὸ τῶν

ON THE CONSUBSTANTIALITY OF THE SON.

cate the divinity of the Word; that the Son, for instance, is Word, and Wisdom, and Power, and that 'I and the Father are one;' lest they, perversely interpreting what is correctly said, should make such statements an occasion for their shameless contentiousness, when they hear [the words], 'I and the Father are one,' and 'He that hath seen Me, hath seen the Father:' but [one should rather] put forward what has been said of the Saviour in respect of His human nature[1], just as he has done; such things, for instance, as His hungering and being wearied, and that He is the Vine, and [that] He prayed, and [that] He suffered. For in proportion as these things which are said are lowly, so much the more is it apparent that it was not the Father who became man. For when the Lord is called a Vine, there must needs be a Vine-dresser also: when He prays, there must be One that hears, and, when He asks, there must be One that gives. And these things shew the madness of the Sabellians much more easily, because He that prays is one, He that hears another; and the Vine is one, and the Vine-dresser another." As to the objection brought against Dionysius by his opponents, that he denied the eternity of the Son, you shall hear the clear reply of the great prelate on that point, in our third book, on the Co-eternity of the Son. But this being the case, certain learned men of the present day need to be seriously reminded, that they imitate not the ways of the false accusers of old time, nor henceforth, suppressing the mention of the very many catholic statements of Dionysius, continue to cast at a very holy man and one who has deserved most highly of the Catholic Church, those two little words "the Vine," and "the Husbandman," as it were stones, and they too moved out of their proper place.

[1] τὰ ἀνθρωπίνως εἰρημένα.

σημαινόντων τὴν θεότητα τοῦ λόγου ποιεῖσθαι τὴν ἀρχήν· ὅτι λόγος, καὶ σοφία, καὶ δύναμίς ἐστιν ὁ υἱός· καὶ ὅτι ἐγὼ καὶ ὁ πατὴρ ἕν ἐσμεν· ἵνα μὴ τὰ καλῶς εἰρημένα παρεξηγούμενοι ἐκεῖνοι, πρόφασιν τῆς ἀναισχύντου φιλονεικίας ἑαυτῶν, τὰ τοιαῦτα πορίσωνται, ἀκούοντες, ὅτι ἐγὼ καὶ ὁ πατὴρ ἕν ἐσμεν· καὶ ὁ ἑωρακὼς ἐμὲ, ἑώρακε τὸν πατέρα· ἀλλὰ τὰ ἀνθρωπίνως εἰρημένα περὶ τοῦ σωτῆρος προβάλλειν, ὥσπερ αὐτὸς πεποίηκεν· οἷά ἐστι, τὸ πεινᾶν, τὸ κοπιᾶν, καὶ ὅτι ἄμπελος, καὶ, ηὔχετο, καὶ πέπονθεν. ὅσῳ γὰρ ταῦτα ταπεινὰ λέγεται, τοσούτῳ δείκνυται μὴ ὁ πατὴρ γενόμενος ἄνθρωπος. ἀνάγκη γὰρ καὶ ἀμπέλου λεγομένου τοῦ κυρίου, εἶναι καὶ γεωργόν· καὶ εὐχομένου αὐτοῦ, εἶναι τὸν ἐπακούοντα· καὶ αἰτοῦντος αὐτοῦ, εἶναι τὸν διδόντα· τὰ δὲ τοιαῦτα μᾶλλον εὐκολώτερον τὴν τῶν Σαβελλιανῶν μανίαν δείκνυσιν· ὅτι ἕτερος ὁ εὐχόμενος, ἕτερος ὁ ἐπακούων, καὶ ἄλλος ἡ ἄμπελος, καὶ ἄλλος ὁ γεωργός.]—tom. i. p. 568. [§ 26. p. 261.]

7. I proceed to the other point, which I think especially
worthy of observation in the history of this Dionysius. It is
then, further, an evident conclusion from it, that in the
Christian Churches in the age of Dionysius, the doctrine
which asserted[1] that the Son of God is of one substance and
co-eternal (*ὁμοούσιος* and *συναΐδιος*) with His Father, was
already commonly received and held, as a certain and catholic [truth], which it were impious to gainsay. For as soon as [403]
certain ill-disposed[2] men had falsely spread abroad a calumny
against Dionysius, as though he had taught, that the Son is
not of one substance with the Father, but created and made,
and that there was a time when the Son was not, nearly the
whole Christian world was moved at it; the complaint was
carried from the East to the West; an appeal was made to
the bishop of Rome, as holding the first seat[3] amongst the
prelates; a council was forthwith held upon the matter in
the diocese of Rome, in which the opinions which were said
to be held by Dionysius of Alexandria, were condemned, and
a synodical epistle was written to Dionysius himself, in which
the fathers enquired of him, whether he had in very deed
published doctrines of such a kind. This Athanasius himself,
the defender of Dionysius, explicitly attests, in his treatise
on the Synods of Ariminum and Seleucia[y], in the following
words; "But when certain persons had laid a charge before
the bishop of Rome against the bishop of Alexandria, as if he
had asserted that the Son was made[4], and was not of one substance with the Father, the council which was convened at
Rome was deeply moved with indignation, and the bishop of
Rome expressed the sentiments of them all in a letter to his
namesake." Hence arose the Refutation and Defence of Dio- 146
nysius of Alexandria, addressed to Dionysius of Rome, in which
he easily cleared himself with[5] that wise and very fair-minded
man. Furthermore, it is a certain conclusion from this history, (as I have, indeed, already observed elsewhere[z],) that
in the times of this Dionysius, i. e., at least sixty years before
the council of Nice, the very word *ὁμοούσιος* (of one sub- [404]

[1] sententiam quæ statuit.
[2] malefe-riati.
[3] cathedram.
[4] *ποίημα.*
[5] apud.

[y] ἀλλὰ τινῶν αἰτιασαμένων παρὰ τῷ ἐπισκόπῳ Ῥώμης τὸν τῆς Ἀλεξανδρείας ἐπίσκοπον, ὡς λέγοντα ποίημα, καὶ μὴ ὁμοούσιον τὸν υἱὸν τῷ Πατρὶ, ἡ μὲν κατὰ Ῥώμην σύνοδος ἠγανάκτησεν, ὁ δὲ τῆς Ῥώμης ἐπίσκοπος τὴν πάντων γνώμην γράφει πρὸς τὸν ὁμώνυμον ἑαυτοῦ.—Tom. i. p. 918. [§ 43. p. 757.]

[z] Above in chapter 1. of this book. § 8. [p. 65.]

ON THE CONSUBSTANTIALITY OF THE SON.

stance), was ordinarily used, received and approved amongst Catholics, in stating[1] the doctrine of the divinity of the Son. For it was expressly objected to Dionysius, as he himself admits, that he did not say that the Son was of one substance[2] with the Father; and to this objection the excellent man replied, that he had not indeed read the word in the Scriptures, but that, nevertheless, he had not on that account shrunk from it; (indeed, in his epistle against Paul of Samosata, as has been shewn above[a], he expressly approves of that word as one that was used by catholic fathers who had lived before him;) whilst the reality itself, which is represented by the word, he had repeatedly and most explicitly affirmed[3], both in his other writings, and in the very epistle from which his adversaries had constructed their charges against him.

[1] in explicatione.
[2] ὁμοούσιος.
[3] confirmasse.

8. Now what does Sandius say[b] to all this? Hear and wonder at the extreme ignorance or impudence of the man, whichever it be; "The Apology," he says, "of this Dionysius, which is said to have been written to Dionysius of Rome, is in my opinion spurious, and forged by those who would have all controversies of the faith to be decided by the Roman pontiff, as supreme judge." But who in the world ever suspected this before himself? Perhaps, however, this unkerneller of ecclesiastical history has his own reasons for this judgment, which we, "simple and old-fashioned folk," do not as yet apprehend. For he openly gives it out[c] that he had proposed "to write the matters which are, as it were, omitted[4] in ecclesiastical history, and which are very different from the notions of the ordinarily learned[5]." Well, let us see, whether he has aught to produce worthy of being opposed to the consent of all, not only of those who are "ordinarily
[405] learned," but of those who rise above the ordinary class. "First," he says, "neither Eusebius nor Jerome have mentioned this Apology." I reply; granting this to be true, still Athanasius has mentioned it, who had the best acquaintance with the writings of his own predecessor in the see of Alexandria: and he has so mentioned it as to cite pretty long extracts from it in the very words[6] of the original, extracts which he

[4] paralipomena.
[5] παρὰ δόξαν vulgariter eruditorum.
[6] αὐτολεξεὶ.

[a] [chap. i. 8. p. 65.]
[b] De Script. Eccles., p. 42, 43.
[c] Enucl. Hist. Eccles. i. p. 121.

boldly opposed to the Arians, when they boasted of Dionysius's agreeing in opinion with them. Basil the Great has also mentioned it in his treatise on the Holy Spirit, c. 29[d], where he likewise produces out of it a remarkable testimony on the divinity of the Holy Ghost. But further, it is quite untrue, that neither Eusebius nor Jerome have mentioned this Apology: both have made clear enough mention of it. Eusebius, in his Ecclesiastical History, vii. 26, in enumerating the epistles, and treatises in the form of epistles, which Dionysius of Alexandria composed against Sabellius, writes thus concerning this Apology[e]: "And he also composed four other treatises on the same subject; which he addressed to his namesake, Dionysius of Rome." These words of Eusebius manifestly designate the books Of Refutation and Apology, portions of which were brought forward by Athanasius. For all points coincide, whether you regard the form, the argument, the title, or the division of the books. The form of both was the same, namely, the epistolary. The work which Eusebius mentions, was written upon the Sabellian controversy; and the work Of Refutation and Apology, cited by Athanasius and Basil, treated of the same argument. Both were alike addressed to Dionysius, bishop of Rome. The epistolary work, which Eusebius mentions, was divided [406] into different portions[1]; so was the apologetic epistle mentioned by Athanasius. The epistle of which Eusebius speaks, consisted, as he himself testifies, of four parts in all; whilst Athanasius brought forward testimonies out of the first, second, and third books, by name, of the Apology of Dionysius. See the annotations of the very learned Valesius on this passage of Eusebius. And as for Jerome, he also expressly mentions this quadripartite epistle, in his Catalogue of Ecclesiastical Writers, under Dionysius of Alexandria, in these words[f], "There are also four books of his addressed to Dionysius, bishop of Rome."

[1] volumina.

9. Sandius' second argument is to this effect; "It is evident," he says, "from the Chronicle and Ecclesiastical History of Eusebius, that Dionysius of Alexandria had died at a very

[d] Tom. ii. p. 358. [vol. iii. p. 60.]

[e] *συντάττει δὲ περὶ τῆς αὐτῆς ὑποθέσεως καὶ ἄλλα τέσσαρα συγγράμματα· ἃ τῷ κατὰ Ῥώμην ὁμωνύμῳ Διονυσίῳ προσφωνεῖ.*—[H. E. vii. 26.]

[f] Ejus [sunt] . . . et quatuor libri ad Dionysium Romanæ urbis episcopum. —[vol. ii. p. 897-8.]

ON THE CONSUBSTANTIALITY OF THE SON.

147 advanced age, and his successor Maximus had been appointed, (A.D. 268,) before Dionysius became bishop of Rome, (A.D. 269.)" An argument, indeed, worthy of such an unkerneller of ecclesiastical history; seeing that all, who possess even a moderate acquaintance with this branch of learning, know that in this place Eusebius made a gross mistake in his chronology. The source of his error was, that he was ignorant of the number of years of the pontificate of Xystus, who was the predecessor of Dionysius of Rome; since he states that he presided over the Roman Church eleven years, whereas it is certain that Xystus did not govern that Church for the whole of three years. On this gross mistake of Eusebius the excellent Valesius writes thus[g]; "Eusebius," he says, "is here grievously mistaken; for Xystus did not rule the Church of Rome eleven years, but only two years and eleven months,
[407] as is stated in the book upon the Roman pontiffs, which was first published by Cuspinian[h]. In that book the years of the popes of Rome, from Pope Callixtus to the pontificate of Liberius, are very well arranged. And of Xystus it states thus: 'Xystus two years, eleven months, and six days. He began from the consulate of Maximus and Glabrio and continued to that of Tuscus and Bassus, and suffered on the eighth day before the ides of August.' Cyprian, who himself suffered martyrdom under the same consuls, but in the following month, gives the same testimony in his epistle to Successus. Eusebius, however, says nothing of the martyrdom of Xystus, either in his Chronicle or in his Ecclesiastical History, which greatly astonishes me, though I should be much more astonished, did I not know that Eusebius was rather careless respecting what was transacted in the West. Besides, in his Chronicle, he states that Xystus occupied the see eight years, though here he assigns eleven years to him. He also makes Dionysius succeed Xystus as Pope in the twelfth year of Gallienus, whilst he says that Maximus succeeded Dionysius of Alexandria, in the eleventh year of the same emperor; which is most absurd, since it is certain that Dionysius of Alexandria addressed four books against Sabel-

[g] In his notes on Eusebius' Eccl. History, vii. 27.

[h] [Pseudo-Damasi Catalogus Pontificum Romanorum, ap. Cuspiniani de Consulibus Romanorum Commentarios, p. 385. ed. Francof. 1601.]

lius to Dionysius, bishop of Rome, as Eusebius states above, c. 26."

DIONYSIUS ALEX.

10. The third and last cavil of Sandius remains to be disposed of by us, in a few words; "This Apology," he says, "is at variance with the sentiments of Dionysius of Alexandria, and agrees with the heresy of Paul of Samosata, of which we shall treat in Book I. of our Ecclesiastical History." But first, from what does he prove that this Apology is, as he says, at variance with the sentiments of Dionysius of Alexandria? Dionysius, forsooth, [as he says], taught that the Son of God, even in that He is properly the Son of God, is a creature and made, &c., which doctrines the author of the Apology professedly impugns. This, however, is begging the question[1]. For we assert, that Dionysius never in reality taught [408] such things, but that they were calumniously fastened on this good man by his adversaries; and of this assertion of ours we give solid proofs from the Apology itself, which, as is clear from the surest evidence, is the genuine work of Dionysius. With these calumnies the Apology is, indeed, at variance; but if it had not been at variance with them, it ought by no means to have been entitled a Refutation and an Apology. Secondly, who is not thoroughly astonished at what Sandius affirms,—that the sentiments, I mean, of the author of the Apology agree with the heresy of Paul of Samosata? For throughout that Apology, the divinity of the Word or Son of God, which Paul of Samosata denied, is clearly asserted. But Sandius perhaps meant, that the author of the Apology was a thorough Sabellian: and that Sabellius and Paul of Samosata were of one opinion[2] on the article respecting the Son of God; as he eagerly maintains in the first book of his Ecclesiastical History[i] Unkernelled, under [the head of] Paul of Samosata. But suppose we allow to this trifler, that the heresy of Sabellius and of Paul of Samosata was the same, or at least came to the same thing; still, whence and by what argument, I ask, will he prove, that the author of the Apology agreed with the heresy of Sabellius. Certainly Eusebius, Athanasius, and others attest that that Apology was written especially against the Sabellian heresy: nay, Athanasius says

[1] τὸ ἐν ἀρχῇ λαμβάνειν.

[2] ὁμοδόξους.

[i] Page 114.

that in that work Dionysius overthrows Sabellius (Σαβέλλιον ἀνατρέπειν). Besides, we have already cited out of the fragments of the Apology, which are extant in Athanasius, statements diametrically opposed to the Sabellian heresy. Of this kind,—I say nothing of the rest, lest I should weary the reader with tedious repetition,—is his illustration of the distinction between God the Father and the Son by a simile derived from a human birth, with this remark subjoined;
[409] "That parents are other than their children only in this, that they are not themselves their children." What man in his sober senses would say that these are the words of one who agrees with Sabellius, or even with Paul of Samosata? I think it probable, however, that Sandius had never read through those fragments of the Apology, which are extant in Athanasius; but had heard from others, that the consubstantiality of the Son was maintained in that work, and thence had inferred that the writer was a thorough Sabellian. Perhaps this conjecture of mine will, at first sight, appear strange to the sound-minded reader, who has not yet seen the cento of Sandius[1]; but it is plain[2] that this author does everywhere in his book regard it as a certain and settled point, that the doctrine of the Homousians, as he calls them,
148 and of the Sabellians, was entirely the same respecting the Son of God; than which nothing is farther from the truth, inasmuch as we have already clearly shewn that no one who holds the same views as Sabellius[j], can say that the Son of God is of one substance with the Father, except in a most absurd and improper sense. So much respecting the Apology of Dionysius of Alexandria.

11. Besides this, the same Dionysius, a short time before his death, at the request of the fathers who were assembled at Antioch in the case of Paul of Samosata, wrote a remarkable epistle against this same Paul, which is extant at this day[k]. In it the divine soul, on the point of departing hence to God, discourses on the true divinity of the Lord Jesus in a manner altogether divine. There are very many passages which bear on this subject; but we will only extract[3] a few. He there expressly calls Christ "uncreated and Creator[l];"

[1] Sandii centonem.
[2] nimirum.
[3] delibabimus.

[j] ii. 1. 9, towards the end. [p. 70.]
[k] Bibl. Patr., tom. ii. [Op., p. 203, &c.]
[l] p. 266. [p. 212.]

(*ἄκτιστον καὶ δημιουργὸν*;) and a little after[m], "Him who is Lord by nature, and the Word of the Father, through whom the Father made all things, and who is said by the holy fathers to be of one substance with the Father." Afterwards we read these words[n]; "Christ is unchangeable, as being God the Word." And one page after, Christ is designated by him[o], "He who is God over all, our refuge." Parallel to this is what we read in the next page respecting our Saviour[p]; "He who is God over all, the Lord God of Israel, Jesus the Christ." What is to be said of the fact, that Dionysius explicitly acknowledges the entire Trinity of one substance? in his replies to the questions[q] of Paul of Samosata, Reply to Quest. IV., he says; "Christ the Word is of one nature[1] with the Holy Spirit in the form of the dove; and the Spirit is of one nature with the Father." This I observe in opposition to those, who think that Dionysius entertained wrong views, at least, respecting the Holy Ghost. But in the same place he also makes these excellent statements respecting the Godhead of the Son and of the Holy Ghost alike[r]; "For Jesus," he says, "the Word before the worlds, is God of Israel; as is likewise the Holy Ghost." Again in the same tract[2] he thus speaks concerning the Holy Ghost[s]; "For he who blasphemes against the Holy Spirit, who is loving unto man[3], shall not go unpunished, and God is a Spirit[4]."

[410]

12. What on the other hand does Sandius say to this? he once more lays aside all shame[5] and audaciously rejects

[411]

[1] ὁμοειδής.

[2] opusculo.

[3] τοῦ φιλάνθρωπου Πνεύματος.

[4] Spiritus est Deus.

[5] frontem perfricat.

[m] τὸν φύσει Κύριον, καὶ λόγον τοῦ Πατρὸς, δι' οὗ τὰ πάντα ἐποίησεν ὁ Πατὴρ, καὶ ὁμοούσιον τῷ Πατρὶ εἰρημένον ὑπὸ τῶν ἁγίων πατέρων.—p. 267. [p. 214.]

[n] ἀναλλοίωτος γὰρ ὁ Χριστὸς, ὡς Θεὸς λόγος.—p. 288. [p. 242.]

[o] ὁ ὢν ἐπὶ πάντων Θεὸς, ἡ καταφυγὴ ἡμῶν.—p. 289. [p. 246.]

[p] ὁ ὢν ἐπὶ πάντων Θεὸς, Κύριος ὁ Θεὸς Ἰσραὴλ, Ἰησοῦς ὁ Χριστός.—p. 290. [p. 248.]

[q] ὁμοειδὴς ἐν τῷ εἴδει τῆς περιστερᾶς ὁ Χριστὸς λόγος τῷ Πνεύματι τῷ ἁγίῳ· ὁμοειδὲς τῷ Πατρὶ τὸ Πνεῦμα.—p. 284. [p. 232.]

[r] Θεὸς γὰρ Ἰσραὴλ Ἰησοῦς ὁ πρὸ αἰώνων λόγος, ὡς καὶ τὸ ἅγιον Πνεῦμα. —[Resp. ad Quæst. vi. p. 244.]

[s] [The Greek words as given by Bp. Bull are; οὐ γὰρ ἀθῷος ἀπελεύσεται βλασφημῶν κατὰ τοῦ φιλανθρώπου Πνεύματος τοῦ ἁγίου· Πνεῦμα δὲ ὁ Θεός: on which Dr. Burton observes; "In p. 245 we read οὐκ ἀθῳώσει, φησὶ, βλάσφημον ἀπὸ χείλεων αὐτοῦ τὸ φιλάνθρωπον Πνεῦμα· ἀλλ' ἐτάζει καρδίας καὶ νεφροὺς, ὅτι καὶ τὰ βάθη τοῦ Θεοῦ, ὡς Θεὸς, τὸ Πνεῦμα ἐπίσταται, ("him, who blasphemes with his lips the Spirit that is loving unto man, He says, He will not let go unpunished: but He searcheth the hearts and reins, for the Spirit, as God, knoweth the deep things of God.") which, if I am not mistaken, Bp. Bull thus altered through fault of memory.]

ON THE CONSUBSTANTIALITY OF THE SON.

this epistle also, which bears the name of Dionysius, as spurious. "There is also circulated," he says[t], "under the name of Dionysius of Alexandria an epistle against Paul of Samosata, but it is supposititious." Now who can, without impatience, endure the shamelessness of this poor creature[1], who thus pronounces his decretory sentence on the writings of the holy fathers, out of his own brain and according to his own pleasure, in contempt of the judgment, trustworthiness, and authority of all writers who have gone before him. At any rate Eusebius mentions, in express terms, this epistle of Dionysius of Alexandria, written to the Church of Antioch against Paul of Samosata, (Hist. Eccles. vii. 27[u]): "Dionysius, bishop of Alexandria," he says, "having been invited to attend the council, declined to be present, alleging in excuse alike his old age and his bodily infirmity, setting before them, [however,] in a letter, the opinion which he held on the question under consideration." The same epistle is mentioned by the fathers of Antioch themselves in their synodical epistle, in Eusebius, Hist. Eccl. vii. 30[x]. "At the same time we sent letters," they say, "and exhorted many even of the distant bishops, to come for the remedying[2] of the pestilential teaching: for instance, to Dionysius the bishop of Alexandria, and to Firmilian of Cappadocia, both of blessed memory: of whom the former sent an epistle to Antioch, not considering the leader of the heresy worthy even of salutation, nor
[412] writing to him in person, but to the whole diocese[3], of which epistle we have also subjoined the copy." Lastly, Jerome,
149 (not to speak of others,) makes mention of this epistle, in his Catalogue of Ecclesiastical Writers, under Dionysius of Alexandria[y]; "There is also circulated," he says, "a notable epistle of his against Paul of Samosata, [written] a few days

1 homuncionis.

2 ἐπὶ τὴν θεραπείαν.

3 παροικία.

t De Script. Eccles., p. 42.

u ὁ μὲν κατ' Ἀλεξάνδρειαν Διονύσιος, παρακληθεὶς ὡς ἂν ἐπὶ τὴν συνόδον ἀφίκοιτο, γῆρας ὁμοῦ καὶ ἀσθένειαν τοῦ σώματος αἰτιασάμενος, ἀνατίθεται τὴν παρουσίαν, δι' ἐπιστολῆς τὴν αὐτοῦ γνώμην, ἣν ἔχοι περὶ τοῦ ζητουμένου, παραστήσας,—[E. H. vii. 27.]

x ἐπεστέλλομεν δὲ ἅμα καὶ παρεκαλοῦμεν πόλλους καὶ τῶν μακρὰν ἐπισκόπων, ἐπὶ τὴν θεραπείαν τῆς θανατηφόρου διδασκαλίας· ὥσπερ καὶ Διονύσιον τὸν ἐπὶ τῆς Ἀλεξανδρείας, καὶ Φιρμιλιανὸν τὸν ἀπὸ τῆς Καππαδοκίας, τοὺς μακαρίτας· ὧν ὁ μὲν ἐπέστειλεν εἰς τὴν Ἀντιόχειαν, τὸν ἡγεμόνα τῆς πλάνης οὐδὲ προσρήσεως ἀξιώσας, οὐδὲ πρὸς πρόσωπον γράψας αὐτῷ, ἀλλὰ τῇ παροικίᾳ πάσῃ· ἧς καὶ τὸ ἀντίγραφον ὑπετάξαμεν. [Ibid., c. 30.]

y Sed et adversus Paulum Samosatenum ante paucos dies quam moreretur, insignis ejus fertur Epistola—[vol. ii. p. 879-98.]

BOOK II. CHAP. XI. § 12.

DIONYSIUS ALEX.

before he died." He here applies to it the epithet notable[1], because in it the catholic doctrine respecting the Son of God was excellently explained and established. Let us then briefly examine the argument which Sandius thought worthy of being opposed to so high an authority: "Erasmus Brochmandus," he says, "rejects the epistle as spurious, because in it Christ is said to be ὁμοούσιος (of one substance) with the Father, whereas that word was not in use before the time of Arius." To be sincere and candid in my reply, I confess I do not know who the Brochmandus is whom Sandius here mentions[z], nor does it much matter to know; for I am sure that his opinion, how great soever he be, must be accounted as worth nothing in comparison with the trustworthiness and authority of the fathers of Antioch, of Eusebius, and of Jerome. And as to his argument, I have already[a] in more than one place clearly proved that the expression ὁμοούσιος was in frequent use among Catholics long before [413] the council of Nice, and even before the time of Dionysius of Alexandria. But here is a notable specimen of Sandius's candour! in this place he uses as a weapon of attack an argument which he himself, elsewhere, in express terms confesses to be of no weight. For, in treating of Origen's books on Job, he makes this statement[b]; "They, however, are mistaken, who with Sixtus Senensis, Possevin, Bellarmine, and Rivet do not hold these treatises, as also the commentaries, to be the works of Origen, on the ground that there is mention made in them of the word ὁμοούσιος, which arose long after the times of Origen; for we shall prove in the first book of our Ecclesiastical History that the word ὁμοούσιος was already in use in the time of Origen. So it seems that this was a foolish[2] reason for proving that Origen was not the author of the books on Job[3], which yet learned men agree in thinking are not Origen's: but now it is held valid for proving that Dionysius was not the author of the epistle against Paul of Samosata, which all authorities, both in ancient and modern times, (with the single exception, perhaps, of this Brochmandus,) do with one consent acknow-

[1] insignem.

[2] inepta.

[3] ab Origene abjudicandum.

[z] [He was a Lutheran teacher of theology, and professor in the university of Copenhagen.—B.]

[a] Chap. 1. 8. [pp. 63, sqq.]

[b] De Script. Eccles., p. 30.

ledge to have been written by Dionysius[c]. The truth is: the books on Job are stuffed full of Arian ravings; and therefore it suited the purpose of Sandius, an Arian, that they should be regarded as the genuine production of Origen; on the contrary the epistle against Paul of Samosata which bears the name of Dionysius, excellently establishes the consubstantiality of the Son: and therefore, rightly or wrongly, it must by all means be rejected as spurious. Here is an honest and trustworthy historian[d]!

[414] Thus have we at last (if I mistake not) given abundant proof, that this very great man, Dionysius of Alexandria, did in no wise favour the blasphemy which Arius subsequently maintained, but that he was both in sentiment and in expression entirely catholic concerning the Son of God, and, further, concerning the Holy Trinity. I now pass on to other doctors of the Church.

151
[415]

CHAPTER XII.

ON THE OPINION AND FAITH OF THE VERY CELEBRATED GREGORY THAUMATURGUS, BISHOP OF NEOCÆSAREA IN PONTUS.

1. St. Theodore, alike the scholar and the glory of Origen, called afterwards by the name of Gregory, and surnamed "the Great," and "the Wonder-worker," (Thaumaturgus,) on account of his stupendous and celebrated deeds,—for he wrought many and very great miracles, and converted nations
[416] to the faith of Christ, not by words only, but much more by deeds—was bishop of Neocæsarea, and contemporary with the Dionysii of Rome and Alexandria, but survived Dionysius of Alexandria; for Dionysius died before the last council

[c] This epistle has been suspected by many on the ground that the fathers of Antioch in their synodal epistle (in Eusebius vii. 30.) expressly declare, that Dionysius addressed his letter to the Church at Antioch in general, and did not even deign to give a salutation to Paul. Cave.—Bowyer. [This is the argument of Basnage and Tillemont, but it has been most fully refuted by the editor of the works of Dionysius, in his preface, p. lvi.—B.]

[d] [This epistle of Dionysius against Paul of Samosata is exceedingly well defended in the preface to the works of Dionysius, p. xxii. &c.—B.]

assembled at Antioch against Paul of Samosata: whereas Gregory[e], as is clear from Eusebius[f], was present at that council. He has handed down to posterity a most accurate and complete Confession of faith, respecting the most holy Trinity of one substance, expressed in the following words[g]; "There is one God, Father of [Him who is] the living Word, subsisting Wisdom[1] and Power and [His] eternal Impress[2]; perfect Begetter of the Perfect; Father of the Only-begotten Son. [There is] one Lord, Alone of the Alone, God of God; Impress[3] and Image[4] of the Godhead, the operative Word; Wisdom, comprehensive of the system of the universe, and Power, productive of the whole creation; True Son of True Father, Invisible of Invisible, and Incorruptible of Incorruptible, and Immortal of Immortal, and Eternal of Eternal. And [there is] one Holy Ghost, who hath His being of God[5], and who hath appeared (that is to mankind) through the Son, Image of the Son, Perfect of the Perfect; Life, the cause of [all] them that live; Holy Fountain, Holiness, the Bestower of Sanctification; in whom is manifested God the Father, who is over all and in all, and God the Son, who is through all. A perfect Trinity, not divided nor alien in glory, and eternity, and dominion[h]. There is therefore nothing created, or servile in the Trinity; nor any thing superinduced, as though previously not-existent, and introduced afterwards. Never therefore was the Son wanting to the Father, nor the Spirit to the Son; but there is ever the same Trinity unchangeable and unalterable."

[1] σοφίας ὑφεστώσης.
[2] χαρακτὴρ, Heb. i. 3.
[3] χαρακτὴρ.
[4] εἰκών.
[5] ὕπαρξιν.

[e] He died in the same year, namely, A.D. 265. Cave.—BOWYER.

[f] Hist. Eccl. vii. 28; compare c. 30.

[g] εἷς Θεὸς, Πατὴρ λόγου ζῶντος, σοφίας ὑφεστώσης, καὶ δυνάμεως, καὶ χαρακτῆρος ἀϊδίου· τέλειος τελείου γεννήτωρ· Πατὴρ υἱοῦ μονογενοῦς. εἷς Κύριος, μόνος ἐκ μόνου, Θεὸς ἐκ Θεοῦ· χαρακτὴρ καὶ εἰκὼν τῆς θεότητος, λόγος ἐνεργός· σοφία τῆς τῶν ὅλων συστάσεως περιεκτικὴ, καὶ δύναμις τῆς ὅλης κτίσεως ποιητική· υἱὸς ἀληθινὸς ἀληθινοῦ Πατρὸς, ἀόρατος ἀοράτου, καὶ ἄφθαρτος ἀφθάρτου, καὶ ἀθάνατος ἀθανάτου, καὶ ἀΐδιος ἀϊδίου. καὶ ἓν πνεῦμα ἅγιον, ἐκ Θεοῦ τὴν ὕπαρξιν ἔχον, καὶ δι' υἱοῦ πεφηνὸς, δηλαδὴ τοῖς ἀνθρώποις, εἰκὼν τοῦ υἱοῦ, τελείου τελεία· ζωὴ, ζώντων αἰτία· πηγὴ ἁγία, ἁγιότης, ἁγιασμοῦ χορηγός· ἐν ᾧ φανεροῦται Θεὸς ὁ Πατὴρ, ὁ ἐπὶ πάντων καὶ ἐν πᾶσι, καὶ Θεὸς ὁ υἱὸς, ὁ διὰ πάντων. τριὰς τελεία, δόξῃ καὶ ἀϊδιότητι καὶ βασιλείᾳ μὴ μεριζομένη, μηδὲ ἀπαλλοτριουμένη. οὔτε οὖν κτιστόν τι, ἢ δοῦλον ἐν τῇ τριάδι, οὔτε ἐπείσακτόν τι, ὡς πρότερον μὲν οὐχ ὑπάρχον, ὕστερον δὲ ἐπεισελθόν· οὔτε οὖν ἐνέλιπέ ποτε υἱὸς Πατρὶ, οὔτε υἱῷ πνεῦμα, ἀλλ' ἄτρεπτος καὶ ἀναλλοίωτος ἡ αὐτὴ τρίας ἀεί.—See the works of Gregory Thaumat., p. 1. edit. Paris. 1622. [and those of Greg. Nyss., vol. iii. p. 546. After the Greek Bp. Bull gives the Latin version, published by Vossius.]

[h] [Here the Creed ends: the remaining words are Gregory Nyssen's.—B. This is not the case: see the notes in Gallandii Bibl. Patr., t. iii. p. 386, where St. Gregory Nazianzen's references to this Creed will also be found.]

ON THE CONSUBSTANTIALITY OF THE SON.

[417]

2. This Confession of faith was delivered, it is said, to Gregory by revelation from heaven, when, being wholly intent upon discharging his pastoral charge in the best way, he was one night considering the mode of preaching the pure faith to his people, and revolving in his mind the various questions which were then in controversy respecting the Holy Trinity.
152 And certainly no one ought to think it incredible that such an event should have happened to a man, whose whole life
[418] was illustrious from revelations and miracles, as all ecclesiastical writers who have mentioned him—and there is scarcely one who has not—unanimously attest. But however that may be, it is certain that this formula of catholic confession respecting the most Holy Trinity did really proceed from Gregory. For it is attributed to him not only by Ruffinus[i], but also by his namesake, Gregory of Nyssa[k], who had a thorough and accurate knowledge of what the admirable man did and wrote, and who also composed his life. Moreover this excellent man narrates the matter in such a way, that scarcely any sensible person can doubt about it. I mean that, being about to recite the Confession, he premises the following words[l]; "By which (Confession) the people of that city (Neocæsarea) are to this day initiated [in the faith[1]], having continued unaffected by all heretical pravity." So certain, you see, was it that this Confession of faith proceeded from Gregory Thaumaturgus, that all the people of the city of Neocæsarea, of which he was the bishop and the immortal glory, embraced it as the undoubtedly genuine work of Gregory, and had been used to be instructed by means of it, from so far back as their fathers could remember down to the age of Nyssen; and hence it came to pass that, when the whole world became Arian, the Church of Neocæsarea kept itself untainted by heretical pravity. Again, after having recited the Confession, Nyssen subjoins these words[m]: "And whoever wishes to be convinced on this point, let him hear the Church in which he used to preach the Word, among whom the very handwriting of that blessed hand is preserved even at the present

[1] μυσταγωγεῖται, i. e. it was their baptismal Creed.

[i] Hist. Eccl. ii. 25.

[k] In his life of Gregory Thaum., Oper., tom. ii. p. 978, 979. [vol. iii. p. 546.]

[l] δι' ἧς μυσταγωγεῖται μέχρι τοῦ νῦν ὁ ἐκείνης λαὸς, πάσης αἱρετικῆς κακίας διαμείνας ἀπείρατος.—[Ibid.]

[m] ὅτῳ δὲ φίλον περὶ τούτου πεισθῆναι, ἀκουέτω τῆς ἐκκλησίας, ἐν ᾗ τὸν λόγον ἐκήρυττεν, παρ' οἷς αὐτὰ τὰ χαράγματα τῆς μακαρίας ἐκείνης χειρὸς εἰς ἔτι καὶ νῦν διασώζεται.—[Ibid., p. 547.]

day." He appeals to the very autograph of Thaumaturgus, which was religiously kept by the Neocæsareans down to his own day. I know not, certainly, that any thing more can be required for the confirmation of a tradition of this nature. Gregory Nyssen's testimony, however, is explicitly supported, [419] as it seems to me, by his brother Basil the Great, who, in his seventy-fifth epistle to the people of Neocæsarea, testifies, that he had learnt from his grandmother, in his tender age, the very words of Gregory Thaumaturgus, by which he had been instructed aright respecting the faith in the most Holy Trinity. His words are these[n]: "What can be a more manifest demonstration of our faith, than this, that we, having been brought up under the nurture[1] of a woman of blessed memory[2], who came forth from you—I mean the illustrious Macrina;—by whom we were taught the words of the most blessed Gregory, whatsoever, having been preserved to her by the tradition of memory[3], she both herself kept treasured up, and used to mould and fashion us, whilst we were yet infants, in the doctrines of religion[o]?" Here, I say, it seems to me, that the Confession of Thaumaturgus is certainly referred to; for Basil expressly testifies that he had, in his infancy, learned of his grandmother Macrina, a native of Neocæsarea, the form[4] of faith touching the most Holy Trinity, (for of that he is [420] there treating,) as it had been delivered in so many words by Gregory. Reader, observe: Nyssen relates that the people of Neocæsarea used to be instructed by means of the Confession of Thaumaturgus, from so far back as their fathers could remember down to his own age; whilst Basil says that he had learned, in his tender age, (that is, before the council of Nice,) from his grandmother, (whilst he, that is, with his parents, was living with her at Neocæsarea in Pontus,) the right faith

[1] τίτθῃ.

[2] μακαρίᾳ.

[3] ἀκολουθίᾳ μνήμης.

[4] ὑποτύπωσιν.

[n] πίστεως δὲ τῆς ἡμετέρας τίς ἂν γένοιτο ἐναργεστέρα ἀπόδειξις, ἢ ὅτι τραφέντες ἡμεῖς ὑπὸ τίτθῃ μακαρίᾳ γυναικὶ, παρ' ὑμῶν ὡρμημένῃ; Μακρίναν λέγω τὴν περιβόητον· παρ' ἧς ἐδιδάχθημεν τὰ τοῦ μακαριωτάτου Γρηγορίου ῥήματα, ὅσα πρὸς αὐτὴν ἀκολουθίᾳ μνήμης διασωθέντα αὐτή τε ἐφύλασσε, καὶ ἡμᾶς ἔτι νηπίους ὄντας ἔπλαττε καὶ ἐμόρφου τοῖς τῆς εὐσεβείας δόγμασι.—Basil. Opera, tom. iii. p. 131. edit. Paris, 1638. [Ep. cciv. 6. vol. iii. p. 306.]

[o] [From these very words Lardner contends that Basil had neither seen nor referred to any confession of faith "written by the hand of Gregory."—B.—The existence of an autograph of St. Gregory's Confession would not cause the Church to depart from the ordinary practice of not circulating the Creed in writing. It would be taught and known to the people and preserved among them by oral transmission. And as no question was raised about the terms of the Confession, St. Basil had no need to refer to such original, supposing it existed.]

ON THE CONSUBSTANTIALITY OF THE SON.

respecting the most Holy Trinity, expressed in so many words of Gregory. Who would not suppose, that they both are speaking of the same Confession of faith? Further, also, the same Basil, in his book on the Holy Spirit, chap. 29, testifies that so great was the reputation of this Gregory amongst the people of Neocæsarea down to his own times, that they would admit in their Church nothing, whether in doctrine or rite, but what they had received by tradition from that their great founder. The words of Basil are these[p]: "Great is the admiration of this man (Gregory) still, even at this day, amongst the people of the country, and the remembrance of him is established in the Churches—fresh, and ever recent, not obscured by any lapse of time. They have not, therefore, added to their Church any practice, or word, or any sacred form[1] beyond what he left to them." If the Church of Neocæsarea refused
153 to admit any word beyond what was left to them by Gregory, certainly much less would they have admitted any Creed or Confession of faith, which they had not received from him. And yet it is most certain, that in the time of Basil, the Confession of faith of which we are speaking, was received in that Church, and that too as having been delivered by
[421] Gregory. To these facts may be added, that this Confession is delivered, as without doubt the genuine work of Thaumaturgus, by the whole of the fathers who were assembled at the fifth œcumenical synod. Lastly, the Confession itself quite bears the character[2] of the age of Gregory Thaumaturgus; in that it is manifestly opposed to the heresies, which were especially disturbing the Church of Christ at that period. Two heresies were particularly prevalent at that time, as is clear from the epistle of Dionysius of Rome, found in Athanasius, which we have already mentioned; one, that of Sabellius, which laid down that the Father, the Son, and the Holy Ghost differed in name only, not in hypostasis[3] (person;) the other as it were diametrically opposed to the Sabellian, that, I mean of those, who divided the most Holy Trinity into three hypostases, separate, foreign to, and mutually alien from each other, and who further affirmed,

[1] *τύπον τινὰ μυστικόν.*

[2] redolet.

[3] *ὑποστάσει.*

[p] *τούτου μέγα ἔτι καὶ νῦν τοῖς ἐγχωρίοις τὸ θαῦμα, καὶ νεαρὰ καὶ ἀεὶ πρόσφατος ἡ μνήμη ταῖς ἐκκλησίαις ἐνίδρυται, οὐδενὶ χρόνῳ ἀμαυρουμένη· οὐκοῦν οὐ πρᾶξίν τινα, οὐ λόγον, οὐ τύπον τινὰ μυστικὸν, παρ' ὃν ἐκεῖνος κατέλιπε, τῇ ἐκκλησίᾳ προσέθηκαν.*—Basil. Oper., tom. ii. p. 360. edit. Paris. 1638. [vol. iii. p. 63.]

BOOK II. CHAP. XII. § 2, 3.

GREGORY THAUMAT.

that the Son and the Holy Ghost were creatures, and that there was a time, when God the Father existed without them[1]. These words at the beginning of the Confession plainly strike at the former heresy: "Father of [Him, who is] the living Word, subsisting Wisdom:" and also these, "True Son of True Father;" (for Sabellius acknowledged neither a true Father nor a true Son, but both only in name:) and, lastly, these respecting the Holy Ghost; "who hath His being of God." The following words, besides others, certainly give a death-blow to the latter heresy: "Perfect Trinity, not divided nor alien in glory, and eternity, and dominion;" as do those which follow[q]: "There is, therefore, nothing created, or servile in the Trinity," &c. In a word, let the attentive reader compare the profession of Dionysius of Rome respecting the most Holy Trinity (which we quoted in the last chapter, § 1. [page 303,] from Athanasius) with this Confession of his contemporary, Gregory, of whom we are speaking, and he will immediately see the wonderful agreement between the two.

[1] et aliquando Deo patri defecisse.

3. Now, what does Sandius[r] say to these facts? "Of this Confession of faith," he says, "I say nothing else than that Eusebius, Jerome, and Sophronius are silent about it;" as [422] if, forsooth, Eusebius and Jerome mentioned every thing which the ancient fathers wrote and did. Eusebius, certainly, in his Ecclesiastical History, by what chance I know not, (for I cannot prevail on myself to believe that it was done, as Anastasius the Librarian[s] thought, with any evil design,) has suppressed almost all mention of the praises of Gregory Thaumaturgus, and says nothing about his miracles, which were celebrated throughout the Christian world. I imagine that, in some other work which has been lost, Eusebius had related more concerning Gregory Thaumaturgus; at any rate, in the Apology[t] for Origen he makes mention of his disciple Gregory Thaumaturgus, and also inserted in that work a panegyrical oration of his in praise of Origen, as Socrates attests, Eccl. Hist. IV. 27. As for Jerome, he trod generally in the very steps of Eusebius's history, whilst So-

[q] [These words, however, as we have already observed, are Gregory Nyssen's. —B. But see above, p. 323, note h.]

[r] De Script. Eccl., p. 39.

[s] Anastasius on the year of Christ 246.

[t] [i. e. the Apology of Pamphilus and Eusebius.—B.]

ON THE CONSUBSTANTIALITY OF THE SON.

phronius was merely a translator of Jerome. I wonder, however, what came into Philip Labbé's mind, when he wrote the following passage in his Dissertation upon the Ecclesiastical Writers[u]; "It is certain, indeed, as St. Gregory Nyssen witnesses in his Life of Thaumaturgus, that the Mother of God appeared with St. John the Evangelist, and commanded John to deliver to him an Exposition of the catholic faith. But whether this be that, which Vossius has published[x], Bellarmine with good reason doubted; see his words, as well as those of Petavius, who denies it, (Dogm. Theol., vol. ii.)" For Bellarmine never doubted, whether the Confession of faith published by Vossius were in reality that of Gregory Thaumaturgus; nay, he held this to be certain, as will be manifest to any one who consults Bellarmine himself. Concerning the ἔκθεσις or longer Exposition of faith, which is
[423] called κατὰ μέρος, which was also published by Vossius, Bellarmine does indeed doubt, and that with very good reason. It is also untrue, that Petavius denied the Confession, as it was published by Vossius, to be the genuine work of Gregory; nay, he cites it as Gregory's, and expressly calls it, "An illustrious monument of the tradition of which we are now treating, and of the ecclesiastical and catholic profession concerning the Trinity;" (Preface to vol. ii. chap. 4. n. 5.) But unquestionably he also, when speaking of the longer Exposition of faith, (which Labbé here confounded with the shorter Confession of Gregory,) does deny, and not without very grave reasons, that it is the genuine work of Gregory; on the Trinity, i. 4. 10. However, Labbé's statement that there is just ground for doubting, whether the Confession of faith, which Gregory Nyssen ascribes to Gregory Thaumaturgus, is the same as that which Vossius published, must astonish every one: for the Confession of faith, which Vossius published, corresponds word for word with that which Gregory Nyssen ascribes to Gregory Thaumaturgus. If Labbé had caught any one of the heterodox critics, as he calls them, so shamefully tripping, how would he (as his way is) have insulted over him! But this by the way[y].

u [Vol. i. p. 373.]

x [That is, that which Bp. Bull has cited; see above, p. 323, note h.]

y [Lardner shews by many arguments not to be despised that this formula of faith is not by any means a

4. Furthermore, there is still extant among the works of Gregory, as published by Vossius, a panegyric Oration upon Origen, which all agree, and which Sandius himself allows, is the genuine production of that very great man. In that Oration, after saying that God the Father cannot worthily be praised by any creature, He subjoins these truly magnificent words concerning the Son of God[z]; "But our praises 154
and hymns unto the King and Ruler of all, the continual fountain of all good things, we will commit to Him who even herein healeth our infirmities, and who alone is able to fill up what is wanting in us—the Guardian[1] and Saviour of our souls, His first-born Word, the Creator and Governor of all things, He Himself alone being able to offer up the perpetual and unceasing thanksgivings unto the Father both for Himself and for all, both for each individually by himself and for the whole body, because He Himself, being the Truth, and the Wisdom and Power of the Father Himself of all things, and, besides, both being in Him and absolutely united[2] to Him, it is not possible that, either through forget- [424]

[1] τῷ προστάτῃ.

[2] ἀτεχνῶς ἡνώμενος

genuine work of Gregory, but a composition of the fourth century.—B.—Lardner's arguments seem to be of two sorts; 1. Internal improbabilities. 2. Want of external evidence. In the first he, (i.) argues as if the genuineness of the *Creed* were disproved by the *vision* being proved legendary: and (ii.) goes upon his own notions of the small importance of the doctrine of the Trinity. In the second he alleges (i.) St. Jerome's omission; but St. Jerome does not profess to enumerate all the writings of the persons he mentions. (ii.) St. Basil's criticising St. Gregory, but this is only with respect to his expressions in an argument. See below, p. 333. (iii.) St. Basil's omitting to appeal to the autograph. On this see above, p. 325. note o. And Lardner omits to notice that it is the baptismal Creed of Neocæsarea of which St. Gregory Nyssen professedly speaks: which must have been too well known to allow of a recent composition being passed off instead of it.]

[z] ἀλλὰ τὰς μὲν εἰς τὸν πάντων βασιλέα καὶ κηδεμόνα, τὴν διαρκῆ πηγὴν πάντων ἀγαθῶν, εὐφημίας καὶ ὕμνους, τῷ κᾀν τούτῳ τὴν ἀσθένειαν ἡμῶν ἰωμένῳ, καὶ τὸ ἐνδέον ἀναπληροῦν μόνῳ δυναμένῳ ἐπιστρέψομεν[1], τῷ προστάτῃ τῶν ἡμετέρων ψυχῶν, καὶ σωτῆρι, τῷ πρωτογενεῖ αὐτοῦ λόγῳ, τῷ πάντων δημιουργῷ, καὶ κυβερνήτῃ. αὐτῷ μόνῳ ὑπέρ τε ἑαυτοῦ, καὶ ὑπὲρ πάντων, ἰδίᾳ τε καὶ καθ' ἕκαστον[2] καὶ ἀθρόον ἅμα δυνατὸν ὂν ἀναπέμπειν διηνεκεῖς καὶ ἀδιαλείπτους τῷ Πατρὶ τὰς εὐχαριστίας· ὅτι αὐτὸς ἡ ἀλήθεια ὢν, καὶ ἡ αὐτοῦ τοῦ Πατρὸς τῶν ὅλων καὶ σοφία καὶ δύναμις, πρὸς δὲ καὶ ἐν αὐτῷ ὢν, καὶ πρὸς αὐτὸν ἀτεχνῶς ἡνωμένος, οὐκ ἔστιν ὅπως ἢ διὰ λήθην, ἢ ἀσόφως, ἢ ὑπ' ἀσθενείας τινὸς, ὥσπέρ τις ἀπεξενωμένος αὐτοῦ, ἢ οὐκ ἐφίξεται τῇ δυνάμει τῆς δυνάμεως, ἢ ἐφίξεται μὲν, ἑκὼν δὲ, ὃ μὴ θεμὶς εἰπεῖν, ἐάσῃ[3] τὸν Πατέρα ἀνευφήμητον. μόνῳ τούτῳ δυνατὸν ὂν τελειότατα πᾶσαν ἀποπληρῶσαι τὴν ἀξίαν τῶν αὐτῷ προσηκόντων αἴνων· ὃν τινα αὐτὸς ὁ τῶν ὅλων Πατὴρ ἓν πρὸς αὐτὸν ποιησάμενος, δι' αὐτοῦ μονονουχὶ αὐτὸς αὐτὸν ἐκπεριιὼν, τῇ ἴσῃ πάντῃ δυνάμει τῇ αὐτοῦ τρόπον τινὰ τιμῴη καὶ τιμῷτο· ὅπερ πρῶτος καὶ μόνος ἔχειν ἔλαχεν ἐκ πάντων τῶν ὄντων ὁ μονογενὴς αὐτοῦ, ὁ ἐν αὐτῷ Θεὸς λόγος. [[1] The Bened. ed. reads ἐπιτρέψομεν. [2] Vossius read ἰδίᾳ τε καὶ ἑκάστου, but conjectured in the margin, καθ' ἕκαστον, which Bull inserted, retaining the καὶ also; the Bened. ed. τε καθ' ἕκαστον. [3] ἐάσει, ed. Ben.]—P. 53, 54. [In vol. iv. Op. Origenis, p. 59. Append. § 4.]

ON THE CONSUBSTANTIALITY OF THE SON.

fulness or from defect of wisdom, or from any infirmity, (as one who was alien [b] from Him,) He shall either not attain by His own power unto the power of the Father, or shall attain unto it indeed, and yet (which it were impious to say) shall willingly allow the Father to be unpraised; He alone being able to fill up most perfectly the due praises which belong to Him; whom the Father of the universe Himself, having
[1] ἓν. made One [1] with Himself, Himself by Him all but going forth
[2] ἐκπερίων (qu. ἐκπεριϊών.) and encircling Himself [c] [2], in a certain manner honours Him, and is honoured by Him, with power every way equal to His
[425] own; which [honour] His only-begotten Son, God the Word, who is in Him, first and alone of all beings obtained." Shortly afterwards in the same passage, he calls the Son [d] "the most perfect, and living, and animate Word of the primal Mind Himself[e]." In these words how many titles are heaped up concerning the Son of God, which eminently set forth His true Godhead! He calls the Son of God the Guardian of our souls, the first-born Word of God, the Creator and Governor of all things, the Truth, Wisdom and Power of the Father Himself: who is in the Father Himself, and truly united unto Him; who is subject to no forgetfulness, no lack of wisdom, no infirmity; who is in no wise alien from God the Father; who by His own power attains unto the Father's power; whom God the Father made one with Himself, and in whom He, as it were, circumscribed His own infinite Majesty; (clearly in the same sense as the very ancient writer in Irenæus, as
[426] we saw above[f], declared that the immeasurable Father Himself is measured in the Son:) who is in very truth endued with power in every way equal to that of the Father; who lastly, subsists in God Himself, as God the Word, and that the most perfect Word, as being sprung from the primal and eternal Mind. Could any one of the Arian herd, sincerely and from his heart, utter these things of the Son of God? Nor ought it to be the slightest difficulty to any one that

[b] So in the Confession Gregory denies that there is any thing alien (ἀπαλλοτριούμενον) in the Trinity.

[c] δι' αὐτοῦ μονονουχὶ αὐτὸς αὐτὸν ἐκπεριών. This clause he added by way of safeguard, (caute,) for, properly speaking, if the Son encircled (circumambiet) the Father, He would be greater than the Father, whereas he meant only to say that he was by nature equal to Him.

[d] τελειότατον καὶ ζῶντα, καὶ αὐτοῦ τοῦ πρώτου νοῦ λόγον ἔμψυχον.—[Ibid.]

[e] In like manner in the Confession he calls the Son "perfect, of the perfect Father," as also "living Word."

[f] Chap. v. § 4. [p. 164.]

Thaumaturgus says, that the Son honours and praises His Father, seeing that he also at the same time says, that the Father has honoured the Son, by imparting to Him power, in every way equal to His own. The truth is, the Son praises and honours the Father, as the Author and Principle of Himself; the Father, on the other hand embraces, and in a manner even honours, the Son, as the lively and most perfect Image and Offspring of Himself. Hence also, catholic writers who lived after the Nicene council, throughout spake in like manner concerning the Son of God. Although in this passage Gregory may seem also to have in view the economy of the Son[1], in so far as He, as Mediator, presents unto God the Father the prayers and thanksgivings of the faithful, and by His own intercession makes them pleasing and acceptable. Nay, he expressly speaks of the Son as, in this matter, "healing our infirmity." For this mediatorial office he shews that the Son is altogether sufficient, inasmuch as, in respect to His higher nature, He is entirely one with the Father, and possesses a power[2] in every respect equal to that of the Father.

[1] Filii οἰκονομίαν.

[2] virtute polleat.

5. Finally, if there were extant at this day no written 155
monument of Gregory's belief respecting the most holy Trinity, the great Basil alone would be a most ample testimony that his sentiments on that article were sound, uncorrupt, and catholic. For Basil, as often as his heretical opponents called in question[3] his faith respecting the Trinity, so often almost did he appeal to the tradition of Gregory Thaumaturgus, and professed, that he had held from a boy altogether the same views respecting the Trinity, as that admirable man [427] taught. Thus, in his seventy-fifth epistle, to the people of Neocæsarea[g], he makes it his boast, as has been already shewn, that he had learnt the catholic doctrine respecting the most holy Trinity in his boyhood from the words of Thaumaturgus, which had been taught him by[4] his grandmother Macrina. Moreover he also distinctly attests in his seventy-ninth epistle, to Eustathius, that he had never changed that faith concerning God, which he had received through his grandmother; these are his words[h]; "For even if all the rest of my life[5] deserve lamentation; yet still this one thing,

[3] litem ipsi intenderent.

[4] ipsi traditas per.

[5] τἄλλα ἡμῶν.

[g] [Ep. cciv.]

[h] εἰ γὰρ καὶ τἄλλα ἡμῶν στεναγμῶν ἄξια, ἀλλ' οὖν ἕν γε τοῦτο τολμῶ καυχᾶσθαι ἐν Κυρίῳ, ὅτι οὐδέποτε πεπλα-

at least, I am bold to glory of in the Lord, that my conceptions concerning God were never at any time led astray; nor having at one time held different opinions, did I afterwards unlearn them; but the notion of God which from a child I received from my mother of blessed memory[1], and from my grandmother, Macrina, this have I retained within me, [only] grown and enlarged[2]." Thus, if the sentiments of Basil on the Trinity were (as no one doubts) orthodox and religious, Gregory also, on the testimony of Basil himself, was catholic in that article. Basil also, on the authority of the Gregory of whom we are speaking, defends that form of doxology, by which the most Holy Trinity was glorified in the Churches subject to his government, and to which the heretics were so vehemently averse, in his Treatise on the Holy Spirit addressed to Amphilochius, chapter 29[i]; where, after he had brought together the highest praises of that very great man, he subjoins these words, which bear on our sub-
[428] ject; "One therefore of the [institutions] of Gregory is that form of doxology, which is now spoken against; preserved from his tradition by the Church;" that is, of Neocæsarea, which he all but founded. It was with good reason, therefore, and in reliance on the testimony of Basil[k], that Anastasius the librarian, in his history, pronounced that this Gregory especially was entirely free[3] from the ravings of Arius.

6. Now, this being the case, I cannot sufficiently wonder at those very learned men, who have ventured to bring a charge of Arianism against this great doctor of the Church, and even to put forward the authority of Basil as supporting their charge. Petavius[1] declares that two errors (not more inconsistent with the truth than with each other) are attributed to Gregory Thaumaturgus by Basil, in his seventy-fifth epistle; one the Sabellian, which taught that the Father and the Son differed only in our mode of conception[4], but not in hypostasis[5]; the other the Arian, which affirmed the Son to be "a creature and a work," (*κτίσμα καὶ ποίημα.*) And with re-

[1] μακαρίας.

[2] αὐξηθεῖσαν.

[3] alienum.

[4] cogitatione nostra.

[5] hypostasi.

νημένας ἔσχον τὰς περὶ Θεοῦ ὑπολήψεις, ἢ ἑτέρως φρονῶν μετέμαθον ὕστερον· ἀλλ' ἣν ἐκ παιδὸς ἔλαβον ἔννοιαν περὶ Θεοῦ παρὰ τῆς μακαρίας μητρός μου καὶ τῆς μάμμης Μακρίνης, ταύτην αὐξηθεῖσαν ἔσχον ἐν ἐμαυτῷ.—tom. iii. p. 141. [Ep. ccxxiii. 3. vol. iii. p. 338.]

[i] *ἓν τοίνυν τῶν Γρηγορίου καὶ ὁ νῦν ἀντιλεγόμενος τρόπος τῆς δοξολογίας ἐστὶν, ἐκ τῆς ἐκείνου παραδόσεως τῇ ἐκκλησίᾳ πεφυλαγμένος.*—[§ 74. p. 63.]

[k] Anastasius, on the year of Christ, 246.

[1] De Trin. i. 4. 10.

spect to the former, Petavius endeavours to shew that
Gregory's statements were correct; whilst in the latter he
thinks that Thaumaturgus did Arianize. Huet[m] also, relying too much, as it seems, on the candour and judgment of
Petavius, writes, "that Gregory Thaumaturgus was censured[1]
by Basil, for openly affirming that the Son was created."
Afterwards he does not hesitate to say, that that admirable
man was "a follower of the ravings of Arius." The Arian
Sandius[n], relying on the authority of these very learned
men, glories greatly in the fact, that one who was so great
a glory and ornament of the Christian Church, by the confession of us Catholics ourselves, agreed in opinion with [429]
Arius. If, however, we consider with a little more attention the words of Basil themselves, from which the mate-
rials of this accusation have been derived, it will presently
appear, that the charge of Arianism is made on Gregory
against the mind[2] of Basil. Basil then, in his seventy-fourth
epistle[o], to the people of Neocæsarea, after he had said that
the revivers of Sabellianism amongst them, with whom he
was in controversy, had even consigned their follies to published works, having mentioned an epistle of theirs to Meletius, presently animadverts on another epistle, addressed by
them to Anthimus, a bishop, in which they put forward the
great Gregory's authority for their ravings. These are the
words of Basil[p]; "They made an attempt by letter on Anthimus also, bishop of Tyana, who is of one mind with us,
as if forsooth Gregory, in an exposition of the faith, had said
that the Father and the Son are indeed two in [our] mode 156
of conception[3], but in hypostasis, one[4]. And these men who
congratulate themselves on the subtilty of their minds, were
[yet] unable to perceive that this was not said dogmatically,
but in the way of argument in his disputation with Ælian:
in which many [expressions] are errors of the transcribers,"
(that is to say, many things have been wrongly[5] copied from
the original MS.,) "as we shall shew, if God will, on the

[1] castigatum fuisse.

[2] ingratiis.

[3] ἐπινοίᾳ.

[4] ἕν.

[5] perperam.

[m] Huet. Origenian., p. 36. [lib. ii. Quæst. 2. 10. p. 122.]

[n] Enucl. Hist. Eccl. i. p. 111.

[o] [Ep. ccx. 5.]

[p] καθῆκαν δέ τινα πεῖραν δι' ἐπιστολῆς καὶ πρὸς τὸν ὁμόψυχον ἡμῶν Ἄνθιμον τὸν Τυάνων ἐπίσκοπον, ὡς ἄρα Γρηγορίου εἰπόντος ἐν ἐκθέσει πίστεως, πατέρα καὶ υἱὸν ἐπινοίᾳ μὲν εἶναι δύο, ὑποστάσει δὲ ἕν. τοῦτο δὲ ὅτι οὐ δογματικῶς εἴρηται, ἀλλ' ἀγωνιστικῶς ἐν τῇ πρὸς Αἰλιανὸν διαλέξει, οὐκ ἠδυνήθησαν συνιδεῖν οἱ ἐπὶ λεπτότητι τῶν φρενῶν ἑαυτοὺς μακαρίζοντες· ἐν ᾗ πολλὰ τῶν

words themselves[1]. Further, in using persuasion to a heathen, he did not think it necessary to be exact in his words, but [thought that he ought] in certain cases to adapt himself[2] to what he whom he was seeking to persuade had been accustomed to[3], in order that he might not offer opposition on the most important points[4], on which very account you will also find there many expressions, which now give the greatest strength to the [cause of the] heretics, such as 'creature' (*κτίσμα*,) and 'work' (*ποίημα*,) and others which there may be of that kind. Besides, they who hear what he has written without previous instruction[5], refer to the subject of the Godhead much of what is said with reference to the union with the manhood[6]; and of this kind is that also, which these [heretics] are circulating." In the passage Basil informs us,
[430] that the Sabellians understood those words in Gregory's exposition, "that the Father and the Son are indeed two in [our] mode of conception[7], but in hypostasis one,"—which he had brought forward in the course of discussion only on the hypothesis of his opponents—as the doctrine of Gregory himself; and for this he ridicules the want of perception of the witlings[8], who were unable to discern what was so obvious. Basil therefore, does not say that it was the actual opinion of Gregory, that the Father and the Son differed simply in [our] conception [of Them[9],] but he says the precise contrary. Petavius accordingly lost his labour and his time[10], when he
[431] endeavoured by I know not what subtleties to defend that statement, as if it were made by Gregory in a right and catholic sense, and censured Basil, as if he had without good grounds found fault with the same declaration of Gregory. For Gregory never wrote this as his own opinion; nor did Basil anywhere attribute that foolish heresy to him. Basil, moreover, says that faulty copies of that work of Gregory had been circulated by the heretics, in which many things

1 *ἐπ' αὐτῶν τῶν λέξεων* ex ipsis verbis.
2 *συνδιδόναι.*
3 *τῷ ἔθει.*
4 *ἀντιτείνοι πρὸς τὰ καίρια.*
5 *ἀπαιδεύτως.*
6 *πρὸς τὸν ἄνθρωπον συναφείας.*
7 cogitatione.
8 homunciorum *ἀβλεψίαν.*
9 *διανοίᾳ.*
10 operam et oleum.

ἀπογραψαμένων ἐστὶ σφάλματα, ὡς ἐπ' αὐτῶν τῶν λέξεων δείξομεν ἡμεῖς, ἐὰν ὁ Θεὸς θέλῃ. ἔπειτα μέντοι τὸν Ἕλληνα πείθων, οὐχ ἡγεῖτο χρῆναι ἀκριβολογεῖσθαι περὶ τὰ ῥήματα· ἀλλ' ἔστιν ὅπη καὶ συνδιδόναι [*συνδιδόντα* ed. Bened.] *τῷ ἔθει τοῦ ἐναγομένου, ὡς ἂν μὴ ἀντιτείνοι πρὸς τὰ καίρια. διὸ δὴ καὶ πολλὰς ἂν εὕροις ἐκεῖ φωνὰς, τὰς νῦν τοῖς αἱρετικοῖς μεγίστην ἰσχὺν παρεχομένας· ὡς τὸ κτίσμα, καὶ τὸ ποίημα, καὶ εἴτι τοιοῦτον. πολλὰ δὲ καὶ περὶ τῆς πρὸς τὸν ἄνθρωπον συναφείας εἰρημένα εἰς τὸν περὶ τῆς θεότητος ἀναφέρουσι λόγον, οἱ ἀπαιδεύτως τῶν γεγραμμένων ἀκούοντες· ὁποῖόν ἐστι καὶ τοῦτο, τὸ παρὰ τούτων περιφερόμενον.*—Oper. Basil., tom. iii. p. 101. [p. 316.]

were wrongly transcribed; and pledges himself to shew those mistakes evidently. This is the manifest meaning of the words, "in which many [statements] are errors of the transcribers," &c., and to this, it seems, we ought to refer what Evagrius observes in his Eccles. Hist. iii. 31, that heretics had obtruded their insanities on the world under the name of the great Gregory. Lastly, Basil allows that Gregory, in what was really his own in that work, (as he did not think it necessary, in delivering a simple outline of Christian doctrine to a heathen, to be exact in his expressions,) had himself used many expressions, from which the followers of the heresy which was the opposite to the Sabellian, endeavoured to establish their doctrines[q]. But does Basil say that they were right in so doing? Any thing but that; for shortly after he adds, that what Gregory had said of Christ in reference to His human nature, the heretics had ignorantly applied to His divinity. And to this class he expressly refers that saying, *κτίσμα καὶ ποίημα* ("creature and work,") which the sophists made so much boast of. Basil, therefore, does not say, (as Petavius would have him say,) that Gregory had in reality either thought or written, that the Son of God, in that He is properly the Son of God, is a creature or work; rather he intimates the very contrary.

7. But why need we say so much? So far is Basil in this [432]
passage from allowing that the Antitrinitarian heretics, of whatever kind, had with good reason put forward Gregory as sanctioning their tenets, that even in this very epistle he himself confidently appeals to his view on the Holy Trinity, in the first place after the Holy Scriptures. His words[r], not
far from the beginning of the epistle, are these; "There is 157
a perversion of the faith studiously pursued[1] among you, which is opposed to the doctrine of the Apostles and Evangelists, and also opposed to the tradition of Gregory the truly great, and of his successors down to the blessed Mu-

[1] μελετᾶται.

[q] Namely the Anomœans, who were also causing disturbances in the Church at Neocæsarea, as is evident from the words of Basil in this epistle; "For on one side the Anomœan is rending us, on another, as it seems, Sabellius." (ἐντεῦθεν γὰρ ἡμᾶς ὁ Ἀνόμοιος σπαράσσει· ἑτέρωθεν δὲ, ὡς ἔοικεν, Σαβέλλιος.) Ibid.

[r] πίστεως διαστροφὴ παρ' ὑμῖν μελετᾶται, ἐχθρὰ μὲν τοῖς ἀποστολικοῖς καὶ εὐαγγελικοῖς δόγμασιν, ἐχθρὰ δὲ τῇ παραδόσει τοῦ μεγάλου ὡς ἀληθῶς Γρηγορίου καὶ τῶν ἐφεξῆς ἀπ' ἐκείνου, μέχρι τοῦ μακαρίου Μουσωνίου· οὗ τὰ διδάγματα ἔναυλα ὑμῖν ἐστιν ἔτι καὶ νῦν δηλονότι.—p. 99. [§ 3. p. 314.]

ON THE CONSUBSTANTIALITY OF THE SON.

sonius, whose instructions are even yet sounding in your ears." The fact is this: both the sentiments and expressions of Gregory with respect to the Persons of the Godhead, were altogether correct and catholic; but the heretics of Neocæsarea, being pressed by his authority especially, either corrupted, or altogether wrongly interpreted, his words. Hence Basil, at the end of the preceding epistle[s], the seventy-third, thus addresses them, not without great emotion of mind; "Be silent as to these innovations respecting the faith; do not reject the [divine] hypostases; deny not the name of Christ; misinterpret not the words of Gregory. Otherwise it is impossible for us, so long as we continue to breathe and have the power of speech, to keep silence in the case of so great perdition of souls." Thus have we at length delivered Gregory of Neocæsarea, the greatest teacher of Christianity, after the Apostles, out of the camp of the Arians, (where certain learned men were detaining him by force, and as if a captive,) and have restored him to the Catholic Church.

158
[434]

CHAPTER XIII.

WHEREIN THE VIEWS RESPECTING THE CONSUBSTANTIALITY OF THE SON, OF THE SIX BISHOPS OF THE COUNCIL OF ANTIOCH, WHO WROTE AN EPISTLE TO PAUL OF SAMOSATA, AS WELL AS OF THE MARTYRS PIERIUS, PAMPHILUS, LUCIAN, AND METHODIUS, IS SHEWN TO BE CATHOLIC, AND QUITE IN HARMONY WITH THE NICENE CREED.

1. IN the days of Gregory Thaumaturgus there arose the heresy of Paul of Samosata, who denied the divinity of Christ, in opposition to whom the catholic bishops repeatedly assembled at Antioch. Of these bishops, the six chief (whose names were Hymenæus, Theophilus, Theotecnus, Maximus, Proclus, and Bolanus) wrote a remarkable epistle to Paul[t], before he was expelled from the Church by the anathema of the last and fullest synod, which is still extant

[s] *τὰς περὶ τὴν πίστιν καινοτομίας κατασιγάσατε, τὰς ὑποστάσεις μὴ ἀθετεῖτε, τὸ ὄνομα τοῦ Χριστοῦ μὴ ἀπαρνεῖσθε, τὰς τοῦ Γρηγορίου φωνὰς μὴ παρεξηγεῖσθε. εἰ δὲ μὴ, ἕως ἂν ἐμπνέωμεν, καὶ δυνώμεθα φθέγγεσθαι, ἀμήχανον ἡμᾶς ἐπὶ τοσαύτῃ λύμῃ ψυχῶν σιωπᾷν.*—[Ep. ccvii. p. 312.]

[t] In the year 270. Cave.—BOWYER.

in the 11th vol. of the Bibliotheca Patrum[u]. In that epistle the holy prelates expressly teach, that the Son of God is in His very essence and substance God. For after professing that they are delivering[x] "the faith which they had received by tradition from the beginning, and held [as it had been] handed down and preserved in the Catholic Church until that very day by succession from the blessed Apostles, who were both eye-witnesses and ministers of the Word, the faith which is preached out of the Law, and the Prophets, and the New Testament:" after premising this profession, I say, they next assert that the true and apostolic faith respecting Christ is this[y]; ["That He is] the Wisdom, and Word, and Power of God, existing before the worlds[1], not in foreknowledge (alone[2]), but in essence and subsistence[3] God, the Son of God." Nevertheless, Petavius does not suffer even these bishops to slip out of his hands without some brand of heterodoxy: although, as we have said, they were in the front rank of the great council of Antioch, and wrote their epistle, as is probable, with the cognizance of the whole synod. For in his first book on the Trinity, c. iv. § 10, the Jesuit writes thus of them; "Moreover, those six bishops who sent the epistle to Paul of Samosata before he was degraded[4], set forth in it certain statements respecting the Son, somewhat discordant from the rule of the catholic faith: for instance, when they say that the Son, in creating the world, fulfilled the Father's will, and that the Father gave Him commandment so to do. Hence also they prove the Son to be different[5] from the Father; inasmuch as he who commands, must necessarily be another from him whom he commands. They add, that He appeared to the patriarchs also in fulfilment of the Father's will, and that on account of this ministerial service He obtained the name of 'the Angel.'" This censure of Petavius was greedily caught at by Sandius[z], that he might fill his bag with these great names also, as abettors of Arian-

1 πρὸ αἰώνων.

2 præscientiâ solâ. Bull.

[435]

3 ὑποστάσει.

4 in ordinem redigeretur.

5 diversum.

u [It is also given in Routh's Reliq. Sacr., vol. ii. p. 465.—B.]

x [ἔδοξεν ἡμῖν ἔγγραφον τὴν πίστιν ἣν ἐξ ἀρχῆς παρελάβομεν, καὶ ἔχομεν παραδοθεῖσαν, καὶ τηρουμένην ἐν τῇ καθολικῇ καὶ ἁγίᾳ ἐκκλησίᾳ, μέχρι τῆς σήμερον ἡμέρας ἐκ διαδοχῆς ὑπὸ (for. ἀπὸ, Routh.) τῶν μακαρίων ἀποστόλων, οἳ καὶ αὐτόπται καὶ ὑπηρέται γεγόνασι τοῦ λόγου, καταγγελλομένην ἐκ νόμου καὶ προφητῶν καὶ τῆς καινῆς διαθήκης, ταύτην ἐκθέσθαι.—Ibid.]

y σοφίαν, καὶ λόγον, καὶ δύναμιν Θεοῦ, πρὸ αἰώνων ὄντα, οὐ προγνώσει, ἀλλ' οὐσίᾳ καὶ ὑποστάσει Θεὸν, Θεοῦ υἱόν. [Ibid.]

z Enucl. Hist. Eccles. i. 123, 124.

ON THE CONSUBSTANTIALITY OF THE SON.

ism. But, though Petavius or any one else bring forward a thousand passages of this kind out of the ancients, he will never thereby persuade me, that they agreed in opinion with Arius. For I know, that all those passages, so far as they refer either to the subordination of the Son to the Father, as His Principle and Author, or to the economy which the Son of God undertook immediately after the fall of man, (and the last passage ought to be referred to this,) do admit of a sound and orthodox sense, and are not discordant[a] from the rule of the catholic faith, as set forth by the Nicene fathers; although they do perhaps exhibit some discrepancy from the scholastic theology, to which Petavius deferred too
[436] much in respect to these mysteries. But, as for these six bishops, I shall hereafter[b] shew by a marked testimony
159 out of this their own epistle, that they held, that the Son of God in respect of nature[1] is altogether equal to the Father. Meanwhile let us pass on to other doctors of the Church.

[1] κατὰ φύσιν.

PIERIUS.

2. Pierius, a presbyter of the Church of Alexandria, and the teacher of Pamphilus the martyr, flourished[c] (according to Jerome[d]) under Clarus and Diocletian, at the time that Theonas presided over that Church. So great was the elegance of his style, and diversity of his treatises, that, as Jerome also states, he was called the younger Origen. He was a man of wonderful asceticism[2], and affected[3] voluntary poverty. It is also reported, as Photius affirms, that he suffered martyrdom for the name of Christ, together with his brother Isidore. The works that he sent out have now all been lost; but we learn from Photius, who had read a volume of his in twelve books, that he was quite a catholic writer on this article of the divinity of the Son. For, in cod. 119[e], he thus says of him: "Many things he sets forth in a way different from what now obtains[4] in the Church, perhaps after the ancient manner[5]: touching the Father and the Son, however, he treats religiously[6], except that he calls Them two substances and two natures[7]; using

[2] ἀσκήσεως.
[3] appetitor erat.
[4] ἔξω τῶν νῦν καθεστηκότων.
[5] ἀρχαιοτρόπως ἴσως.
[6] εὐσεβῶς πρεσβεύει.
[7] οὐσίας δύο καὶ φύσεις δύο.

[a] See this book, chap. 5. § 6. [p. 170.]

[b] See book iv. chap. 2. § 7.

[c] About the year 283. Cave.—BOWYER.

[d] Catalog. Script. Eccles., c. 87. [vol. ii. p. 901.]

[e] πολλὰ δὲ ἔξω τῶν νῦν ἐν τῇ ἐκκλησίᾳ καθεστηκότων, ἀρχαιοτρόπως ἴσως, ἀποφαίνεται· ἀλλὰ περὶ μὲν Πατρὸς καὶ υἱοῦ εὐσεβῶς πρεσβεύει, πλὴν ὅτι οὐσίας δύο καὶ φύσεις δύο λέγει· τῷ τῆς οὐσίας

BOOK II. CHAP. XIII. § 1, 2.

PIERIUS.

the words substance and nature, as is plain from what precedes and follows, instead of person (ὑποστάσις,) and not as the followers of Arius [use them]." What Pierius had written concerning the Son of God, must indeed have been [437] in the highest degree catholic, since his statements are commended as very religious[1] and alien from Arianism, even by Photius himself, who was in other instances a rigid and severe critic of the earlier writers, and was wont to bring even their most harmless expressions under the suspicion of Arianism. Besides, when Photius says, that Pierius had set forth many things after the ancient manner, and differently from what in his age obtained in the Church, and then immediately adds, that the same Pierius did, nevertheless, believe religiously concerning the Son of God, he therein plainly indicates, that the doctrine of Pierius respecting the Son of God, altogether agreed with the theology which in his own age was regarded as catholic. Now all who know any thing of Ecclesiastical History, are aware how widely removed from Arianism was the doctrine of the Greek Church concerning the Son of God, in the time of Photius; with respect however to what Photius further states in the same place, that Pierius's teaching respecting the Holy Ghost was not religious[2], inasmuch as he affirmed that the Holy Ghost is inferior to the Father and the Son, it is very easily defended from the suspicion of heresy. For the Holy Ghost is less[3] than the Father and the Son in the same respect, in which the Son Himself is acknowledged by all Catholics to be less[4] than the Father; I mean in respect of origin[5]. The Son has His origin from the Father alone; whilst the Holy Ghost derives His origin from the Father and the Son, as the Western Church defined; or from the Father through the Son[6], as the Orientals loved to express themselves. This I am quite persuaded is all that Pierius meant. But it is clear from this how falsely, and, as his way is, how impudently Sandius wrote that[f]; "Pierius (as Photius attests) taught that the Son and the Father are two essences and natures," the words essences and natures, that is, being taken in the sense in [438]

[1] pie admodum scripta.

[2] minus pie [δυσσεβῶς, Phot.]

[3] minor.

[4] minor.

[5] originis respectu.

[6] per Filium.

καὶ φύσεως ὀνόματι, ὡς δῆλον ἔκ τε τῶν ἑπομένων καὶ προηγουμένων τοῦ χωρίου, ἀντὶ τῆς ὑποστάσεως, καὶ οὐχ ὡς Ἀρείῳ προσανακείμενοι, χρώμενος. — [Phot. Bibl. cod. 119.]

[f] Enucl. Hist. Eccles. i. p. 126.

ON THE CONSUBSTANTIALITY OF THE SON.

which they are distinguished from person. Photius does not attest this, but the direct contrary, namely that Pierius's belief respecting the Father and the Son was religious; and that, in the place where he said, that the Father and the Son are two substances, it is manifest from the context of the passage, that he used the word *οὐσια* (substance) instead of *ὑπόστασις* (person); and that he, consequently, meant no more than that the Father and the Son are two persons; and that this is catholic, all Catholics will, I suppose, readily allow. But from the master let us come to his scholar.

PAMPHILUS.

3. St. Pamphilus[g], a disciple of Pierius, and presbyter of the Church of Cæsarea in Palestine, a celebrated man, who was crowned[h] with martyrdom in the persecution under Maximinus, a little before his death[1], being in prison along with Eusebius, wrote an Apology for Origen, consisting of five parts, to which, after the death of Pamphilus, Eusebius himself added a sixth. The first of these five books of Pamphilus, is still extant in a Latin translation by Ruffinus, among the works of Jerome, published by Marianus Victorinus[i]. It can be easily proved, in opposition to Jerome, who advances various and inconsistent arguments on this point, that this book does not wrongly bear the martyr's name. At all events the statement is palpably false which Jerome makes, (in book iii. of his Apology against Ruffinus, chapter 4[k],) that "Ruffinus was the only person who had published" that Apology "under the martyr's name;" since the Greek copies also, (as is attested by Photius, cod. 118, and by the ancient Greek author of an Apology for Origen, mentioned in Photius, cod. 117,) attributed it to Pamphilus. It is in a crafty way also that Jerome repeatedly contends that the Apology is the work of Eusebius; for it is, indeed, Eusebius's, but not Eusebius's alone; inasmuch as it was composed by the joint labours of both, of Pamphilus as well as of Eusebius.
[439] This fact is expressly asserted by Eusebius himself, who best knew the circumstances, in his Ecclesiastical History,

[1] τελείωσιν.

[g] He flourished about the year 294. Cave.—BOWYER.

[h] About the year 309. Cave.—BOWYER. [See above, p. 65.]

[i] [And in the appendix to the fourth volume of the Benedictine edition of Origen.]

[k] [Jerome's words are "quem tu solus sub martyris nomine edidisti." § 12. vol. ii. p. 541.]

vi. 33, he says[l]; "But what is necessary to be known concerning him (Origen), you may gather from the Apology on his behalf, composed by me and Pamphilus, the holy martyr of our times; which we wrote on account of his censorious accusers, labouring together with care and diligence." Photius, cod. 118, explains this passage of Eusebius thus[m]; "I read the work of Pamphilus the martyr and Eusebius in defence of Origen; the book consists of six parts[1], of which five were the work of Pamphilus, when he was in prison, Eusebius being with him there, and the sixth was finished by Eusebius, after the martyr was removed from this life by the sword, and departed[2] to God for whom he longed." It is, strange, however, that Jerome, in the passage quoted above, should endeavour to prove that this Apology was not written by Pamphilus, by this argument especially[n]; "that Eusebius writes that Pamphilus published nothing of his own." For here, it seems, he sets Eusebius against Eusebius; inasmuch as the same Eusebius, as we have seen, expressly testifies that Pamphilus employed his labours in that defence. But Jerome might, if he had wished, very easily have solved this difficulty; for the Apology could not properly be called Pamphilus' own work, since he wrought it out with the [440]
assistance of another, namely Eusebius. Of the fidelity of Ruffinus's version of Pamphilus's Apology, we have spoken already, [pages 272, 273.] Now it is abundantly clear from that Apology, that the opinion of Pamphilus was orthodox concerning the divinity of Christ. For while in that work the holy man endeavours to prove that Origen was catholic, from the circumstance that in his writings he taught[o], "that the Holy Ghost is unchangeable, equally as the Father and the Son; that the Trinity is equal, and that the Holy

[1] τόμοι.

[2] ἀνέλυσε.

l ὅσα δὲ ἀναγκαῖα τῶν περὶ αὐτὸν διαγνῶναι ἦν, ταῦτα καὶ ἐκ τῆς ὑπὲρ αὐτοῦ πεπονημένης ἡμῖν τε καὶ τῷ καθ' ἡμᾶς ἱερῷ μάρτυρι Παμφίλῳ ἀπολογίας πάρεστιν ἀναλέξασθαι· ἣν τῶν φιλαιτίων ἕνεκα συμπονήσαντες ἀλλήλοις, διὰ σπουδῆς πεποιήμεθα.—[Euseb. H. E. vi. 33.]

m ἀνεγνώσθη Παμφίλου τοῦ μάρτυρος καὶ Εὐσεβίου ὑπὲρ Ὠριγένους· τόμοι δὲ τὸ βιβλίον ἕξ· ὧν οἱ μὲν πέντε Παμφίλῳ τὸ δεσμωτήριον οἰκοῦντι, συμπαρόντος καὶ Εὐσεβίου, ἐξεπονήθησαν· ὁ δὲ ἕκτος, ἐπεὶ ὁ μάρτυς ξίφει τοῦ ζῆν ἀπαχθεὶς ἀνέλυσε πρὸς ὃν ἐπόθει Θεὸν, Εὐσεβίῳ λοιπὸν ἀπαρτίζεται. [Phot. cod. 118.]

n [cum . . .] Eusebius scribat Pamphilum nihil proprii operis edidisse.—[S. Hieron. ubi supra, p. 541.]

o [Quod eadem sit inconvertibilitas Spiritus Sancti, quæ et Patris et Filii (c. 4. p. 26); . . . . Quod æqualis sit sibi Trinitas, et quod Spiritus Sanctus non sit creatura (p. 27); . . . . Quod sicut

ON THE CONSUBSTANTIALITY OF THE SON.

Ghost is not a creature; that as the Father knows the beginnings and the limits of all things which exist, so does the Son, and so does the Holy Ghost know them; that the Son is ὁμοούσιος, (consubstantial,) that is, of one substance with the Father;" while, I say, he endeavours to shew that Origen was orthodox on these heads, he most plainly declares that he himself held the same propositions to be true and catholic. Besides, it is no contemptible argument for the orthodoxy of Pamphilus on this point, that he was taught his theology by St. Pierius; and that Pierius held entirely orthodox opinions concerning the Father and the Son, Photius himself, as we have seen, allows. It follows that the shameless sophist, Sandius[p], has most unjustly classed this blessed martyr among those who favoured and supported the heresy which was afterwards called Arian.

LUCIAN.

4. With St. Pamphilus must be joined St. Lucian[q]. He was a presbyter of the Church of Antioch and a very eloquent man, who laboured so much in the study of the Scriptures, that even in the age of Jerome, as he himself testifies[r], certain copies of the Scriptures were called Lucianean[1]. He wrote some short treatises[2] concerning the faith, and brief epistles to some persons, which are all lost. He suffered at Nicomedia in maintaining the cause of Christ, during the persecution of Maximinus[s], and was buried at Helenopolis in Bithynia. This blessed man, also, Petavius has branded with the mark of heterodoxy, in the article concerning the divinity of the Son[t]; and he is [herein] followed by Sandius[u], who boasts much of Lucian as a patron of the Arians. Nay, even Huet himself, misled, I suppose, by Petavius, enumerates this martyr amongst those who devised false and absurd notions respecting the Trinity[x]. Let us, however, examine the arguments, on which this censure of theirs is grounded. First, they say, that the Arians used to call themselves Lucianists, because, that is, of their agreeing in

[1] exemplaria Scripturarum Lucianæa.

[2] libellos.

[441]

Pater novit initia omnium quæ sunt, et fines, sic et Filius, sic et Spiritus Sanctus sciat (p. 28); .... ὁμοούσιος est cum Patre Filius, id est, unius substantiæ (p. 33.)

[p] Enucl. Hist. Eccles. i. p. 126.

[q] He flourished about the year 290. Cave.

[r] Hieron. Catal. Script. Eccles., c. 88. [vol. ii. p. 903.]

[s] In the year 311. Cave.—BOWYER.

[t] De Trin. i. 4. 13.

[u] Enucl. Hist. Eccles. i. p. 127.

[x] Pag. 187. Origenian. ii. 3. § 6. [p. 253.]

belief with Lucian the martyr. I grant it; but what man of sense will give credit to this most mendacious class of men? They boasted just in the same way of Origen and Dionysius of Alexandria as being of one mind with them[1]. But how utterly vain and shameless this boasting of theirs was, I have given, if I mistake not, abundant proof in the preceding chapters. As regards the martyr Lucian, however, what Sozomen, Hist. Eccl. iii. 5[y], relates respecting the council which was convened at Antioch, by the mandate of the emperor Constantius, for the Dedication [of the Golden church,] 161
is worthy of being noted. The bishops of this synod (of whom the largest part were either simply Arians, or at any rate only too favourable to Arius) first published a Confession of faith, which was widely different from the Nicene faith. But since in this formulary they were thought to have treated in too meagre a way of the divinity of the Son, they published another more full, seizing the following circumstance as an occasion for it. Having somewhat prolonged their stay at Antioch, they discovered a Confession of faith which had been drawn up by the martyr Lucian; this, in- [442]
asmuch as the word ὁμοούσιος was not found in it, and some of its phrases seemed to favour their heresy, they greedily embraced, and published it as the explication of their own belief; for the purpose, no doubt, of persuading the ignorant that they held the belief of the famous martyr Lucian. For thus Sozomen writes in the passage cited[z]; "And they said that they had discovered this Creed, all written in the hand of Lucian himself, who suffered martyrdom at Nicomedia."

5. This formulary is given by Athanasius, Socrates[a], and others, and for the sake of the reader who may not have these authors by him, I shall not hesitate to transcribe here such portions of it as relate to the Trinity. The Creed of Lucian, then, so much talked of by the Arians, makes this profession respecting the most Holy Trinity: "In agreement with the teaching[2] of the Gospels and the Apostles we believe in one God the Father Almighty, the Creator[3] and Maker [and

[1] ὁμοψύχοις.

[2] παραδόσει.

[3] δημιουργὸν τε καὶ ποιητὴν.

[y] See also Niceph. Hist. Eccles. ix. 5.

[z] ἔλεγον δὲ ταύτην τὴν πίστιν ὁλόγραφον εὑρηκέναι Λουκιανοῦ, τοῦ ἐν Νικομηδείᾳ μαρτυρήσαντος.—[H. E. iii. 5.]

[a] πιστεύομεν ἀκολούθως τῇ εὐαγγελικῇ καὶ ἀποστολικῇ παραδόσει εἰς ἕνα Θεὸν Πατέρα παντοκράτορα, τὸν τῶν ὅλων δημιουργόν τε καὶ ποιητὴν [καὶ

ON THE CONSUBSTANTIALITY OF THE SON.

Providential Ruler] of all things, [from whom are all things]; and in one Lord Jesus Christ, His Son, the only-begotten, God; through whom were all things (made); who was begotten of[1] the Father before (all) the worlds, God of[2] God, Whole of Whole, Sole of Sole, Perfect of Perfect, King of King, Lord from[3] Lord; the living Word, Wisdom, Life[4], true Light, Way of Truth[5], Resurrection, Shepherd, Door, both unalterable and unchangeable, the unvarying[6] Image of the Godhead, both of the substance and power, and counsel and glory of the Father; the first-born of every creature; Him, who was in the beginning with God, God the Word, according to that which is said in the Gospel, 'And the Word was God;' through whom all things were made, and in
[443] whom all things consist; Him who in the last days came down from above, and was born of a virgin, according to the Scriptures; . . . . And in the Holy Ghost, who is given to them that believe for consolation and sanctification, and (for) perfection[7]: even as our Lord Jesus Christ gave commandment to His disciples, saying, Go ye and make disciples of all nations, baptizing them into the name of the Father, and of the Son, and of the Holy Ghost; that is, of the Father, being truly Father, the Son, being truly Son, and the Holy Ghost, being truly Holy Ghost; the names not being used as mere [names[8],] and without [corresponding] realities[9], but expressing accurately the proper Person[10] (hypostasis), and glory, and order of Each of Those that are named; so that They are in Person[11] (hypostasis) Three, but in agreement One."

1 ἐκ.
2 ἐκ.
3 ἀπὸ.
4 Living Wisdom. S. Ath.
5 Way, Truth. S. Ath.
6 ἀπαράλλακτον.
7 τελείωσιν.
8 οὐκ ἁπλῶς.
9 οὐδὲ ἀργῶν κειμένων [ἀργῶς Ath.]
10 ὑπόστασιν.
11 τῇ ὑποστάσει.

προνοητὴν ἐξ οὗ τὰ πάντα]· καὶ εἰς ἕνα Κύριον Ἰησοῦν Χριστὸν, τὸν υἱὸν αὐτοῦ τὸν μονογενῆ Θεὸν, δι' οὗ τὰ πάντα (ἐγένετο)· τὸν γεννηθέντα πρὸ (πάντων) τῶν αἰώνων ἐκ τοῦ Πατρὸς, Θεὸν ἐκ Θεοῦ, ὅλον ἐξ ὅλου, μόνον ἐκ μόνου, τέλειον ἐκ τελείου, βασιλέα ἐκ βασιλέως, Κύριον ἀπὸ Κυρίου· λόγον ζῶντα, σοφίαν, ζωὴν [l. ζῶσαν], φῶς ἀληθινὸν, ὁδὸν ἀληθείας [l. ὁδὸν, ἀλήθειαν], ἀνάστασιν, ποιμένα, θύραν· ἄτρεπτόν τε καὶ ἀναλλοίωτον· (τὴν) τῆς θεότητος, οὐσίας τε καὶ δυνάμεως, καὶ βουλῆς, καὶ δόξης τοῦ Πατρὸς ἀπαράλλακτον εἰκόνα· τὸν πρωτότοκον πάσης κτίσεως· τὸν ὄντα ἐν ἀρχῇ πρὸς τὸν Θεὸν, λόγον Θεὸν, κατὰ τὸ εἰρημένον ἐν τῷ εὐαγγελίῳ, Καὶ Θεὸς ἦν ὁ λόγος, δι' οὗ τὰ πάντα ἐγένετο, καὶ ἐν ᾧ τὰ πάντα συνέστηκε· τὸν ἐπ' ἐσχάτων τῶν ἡμερῶν κατελθόντα ἄνωθεν, καὶ γεννηθέντα ἐκ παρθένου κατὰ τὰς γραφάς. . . . καὶ εἰς τὸ πνεῦμα τὸ ἅγιον, τὸ εἰς παράκλησιν καὶ ἁγιασμὸν, καὶ (εἰς) τελείωσιν τοῖς πιστεύουσι διδόμενον· καθὼς καὶ ὁ Κύριος ἡμῶν Ἰησοῦς Χριστὸς διετάξατο τοῖς μαθηταῖς, λέγων, Πορευθέντες μαθητεύσατε πάντα τὰ ἔθνη, βαπτίζοντες αὐτοὺς εἰς τὸ ὄνομα τοῦ Πατρὸς, καὶ τοῦ υἱοῦ, καὶ τοῦ ἁγίου πνεύματος. δῆλον ὅτι Πατρὸς ἀληθινῶς ὄντος Πατρὸς, καὶ υἱοῦ ἀληθινῶς υἱοῦ ὄντος, καὶ πνεύματος ἁγίου ἀληθῶς ὄντος πνεύματος ἁγίου· τῶν ὀνομάτων οὐχ ἁπλῶς, οὐδὲ ἀργῶν [l. ἀργῶς] κειμένων, ἀλλὰ σημαινόντων ἀκριβῶς τὴν ἰδίαν [l. οἰκείαν] ἑκάστου τῶν ὀνομαζομένων ὑπόστασίν τε καὶ δόξαν καὶ τάξιν· ὡς εἶναι τῇ μὲν ὑποστάσε, τρία, τῇ δὲ συμφωνίᾳ ἕν.—

6. That this was really the Creed of Lucian, and was not palmed upon him by the Arians, is proved by many considerations. In the first place, those bishops would have
acted very imprudently, and even shamelessly, if they had [444]
published any Confession of faith at Antioch in the name
of Lucian, which was not really his; [in a place] where the 162
memory of the holy martyr was justly sacred, and his writings were preserved with the most religious care; so that any fraud might have been detected with the greatest ease by any one. Secondly, suppose it had been possible for them to practise deceit on one single occasion[1] in safety, still the imposture could not have been long concealed. Yet the Arians put forward this Creed, and that with the greatest confidence, as the undoubted production of Lucian the martyr, many years afterwards, when, in the reign of Valentinian and Valens, a synod was to be assembled[2] in the city of Tarsus in Cilicia, as Sozomen states in his Ecclesiastical History vi. 12. For then, he says, in the same passage[b], "about thirty-four bishops of Asia, having assembled in Caria of Asia, commended the zeal [shewn] for the concord of the Churches; but declined the word *ὁμοούσιος*; and strenuously maintained that the faith which had been put forth at Antioch and Seleucia, ought to hold, both as being that of the martyr Lucian, and as having been approved by their predecessors amid dangers and many labours." Moreover, if the [445]
Arians had themselves patched together this Creed, they would certainly have made it more closely conformed to their own opinions; at least they would not have inserted such things as would be quite a death-blow to their own heresy; and that some things of this kind are found in it, we shall presently shew. Lastly, this Confession of faith is chiefly directed against the Sabellian heresy, as is most manifest from

[1] semel.

[2] congreganda esset.

Socrat. Hist. Eccles. ii. 10. S. Athan. Lib. de Synod. Arim. et Seleuc., tom. i. p. 892. [§ 23. vol. i. p. 735-6. The words omitted in St. Athanasius are included in ( ), his additions and variations in [ ]. In the concluding clauses he has *ἀληθῶς* for *ἀληθινῶς*, and some slight variations in the arrangement of the words.]

[b] *συνελθόντες ἐν Καρίᾳ τῆς Ἀσίας ἀμφὶ τριάκοντα τέσσαρες τῶν Ἀσιανῶν ἐπισκόπων, τὴν μὲν ἐπὶ τῇ ὁμονοίᾳ τῶν ἐκκλησιῶν σπουδὴν ἐπῄνουν· παρῃτοῦντο δὲ τὸ τοῦ ὁμοουσίου ὄνομα· καὶ τὴν ἐν Ἀντιοχείᾳ καὶ Σελευκείᾳ ἐκτεθεῖσαν πίστιν χρῆναι κρατεῖν ἰσχυρίζοντο, ὡς καὶ Λουκιανοῦ τοῦ μάρτυρος οὖσαν, καὶ μετὰ κινδύνων καὶ πολλῶν ἱδρώτων παρὰ τῶν πρὸ αὐτῶν δοκιμασθεῖσαν.*—[H. E. vi. 12.]

ON THE CONSUBSTANTIALITY OF THE SON.

what it contains towards the end[c]. For after giving a full explanation of the faith respecting the most holy Trinity, the Creed at last concludes with this, as a sort of epilogue, explaining the sum and scope of all that had been stated before; "Of the Father, that is, being truly Father, *and of the Son, being truly Son,* and of the Holy Ghost, being truly Holy Ghost; the names not being used as mere [names,] and without [corresponding] realities, but expressing accurately the proper person, glory, and order of Each; so that They are in Person Three, but in agreement One." Now what had these assertions to do with the Arian controversy, which was the subject of discussion at the council of Antioch? In the days of Lucian, however, the doctrine of Sabellius was especially prevalent; and Lucian himself is said to have been a most energetic opponent of it. To this I will subjoin, by way of addition[1], an observation of Philostorgius, Hist. Eccl. ii. 15, where, speaking of the disciples of Lucian the martyr, who had not maintained their master's doctrine unimpaired, he writes that[d] "Asterius had perverted his views[2], testifying [as he does] in his words and writings that the Son is the unvarying Image of the substance of the Father." Asterius, however, borrowed this statement in so many words from the Creed of Lucian, as will be evident on comparing them.

[1] mantissæ loco.

[2] παρατρέψαι τὸ φρόνημα.

[446]

7. Now, if this Creed be really Lucian's, he must have been altogether catholic in the article of the divinity of the Son. For this Confession, except that the word *ὁμοούσιος* is wanting in it, does in all other points quite agree with the Nicene Creed, as Sozomen rightly observed in the passage cited above. It follows that, if we look to the thing itself, putting aside all controversy about words, the Arians might with as good reason have called themselves the maintainers of the Nicene Creed, as Lucianists. Nay, I may almost venture to affirm, that the absolute divinity of the Son is up to a certain point more effectually and significantly expressed in the Creed of Lucian, than in the Nicene Creed itself. For the words, "God of God, Whole of Whole, Per-

[c] An observation which has also been made by Hilary, as the reader will see in § 7.

[d] καὶ τὸν Ἀστέριον παρατρέψαι τὸ φρόνημα, ἀπαράλλακτον εἰκόνα τῆς τοῦ Πατρὸς οὐσίας εἶναι τὸν υἱὸν, ἐν τοῖς αὐτοῦ λόγοις καὶ γράμμασι διαμαρτυρόμενον. [Philost. H. E. ii. 15.]

BOOK II. CHAP. XIII. § 6, 7. LUCIAN.

fect of Perfect," which occur in the Confession of Lucian, do more expressly enunciate the perfect Divinity of the Son, and the equality of His nature with the Father's, than those of the Nicene Creed, "God of God, Light of Light, very God of very God." Such statements, however, in the Creed of Lucian, as have the appearance of favouring the Arians in some degree, Hilary, in his book on the Synods against the Arians, admirably demonstrates to be quite catholic. These are his words[e]; "The assembled synod of holy men therefore," (for so catholic did this Creed appear to Hilary, that he believed it had issued forth from catholic men assembled at Antioch,)—"wishing to put an end to that impiety, which would elude the real existence[1] of the Father, and of the Son, and of the Holy Ghost, by representing these as so many names[2],—that so a threefold denomination without a subsistent reality corresponding to each name[3], might uphold [their doctrine of] oneness[4][f] under an unreality[5] of names, and the Father being alone and single, the same and by Himself, might have the name of Holy Spirit and of Son—on this account asserted that They are three substances (*substantias*, [ὑποστάσεις]), indicating by *substances* the persons of those that exist substantively, not separating the substance of the Father and the Son by the difference of dissimilar essence. Moreover the statement that They are indeed in substance (*per substantiam*, [ὑποστάσει]) three[6], but in agreement one[7], contains no ground for injurious accusation; because the Spirit, that is, the Comforter, being named along with Them, it was fitting to set forth the unity of agreement, rather than that of essence arising from likeness of substance[g]. Besides, the whole preceding statement did not in any one point distinguish the Father and the Son by difference of essence

[1] veritatem.

[2] nominum numero.

[447]

[3] non subsistente causa nominis.

[4] unionem.

[5] falsitate.

[6] tria.

[7] unum.

[e] Volens igitur congregata sanctorum synodus impietatem eam perimere, quæ veritatem Patris et Filii et Spiritus Sancti nominum numero eluderet, ut non subsistente causa uniuscujusque nominis, triplex nuncupatio obtineret sub falsitate nominum unionem, et Pater solus atque unus idem atque ipse haberet (et Spiritus Sancti) nomen et Filii; idcirco tres substantias esse dixerunt, subsistentium personas per *substantias* edocentes, non substantiam Patris et Filii diversitate dissimilis essentiæ separantes. Quod autem dictum est, *ut sint quidem per substantiam tria, per consonantiam vero unum*, non habet calumniam; quia connominato Spiritu, id est Paracleto, consonantiæ potius quam essentiæ per similitudinem substantiæ prædicari convenit unitatem. Cæterum omnis superior sermo in nullo Patrem et Filium es-

ON THE CONSUBSTANTIALITY OF THE SON.

and nature. For where it is said, 'God of God, Whole of Whole[1],' there is no doubt, that Whole God is begotten of Whole God. For neither is there difference in the nature of [Him who is] God from God; and [He that is] Whole from Whole, is Himself in [all] those things in which the Father is[2]. 'One from One' (*unum ex uno*, [*μόνον ἐκ μόνου*]) excludes the affections of human birth and conception; so that, being One from One, He is not from any other source, nor different, nor other[h], Who is 'One from One, Perfect from Perfect;' the condition of the begotten[3] differs not from that of the unbegotten[4], excepting the cause of origin, seeing that the perfection of each is not different. 'King from King;' power named together under one and the same name, admits not of dissimilarity of power. 'Lord of Lord;' lordship also is made equal by [the word] Lord; nor does lordship [thus] confessed in each, without difference, admit of diversity. But that which is added after many other statements, 'the unalterable and unchangeable (unvarying) Image of the Godhead, both of the essence, and power, and glory,' is absolute. For, being of God, God, of Whole Whole, of One One, of Perfect Perfect, and of King King, and of Lord Lord, seeing that in all that glory and nature of the Godhead, in which
[448] the Father abides, the Son also being born (begotten) does also subsist, He hath this likewise from the substance of the Father, that He be not capable of change. For that nature of which He was born, (begotten,) was not changed in Him in His being born, (begotten,) but being born (begotten) He obtained an unchangeable nature, from an original[5] of un-

[1] totum ex toto.

[2] in iis est ipse in quibus Pater est.

[3] nativitas.

[4] ab innascibilitate.

[5] ex auctoritate.

sentiæ ac naturæ diversitate discrevit. Ubi enim dicitur, *Deum de Deo, totum ex toto;* non ambigitur totum Deum ex toto Deo natum. Nam et Dei de Deo natura non differt; et totus ex toto in iis est ipse, quibus pater est. *Unus ex uno* passiones humani partus et conceptionis excludit: ut dum unus ex uno est, non aliunde, nec diversus, aut alius sit, qui est *unus ex uno, perfectus a perfecto;* non differt præter originis causam ab innascibilitate nativitas, cum perfectio utriusque non differat. *Rex de Rege;* non admittit uno atque eodem nomine potestas connuncupata dissimilitudinem potestatis. *Dominum de Domino;* dominatus quoque æquatur in Domino; nec recipit differentiam confessa in utroque sine diversitate dominatio. Illud vero quod post multa alia subjectum est, *inconvertibilem et immutabilem, divinitatis et essentiæ et virtutis et gloriæ imaginem,* absolutum est. Nam ex Deo Deus, ex toto totus, ex uno unus, et ex perfecto perfectus, et ex Rege Rex, et ex Domino Dominus, cum in ea omni divinitatis gloria atque natura, in qua Pater permanet, natus quoque subsistat et Filius, etiam hoc ex paterna substantia habet, ne demutabilis fiat. Non enim in eo nascente ea, de qua est natus, demutata natura est; sed indemutabilem essentiam natus obtinuit, ex indemutabilis auctoritate naturæ. Nam quamvis imago est, tamen incommutabilis est imago; (non

changeable nature. For though He is an Image, still He is an unchangeable Image; (the nature, that is to say, of the Father's essence, of which He was begotten, not being changed in Him by means of[1] dissimilitude) because in Him an image of the Father's essence must be produced. Again, when He is declared to be the first-born (*primus editus*) of the whole creation, and [at the same time] He Himself is said to have been ever in the beginning with God, God the Word; in that He is first put forth (*primus editur*), He is shewn to have been born (*natus*), and in that He ever has been, He is not separated in time from the Father. The division of the substances, therefore, (which aimed at nothing else, than, by the name of three subsisting[2] [Persons],) to exclude [their doctrine of] oneness under a threefold appellation, cannot be thought to have been introduced with a view to the separation of the substance, [as if] different in the Father and the Son; since what is set forth in the statement of the whole Creed distinguishes not the Father and the Son, the Unbegotten and the Only-begotten, either in time, or name, or essence, or dignity, or dominion." And thus have we fully refuted the first argument, by which some persons have endeavoured to prove that the martyr Lucian favoured the Arian heresy, drawn from the Arians' boasting about their agreement in opinion with Lucian.

[1] per.

[2] trium subsistentium (al. substantiarum.)

8. But learned men rely chiefly on the testimony of Alexander, bishop of Alexandria, who, in an epistle to his namesake, Alexander of Constantinople, after mentioning Paul

commutata in eo scilicet per dissimilitudinem paternæ essentiæ, ex qua est genitus, natura,) quia in eo imago paternæ essentiæ nasceretur. Jam vero cum *primus editus* esse *totius creaturæ* docetur, et ipse ille *semper fuisse in principio apud Deum Verbum Deus* dicitur; dum *primus editur*, natus fuisse ostenditur, dum *semper fuit*, nec tempore separatur a Patre. Non ergo videri potest divisio substantiarum, (quæ nihil aliud studuit, quam ut per trium subsistentium nomen triplicis vocabuli excluderet unionem,) ad separationem diversæ in Filio et in Patre substantiæ introducta; cum totius fidei expositio Patrem et Filium, innascibilem et unigenitum, nec tempore, nec nomine, nec essentia, nec dignitate, nec dominatione discernat.—Pag. 228. [§ 32. p. 1170. ed. Ben. The punctuation of the Benedictine edition has been in some cases substituted for that of the earlier editions followed by Bp. Bull; and *unus ex uno, perfectus a perfecto*, has been printed in italics as being, like the other portions, an extract from the Confession.]

[f] [Unio was used to express the Sabellian doctrine of one Person in the Godhead.]

[g] [This probably relates to the notion of the Holy Spirit as the Love of the Father and the Son: as in S. Aug. de Trin. vi. 7.]

[h] [Alius, used by St. Hilary in the masculine for distinct in substance.]

ON THE CONSUBSTANTIALITY OF THE SON.

[449] of Samosata, adds this remark[h]; "Lucian having succeeded him," (that is, in his error,) "continued for the space of many years excluded from communion by three bishops." My reply is, that Alexander is either speaking of another Lucian in that place, (which is indeed probable even from this circumstance, that he does not call his Lucian a martyr,) or that he was simply mistaken. For it is inconsistent with the trust-worthiness of all ecclesiastical history, that Lucian the martyr embraced the blasphemy of Paul of Samosata, and that, on that account, he continued excommunicated[i] under three successive bishops, which Alexander testifies concerning his Lucian. Certainly Eusebius, who lived in the time of Lucian the martyr, tells a very different tale of him, in his Ecclesiastical History, viii. 13. "Of the martyrs of Antioch," he says[j], "was Lucian, a presbyter of that diocese[1], most excellent through his whole life; who had himself also, in the presence of the Emperor[2] at Nicomedia, proclaimed the heavenly empire[3] of Christ, first by word in an Apology, and afterwards also by deeds." How was it that Eusebius described him as a presbyter most excellent through his whole life, if, for many years, that is, under three bishops in succession[4], (as they express it,) he continued out of the communion of the Church, for maintaining the heresy of the Samosatene? Eusebius, Eccl. Hist. v. 28, mentions the excommunication of Theodotus
[450] the Currier by Victor, on account of the same heresy. He also mentions, in the same passage, Natalis a confessor, who was seduced by Theodotus, and therefore put out of the communion of the Church. Lastly, in book vii. ch. 27, and following chapters, he narrates at length the history of Paul of Samosata's lapsing into heresy, and of his being in consequence anathematized by the council of Antioch. Who then can suppose, that, if Lucian the martyr had,

[1] τῆς αὐτόθι παροικίας.
[2] βασιλέως.
[3] βασιλείαν.
[4] successive (ut loquuntur.)

[h] ὃν διαδεξάμενος Λουκιανὸς ἀποσυνάγωγος ἔμεινε τριῶν ἐπισκόπων πολυετεῖς χρόνους.—Theodoret. H. E. i. 4. [p. 15.]

[i] [Valesius (on this place of Theodoret) intimates that the translators have not understood the meaning of the word ἀποσυνάγωγος: Alexander "only says that Lucian caused a schism in the Church of Antioch, and under three successive bishops celebrated the Eucharist apart from the rest of the Church."—B.]

[j] τῶν δ' ἐπ' Ἀντιοχείας μαρτύρων τὸν πάντα βίον ἄριστος πρεσβύτερος τῆς αὐτόθι παροικίας Λουκιανός. ἐν τῇ Νικομηδείᾳ καὶ αὐτὸς, βασιλέως ἐπιπαρόντος, τὴν οὐράνιον τοῦ Χριστοῦ βασιλείαν λόγῳ πρότερον δι' ἀπολογίας, εἶτα δὲ καὶ ἔργοις ἀνακηρύξας. [H. E. viii. 13.]

under three [successive] bishops, persevered in the heresy of the Samosatene, out of the communion of the Church, Eusebius chose to be silent about so remarkable a circumstance, occurring in his own times; nay more, that he would have been willing himself to commend Lucian as a presbyter most excellent through his whole life, and as one, who had much advanced the kingdom of Christ, both in word and in deed? Besides, as we have seen, Jerome in his catalogue wonderfully praises Lucian the martyr, not only for the sanctity of his life, but also for his learning and his acquaintance with the Holy Scriptures; and, when he makes mention of his books concerning the faith, he does not note any thing in them as different from the catholic faith. Moreover, in his preface to the books of Chronicles, 164
he says that, in his own time, Lucian's version of the Scriptures was received and approved among Catholics from Constantinople even to Antioch. Further, Sozomen, in his Eccl. Hist., iii. 5, declares that Lucian[k] "was both in all other respects a man most approved, and most accurately acquainted with the Holy Scriptures." It is, therefore, plain, that neither Eusebius, nor Jerome, nor Sozomen, had ever heard any thing of any heresy or schism of Lucian the martyr. Therefore, although I would not over obstinately deny that the same thing might have happened to Lucian the martyr in his contests with the Sabellians, which befel Dionysius of Alexandria: namely, to be accused by the Sabellians, before the bishops of the Church, of denying the true divinity of Christ, because he endeavoured to prove, from the [properties] which belong to Christ as Man, that He is not the Father Himself; [451]
yet I could not easily be induced to believe, that this most blessed man did in truth embrace the blasphemies of Paul the Samosatene, or Arius, and did in consequence dissever himself, (for this is what Alexander says of his Lucian,) under three successive bishops, from the communion of the Catholic Church. For against such a story all ecclesiastical history, as I have said, cries out, as well as that confession of faith, which the Arians themselves have attributed to Lucian. I will, however, in conclusion, add this *ex abun-*

[k] ἀνδρὸς τά τε ἄλλα εὐδοκιμώτατου, καὶ τὰς ἱερὰς γραφὰς εἰς ἄκρον ἠκριβωκότος.—[H. E. iii. 5.]

ON THE CONSUBSTANTIALITY OF THE SON.

danti, that, should we grant that Alexander did write this of Lucian the martyr, and that with truth, it can afford very little help to the cause of the Arians. For it was the Samosatene heresy, which Alexander declares that his Lucian embraced, and this the Arians themselves condemn. But could they allege, that in this one particular Alexander was wrong, in having considered the doctrine of Paul of Samosata and of Lucian as identical, as well as that of Arius also; they will not even in this way gain any thing. For then, in return for the support of a single Lucian, they will have the Catholic Church of Lucian's age opposed to their heresy; for the doctrine of that Lucian (whoever he was, and whatever were his opinions) was so opposed to the catholic, that he was unable, according to the testimony of Alexander, to retain his heresy and the communion of the Church together. And thus much for Lucian the martyr.

METHODIUS.

9. I shall conclude this chapter with a brief examination of the doctrine and faith of St. Methodius. According to Jerome[l], St. Methodius, bishop first of Olympus in Lycia, and afterwards of Tyre, and famous[m] for some writings in an elegant and elaborate style, against Porphyry and Origen, and for many other works, was crowned with martyrdom
[452] at Chalcis, a city of Greece, towards the end of the last persecution under Diocletian and Maximian. Of his many writings, the Symposium, [The Banquet of the Ten Virgins,] is, I may say, the only work which has come down to us entire; if at least it be entire; for we shall presently shew that this work also has been interpolated and altered by heretics. We find very many fragments and extracts from him in Photius and other authors; from which, especially, we shall gather his opinion and belief touching the Son of God. In his book on the martyrs, as quoted by Theodoret[n], he calls Christ, "Lord, and Son of God, who thought it not robbery to be equal with God." A statement which, in the judgment even of Petavius[o], can only apply to the true God. Likewise in a book 'Concerning the Creation,'

[l] Catalog. Scriptor. Eccles., c. 94. [vol. ii. p. 90.]

[m] He flourished about the year 290. Cave.—BOWYER.

[n] [αὐτὸς ὁ Κύριος Ἰησοῦς Χριστὸς, ὁ υἱὸς τοῦ Θεοῦ, τιμὴν αὐτὸς ἐμαρτύρησεν, οὐχ ἁρπαγμὸν ἡγησάμενος τὸ εἶναι ἴσα Θεῷ.]—Dial. i. p. 37.

[o] Præfat. in tom. ii. 4, 5.

BOOK II. CHAP. XIII. § 8, 9.

METHODIUS.

(*περὶ τῶν γενητῶν*,) in Photius, cod. 235, he gives this comment on the words of St. John, chap. i.[p]: "In the beginning was the Word," &c. "For we must say that the Beginning, from which the most true Word[1] sprang, is the Father and Maker of all things, in whom He was; and in the words, 'He was in power (*ἐν ἀρχῇ*, in the beginning, E. V.),' with God, he appears to signify the power or dominion[2] of the Word, which He had with the Father even before the world was created; calling His power *ἀρχὴ*, (beginning, E. V.)" In this passage where he says that the Word sprang from God the Father Himself, as from His root, that in Him He both is and was, and that with Him He possessed power[3], authority, or dominion, before created beings came into existence, He absolutely declares the consubstantiality of the Word, and exempts that Word from the class of things which were [453]
created out of nothing and placed in a servile state. But it should also be observed, that Methodius, in this book, is professedly impugning the error attributed to Origen, in which he was said to have proved that created beings existed with God from eternity, by this argument, that otherwise, God would not have been Lord from eternity, seeing that in that case nothing would exist from eternity over which He could exercise lordship. In opposition to this conceit, Methodius excellently shews that power[4] pertained to God the Father and the Son, even before any one created being came into existence; forasmuch as from eternity, God the Father, with His Word, was in possession of Almighty power, by which, whenever He willed, He was able to produce creatures, over which to exercise dominion: and that meanwhile nothing was lacking to the very God; forasmuch as from eternity He was most perfectly blessed, and needed none of those things which were afterwards to be created, to consummate His happiness. Methodius likewise declares in his Symposium[q], that Christ "is, not, is made, (*εἶναι, οὐ γεγονέναι*,)" the Son of God; i. e. that He is the Son of God by nature, not through 165
creation, or by right of adoption. Moreover he also says

[1] *ὁ ὀρθότατος λόγος.*

[2] *τὸ ἐξουσιαστικὸν*, potestatem sive dominationem.

[3] *τὸ ἐξουσιαστικὸν.*

[4] *τὸ ἐξουσιαστικὸν.*

[p] *τὴν μὲν γὰρ ἀρχὴν, ἀφ' ἧς ἀνεβλάστησεν ὁ ὀρθότατος λόγος, τὸν πατέρα καὶ ποιητὴν τῶν ὅλων φατέον, ἐν ᾧ ἦν. τὸ δὲ, Οὗτος ἦν ἐν ἀρχῇ πρὸς τὸν Θεὸν, τὸ ἐξουσιαστικὸν τοῦ λόγου, ὃ εἶχε παρὰ τῷ Πατρὶ, καὶ πρὸ τοῦ τὸν κόσμον εἰς γένεσιν παρεχθεῖν, ἔοικε σημαίνειν, τὴν ἐξουσίαν ἀρχὴν εἰπών.*—[Phot. cod. 235.]

[q] Apud Photium, cod. 237. p. 959.

in the same place, that the Son of God neither had a beginning, nor will have an end of His existence, but "is ever the same, (*εἶναι ἀεὶ τὸν αὐτὸν,*)" which certainly, at least in the judgment of Methodius, is a property of the true God alone; for in the work which has been cited On the Creation, in opposition to Origen, or rather the interpolator of Origen, who asserts the eternity of the world, he contends by several arguments, that whatsoever is without any beginning is uncreated, (*ἀγένητον,*) and that nothing is eternal but God[r].
[454] The entire passage we shall quote in Book iii. on the coeternity of the Son, c. 4. § 7.

10. To these statements so express, Petavius[s] opposes one sentiment of Methodius, which Photius, cod. 235, quotes out of his work On the Creation[1], expressed in the following words[t]; "In what has been already said, we stated that there are two creative powers. One, out of what is not[2], by His mere will, without delay, simultaneously with the act of will, of Himself working[3] whatsoever He wishes to create; and this is the Father; the Other setting in order and varying what has already been called into being, in imitation of the former; this is the Son, the all-powerful and mighty Hand of the Father, by which, after He had produced matter out of what was not[4], He sets it in order." In this passage, there are three statements which Petavius censures, as at variance with the rule of the catholic faith: first, that Methodius calls the Father and the Son two powers, (*δυνάμεις;*) secondly, that he says that the former power, namely the Father, of Himself works and creates[5], *αὐτουργεῖν,* whilst the Son works from the Father[6], and in imitation of Him; and lastly, that he attributes to the Father the creation of the world out of nothing, to the exclusion as it were of the

[1] περὶ τῶν γενητῶν.

[2] ἐξ οὐκ ὄντων.

[3] αὐτουργοῦσαν.

[4] ἐξ οὐκ ὄντων.

[5] a se moliri et creare.

[6] a Patre.

[r] *πῆ δὴ οὖν, ὦ ἠλίθιοι, οἴεσθε τὴν κτίσιν, συναπέραντον οὖσαν τῷ δημιουργῷ, μὴ δεῖσθαι τοῦ δημιουργοῦ; τὸ γὰρ συναπέραντον, μηδαμῶς ἀρχὴν γενέσεως ἔχον, καὶ συναγένητον, καὶ ἰσοδύναμον ἀνάγκη τυγχάνειν.* Methodius apud Photium, cod. 235. p. 938.

[s] De Trinit. i. 4. 12.

[t] *δύο δὲ δυνάμεις ἐν τοῖς προωμολογημένοις ἔφαμεν εἶναι ποιητικάς· τὴν ἐξ οὐκ ὄντων γυμνῷ τῷ βουλήματι χωρὶς μελλησμοῦ*[1], *ἅμα τῷ θελῆσαι, αὐτουργοῦσαν ὃ βούλεται ποιεῖν· τυγχάνει δὲ ὁ Πατήρ· θατέραν δὲ κατακοσμοῦσαν καὶ ποικίλλουσαν κατὰ μίμησιν τῆς προτέρας τὰ ἤδη γεγονότα· ἔστι δὲ ὁ υἱὸς, ἡ παντοδύναμος καὶ κραταιὰ χεὶρ τοῦ Πατρὸς, ἐν ᾗ μετὰ τὸ ποιῆσαι τὴν ὕλην ἐξ οὐκ ὄντων κατακοσμεῖ.*—Pag. 938.

[1] [In the edition which Bp. Bull used, we read *μελισμοῦ,* "distinction of parts." I do not know whether *μελλησμοῦ,* "delay," is his own conjecture.—B. The reading of Bekker's edition (ed. Berlin. 1824) according to the MSS. A. B. is *μελλησμοῦ.*]

Son, to whom he allows only the adorning what are already created. But all this easily admits, and even requires a catholic sense; accordingly, even Photius did not find any thing to blame in that passage. As to the first point, the [455]
Father and the Son are with better right called two powers by Methodius, than two natures or essences by other fathers, who yet are regarded as catholic and orthodox in this article: the truth is, these words, as we have shewn above, are taken altogether in a personal sense, as it is called. As to the second, that the Father alone works of Himself, *αὐτουργεῖν*, what Catholic would deny it? For it is the property of the Father to exist and to work of Himself; whereas the Son refers both His being and His working[1] (as they express it) [as if] received, to the Father as His Author. In this respect also the Son is said to do His works in imitation as it were of the Father. See John v. 19, and Maldonatus on the passage. The meaning of Methodius and other fathers, as also of Holy Scripture, is very well expressed by Gregory Nazianzen, Oration xxxvi.[u], in these words; "It is manifest that with respect to the same objects the Father imprints the forms [of them], and the Word finishes them, not as a servant, or without intelligence, but with knowledge and as a master, and (to speak more properly) as the Father[2]." You may read in the same passage more that is worthy of observation on this subject. This statement of Nazianzen, however, Petavius himself somewhere[x] expresses approbation of, and further remarks thus on it; "Whence it is plain, that the Father's shewing to the Son, or teaching Him what He has to do, and as it were going before Him to shew Him the way, is nothing else than communicating to Him by generation, together with His nature and essence, the understanding of [456]
things to be made, and the forms and types of them." Then with regard to the last point which is censured, namely, that Methodius attributes to the Father, to the exclusion as it were of the Son, the creation of things out of nothing, the answer is not difficult. The truth is, He no more excludes the Son from the act of creating things, than He does the

[1] et esse et operari suum.

[2] πατρικῶς.

[u] δῆλον ὅτι τῶν αὐτῶν πραγμάτων τοὺς τύπους ἐνσημαίνεται μὲν ὁ Πατὴρ, ἐπιτελεῖ δὲ ὁ λόγος, οὐ δουλικῶς, οὔτ' [οὐδὲ] ἀμαθῶς, ἀλλ' ἐπιστημονικῶς τε καὶ δεσποτικῶς, καὶ, οἰκειότερον εἰπεῖν, πατρικῶς.—Tom. i. p. 584. ed. Par. 1630. [Orat. xxx. 11. p. 547.]

[x] De Trin. ii. 4. 6.

Father from that of putting them in order when created; indeed in the last words of the passage quoted, he says in no obscure terms, that the Father both created matter and put it in order through the Son, or in the Son. Besides, how is it to be supposed that Methodius declared that the Father created all things out of nothing without the Son, in the very same passage in which he expressly calls the Son the almighty Hand of the Father? Did the Father create or make any thing without His own almighty Hand? What then? we must here, by all means, repeat what we adduced before[y] from Huet for the purpose of illustrating a similar passage from Origen? The substance of it is this: Although the external works of the Holy Trinity are one and the same, still both in the sacred Scriptures and in the writings of the ancients, some are usually assigned to the Father, others to the Son, and others to the Holy Ghost. So in this passage Methodius attributes to the Father especially, as the fountain
166 of Godhead, the creation of things, whilst to the Son he ascribes the wise ordering, disposition and adornment of what were already created; inasmuch as He is usually called the Reason, the Counsel, and the Wisdom of the Father. In what sense indeed this is said, it is impossible for us fully to understand; but it is utterly foolish and rash at once to reject those points in these mysteries which we puny mortals[1] cannot adequately explain. It is certain however that Methodius never dreamt of attributing to the Father the creation of the world, in such sense as to exclude the Son. For from this very work On the Creation, Photius in the same place
[457] cod. 235[z], and that immediately after the words which Petavius carps at, quotes a passage of Methodius in which the creation of the world is expressly attributed to the Son. For even in the same passage Methodius thus comments on those words of Genesis, "In the beginning God created the heaven and the earth;" "If by 'the beginning' any one should understand Wisdom Herself, he would not err. For She is

[1] homunciones.

[y] See c. 10. § 9. of this book, [p. 300.]

[z] ἀρχὴν δὲ αὐτὴν τὴν σοφίαν λέγων τις, οὐκ ἂν ἁμάρτοι. λέγεται γὰρ παρά τινι τῶν ἐκ τοῦ θείου χοροῦ λέγουσα περὶ αὐτῆς τὸν τρόπον τοῦτον· Κύριος ἔκτισέ με ἀρχὴν ὁδῶν αὐτοῦ, εἰς ἔργα αὐτοῦ, πρὸ τοῦ αἰῶνος ἐθεμελίωσέ με. ἦν γὰρ ἀκόλουθον καὶ πρεπωδέστερον, πάντα ἃ εἰς γένεσιν ἦλθον, εἶναι ταύτης νεώτερα, ἐπεὶ καὶ δι' αὐτῆς γεγόνασιν. —[Phot. cod. 235.]

BOOK II. CHAP. XIII. § 10, 11.

METHODIUS.

introduced by one of the band of inspired writers[1] speaking of Herself after this manner, The Lord created[2] Me, the Beginning of His ways, for His works, He founded Me before the worlds[3]. For it was natural and more becoming, that all things that were created[4] should be younger than She, since also it was through Her that they came into being." And it is clear that by Wisdom is here meant the Son of God.

11. Sandius[a] also objects to Methodius some unseemly sentiments[5] concerning the Trinity, which his editor Possinus noted in the Symposium. But Photius supplies us with an answer to this objection; for in cod. 237, he expressly cautions us respecting the work of Methodius, entitled the Symposium, that even in his time it had been to a very great degree altered and interpolated by heretics. These are Photius's words[b]; "It is to be noted, that this Dialogue, which is entitled the Symposion, or Concerning Chastity, is very much corrupted; for you will find it interpolated both with Arian imaginations[6], and the fables[7] of other heterodox persons." Here, the reader will also observe, as I have done, that, whereas Photius thought it necessary to inform us about the Symposium of Methodius only, that there were found in [458] it many Arian additions, as also absurdities of other heretics, he hereby pretty plainly intimates that nothing of the kind occurred in his other writings, as they were extant in his own day. For how could Photius have gathered, that the Symposium of Methodius was corrupted, on the ground of the vain opinions of Arius occurring in it throughout, unless it had been clear to him from Methodius's other writings, (and they were numerous,) that his uniform teaching concerning the Son of God was entirely repugnant to the wild notions of the Arians? This surely is a striking argument for the orthodoxy of Methodius on this article. Meanwhile, in this very Symposium there remain even at this day vestiges not a few, of Methodius's genuine teaching respecting the Son of God; some of which we have already pointed out from Photius, and could easily point out more,

[1] τοῦ θείου χοροῦ.
[2] ἔκτισε.
[3] πρὸ τοῦ αἰῶνος.
[4] ἃ εἰς γένεσιν ἦλθον.
[5] incommodas.
[6] δοξοκοπίας.
[7] μυθολογήματα.

[a] Enucl. Hist. Eccles. i. p. 128.

[b] σημειωτέον, ὡς οὗτος ὁ διάλογος, ᾧ ἐπιγραφὴ Συμπόσιον, ἢ Περὶ ἁγνείας, παρὰ πολὺ νενοθευμένος ἐστίν. εὑρήσεις γὰρ ἐν αὐτῷ παραβεβλημένας καὶ Ἀρειανικὰς δοξοκοπίας, καὶ ἑτέρων τινῶν κακοδοξούντων μυθολογήματα.—Pag. 963.

ON THE CONSUBSTANTIALITY OF THE SON.

if we had thought it worth our while. Enough however, concerning Methodius.

[460]
168

CHAPTER XIV.

THE OPINION AND FAITH OF ARNOBIUS THE AFRICAN, AND LACTANTIUS, RESPECTING THE TRUE DIVINITY OF THE SON, IS DECLARED; THE SECOND BOOK, ON THE CONSUBSTANTIALITY, IS BROUGHT TO A CLOSE, WITH A BRIEF CONCLUSION.

ARNOBIUS.

1. THERE are two other authors left, who lived shortly before the Nicene council, Arnobius and Lactantius, the master and the scholar. The former of these, Arnobius, had a very flourishing school of rhetoric at Sicca, in Africa, in the reign of the emperor Diocletian[c], as is related by Jerome in his Catalogue of Eccles. Writers, chap. 90[d]; who also tells us in his Chronicon, on the twentieth year of Constantine, that this Arnobius, when engaged in instructing youths in declamation at Sicca, being as yet a heathen, was constrained by dreams to become a believer, and yet could not
[461] obtain from the bishops, [admission to] that faith which he had always impugned; whereupon he composed with great pains some very clear works against his old religion, and at length having given these hostages, as it were, of his piety, was admitted into the covenant. These books were seven in number, entitled Against the Heathen[1]. After passing through various editions, they have at length been published in 4to., with very learned *Variorum* notes, in very elegant type, at Leyden, A.D. 1651. This is the edition which we shall follow. In this work he frequently, and in most express terms, acknowledges the true divinity of the Son. In the first book, in treating of the miracles of Christ, he thus writes[e]; "But it was evident that Christ wrought all those things which He wrought by the power of His own Name,

[1] Adversus Gentes.

[c] He flourished about the year 303. Cave.—BOWYER.

[d] [Vol. ii. p. 903.]

[e] Atqui constitit Christum sine ullis adminiculis rerum, sine ullius ritus observatione, vel lege, omnia illa quæ

BOOK II. CHAP. XIV. § 1. ARNOBIUS.

without any helps from [external] things, without the observance of any rite, or rule, and, (what was the special property, suitable to and worthy of the true God,) He bestowed nothing injurious or hurtful, but what was helpful, salutary, and full of aiding blessings, in the bountifulness of munificent power." Here he expressly declares Christ to be true God. There is a passage parallel to this, which follows some way after in the same book, in which, after saying that Christ "equally relieved[f] the good and the bad," he adds these words; "For this is the property of the true God and of regal power, to deny His bounty to none." In the same book, upon a heathen's enquiring, "If Christ were God, why did He appear in the form of man, and why was He put to death after the manner of man?" he answers thus[g]; "Could that power which is invisible and has no corporeal substance, present and lend Itself to the world, be present in the assemblies of men, otherwise than by assuming some covering of more solid matter, such as might meet the glance of the eye, and on which the gaze of the dullest contemplation might be able to fix? For what mortal is there [462] that could have been able to see Him, or to discern Him, if He had willed to present Himself on earth such as is His original[1] nature, and such as He has willed to be in His own quality or Deity[2]? He therefore took on Him the form of man, and enclosed His power under the likeness of our race, in order that He might be both seen and beheld." In the same place after a few intervening words these follow; "But He was put to death after the manner of man; not He Himself; for to perish by death[3] is not incident to

[1] primigenia.
[2] numine.
[3] mortis occasus.

fecit, nominis sui possibilitate fecisse; et quod proprium, consentaneum, dignum Deo fuerat vero, nihil nocens, aut noxium, sed opiferum, sed salutare, sed auxiliaribus plenum bonis, potestatis munificæ liberalitate donasse.—[Pag. 25, 26.]

[f] Christus æqualiter bonis malisque subvenit. . . . Hoc est enim proprium Dei veri potentiæque regalis, benignitatem suam negare nulli.—Pag. 29.

[g] [Sed] . . . si Deus fuit Christus, cur forma est in hominis visus, et cur more est interemptus humano? An aliter potuit invisibilis illa vis, et habens nullam substantiam corporalem, inferre et commodare se mundo, conciliis interesse mortalium, quam ut aliquod tegmen materiæ solidioris assumeret, quod oculorum susciperet injectum, et ubi se figere inertissimæ posset contemplationis obtutus? quis est enim mortalium, qui quiret eum videre, quis cernere, si talem voluisset inferre se terris, qualis ei primigenia natura est, et qualem se ipse in sua esse voluit vel qualitate vel numine? Assumpsit igitur hominis formam, et sub nostri generis similitudine potentiam suam clausit, ut et videri posset et conspici. . . . Sed more est hominis interemptus; non ipse; neque enim

what is divine[1], nor can that go to pieces by being dissolved in destruction, which is one, and simple, and not made up of the combination of any parts. Who then was seen to hang upon the cross? who died? The manhood which[2] He had put on, and bore about with Him." Here he calls the higher nature of Christ, "a thing divine, incorruptible, one and simple, made up of no combination of parts," [qualities] which cannot be attributed to any created nature.

[1] divinas res.
[2] homo quem.

2. It is, however, unnecessary to lead the reader by these circuitous ways[3]. I will bring forward two passages, in which Arnobius professedly, and in terms as clear as if written with a sunbeam, declares the absolute divinity of the Son. In the first book, he replies to the objection of the heathen "You worship a man that was born," in these words[h]; "Even if that were true, still on account of the many and so liberal gifts which have come from Him unto[4]
169 us, He ought to be called and entitled *God.* But seeing that He is really and certainly God, without ambiguity or doubt of any kind[5], do you suppose that we shall disown that we pay Him the highest worship, and call Him the Guardian[6] of our body? What then, some one will say, raging, angry, and excited, 'Is Christ that God?' He is God, our reply will be, even God of the inner powers[i];
[463] and, what yet more torments unbelievers with most bitter pangs, sent to us by the supreme King for a matter of the highest moment." The other passage also occurring in the same book[j], runs thus: "There was nothing magical, as you suppose, nothing human, illusive, or deceitful, nothing of

[3] ambages.
[4] in nobis.
[5] ullius redubitationis ambiguo.
[6] præsidem.

cadere divinas in res potest mortis occasus, nec interitionis dissolutione dilabi id, quod est unum et simplex, nec ullarum partium congregatione compactum. Quis est ergo visus in patibulo pendere, quis mortuus est? homo, quem induerat, et secum ipse portabat. —Pag. 37, 38.

[h] Natum hominem colitis? Etiamsi esset id verum, tamen pro multis et tam liberalibus donis, quæ ab eo profecta in nobis sunt, *Deus* dici appellarique deberet. Cum vero Deus sit re certa, et sine ullius rei dubitationis (leg. redubitationis, Bull.) ambiguo, inficiaturos arbitramini nos esse, quam maxime illum a nobis coli, et præsidem nostri corporis nuncupari? Ergone, inquiet aliquis furens, iratus et percitus, Deus ille est Christus? Deus, respondebimus, et interiorum potentiarum Deus; et quod magis infidos acerbissimis doloribus torqueat, rei maximæ causa a summo rege ad nos missus.—Pag. 24. [Herald conjectured redubitationis; Orelli, following Ursinus, would omit rei, there being no such word as redubitationis.]

[i] interiorum potentiarum, [i. e. over the highest angelic powers in the innermost courts of heaven.]

[j] Nihil, ut remini, magicum, nihil humanum, præstigiosum, aut subdolum, nihil fraudis delituit in Christo, derideatis licet ex more atque in lasciviam dissolvamini cachinnorum. Deus

fraud concealed in Christ, although you deride, as your way is, and burst out into unrestrained laughter. He was the High[1] God, God from the inmost root, God from the unknown realms, and sent as God the Saviour from the Sovereign of all; with regard to whom neither the sun itself, nor any of the stars, if they have perception, not the rulers, not the princes of this world, nor lastly the great gods, or those who, pretending to be gods, terrify the whole race of mortals, could know or imagine whence He came, or who He was." In these passages, Arnobius expressly teaches, that the Son is called God, not simply by a figure of speech[2], (as angels, rulers, and very excellent men are sometimes called gods,) but in very reality and without ambiguity, that is, most truly and most properly; and this is a plain condemnation of the craftiness of the impious Arians, who did not refuse to call the Son God, but deceived good men by an ambiguous use of the name. Furthermore He designates Him the High God, God from the inmost root, God the Saviour, God the object of the very highest worship[3], lastly, God incomprehensible, whom no creature can comprehend[4]. What could have been set forth concerning the Son of God more majestic than this? If however, it be a difficulty to any one, that Arnobius does still call the Father the supreme King and the Sovereign[5] of all; let him know and remember, (what I am obliged to repeat again and again,) that this is by all means to be referred to that pre-eminence[6] which belongs[7] to the Father, in so far as He is the fountain and head of Divinity, which both the sacred writers and the fathers, whether Nicene or Antenicene, wished to present whole and entire[8], and concerning which we shall treat more largely in its proper place[k].

3. And yet Sandius classes this Arnobius among those Antenicene writers who preceded Arius in his heresy. For [464] in the Index[9] of his book he writes, "Arnobius was of the same opinion as Arius." And he there refers his reader to the 127th page of his book. Come then, let us see how

1 sublimis.
2 abusive.
3 quam maxime colendum.
4 capere.
5 Principem.
6 ἐξοχήν.
7 competit.
8 sartam tectam conservatam voluere.
9 Indice sive Elencho.

ille sublimis fuit, Deus radice ab intima, Deus ab incognitis regnis, et ab omnium Principe Deus Sospitator est missus; quem neque sol ipse, neque ulla, si sentiunt (sentiant, Bull), sidera, non rectores, non principes mundi, non denique dii magni, aut qui fingentes se deos genus omne mortalium territant, unde aut qui fuerit, potuerunt noscere vel suspicari.—Pag. 32.

k [See book iv.]

ON THE CONSUBSTANTIALITY OF THE SON.

he there proves that Arnobius was of the same opinion as Arius? "Arnobius," he says, "taught that it was a matter of religion to worship a God unbegotten, that the true God must never have been begotten, that God alone is unbegotten; that there is one Father of the universe, who is alone immortal, and unbegotten, and that nothing whatever existed before Him; that hence it follows, that all those whom men have supposed to be gods, are either begotten of Him, or brought forth at His command: and that, if they have been brought forth and begotten, they are posterior in order and time; if they be posterior in order and time, they must have had an origin, and commencement of birth and life; that he is not true God, who has father or mother, grandfathers, grandmothers, brothers, and was only lately formed in his mother's womb, and finished and perfected in ten months, who was conceived and born of a woman's womb, who arrived at that limit of life by the stages of years; for that the Almighty God is not begotten, but unbegotten[k]." But in this passage, assuredly, Sandius shews himself to be either a most negligent reader of Arnobius's writings, or at any rate an egregious sophist and prevaricator. For what person of sound mind, who ever attentively read through that master of African eloquence, can be ignorant, that all this was spoken by him against the superstition of the heathen, who used to pay divine honours to mere men, that were born and died just like themselves? How then does this make any thing against the true divinity of Christ, God [and] Man[1]? Nay, it confirms it. For when Arnobius taught, as Sandius allows, in the passages cited, that the true God must be unbegotten, that is, uncreated, and have no beginning by birth, that is, that He must be eternal; and yet he affirmed repeatedly and most plainly, (as we have seen,) that Christ is altogether true God; it follows clearly from this that Christ in His higher nature, in respect of which He is called true God, is, according to the opinion of Arnobius, altogether uncreated and eternal. So from the fact that Arnobius taught that the true God is one, and yet at the same time taught that the Son equally with the Father is true God, we may conclude for certain, that he believed that the Son is

[1] θεάνθρωπος.

[465]

[Sandius refers generally to lib. 1, 2, and 8. Adv. Gentes.]

BOOK II. CHAP. XIV. § 3, 4.

ARNOBIUS.

one God with the Father, although different in person. As for what Sandius adds in the same passage, namely, that Arnobius taught "that Christ came into the world to preserve the empire of the supreme King," it is entirely catholic; so far forth, that is, as it is referred, as it ought by all means to be referred, to the humiliation[1] of the Son, by which, having taken upon Himself the form of a servant, He became obedient to God the Father. It certainly gives one both pain and shame to have so often to refute such senseless cavils.

[1] exinanitio [κένωσις Phil. ii. 6.]

LACTANTIUS.

4. We will now briefly treat of the doctrine of Lactantius[1], the explaining of which will bring this second book, now more than long enough, to a close. That writer was almost unacquainted with the Christian system[2], and better skilled in rhetoric than in theology. Hence Pope Damasus regarded him as belonging more to the school than to the Church[3]; and Jerome commended him rather for his elegant style, than for his accurate knowledge of gospel doctrine. He certainly was never reckoned among the doctors of the Church; so that it may scarcely seem worth while to enquire what he either thought or wrote on this point. I request the reader, however, to observe and to admire the influence of catholic tradition. This very Lactantius, although in other parts of his writings, through his ignorance of the Holy Scriptures and of the doctrine of the Church, he has made some very absurd, and utterly ridiculous statements[4] [m], (if indeed it be Lactantius who has made those statements,) respecting the manner of the generation of the Son, nevertheless was not ignorant of the chief point itself[5] of this doctrine, and consequently taught in his works what is especially catholic, and diametrically opposed to the Arian heresy. For he clearly affirms that the Son of God is of one substance with the Father, and is one God, and contains and comprehends the whole of the Father. These are his very words. In book iv. 29, he proposes the heathen objection against the Christian doctrine concerning the Son of God in these terms[n]; "Perhaps some one may enquire how it is,

170

[2] disciplinæ.

[3] scholasticum magis quam ecclesiasticum.

[466]

[4] tradiderit.

[5] ipsum τὸ ὑπέρεχον.

[1] Lactantius flourished in the year 303. Cave.—BOWYER.

[m] Vid. book iii. chap. 10. § 20.

[n] Fortasse quærat aliquis, quomodo, cum Deum nos unum colere dicamus, duos tamen esse asseveremus, Deum Patrem et Deum Filium; quæ asseveratio plerosque in maximum impegit errorem. Quibus cum probabilia videantur esse quæ dicimus, in hoc uno

ON THE CONSUBSTANTIALITY OF THE SON.

that when we say we worship one God, we yet assert that there are two, God the Father, and God the Son: an assertion which has driven very many into the greatest error; who whilst they think what we say probable, still conceive that we are wrong on this one point, that we acknowledge a second, and that a mortal God." To this objection he answers as follows, word for word: "Of the mortality we have already spoken; let us now inform you respecting the unity. When we speak of God the Father and God the Son, we do not speak of a different God, nor do we separate Each [from the Other]; because neither can the Father exist without the Son, nor can the Son be separated from the Father; since neither can the Father be [so] called [1] without the Son, nor can the Son be begotten without the Father. Since then both the Father implies[2] the Son, and the Son the Father, Both have one mind, one spirit, one substance; but the One is, as it were, an overflowing fountain, the Other is like a stream issuing from it: the One is as the
[467] sun, the Other as a ray darted from the sun; who, because He is both faithful and dear to the supreme Father, is not separated from Him, as is neither a river from its fountain, nor a ray from the sun; inasmuch as both the water of the fountain is in the stream, and the light of the sun is in the ray." If Lactantius had agreed in opinion with Arius, his answer to this objection would certainly have been very different: I mean, very much to this effect; "You, philosophers, are much mistaken in supposing that we Christians, in setting forth God the Father and God the Son, are really introducing two Gods; seeing that we give the name of God to the Father and to the Son in entirely different senses; for the Father alone we call God truly and properly, the Son metaphorically and improperly; since the latter is in truth a mere

[1] nuncupari.

[2] faciat.

labare nos arbitrantur, quod et alterum et mortalem Deum fateamur. De mortalitate jam diximus; nunc de unitate doceamus. Cum dicimus Deum Patrem et Deum Filium, non diversum dicimus, nec utrumque secernimus; quia nec Pater sine Filio esse potest, nec Filius a Patre secerni; siquidem nec Pater sine Filio nuncupari, nec Filius potest sine Patre generari. Cum igitur et Pater Filium faciat, et Filius Patrem, una utrique mens, unus Spiritus, UNA SUBSTANTIA est; sed ille quasi exuberans fons est, hic tanquam defluens ex eo rivus: ille tanquam sol, hic quasi radius a sole porrectus; qui quoniam summo Patri et fidelis et carus est, non separatur, sicut nec rivus a fonte, nec radius a sole; quia et aqua fontis in rivo est, et solis lumen in radio.—[Lactant. Divin. Instit. iv. 29. vol. i. p. 350, 351.]

BOOK II. CHAP. XIV. § 4.

LACTANTIUS.

creature, alien from the essence of God and made out of nothing, being admitted by adoption and grace only unto the honour and dignity of the divine name." Lactantius, however, did not dream of any thing of this sort; the catholic doctrine respecting the Son of God was too well known for even him to publish such ravings as the tenets of Christians. How then does he untie the knot? he confesses according to the belief of the Christians, that the Son equally with the Father is truly and properly called God; inasmuch as He has not only one mind, but one Spirit also, and one substance with the Father, (the very thing which the Nicene fathers meant, when they decreed that God the Father and God the Son were of one substance[1],) though he strenuously contends that it is by no means true that two Gods are preached among the Christians. And this he explains in two ways; first, God the Father and God the Son exist, not separately, as two men, but undivided the One from the Other, so that the Father is in the Son and the Son in the Father; exactly as the sun and the ray, or the fountain and the stream, are no way separated the one from the other. Secondly, there is one fountain and principle of Godhead, namely, the Father, from whom the Son is derived, like the ray from the sun, or the stream from the fountain. What could have been said in a way more agreeable to catholic truth? that is to say, it was precisely in the [468] same way that all the orthodox fathers, both the Antenicene and those who flourished after the Nicene council, explained the unity of the Father and the Son, as we shall shew hereafter. Here, indeed, some persons find fault with this, that Lactantius compares God the Father to an overflowing fountain, as if, that is, the Son were only a rivulet issuing from that fountain, and a diminished portion of the Father's substance. They, however, have always appeared to me to be most unfair, who would thus cut to the quick[2] [o]whatever similes the ancients employed to illustrate, as well as they might[3], the ineffable mystery of the divine generation. That Lactantius certainly did not mean any thing of that kind is clear from his own express words, which follow in the same

[1] ὁμοούσιους.

[2] ad vivum resecant.

[3] utcunque.

[o] See what we have observed on Tertullian in the 7th chap. of this book, § 5. [p. 199.]

ON THE CONSUBSTANTIALITY OF THE SON.

chapter[p]: "Wherefore," he says, "since the mind and will of Each is in the Other, or rather is one in Both, Both are justly called one God; because whatsoever is in the Father flows[1] over to the Son, and whatsoever is in the Son, descends from the Father." If whatsoever is in the exuberant fountain of Godhead, which is called the Father, does all flow over to the Son, (which Lactantius expressly asserts,) then certainly the Son is not, properly speaking, a portion of the Godhead, but God of God, Whole of Whole, Perfect of Perfect, as we have already heard the Creeds of Gregory Thaumaturgus and Lucian the martyr declare. Parallel to this is what Lactantius says respecting the Son of God, book ii. 9[q]; namely, that God the Father "employed" Him "as His counsellor and artificer, in devising, adorning, and perfecting the universe[2]; seeing that He is perfect in providence, in reason, and in power." Lactantius, therefore, did not dream of any thing diminished or imperfect in the Son of God. So far of Lactantius.

[1] transfluit.

171

[2] rebus.

[469] 5. And thus have we at length, by the clearest testimonies adduced from each one of the Antenicene writers, of whom we had been able to discover either entire works, or even any fragments,—abundantly proved our second proposition, which was this; "It was the settled and unanimous opinion of the catholic doctors, who flourished in the first three centuries, that the Son of God was of one substance[3] or consubstantial with God the Father, that is, that He was not of any created or mutable essence, but of altogether the same divine and unchangeable nature with His Father, and, therefore, Very God of Very God." If, however, any one wonder that our second book has grown to this length, I would wish him to reflect, that herein we have explained out of the writings of the ancients the chief point[4] of the doctrine respecting the divinity of the Son; and that in the remaining books we shall only have to treat of the consequences of that doctrine, and of its collateral points[5]. On this the hinge of

[3] ὁμοούσιος.

[4] τὸ ὑπερέχον.

[5] de ejusdem consectariis et consentaneis.

[p] Quapropter cum mens et voluntas alterius in altero sit, vel potius una in utroque, merito unus Deus uterque appellatur; quia quicquid est in Patre ad Filium transfluit, et quicquid in Filio, a Patre descendit.—[ubi supr. iv. 29. p. 352.]

[q] Et consiliatore usus est et artifice in excogitandis, ornandis perficiendisque rebus; quoniam is et providentia, et ratione, et potestate perfectus est.—[Ibid., ii. 9. p. 145.]

CONCLUSION.

the controversy turns: on this therefore it was necessary for us to bestow the greatest pains. Besides in this book most of the writers of the first three centuries come to be spoken of for the first time, and it was important that the reader should in some degree be made acquainted with their history; and when this is done once, there will be no occasion in what follows to make any mention of their age, authority, or other matters connected with them. Many writings also of the ancients are here for the first time cited, about which it is matter of controversy among the learned whether they are really the works of the authors whose names they bear; much of our labour therefore in this book has been spent in critical discussions of this kind, which are of especial need for deciding the question of which we are treating. Now, however, that the genuine writings of each author have been once for all vindicated, and the spurious rejected, it will hereafter be hardly necessary, when we have occasion again to quote these writers or their works, to detain the reader by controversies of this nature. In a word, as I do not see how I [470]
could have given full satisfaction to the studious reader, if I had used greater brevity in elucidating and establishing the subject of this second book, so I trust that in what relates to the following books, I shall say what may suffice at least for the impartial reader. To the remainder of our subject, therefore, let us now, with God's blessing, proceed.

www.ingramcontent.com/pod-product-compliance
Lightning Source LLC
LaVergne TN
LVHW020525100826
845148LV00010B/1340
9781606081372